Correspondence of
THOMAS GRAY

Thomas Gray
from a painting by Benjamin Wilson
in the possession of Sir John Murray

Correspondence of
THOMAS GRAY

Edited by the late
PAGET TOYNBEE
and
LEONARD WHIBLEY

With Corrections and Additions
by
H. W. STARR

IN THREE VOLUMES
Volume III. 1766–1771

OXFORD
AT THE CLARENDON PRESS

Oxford University Press, Ely House, London W. 1

GLASGOW NEW YORK TORONTO MELBOURNE WELLINGTON
CAPE TOWN SALISBURY IBADAN NAIROBI DAR ES SALAAM LUSAKA ADDIS ABABA
BOMBAY CALCUTTA MADRAS KARACHI LAHORE DACCA
KUALA LUMPUR SINGAPORE HONG KONG TOKYO

FIRST PUBLISHED 1935
REPRINTED LITHOGRAPHICALLY IN GREAT BRITAIN
(WITH CORRECTIONS AND ADDITIONS)
AT THE UNIVERSITY PRESS, OXFORD
BY VIVIAN RIDLER
PRINTER TO THE UNIVERSITY
1971

CONTENTS

v

Contents

LIST OF LETTERS

THE list of letters indicates the dates when, the places at which the letters were written, and the names of Gray's correspondents to whom, or by whom, each letter was written. Letters to Gray from his correspondents are shown as '*From* Walpole', &c.; non-extant letters of which note has been taken in the text have the names of the correspondent in italics.

A further purpose served by the list is to give the source from which the text of each of the letters has been derived. Nearly three-fourths of the letters have been printed from the original manuscripts, (see Introduction). Other letters come from printed sources or from manuscript transcripts of letters of which the originals cannot now be traced.

In the Introduction an account has been given of the chief manuscripts, and acknowledgement has been made to the owners who have allowed their manuscripts to be photographed or copied. A reference to the account will explain the abbreviated form under which the names of institutions or individual owners are indicated in the list.[1]

Of the printed sources the most important are William Mason's *Memoirs of the Life and Writings of Mr. Gray* (1775), *The Works of Lord Orford* (1798), and the editions in which, at different times, Mitford published Gray's correspondence. Other printed sources include books not directly connected with Gray, Magazines, and Sale Catalogues. Precise indications of the particular editions of Mitford and of other printed sources are given in the preliminary notes to the letters. The transcripts (indicated by T in the sixth column of the list) include two made by Gray himself (58**, 261 A), others made by Cole, Fess, copyists whose names are not known, and seven by Mitford (in one of his note-books now in the British Museum).

[Two numbers survive in the list (387, 396) with no letters attached to them. The letters were transposed in date after the general order had been settled.]

---

[1] See Introduction to reprint of 1971.

No. of Letter	Date	Place	Correspondent	Original Source	Printed Source or Transcript
	1734				
1	16 Apr.		Walpole	Waller	
2	31 Oct.	Cambridge	,,	,,	
3	17 Nov.	,,	,,	,,	
4	8 Dec.	,,	,,	,,	
5	Dec.	,,	,,	,,	
6	23 Dec.	,,	,,	,,	
	1735				
7	6 Jan.	,,	,,	,,	
8	12 Jan.	,,	,,	,,	
9	14 Jan.	,,	,,	,,	
10	19 Jan.	,,	,,	,,	
11	21 Jan.	,,	,,	,,	
12	27 Jan.	,,	,,	,,	
13	4 Feb.	,,	,,	,,	
14	25 Feb.	,,	,,	,,	
15	5 Mar.	,,	,,	,,	
15*	c. 1 July	,,	From West		
16	3 July	,,	Walpole	Waller	
17	c. 15 Oct.	,,	From Walpole		Mrs. Toynbee
18	14 Nov.	Oxford	From West		Mason
19	c. 20 Dec.	Cambridge	West		,,
	1736				
20	3 Jan.	London	Walpole	Waller	
21	11 Mar.	Cambridge	,,	,,	
22	8 May		West	Loyd	
22*	9 May	Oxford	From West		
22**	May	Cambridge	West		Mason
23	24 May	Oxford	From West		,,
24	11 June	London	Walpole	Waller	
25	15 July	,,	,,	,,	
26	Aug.	Burnham	,,	,,	
27	26 Sept.	,,	,,	,,	
28	3 Oct.	London	,,	,,	
29	8 Oct.	,,	Birkett	Pemb. Coll.	
30	Oct.	Cambridge	From Birkett	,,	
31	12 Oct.	London	Walpole	Waller	
32	27 Oct.	Cambridge	,,	,,	
33	Dec.	,,	West		Mason
34	22 Dec.	Oxford	From West		,,
35	29 Dec.	Cambridge	Walpole	Waller	
	1737				
36	16 Jan.	,,	,,	,,	
37	March	,,	West		Mason
38	4 July	Oxford	From West		,,
39	July	Cambridge	Walpole	Waller	
40	22 Aug.	London	West		Mason
41	c. 22 Aug.	,,	Walpole	Waller	

No. of Letter	Date	Place	Correspondent	Original Source	Printed Source or Transcript
	1737				
41*	Oct. or Nov.	London	*From West*		
·42	c. 12 Nov.	London	Walpole	Waller	
43	2 Dec.	Oxford	*From* West		Mason
44	29 Dec.	Cambridge	Walpole	Waller	
	1738				
45	10 Jan.	,,	,,	,,	
46	15 Jan.	,,	,,	,,	
47	22 Jan.	,,	West		Mason
48	21 Feb.	London	*From West*		,,
49	23 Feb.	Cambridge	Walpole	Waller	
50	7 Mar.	,,	,,	,,	
51	20 Mar.	,,	,,	,,	
52	28 Mar.	,,	,,	,,	
53	June	,,	West		Mason
54	30 June	,,	Ashton		Mitford (T)
55	29 Aug.	London	*From* West		Mason
55*	c. 7 Sept.	Cambridge	*Ashton*		
56	Sept.	,,	West		Mason
57	17 Sept.	London	*From* West		,,
58	19 Sept.	,,	Walpole	Waller	
58*	Dec.	,,	West		Mitford (T)
	1739				
58**	Jan.	Epsom	*From West*		Gray (T)
59	1 Apr.	Amiens	Mrs. Gray		Mason
60	12 Apr.	Paris	West		,,
61	24 Apr.		Ashton		Mitford (T)
61*	Apr. or May		*West*		
62	c. 15 and 22 May		West		Mason
63	29 May		Ashton	Huntington	
63*	June	London	*From West*		
63**	June	Rheims	*West*		
64	21 June	,,	Mrs. Gray		Mason
65	July	,,	Gray and Walpole to Ashton		Mitford (T)
66	25 Aug.	,,	Ashton		,,
67	11 Sept.	Dijon	Philip Gray		Mason
68	18 Sept.	Lyons	West		,,
69	24 Sept.	London	*From* West to Gray and Walpole	Waller	
70	28 Sept.	,,	*From* West		Mason
71	13 Oct.	Lyons	Mrs. Gray		,,
72	25 Oct.	,,	Philip Gray		,,
73	7 Nov.	Turin	Mrs. Gray		,,
74	16 Nov.	,,	West		,,
75	21 Nov.	Genoa	,,		,,
76	9 Dec.	Bologna	Mrs. Gray		,,
77	19 Dec.	Florence	,,		,,

Note. The dates of letters written by Gray from France and Italy were New Style.

No. of Letter	Date	Place	Correspondent	Original Source	Printed Source or Transcript
	1740				
78	15 Jan.	Florence	West		Mason
78*	Feb. or Mar.	London	*From West*		
78**	Mar. or Apr.	Florence	*West*		
79	12 Mar.	,,	Wharton	Egerton	
80	19 Mar.	,,	Mrs. Gray		Mason
81	2 Apr.	Rome	,,		,,
82	15 Apr.	,,	,,		,,
83	16 Apr.	,,	Walpole and Gray to West		Orford
84	Apr.	London	*From* West		Mason
85	14 May	Rome	Walpole and Gray to Ashton	Quaritch	
86	20 and 21 May	Tivoli	West		Mason
87	May	Rome	,,		,,
88	14 June	Naples	Mrs. Gray		,,
89	5 June (o.s.)	London	*From West*		,,
90	10 July	Florence	Philip Gray		,,
91	16 July	,,	West		,,
92	31 July	,,	Walpole and Gray to West		Orford
93	21 Aug.	,,	Mrs. Gray		Mason
93*	Aug.	London?	*From West*		
94	25 Sept.	Florence	West		Mason
95	9 Oct.	,,	Philip Gray		,,
	1741				
96	12 Jan.	,,	,,		,,
96*	c. Apr.	,,	*West*		
96**	Apr.	London?	*From West*		
97	21 Apr.	Florence	West		Mason
98	c. 1 Sept.	Dover	*Chute*		
99	7 Sept.	London	Chute	Chute	
99*	Sept.		*From Conway*		
	1742				
100	28 Mar.	Popes	*From West*		Mason
101	c. 1 Apr.	London	West		,,
102	4 Apr.	Popes	*From West*		,,
103	8 Apr.	London	West		,,
104	c. 12 Apr.	Popes	*From West*		,,
105	23 Apr.	London	West	Loyd	
106	5 May	Popes	*From West*		Mason and Prideaux
107	8 May	London	West		Mason
108	11 May	Popes	*From West*		,,
108*	c. 20 May	London	*Chute*		
109	24 May	,,	Chute	Chute	
110	27 May	,,	West		Mason
110*	c. 3 June	Stoke	*West*		
111	17 June	,,	Ashton		Mitford (T)
112	July	London	Chute and Mann	Chute	

No. of Letter	Date	Place	Correspondent	Original Source	Printed Source or Transcript
	1743				
113	25 Oct. (1743 or 1744)	Cambridge	Chute	Chute	
114	27 Dec.	,,	Wharton	Egerton	
	1744				
115	26 Apr.	,, Cambridge	,,	Egerton	
	1745				
116	14 Nov.	Stoke	,,	,,	
	1746				
117	3 Feb.	Cambridge	Walpole	Waller	
118	28 Mar.	,,	,,	,,	
119	7 July	,,	,,	Haverford	
120	10 Aug.	Stoke	Wharton	Egerton	
121	11 Sept.	,,	,,	,,	
122	c. 6 Oct.	London	Chute	Chute	
123	8 Oct.	,,	Wharton	Egerton	
124	12 Oct.	Cambridge	Chute	Chute	
125	20 Oct.	,,	Walpole	Waller	
126	23 Nov.	,,	Chute	Chute	
127	11 Dec.	,,	Wharton	Egerton	
128	22 Dec.	,,	Walpole		Orford
129	27 Dec.	,,	Wharton	Egerton	
	1747				
130	Jan.	,,	Walpole		Orford
131	8 Feb.	,,	,,	Waller	
132	c. 15 Feb.	,,	,,	,,	
133	c. 22 Feb.	,,	,,		Mason
134	1 Mar.	,,	,,	,,	
135	17 Mar.	,,	Wharton	Egerton	
136	26 Mar.	,,	,,	,,	
137	c. 10 Apr.	,,	,,	,,	
138	13 May	Stoke	Walpole	Waller	
139	c. 15 June	Cambridge	,,		Mitford
140	Aug.	Stoke	,,	Waller	
141	9 Sept.	,,	,,	,,	
142	Nov.	Cambridge	,,		Orford
143	30 Nov.	,,	Wharton	Egerton	
143*	c. Dec.	,,	Whalley		
	1748				
144	Jan. or Feb.	,,	Walpole	Waller (part)	Orford (part)
145	5 June	London	Wharton	Egerton	
146	19 Aug.	Stoke	,,	,,	
147	c. 1748	Cambridge	Cole	R. B. Adam	
147*	c. 1748?	,,	Chute	Chute	
	1749				
148	9 Mar.	,,	Wharton	Egerton	
149	25 Apr.	,,	,,	,,	
150	8 Aug.	,,	,,	,,	
151	7 Nov.	,,	Mrs. Gray		Mason
152	12 Nov.	,,	Walpole	Waller	

List of Letters

No. of Letter	Date	Place	Correspondent	Original Source	Printed Source or Transcript
	1750				
153	12 June	Stoke	Walpole		Orford
154	9 Aug.	,,	Wharton	Egerton	
154*	Sept.	,,	*From* Lady Schaub		Mason
155	Oct.	,,	*From* Miss Speed		Mitford (T)
156	18 Dec.	Cambridge	Wharton	Egerton	
	1751				
157	11 Feb.	,,	Walpole	Waller	
158	20 Feb.	,,	,,		Orford
159	3 Mar.	,,	,,		,,
160	16 Apr.	,,	,,	Waller	
161	8 Sept.	,,	,,	,,	
162	29 Sept.	,,	,,	,,	
163	10 Oct.	,,	Wharton	Egerton	
164	26 Nov.	,,	Walpole	Waller	
165	31 Dec.	,,	,,	,,	
165*	c. Dec.	,,	Mason		Mitford
	1752				
166	9 Apr.	London	Wharton	Egerton	
167	28 May	Cambridge	Walpole		The Times
168	8 July	Stoke	,,	Waller	
169	July	,,	,,		Orford
169*	29 Sept.	,,	Wharton	Egerton	
169**	Nov.	London	*From* Robert Dodsley		
169*∗*	Nov.	Cambridge	Dodsley		
169‡‡	c. 15 Dec.	London	*From* Dodsley		
170	17 Dec.	Cambridge	Walpole	Waller	
171	19 Dec.	,,	Wharton	Egerton	
	1753				
171*	c. 11 Feb.	London	*From Walpole*		
172	12 Feb.	Cambridge	Dodsley	Eton	
173	13 Feb.	,,	Walpole	Waller	
173*	c. 15 Feb.	London	*From Walpole*		
173**	c. 17 Feb.	Cambridge	*Walpole*		
174	20 Feb.	London	*From* Walpole	Waller	
175	27 Feb.	Stoke	Walpole	,,	
176	15 Mar.	,,	Wharton	Egerton	
177	28 June	Cambridge	,,	,,	
178	14 July	,,	,,	,,	
179	24 July	Durham	Brown	Morgan	
180	21 Sept.	,,	Mason	Loyd	
181	23 Sept.	Hull	*From* Mason	,,	
182	26 Sept.	Durham	Mason	,,	
183	18 Oct.	Stoke	Wharton	Egerton	
184	5 Nov.	,,	Mason	Loyd	
184*	c. 1754	Cambridge	Brockett	Brit. Mus.	

No. of Letter	Date	Place	Correspondent	Original Source	Printed Source or Transcript
	1754				
185	15 Feb.	Cambridge	Walpole	Waller	
186	3 Mar.	,,	,,	,,	
187	17 Mar.	,,	,,	,,	
188	11 Apr.	,,	,,	,,	
189	23 May	,,	,,	,,	
189*	23 May	,,	Chute		
190	20 July	Stoke	Wharton		
191	13 Aug.	,,	Wharton	Egerton	
192	18 Sept.	,,	,,	,,	
193	10 Nov.	Cambridge	,,	,,	
194	26 Dec.	,,	,,	,,	
	1755				
195	1 Mar.	London	*From* Mason	Loyd	
196	9 Mar.	Cambridge	Wharton	Egerton	
197	27 June	Hanover	*From* Mason	Loyd	
198	22 July	The Vyne	Walpole	Waller	
199	6 Aug.	Stoke	Wharton	Egerton	
200	8 Aug.	,,	Walpole	Waller	
201	10 Aug.	,,	,,	,,	
202	14 Aug.	,,	,,	,,	
203	14 Aug.	,,	Chute	Chute	
204	21 Aug.	,,	Stonhewer		Mason
205	21 Aug.	,,	Wharton	Egerton	
205A			Text of the Bard		,,
206	10 Sept.	Tonbridge	*From* Mason	Loyd	
207	14 Oct.	Stoke	Walpole	Waller	
208	18 Oct.	,,	Wharton	Egerton	
209	26 Nov.	Wadworth	*From* Mason	Loyd	
210	25 Dec.	Cambridge	Bedingfield	Huntington	
211	25 Dec.	London	*From* Walpole	Waller	
212	25 Dec.	Chiswick	*From* Mason	Loyd	

xiii

VOLUME II

No. of Letter	Date	Place	Correspondent	Original Source	Printed Source or Transcript
	1756				
213	9 Jan.	Cambridge	Wharton	Egerton	
214	25 Jan.	,,	,,	,,	
215	29 Apr.	,,	Bedingfield	Huntington	
216	8 June	,,	Mason	Loyd	
217	14 June	,,	*Wharton*		
218	23 July	Stoke	Mason	Loyd	
219	30 July	,,	Walpole	Waller	
220	30 July	,,	Mason	Loyd	
221	4 Aug.	,,	Walpole	Waller	
222	27 Aug.	,,	Bedingfield	Huntington	
223	29 Aug.	,,	Walpole	Waller	
224	8 Sept.	The Vyne	,,	,,	
225	12 Sept.	,,	,,	,,	
226	19 Sept.	,,	,,	,,	
227	21 Sept.	,,	,,	,,	
228	15 Oct.	Stoke	Wharton	Egerton	
229	12 Nov.	,,	,,	,,	
230	19 Dec.	Cambridge	Mason	Loyd	
231	29 Dec.	,,	Bedingfield	Huntington	
	1757				
231*	7 Jan.	,,	*From* Hurd	Hartlebury	
232	12 Feb.	,,	Bedingfield	Huntington	
233	17 Feb.	,,	Wharton	Egerton	
234	3 Mar.	,,	,,	,,	
235	11 Mar.	London	Walpole	Waller	
236	17 Apr.	Cambridge	Wharton	Egerton	
237	23 Apr.	,,	Mason	Loyd	
237*	c. Apr.	,,	*From* Hurd	Hartlebury	
238	24 or 31 May	,,	Mason	Loyd	
239	11 June	,,	,,	,,	
240	11 July	Stoke	Walpole		Orford
241	25 July	,,	Brown	Loyd	
242	1 Aug.	,,	Mason	,,	
243	10 Aug.	,,	Walpole	Waller	
244	10 Aug.	,,	Bedingfield	Huntington	
245	14 Aug.	,,	Brown	Morgan	
245*	16 Aug.	Cambridge	*From* Hurd	Hartlebury	
246	17 Aug.	Stoke	Wharton	Egerton	
247	25 Aug.	,,	Hurd		Mitford
247*	28 Aug.	Cambridge	*From* Hurd	Hartlebury	
248	7 Sept.	Stoke	Mason	Loyd	
249	7 Sept.	,,	Wharton	Egerton	
250	28 Sept.	,,	Mason	Loyd	
251	7 Oct.	,,	Wharton	Egerton	
252	13 Oct.	,,	Walpole	Waller	
253	13 Oct.	,,	Mason	Loyd	
254	21 Oct.	,,	Walpole	Waller	
255	31 Oct.	,,	Wharton	Egerton	
256	31 Oct.	,,	Bedingfield	Huntington	

No. of Letter	Date	Place	Correspondent	Original Source	Printed Source or Transcript
	1757				
256*	c. 2 Dec.	Andover	*From* Butler		Mason
257	8 Dec.	Cambridge	Wharton	Egerton	
258	12 Dec.	,,	,,	,,	
258*	c. 13 Dec.	London	*From Mason*		
258**	c. 15 Dec.	Cambridge	*Mason*		
258*₊*	c. 17 Dec.	London	*From Mason*		
259	19 Dec.	Cambridge	Mason	Loyd	
260	c. 27 Dec.	,,	*Mason*		
	1758				
261	5 Jan.	Syon Hill	*From* Mason	Loyd	
261A			Gray's Copy of Mason's Ode		Gray (T)
262	13 Jan.	Cambridge	Mason	Loyd	
263	16 Jan.	Syon Hill	*From* Mason	,,	
263*	c. 16 Jan.	Cambridge	*Butler*		
264	17 Jan.	,,	Walpole	Waller	
265	22 Jan.	,,	Mason	Loyd	
265*	c. 23 Jan.	Andover	*From* Butler		Mason
266	31 Jan.	Cambridge	Bedingfield	Huntington	
266*	3 Feb.	,,	Mason	Loyd	
267	21 Feb.	,,	Wharton	Egerton	
268	8 Mar.	,,	,,		Mason
269	24 Mar.	,,	Mason	Loyd	
270	9 Apr.	,,	Wharton	Egerton	
271	18 June	,,	,,	,,	
272	20 June	,,	Mason	Loyd	
273	22 July	Stoke	Walpole	Waller	
273*	Aug.	,,	Palgrave	Lady Charnwood	
274	9 Aug.	,,	Wharton	Egerton	
275	11 Aug.	,,	Mason	Loyd	
276	18 Aug.	,,	Stonhewer		Mason
277	31 Aug.	,,	Wharton	Egerton	
278	6 Sept.	,,	Palgrave		Mason
279	7 Sept.	,,	Brown	Harvard	
280	16 Sept.	,,	Wharton	Egerton	
281	28 Oct.	,,	Brown		Mitford
282	9 Nov.	,,	Wharton	Egerton	
283	9 Nov.	,,	Mason	Loyd	
283*	Nov.?	,,	Mary Antrobus		Maggs
284	Nov.	Aston	*From* Mason	Loyd	
284*	c. 28 Nov.	Stoke	Mason	,,	
285	2 Dec.	,,	Wharton	Egerton	
	1759				
286	18 Jan.	London	Mason	Loyd	
287	22 Jan.	Aston	*From* Mason	,,	
288	25 Jan.	,,	,, ,,	,,	
289	14 Feb.	London	Walpole	Waller	

xv

B

List of Letters

No. of Letter	Date	Place	Correspondent	Original Source	Printed Source or Transcript
	1759				
290	15 Feb.	London	*From* Walpole	Waller	
291	1 Mar.	Cambridge	Mason	Loyd	
292	10 Apr.	London	,,	,,	
293	3 May	,,	Mary Antrobus	A. E. Newton	
294	28 May	,,	Brown	Fitzwilliam Museum	
295	c: May?	,,	*Mary Antrobus*		
296	21 July	,,	Wharton	Egerton	
297	23 July	,,	Mason	Loyd	
298	24 July	,,	Palgrave		Mason
299	8 Aug.	,,	Brown	Loyd	
299*	11 Aug.	,,	,,	,,	
299**	c. 20 Aug.	,,	*Miss Speed*		
300	25 Aug.	Stoke	*From* Miss Speed	Morgan	
301	c. 15 Sept.	London	Mary Antrobus	Rosenbach	
302	8 Sept.	,,	Mrs. Antrobus	Rochester	
303	18 Sept.	,,	Wharton	Egerton	
304	6 Oct.	Stoke	Mason	Loyd	
304*	27 Oct.	London	Mrs. Jennings	Antiquaries	
305	24 Nov.	,,	Mary Antrobus	Rosenbach	
306	28 Nov.	,,	Wharton	Egerton	
307	1 Dec.	,,	Mason	Loyd	
	1760				
308	23 Jan.	,,	Wharton	Egerton	
309	c. 28 Mar.	,,	Brown	Pennsylvania	
310	c. Apr.	,,	Walpole		Orford
311	22 Apr.	,,	Wharton	Egerton	
311*	May	,,	*Macpherson*		
312	7 June	,,	Mason	Loyd	
313	c. 20 June	,,	Wharton	Egerton	
314	27 June	,,	Mason	Loyd	
315	29 June	[London]	Stonhewer		Mason
316	26 July	London	Brown		Mitford
317	7 Aug.	Cambridge	Mason	Loyd	
318	12 Aug.	,,	Clerke		Mason
319	Aug.	Strawberry Hill	*From* Walpole	Waller	
319*	c. 31 Aug.	Cambridge	Mason	Loyd	
320	2 Sept.	,,	Walpole	Waller	
321	21 Oct.	London	Wharton	Egerton	
322	23 Oct.	,,	Brown	Pennsylvania	
323	25 Oct.	,,	,,	Quaritch	
324	c. 28 Oct.	,,	Walpole	Waller	
324*	c. Oct.	,,	Mrs. Jennings	Last	
325	8 Nov.	,,	Brown	Eton	
326	28 Nov.	Aston	*From* Mason	Loyd	

Note. For Letters 301, 302 see Addendum in Vol. II.

No. of Letter	Date	Place	Correspondent	Original Source	Printed Source or Transcript
	1760				
327	10 Dec.	London	Mason	Loyd	
328	Dec.	,,	Walpole		Orford
	1761				
329	8 Jan.	Aston	*From* Mason	Loyd	
330	22 Jan.	London	Mason	,,	
331	31 Jan.	,,	Wharton	Egerton	
332	9 Feb.	,,	Brown	Eton	
333	9 May	,,	Wharton	Egerton	
333*	May?	,,	Walpole	Waller	
334	26 May	,,	Brown	Pemb. Coll.	
335	13 June	,,	,,		Mitford
336	23 June	Cambridge	Wharton	Egerton	
337	19 July	,,	,,	,,	
338	20 July	Aston	*From* Mason	Loyd	
339	Aug.	Cambridge	Mason	,,	
340	2 Sept.	,,	Percy	Brit. Mus.	
341	Sept.?		Anstey		Anstey
342	8 Sept.	London	Wharton	Egerton	
343	10 Sept.	,,	Walpole	Waller	
344	19 Sept.	,,	Brown		Morrison Catalogue
345	24 Sept.	,,	,,		K. Fess (T
346	c. 20 Oct.	,,	Mason	Loyd	
347	22 Oct.	,,	Brown		Transcript at Pemb. Coll.
348	22 Oct.	,,	Wharton	Egerton	
349	7 Nov.	,,	Brown	Loyd	
350	13 Nov.	,,	Wharton	Egerton	
351	8 Dec.	Cambridge	Mason	Loyd	
351*	Dec.	,,	Stonhewer		Mason
351**	Dec.	,,	Walpole	Waller	
	1762				
352	11 Jan.	Cambridge	Mason	Loyd	
353	11 Jan.	,,	Wharton	Egerton	
354	5 Feb.	,,	Mason	Loyd	
355	11 Feb.	,,	Walpole	Waller	
356	28 Feb.	,,	,,		Orford
357	17 Mar.	,,	Mason	Loyd	
358	4 June	,,	Wharton	Egerton	
359	21 June	,,	Mason	Loyd	
360	10 July	York	Wharton	Egerton	
361	19 July	Old Park	Brown		Mitford
362	1 Sept.?	,,	Mason	Loyd	
363	4 Dec.	Cambridge	Wharton	Egerton	
364	21 Dec.	,,	Mason	Loyd	
	1763				
365	15 Jan.	Aston	*From* Mason	,,	
366	8 Feb.	Cambridge	Mason	,,	
367	Feb.	,,	Brown	Brit. Mus.	
368	6 Mar.	,,	Mason	Loyd	

List of Letters

No. of Letter	Date	Place	Correspondent	Original Source	Printed Source or Transcript
	1763				
369	24 Apr.	Pisa	*From* Algarotti	Loyd	
370	25 Apr.	,,	*From* How	Brit. Mus.	
371	28 June	York	*From* Mason	Loyd	
372	July	Cambridge	Mason	,,	
373	5 Aug.	,,	Wharton	Egerton	
374	9 Sept.	,,	Algarotti		Transcript in Brit. Mus.
375	10 Sept.	,,	How	Brit. Mus.	
376	12 Sept.	,,	Walpole	Waller	
377	19 Sept.	,,	,,	,,	
378	29 Sept.	Spa	*From* How	Brit. Mus.	
379	8 Oct.	Cambridge	Mason	Loyd	
380	10 Oct.	,,	Robinson		Gent. Mag.
381	8 Nov.	Brussels	*From* How	Brit. Mus.	
382	Nov.	London	How	,,	
	1764				
383	27 Jan.	Cambridge	Walpole	Waller	
384	31 Jan.	,,	,,	,,	
385	21 Feb.	,,	Wharton	Egerton	
386	18 Mar.	,,	Walpole	Waller	
387	No letter corresponding to this number				
388	25 Apr.	Cambridge	Walpole	Waller	
389	10 July	,,	,,	,,	
390	10 July	,,	Wharton	Egerton	
391	17 Aug.	,,	Walpole	Waller	
391*	Sept. or Oct.	London	Mary Antrobus	Pennsylvania	
392	1 or 8 Oct.	Southampton	Brown	Brit. Mus.	
393	13 Oct.	,,	,,	Pennsylvania	
394	25 Oct.	London	,,		Mitford
395	29 Oct.	,,	,,		,,
396	No letter corresponding to this number				
397	19 Nov.	London	Nicholls	Eton	
398	30 Dec.	Cambridge	Walpole	Waller	
	1765				
399	17 Jan.	,,	Mason	Loyd	
399*	March	,,	Bentham		Gent. Mag.
400	March	,,	Palgrave		Mason
400*	14 Apr.	,,	Walpole	Waller	
401	29 Apr.	,,	Wharton	Egerton	
402	May?	London	Brown	Pemb. Coll.	
403	20 May	,,	,,	Bodleian	
404	23 May	,,	Mason	Loyd	
405	4 June	York	Bedingfield	Huntington	
406	6 June	,,	Wharton	Egerton	
407	8 July	Old Park	Mason	Loyd	
408	22 July	Aston	*From* Mason	,,	
409	15 Aug.	Old Park	Brown		Tovey
410	30 Aug.	Aberdeen	*From* Beattie		Forbes
411	8 Sept.	Glamis	Beattie	Aberdeen	

xviii

No. of Letter	Date	Place	Correspondent	Original Source	Printed Source or Transcript
	1765				
412	30 Sept.	Glamis	Wharton	Egerton	
413	2 Oct.	,,	Beattie	Aberdeen	
414	2 Nov.	London	Brown	Bodleian	
415	8 Nov.	,,	Mason	Loyd	
416	10 Nov.	,,	Walpole	Waller	
417	19 Nov.	Paris	*From* Walpole	,,	
418	13 Dec.	Cambridge	Walpole		Orford
418*	Dec.	,,	Mary Antrobus	Rosenbach	

VOLUME III

List of Letters

No. of Letter	Date	Place	Correspondent	Original Source	Printed Source or Transcript
	1768				
463	17 Jan.	Cambridge	Wharton	Egerton	
464	28 Jan.	,,	Nicholls	Eton	
465	c. 1 Feb.	,,	James Dodsley	Brit. Mus.	
466	1 Feb.	,,	Beattie	Aberdeen and A. H. H. Murray	
467	3 Feb.	,,	Nicholls	Eton	
468	14 Feb.	,,	Walpole		Orford
469	16 Feb.	Aberdeen	From Beattie	Aberdeen	
470	18 Feb.	London	From Walpole		Orford
471	25 Feb.	Cambridge	Walpole		,,
472	26 Feb.	London	From Walpole		,,
473	6 Mar.	Cambridge	Walpole		,,
474	8 Mar.	London	From Walpole	Waller	
475	15 Mar.	Cambridge	Wharton	Egerton	
476	27 Apr.	London	Brown		Gosse
477	29 May	,,	Nicholls		Mitford
477*	27 July	,,	From Duke of Grafton		
478	27 or 28 July	,,	Duke of Grafton		Mason
479	29 July	,,	Mary Antrobus		Mitford
480	1 Aug.	,,	Wharton	Egerton	
481	1 Aug.	,,	Mason	Loyd	
482	3 Aug.	,,	Nicholls	Eton	
483	6 Aug.	Blundeston	From Nicholls		Mitford
484	8 Aug.	Hornby Castle	From Mason	Loyd	
485	27 Aug.	London	Nicholls	Eton	
486	7 Sept.	Cambridge	Mason	Loyd	
487	31 Oct.	,,	Beattie	Aberdeen	
488	8 Nov.	,,	Nicholls	Eton	
488*	Dec.	,,	Palgrave		
489	29 Dec.	,,	Mason	Loyd	
	1769				
490	2 Jan.	,,	Nicholls	Eton	
491	26 Jan.	,,	,,	,,	
491*	end Jan.		Percy [?]	Brit. Mus.	
492	Apr.	London	Walpole	Waller	
493	20 Apr.	,,	Wharton	Egerton	
494	c. 20 Apr.		Brown		Mitford
495	26 May	Cambridge	Walpole	Waller	
496	7 June	,,	Nicholls	Eton	
497	12 June		Stonhewer		Mason
498	14 June	Blundeston	From Nicholls		Mitford
499	24 June	Cambridge	Nicholls	Eton	
500	3 July	Blundeston	From Nicholls		Mitford
501	16 July	Cambridge	Beattie	Aberdeen	
502	17 July	,,	Wharton	Egerton	
503	26 Aug.	Old Park	Mason	Loyd	
504	10 Oct.	Lancaster	Brown		Mitford

List of Letters

List of Letters

No. of Letter	Date	Place	Correspondent	Original Source	Printed Source or Transcript
	1770				
538	22 Dec.	Milton	*From Cole*		
539	22 Dec.	Cambridge	Cole		Cole (T)
	1771				
540	26 Jan.	,,	Nicholls	Eton	
541	31 Jan.	Blundeston	*From* Nicholls		Mitford
541*	Jan. or Feb.	Cambridge	Ashby	Pemb. Coll.	
542	2 Feb.	,,	Wharton	Egerton	
543	24 Feb.	,,	Nicholls	Eton	
544	8 Mar.	,,	Beattie		Forbes
545	16 Mar.	Blundeston	*From* Nicholls		Mitford
545*	17 Mar.	Cambridge	Walpole		Mason
545**	c. 23 Mar.	,,	*Walpole*		
546	25 Mar.	London	*From* Walpole	Waller	
547	27 Mar.	,,	*From* Mason	Loyd	
547*	c. 13 Apr.	Cambridge	*Stonhewer*		
548	15 Apr.	London	*From* Mason	Loyd	
549	29 Apr.	Blundeston	*From* Nicholls		Mitford
550	3 May	Cambridge	Nicholls	Eton	
551	14 May	Blundeston	*From* Nicholls		Mitford
552	20 May	London	Nicholls	Eton	
553	24 May	,,	Wharton	Egerton	
554	27 May	Blundeston	*From* Nicholls		Mitford
555	22 June	London	Brown	Bodleian	
556	28 June	,,	Nicholls	Eton	
557	29 June	Paris	*From* Nicholls		Mitford

CHRONOLOGICAL TABLE

THE following table serves a double purpose.

The first column shows where Gray was at different dates: it records his places of residence, his journeys, and where he stayed. By a reference to this column the place from which any particular letter was written can be traced.

The second column gives the more important events in Gray's uneventful life and records the dates of the composition and publication of his works. The numbers of the letters are given for some of the entries. It should be noted that some of the dates are approximate, and that the time spent on Gray's journeys from place to place is not always stated.

1716 26 Dec. to *c.* **1725** } Living in Cornhill.	26 Dec. Born at his father's house in Cornhill.
c. **1725** to **1734** Sept. } At School at Eton.	4 July. Entered at Peterhouse.
9 Oct. to **1735** 31 July } Cambridge.	9 Oct. Admitted at Peterhouse.
31 July to 18 Oct. } London and elsewhere.	
18 Oct. to 24 Dec. Cambridge	22 Nov. Admitted at Inner Temple.
24 Dec. to **1736** 23 Jan. } London.	
23 Jan. to } Cambridge. 12 Feb.	9 Feb. Dr. Audley's Opinion (App. A). 12 Feb. His Aunt Sarah Gray died and left him her property.
12 Feb. to 5 Mar. London.	
5 Mar. to } Cambridge. 6 June	May. *Hymeneal* on the Marriage of the Prince of Wales in the Cambridge *Gratulatio* (23).
6 June to 22 Oct. } London and Burnham.	
23 Oct. to **1737** 28 July } Cambridge.	Mar. *Luna est habitabilis* (Tripos Verses, 35).
28 July to 15 Nov. } London and elsewhere.	
15 Nov. to **1738** 27 Apr. } Cambridge.	
27 Apr. to 26 May. London(?).	
26 May to 14 Sept. Cambridge.	
14 Sept. to **1739** 18 Mar. (O.S.) } London.	
29 Mar. (N.S.)[1] to } Journey to 4 Apr. } Paris.	29 Mar. Began his tour to France and Italy with Walpole (59).

[1] The dates during Gray's journey are in New Style.

xxiv

1739 4 Apr. to 2 June. Paris.

2 June to 7 Sept. Rheims.

7–15 Sept. Journey to Lyons.

13 Sept. to ⎱ Lyons with excur-
31 Oct.   ⎰ sion to Geneva.

31 Oct. ⎫ Journey from Lyons
  to   ⎬ by Turin, Genoa,
16 Dec. ⎭ Bologna to Florence.

16 Dec. to ⎫
1740 21 Mar. ⎬ Florence.

21–25 Mar. Journey to Rome.

25 Mar. ⎫ Rome with excursions
  to   ⎬ to Tivoli and Naples.
4 July ⎭

4–7 July. Journey to Florence.

7 July ⎫ Florence with excur-
  to   ⎬ sion to Bologna in
1741 24 Apr.⎭ Aug. 1740.

24 Apr. to 3 May. To Bologna and Reggio, and at Reggio.

3 May to 15 July. Venice.

15 July ⎫ Journey by Padua,
  to   ⎬ Verona, Milan, Lyons,
12 Sept.⎭ and Paris to London.

1 Sept. (O.S.) ⎫ London with
  to   ⎬ visits (prob-
1742 28 May ⎭ ably to Stoke).

28 May to ⎫
19 June   ⎬ Stoke.

19 June to *c.* 15 July. London.

c. 15 July to ⎫ Stoke and Lon-
15 Oct.   ⎬ don.

15 Oct. ⎫
        ⎪
  to   ⎬ Cambridge.
        ⎪
1743 23 June⎭

23 June to ⎫
30 Sept.   ⎬ Stoke and London.

30 Sept. ⎫
  to   ⎬ Cambridge.
1744 8 July ⎭

8 July to ⎫
5 Oct.   ⎬ Stoke and London.

5 Oct. to ⎫ Cambridge.
1745 12 May ⎭

12 May to ⎫
13 Sept. ⎬ Stoke and London.

De Principiis Cogitandi begun (sometime in 1740).

c. 3 May. Quarrel with Walpole at Reggio.

21 Aug. *Ode* written in the album at the *Grande Chartreuse.*

6 Nov. Philip Gray died.
Winter (1741–2). *Agrippina* begun (101).
Mar.(?). *Hymn to Ignorance* written.
1 June. West died (110*).
3 June. *Ode on the Spring* sent to West.

Aug. *Eton Ode, Sonnet on the death of West,* and *Hymn to Adversity* composed.

15 Oct. Returned to Peterhouse as a Fellow-commoner.
21 Oct. Jonathan Rogers died.
Dec.(?). Mrs. Gray and Mary Antrobus retired from Cornhill to Stoke.

Dec. Admitted to degree of Bachelor of Laws (114).

1745 13 Sept. to 7 Nov. Cambridge.
7–22 Nov. London and Stoke.

    8 Nov. Reconciliation with Walpole and Ashton (116).

22 Nov. to ⎫
1746 13 July ⎬ Cambridge.
13 July to 10 Oct. London and Stoke (with an excursion to Hampton Court and other places (120)).
10–30 Oct. Cambridge.
30 Oct. to 15 Nov. London.

15 Nov. ⎫ Cambridge (with a
      to ⎬ few days' absence in
1747 8 May ⎭ February).

    1 Mar. *Ode on the Cat* sent to Walpole (134).

8–22 May. Stoke and London.
22 May to 16 Aug. Cambridge.
16 Aug. to 23 Oct. London, Stoke, Strawberry Hill, &c.

    30 May. *Eton Ode* published (139).

23 Oct. to ⎫
1748 8 Apr.   ⎬ Cambridge.

    15 Jan. Dodsley's *Collection of Poems* (containing three poems by Gray) published (144).
    25 Mar. Fire in Cornhill. Gray's house burnt (145).

8 Apr. to 5 Nov. London and Stoke with visit to Strawberry Hill and perhaps visit to Cobham &c. (191, n. 22).

    Aug.(?). *Alliance of Education and Government* begun (146).

5 Nov. to ⎫
1749 21 May ⎬ Cambridge.
21 May to ⎫
27 June   ⎬ Stoke and London.
27 June to 14 Sept. Cambridge.
14–26 Sept. Stoke(?).
26 Sept. to 23 Nov. Cambridge.

    5 Nov. Mary Antrobus died (151).

23 Nov. to ⎫
1750 5 Jan.   ⎬ Stoke and London.
5 Jan. to ⎫
3 June   ⎬ Cambridge.
3 June ⎫
    to   ⎬ Stoke.
15 Nov. ⎭
15 Nov. to 7 Dec. London.

    12 June. The *Elegy* finished and sent to Walpole (153).
    Oct.(?). The *Long Story* sent to Lady Cobham (155).

7 Dec. to ⎫
1751 10 Mar. ⎬ Cambridge.
10–29 Mar. London.
29 Mar. to 6 June. Cambridge.

    15 Feb. The *Elegy* published (157).

1751	6 June to 2 Sept. } Stoke and London.	
	2 Sept. to } Cambridge (with brief visit to Abbots Ripton in Sept.	
1752	2 Apr.	
	2–15 Apr. London.	
	15 Apr. to 21 June. Cambridge.	
	21 June } Stoke (with visits to to } Strawberry Hill and 13 Oct. } London.	July or (before). *Progress of Poesy* begun (169).
1753	13 Oct. to } 22 Feb. } Cambridge.	
	22 Feb. to } Stoke. 13 Apr.	11 Mar. Mrs. Gray died (176). 29 Mar. *Six Poems with Bentley's Designs* published (175).
	13 Apr. to 16 July. Cambridge.	
	16 July to 3 Oct. Trip to the north and visit to Durham.	
	3–4 Oct. Cambridge.	
	4 Oct. to } 21 Dec. } Stoke and London.	
1754	21 Dec. to } 21 Jan. } Cambridge.	
	21 Jan. to 8 Feb. London(?).	
	8 Feb. to 16 June. Cambridge.	
	16 June } Stoke (with tour to to } Northants, Warwick, 27 Sept. } &c.) and London.	
	27 Sept. to } 20 Dec. } Cambridge	Dec. (or before). *Progress of Poesy* finished (194).
	20–27 Dec. Away from Cambridge.	
1755	27 Dec. to } 24 Apr. } Cambridge.	1754–5. The *Bard* and *Ode on Vicissitude* begun (196). 1755.[1] Offer of Secretaryship to Earl of Bristol at Lisbon declined.
	24 Apr. to 15 July. London, Stoke, the Vyne, &c.	
	15–31 July. The Vyne with trip to Portsmouth, Southampton, Winchester, &c.	
	1 Aug. } Stoke (with visit to to } Strawberry Hill) and 26 Nov. } London.	
1756	26 Nov. to } 3 Apr. } Cambridge.	5 Mar. Migration from Peterhouse to Pembroke (214).

[1] Walpole in his brief *Memoir of Gray* (App. Y) says in the winter of 1755: the winter of 1754–5 seems to have been meant.

1756 3–8 Apr. London.
8 Apr. to 16 June. Cambridge.
16 June to 3 Dec. London and
Stoke (with visit to Straw-
berry Hill).

1757 3 Dec. to ⎱ Cambridge.
5 Mar. ⎰

                                         Feb. Tuthill deprived of his Fellowship
at Pembroke (App. G).

5 Mar. to 2 Apr. London.
2 Apr. to 17 June. Cambridge.
17 June ⎱ London and Stoke
to ⎰ with visit to Straw-   8 Aug. *Odes* published (240, n. 2).
4 Dec. ⎰ berry Hill.

4 Dec. ⎱ Cambridge (with a   15 Dec. Poet Laureateship offered to
to ⎰ brief visit to Abbots   Gray and declined (258*).
⎰ Ripton at the end of
1758 16 Apr. ⎰ Jan).   Jan. (or before). *Epitaph on Mrs. Clerke*
composed (266).

16 Apr. to 15 May. London.
15 May ⎱ Cambridge (with tour
to ⎰ to Ely, Peterborough,
29 June ⎰ &c.).

29 June ⎱ London and Stoke,   July(?). *Epitaph on a Child* written for
to ⎰ Hampton Court and   Wharton (271).
31 July ⎰ Strawberry Hill, &c.

31 July to ⎱ Stoke with brief visit   Sept. Mrs. Rogers died (281).
12 Dec. ⎰ to London in Oct.

1759 12 Dec. to ⎱ London.
15 Feb. ⎰
15 Feb. to 4 Mar. Cambridge.
4 Mar. to 29 June. London.
29 June to 9 July. Cambridge.
9 July ⎱ London with excur-   July. Gray took up his residence in
to ⎰ sion to Strawberry   London (296).
23 Sept. ⎰ Hill, &c.

23 Sept. to ⎱ Stoke (at Lady   Sept. Alderman Nutting died (302).
15 Oct. ⎰ Cobham's).

15 Oct. ⎱ London with visit to
to ⎰ Strawberry Hill in   Mar. Lady Cobham died (311).
1760 28 June ⎰ June, &c.   June to July. Gray and Miss Speed
28 June to ⎱ Shiplake.   stayed with Mrs. Jennings (318).
21 July ⎰
21–29 July. London.
29 July to 6 Oct. Cambridge.

1761 6 Oct. to ⎱ London.
15 June ⎰   Apr. (or before). *The Fatal Sisters* and
The Descent of Odin composed (471,
n. 1a).

15–29 June. Cambridge.

1761 29 June to⎫ Tour in Suffolk
      11 July ⎭ and Norfolk.
      11 July to⎫ Cambridge.
      8 Sept. ⎭
      8 Sept. to⎫ London.
      19 Nov. ⎭

      19 Nov.⎫
         to ⎬ Cambridge.
1762 22 Mar.⎭

      22 Mar. to 30 May. London.
      30 May to 1 July. Cambridge.
      1 July to⎫ York and Old Park.
      11 Nov. ⎭
      11–18 Nov. Journey to London.
      18–25 Nov. London.

      25 Nov. to⎫ Cambridge.
1763 6 May ⎭
      6 May ⎫ London with 'a little
        to ⎬ jaunt to Epsom and
      16 June⎭ Boxhill'.
      16 June to 19 Sept. Cambridge.
      19 Sept. to⎫ 'A ramble away
      4 Oct. ⎭ from Cambridge.'
      4 Oct. to 4 Nov. Cambridge.
      4 Nov. to 8 Dec. London.

      8 Dec. to⎫ Cambridge.
1764 16 May ⎭

      16 May to 25 June. London.
      25 June to 4 Sept. Cambridge.
      4 to 25 Sept. London.
      25 Sept. to 22 Oct. Winchester,
        Southampton, Salisbury, Wil-
        ton, Stonehenge, &c.
      22 Oct. to 21 Nov. London.

      21 Nov. to⎫ Cambridge.
1765 30 Apr. ⎭
      30 Apr. to⎫ London with visit
      27 May ⎭ to Windsor.
      27 May⎫ York and Old Park
        to ⎬ with visits to Hartle-
      18 Aug.⎭ pool.

Aug. *Epitaph on Sir W. Williams* com-
  posed (339).
Oct. Song (*Thyrsis*) written for Miss
  Speed.
12 Nov. Miss Speed married to Baron
  de la Perrière (353).
Nov. Gray gave up his lodgings in
  London (347).
Sometime in this year *The Triumph of
  Owen* and other imitations of Welsh
  poetry composed (App. M).

Nov. Gray's name suggested for the
Regius Professorship of Modern History
(363).

March(?). *The Candidate* composed
(App. P).

1765 18 Aug. to 17 Oct. Journey to Glamis, stay at Glamis, with excursion to the Highlands.

7–14 Oct. Journey by Perth, Stirling, and Edinburgh to Old Park.

14–28 Oct. Old Park.

28 Oct. to 2 Dec. London.

2 Dec. to
1766 16 Apr. } Cambridge.

16 Apr. to 16 May. London.

16 May to 4 July } Canterbury and Denton with excursion to Margate and Dover.

4–17 July. London.

17–24 July. Cambridge.

24 July to 3 Aug. Away from Cambridge.

3 Aug. to 11 Sept. Cambridge.

11–22 Sept. Suffolk and Norfolk.

22 Sept. to 6 Oct. Cambridge.

6 Oct. to 5 Dec. London.

5 Dec. to
1767 20 Apr. } Cambridge.

20 Apr. to 13 June. London with excursion to Chiswick, Strawberry Hill, &c., at the end of May.

13–15 June. Cambridge.

15 June to 1 July. Aston (with a visit to Dovedale and the Peak) and York.

1 July to 24 Oct. Old Park with visits to Rokeby and Richmond, Hartlepool, Carlisle, Keswick, &c.

24 Oct. to 2 Nov. York.

2 Nov. to 14 Dec. London.

14 Dec. to
1768 7 Apr. } Cambridge.

7 Apr. to 15 July(?) } Ramsgate, Denton, and other places in Kent.

15 July(?) to 31 Aug. } London.

1–15 Sept. Cambridge.

15 Sept. to 6 Oct. Lovingland, Norwich, and Newmarket.

6 Oct. to 10 Nov. } Cambridge.

12 Mar. *Poems* published by Dodsley (470).

4 May. Poems published by Foulis (487).

July. *Verses on Lord Holland's Villa* composed (App. T).

28 July. Appointed Regius Professor of Modern History (477* ff.).

Oct.(?). New edition of *Poems* published by Dodsley (487).

1768   10 Nov. to 23 Dec. London.

1769   23 Dec. to ⎫ Cambridge.
       3 Apr. ⎭

       3 Apr. to ⎫ London and else-   Apr. *Installation Ode* composed (493).
       16 May ⎭ where.

       16 May to ⎫ Cambridge.   1 July. Installation of Chancellor.
       8 July   ⎭

       8–16 July. London.
       18–23 July. York.
       23 July to 29 Sept. Old Park
         with excursion to Hartlepool.
       29 Sept. ⎫ Tour in the Lakes,
         to   ⎬ Lancashire and
       15 Oct. ⎭ Yorkshire.
       15–22 Oct. Journey to Cam-
         bridge by Leeds, Aston, &c.
       22 Oct. to 4 Dec. Cambridge.
       4–21 Dec. London.   Dec. Made acquaintance of Bonstetten
                                              and took him to Cambridge (508,512).

       21 Dec. to ⎫ Cambridge.
1770   21 Mar. ⎭
       21 Mar. to 2 Apr. London.   Mar. Bonstetten left England (514).
       2–23 Apr. Cambridge.
       23 Apr. to ⎫ Thrapston and
       7 May   ⎭ Lovingland.
       7–10. May. Cambridge.   2 July. Made his will (App. X).
       10–31 May. London.
       31 May to 3 June. Cambridge.
       3–19 June. Aston.
       19 June to 2 July. Cambridge.
       2 July to 3 Aug. Tour in Wor-
         cestershire, Gloucestershire,
         Monmouthshire, Hereford-
         shire, &c.
       3–17 Aug. London.

       17 Aug. to ⎫ Cambridge.   Dec. James Brown elected Master of
1771   1 Jan.   ⎭   Pembroke (540).
       1–17 Jan. London.
       17 Jan. to 16 May. Cambridge.
       16 May to 22 July. London.
       22–30 July. Cambridge.   30 July. Died (App. W).

LIST OF ILLUSTRATIONS

VOLUME III

List of Illustrations

*** *Grateful acknowledgement is made to the owners of the original pictures
and letters, for permission to reproduce them.*

419. WALPOLE TO GRAY

Paris, January 25, 1766.

I AM much indebted to you for your kind letter and advice; and though it is late to thank you for it, it is at least a stronger proof that I do not forget it. However, I am a little obstinate, as you know, on the chapter of health, and have persisted through this Siberian winter in not adding a grain to my clothes, and in going open-breasted without an under-waistcoat. In short, though I like extremely to live, it must be in my own way, as long as I can: it is not youth I court, but liberty; and I think making one's self tender, is ifsuing a *general warrant* against one's own person. I suppose I shall submit to confinement, when I cannot help it; but I am indifferent enough to life not to care if it ends soon after my prison begins.

I have not delayed so long to answer your letter, from not thinking of it, or from want of matter, but from want of time. I am constantly occupied, engaged, amused, till I cannot bring a hundredth part of what I have to say into the compafs of a letter. You will lose nothing by this: you know my volubility, when I am full of new subjects; and I have at least many hours of conversation for you at my return. One does not learn a whole nation in four or five months; but, for the time, few, I believe, have seen, studied, or got so much acquainted with the French as I have.

By what I said of their religious or rather irreligious opinions, you must not conclude their people of quality, atheists—at least not the men—Happily for them, poor souls! they are not capable of going so far into thinking. They afsent to a great deal, because it is the fashion, and because they don't know how to contradict. They are ashamed to defend the Roman catholic religion, because it is quite exploded; but I am convinced they believe it in their hearts. They hate the parliaments and the philosophers, and are rejoiced that they may still idolize royalty. At present too they are a little triumphant: the court has shown a little spirit, and the parliaments much lefs: but as the duc de Choiseul,[1] who is very fluttering, unsettled, and inclined to the

LETTER 419.—First printed in *Works of Lord Orford*, vol. v, pp. 361–7.

[1] Étienne François de Choiseul-Stainville (1719–85), Duc de Choiseul, who became Minister for Foreign Affairs in this year. He was disgraced and exiled in 1770, owing to the intrigues of Madame du Barry.

philosophers, has made a compromise with the parliament of Bretagne, the parliaments might venture out again, if, as I fancy will be the case, they are not glad to drop a cause, of which they began to be a little weary of the inconveniences. The generality of the men, and more than the generality, are dull and empty. They have taken up gravity, thinking it was philosophy and English, and so have acquired nothing in the room of their natural levity and cheerfulness. However, as their high opinion of their own country remains, for which they can no longer afsign any reason, they are contemptuous and reserved, instead of being ridiculously, consequently pardonably, impertinent. I have wondered, knowing my own countrymen, that we had attained such a superiority.—I wonder no longer, and have a little more respect for English *heads* than I had.

The women do not seem of the same country: if they are lefs gay than they were, they are more informed, enough to make them very conversable. I know six or seven with very superior understandings; some of them with wit, or with softnefs, or very good sense.

Madame Geoffrin,[2] of whom you have heard much, is an extraordinary woman, with more common sense than I almost ever met with. Great quicknefs in discovering characters, penetration in going to the bottom of them, and a pencil that never fails in a likenefs—seldom a favourable one. She exacts and preserves, spite of her birth and their nonsensical prejudices about nobility, great court and attention. This she acquires by a thousand little arts and offices of friendship; and by a freedom and severity, which seems to be her sole end of drawing a concourse to her; for she insists on scolding those she inveigles to her. She has little taste and lefs knowledge, but protects artisans[3] and authors, and courts a few people to have the credit of serving her dependents. She was bred under the famous madame Tencin,[4] who advised her never to refuse any man; for, said her mistrefs, though nine in ten should not care a farthing for you, the tenth may live to be an useful friend. She

[2] Marie Thérèse Geoffrin, *née* Rodet (1699–1777), widow of a wealthy manufacturer, who for many years presided over a *salon* in Paris.

[3] 'Artisan' was used until the end of the eighteenth century in the sense of 'artist'. Philemon Holland in his translation of Pliny (p. 535) describes Zeuxis as 'a professed artisane'.

[4] Claudine Alexandrine Guérin (1681–1749), Marquise de Tencin, at one time mistress of the Regent, famous for her *salon*, and as an authoress of novels.

did not adopt or reject the whole plan, but fully retained the purport of the maxim. In short, she is an epitome of empire, subsisting by rewards and punishments. Her great enemy, madame du Deffand,[5] was for a short time mistrefs of the regent, is now very old and stone blind, but retains all her vivacity, wit, memory, judgment, pafsions, and agreeablenefs. She goes to operas, plays, suppers, and Versailles; gives suppers twice a week; has every thing new read to her; makes new songs and epigrams, aye, admirably, and remembers every one that has been made these fourscore years. She corresponds with Voltaire, dictates charming letters to him, contradicts him, is no bigot to him or any body, and laughs both at the clergy and the philosophers. In a dispute, into which she easily falls, she is very warm, and yet scarce ever in the wrong: her judgment on every subject is as just as pofsible; on every point of conduct as wrong as pofsible: for she is all love and hatred, pafsionate for her friends to enthusiasm, still anxious to be loved, I don't mean by lovers, and a vehement enemy, but openly. As she can have no amusement but conversation, the least solitude and ennui are insupportable to her, and put her into the power of several worthlefs people, who eat her suppers when they can eat nobody's of higher rank; wink to one another and laugh at her; hate her because she has forty times more parts—and venture to hate her because she is not rich. She has an old friend whom I must mention, a monsieur Pondevelle,[6] author of the Fat Puni, and the Complaisant, and of those pretty novels, the Comte de Cominge, the Siege of Calais, and les Malheurs de l'Amour. Would not you expect this old man to be very agreeable? He can be so, but seldom is: yet he has another very different and very amusing talent, the art of parody, and is unique in his kind. He composes tales to the tunes of long dances: for instance, he has adapted the Regent's Daphnis and Chloe to one, and made it ten times more indecent; but is so old and sings it so well, that it is permitted in all companies. He has succeeded still better in les characteres de la danse, to which he has adapted words that express all the characters of love. With all this, he

---

[5] See Letter 417, n. 4. Madame du Deffand never forgave Madame Geoffrin for her protection of Mademoiselle de Lespinasse after the rupture of the latter with the Marquise.

[6] Antoine de Ferriol (1697–1774), Comte de Pont-de-Veyle. He wrote the two comedies, the *Fat Puni* and the *Complaisant*, but was only part author (with Madame de Tencin, his aunt) of the three novels, the *Mémoires du Comte de Comminge, Siège de Calais*, and *Malheurs de l'Amour*.

has not the least idea of cheerfulnefs in conversation; seldom speaks but on grave subjects, and not often on them; is a humourist, very supercilious, and wrapt up in admiration of his own country, as the only judge of his merit. His air and look are cold and forbidding; but ask him to sing, or praise his works, his eyes and smiles open and brighten up. In short, I can show him to you: the self-applauding poet in Hogarth's Rake's Progrefs, the second print, is so like his very features and very wig, that you would know him by it, if you came hither—for he certainly will not go to you.

Madame de Mirepoix's[7] understanding is excellent of the useful kind, and can be so when she pleases of the agreeable kind. She has read, but seldom shows it, and has perfect taste. Her manner is cold, but very civil; and she conceals even the blood of Lorrain, without ever forgetting it. Nobody in France knows the world better, and nobody is personally so well with the king. She is false, artful, and insinuating beyond measure when it is her interest, but indolent and a coward. She never had any pafsion but gaming, and always loses. For ever paying court, the sole produce of a life of art is to get money from the king to carry on a course of paying debts or contracting new ones, which she discharges as fast as she is able. She advertised devotion to get made dame du palais to the queen; and the very next day this princefs of Lorrain was seen riding backwards with madame Pompadour in the latter's coach. When the king was stabbed and heartily frightened, the mistrefs took a panic too, and consulted d'Argenson,[8] whether she had not best make off in time. He hated her, and said, By all means. Madame de Mirepoix advised her to stay. The king recovered his spirits, d'Argenson was banished, and la marechale inherited part of the mistrefs's credit.—I must interrupt my history of illustrious women with an anecdote of monsieur de Maurepas,[9] with whom

---

[7] Anne Marguerite Gabrielle de Beauvau-Craon, Maréchale-Duchesse de Mirepoix; she was dame d'honneur to Queen Marie Leszczynska, and took a prominent part in Court intrigues. She paid great court to Madame de Pompadour, and subsequently countenanced Madame du Barry.

[8] Marc Pierre de Voyer (1696–1764), Comte d'Argenson, Minister of War, in which capacity he reorganized the French army. Having incurred the resentment of Madame de Pompadour, he was disgraced and exiled in 1757.

[9] Jean Frédéric Phélypeaux (1701–81), Comte de Maurepas; he had been exiled by Louis XV, but was recalled by Louis XVI and appointed minister of finance.

I am much acquainted, and who has one of the few heads that approach to good ones, and who luckily for us was disgraced, and the marine dropped, because it was his favourite object and province. He employed Pondevelle to make a song on the Pompadour: it was clever and bitter, and did not spare even majesty. This was Maurepas absurd enough to sing at supper at Versailles. Banishment ensued; and lest he should ever be restored, the mistrefs persuaded the king that he had poisoned her predecefsor madame de Chateauroux.[10] Maurepas is very agreeable, and exceedingly cheerful; yet I have seen a transient silent cloud when politics are talked of.

Madame de Boufflers,[11] who was in England, is a sçavante, mistrefs of the prince of Conti,[12] and very desirous of being his wife. She is two women, the upper and the lower. I need not tell you that the lower is galant, and still has pretensions. The upper is very sensible too, and has a measured eloquence that is just and pleasing—but all is spoiled by an unrelaxed attention to applause. You would think she was always sitting for her picture to her biographer.

Madame de Rochfort[13] is different from all the rest. Her understanding is just and delicate; with a finefse of wit that is the result of reflection. Her manner is soft and feminine, and though a sçavante, without any declared pretensions. She is the *decent* friend of monsieur de Nivernois;[14] for you must not believe a syllable of what you read in their novels. It requires the greatest curiosity, or the greatest habitude, to discover the smallest connection between the sexes here. No familiarity, but under the veil of friendship, is permitted, and love's dictionary is as much prohibited, as at first sight one should think his ritual was. All you hear, and that pronounced with nonchalance, is, that *monsieur un tel* has had *madame une telle*. The duc de Niver-

---

[10] Marie Anne de Mailly-Nesle (1717–44), Duchesse de Châteauroux, mistress of Louis XV.

[11] Marie Charlotte Hippolyte de Campet-de-Saujeon (1725–1800), Comtesse de Boufflers; she was in England in 1763, when she visited Strawberry Hill, of which she disapproved, as being 'peu digne de la solidité anglaise'. Topham Beauclerk's account of her visit to Dr. Johnson at his chambers in the Temple is recorded in Boswell's *Life of Johnson*.

[12] Louis François de Bourbon (1717–76), Prince de Conti.

[13] No doubt Marie Élisabeth de Talleyrand, wife (1736) of Charles de Chabannes, Comte de Rochefort; she subsequently married the Duc de Nivernais.

[14] Louis Jules Barbon Mancini-Mazarini, Duc de Nivernais, French Ambassador in England, 1762–3 (see Letter 382, n. 12).

nois has parts, and writes at the top of the mediocre, but, as madame Geoffrin says, is *manqué par tout; guerrier manqué, ambafsadeur manqué, homme d'affaires manqué,* and *auteur manqué*— no, he is not *homme de naifsance manqué.* He would think freely, but has some ambition of being governor to the dauphin,[15] and is more afraid of his wife[16] and daughter,[17] who are ecclesiastic fagots. The former out-chatters the duke of Newcastle; and the latter, madame de Gisors, exhausts Mr. Pitt's eloquence in defence of the archbishop[18] of Paris. Monsieur de Nivernois lives in a small circle of dependent admirers, and madame de Rochfort is high priestefs for a small salary of credit.

The duchefs of Choiseul,[19] the only young one of these heroines, is not very pretty, but has fine eyes, and is a little model in wax-work, which not being allowed to speak for some time as incapable, has a hesitation and modesty, the latter of which the court has not cured, and the former of which is atoned for by the most interesting sound of voice, and forgotten in the most elegant turn and propriety of expression. Oh! it is the gentlest, amiable, civil, little creature that ever came out of a fairy egg! So just in its phrases and thoughts, so attentive and good-natured! Every body loves it, but its husband, who prefers his own sister the duchefse de Grammont,[20] an amazonian, fierce, haughty dame, who loves and hates arbitrarily, and is detested. Madame de Choiseul, pafsionately fond of her husband, was the martyr of this union, but at last submitted with a good grace; has gained a little credit with him, and is still believed to idolize him—But I doubt it—she takes too much pains to profefs it.

I cannot finish my list without adding a much more common character—but more complete in its kind than any of the foregoing, the marechale de Luxembourg.[21] She has been very

[15] Afterwards Louis XVI.
[16] Hélène Angélique Françoise Phélypeaux de Pontchartrain, married in 1730.
[17] Hélène Julie Rosalie (1740–80), styled Mademoiselle de Nevers, married (1753) Louis Marie Fouquet, Duc de Gisors (d. 1758).
[18] Christophe de Beaumont du Repaire (1703–81), Archbishop of Paris, 1746–81.
[19] Louise Honorine Crozat du Châtel (1736–1801), married in 1750.
[20] Béatrix de Choiseul-Stainville (1730–94), married (1759) Antoine Antonin, Duc de Gramont.
[21] Madeleine Angélique de Neufville (1707–86), married (1750) Charles François Frédéric de Montmorency, Maréchal-Duc de Luxembourg.

handsome, very abandoned, and very mischievous. Her beauty is gone, her lovers are gone, and she thinks the devil is coming. This dejection has softened her into being rather agreeable, for she has wit and good-breeding; but you would swear, by the restlefsnefs of her person and the horrors she cannot conceal, that she had signed the compact, and expected to be called upon in a week for the performance.

I could add many pictures, but none so remarkable. In those I send you, there is not a feature bestowed gratis or exaggerated. For the beauties, of which there are a few considerable, as mesdames de Brionne,[22] de Monaco,[23] et d'Egmont,[24] they have not yet lost their characters, nor got any.

You must not attribute my intimacy with Paris to curiosity alone. An accident unlocked the doors for me. That *pafse-partout*, called the fashion, has made them fly open—and what do you think was that fashion?—I myself—Yes, like queen Elinor in the ballad, I sunk at Charing-crofs,[25] and have risen in the

[22] Louise Julie Constance de Rohan-Montauban, married (1748) Charles Louis de Lorraine, Comte de Brionne.

[23] Marie Christine de Brignole, married (1757) Honoré Camille Léonor Grimaldi, Prince de Monaco.

[24] Jeanne Sophie Élisabeth Louise Armande Septimanie de Richelieu, married (1756) Casimir Pignatelli d'Egmont, Comte d'Egmont.

[25] The ballad referred to is that known as 'The Fall of Queen *Eleanor*, wife to *Edward* the First, King of *England*; who, for her Pride, by God's Judgments, sunk into the Ground at *Charing-Cross*, and rose at *Queen-Hithe*'. According to the ballad, the Queen, among other barbarous crimes, cruelly did to death 'the Mayor of *London*'s Wife', which brought down a judgement upon her:

> A Judgment lately sent from Heav'n,
>   For shedding guiltless Blood,
> Upon this sinful Queen, that slew
>   The *London* Lady good!
>
> King *Edward* then, as Wisdom will'd,
>   Accus'd her of that Deed:
> But she deny'd; and wish'd, that God
>   Would send his Wrath with Speed;
>
> If that upon so vile a Thing
>   Her Heart did ever think,
> She wish'd the Ground might open wide,
>   And she therein might sink!
> With that, at *Charing-Cross* she sunk
>   Into the Ground alive;
> And after rose with Life again,
>   In *London*, at *Queen-Hithe*.

(See *A Collection of Old Ballads*, London, 1723, vol. i, pp. 97 ff.)

fauxbourg St. Germain. A *plaisanterie* on Roufseau,[26] whose arrival here in his way to you brought me acquainted with many anecdotes conformable to the idea I had conceived of him, got about, was liked much more than it deserved, spread like wildfire, and made me the subject of conversation. Roufseau's devotees were offended. Madame de Boufflers, with a tone of sentiment, and the accents of lamenting humanity, abused me heartily, and then complained to myself with the utmost softnefs. I acted contrition, but had like to have spoiled all, by growing dreadfully tired of a second lecture from the prince of Conti, who took up the ball, and made himself the hero of a history wherein he had nothing to do. I listened, did not understand half he said (nor he neither), forgot the rest, said Yes when I should have said No, yawned when I should have smiled, and was very penitent when I should have rejoiced at my pardon. Madame de Boufflers was more distrefsed, for he owned twenty times more than I had said: she frowned, and made him signs; but she had wound up his clack, and there was no stopping it. The moment she grew angry, the [lord of the house][27] grew charmed, and it has been my fault if I am not at the head of a numerous sect:—but when I left a triumphant party in England, I did not come hither to be at the head of a fashion. However, I have been sent for about like an African prince or a learned canary-bird, and was, in particular, carried by force to the princefs of Talmond,[28] the queen's cousin, who lives in a charitable apartment in the Luxembourg, and was sitting on a small bed hung with saints and Sobieskis, in a corner of one of those vast chambers, by two blinking tapers. I stumbled over a cat, a foot-stool, and a chamber-pot in my journey to her presence. She could not find a syllable to say to me, and the visit ended with her begging a lap-dog. Thank the Lord! though this is the first month, it is the last week, of my reign; and I shall resign my crown with great satisfaction to a bouillie of chestnuts, which is just invented, and whose annals will be illustrated by so many indigestions, that Paris will not want any thing else these three weeks. I will enclose the fatal letter after I have finished this enormous one; to which I will only add, that

[26] A letter which Walpole wrote to Rousseau in the name of the King of Prussia. It is printed in Walpole's letter to Conway of 12 Jan. 1766.
[27] Miss Berry printed by mistake 'the house of the lord'.
[28] Marie Louise Jablonowska (1710–73), married (1730) Antoine Charles Frédéric de la Trémoille, Prince de Talmond.

nothing has interrupted my Sevigné-researches but the frost. The abbé de Malesherbes has given me full power to ransack Livry. I did not tell you, that by great accident, when I thought on nothing less, I stumbled on an original picture of the comte de Grammont.[29] Adieu! You are generally in London in March: I shall be there by the end of it.

Yours ever,
HOR. WALPOLE.

420. GRAY TO WHARTON

March 5. 1766. Pemb: C:

Dear Doctor

I AM amazed at myself, when I think I have never wrote to you:[1] to be sure it is the sin of witchcraft or something worse. something indeed might be said for it, had I been married like Mason, who (for the first time since that great event) has just thought fit to tell me, that he never pafs'd so happy a winter as the last, & this in spite of his anxieties, wch perhaps (he says) might even make a part of his happinefs: for his Wife is by no means in health, she has a constant cough, yet he is afsured, her lungs are not affected, & that it is nothing of the consumptive kind. what say you to this case? may I flatter him, that breeding will be a cure for this disorder? if so, I hear she is in a fair way to be well. as to me I have been neither happy, nor miserable: but in a gentle stupefaction of mind, & very tolerable health of body hitherto. if they last, I shall not much complain. the accounts one has lately had from all parts make me suppose you buried under the snow,[2] like the old Queen of Denmark:[3] as soon as you are dug out, I should rejoice to hear your voice from the battlements of Old-Park. the greatest cold we have felt here was Jan: 2, Thermom: (in the garden) at 4 in the afternoon standing at 30 Deg: $\frac{1}{2}$, and next day fell a little snow, wch did not lie. it was the first we had had during the winter. again,

[29] Philibert (1621–1707), Comte de Gramont, subject of Hamilton's famous *Mémoires*, in Walpole's edition of which, printed at Strawberry Hill in 1772, an engraving of this portrait was inserted.

LETTER 420.—First printed in part (in a garbled text) in Mason's *Memoirs*, pp. 320–1; first printed in full by Mitford (1816), vol. ii, pp. 468–72; now reprinted from original.

[1] His last extant letter to Wharton was written at the end of Sept. 1765 (Letter 412).

[2] Walpole, writing to Montagu from Paris on 3 Mar., speaks of 'this Siberian winter'.   [3] This allusion has not been explained.

Feb: 5 toward night, Therm: was down at 30 D: with a clear sky; the snow-drops then beginning to blow in the garden: next day was a little snow. but on the 11th & 12th fell a deep snow (the weather not very cold) wch however was melted on ye 15th, & made a flood in the river. next day the Thrush was singing, & the Rooks building. at & about London instead of snow they had heavy rains. on the 19th the red Hepatica blew, & next day the Primrose. the Crocus is now in full bloom. so ends my chronicle.

My oracle[4] of state (who now & then utters a little, as far as he may with discretion) is a very slave & pack-horse, that never breaths any air better than that of London, except like an Apprenticc, on Sundays with his Master[5] and Co:. however he is in health, & a very good Boy. it is strange, the turn that things have taken. that the late Ministry should negociate a reconciliation with L^d B:,[6] & that Ld Temple should join them; that they should after making their (bad) apologies be received with a gracious kind of contempt, & told that his L^{dp}: could enter into no political connections with them: that on the first division on the American businefs[7] that happen'd in the H: of Lords they should however all join to carry a point against the Ministry by a majority indeed of four only, but the D: of Y—k[8] present & making one: that when the Ministers expostulated in a proper place, they should be seriously afsured the K: would support them. that on a division on an insignificant point to try their strength in the H: of Commons they should again lose it by 12 majority: that they should persist neverthelefs: that Mr Pitt should appear *tanquam e machinâ*, speak for 3 hours & ½, & afsert the rights of the Colonies in their greatest latitude:[9] that the

---

[4] Stonhewer, Under-Secretary of State (see Letter 408, n. 8).

[5] The Duke of Grafton, Secretary of State for the Northern Department.

[6] 'From being persecuted by both factions of the old and new Administrations, Lord Bute began to assume the style of holding the balance between both. The farce was carried on by the King. His Majesty told them (those members of the administration, who voted against its measures) that they *were at liberty to vote against him and keep their places*. This was, in effect, ordering his servants to oppose his Ministers' (Walpole, *Memoirs*, vol. ii, pp. 182–3).

[7] The Government had made known their intention to repeal the Stamp Act.

[8] The Duke of York, the King's next brother (see Letter 228, n. 9): 'In the House of Lords the Opposition . . . even carried one or two questions by majorities of four and five' (Walpole, *op. cit.*, vol. ii, pp. 200).

[9] Parliament met again on 14 Jan.; while the debate on the Address was in progress 'Mr Pitt appeared in the House, and took the first opportunity

Minister[10] should profefs himself ready to act with & even serve under him: that he should receive such a compliment with coldnefs, & a sort of derision: that Norton[11] should move to send him to the Tower: that when the great questions came on, the Min^y: should always carry their point at one, two, three in the morning by majorities of 110 & 170 (Mr Pitt entirely concurring with them, & the Tories, People of the Court, & many Placemen, even L^d G: Sackville,[12] constantly voting against them) all these events are unaccountable on any principles of common-sense. I attribute much of the singular part to the interposition of *Women*[13] as rash as they are foolish. on Monday[14] (I do not doubt, tho' as yet I do not certainly know it) the Bill to repeal the Stamp-act went thro' that House, & to-day it is before the Lords, who surely will not venture to throw it out.[15]

of opening his mind . . . on the Stamp Act. . . . Though he had on other occasions, perhaps, exerted more powers of eloquence . . . yet the novelty and boldness of his doctrines, the offence he gave by them at home, and the delirium which they excited in America, made his speech rank in celebrity with his most famous orations. . . . The repeal of the Stamp Act was the last great question on which he figured in the House of Commons' (Walpole, *op. cit.*, vol. ii, pp. 184–5).

[10] This was General Conway, Secretary of State for the South, who was in charge of the bill for the Repeal of the Stamp Act. Walpole does not mention Conway's alleged offer to serve under Pitt; he reports him as saying that 'he had the honour of agreeing with almost every word that had fallen from Mr Pitt'; and that, 'he had not studiously thrust himself into employment, and could assure the right honourable gentleman that he should think himself happy to resign it to him whenever he should please to take it' (*op. cit.*, vol. ii, p. 186).

[11] Sir Fletcher Norton, Attorney-General in the Grenville Ministry (see Letter 390, n. 8). Gray's informant seems to have been mistaken; according to Walpole, what Norton said to Pitt was, 'if the House go along with me, the gentleman will go to another place'—which Walpole explains as meaning 'to the bar of the House, whither members are ordered when they violate the rules or privileges of Parliament' (*op. cit.*, vol. ii, p. 193).

[12] On 31 Jan. 1766 Ministers narrowly escaped defeat in a division in which, among other placemen, Lord George Sackville voted against them, in spite of the fact that his name, which had been struck from the list of Privy Councillors in Apr. 1760 (see Letter 311, n. 12), had been restored on 20 Dec. 1765, and that only ten days before the division he had been appointed a Vice-Treasurer of Ireland.

[13] Perhaps, as Tovey suggests, Gray meant the Princess of Wales (the King's mother) and the Duchess of Bedford.

[14] Not on Monday, but on Tuesday, Mar. 4, the Bill passed in the House of Commons by 250 to 122.

[15] The Bill was passed in the House of Lords on 7 Mar. by 105 to 71. It received the royal assent on 18 Mar.

oh, that they would!—but after this important busineſs is well over, there must be an eclairciſsement: some amends must be made & some gracious condescensions insisted on, or else who would go on, that really means to serve his country! The D: of Bedford & Ld Temple were gone down to their Villas, & I believe are not likely to come back. Ld Chesterfield, who had not been for many years at the house, came the other day to qualify himself in order to leave a proxy, that should vote with the Ministry.[16] some body (I thought) made no bad application of those lines in Virgil L: 6. v: 489

At Danaum proceres, Agamemnoniæq phalanges &c:

to Mr Pitt's first appearance (for no one expected him) in the house. turn to the place.[17]

Every thing is politicks. there are no literary productions worth your notice, at least of our country. the French have finish'd their great Encyclopedie[18] in 17 Volumes: but there[19] are many flimsey articles very hastily treated, & great incorrect-neſs of the Preſs. there are now 13 Vol: of Buffon's Natural History,[20] & he is not come to the Monkies yet, who are a very numerous people. the Life of Petrarch has entertain'd me: it is not well written, but very curious & laid together from his own letters & the original writings of the 14th Century: so that it takes in much of the history of those obscure times, & the characters of many remarkable persons. there are 2 vol^s: 4to, & another (unpublish'd yet) that will compleat it.[21]

M^r W:[22] writes me now & then a long and lively letter from Paris, to wch place he went the last summer with the gout upon him sometimes in his limbs, often in his stomach & head. he has got somehow well (not by means of the climate, one would

[16] Chesterfield wrote to his son on 17 Mar.: 'The repeal of the Stamp-Act is at last carried through. I am glad of it, and gave my proxy for it; because I saw many more inconveniences from the enforcing, than from the repealing it. The repeal of it was carried in both Houses by the Ministers against the King's declared inclinations.'

[17]   At Danaum proceres Agamemnoniæque phalanges
     Ut videre virum fulgentiaque arma per umbras,
     Ingenti trepidare metu.

[18] It was not actually completed till 1772, when it consisted of 28 volumes (see Letter 245, n. 4).   [19] MS. 'their'.   [20] See Letter 154, n. 6.
[21] This was *Mémoires pour la vie de François Pétrarque, tirés de ses œuvres et des auteurs contemporains, avec des notes ou dissertations, & les pièces justificatives* (Amsterdam, 1764–7, 3 vols. 4to). The author, the Abbé Jacques François de Sade (1705–80), identifies Petrarch's Laura with Laura de Noves, who married Hugh de Sade.   [22] See Letters 417, 419.

think) goes to all publick places, sees all the best company & is very much in fashion. he says, he sunk like Queen Eleanour[23] at Charing-Crofs, & has risen again at Paris. he returns again in April: but his health is certainly in a deplorable state. Mad: de la Perriere[24] is come over from the Hague to be Ministrefs at London. her Father-in-law Viry[25] is now first Minister at Turin. I sate a morning with her before I left London. she is a prodigious fine Lady, & a Catholick[26] (tho' she did not exprefsly own it to me) not fatter than she was: she had a cage of foreign birds & a piping Bullfinch at her elbow, two little Dogs on a cushion in her lap, a Cockatoo on her shoulder, & a sl[ight][27] suspicion of Rouge on her cheeks. They were all exceeding glad to [see][27] me, & I them.

Pray tell me the history of your winter, & present my respects to M[rs] Wharton. I hope Mifs Wharton & Mifs Peggy with the afsistance of Sister Betty[28] make a great progrefs in Natural History: recommend me to all their good graces, & believe me ever

Truly Yours

If you chance to see or send to M[r] & M[rs] Leighton,[29] I will trouble you to make my compliments: I have never received the box of shells, tho' pofsibly it may wait for me at M[r] Jonathan's in Town, where I shall be in April. M[r] Brown is well & desires to be remember'd to you & M[rs] Wharton. I have just heard, there are like to be warm debates in the house of Lords, but that the Ministry will undoubtedly carry it[30] in spite of them all. they say, L[d] Cambden[31] will soon be Chancellour.

Addressed: To D[r] Wharton M:D: at Old-Park near Darlington, Durham
Postmark: CAMBRIDGE

[23] See Letter 419, n. 25.   [24] See Letter 353, n. 13.   [25] See Letter 353, n. 14.

[26] She had been married as a Catholic (see Letter 353, n. 12) and, as appears from an unpublished letter to Sir Joseph Yorke, British Minister at The Hague, to his brother the Earl of Hardwicke, written on 1 June 1764, 'when she first went to Turin, she had been an occasional Conformist, but upon her return to England, she had returned to the Church of England. This offended his Sardinian Majesty, and [at some time before the date of the letter] she had enter'd into the Pale of the Romish Church' (British Museum, *Add. MS.* 35367, ff. 96–7).

[27] MS. torn.   [28] See Letter 414, n. 4.

[29] Wharton's youngest sister, who married Rev. Thomas Leighton (see Genealogical Table).   [30] The Repeal of the Stamp Act (see n. 9).

[31] Sir Charles Pratt (see Letter 308, n. 27) had been created Baron Camden on 17 July 1765. He became Lord Chancellor, in the place of Lord Northington, on 30 July 1766, on the formation of Chatham's Ministry.

421. GRAY TO BROWN

Jermyn Street, May 15, 1766.

Dear Sir

TO-MORROW morning I set out for Canterbury.[1] If any letter comes, I believe it will be better to direct to me as usual at Mr. Roberts's[2] here, and he will take care to send it. I know not how long my stay in Kent may be: it depends on the agreeability of Mr. Robinson[3] and his wife.

You expect to hear who is Secretary of State.[4] I cannot tell. It is sure this morning it was not determined; perhaps Lord Egmont;[5] perhaps Lord Hardwicke[6] (for I do not believe he has refused, as is said); perhaps you may hear of three instead of

LETTER 421.—First printed by Mitford in *Gray–Mason* (1853), pp. 356–8.

[1] In one of Gray's pocket-books in possession of Sir John Murray are the following dates, which throw light on Gray's movements: 'In London 10 May 1766.—Denton in Kent, May 20 1766. June 5 Margate, & the Coast to Dover. Denton, 7 June. June 19, to Canterbury.' As he set out for Canterbury on 16 May, and apparently did not arrive at Denton till 20 May, he probably spent the intervening days at Canterbury, perhaps with a cousin of his own name who was resident there. (Sir Egerton Brydges, *Imaginative Biography*, vol. i, p. 78, says of Philip Gray: 'He had a cousin, an Alderman Gray, a grocer, at Canterbury, whom Gray sometimes visited.')

[2] See Letter 176, n. 3. In the pocket-book mentioned in n. 1 there is a note, dated 10 May 1766, headed 'Mr Roberts's Collection' and containing a list of thirty-nine insects, with Latin descriptions. It may be inferred that Gray encouraged Mr. Roberts, with whom he lodged, to take an interest in natural history, and to observe flies and bees and beetles including 'blatta, the *Cockroach*'.

[3] Rev. William Robinson, Rector of Denton, about eight miles east of Canterbury (see Letter 304, n. 4).

[4] Walpole wrote to Mann on 22 May 1766: 'The Duke of Grafton . . . has resigned the Seals, which are given to the Duke of Richmond, who kisses hands tomorrow.' Grafton stated in the House of Lords that he had resigned office not 'from a love of ease and indulgence to his private amusements, as had falsely been reported, but because they wanted strength, which one man only [Pitt] could supply'.

[5] John Perceval (1711–70), second Earl of Egmont (1748); he was at this time First Lord of the Admiralty. It was his eldest son, afterwards third Earl, who was concerned in the escapade which led to Gray's removal from Peterhouse to Pembroke (see Appendix J).

[6] See Letter 297, n. 5. By desire of the King, who objected to the Duke of Richmond, the Secretaryship was first offered successively to the Earl of Hardwicke, whom Walpole in his *Memoirs* (vol. ii, p. 230) describes as 'a bookish man, conversant only with parsons, ignorant of the world, and void of breeding', and to his brother, Charles Yorke (see Letter 308, n. 28), the Attorney-General, by both of whom the offer was declined.

two. Charles Townshend[7] affirms he has rejected both that office and a peerage; doubtlefs from his firm adherence to Mr. Pitt—a name which the court, I mean Lord Tt.,[8] Lord Nd.,[9] and even Lord B.[10] himself, at present affect to celebrate, with what design you are to judge. You have doubtlefs heard of the honour done to your friend Mrs. Macaulay.[11] Mr. Pitt has made a panegyric of her *History* in the house.[12] It is very true Wilkes has arrived.[13] The tumults in Spain[14] spread wider and wider, while at Naples they are publicly thanking God for their cefsation; perhaps you may hear. All is not well in Ireland.[15] It is very late at night. Adieu. Pa.[16] went home to-day and Mr. Weddell[17] with him. J. Wheeler[18] has returned from Lisbon. The great match[19] will not be till after Christmas. Tom[20] is

[7] See Letter 212, n. 4. He was at this time Paymaster-General, an office to which he had been appointed by Grenville in May 1765, and which he retained throughout Rockingham's administration. In August of this year he became Chancellor of the Exchequer in Chatham's administration.

[8] Lord Talbot, Lord Steward of the Household (see Letter 345, n. 13).

[9] Lord Northumberland, recently Lord Lieutenant of Ireland (see Letter 408, n. 7).   [10] Lord Bute.

[11] Catherine Sawbridge (1731–91) who married, in 1760, Dr. George Macaulay, a Scottish physician, who died in 1766. Her fame was made by her *History of England from the Accession of James I to that of the Brunswick Line*, in eight volumes, the first of which was published in 1763, the last in 1783. She wrote with a republican bias, which Horace Walpole affected to approve: in a letter to Mason, written on 29 Dec. 1763, soon after the appearance of the first volume, he said: 'Have you read Mrs Macaulay? I am glad again to have Mr Gray's opinion to corroborate mine, that it is the most sensible, unaffected, and best history of England that we have had yet.'

[12] There appears to be no other record of Pitt's panegyric.

[13] On the return of the Whigs to power Wilkes had hopes of obtaining a pardon and a pension or place; but a visit to London in May 1766 disillusioned him, and he returned to Paris.

[14] Of the disorders in Madrid Walpole gives an account in his letter to Conway of 8 Apr. from Paris. The King had been forced to consent to the banishment of his minister Squillaci, an Italian who fled to Naples.

[15] Owing to the agrarian riots of the Whiteboys (Roman Catholics) in Tipperary and Limerick, and of the Oakboys (Protestants) in the north.

[16] Palgrave.   [17] See Letter 400, n. 13.

[18] John Wheler, younger son of Sir William Wheler, 5th Bart., of Leamington Hastings, Warwick; educated at Rugby; admitted pensioner at Clare Hall, Cambridge, 1752; LL.B. 1759; Rector of Mercham le Fen (otherwise Marrow), Lincs. He was no doubt the same as Norton Nicholls's friend 'Wheeler', of Letters 508, 512, 537, and 550. Sixty letters from Nicholls to the Rev. J. Wheler were included in the eight volumes of Nicholls's literary correspondence in the sale of Dawson Turner's library in June 1859.

[19] Between Lord Strathmore and Miss Bowes (see Letter 431, n. 6).

[20] Lord Strathmore's brother.

gone to Scotland. It is sure the lady[21] did refuse both Lord Mountstuart[22] and the Duke of Beaufort.[23] Good-night.

I came away in debt to you for two post-chaises. Pray set it down.

422. GRAY TO NICHOLLS

Aug: 26. 1766. Pemb: Hall.

Dear S[r]

IT is long since that I heard you were gone in hast into York-shire[1] on account of your Mother's illnefs, & the same letter inform'd me, that she was recover'd. otherwise I had then wrote to you only to beg you would take care of her, & to inform you, that I had discover'd a thing very little known, w[ch] is, that in one's whole life one never can have any more than a single Mother. you may think this is obvious, & (what you call) a trite observation. you are a green Gofsling! I was at the same age (very near) as wise as you, & yet I never discover'd this (with full evidence & conviction, I mean) till it was too late. it is 13 years ago,[2] & seems but yesterday, & every day I live it sinks deeper into my heart.[3] many a corollary could I draw from this axiom for your use (not for my own) but I will leave you the merit of doing it yourself. pray, tell me how your own health is. I conclude it perfect, as I hear you offer'd yourself for a guide to M[r] Palgrave into the Sierra-Morena of Yorkshire. for me I pafs'd the end of May & all June in Kent not disagreeably. the country is all a garden, gay, rich, & fruitfull, & (from the rainy season) had preserved, till I left it, all that emerald ver-

[21] Miss Bowes (see n. 19).

[22] John Stuart (1744–1814), eldest son of third Earl of Bute, whom he succeeded in 1792; he married, on 1 Nov. 1766, 'a rich ugly Miss Windsor', as Walpole writes to Mann on 13 Nov., namely, Charlotte Jane, eldest daughter and coheiress of first Viscount Windsor.

[23] Henry Somerset (1744–1803), fifth Duke of Beaufort (1756), married, on 2 Jan. 1766, Elizabeth, youngest daughter of Admiral Hon. Edward Boscawen.

LETTER 422.—First printed in part (in a garbled text) in Mason's *Memoirs*, pp. 391–2; first printed in full by Mitford (1835–43), vol. v, pp. 60–2; now reprinted from original.   [1] See Letter 397, n. 13.

[2] Mrs. Gray died on 11 Mar. 1753 (see Letter 176).

[3] He seldom mentioned his Mother without a sigh. After his death, her gowns and wearing apparel were found in a trunk in his apartments just as she had left them; it seemed as if he could never take the resolution to open it, in order to distribute them to his female relations, to whom, by his will, he bequeathed them. *Mason.*—There is no specific mention in Gray's will of his mother's wearing apparel.

dure, wch commonly one only sees for the first fortnight of the spring. in the west part of it from every eminence the eye catches some long winding reach of the Thames or Medway with all their navigation. in the east the sea breaks in upon you, & mixes its white transient sails & glittering blew expanse with the deeper & brighter greens of the woods & corn. this last sentence is so fine[4] I am quite ashamed. but no matter! you must translate it into prose. Palgrave, if he heard it, would cover his face with his pudding-sleeve.[5] I went to Margate for a day:[6] one would think, it was Bartholomew Fair that had *flown* down: From Smithfield[7] to Kent in the London machine like my Lady Stuffdamask (to be sure you have read the New Bath Guide,[8] the most fashionable of books) so then I did *not* go to Kingsgate,[9] because it belong'd to my Ld Holland: but to Ramsgate I did, & so to Sandwich & Deal & Dover & Folk-

[4] Gray had referred to his own 'well-turn'd' and 'fine' periods in his letter to Nicholls of 19 Nov. 1764 (Letter 397).

[5] Such as Palgrave, as a parson, would wear. In Swift's *Baucis and Philemon* the old yeoman Philemon, having been told 'to ask for what he fancied most', says:

> 'I'm old, and fain would live at ease;
> Make me the parson if you please.'
> He spoke, and presently he feels
> His grazier's coat fall down his heels;
> He sees, yet hardly can believe,
> About each arm a pudding sleeve . . .

[6] On 5 June (see Letter 421, n. 1).

[7] Where the Fair was held 'at Bartholomew Tide, within the precinct of the Priory of St. Bartholomew'.

[8] *The New Bath Guide: or Memoirs of the Bl-n-d-r-d Family, in a Series of Poetical Epistles* (Cambridge, 1766, 4to), by Christopher Anstey (see Letter 341, n. 1). Walpole wrote to Montagu on 20 June 1766: 'There is a new thing published . . . called the *New Bath Guide*. . . . so much wit, so much humour, fun, poetry, so much originality, never met together before.' The passage to which Gray refers comes from Letter XIII in which Simkin Blunderhead sends his mother a description of a public breakfast:

> I freely will own I the Muffins preferr'd
> To all the genteel Conversation I heard;
> E'en tho' I'd the Honour of sitting between
> My Lady Stuff-Damask, and Peggy Moreen,
> Who both flew to *Bath* in the *London* Machine.

[9] About three miles from Margate, near the North Foreland. In May 1762 Fox had taken a long lease of a small house there on the edge of the cliffs, where a few years later he erected a great pile, with 'a lofty Doric portico of twelve columns of Portland stone', and sham ruins of a castle, &c. It was on his second visit to Denton in 1768 that Gray wrote his verses on Lord Holland's Villa (see Appendix T).

stone & Hithe all along the coast very delightful. I do not tell you of the great & small beasts & creeping things innumerable that I met with, because you do not suspect, that this world is inhabited by any thing but Men & Women, & Clergy, & such two-legged cattle. now I am here again very disconsolate & all alone: even Mr Brown is gone, & the cares of this world are coming thick upon me, I do not mean Children. you I hope are better off, riding & walking with Mr Aislaby,[10] singing Duets with my Cousin Fanny,[11] improving with Mr Weddell,[12] conversing with Mr Harry Duncomb.[13] I must not wish for you here: besides I am going to Town at Michaelmas, by no means for amusement. do you remember, how we are to go into Wales[14] next year? well!—Adieu, I am

Sincerely Yours,
T G:

Pray how does poor Temple[15] find himself in his new situa-

[10] William Aislabie, of Studley Royal near Ripon; M.P. for Ripon from 1721 to 1781. He was the only son of the notorious John Aislabie (1670–1742), who was Chancellor of the Exchequer at the time of the South Sea scheme.

[11] Nicholls's cousin, Frances, only daughter of Charles Floyer (see Letter 397, n. 13), and sister of Augustus Floyer (see Letter 425, n. 4). She eventually married John Erskine, of Alloa (see Letter 533, n. 9).

[12] Weddell, at this time adding two wings to Newby Hall (see Letter 400, n. 13).

[13] Henry Duncombe, of Copgrove, near Boroughbridge, about six miles from Ripon; he was subsequently M.P. for York County, 1780–96.

[14] In an unpublished letter to Temple of 2 Apr. 1767 (owned by Professor Tucker) John Clarke (see Letter 513, n. 1) says: 'Mr G. and our friend N. think of going into Wales together this summer.'

[15] William Johnson Temple (1739–96), friend of Boswell, Gray, and Norton Nicholls, was born at Allerdean, near Berwick-on-Tweed, where his father had a post in the Customs. His mother had been a Miss Stow, of Northumberland. He was educated at Edinburgh University (where he was a fellow student with Boswell), and at Trinity Hall, Cambridge, where he was admitted in May 1758. In Nov. 1761 he went to London, where he took chambers in order to read for the Bar. Having contributed more than half the small estate which he had inherited from his mother, to satisfy his father's creditors, he had to seek a livelihood, and in 1763 he returned to Trinity Hall, as a Fellow-commoner, with the intention of being ordained. It was apparently during his residence at this time that he became acquainted with Gray. In June 1765 he graduated LL.B. While on a visit to London in 1766 he was introduced by Boswell to Dr. Johnson at the Mitre Tavern. On 14 Sept. of the same year he was ordained deacon at Exeter and priest a week later, and the next day he was presented by his cousin Lord Lisburne to the Rectory of Mamhead, near Exeter.

Shortly after Gray's death Temple, in a letter to Boswell, wrote a character

tion?[16] is L^d L:[17] as good as his letters were? what is come of the Father[18] & Brother?[19] Have you seen Mason?

Addressed: To Norton Nicholls Esq at Charles Floyers Esq of Hollinclose near Rippon Yorkshire

423. GRAY TO WHARTON

Dear Doctor

WHATEVER my pen may do, I am sure my thoughts expatiate no where oftener or with more pleasure than to Old-Park. I hope you have made my peace with Mifs Debo:.[1] it is certain, whether her name were in my letter[2] or not, she was as present to my memory, as the rest of the little family, & I desire you would present her with two kifses in my name, & one apiece to all the others: for I shall take the liberty to kifs them all (great & small) as you are to be my proxy.

In spite of the rain, wch I think continued with very short intervals till the beginning of this month, & quite effaced the summer from the year, I made a shift to pafs May & June not disagreeably in Kent. I was surprised at the beauty of the road to Canterbury, w^{ch} (I know not why) had not struck me in the

of Gray, which was incorporated in part by Mason in his *Memoirs* (pp. 402–4), and by Johnson in his account of Gray in his *Lives of the Poets*. Temple there spoke of Gray as 'perhaps the most learned man in Europe'. A collection of nearly 100 letters, written by Boswell to Temple between 1758 and 1795, was discovered at Boulogne in 1850, and was published in 1857. Temple's *Diaries* (1780–96), edited by Lewis Bettany, were published in 1929.

[16] Gray is writing in August, and Temple was not ordained until 14 Sept. (see n. 15). Gray is therefore unwittingly anticipating his ordination and presentation to his living.

[17] Temple's cousin, Wilmot Vaughan (1728–1800), fourth Viscount (1766), and first Earl of Lisburne (1776) in the Peerage of Ireland; M.P. for Berwick-on-Tweed, 1765–8; he had succeeded to his father's title in January of this year. For the strained relations between Nicholls and Lord and Lady Lisburne in 1767 see Letter 456, n. 2.

[18] In a letter to Andrew Mitchell, British Envoy at Berlin, of 26 Dec. 1764, Boswell appeals for an employment for Temple's father (*Letters of James Boswell*, pp. 64–5).

[19] Temple's younger brother, Robert, had been lieutenant in General Crawfurd's regiment and was retired on half pay (see Boswell's letter to Andrew Mitchell referred to in n. 18).

LETTER 423.—First printed in part (in a garbled text) in Mason's *Memoirs*, pp. 322–4; first printed in full by Mitford (1816), vol. ii, pp. 473–6; now reprinted from original.

[1] This was Wharton's third daughter, born in 1755 (see Letter 209, n. 17).

[2] That of 5 Mar. (Letter 420). Deborah's name does not appear with those of the other three sisters in the message at the end of the letter.

same manner before. the whole county is a rich & well-cultivated garden, orchards, cherry-grounds, hop-gardens, intermix'd with corn & frequent villages, gentle risings cover'd with wood, and every where the Thames & Medway breaking in upon the Landscape with all their navigation. it was indeed owing to the bad weather, that the whole scene was drefs'd in that tender emerald-green, wch one usually sees only for a fortnight in the opening of spring, & this continued till I left the country. my residence was eight miles east of Canterbury in a little quiet valley on the skirts of Barham-down.[3] in these parts the whole soil is chalk, and whenever it holds up, in half an hour it is dry enough to walk out. I took the opportunity of three or four days fine weather to go into the Isle of Thanet, saw Margate (wch is Bartholomew-Fair by the seaside) Ramsgate, & other places there, & so came by Sandwich, Deal, Dover, Folkstone, & Hithe back again. the coast is not like Hartlepool: there are no rocks, but only chalky cliffs of no great height, till you come to Dover. there indeed they are noble & picturesque, & the opposite coasts of France begin to bound your view, wch was left before to range unlimited by any thing but the horizon: yet it is by no means a *shiplefs* sea, but every where peopled with white sails & vefsels of all sizes in motion; and take notice (except in the Isle, wch is all corn-fields, & has very little inclosure) there are in all places hedge-rows & tall trees even within a few yards of the beach, particularly Hithe stands on an eminence cover'd with wood. I shall confefs we had fires of a night (ay, & a day too) several times even in June: but don't go & take advantage of this, for it was the most untoward year that ever I remember.

Your Friend Roufseau (I doubt) grows tired of Mr Davenport & Derbyshire.[4] he has pick'd a quarrel with David Hume & writes him letters of 14 pages Folio upbraiding him with all his *noirceurs*. take one only as a specimen, he says, that at Calais

[3] See Letter 421, n. 3.
[4] Rousseau, having been offered by Hume towards the end of 1765 an asylum in England, accepted the offer, and after a brief stay in Paris landed in England with Hume on 13 Jan. of this year (1766). He spent some weeks in London where he was made much of; and when he became dissatisfied with London Hume procured for him a retreat in the country in the house of a Mr. Davenport at Wootton in Derbyshire. At Wootton, where he wrote the greater part of his *Confessions*, he remained till May 1767, when he hastily departed and returned to France (see Letter 441, n. 15), leaving behind him a letter full of abuse addressed to his host (see *Gent. Mag.* for 1767, p. 275).

they chanced to sleep in the same room together, & that he overheard David talking in his sleep, & saying, *Ah! Je le tiens, ce Jean-Jacques là.* In short (I fear) for want of persecution & admiration (for these are his real complaints) he will go back to the continent. What shall I say to you about the Ministry?[5] I am as angry as a Common-council Man of London about my Ld Chatham:[6] but a little more patient, & will hold my tongue till the end of the year. in the mean time I do mutter in secret & to you, that to quit the house of Commons, his natural strength; to sap his own popularity & grandeur (which no one but himself could have done) by afsuming a foolish title; & to hope that he could win by it & attach to him a Court, that hate him, & will dismifs him, as soon as ever they dare, was the weakest thing, that ever was done by so great a Man. had it not been for this, I should have rejoiced at the breach between him & Ld Temple,[7] & at the union between him & the D: of Grafton & Mr Conway: but patience! we shall see! St:[8] perhaps is in the country (for he hoped for a month's leave of absence) & if you see him, you will learn more than I can tell you.

Mason is at Aston. he is no longer so anxious about his Wife's health, as he was, tho' I find she still has a cough, & moreover[9] I find she is not with child: but he made such a bragging, how could one chuse but believe him.

When I was in town, I mark'd in my pocket-book the utmost limits & division of the two columns in your Thermometer, &

[5] The Chatham ministry. On 30 July Pitt kissed hands as Lord Privy Seal; the Duke of Grafton being appointed First Lord of the Treasury; Lord Camden, Lord Chancellor; Earl of Shelburne and General Conway, Secretaries of State; and Charles Townshend, Chancellor of the Exchequer. On 4 Aug. Pitt was created Earl of Chatham, with a pension of £3,000 a year for three lives.

[6] 'The City of London had intended to celebrate Mr Pitt's return to employment, and lamps for an illumination had been placed round the Monument. But no sooner did they hear of his new dignity, than the festival was countermanded' (Walpole, *Memoirs*, vol. ii, p. 255).

[7] Pitt had advised the King to send for Lord Temple, who, however, made such extravagant demands that they were peremptorily refused. The breach between Temple and Pitt was due to Temple's demand that his brother (George Grenville) and Lord Lyttelton should be included in the ministry, to which Pitt would not consent.

[8] Stonhewer had just been appointed Private Secretary to the Duke of Grafton (the appointment was officially announced in the papers of 15 Aug.).

[9] Gray wrote 'morever'.

ask'd Mr. Ayscough[10] the Instrument-Maker on Ludgate Hill, what scales they were. he immediately afsured me, that one was Fahrenheit's, & shew'd me one exactly so divided. the other he took for Reaumur's, but, as he said there were different scales of his contrivance, he could not exactly tell, wch of them it was. your Brother[11] told me, you wanted to know, who wrote Duke Wharton's[12] Life in the Biography:[13] I think, it is chiefly borrowed from a silly book enough call'd *Memoirs of that Duke*:[14] but who put it together there, no one can inform me. the only person certainly known to write in that vile collection (I mean these latter volumes) is Dr Nicholls,[15] who was expell'd here for stealing books.

Have you read the *New Bath-Guide?*[16] it is the only [thing][17] in fashion, & is a new & original kind of humour. Mifs Prue's Conversion[18] I doubt you will paste down, as S^r W: St Quintyn[19] did, before he carried it to his daughter. yet I remember you all read *Crazy Tales*[20] without pasting. Buffon's first collection of Monkies are come out (it makes the 14th volume)[21] something, but not much, to my edification: for he is pretty well acquainted with their persons, but not with their manners.

I shall be glad to hear, how far Mrs Ettrick[22] has succeeded,

[10] Kent's *Directory* (1759) has: 'Ayscough, James, Optician, Ludgate-Street.'

[11] Jonathan Wharton (see Letter 116, n. 15).

[12] Philip Wharton (*c.* 1698–1731), second Earl and Marquis (1715), and first Duke (1718) of Wharton, only son of Thomas, first Earl and Marquis. His character is summed up by Pope in the first Epistle (ll. 180–209) of his *Moral Essays*, in which he is introduced as

Wharton, the scorn and wonder of our days.

[13] The *Biographia Britannica: or the Lives of the most eminent Persons of Great Britain and Ireland* (Lond. 1747–66, 7 vols. fol.), the last volume of which had recently been published (see Letter 170, n. 7).

[14] Probably *A Memoir of Philip, Duke of Wharton* (Lond. 1731, 8vo).

[15] Philip Nicholls, late Fellow of Trinity Hall, LL.D. 1729, who had been guilty of stealing valuable books from St. John's Library and elsewhere, was, by a Grace of the Senate passed on 6 Aug. 1731, deprived of all degrees and privileges (dejectus omni de gradu): see Cooper, *Annals of Cambridge*, vol. iv, p. 209.   [16] See Letter 422, n. 8.

[17] MS. damaged—restoration conjectural.

[18] This is contained in Letter xiv in which 'Miss Prudence B-N-R-D informs Lady Betty that she has been elected to Methodism by a Vision'. It is accompanied by a 'very humorous and whimsical Translation' (into Latin) by the author.

[19] Sir William St. Quintin (*c.* 1700–70), fourth Baronet (1723) of Harpham, Yorks.   [20] By John Hall-Stevenson (see Letter 311, n. 37).

[21] See Letter 154, n. 6.   [22] See Letter 401, n. 1.

& when you see an end to her troubles. my best respects to Mrs. Wharton, & compliments to all your family: I will not name them, least I should affront any body. Adieu, dear S^r,

I am most sincerely Yours,

T G:

26 Aug: 1766. Pemb: Coll:

Mr. Brown is gone to see his Brother near Margate. when is Ld Str: to be married?[23] if M^r & Mrs Jonathan are with you, I desire my compliments.

Addressed: To Dr Wharton M:D: at Old-Park near Darlington Durham to be left at Sunderland-Bridget[24]

424. GRAY TO MASON

[c. August 26, 1766.][1]

Dear Mason

I REJOICE to find you are both in health, & that one or other of you at least can have your teeming-time.[2] you are wise as a serpent, but the devil of a dove, in timing both your satire, & your compliment.[3] when a Man stands on the very verge of Legislation[4] with all his *unblushing* honours thick upon him; when the Gout has nip'd him in the bud, & blasted all his hopes at least for one winter: then come you buzzing about his nose, & strike your sting deep into the reddest angriest part of his

---

[23] Lord Strathmore (see Letter 421, n. 19).

[24] About four miles south of Durham, where the great north road crosses the Wear.

LETTER 424.—First printed by Mitford in *Gray–Mason* (1853), pp. 353–5; now reprinted from original.

[1] This letter is dated 1765 by Mason, which is certainly wrong; it was obviously written at about the same time as (perhaps a few days earlier than) the preceding letter.

[2] Mrs. Mason had been supposed to be with child but this was not so (see Letter 423). Mason himself, as appears from what follows, had been writing a satirical ode on two public characters, which he had sent to Gray.

[3] Gray is undoubtedly alluding to a satirical poem, which appeared in the *St. James's Chronicle* for 26–8 Aug., with the title *Extract from an Ode to the Legislator Elect of Russia, on his being prevented from entering on his high Office of Civilisation by a Fit of the Gout*. From what he says in this letter it appears that the poem was by Mason. The 'satire' was directed against Dr. John Brown (see Letter 144, n. 27), and the 'compliment' was paid to Chatham (see Appendix R where the text of the Ode is given).

[4] The mention of legislation, and of gout in the next line, are allusions to the title of Mason's satire.

toe, wch will surely mortify. when another[5] has been weak enough in the plenitude of power to disarm himself of his popularity; & to conciliate a Court, that naturally hates him, submits to be deck'd in their trappings, & fondle their lap-dogs: then come you to lull him with your gentlest hum, recalling his good deeds,[6] & *hoping*[7] what I (with all my old partialities) scarce should dare to hope, if I had but any one else to put my trust in. let you alone, where *Spite* & *Interest* are in view!—ay, ay, M^rs M: (I see) will be a Bishopefs.

Well, I transcribed your wickednefs in a print-hand & sent it by last Sunday's post to D^r G:[8] with your orders about it, for I had heard St: say, that he hoped for a month's respite[9] to go into the North, & did not know, but he might be gone. G: was to send me word, he had received it, but has not yet done so, and (Lord blefs me!) who knows, but he may be gone into Derbyshire,[10] & the Ode gone after him! if so, mind, I am innocent, & meant for the best. I liked it vastly, & thought it very well-turn'd & easy, especially the *diabolical*[11] part of it: I fear, it will not keep, & would have wish'd the Publick might

[5] Here the reference is to Chatham, whose recent acceptance of a peerage and a pension had disgusted his admirers (see Letter 423, nn. 5, 6).
[6] In the concluding stanzas of the satire the eulogy of Chatham begins:
> Quote we then Pitt, who once had Worth
> Was wise—a Patriot—and so forth.

[7] Mason's final stanza expresses his hopes:
> And still I'll hope, thought Fools may flout,
> That this same Pitt, in spite of Gout,
> And what is worse, of Peerage,
> Will do his best to save from Fate
> That leaky Skiff we call the State,
> Now he is at the Steerage.

[8] Mitford printed 'Gisborne', which was no doubt the name intended. It seems to have been Mason's practice in order to preserve his anonymity to get his effusions copied in a strange hand and sent to Gisborne or Stonhewer or some other intermediary for insertion in one of the London papers.
[9] See Letter 423.
[10] The Gisbornes were a Derbyshire family (see Letter 299, n. 10).
[11] The allusion is to the concluding stanza of the apostrophe supposed to be addressed to the Empress by Brown:
> ' Meanwhile, dread Empress, I to thee
> Will Solon and Lycurgus be,
> And Montesquieu also.'
> And scarce these Words were well got out,
> When lo! a Dæmon, call'd the Gout,
> Did tweak him by the Toe.

have eat it fresh: but if any untoward accident should delay it, it will be still better than most things, that appear at their table.
I shall finish, where you begun, with my apology. you say you have *neglected* me, & (to make it relish the better) *with many others.* for my part I have not neglected you: but I have always consider'd the *Happy*, that is, new-married People, as too sacred, or too profane, a thing to be approach'd by me: when the year is over, I have no longer any respect or aversion for them. Adieu! I am in no spirits, & perplex'd besides with many little cares, but always sincerely

Yours
T G:

P:S: My best respects to Madam in her grogram gown.[12] I have long since heard, that you were out of pain with regard to her health. Mr Brown is gone to see his Brother near Margate.

425. GRAY TO NICHOLLS

My dear S^r

I WAS absent in Suffolk,[1] & did not receive your melancholy letter till my return hither yesterday: so you must not attribute this delay to me, but to accident. to sympathize with you in such a lofs[2] is an easy task for me: but to comfort you not so easy. can I wish to see you unaffected with the sad scene now before your eyes, or with the lofs of a person, that thro' a great part of your life has proved himself so kind a Friend to you? he who best knows our nature (for he made us, what we are) by such afflictions recalls us from our wandering thoughts & idle merriment, from the insolence of youth & prosperity, to serious reflection, to our duty & to himself: nor need we hasten to get rid of these imprefsions; Time (by appointment of the same

---

[12] Another reminiscence (see Letter 422, n. 5) of Swift's *Baucis and Philemon*:

> Plain 'Goody' would no longer down,
> 'Twas 'Madam', in her grogram gown.

Later on Gray applies the phrase to Mrs. Nicholls (see Letter 455).

LETTER 425.—First printed in part (in a garbled text) in Mason's *Memoirs*, pp. 343–5; first printed in full by Mitford (1835–43), vol. v, pp. 63–4; now reprinted from original.

[1] The College records show that Gray left Cambridge 12 Sept. He had probably been to see Palgrave, who was Rector of Thrandeston and Palgrave in Suffolk. He also went into Norfolk (Letter 426).

[2] Charles Floyer (see Letter 397, n. 13), uncle of Norton Nicholls, died on 7 Sept. this year.

Power) will cure the smart, & in some hearts soon blot out all the traces of sorrow: but such as preserve them longest (for it is left partly in our own power) do perhaps best acquiesce in the will of the Chastiser.

For the consequences of this sudden lofs[3] I see them well, & (I think) in a like situation could fortify my mind so as to support them with chearfulnefs & good hopes, tho' not naturally inclined to see things in their best aspect. your Cousins[4] seem naturally kind & well-disposed worthy young People: your Mother & they will afsist one another. you too (when you have time to turn you round) must think seriously of your profefsion.[5] you know I would have wish'd to see you wear the livery of it long ago. but I will not dwell on this subject at present. to be obliged to those we love & esteem is a pleasure: but to serve & to oblige them is a still greater, & this with independence (no vulgar blefsings) are what a Profefsion at your age may reasonably promise. without it they are hardly attainable. remember, I speak from experience!

Poor Mr. W: is struck with a paralytick disorder.[6] I know it only from the papers, but think it very likely. he may live in this state, incapable of afsisting himself, in the hands of servants or relations, that only gape after his spoils, perhaps for years to come. think, how many things may befall a man far worse than death. Adieu! I sincerely wish your happinefs, & am

Faithfully Yours

Pemb: C: Sept: 23. 1766.   T G:

P:S: I must go soon to London: but if you direct to me here, I shall have your letters. let me know soon, how you go on.

Addressed: To Norton Nicholls Esq at Hollin-close Hall near Rippon Yorkshire *Postmark:* SAFFRON WALDEN 24 SE

[3] It appears that Nicholls and his mother had hitherto benefited by the generosity of his uncle. In his will (dated 15 June 1764) Charles Floyer bequeathed 'to my sister-in-law (*sic*) Nicholls £300, but it must be settled so that Norton Nicholls her husband shall receive none' (see Letter 432, n. 9). He further bequeathed '£200 to my nephew Norton Nicholls'.

[4] Charles Floyer's son, Augustus, and his daughter, Frances (see Letter 422, n. 11). Augustus Floyer, for whom his father had purchased a troop of Dragoon Guards, subsequently married a Miss Lisle and resided at Upwey, near Dorchester (Letter 500, n. 3).

[5] Gray expected Nicholls to be ordained (see Letters 429 and 432).

[6] This was a false alarm; it was not paralysis, but gout (see Letters 426 and 429). In a note to Lady Mary Coke, written on 17 Sept., Walpole says: 'I have had a violent attack in my stomach, bowels, and back, of what Dr. Pringle says is the gout, accompanied with intolerable sickness.'

426. GRAY TO WALPOLE

Dear S^r

I HAPPEN'D to be in Norfolk on the way to Houghton, when I read an article in a news-paper relating to you, that shock'd me. I wrote to Dr Gisburne[1] (who lives very near you) to beg he would inform himself of your health: but I fear he is out of Town, for I have received no answer. today by accident I received a letter from Cole,[2] from whence I learn, thank God! that the worst part of that news was false: but that you have suffer'd much from a return of the gout, & are prevented only by weaknefs from going to Bath. it would be a singular satisfaction to me, if I might see three lines in your own hand: but it is impofsible for me to judge, whether this is a reasonable request. I flatter myself, if you can, you will indulge me in it, especially when you know, that of those who are most about you, there is no one I can well write to. in a fortnight or lefs I hope to be in Town. Heaven preserve you, & restore you to health & ease. I hope this severe lefson will warn you against that carelefs regimen, to wch you were so unreasonably attach'd. I am ever

Yours

T GRAY.

Sept: 24. 1766 Pemb: Hall.

Addressed: To The Honble Horace Walpole in Arlington Street London

426* Gray to Stonhewer

[Cambridge, c. 23 Sept. 1766]

[In his letter to Mason of 5 Oct. 1766 (Letter 427) Gray refers to a letter which he wrote to Stonhewer on receiving from him the news of Dr. John Brown's suicide. As Gray heard from Stonhewer on 23 Sept., Gray's letter must have been written about 23 Sept. Both letters are missing, as well as others mentioned in the same letter to

LETTER 426.—First printed by Toynbee (1915), No. 236.
[1] See Letter 299, n. 10.
[2] No doubt Cole had passed on to Gray the news he had received from Walpole who wrote to him on 18 Sept.: 'I am exceedingly obliged to you for your very friendly letter, and hurt at the absurdity of the newspapers that occasioned the alarm. Sure I am not of consequence enough to be lied about? It is true I am ill, have been extremely so, and have been ill long, but with nothing like paralytic, as they have reported me. . . . I have been to take the air to-day for the first time, but bore it so ill that I don't know how soon I shall be able to set out for Bath, whither they want me to go immediately.'

Mason. Stonhewer had written a second letter on 27 Sept. Gray had also received a letter from Walpole in reply to his letter of 24 Sept. (Letter 426).]

427. GRAY TO MASON

5 Oct: 1766. P: Hall.

Dear Mason

I WAS going to write to you, when I received your letter, and on the same subject.[1] the first news I had was from St:[2] on the 23ᵈ. of Sept: in these words:

'This morning Dʳ B: dispatch'd himself: he had been for several days past very low-spirited, & within the last two or three talk'd of the necefsity of dying in such a manner as to alarm the people about him: they removed as they thought every thing, that might serve his purpose. but he had contrived to get at a razor unknown to them, & took the advantage of a minute's absence of his servants to make use of it.' I wrote to him again (I suspect, he knows our secret,[3] tho' not from me) to make farther enquiries, & he says, 27 Sept:, 'I have tried to find out, whether there was any appearance or cause of discontent in B:, but can hear of none. a bodily complaint of the gouty kind, that fell upon his nerves & affected his spirits in a very great degree is all that I can get any information of; & I am told besides, that he was some years ago in the same dejected way, & under the care of *proper attendants*.' Mr. W: too in answer to a letter I had written to enquire after his health after giving an account of himself, while under the care of Pringle,[4] adds, 'He (Pringle) had another Patient at the same time, who has ended very unhappily, that poor Dʳ B:. the unfortunate Man appre-

LETTER 427.—First printed by Mitford in *Gray–Mason* (1753), pp. 359–62; now reprinted from original.

[1] The subject was the suicide of Dr. John Brown on 23 Sept. *Lloyds Evening Post*, Wednesday, 24 Sept. to Friday, 26 Sept. 1766 reports: 'On Tuesday the Coroner's Inquest sat on the body of a Gentleman of distinguished literary merit, who had cut a jugular vein with a razor, at his lodgings in Pall Mall; and brought in their verdict Lunacy.'
This letter is a sequel to Gray's letter to Mason of *c.* 26 Aug. (Letter 424). The receipt of the news of his death had evidently caused much concern to both Mason and Gray, who feared that Mason's recently published satire might have been a contributory cause to his suicide (see Appendix R).

[2] Stonhewer (see Letter 426*).

[3] 'Our secret' was that Mason was the author of the Ode on John Brown.

[4] Sir John Pringle, Bart., an eminent physician (see Letter 425, n. 6). He was an intimate friend of Boswell.

hended himself going mad, & two nights after cut his throat in bed.' this is all I know at present of the matter. I have told it you literally, & I conceal nothing. as I go to town tomorrow, if I learn any thing more, you shall soon hear from me. in the mean time I think we may fairly conclude, that if he had had *any other* cause added to his constitutional infirmity, it would have been uppermost in his mind: he would have talk'd or raved about it, & the first thing we should have heard of, would have been this, w^{ch} (I do afsure you) I have never heard from any body. there is in this neighbourhood a Mr Wale,[5] who once was in the Rufsia-trade & married a Woman of that country: he always maintain'd, that D^r B: would never go thither, whatever he might pretend; & that tho' fond of the glory of being invited thither, he would certainly find or make a pretence for staying at home. very pofsibly therefore he might have engaged himself so far, that he knew not how to draw back with honour; or might have received rough words from the Rufsian Minister offended with his prevarication. this supposition[6] is at least as likely as yours; added to what I have said before, much more so: if it be necefsary to suppose any other cause than the lunatick disposition of the Man. and yet I will not disguise to you, that I felt as you do on the first news of this sad accident, & had the same uneasy ideas about it.

I am sorry the cause you mention[7] should be the occasion of your coming to London: tho' perhaps change of air may do more than medicine. in this length of time I should think you must be fully apprised, whether her looks or strength or embonpoint have suffer'd by this cough: if not; surely there is no real danger. yet I do not wonder, she should wish to get rid of so troublesome a companion.

When I can meet with the book, I will transcribe what you mention from *Mallet*.[8] I shall write again soon. do you know of any great, or at least rich, family that want a young Man worth his weight in gold to take care of their eldest hope. if you do, remember I have such a one,[9] or shall have (I fear) shortly

[5] Thomas Wale (1701–96) (father of General Sir Charles Wale), who lived at Shelford a few miles from Cambridge, and was long engaged in the Russian trade. He married, in Riga, a daughter of Nicholas Rahten of Lüneburg. (See H. J. Wale's *My Grandfather's Pocket Book*.)

[6] Disappointment at the failure of his Russian scheme was generally supposed to have been the cause of his suicide.   [7] Mrs. Mason's ill health.

[8] Presumably the book referred to by Gray in Letter 262 (see n. 3).

[9] Norton Nicholls (see Letter 425).

to sell: but they must not stand haggling about him, & besides
they must be very good sort of people too, or they shall not have
him. Adieu! my respects to Mrs Mason. I am ever

Sincerely Yours.

Mr Brown desires his best compliments to you both.

428. GRAY TO MASON

Oct: 9. 1766. Jermyn-Street at Mr Roberts's.

Dear Mason

I AM desired to tell you, that if you *still* continue to be tired of
residence, or are in any way moderately ambitious, or
covetous, there never was a better opportunity. the D: of G:[1]
is extremely well inclined, & you know, who is at hand[2] to give
his afsistance: but the apparent channel should be your Friend,
L^d H:^fse,[3] who is upon good terms. this was said to me in so
friendly a way, that I could not but acquaint you of it im-
mediately.

I have made enquiry, since I came hither on a subject,[4] that
seem'd much to take up your thoughts, & (I do afsure you) find
not the least grounds to give you uneasinefs. it was mere dis-
temper & nothing more. Adieu! I am sincerely

Yours

My respects to M^rs M: T G:

429. GRAY TO NICHOLLS

[Oct. 13, 1766][1]

My Dear S^r

I HAVE received a second instance of your kindnefs & confi-
dence in me. and surely you hazard nothing in trusting me
with the whole of your situation. it appears not to me so new,
as it does to you. you well know, the tenour of my conversation

LETTER 428.—First printed by Mitford in *Gray–Mason* (1853), pp. 362–3;
now reprinted from original.
    [1] The Duke of Grafton was now First Lord of the Treasury in the Chatham
ministry (see Letter 423, n. 5).
    [2] Stonhewer.   [3] Lord Holdernesse.   [4] See Letter 427, n. 1.
    LETTER 429.—First printed in part (in a garbled text) in Mason's *Memoirs*,
pp. 344–5; first printed in full by Mitford (1835–43), vol. v, pp. 65–6; now
reprinted from original.
    [1] The letter is undated—the date of the month is determined by the post-
mark; that of the year, by the references to Nicholls's loss through his uncle's
death, and to Walpole's illness (see Letter 425).

(urged perhaps at times a little farther than you liked) has been intended to prepare you for this event, to familiarize your mind with this spectre, that you call by its worst name: but remember, that *Honesta res est læta paupertas.*[2] I see it with respect, & so will every one, whose poverty is not seated in their mind. there is but one real evil in it (take my word, who know it well) & that is, that you have lefs the power of afsisting others, who have not the same resources to support them. it is this consideration, that makes me remind you, that *Ansel*[3] is lately dead, a Lay-fellow of your college. that if D^r M:[4] (whose follies let us pardon, because he has some feeling & means us well) be of little use, & if D^r H:[5] (another simple Friend of ours, perhaps with lefs sensibility) can not serve us in this: yet D^r R:[6] is not immortal, you have always said to succeed him was not impracticable. I know it would be creditable, I know it would be profitable, I know it would in lieu of a little drudgery bring you freedom. that drudgery would with a little use grow easy. in the mean time, if any better prospect present itself, there you are ready to take advantage of the opportunity. in short this was always my favourite project, & now more than ever for reasons, that will occur to yourself. in waiting for the accomplishment of it, you will take orders, & if your Uncles[7] are slow in their motions, you will accept a Curacy (for a title will be requisite) not under every body, that offers, but under some gentlemanlike friendly Man, & in a christian country. a profefsion you must have: why not then accommodate yourself chearfully to its beginnings.

[2] Seneca, *Epist.* ii: 'Honesta, inquit [Epicurus], res est, laeta paupertas. Illa vero non est paupertas, si laeta est.' The first sentence is quoted by Gray, with a reference to Seneca, in his Commonplace-book.

[3] Thomas Ansell (d. 1766), admitted Scholar at Trinity Hall, 1739; Fellow, 1747–66. Ansell, who graduated LL.B. in 1744, the same year as Gray, played a prominent part in the affair of the Westminster Club in Nov. 1750 (see Letter 156, n. 24).

[4] Marriott, see Letter 397, n. 12.

[5] Hallifax, see Letter 409, n. 10.

[6] Ridlington, see Letter 399, n. 13. Mitford supposes that Gray had in mind the possibility of Nicholls's succeeding Ridlington as Tutor of Trinity Hall.

[7] Charles Floyer, his mother's brother, the uncle he had just lost, was Nicholls's only Floyer uncle. Presumably the references here, and in Letters 432, 488, 541, and 551, are to his Turner uncles or great uncles. Charles Floyer in his will mentions three maternal uncles of his, and an aunt, of the name of Turner. It was to one of these, William Turner, of Richmond, that Nicholls was indebted in 1767 for the living of Lound and Bradwell.

you have youth, you have many kind well-intention'd people belonging to you, many acquaintance of your own, or familie's, that will wish to serve you. consider, how many have had the same, or greater cause for dejection with none of these resources before their eyes.

I am in Town for a month or more, & wish to hear from you soon. Mr. W: has indeed been dangerously ill with the gout in his stomach, but nothing paralytick, as was said. he is much recover'd, & gone to Bath.[8] Adieu, Dear S^r, I am faithfully Yours,

T G.

I will write again soon.

Addressed: To Norton-Nicholls Esq at Hollin-close near Rippon Yorkshire
Postmark: 14 oc

430. GRAY TO BROWN

Jermyn Street, October 23, 1766.

Dear Sir

I OBSERVED that Ansel[1] was dead, and made the same reflection about it that you did. I also wrote to remind N:[2] of it, but have heard nothing since. We have great scarcity of news here. Everything is in Lord Ch.'s[3] breast. If what lies hid there be no better than what comes to light, I would not give sixpence to know it. Spain was certainly offered to Lord Weymouth,[4] and in the second place, some say to Sandwich; at last, perhaps, Sir

[8] Walpole arrived in Bath on 1 Oct.; Lord Chatham, who was there also, called on him, and they had 'a conversation of two hours', in the course of which apparently Chatham proposed that Walpole should move the address in the House of Commons (see Walpole's letters to Conway of 2 and 18 Oct.; and *Memoirs*, vol. ii, pp. 261–2).

LETTER 430.—First printed by Mitford in *Gray–Mason* (1853), pp. 363–7.
[1] See Letter 429, n. 3.
[2] Norton Nicholls.
[3] Lord Chatham. Walpole wrote to Mann on 26 Oct.: 'I left Lord Chatham at Bath, in great health and spirits. He does not seem to dread his enemies, nor respect them.'
[4] See Letter 292, n. 6. Walpole reports Chatham as saying during their interview at Bath (see Letter 429, n. 8): 'He wished to take some of all parties. The Duke of Bedford, indeed, had made himself nobody. Lord Gower was considerable, and ought to be high. If the Duke and Duchess desired it, Rigby might be taken care of; but when Cabinet places were so scarce, they wanted one for Lord Weymouth—a pretty man, Lord Weymouth!—but that could not be. He had been offered the embassy to Spain, but would not accept it; nor Post-master, though it had been held by Lord Grantham, who had been Secretary of State' (*Memoirs*, vol. ii, p. 261).

James Gray[5] may go. But who goes Secretary[6] do you think? I leave Mr. T.[7] and you ten guefses a-piece, and yet they will be all wrong. Mr. Prowse[8] has refused the Post Office. I do not believe in any more dukes,[9] unlefs, perhaps, my Lord Marquis of Rockingham should like it. The Prince of Wales has been ill of what they call a fever. They say he is better, but Sir J. Pringle[10] continues to lie every night at Kew. My Lady —— has discarded Thynne[11] and taken to Sir T. Delaval,[12] they say. The clothes are actually making, but pofsibly she may jilt them both. The clerk who was displaced in the Post Office lost 1,700*l* a year. Would you think there could be such under-offices there? Have you read Mr. Grenville's Considerations[13]

[5] In a PS. to his letter to Mann of 26 Oct. 1766 Walpole says: 'Sir James Gray goes to Madrid. The embassy has been sadly hawked about; not a peer would take it.' Sir James Gray (*c.* 1708–73), second baronet (1722), was Ambassador at Madrid, 1766–70.

[6] Lord Cardross, through the interest of Chatham, was by him named Secretary to the Embassy for Spain, under Sir James Gray. He is said to have refused the appointment on the ground that the Ambassador was of inferior rank to himself. Lord Cardross was David Stuart Erskine (1742–1829), eldest surviving son of the tenth Earl of Buchan, whom he succeeded as eleventh Earl in Dec. 1767. Why Gray and his friends should have been interested in the nomination to this particular post does not appear.

[7] No doubt Talbot (see Letter 241, n. 15).

[8] This was Thomas Prowse, M.P. for Somerset County from 1740 till his death on 1 Jan. 1767. Walpole writes: 'Lord Grantham was removed from the Post-office in favour of Mr Prowse, who would not accept it' (*Memoirs*, vol. ii, p. 261).

[9] Walpole wrote to Mann on 26 Oct. 1766: 'Lord Northumberland and Lord Cardigan are made Dukes.'

[10] See Letter 427, n. 4. He had been appointed Physician to the Queen in 1761.

[11] Probably Hon. Henry Frederick Thynne (1735–1826), second son of second Viscount Weymouth, and next brother of the third Viscount (see n. 4); he was Master of the Household, 1768–70; Joint Post-Master General, 1770–89.

[12] There is no evidence that there was any 'Sir T. Delaval' at this time. It is probable that Mitford misread, or miscopied, 'Sir F. Delaval' and that the reference was to Sir Francis Blake Delaval, the eldest son of 'old Delaval of Northumberland' (see Letter 163), and elder brother of John Blake Hussey and Edward Hussey Delaval (Letters 127 and 163). He was created Knight of the Bath in 1761. If Gray was referring to him, the intended marriage does not seem to have taken place, and there is nothing to show the identity of the lady, whose name was presumably obliterated.

[13] *Considerations on the Trade and Finances of this Kingdom, and on the Measures of Administration with respect to those great National Objects, since the Conclusion of the Peace* (1766), written in defence of Grenville's administration by Thomas Whately, M.P., who had been Secretary to the Treasury under Grenville.

on the merits of his own Administration? It is all figures; so, I suppose, it must be true. Have you read Mr. Sharp the surgeon's Travels into Italy?[14] I recommend these two authors to you instead of Livy and Quintilian.[15]

Palgrave, I suppose, you have by this time seen and sifted; if not, I must tell you, his letter was dated from Glamis, 30th Sept., Tuesday night. He was that day returned from my tour in the Highlands, delighted with their beauties, though he saw the Alps last year. The Friday following he was to set out for Hetton,[16] where his stay would not be long; then paſs four days at Newby,[17] and as much at York, and so to Cambridge, where, ten to one, he has not yet arrived. Tom[18] outstripped Lord Panmure[19] at the county court at Forfar all to nothing. Dr. Richmond[20] is body chaplain to the Duke of Athol, lives at Dunkeld,[21] and eats muir-fowls' livers every day. If you know this already, who can help it?

Pray tell me, how do you do; and let me know the sum total of my bill.[22] Adieu.

I am ever yours,
T. G.

[14] *Letters from Italy, describing the Customs and Manners of that Country, in the Years 1765, and 1766*, by Samuel Sharp (*c.* 1700–78), who was surgeon to Guy's Hospital, 1733–57; in 1765 he set out on a tour through Italy, and on his return in 1766 published the above *Letters from Italy*, which were approved by Dr. Johnson, but aroused the wrath of Baretti, who in 1768 published a counterblast in his *Account of the Manners and Customs of Italy*, to which Sharp replied.   [15] See Letter 406, n. 4.   [16] See Letter 409, n. 6.

[17] Newby Hall, the residence of Palgrave's friend Weddell (see Letter 400, n. 13).

[18] Lord Strathmore's brother, Hon. Thomas Lyon.

[19] William Maule (1700–82), nephew of James Maule, fourth Earl of Panmure (1686) (who took part in the Jacobite rising of 1715, in consequence of which his honours and estates were forfeited to the Crown), was M.P. for Forfar, 1735–82, and in 1743 was created an Irish Peer as Earl of Panmure of Forth. The forfeited Panmure estates were purchased from the Crown by the York Buildings Company, from whom the estates in Forfarshire were repurchased by William, Earl of Panmure in 1764. It was perhaps in connexion with these estates that Thomas Lyon's dispute with Lord Panmure, which in 1768 came before the House of Lords (see Letter 475, PS.), arose.

[20] Richard Richmond (1727–80), admitted at St. John's, Cambridge, 1746; LL.B. 1752; LL.D. 1758; Chaplain to Duke of Athol; Bishop of Sodor and Man, 1773–80.

[21] As Gray mentions in his letter to Wharton from Glamis (Letter 412), the Duke of Athol had 'a large house' at Dunkeld.

[22] See Letter 281, n. 8.

Commend me to Mr. Talbot and Dr. Gisborne. Delaval is coming to you. Is Mr. Mapletoft there? If not, he will lie in my rooms.

431. GRAY TO BROWN

18 Nov: 1766. Jermyn-Street.

Dear S^r 5^l

I PAID the sum abovemention'd this morning at Gillam's Office in Bishopsgate-Street:[1] the remittance you will please to pay out of it. I have not time to add all the bad news of the times,[2] but in a few days you shall have some of it; tho' the worst of all is just what I can not write. I am perfectly out of humour, & so will you be.

Mason is here, & has brought his Wife, a pretty, modest, innocent, interesting figure, looking like 18, tho' she is near 28. she does not speak, only whispers, & her cough as troublesome as ever: yet I have great hopes, there is nothing consumptive. she is strong & in good spirits. we were all at the Opera together on Saturday last.[3] they desire their loves to you. I have seen Mr Talbot, & Delaval lately. Adieu! I am ever

Yours

T G:

I can not find Mons: de la Chalotais[4] in any of the shops.

LETTER 431.—First printed by Mitford in *Gray–Mason* (1853), pp. 367–8; now reprinted from original.

1 Gillam was the Cambridge carrier (see Letter 347, n. 1).

2 Gray is presumably referring to the political situation, which Walpole in his letter to Mann of 8 Dec. 1766 speaks of as 'the late hurricane'. In this same letter Walpole gives an account of the crisis. Chatham had offended those of his colleagues who had been members of the Rockingham Ministry. The Duke of Portland and other Ministers had resigned. Henry Conway, who was pressed by Rockingham and the Cavendishes to retire, remained in the Government. Pitt filled the vacant offices, and on 12 Dec. Walpole wrote to George Montagu: 'We have had a busy month, and many grumbles of a State-quake; but the session has however ended very triumphantly for the Great Earl—I mean, we are adjourned . . . after two divisions of 166 to 48, and 140 to 56.'

3 15 Nov. In the *Public Advertiser* for that day is the following announcement: 'Haymarket. By Command of Their Majesties. At The King's Theatre in the Haymarket, this Day will be performed a new serious opera call'd Trakebarne Gran Mogul.' This was the first performance. Burney describes it as 'a serious pasticcio' (*Hist. Music*, vol. iv, p. 489).

4 Louis René de Caradeuc de La Chalotais (1701–85), Procureur Général

L^d St:[5] I am told is to be married here. I know nothing of Pa:, but that he was still at Mr Weddell's[6] a fortnight since. Be so good to tell me you have received this (if you can) by the return of the Post.

Addressed: [To The Rev^d M^r][7] Brown, President of Pembroke Hall, Cambridge *Postmark:* 18 NO

432. GRAY TO NICHOLLS

Dear S^r

DO not think, I forget you all this time: nothing lefs! I have daily thought on you, tho' to little purpose. perhaps the sense of my own inutility has been the reason of my silence, it is certain I have been well enough, & enough alone for the 7 or 8 weeks that I have pafs'd here, the last three of them indeed (during this dreadful weather) I have been nursing Mr Brown, who has been under the Surgeon's hands, & now just begins to go acrofs the room. the moral of this is, that when you break your shin, you should not put the black sticking-plaister to it, wch has been the cause of our sufferings; & thus at other people's expence we become wise, & thank heaven, that it is not at our own.

I have often wish'd to talk to D^r H:[1] about you, but have been restrain'd by the fear, that my interposition, like your friend

of the Parlement of Brittany. He was an ardent opponent of the Jesuits, the edict for whose suppression in France in 1764 was largely due to his *Comptes rendus des Constitutions des Jésuites* (1762). In 1763 he published his *Essai d'Éducation nationale*, advocating a system of scientific studies in the place of those taught by the Jesuits. In the same year there arose a conflict between the Estates of Brittany and the Governor of the Province, the Duc d'Aiguillon, in which La Chalotais, who was a personal enemy of the latter, became involved. In Nov. 1765 he and his son, and four others, were arrested on a false charge, tried, and sentenced to be exiled. Eventually, in consequence of the popular indignation, the sentence was quashed, and La Chalotais was reinstated.

The work for which Gray had been inquiring on Brown's behalf was presumably either one of the two mentioned above, or the first instalment of the *Exposé justificatif de la conduite de Caradeuc de la Chalotais*, written by himself, and published in 1766–7.

[5] Lord Strathmore's marriage took place at St. George's, Hanover Square, on 24 Feb. 1767.

[6] See Letter 430, n. 17.

[7] Partly cut away.

LETTER 432.—First printed by Mitford (1835–43), vol. v, pp. 67–9; now reprinted from original.

D^r M:ˢ,¹ might do more hurt than good. in the mean time I do suspect a little, that our acquaintance at Nice¹ is by no means so near his end, as all good Christians might wish. my reasons are twofold. First, because I do not remember ever to have read in any news-paper that Lady Betty Beelzebub or Master Moloch, or even old Sr Satan himself, or any of the good family, were dead:² therefore I may be allow'd to doubt a little of their mortality. Secondly, is it not very poſsible, that he may think, his Substitute³ here will not so readily go on without rising in his terms; nor do his drudgery so patiently, unleſs he thought him likely soon to return? and as he has no such intention, what else can he do, but make himself worse than he is, & order his Nurse to write melancholy accounts of him to her friends here?

Had it not been for this ill-contrived notion of mine,⁴ I should have been glad to hear my⁵ Uncles were off their bargain.⁶ it is sure, that the situation you mention is reckon'd as good as any part of the county. I, who lately was in the county,⁷ know, that this is not saying a vast deal. but however⁸ now I wish it had succeeded. this at least we seem to learn from it, that they are in earnest, wch is the great point: and I hope you have not been wanting in acknowledgements, nor shew'd the least sulkineſs at seeing the negotiation drop, because the purchase was dear. I desire, you would give yourself no airs!

The letter to your Father⁹ was the very thing I meant to

---

¹ Gray is alluding to Hallifax, Marriott, and Ridlington ('our acquaintance at Nice'). See Letter 429.

² Meaning that Ridlington was as little likely to oblige them by dying as any of the Satanic brood.

³ Hallifax (see Letter 409, n. 10).   ⁴ See n. 6.

⁵ Gray is, as often, adopting the relations and interests of his correspondent as his own. For Nicholls's uncles see Letter 429, n. 7.

⁶ Gray does not express himself very clearly. He apparently meant: 'If I could have got you a post at Trinity Hall I should have been glad that your uncles had not succeeded in purchasing the living for which they were negotiating.'   ⁷ Suffolk or Norfolk (see Letter 425, n. 1).

⁸ 'But however' seems to haVe been a colloquial combination of words. It occurs in Dr. Johnson's letter to Mrs. Thrale of 23 June 1775 and was used frequently by Jane Austen in the conversation of her more illiterate characters. (See *The Novels of Jane Austen*, edited by R. W. Chapman, vol. i, p. 392.)

⁹ There was evidently some mystery connected with Nicholls's father. Mathias, who was intimate with Nicholls, speaks in his letter on the death of Nicholls (printed by Mitford in *Works of Gray*, 1835–43, vol. v, pp. 3–21) of his 'having lost his father so very early in life as scarcely to have seen him'. This may mean that his father died soon after marriage; but it may also

write to you about. if he is really dead, or dead to shame or humanity, it is no matter: a few words are lost. if he lives, who knows what may be the consequence? why are you not in orders yet, pray!¹⁰ how have you pafs'd this frightful piece of a winter? better I dare say, & more comfortably than I. I have many *desagrémens*, that surround me: they have not dignity enough to be called *misfortunes:* but they feel heavy on my mind. Adieu! I wish you all happinefs, & am

Sincerely Yours
T G:

Jan: 19. 1767. Pemb: C:

Addressed: To Norton Nicholls Esq at Hollinclose near Rippon Yorkshire
Postmark: illegible

mean, and this is the impression given by Gray's reference to him, that he left Mrs. Nicholls and disappeared at an early date, and had been looked upon as dead. Nicholls apparently had some grounds for believing that he was still alive, and in his altered circumstances may have written to him to appeal to him on behalf of his mother and himself. No further mention of him occurs in the correspondence. Charles Floyer, in his will, dated 15 June 1764, seems to have assumed that the elder Nicholls was then alive (see Letter 425, n. 3).

¹⁰ See Letter 425, n. 5. Nicholls was ordained a month later. He had applied in the first instance to the Archbishop of York, and in the York Diocesan Registry (at a date not specified) there is an entry: 'Letters dimissory were granted to Norton Nicholls, LL.B. of Trinity Hall in Cambridge to be ordained deacon by the Right Rev. the Lord Bishop of London.' The Bishop of London's Registry has a record of his ordination as deacon on 15 Feb. 1767 and as priest on the 24th of the same month by the Bishop of London.

According to Boswell he took a flippant view of his profession. Writing to Temple on 3 Nov. 1780 (thirteen years later) Boswell mentions Nicholls's visit to Edinburgh at that time: 'Nichols was some days here in his way home. His foppery is unbecoming in a clergyman. But I was really much offended with him one night when he supt with me. McLaurin, who, I fear, is an infidel, was the only other person in company. Nichols gave a ludicrous account of his ordination. Said he applied to the Archbishop of York (Drummond) who asked him what books he had read on divinity. "Why, truly, my Lord," said he, "I must tell you frankly, none at all, though I have read other books enough." "O very well," said the Archbishop, "I'll give you a letter to one who will examine you properly."—Accordingly he got a letter to a clergyman in London, who examined him—and, to cut short this dissagreeable story, Nichols said that he did not well understand what was meant when desired to write on the necessity of a Mediator—that he wrote some strange stuff, as fast as he could do a card to a lady, and that he had never read the Greek New Testament. He made a very profane farce of the whole. McLaurin laughed exceedingly. I could only be grave' (*Letters of James Boswell*, vol. ii, p. 308).

433. GRAY TO MASON

Dear Mason   Jan: 27. 1767. Pemb: Hall.

Dr SWIFT says, one never should write to one's Friends but in high health & spirits.[1] by the way it is the last thing people in those circumstances usually think of doing: but it is sure, if I were to wait for them, I never should write at all. at present I have had for these six weeks a something growing in my throat, wch nothing does any service to, & wch will, I suppose, in due time stop up the pafsage. I go however about, & the pain is very little. you will say perhaps, the malady is as little, & the stoppage is in the imagination. no matter for that! if it is not sufficient to prove want of health (for indeed this is all I ail) it is so much the stronger proof of the want of spirits. so take it as you please, I carry my point, & shew you, that it is very obliging in me to write at all. indeed perhaps on your account, I should not have done it: but after three such weeks of Lapland-weather I can not but enquire after Mrs Mason's health. if she has withstood such a winter & her cough never the worse: she may defy the Doctors & all their works. pray, tell me how she is, for I interest myself for her not merely on your account, but on her own. these three last mornings have been very vernal & mild: has she tasted the air of the new year at least in Hyde-Park?

Mr Brown will wait on her next week, & touch her.[2] he has been confined to lie on a couch, & under the Surgeon's hands eversince the first of January with a broken shin ill-doctor'd. he is just now got abroad, & obliged to come to Town about Monday on *particular* businefs.

Stonhewer was so kind as to tell me the mystery now accomplish'd, before I received your letter. I rejoice in all his accefsions:[3] I wish, you would persuade him to take unto him a Wife: but don't let her be a fine Lady. Adieu. present my respects & good wishes to Argentile.[4] I am truly

Yours
T G

LETTER 433.—First printed by Mitford in *Gray–Mason* (1853), pp. 369–70; now reprinted from original.

[1] See Swift's letter to Pope, 9 Feb. 1735–6: 'Perhaps you would have fewer complaints of my ill health and lowness of spirits, if they were not some excuse for my delay of writing even to you' (*Works of Pope*, 1764, vol. iv, p. 362).   [2] See Letter 379, n. 4.
[3] Stonhewer had just been appointed Commissioner of Excise (*Gentleman's Magazine*, Jan. 1767, p. 49).
[4] Mrs. Mason (see Letter 408, n. 3).

434. MASON TO GRAY

Cleveland row[1] Feb. 2[d] 1767

Dear M[r] Gray

NO, alafs, she has not withstood the Severity of the Weather. It nipt her as it would have done a flower half witherd before, & she has been this last month in a most weak condition. Yet this present fine season has enabled me to get her three or four times out into the air, & it seems to have had some good effect, yet not enough to give me any substantial hopes of her recovery.[2] There are few Men in the world that can have a competent Idea of what I have of late felt, & still feel, yet you are one of those few, & I am sure will give me a full share of your pity. Was I to advise Stonehewer to a Wife it should certainly be to a fine Lady, It should not be to one he could Love to the same degree that I do this gentle this innocent creature.

I hope she will be well enough to see M[r] Brown when he comes—pray tell him we have changd our Lodgings & are to be found at M[r] Mennis's a Taylor at the Golden Ball in Cleveland row the last door but one nearest the green park Wall. Would to God he would persuade you to come with him.

If I had spirits for it, I would congratulate You on the New Bishop of Cloyne.[3] Is it not think you according to the order of things, I mean not the general but the peculiar order of our own times, That the Mitre w[ch] so lately was on the Brows of the Man[4] with every Virtue under heavn should now adorn those of our *friend* Frederic?

LETTER 434.—First printed by Mitford in *Gray–Mason* (1853), pp. 371–2; now reprinted from original.

[1] The passage in front of St. James's Palace, forming the continuation westward of Pall Mall.

[2] Warburton wrote to Hurd from Grosvenor Square on 20 Feb. 1767: 'M[r] Mason called on me the other day. He is grown extremely fat, and his wife extremely lean. Indeed in the last stage of a consumption. I enquired of her health. He said she was something better: and that, I suppose, encouraged him to come out. But D[r] Balguy tells me, that Heberden says she is irretrievably gone; and has touched upon it to him, and ought to do it to her' (*Letters of a late eminent Prelate*, p. 291).

[3] Hon. Frederick Augustus Hervey (see Letter 329, n. 5).

[4] George Berkeley, Bishop of Cloyne, 1734–53. The allusion is to Dialogue II of Pope's *Epilogue to the Satires*:

> Manners with Candour are to *Benson* giv'n,
> To *Berkeley*, ev'ry Virtue under Heav'n.

(ll. 72–3.)

I think it probable that the Swelling You complain of in your throat is owing to some little swelling in a Gland. I had a complaint of the same kind a great while & after I used myself first to a flannel round my neck at Night & afterwards constantly lying in my stock the disorder left me. I wish you would try the same method, if you have not tryd it already. Dear Mr Gray beleive me to be,

Yours most cordially
W MASON

My Wife sends her kindest Compliment.

435. GRAY TO MASON

Dear Mason   Sunday. 15 Feb: 1767.

IT grieves me to hear the bad account you give of our poor Patient's health. I will not trouble you to enquire into the opinions of her Physicians: as you are silent on that head, I doubt you are grown weary of the inutility of their applications. I (you will remember) am at a distance, & can not judge (but by conjecture) of the progre∫s her disorder seems to make, & particularly of that increasing weakne∫s, wch seems indeed an alarming symptom. I am told, that the sea-air is advised as likely to be beneficial, & that L^d H: offers you the use of Walmer-Castle,¹ but that you wait till the spring is more advanced to put this in execution. I think, I should by no means delay at all. the air of the coast is at all seasons warmer, than that of the inland-country: the weather is now mild & open, & (unle∫s the rains increase) fit for travelling. remember, how well she bore the journey to London; & it is certain, that sort of motion in her case instead of fatigue often brings an acce∫sion of strength. I have lately seen that coast,² & been in Deal-Castle, wch is very similar in situation to Walmer & many other little neighbouring forts. no doubt, you may be very well lodged & accommodated there: the scene is delightful in fine weather, but in a stormy day & high wind (and we are but just

LETTER 435.—First printed by Mitford in *Gray–Mason* (1853), pp. 373-7; now reprinted from original.

¹ On his dismissal from the Secretaryship of State in Mar. 1761, Holdernesse was given the reversion of the Wardenship of the Cinque Ports for life, after the Duke of Dorset, at that time Constable of Dover and Warden, who was very infirm. Holdernesse had become Constable and Warden on the Duke's death in Oct. 1765. Walmer Castle was his official residence.

² In May and June 1766 (see Letters 422 and 423).

got so far in the year as the middle of February) exposed to all the rage of the sea, & full force of the East: so that to a Person unused to the sea, it may be even dreadful. my idea therefore is, that you might go at present to Ramsgate, wch is shelter'd from the North, & opening only to S: & S:E:, with a very fine pier to walk on.³ it is a neat Town, seemingly with very clean houses to lodge in, & one end of it only running down to the shore. it is at no season much pester'd with company, & at present I suppose there is no body there. if you find Mrs Mason the better for this air & situation (wch God send) when May & fine settled weather come in, you will easily remove to Walmer, wch at that season will be delightful to her. if—forgive me for supposing the worst: your letter leaves me too much reason to do so, tho' I hope it was only the effect of a melancholy imagination. if it should be necefsary to meet the spring in a milder climate than ours is: you are very near Dover, & perhaps this expedient (if she grow very visibly worse) may be preferable to all others, & ought not to be defer'd. it is usually too long delay'd.

There are a few words in your letter, that make me believe, you wish I were in Town. I know myself, how little one like me is form'd to support the spirits of another, or give him consolation: one that always sees things in their most gloomy aspect. however be afsured, I should not have left London while you were in it, if I could well have afforded to stay there till the beginning of April, when I am usually there. this however shall be no hindrance, if you tell me, it would signify any thing to you, that I should come sooner. Adieu! you (both of you) have my best & sincerest good wishes. I am ever

Yours
T G:

P:S:—Remember, if you go into Kent, that W. Robinson lives at Denton (8 miles from Dover) perhaps he & his Wife⁴ might be of some little use to you. him you know; & for her she is a very good-humour'd, chearful Woman, that (I dare swear) would give any kind of afsistance in her power. remember too

---

³ Mitford notes: 'Sir Egerton Brydges told me that when Gray was staying in Kent with his friend the Rev. W. Robinson, they went over to Ramsgate. The stone pier had just been built. Some one said, "For what did they make this pier?" Gray immediately said, *"For me to walk on"*, and proceeded, with long strides, to claim possession of it.'

⁴ See Letter 316, n. 5.

to take whatever medecines you use with you from London: a countrey Apothecarie's shop is a terrible thing.[5]

‚My respects to Dr Gisburne, & love to Stonhewer. when you have leisure & inclination, I should be very glad to hear from you. need I repeat my kindest good wishes to Mrs Mason!

Addressed: To The Revd Mr Mason at Mr Mennis's in Cleveland Row St James's London *Postmark:* SAFFRON WALDEN 16 FE

436. GRAY TO MASON

My Dear Mason   March. 28. 1767.

I BREAK in upon you at a moment, when we least of all are permitted to disturb our Friends, only to say, that you are daily & hourly present to my thoughts. if the *worst* be not yet past: you will neglect & pardon me. but if the last struggle be over: if the poor object of your long anxieties be no longer sensible to your kindnefs, or to her own sufferings: allow me (at least in idea, for what could I do, were I present, more than this?) to sit by you in silence, & pity from my heart not her, who is at rest; but you, who lose her. may He, who made us, the Master of our pleasures, & of our pains, preserve & support you! Adieu

I have long understood, how little you had to hope.[1]

437. BEATTIE TO GRAY

March 30, 1767.

*   *   *   *   *
*   *   *   *   *
*   *   *   *   *

A PROFESSOR at Edinburgh[1] has published an Efsay on the History of Civil Society, but I have not seen it. It is a fault

[5] So it was in those days, for Adam Smith computes the value of all the drugs in the shop of a country apothecary at no more than 25*l*. *Mitford.*

LETTER 436.—First printed by Mason in *Memoirs*, p. 324; now reprinted from original.

[1] In the blank space at the end of the letter in the original Mason has appended the following note (which he printed in the *Memoirs*): 'as this little Billet wch I rec^d at the Hot Wells almost at the precise moment when it would be most affecting, then breathd & still seems to breathe the voice of Friendship in its tenderest & most pathetic note, I cannot refrain from Publishing it in this place.' Mrs. Mason died on 27 March, 1767.

LETTER 437.—Extract from letter, first printed in Mason's *Memoirs*, p. 326 n.

[1] This was Adam Ferguson (1723–1816). Having been ordained, in

common to almost all our Scotch authors, that they are too metaphysical: I wish they would learn to speak more to the heart, and less to the understanding; but alas! this is a talent which heaven only can bestow: Whereas the philosophic spirit (as we call it) is merely artificial and level to the capacity of every man, who has much patience, a little learning, and no taste.[2] . . .

438. MASON TO GRAY

Dear M[r] Gray   Bath April 1st 1767

THE dear testimonial of your friendship reachd Bristol about the time when the last offices were done to my lost angel at the Cathedral & was brought to me hither just now; Where I had fled to My Wadworth[1] relations a few Hours before the Ceremony. I cannot exprefs the State of my Mind or health, I know not what either of them are. But I think that I mean at present to steal thro London very soon & come to you at Cambridge, tho I fear it is about the time you are going to Town. I have businefs there with Sidney College. I can add no more. But that I am as much Yours as I am my own

W. M.

Addressed: To Thomas Gray Esq[r] at Pembroke Hall Cambridge

439. GRAY TO MARY ANTROBUS

Dear Mary   May . . 1767. Jermyn-Street

THE note I inclose to you is for money lent by poor Graves,[1] while he lived with me, to a pot-companion of his. we look'd upon it long as a desperate debt, but of late have

1745 he was appointed chaplain to the Black Watch, in which capacity he was present at the battle of Fontenoy (May 1745). About 1754 he abandoned the clerical profession; and after being Librarian to the Faculty of Advocates he became Professor of Natural Philosophy at Edinburgh in 1759; of Moral Philosophy in 1764. His *Essay on the History of Civil Society* was published at Edinburgh in 1767.

² He has since dilated on this just sentiment in his admirable Essay on the Immutability of Truth. *Mason.* (See Letter 522, n. 3.)

LETTER 438.—First printed by Mitford in *Gray–Mason* (1853), p. 379; now reprinted from original.

¹ Mitford printed 'Wadsworth' and in the Additional Notes in his second edition (p. 529) corrected it to 'Wadworth' and added a note that Mason's relations were Mr. and Mrs. Wordsworth, who lived at Wadworth, near Doncaster (see Letter 209, n. 1). Mrs. Wordsworth was a first cousin of Mason, and her brother was the Rev. Arthur Robinson. He and his wife are the Robinsons mentioned in Letter 450. (See Genealogical Table.)

LETTER 439.—Now first printed from the original.

learn'd, that the Man is set up in a way of businefs, & very capable of paying it. the reason I trouble you with it is this. your Cousin *T: Hide*[2] has several times mention'd it to my Servant *Stephen,*[3] & was so obliging to offer his afsistance in getting the money. if he will really give himself that trouble, it will be a deed of charity, & I should be very glad of his succefs. you will take care of the note, wch is already torn & tatter'd with age: if any little expence is incur'd, Graves will gladly satisfy it out of the money, & be very thankful.

My shirts[4] begin exceedingly to want company, w^ch (I hope) they may shortly expect, & I as much want to get into the North. when you send them, you will please to add a bill of my debts to you, & insert the expence you were at for what you bought the morning I set out for Hadham:[5] and I will send the money, & thank you. I know not, whether Dolly[6] will want any farther intelligence from me, before I go. if she does, let her tell me soon. she has already an account of the rents of Hand-Alley;[7]

[1] Graves Tokeley, a former servant of Mrs. Rogers, and, after her death, of Gray (see Letter 305, n. 10).

[2] Thomas Hide, son of Mrs. Antrobus's sister, Anne Nutting (d. 1759), who married John Hide, Alderman Nutting's book-keeper, according to Cole (see Genealogical Table).

[3] Stephen Hempsted, as appears from the following clause in Gray's will (dated 2 July 1770): 'I give to my Servant, Stephen Hempsted, the sum of fifty pounds Reduced Bank-annuities, and (if he continue in my service to the time of my death) I also give him all my wearing-apparel and linnen.' Stephen apparently married a few months before Gray's death (see Letter 548, n. 15), and may have left his service; he was, however, in attendance upon Gray during his last illness, for in a letter to Wharton, written on Monday night, 29 July 1771 (the night before Gray died), Brown says: 'Stephen his old servant is very diligent and handy in his attendance upon him, & Mr Gray is well satisfied with it' (see Appendix W).

[4] Gray had recourse to Mary Antrobus for help in replenishing his wardrobe, and in other domestic matters. In his pocket-book for 1760 is the entry: 'M. Antrobus for Linen & Ruffles 5 shirts & making 5. 9. 0'; and in his letter to her of 24 Nov. 1759 (Letter 305) he asks her advice as to material for curtains.

[5] See Letter 305, n. 4. Gray's journey to Hadham was probably to attend the funeral of Mary's brother, Robert, who died on 29 Mar. 1767 (see Letter 283*, n. 7).

[6] Her sister Dorothy (see Letter 293, n. 3).

[7] By her will Mrs. Rogers left to Gray 'one Moiety or half part of all that my Moiety or half part of the several Messuages or Tenements Hereditaments and Premises situate in Hand Alley in the parish of Saint Botolph Without, Bishopsgate'; and to her sister, Jane Olliffe 'the other Moiety or half part of the said Moiety of the said several Messuages etc.'. For an

a state of the case with regard to the Conveyance, wch Worlidge[8] ought to have got ready & sign'd; & the Extract from Mrs Rogers's Will. I would wish to send her an account of the Taxes, but have it not perfect myself. in the mean time I send her, what appears from the last account (turn over). you will give my service to your Mamma, & love to Dolly. I am sincerely

Yours
T G:

			£ .. s .. D:
1.	Tho: Tilson (has a Lease, & pays the Taxes himself)		
2.	Hurst.		
3.	Tho: Abbis.		
4.	Mrs Humphreys - - - - - - - - - - - - -		0 -- 12 -- 0
5.	West - - - - - - - - - - - - - - -		0 -- 14 -- 0
6.	Crack - - - - - - - - - - - - - -		
7.	Mrs Burgefs - - - - - - - - - - - - -		0 -- 10 -- 0
8.	Terry - (will pay no rent, nor quit the house)		
9.	Leach - - - - - - - - - - - - - - -		0 -- 10 -- 0
10.	Davis - - - - - - - - - - - - - - -		0 -- 10 -- 0
11.	Munt, for his house, & stable-yard, has no lease, but pays taxes himself - - - -		
12.	Hatton (no house, but a saw-yard) - - -		
13.	Mrs Richardson (has a Lease)- - - - - - - -		2 -- 0 -- 0

They all (I think) are allow'd the Tax, except *Tilson, Munt,* & *Hatton,* but in some cases I really do not know to what it amounts. observe, that what I set down belongs to Mrs Olliffe & myself jointly: so that you are only to reckon the half of it, as deducted from your part of the rents.[9] the bills brought in by the Workmen amount in the whole (Mr Eyres[10] included) to about 105£.

account of the property and an explanation of the conveyance to which Gray refers see Appendix U.

[8] Worlidge was no doubt a solicitor. Philip and John Worlidge were the witnesses to Mrs. Rogers's will.

[9] If Mrs. Olliffe was at the time living with her sister at Cambridge 'your part of the rents' might refer to the share due to her, of which her niece Dorothy was keeping account. Another possible explanation is that Gray had made over to his nieces his share of the income from the estate.

[10] This was no doubt Joseph Eyre, who, with a partner, subsequently purchased the property (see Letter 479, n. 6, and Appendix U).

William Mason
(*holding a copy of the epitaph on his wife*)
from a painting at Nuneham Park

440. GRAY TO MASON

Jermyn-Street. 23 May. 1767.

Dear Mason

ALL this time have I been waiting to say something to the purpose, & now am just as far off as at first. Stuart[1] appointed Mr Weddell an hour, when I was to meet him, & (after staying an infinite while at his lodgings in expectation) he never came: indeed he was gone out of Town. the *drawing* & your *questions* remain in Weddell's hands to be shew'd to this Rogue, as soon as he can meet with him: but I firmly believe, when he has got them, he will do nothing. so you must tell me, what I am to do with them. I have shew'd the Epitaph to no one but Hurd, who entirely approves it. he made no objection, but to one line (& that was mine) *Heav'n lifts* &c:[2] so if you please to make another, you may: for my part I rather like it still.

I begin to think of drawing northwards (if my wretched matters will let me) & am going to write to Mr Brown about it. you are to consider, whether you will be able or willing to receive us at Aston about a fortnight hence, or whether we are to find you at York, where I suppose you to be at present. this you will let me know soon, & if I am disappointed, I will tell you in time. you will tell me, what to do with your *Zumpe*,[3] wch has

LETTER 440.—First printed by Mitford in *Gray–Mason* (1853), pp. 380–1; now reprinted from original.

[1] James Stuart, the architect (see Letter 267, n. 8). Mason desired to have Stuart's opinion of his sketch for the memorial tablet to Mrs. Mason, which was to be set up in Bristol Cathedral (see Letter 444).

[2] Norton Nicholls in his *Reminiscences of Gray* (see Appendix Z) says: 'The last four lines of Mason's epitaph on his wife were written by Gray, I saw them in his hand-writing interlined in the Mss. which he shewed me. The words of Mrs Mason when she had given up all hope of life:

> "Tell them tho' 'tis an awful thing to die,
> 'Twas e'en to thee, yet the dread path once trod
> Heaven lifts its everlasting portals high,
> And bids the pure in heart behold their God."

I do not now remember the lines of Mason which were effaced & replaced by these which have the genuine sound of the lyre of Gray. I remember that they were weak, with a languid repetition of some preceding expressions. Mr Gray said "That will never do for an ending, I have altered them thus."'

[3] In the (posthumous) article on 'Harpsichord' in Rees's *Cyclopædia* Burney wrote: 'Zumpe, a German who had long worked under Shudi, constructed small piano-fortes of the shape and size of the virginal, of which the tone was very sweet, and the touch, with a little use, equal to any degree

amused me much here. if you would have it sent down, I had better commit it to its Maker, who will tune it & pack it up. Dr Long has bought the fellow to it. the base is not quite of a piece with the treble, & the higher notes are somewhat dry & sticky: the rest discourses very eloquent musick.[4] Adieu! Dear S^r, I am ever

Yours
T G:

Gisburne, Fraser, & Stonhewer, often enquire kindly after you, with many more.

441. GRAY TO BROWN

[Jermyn Street, c. May 28, 1767][1]

How do you do, good Mr. Brown? Do your inclinations begin to draw northward, as mine do, and may I take you a place soon? I wait but for an answer from Mason how to regulate our journey, which I should hope may take place in a little more than a week. I shall write a line again to settle the exact day, but you may now tell me whether you will come to town, or be taken up at Buckden,[2] or thirdly, whether you will go in a chaise with me by short journeys, and see places in our way. I dined yesterday on Richmond Hill, after seeing Chiswick,[3] and Strawberry, and Sion;[4] and be afsured the face of the country looks an emerald, if you love jewels.

The Westminster Theatre[5] is like to come to a sudden end.

---

of rapidity. These . . . suddenly grew into such favour, that there was scarcely a house in the kingdom, where a keyed instrument had ever had admission, but was supplied with one of Zumpe's piano-fortes' (vol. xvii, 1819).   [4] *Hamlet*, III. ii. 374.

LETTER 441.—First printed by Mitford in *Gray–Mason* (1853), pp. 385–8.

[1] Date conjectural; in his next letter of 2 June (Tuesday) Gray refers to this letter as having been written 'last week'.

[2] In Huntingdonshire, on the Great North Road, where Brown, coming from Cambridge, would await Gray's arrival from London.

[3] The villa built (1730–6) by Richard Boyle, third Earl of Burlington, well known as an amateur architect. It belonged at this date to the Duke of Devonshire, whose mother, the wife of the fourth Duke, was the daughter and heiress of the Earl of Burlington.

[4] Probably Syon House, at Isleworth, belonging to the Duke of Northumberland.

[5] On 12 Dec. 1766 Walpole wrote to George Montagu: 'The Duke of York is erecting a Theatre at his own palace and is to play Lothario in the *Fair Penitent* himself.'

The manager[6] will soon embark for Italy without Callista.[7] The reason is a speech, which his succefs in Lothario emboldened him to make the other day in a greater theatre.[8] It was on the subject of America,[9] and added so much strength to the opposition, that they came within six of the majority. He did not vote, however, though his two brothers did, and, like good boys, with the ministry. For this he has been rattled on both sides of his ears, and forbid to appear there any more.[10] The Houses wait with impatience the conclusion of the East India businefs[11] to rise. The E. of Chatham is mending slowly in his health, but sees nobody on businefs yet, nor has he since he came from Marlborough: yet he goes out daily for an airing.[12]

[6] The Duke of York.

[7] Calista was the heroine of Rowe's *Fair Penitent*. The part of Calista was played by Lady Stanhope, sister of Sir Francis Blake Delaval (see Letter 127, n. 6), and third wife of Sir William Stanhope, K.B.

[8] The House of Lords.

[9] Walpole wrote to Mann on 24 May: 'Last Friday [22 May] the House of Lords examined the rejection by the Privy Council of the Act of Assembly of Massachusetts Bay . . . the motion [of the Opposition] was rejected by only sixty-two voices to fifty-six. . . . A more remarkable event of the day was, that the Duke of York spoke for the first time—and against the court; but did not vote. His two brothers [the Dukes of Gloucester and Cumberland] voted with the ministry. . . . This is not the only walk of fame he has lately chosen. He is acting plays with Lady Stanhope and her family, the Delavals. They have several times played *The Fair Penitent*.'

[10] On 30 May Walpole wrote to Mann: '[The Duke of York] is in great disgrace; he has been thoroughly chid, was not spoken to at a great review on Monday in the face of all England, and, they say, is to go on a pilgrimage with his sister to Spa.' He went to Paris, and thence to Monaco, where he died of a malignant fever on 17 Sept.

[11] Towards the end of 1766 Chatham had determined to institute an inquiry into the affairs of the East India Company. The matter had dragged on for six months and Walpole announced to Mann on 24 May that an accommodation had been made with the Company (the settlement consisting in the agreement of Parliament to accept from the Company £400,000 a year for two years).

[12] After the end of the session in Dec. 1766 Chatham had gone once more to Bath to recruit his health, but was seized with gout, which kept him there for a couple of months. When at last he set out to return, he relapsed on the road, and, being forced to lie up again for several weeks at Marlborough, did not reach London till the beginning of March, when he was forbidden by his physician, Dr. Addington, to do the least business, and there were rumours that his head was disordered. On 24 May Walpole writes: 'Lord Chatham's state, I doubt, is, too clearly, the gout flown up into his head. He may recover, but, as yet, he is assiduously kept from all company.' In this condition, incapacitated from all attention to business, and cut off from all intercourse with the outside world, he remained till Oct. 1768.

I have seen his lordship of Cloyne[13] often. He is very jolly, and we devoured four raspberry-puffs together in Cranbourn-alley[14] standing at a pastrycook's shop in the street; but he is gone, and Heaven knows when we shall eat any more. Roufseau you see is gone too. I read his letter to my Lord Chancellor from Spalding, and hear he has written another long one to Mr. Conway from Dover, begging he might no longer be detained here.[15] He retains his pension.[16] The whole seems madnefs increasing upon him. There is a most bitter satire on him and his Madlle. le Vafseur,[17] written by Voltaire, and called *Guerre de Geneve*.[18] Adieu, and let me hear from you.

I am ever yours,

T. G.

How do our Elmsted friends?[19] Are they married yet? Old Pa. is here, and talks of writing soon to you.

[13] See Letter 434, n. 3.

[14] 'Cranbourne Alley, Leicester Square, a paved thoroughfare for foot-passengers ... leading from Castle Street to the north-east corner of Leicester Square. ... The name was derived from the Cecils, Earls of Salisbury, and Viscounts Cranbourne' (Wheatley's *London*).

[15] Tovey quotes the following: 'Rousseau, while staying at Wootton in Derbyshire [see Letter 423, n. 4], became the victim of insane delusions, believing that the whole English nation was in a plot against him. In a paroxysm of terror he fled away from Wootton. From Spalding, where he was next heard of, he wrote a long letter to the Lord Chancellor, Lord Camden, praying him to appoint a guard, at Rousseau's own expense, to escort him in safety out of the kingdom where enemies were plotting against his life. From Dover, on 18 May, he wrote a letter to General Conway (Secretary of State), setting forth his delusions in full form' (see *Rousseau*, by John Morley, 1873, vol. ii, chap. 15, pp. 306–8).

[16] 'George III, then in the heyday of his youth, was so pleased to have a foreigner of genius seeking shelter in his kingdom, that he readily acceded to Conway's suggestion, prompted by Hume, that Rousseau should have a pension settled on him' (Morley, *op. cit.*). The pension, which was £100 a year, was granted at the beginning of 1766, on Rousseau's first arrival in England.

[17] Marie Thérèse Le Vasseur (1721–1801), the servant at the inn in Paris (the Hôtel Saint-Quentin, in the Rue des Cordiers, near the Sorbonne) where Rousseau lodged in 1742, lived with him as his mistress for more than thirty years, and was the mother, as he alleged, of five children, whom he secretly deposited at the Enfants Trouvés. Thérèse followed Rousseau to England under the escort of Boswell.

[18] *La Guerre Civile de Genève, ou les Amours de Robert Covelle, Poëme Heroïque, Avec des Notes Instructives* (Paris, MDCCLXVII).

[19] On the assumption that 'Mr Talbot', often mentioned in Gray's letters to Brown, was William Talbot, Fellow of Clare (see Letter 241, n. 15), it is suggested that 'Elmstead' was a mistake of Gray (or Mitford) for 'Elmsett'. Elmsett is a parish in Suffolk; the patronage of the living was held by Clare

442. GRAY TO BROWN

Jermyn Street, June 2, 1767.

Dear Sir

WHERE are you? for I wrote to you last week[1] to know how soon we should set out, and how we should go. Mason writes to-day, he will expect us at Aston in Whitsun-week; and has ordered all his lilacs and roses to be in flower. What can you be doing? And so as I said, shall we go in the Newcastle post-coach or the York coach? Will you choose to come to town or be taken up on the way? Or will you go all the way to Bawtry[2] in a chaise with me and see sights? Answer me speedily. In return I will tell you that you will soon hear great news; but whether good or bad is hard to say; therefore I shall prudently tell you nothing more. Adieu.—I am ever yours,

T. G.

Old Pa. is still here, going to Ranelagh and the Opera. Lady Strathmore is with child, and not very well, as I hear.

443. GRAY TO BROWN

Jermyn Street, Saturday, June 6, 1767.

Dear Sir

MY intention is (*Deo volente*) to come to Cambridge on Friday or Saturday next; and shall expect to set out on Monday following. I shall write to Mason by to-night's post, who otherwise would expect us all Whitsun-week. Pray that the Trent

College, and William Talbot was presented to the Rectory in 1766. In the *Gentleman's Magazine* for July 1767 (p. 382) there appeared the announcement of a marriage on 15 July: 'The Rev. Mr. Talbot of Clare-hall to Miss Kirke, a near relative of the late Dr Newcombe's.' 'Our Elmstead friends' would thus be William Talbot and his future wife.

LETTER 442.—First printed by Mitford in *Gray–Mason* (1853), p. 382.
[1] Letter 441.
[2] Mitford printed 'Bantry' in the text and corrected it in his second edition. Bawtry is nine miles south of Doncaster, where the Great North Road enters Yorkshire from Nottinghamshire; here the road to Rotherham and Sheffield branches off to the left across the River Idle. (Gray perhaps wrote Bautry, as he did in Letter 444.)

LETTER 443.—First printed by Mitford in *Gray–Mason* (1853), pp. 383–5.

may not intercept us at Newark,[1] for we have had infinite rain here, and they say every brook sets up for a river.

I said nothing of Lady M. Lyon,[2] because I thought you knew she had been long despaired of. The family I hear now do not go into Scotland till the races[3] are over, nor perhaps then, as my lady will be advancing in her pregnancy, and I should not suppose the Peats[4] or the Firth very proper in her condition; but women are courageous creatures when they are set upon a thing.

Lord Bute is gone ill into the country with an ague in his eye and a bad stomach. Lord Holland is alive and well,[5] and has written three poems; the only line in which, that I have heard, is this:[6]

'White-liver'd Grenville and self-loving Gower.'[7]

Lord Chatham is ———,[8] and the Rockinghams are like the brooks that I mentioned above.[9] This is all the news that I know. Adieu.

I am ever yours,
T. G.

[1] See Letter 475, n. 14.

[2] Lady Mary Lyon, third sister of Lord Strathmore; she had died a fortnight before, on 22 May.

[3] Durham races (see Letter 445).

[4] There does not seem to be any part of the road to Glamis called 'the Peats'. Gray probably meant roads across the moors.

[5] Lord Holland had left England at the end of Sept. 1766 for a tour in Italy for the sake of his health, and had landed at Kingsgate on his return a week or two before the date of this letter.

[6] This line comes from some verses, which he had privately printed, entitled, 'Lord Holland returning from Italy' (see Appendix T).

[7] See Letter 373. Lord Gower became Lord President of the Council in December this year.

[8] What Gray wrote may have been obliterated, or he may have left a blank to imply that Chatham was mad (see Letter 441, n. 12).

[9] With regard to the situation. Walpole wrote to Mann on 20 July: 'You have heard enough . . . of our *interministeriums*, not to be surprised that the present lasts so long . . . the Parliament was scarce separated when a negotiation was begun with the Bedfords, through Lord Gower, with a view to strengthen the remains of administration by that faction.' This negotiation was wrecked by Lord Temple's exorbitant demands. Another was then begun with Lord Rockingham, who, elated with some initial success, assumed that instead of strengthening the existing administration he was to be entrusted with the formation of a new 'comprehensive ministry'. He was, however, soon undeceived by the King, and consequently this negotiation also came to nothing.

444. GRAY TO MASON

Dear Mason   June 6. 1767. Jermyn-street.

WE are a-coming, but not so fast as you think for, because Mr Brown can not think of stirring till Whitsun-week is over. the Monday following[1] we propose to set out in our chaise: do not think of sending Benjamin,[2] I charge you. we shall find our way from Bautry very cleverly.

I shall bring with me a drawing,[3] wch Stuart[4] has made. he approves your sketch highly, & therefore (I suppose) has alter'd it in every particular, not at all for the better in my mind. he says, you should send him an account of the place & position, & a scale of the dimensions; this is what I modestly proposed before, but you give no ear to me. the relief, in artificial stone,[5] he thinks, would come to about eight guineas.

Poor Mr Fitzherbert[6] had a second Son, who was at Caen: he complain'd of a swelling & some pain in his knee, wch rather increasing upon him, his Father sent for him over. the Surgeons agreed, it was a White-swelling, & he must lose his leg. he underwent the operation with great fortitude, but died the second day after it. Adieu! I am ever

Yours
T G:

I rejoice, Mr Wood[7] is well, & present my humble service to him.

LETTER 444.—First printed by Mitford in *Gray–Mason* (1853), pp. 388–9; now reprinted from original.   [1] 15 June.   [2] Mason's servant.

[3] The monument to Mrs. Mason is on the wall of Bristol Cathedral. Above a white tablet containing Mason's epitaph to his wife is a smaller tablet with the note of her death. Surmounting this, in shallow relief, is an urn with a female figure.   [4] See Letter 440, n. 1.

[5] This was no doubt 'Coade's artificial stone', or 'lithodipra', which was made at Lambeth in the factory where the sculptor, John Bacon, worked in his early years. The two statues in the façade of the Soane Museum are of this material, as were the piers of the Gothic gateway into Horace Walpole's garden.

[6] William Fitzherbert (d. 1772), of Tissington, near Ashbourne, in Derbyshire; M.P.; Lord of Trade, 1765–72. He figures frequently in Boswell's *Life of Johnson*, where a 'portrait' of him by Johnson is recorded under 1777. He committed suicide by hanging himself with a bridle in his own stable (see Walpole to Lady Ossory, 5 Jan. 1772). His fourth son, Thomas, the son here in question, born in 1750, was a Lieutenant in the 21st Regiment of Foot, and died unmarried in 1767. The fifth and youngest son, Alleyne, after a distinguished career at Cambridge, and in the Diplomatic Service, was created an Irish Peer as Baron St. Helen's in 1791 (see Letter 535, n. 5).

[7] Rev. John Wood, Mason's former curate at Aston (see Letter 263, n. 7).

445. GRAY TO WHARTON

Sunday. 21 June. 1767. Aston.

Dear Doctor

HERE we are, Mr Brown & I, in a wildernefs of sweets, an Elysium among the coal-pits, a terrestrial heaven. mind, it is not I, but Mason, that says all this, & bids me tell it you. tomorrow we visit Dovedale & the Wonders of the Peak, the Monday following we go to York to reside,[1] & two or three days after set out for Old-Park, where I shall remain upon your hands; & Mr Brown about the time of Durham-races must go on to Gibside,[2] & for ought I know to Glamis:[3] Mason remains tied down to his Minster for half a year.   he & M^r B: desire their best compliments to you & Mrs Wharton. Adieu!

I am ever Yours,

T GRAY.

Mr. B: owns the pleasantest day he ever past was yesterday at Roche-Abbey.[4]   it is indeed divine.

Addressed: To Dr Wharton at Old-Park near Darlington Durham *Postmark:* ROTHERHAM

446. GRAY TO MASON

Old-Park, near Darlington
July 10: 1767.

Dear Mason

WE are all impatient to see you in proportion to our various interests & inclinations.   Old-Park thinks, she must die a maid, if you don't come & lay her out: the River Atom weeps herself dry, & the Minikin[1] cries aloud for a channel.   when you

LETTER 445.—First printed by Mitford (1816), vol. ii, p. 478; now re-printed from original.

[1] That is, he and Brown would accompany Mason to York, where the latter had to go into residence as Canon Residentiary and Precentor.

[2] A property of Lord Strathmore's in the north of Durham, which came to him on his marriage to Miss Bowes (see Letter 194, n. 8).

[3] Brown went to Scotland on 1 Sept. (see Letter 453).

[4] About seven miles from Rotherham, and the same from Aston. Walpole visited it in Aug. 1772, while staying with Mason at Aston, and gave a description of it in his *Journals of Visits to Country Seats, etc.*

LETTER 446.—First printed by Mitford in *Gray–Mason* (1853), pp. 390–1; now reprinted from original.

[1] The 'Atom' and the 'Minikin' (see Letter 390, n. 3) were the names given to two tiny streamlets at Old Park. Mason was to make a plan for improving the grounds. Some months later he sent a sketch for the purpose,

can determine on your own motions, we pray you to give us immediate notice. soon as you arrive at Darlington, you will go to the *King's-Head*,[2] where may be had two Postillons, either of wch know the road hither: it is about 16 miles, & runs by Kirk-Merrington, & Spenny-moor House;[3] a little rough, but not bad or dangerous in any part. your Aunt (I hope) is well again, & little Clough[4] produces a plentiful crop: delay therefore no longer.

M^r Br: is enchanted & beatified[5] with the sight of Durham, whither he went yesterday. I perform'd your commifsion to Mrs Wilkinson,[6] who exprefs'd herself (I thought) like a Woman of a good heart, & wish'd much to see you. Adieu! we really long for you.

447. MASON TO GRAY

York July 15th 1767

Dear S^r

M^Y Old Aunt is dead[1] but she has not left me so much money that I can come and make ducks & drakes in the Minikin.[2] You will say I need not, I have only to teach Dr Wharton how to make them. Perhaps my metaphor was not well chosen, tis

and this included something to be done with 'the water' (see Letters 447, 459, and 484). There was, at one time, a fish-pond in the grounds of Old Park, and this may have been part of Mason's plan.

² The King's Head is mentioned in Paterson's *Road Book* as one of the two principal inns at Darlington. ³ See Letter 407, n. 14.

⁴ This name, which occurs again in Letter 453, was taken by Tovey to be that of a property of Mason. It appears, however, from Mason's unpublished letters to Rev. Christopher Alderson (see Letter 453, n. 7), that the name is that of a man with whom Mason had business relations. This was John Clough, described in the obituary notice of him in the *Gentleman's Magazine* for 31 Dec. 1789 (vol. lix, p. 1215) as 'distributor and collector of stamps for York, and the West riding of that County, Register of the Deanery and Dean and Chapter's Court of York; one of the proctors of the Ecclesiastical Courts there, and a partner in the Bank of Messrs. Garforth and Co.' He was Mason's banker, and probably the agent through whom his stipends as Canon and Precentor of York were paid.

⁵ Evidently an expression used by Brown; Mason in the next letter refers to Brown's 'beatifications'; and Gray in his letter to Mason of 9 Aug. (Letter 451) refers to him as 'our beatified friend'.

⁶ Presumably Wharton's mother-in-law, his wife having been a Miss Wilkinson (see Letter 135, n. 2).

LETTER 447.—First printed by Mitford in *Gray–Mason* (1853), pp. 391–5; now reprinted from original.

¹ Nothing is known of Mason's 'Old Aunt', whether she were real or fictitious. ² See Letter 446, n. 1.

however as good as yours where you say Old Park must die a maid if I dont come & lay her *out.* When Mr Hurd comes to publish our correspondence I know what will be his Note upon this pafsage, "To have made the allusion appear with due congruity the Poet should have written lay her *down* for to lay her *out* supposes her to be already dead ˏw^{ch} the premises inform us this old Maid was not, & therefore only wanted to be *laid down.* As the Pafsage now stands there is an impropriety in it wch evn the freedom of the Epistolary mode of writing will not Justify." Take another Note from Dr Balguy: "There are two Vernacular Phrases wch we apply seperately, & wch indeed will not admit of a reciprocal usage in our tongue. the one we apply constantly where any thing is predicated concerning Gardening & the other we as constantly use as a term in Agriculture. Thus we lay *out* pleasure Grounds but we lay *down* feild Lands. Now had the writer deliverd the above sentiment without a figure he would have simply said Old Park wants to be *laid out,* & here as Old Park means a pleasure ground or Garden, the Phrase would have been just & pertinent. But he chose to personify Old park & to speak of her under the figure of an Old Maid, & hence arose the incongruity which the Critic has so justly stigmatizd, & wch would not have appeard so had Old Park been a common feild; but unhappily for the writer, Old Park was (as we have seen) a pleasure ground, or garden and as such requird to be *laid out* not to be *laid down,* hence it would not admit of the Metaphor in quæstion, & I know no way of reducing this passage into the rules of *chast* Composition but by supposing Old Park *arable;* then the figure will be in its place, & the *Maid* will be *laid down* in a *natural* & even *elegant* manner."

Explicit Nonsense—& now what remains must be serious. I dined lately at Bishopthorpe[3] when the Archbishop[4] took me into his Closet & with many tears, begd me to write an Epitaph on his daughter.[5] In our conversation he touchd so many unison Strings of my heart (for we both of us wept like childern) that I could not help promising him that I would try if pofsible to oblige him. The result you have on the opposite page, if it either is, or can be made a decent thing afsist me with your

[3] A village 2½ miles south of York, where the Archbishop's palace is situated.
[4] Archbishop Drummond (see Letter 344, n. 3).
[5] Her death is recorded in the *Gentleman's Magazine,* 1766, p. 390, as having taken place on 1 Aug. 1766.

Judgment immediatly, for what I do about it I would do quickly, & I can do nothing neither, if this will not do with correction. It cannot be expected, neither would I wish it, to be equal to what I have written from my heart, upon my Hearts heart[6]—Give me I beg your sentiments upon it as soon as pofsible. to conclude I wish heartily to be with you but cannot fix a time For I was obligd to invite Mr Robinson[7] & the Wordsworths[8] hither, & I have not rec^d their answer. In my next perhaps I can speak more detirminately. My best Compliments to D^r & Mrs Wharton & best wishes for the continuance of Mr Browns beatifications.[9]

yours cordially W MASON

EPITAPH ON MISS DRUMMOND

Hence stoic Apathy to hearts of Stone!
A Christian Sage with dignity can weep.
See mitred Drummond heave the heartfelt groan,
Where the cold ashes of his daughter sleep;
Here sleep what once was beauty, once was grace,
Grace that exprefst, in each benignant smile,
*That dearest harmony of soul, & face,
When beauty glories to be virtue's foil.

Such was the Maid, that, in the noon of youth,
In virgin innocence, in natures pride,
Grac'd with each liberal art, & crownd with truth,
Sunk in her fathers fond embrace, & died.
He weeps. O venerate the holy tear!
Faith sooths his sorrows, lightens all their load;
Patient he spreads his child upon her bier,
And humbly yeilds an Angel to his God.

* Or thus:
That sweetest Sympathy of soul & face,
When beauty only blooms as virtue's foil.

Addressed: To Thomas Gray Esqr at Doctor Whartons at Old Park near Darlington　*Postmark:* YORK

[6] His epitaph on Mrs. Mason (see Letter 440).
[7] See Letter 450, n. 2.
[8] See Letter 438, n. 1.　　　　　　[9] See Letter 446, n. 5.

448. GRAY TO MASON

Dear Mason   Sunday. July 19. 1767. Old-Park.

I COME forthwith to the epitaph, wch you have had the charity to write at the A:^p's request. it will certainly do (for it is both touching & new) but yet will require much finishing. I like not the three first lines: it is the Party most nearly concern'd, at least some one closely connected, & bearing a part in the lofs, that is usually supposed to speak on these occasions: but these lines appear to be written by the Chaplain, & have an air of flattery to his Patron. all that is good in them is better exprefsed in the four last verses. *Where the cold ashes* &c: these five verses are well, except the word *benignant,* & the thought (wch is not clear to mc, besides that it is somewhat *hardly* exprefs'd) of *When Beauty only blooms* &c: in gems, that want colour & perfection, a *foil* is put under them to add to their lustre: in others, as in diamonds, the foil is black; & in this sense when a pretty Woman chuses to appear in publick with a homely one, we say she uses her *as a foil.* this puzzles me, as you neither mean, that Beauty sets off Virtue by its contrast & opposition to it: nor that her Virtue was so imperfect, as to stand in need of Beauty to heighten its lustre. for the rest I read, *That sweetest harmony of soul* &c: *Such was the Maid,* &c: all this to the end I much approve, except—*crown'd with truth,* and lightens *all their load.* the first is not precise; in the latter you say too much. *Spreads his child* too is not the word. when you have corrected all these faults, it will be excellent.[1]

I thank you for your Comments on my inaccurate metaphor. in return I will be sure to shew them to the Parties,[2] who should have wrote them; & who doubtlefs, when they see them, will acknowledge them for their own. We are all much in want of you, & have already put off two journeys, because we thought you were to come on Mondays: pray tell us your mind out of hand, least we lose all our future Mondays. Mr Brown has not above another week to stay with us (for L^d St: comes on the 27th out of Scotland) & must go into the third heaven to see nothing-at-all, 'tall—all.[3] Adieu! I am truly

No news of Palgrave [   ]⁴   Yours.

LETTER 448.—First printed by Mitford in *Gray–Mason* (1853), pp. 396–7; now reprinted from original.
    [1] Gray's corrections were ultimately accepted by Mason (see Letter 450, n. 3).   [2] Hurd and Balguy (see Letter 447).
    [3] This was evidently a mannerism of Brown's.   ⁴ MS. torn.

449. GRAY TO MASON

26 July. 1767, Old-Park.

Dear Mason

Y OU are very perverse. I do desire, you would not think of dropping the design you had of obliging the A:ᴾ.[1] I submitted my criticisms to your own conscience, & I allow'd the latter half to be *excellent*, two or three little words excepted. if this will not do, for the future I must say (whatever you send me) that the whole is the most perfect thing in nature, wᶜʰ is easy to do, when one knows it will be acceptable. seriously I should be sorry, if you did not correct these lines; & am interested enough for the *party* (only upon your narrative) to wish, he were satisfied in it, for I am edified, when I hear of so *mundane*[2] a Man, that yet—He has a tear for pity—

By the way I ventured to shew the *other*[3] Epitaph to Dʳ Wh:, & sent him brim-full into the next room to cry: I believe, he did not hear it quite through, nor has he ever ask'd to hear it again. and now will you not come & see him?

We are just come back from a little journey to Barnard-Castle,[4] Rookby,[5] & Richmond[6] (Mʳ Brown & all, all)[7] some thoughts we have of going for two or three days to Hartlepool. then we (Dʳ W: & I), talk of seeing Westm:ᵈ & Cumberland, &

LETTER 449.—First printed by Mitford in *Gray–Mason* (1853), pp. 398–400; now reprinted from original.

[1] Mason's reply to Gray's letter of 19 July has not been preserved. He had resented Gray's criticisms and talked of giving up the epitaph altogether.

[2] Walpole in his *Last Journals*, under date 10 Dec. 1776, describes him as 'a sensible, worldly man, but much addicted to his bottle'.

[3] Mason's epitaph on his wife (see Letter 440).

[4] In Durham, on the Tees, seventeen miles west of Darlington; it takes its name from the ancient castle founded by Barnard Balliol (the principal scene of Scott's *Rokeby*), the remains of which extend over more than six acres. It belonged to the Vane family, who derived thence their titles of Baron and Viscount Barnard.

[5] In Yorkshire, near Greta Bridge, about three miles south-east of Barnard's Castle. The estate passed after the Civil War from the Rokeby family to the Robinsons, one of whom, at this time Archbishop of Armagh, was in 1777 created Baron Rokeby. In 1769 the estate was sold by Sir Thomas Robinson ('Long Sir Thomas'), first Baronet of Rokeby, to the father of J. B. S. Morritt, Scott's friend, to whom he dedicated *Rokeby*.

[6] In Yorkshire on the Swale, seventeen miles south of Darlington, where are the remains of an ancient Norman castle, situated on a perpendicular rock about 100 feet above the Swale.

[7] See Letter 448, n. 3.

perhaps the west of Yorkshire; the mountains I mean, for we despise the plains. then at our return I write to you, not to shew my talent at description, but to ask again, whether you will come or no. Adieu! I wish you health & peace of mind, and am ever

Yours

T G:

Mr Brown & the D^r desire their comp:^{ts} to Mr Robinson.[8]

450. MASON TO GRAY

York July 27th 1767

Dear Mr Gray

IN hopes this may catch you before you set off for Hartlepool I answer yours the moment I receive it (Minster Vespers only intervening) The Dean[1] has disapointed me & is not yet arrivd, the Robinsons[2] I expect every hour. in the meanwhile I will resume the subject of the Epitaph.

Had you given me any hint any *Lueur* how the three first lines might have been alterd, it would have been charitable indeed. But you say nothing, only that I must alter them, Now in my Conscience to wch you appeal I cannot find fault with the Sentiment wch they contain, & yet in dispite of my Conscience if I thought that they implyd the least shadow of flattery to the Æp I would wipe them out with a spunge dipt in the mud of the kennel. But I cannot think they do. I think on the contrary they give the Composition that Unity of Thought wch ought always to run thro compositions of this kind, for in my mind *a Perfect Epitaph is a Perfect Epigram without a sting.* NB this sentence in our Epistolæ Familiares cum notis variorum will be explaind, in a Note of Dr Balguys, to the contentation of every reader; in the meantime if you dont understand it yourself, console yourself with the pleasing Idea that Posterity will, & that is enough in reason.

---

[8] Mason's cousin, Rev. Arthur Robinson (see Letter 450, n. 2).

LETTER 450.—First printed by Mitford in *Gray–Mason* (1853), pp. 400–4; now reprinted from original.

[1] The Dean of York, Dr. John Fountayne (see Letter 353, n. 4).

[2] The Rev. Arthur Robinson and his wife. Arthur Robinson, Mason's first cousin, was the son of a Customs Officer at Sunderland of the same name (see Genealogical Table). He matriculated at Sidney Sussex College, Cambridge, in 1735; B.A. 1738; M.A. 1742; besides holding other livings in Yorkshire he was Vicar of Hull, 1753–83.

However to shew you my Complacency, & in dread that you should ever do as you threaten, & call whatever I send you the most perfect things in Nature, I will sacrifice the first Stanza on Your Critical Altar. & let it consume either in flame or *Smudge* as it chuses. Then we begin, *Here sleeps* a very poetical sort of *Ci git*, or *here lies*, & wch I hope will not lead the reader to imagine a sentence lost.

1   Here sleeps what once was Beauty once was Grace
2   Grace that with native Sentiment combind
3   To form that Harmony of Soul & face
4   Where Beauty shines the mirror of the mind
5   Such was the Maid that in the noon of youth,
6   In Virgin innocence in natures pride
7   Blest with each Art that taste supplies or Truth
8   Sunk in her Fathers fond embrace & died
9   He weeps O venerate the holy tear
10   Faith lends her aid to ease afflictions Load
11   The Parent mourns his child upon her bier
12   The Christian yeilds an Angel to his God.[3]

Various Lections, pick, & chuse,

2 *inborn* sentiment.

3 *displayd* or *diffusd* that Harmony &c.

[3] Mason's final version, first printed in the 'New Edition' of his *Poems* (1771), was as follows:

EPITAPH II

On the Honourable Miss DRUMMOND
In the Church of Brodsworth, Yorkshire.

Here sleeps what once was Beauty, once was Grace;
    Grace that with tenderness and sense combin'd
To form that harmony of soul and face,
    Where beauty shines the mirror of the mind.
Such was the Maid, that in the morn of youth,
    In virgin innocence, in nature's pride,
Blest with each art that owes its charm to truth
    Sunk in her Father's fond embrace and died.
He weeps: O venerate the holy tear:
    Faith lends her aid to ease affliction's load;
The Parent mourns his Child upon her bier,
    The Christian yields an Angel to his God.

It will be seen, by a comparison of the two versions, that Mason had adopted all Gray's suggested amendments; he had sacrificed the first stanza (see Letter 448) on Gray's critical altar. But it was against his own feelings, and in his Commonplace-book he transcribed the stanza at the beginning of the epitaph.

7 that *springs* from taste or Truth *derivd* from taste or Truth, that *charms* with taste & Truth. But, after all I dont know that she was a Metaphysician Blest with each art *that owes its charms* to Truth wch Painting does as well as Logic & Metaphysics.

10 Faith lends her lenient aid to Sorrows Load. Faith lends her Aid & *eases* or *lightens* Sorrows Load

11 Pensive he *mourns* or he *views* or *Gives*

12 *Yet humbly yeilds* or *But* humbly

Now if from all this you can pick out 12 Ostensible Lines, do, & Ill father them, or if you will out of that Lukewarm corner of your heart where you hoard up your poetical Charity, throw out a poor mite to my distresses, I shall take it kind indeed. But if not, Stat prior Sententia, for I will give myself no further trouble about it. I cannot in this uncomfortable place where my Opus Magnum sive didacticum[4] has not advancd ten lines since I saw you.

God bless Dr Wharton & send him (for his Sympathy) never to feel what I feel. I will come to him the moment I can; write be sure you [do] when you return from your longer tour. But I hope to have an answer to this before you set out, because I shall not give the ABp any detirminate answer about the matter till I hear again from you. The Robinsons are just arrivd.

Adieu W. M.

I must needs tell you, as an instance of my enjoyments here that Yesterday Mr Comber[5] preachd again & dind with me & in the afternoon who but Billy Harvey[6] should preach & drink tea with me! The said Billy enquird most Cordially after you & has got your directions how to come at you, by Kirksomething[7] & Spinny moor house, for he is going into Scotland with

[4] His *English Garden*, a work which Gray did not encourage (see Letter 509*, n. 4), the first volume of which was published in 1772.

[5] As Mitford suggested, this was no doubt William Comber, Vicar of Kirkby-Moorside, Yorks., second son of Thomas Comber, LL.D., of Buckworth, Hunts., and grandson of Thomas Comber (1645–99), D.D., Dean of Durham, 1691–9.

[6] Hon. William Hervey (1732–1815), fourth son of John, Lord Hervey, and next younger brother of the Bishop of Cloyne (see Letter 434, n. 3). He was admitted at Corpus Christi College, Cambridge, in 1751, and graduated M.A. in 1754. He subsequently entered the army, and became Major, 1782; Lieut.-General, 1793; and General, 1798. It was doubtless while in residence at Cambridge that he made the acquaintance of Gray and Mason. The latter's reference here to his 'preaching' must have been meant as a joke.

[7] Kirk-Merrington (see Letter 446).

a Scotch Captain, ten times duller than himself. youll have them at Old park almost as soon as this if you dont run away.

ANECDOTE.

The Country Folks are firmly persuaded that the Storm (wch made us get up here) was raisd by the Devil out of revenge to Comber for preaching *at him* the day before in the minster.

Addressed: To Thomas Gray Esq at Old Park near Darlington *Postmark:* YORK

451. GRAY TO MASON
Old-Park. 9 Aug: 1767. Sunday.
Dear Mason

I HAVE been at Hartlepool like any thing, & since that visiting about (wch is the ruin of all my country-expeditions) so that I was not able to write to you sooner. tomorrow I go *vizzing* to Gibside[1] to see the new-married Countefs,[2] whom (blefs my eyes!) I have seen here already: there I drop our beatified Friend,[3] who goes into Scotland with them; & return hither all alone. soon after I hope to go into Cumberland, &c: & when that is over, shall let you know.

I exceedingly approve the Epitaph in its present shape:[4] even what I had best liked before is alter'd for the better. the various readings I do not mind, only perhaps, I should read the 2d line

    Grace, that with tendernefs & sense combined
    To form &c:

for I hate *sentiment* in verse. I will say nothing to *Taste* & *Truth*, for perhaps the A:^p may fancy they are fine things, but to my palate they are Wormwood. all the rest is just as it should be, & what he ought to admire.

Billy Hervey[5] went directly to Durham, & call'd not here. he danced at the Afsembly with a conquering mien, & all the Mifses swear, he is the genteelest thing they ever set eyes on, &

LETTER 451.—First printed by Mitford in *Gray–Mason* (1853), pp. 404–6; now reprinted from original.
  [1] See Letter 445, n. 2.
  [2] Lady Strathmore.
  [3] Brown (see Letter 446, n. 5). It was probably for Brown's use on this journey to Scotland that Gray wrote the itinerary (based upon his notes of his own Scotch tour in the autumn of 1765) which is printed in Appendix Q.
  [4] See Letter 450, n. 3.   [5] See Letter 450, n. 6.

wants nothing but two feet more in height. the Doctor & Mr Brown send their blefsing, & I am ever

Yours
T G:

Addressed: To The Revd Mr Mason, Precentor of York *Postmark:* DARLINGTON

452. GRAY TO BEATTIE

Old-Park, near Darlington, Durham.
12 Aug: 1767.

S^r

I RECEIVED from Mr Williamson[1] that very obliging mark you were pleased to give me of your remembrance. had I not entertain'd some slight hopes of revisiting Scotland this summer, & consequently of seeing you at Aberdeen, I had sooner acknowledged by letter the favor you have done me. those hopes are now at an end: but I do not therefore despair of seeing again a country, that has given me so much pleasure; nor of telling you in person how much I esteem you, & (as you chuse to call them) your *amusements*. the specimen[2] of them, wch you were so good to send me, I think excellent. the sentiments are such as a melancholy imagination naturally suggests in solitude & silence, & that (tho' light & businefs may suspend or banish them at times) return with but so much the greater force upon a feeling heart. the diction is elegant & unconstrain'd, not loaded with epithets & figures, nor flagging into prose. the versification is easy & harmonious. my only objection is to the first part of this line

Perfumed with fresh fragrance &c:

where the consonants are harsh & frequent, tho' the image is good & the words in all other respects well chosen. a Friend[3] of

LETTER 452.—First printed in part in Mason's *Memoirs,* pp. 325–7; now first printed in full from original.

[1] James Williamson, a friend and former pupil of Beattie, who wished to continue his studies at one of the English Universities. He afterwards went to Oxford and became a Fellow of Hertford College. He took orders in the English Church, and held a living near Nottingham. Beattie had given him an introduction to Gray.

[2] Beattie had sent Gray a copy of his poem *The Hermit* written in 1766, first published with the *Minstrel* and a selection of his other poems in 1776.

[3] This was perhaps Mason. *The Hermit* had been written, 'at the request of a young lady, to suit the tune of *Pentland Hills*' (Miss Forbes, *Beattie and his Friends,* p. 26).

mine, to whom I shew'd these verses, rather blames the choice of your measure, as appropriated to comic, or at most to pastoral subjects: but I do not think his criticism of much weight. you see, S^r, I take the liberty you indulged me in, when I first saw you, & therefore I make no excuses for it, but desire you would take your revenge on me in kind.

I have read over (but too hastily) Mr Ferguson's book.[4] there are uncommon strains of eloquence in it, & I was surprised to find not one single idiom of his country (I think) in the whole work. he has not the fault you mention: his application to the heart is frequent, & often succefsful. his love of Montesquiou & Tacitus has led him into a manner of writing too short-winded & sententious, wch those great Men had they lived in better times & under a better government would have avoided.

I know no pretence, that I have, to the honor Lord Gray is pleased to do me:[5] but if his L^{dp} chuses to own me, it certainly is not my businefs to deny it. I say not this merely on account of his quality: but because he is a very worthy & accomplish'd Person. I am truly sorry for the great lofs[6] he has had, since I left Scotland. if you should chance to see him, I will beg you to present my respectful humble service to his Lordship.

I gave Mr Williamson all the information I was able in the short time he stay'd with me. he seem'd to answer well the character you gave me of him: but what I chiefly envied in him was his ability of walking all the way from Aberdeen to Cambridge, & back again, wch if I pofsefs'd, you would soon see

Your obliged & faithful humble Servant
T GRAY.

Addressed: To Mr Profefsor Beattie of the Marischal College Aberdeen
Postmark: DUNDEE

[4] See Letter 437.

[5] Lord Gray had said that our Author was related to his family. *Mason.*— Cole in a note on Mason's *Memoirs* (in Mitford (1835–43), vol. i, p. cviii) explains: 'It might probably arise from his lordship seeing the seal of arms on a letter, which Mr Gray used; and which were Gules, a lion rampant within a bordure, engrailed argent. . . . The Scotch Lord Gray bears these arms.' John Gray (1716–82), eleventh Lord Gray, must have met Gray on his visit to Scotland. Gray desired Foulis to send Lord Gray a copy of the edition printed at Glasgow in 1768 (see Letter 466).

[6] His eldest son, Andrew, born in 1742, died 23 May 1767.

453. GRAY TO MASON

Old-Park. Sept: 11. 1767.

Dear Mason

I ADMIRE you as the pink of perversity.[1] how did I know about York-Races? & how could I be more explicit about our journey. the truth is, I was only too explicit by half, for we did not set out in earnest till the 29th of August, being delay'd partly by the bad weather, & partly by your Cousin my Lord Perrot,[2] & his afsizes, whose train we were afraid to overtake, & still more afraid of being overtaken by it. at last then we went in the sun & dust broiling to Newcastle, & so by the military road to Hexham at night, where it begun to rain, & continued like fury (with very short intervals) all the rest of our way. so we got to Carlisle, pafs'd a day there in raining & seeing delights. next day got to Penrith (more delights) the next dined & lay at Keswick, could not go a mile to see anything. D[r] Wh: taken ill in the night with an asthma. went on however over stupendous hills to Cockermouth: here the D[r] grew still worse in the night, so we came peppering (& raining) back thro Keswick to Penrith. next day lay at Brough,[3] grew

LETTER 453.—First printed by Mitford in *Gray–Mason* (1853), pp. 406–9; now reprinted from original.

[1] 'The pink', denoting the flower of excellence, is found in Shakespeare, Steele, and Goldsmith. Gray applies it to a bad quality.

[2] George Perrot (1710–80), Baron of the Exchequer, 1763–75. Gray gives him the complimentary title of 'my Lord', as a judge: he was not a peer, nor was he even knighted. He belonged to a Yorkshire family and his father had held a living in York. Mason may have been acquainted with him and this would explain why Gray should associate him with Mason, by calling him 'your Cousin', in accordance with his playful habit of bestowing imaginary relationships.

[3] It must have been on this occasion that Gray wrote what Wharton described as: 'Extempore Epitaph on Ann Countess of Dorset, Pembroke and Montgomery, made by M[r] Gray on reading the Epitaph on her mother's tomb in the Church at Appleby, composed by the Countess in the same manner.' The epitaph written by the Countess (in 1617) was as follows:

Who Faith, Love, Mercy, noble Constancy
To God, to Virtue, to Distress, to Right
Observed, expressed, showed, held religiously
Hath here this monument thou seest in sight,
The cover of her earthly part, but passenger
Know Heaven and Fame contains the best of her.

The manuscript of Gray's burlesque epitaph is with the Wharton correspondence:

better (raining still) & so over Stanemoor[4] home, Sept: 5, in a heavy thunder-shower. now you will think from this detail, wch is litterally true, that we had better have staid at home. no such thing! I am charm'd with my journey, & the D^r dreams of nothing but Skiddaw, & both of us vow to go again the first opportunity. I carried Mr Brown to Gibside[5] the 11th of Aug: & took a receipt for him: they did not set out for Scotland till the 1st of September, & as yet I have not heard from him.

If you are not too much afflicted for the lofs of Charles Townshend,[6] now is your time to come & see us. in spite of your coquetry we still wish of all things to see you, & (bating that vice, & a few more little faults) have a good opinion of you, only we are afraid you have a bad heart. I have known purse-proud People often complain of their poverty, wch is meant as an insult upon the real poor. how dare you practise this upon me? don't I know little Clough![6a] here is a fufs indeed about poor threescore miles. don't I go galloping five hundred, whenever I please? have done with your tricks, & come to Old-Park, for the peaches & grapes send forth a good smell, & the voice of the Robin is heard in our land.[6b] my services to Mr. Alderston,[7]

> Now clean, now hideous, mellow now, now gruff,
> She swept, she hissed, she ripened and grew rough
> At Brougham, Pendragon, Appleby and Brough.

The last line alludes to four of her six castles (see Letter 511 A, n. 31).

[4] Stainmoor Fell is on the borders of Westmorland and Yorkshire.

[5] See Letter 451.

[6] Chancellor of the Exchequer in the Chatham Ministry (see Letter 212, n. 4); he died on 4 Sept. 1767. Gray's detestation of him was expressed in the sketch of his own character quoted in Letter 248, n. 2. Walpole says of him in his *Memoirs* (vol. iii, p. 72): 'He had almost every great talent and every little quality. . . . With such a capacity he must have been the greatest man of this age, and perhaps inferior to no man in any age, had his faults been only in a moderate proportion—in short, if he had had but common truth, common sincerity, common honesty, common modesty, common steadiness, common courage, and common sense.'

[6a] See Letter 446, n. 4.   [6b] *Song of Solomon*, ii. 12.

[7] The Rev. Christopher Alderson (whose name is misspelt here and by both Gray and Wharton in Letter 503) became Mason's curate at Aston in 1763. In 1771 he entered Pembroke College, Cambridge, and in 1782 graduated B.D. as a 'ten year man' (without examination or regular residence). After holding other preferment, on the death of Mason in 1797 he succeeded him as Rector of Aston. He was Mason's sole executor, and many of Gray's and Mason's papers and books remained in his possession, and in that of his son William Alderson, who succeeded him in the rectory and whom Mitford visited in 1850.

for he is a good creature: But I forget: you are at York again.
Adieu! I am ever

Yours
T G:

The Doctor presents his compliments to you with great cordiality, & desires your afsistance. one of his daughters[8] has some turn for drawing, & he would wish her a little instructed in the practise. if you have any Profefsor of the art at York, that would think it worth his while to pafs about six weeks here, he would be glad to receive him. his conditions he would learn from you. if he have any merit in his art, doubtlefs so much the better: but *above all* he must be elderly, & if ugly and ill-made, so much the more acceptable. the reasons we leave to your prudence.

454. GRAY TO BROWN

York . . Sat: 31. Oct: 1767.

Dear S^r

I HAVE received a letter from Howe,[1] another from Mr Beattie,[2] & a third, wch was a printed Catalogue, from London. the parcel sent to Cambridge was a set of Algarotti's works[3] for your Library, wch need not be impatient,[4] if it remain unopen'd, till I come. the Doctor & I came hither on Saturday last: he return'd on Wednesday, & I set out for London (pray for me!) at ten o'clock tomorrow night. you will please to direct to me at Roberts's,[5] as usual, & when it is convenient I shall be glad of my Bill.[6] I will trouble you also to give notice of my motions to Mifs Antrobus,[7] as soon as you can.

Here has been Ld Holdernefse's ugly face,[8] since I was here,

---

[8] This, as appears from Letter 459, was Peggy, Wharton's second daughter, at this time about 16 (see Letter 228, n. 5).

LETTER 454.—First printed by Mitford in *Gray–Mason* (1853), pp. 409–11; now reprinted from original.

[1] William Taylor How (see Letter 366, n. 7). The letter from How Gray answered on 12 Jan. 1768 (see Letter 462).

[2] Beattie's letter is not extant.

[3] See Letter 462.

[4] An echo of Mrs. Mincing in Congreve's *Way of the World* (see Letter 288, n. 2).

[5] In Jermyn-Street (Letter 176, n. 3).   [6] See Letter 281, n. 8.

[7] Molly Antrobus, who was resident in Cambridge with her mother, the Postmistress.

[8] These two words have been scored through in the original, but are still decipherable (see Letter 379, n. 11).

& here actually is Mr Weddell,[9] who enquires after you. Pa: is in London with his Brother,[10] who is desperate: if he dies, We shall not be a shilling the better, so we are really very sorrowful. Mason desires his love to you. Adieu! the Minster-bell rings! I am ever

                                             Yours

I rejoice greatly at N:'s good luck.[11]   T G

Addressed: To The Revd Mr Brown, President of Pembroke Hall Cambridge

455. GRAY TO NICHOLLS

Dear S^r

I AM come, & shall rejoice to congratulate you face to face on your good luck,[1] wch is wonderful in my eyes: I hope there are no rubs in the way to prevent my seeing you snug in the rectory, surrounded with fat pigs & stubble-geese, & Madam in her grogram gown[2] doing the honours of Lovingland[3] at the head of your table.

I have much to say, so much that I shall say no more: but come quickly, if the main chance will suffer you, or I will know the reason why. Adieu! I am sincerely

                                             Yours

Jermyn-Street. 5 Nov: 1767.   T G:

Addressed: To The Revd Mr Nicholls at Capt:ⁿ Floyer's[4] in Richmond Surrey
Postmark: 5 NO

[9] See Letter 400, n. 13.

[10] Palgrave's elder brother who took the name of Sayer (see Letter 409, n. 9).   [11] See Letter 455.

LETTER 455.—First printed by Mitford (1835–43), vol. v, p. 69; now reprinted from original.

[1] William Turner, uncle of Norton Nicholls (see Letter 429, n. 7), had purchased the presentation to the livings of Lound and Bradwell in Suffolk. On 28 Oct. 1767 (after the death of his predecessor, the Rev. Samuel Killett) Nicholls was presented to the livings. He had been ordained in February of this year. See Letter 432, n. 10.

[2] See Letter 424, n. 12.

[3] The district of Suffolk in which Nicholls was going to reside, in the neighbourhood of Lowestoft, is called Lothingland, from Lake Lothing, close to Lowestoft. Gray (here, and in Letter 485) and Nicholls (in Letter 508) call it Lovingland. Camden in his *Britannia* (p. 1637) records that both names were in use: 'Waveney drawing nearer unto the Sea . . . by the mere Luthing maketh a pretty big Demy Isle . . . which some name Lovingland, others more truly Luthingland, of Luthing the lake . . .'

[4] See Letter 425, n. 4.

456. GRAY TO NICHOLLS

[Dec. 17, 1767][1]

You have indeed brought yourself into a little scrape. I would, if it were my own case, say to L^d L: (supposing you were prefsed by him) that I had not received yet any letter from T:;[2] in the mean time I would write instantly to him in Devonshire, tell him my difficulty, & how I got into it, & desire his consent to shew L^d L: so much of his letter, as might be proper. I would then (supposing him not averse) have a cold or the tooth-ach, & be detain'd at Richmond,[3] from whence I would (transcribing so much of this very letter as may be fit

LETTER 456.—First printed by Mitford (1835–43), vol. v, pp. 83–5; now reprinted from original.

[1] The letter has hitherto been misplaced among the letters of 1768, because it had been dated in a pencil note: 'Dec 18, 1868' (*sic*). Its contents show that it must belong to 1767 (see n. 2) and the postmark determines the date of the month.

[2] There are references to the strained relations between Temple and his patron and relative, Lord Lisburne (see Letter 422, n. 15) here and in three other letters of Gray to Nicholls (Letters 460, 464, 467). From these letters it is possible to trace the cause and progress of their disagreement. Temple, who had been presented to the living of Mamhead in Devonshire, where Lord Lisburne had his seat (see Letter 422) in Sept. 1766, married his cousin Ann Stow on 6 Aug. 1767, and early in October took his wife to Mamhead. Gray suggests below that her coming began the trouble between Temple and Lord and Lady Lisburne, who 'did not much like her'. In November or December the Lisburnes went away and an acrimonious correspondence ensued. It began apparently with a letter of Temple to Lady Lisburne (see Letter 467), in which he seems to have suggested that he might be presented to a living at Berwick (see n. 4 below). He wrote also to complain of the parsonage-house and of some addition to it, that he had expected Lisburne to make (see n. 5). This produced a *'sensible & manly* answer' (see Letter 467), and Temple's relations with his patron became strained to a dangerous degree. Temple wrote to Nicholls, who was his intimate friend, sending letters from Lisburne and perhaps copies of his own letters. Lisburne probably met Nicholls in town, and consulted him, as a friend of Temple. In this situation Nicholls wrote to Gray, and sent him Temple's last letter to Lisburne: later he sent other letters on both sides. On 31 Dec. Gray wrote (Letter 460): 'There are many letters & things that I never saw', but a month later (see Letters 464, 467) he refers to letters that Nicholls had sent, and which he was returning. The incident reveals Temple as irritable and discontented. In May 1771 there were further difficulties between Temple and Lord Lisburne which were reported to Nicholls, who again consulted Gray (see Letters 551, 552). It is noteworthy that in 1767 Temple does not seem to have imparted his troubles to his bosom friend Boswell. There are letters of Boswell to Temple in Dec. 1767 and Feb. 1768 with no hint that he had any knowledge of Temple's troubles.

[3] The address of the letter shows that Nicholls was staying at Richmond.

for his L^dp to see) send it to him in Town, as the substance of what I had *just then* received in answer to my own. he will have suspicions (you will say) from my not shewing him the original. no matter! you are nothing to L^d L:; perhaps you had written to T: about other affairs, that you can not shew him; he will not be so uncivil as to ask for it; in short let him suspect, what he pleases: any thing is better, than to shew it him. and yet I would omitt nothing in my copy but what relates to *Berwick*[4] and to *the addition* that he should have made to the parsonage-house.[5] the kindnefs exprefs'd for him toward the latter part of the letter will (if he cares for T:) make up for all the rest.

By the way T: does himself much credit with me by this letter, & I did not (begging his pardon) suspect him of writing so well. but yet I must stand up a little for L^d L:. what occasion pray for so many cordial letters (w^ch, if he were good for nothing at bottom, must have cost him some pains of head) & for the bribe of a living, only to gain T:^s vote & interest, wch as a Relation & Friend he would have had for nothing at all. is not the date he sets to the beginning of L^d L:^s coldnefs to him carried a little too far back? did it not really begin a little later, when he had brought his wife to Mamhead, & they did not much like her? these indeed are only conjectures, but they may be true. I have to be sure a little prejudice to Madam; but yet I must be candid enough to own that the parsonage-house sticks a little in my stomach.

My best remembrances to Temple, & tell him, I wish, he would not give too much way to his own sensibilities; & still lefs (in this case) to the sensibilities of *other People*. it is always time enough to quarrel with one's Friends. Adieu!

T G:

It was Mr Bentley[6] indeed.

Addressed: To the Revd Mr Nicholls at Richmond in Surrey　*Postmark:* SAFFRON WALDEN 18 D[E]

[4] Temple must have made some proposal for exchanging his living for one at Berwick. With Berwick Lord Lisburne was connected through his mother's family, and both Temple and his wife had property in the neighbourhood.

[5] Temple is said to have written of 'the wretchedness of the parsonage' in a letter to his future wife, before he was ordained and more than a year before his marriage (see *Diaries of W. J. Temple*, edited by Lewis Bettany, p. xxiv). Mrs. Temple no doubt resented the discomfort and moved him to ask for some improvements. This was done tactlessly. Gray says: 'the parsonage-house sticks a little in my stomach' (he repeats the phrase in Letter 460).

[6] Presumably Richard Bentley (see Letter 162, n. 3). The reference to him has not been explained.

457. GRAY TO BEATTIE

Dec: 24. 1767. Pembroke Hall
Cambridge.

S^r

SINCE I had the pleasure of receiving your last letter,[1] wch did not reach me, till I had left the North, & was come to London, I have been confined to my room with a fit of the gout: now I am recover'd & in quiet at Cambridge, I take up my pen to thank you for your very friendly offers, wch have so much the air of franknefs & real good-meaning, that were my body as tractable & easy of conveyance as my mind, you would see me tomorrow in the chamber you have so hospitably laid out for me at Aberdeen. but, alas! I am a summer-bird, & can only sit drooping, till the sun returns: even then too my wings may chance to be clipp'd, & little in plight for so distant an excursion.

The proposal you make me about printing, what little I have ever written, at Glasgow does me honour. I leave my reputation in that part of the kingdom to your care, & only desire you would not let your partiality to me & mine mislead you. if you persist in your design, Mr Foulis[2] certainly ought to be acquainted of what I am now going to tell you. when I was in London the last spring, Dodsley the Bookseller ask'd my leave to reprint, in a smaller form all I have ever publish'd, to wch I consented; & added, that I would send him a few explanatory notes, & if he would omitt entirely the *Long Story* (wch was never meant for the publick, & only suffer'd to appear in that pompous edition because of Mr Bentley's designs, wch were not intelligible without it) I promised to send him some thing else to print instead of it, least the bulk of so small a volume should be reduced to nothing at all. now it is very certain, that I had rather see them printed at Glasgow (especially as you will condescend to revise the prefs) than at London, but I know not how to retract my promise to Dodsley. by the way you perhaps may imagine, that I have some kind of interest in this publication: but the truth is, I have none whatever. the expence is his & so is the profit, if there[3] be any. I therefore told him the other day in general terms, that I heard, there would be an edition

LETTER 457.—First printed in part in Mason's *Memoirs*, pp. 327–9; now first printed in full from original.
   [1] This was presumably a later letter than the one mentioned by Gray in his letter to Brown of 31 Oct. (see Letter 454).
   [2] See Letter 382, n. 4.   [3] Gray by mistake wrote 'their'.

put out in Scotland by a friend of mine, whom I could not refuse, & that if so, I would send thither a copy of the same notes & additions, that I had promised to send to him. this did not seem at all to cool his courage; M[r] Foulis therefore must judge for himself, whether he thinks it worth while to print, what is going to be printed also at London. if he does I will send him (in a packet[4] to you) the same things I shall send to Dodsley.[5] they are imitations of two pieces of old Norwegian poetry, in w[ch] there was a wild spirit, that struck me: but for my paraphrases I can not say much. you will judge. the rest are nothing but a few parallel pafsages; & small notes just to explain, what People said at the time was wrap'd in total darknefs. you will please to tell me, as soon as you can conveniently, what M[r] F:[s] says on this head,[6] that (if he drops the design) I may save myself & you the trouble of this packet. I ask your pardon for talking so long about it: a little more & my letter would be as big as all *my works*.

I have read with much pleasure an Ode[7] of yours (in w[ch] you have done me the honour to adopt a measure, that I have used) on L[d] Hay's[8] birth-day. tho' I do not love *panegyrick*, I can not but applaud this, for there is nothing mean in it. the diction is

---

[4] See Letter 466.   [5] See Letter 465.

[6] On 6 Jan. 1768, Robert Foulis wrote to Beattie: 'We have a just sense of the honour done us not merely from the reputation of M[r] Gray with people of taste in every rank, but also from the experience we ourselves have had of the power of his sentiments and description, striking the mind and awakening the soul. . . . As to Mr. Dodsley's printing them at the same time, it is no disagreeable circumstance, especially as he knows they are to be printed in Scotland. This may produce emulation without envy.' (Quoted in *Beattie and His Friends*, by Margaret Forbes, p. 36.)

[7] The first stanza of this ode, which is in the metre of Gray's *Ode on the Spring*, runs:

> A muse, unskill'd in venal praise,
>   Unstain'd with flattery's art:
> Who loves simplicity of lays
>   Breath'd ardent from the heart;
> While gratitude and joy inspire
> Resumes the long-unpractis'd lyre,
>   To hail, O Hay, thy natal morn:
> No gaudy wreath of flowers she weaves,
> But twines with oak the laurel leaves,
>   Thy cradle to adorn.

[8] George Hay (1767–98), eldest son of James Boyd (afterwards Hay), fifteenth Earl of Erroll (whom he succeeded as sixteenth Earl in 1778), and grandson of the fourth Earl of Kilmarnock, who was executed as a Jacobite rebel in 1746 (see Letter 120, n. 17).

easy & noble. the texture of the thoughts lyrick, & the versification harmonious. the fourth Stanza[9] is particularly my favourite (*the Muse with joy* &c:) for the contrast of images; & the three follo[wing][10] are excellent: not so the last. it is rather sp[un out][10] & the thoughts repeated. I object a little too to (in St: 2[d]) *All energy of mind.* the word *all* weakens the verse; & again in St: 6, *O yet e'er Luxury.*[11] that word can not be contracted to a difsyllable without harshnefs, tho' *Mem'ry* may. these indeed are Minutiæ, but they weigh for something, as half a grain makes a difference in the value of a diamond.

Adieu! Dear S^r, & believe me
Your Friend & faithful Servant
T Gray.

I am forced to write without a frank, but I will do so no more.

Addressed: To Mr Profefsor Beattie in the University of Aberdeen by Caxton-Bag *Postmark:* CAMBRIDGE

458. GRAY TO WALPOLE

SURELY as the letter is addrefs'd to a *Lady*, & subscribed, Your most humble *Son*, it can be to nobody but his[1] Mother. I do not remember, that there is any superscription to it, for the

9   The Muse with joy attends their way
   The vale of peace along;
  There to its lord the village gay
   Renews the grateful song.
  Yon castle's glittering towers contain
  No pit of woe, nor clanking chain,
  Nor to the suppliant's wail resound;
   The open doors the needy bless,
   Th' unfriended hail their calm recess,
    And gladness smiles around.

10 MS. torn.

11 Beattie substituted 'Pleasure' when he published the poem in 1776 (see Letter 452, n. 2).

LETTER 458.—First printed by Toynbee (1915), No. 237.

1 Richard III. This was evidently the letter of Richard to his mother mentioned by Gray in his letter to Wharton of 18 Sept. 1759 (see Letter 303, n. 14). Walpole was at this time engaged upon his *Historic Doubts on Richard the Third.* Writing to Cole on 19 Dec. he says: 'My *Richard the Third* will go to the press this week . . . Mr Gray went to Cambridge yesterday se'nnight; I wait for some papers from him for my purpose.' The book was published at the beginning of the following year. '1768. Feb. 1. Published my *Historic Doubts on Richard the Third.* I had begun it in the winter of 1767

original is not the letter itself, but a transcript of it set down in a great register-book belonging to the Privy-seal Office, in wch this stands very near to the beginning. I have mark'd the number of the Mſs, & of the article, if you chuse to consult the Musæum about it. I told you false, when I said the letter was dated: but the reason I concluded so was, that the articles, as I remember, go on regularly in the book in order of time & many come after it, that belong to the first year of his reign.

In the page, that contains his letter about Jane Shore, at a little distance below it are some abbreviated words in a cramp hand thus²—ffin by . . . . . . Thom Drury date A° ix° Henrici sept . . per Copiam . . . . wch seem to say something about the 9th year of Henry 7th, but I think they relate not to this letter (wch is directed to the B^p *of Lincoln, his Chaunc:^r*;³ now Rufsel B^p of Lincoln was his Chancellor, & not so to H: 7th.) & the few succeeding articles are really of H: 7th & H: 8th's time, so I suppose the words to relate to them only.

Mr Anstey's⁴ satyr seems to aim chiefly at this University, the patrons that protect it, the clients that make their court to them, their dedications, & clumsy flattery, their method of education, & style of politicks, &c: he has not indeed refused any thing else ridiculous, that came acrofs him. I like it but little: the only things, that made me laugh, were

> Sent venison, wch was kindly taken
> And Woodcocks, wch they boild with bacon.

and the High-Sheriffs frizzled Lady, when she meets her Husband, after he is knighted, at a ball.⁵

[*sc.* Jan.–Feb. 1767] continued it in the summer, and finished it after my return from Paris [in Oct. 1767]. Twelve hundred copies were printed, and sold so very fast that a new edition was undertaken the next day of 1,000 more, & published the next week' (*Short Notes*).

² Gray has here copied the old writing (sixteen words in four lines), which apparently reads as printed above. But see *Yale*, xiv. 160.

³ The letter here in question was that of Richard to his Chancellor mentioned by Gray in his letter to Wharton of 18 Sept. 1759 (see Letter 303, n. 15). It indicates a clerk was paid 6s. for his work as a copyist.

⁴ See Letter 341, n. 1. The satire ('Written at the close of the Duke of Newcastle's Administration') alluded to by Gray was *The Patriot: A Pindaric Epistle, Addressed to Lord Buckhorse* (Buckhorse being a noted pugilist), published in this year.

⁵   In velvet coat array'd, he
> Meets at the ball his frizzled lady,
> Who looks half pleas'd, and half affrighted,
> E'er since her husband has been knighted.

I have been confined to my room, eversince I came hither, but not very ill. Adieu, I am

Ever Yours

[Cambridge] 24 Dec: 1767.   T G:

Addressed: To The Honble Horace Walpole in Arlington Street London
Postmark: SAFFRON WALDEN 25 DE   *Stamped:* FREE

459. GRAY TO WHARTON

Dear Doctor

MANY & various maladies have I labour'd under, since I left the north, but none of them (thanks to my summer expedition) *jusqu' a mourir.* the gout came regularly, while I was in town, first in one, then in the other foot, but so tame[1] you might have stroked it. since I got hither, *another* of my troublesome companions for life has confined me to my room, but abstinence has (I believe) got the better of that too, & to-morrow I go abroad again. I sent to your brother,[2] before I left London, the *maps* you wanted, the *Decouvertes des Rufses,*[3] *Voyage de Gmelin en Siberie,*[4] Mr. Clerke of Chichester *on the Saxon coins,*[5] Lee's *Linnæan Dictionary,*[6] *Verrall's Cookery,*[7] & something else that I

LETTER 459.—First printed by Mitford (1816), vol. ii, pp. 483–7; now reprinted from original.

[1] See Letter 390, n. 2.
[2] Jonathan Wharton (see Letter 116, n. 15).
[3] This was a French translation (*Voyages et Découvertes faites par les Russes,* Amsterdam, 1766, 2 vols. 12mo) of an English work (*Voyages from Asia to America, for completing the discovery of the north-west Coast of America, translated from the German,* London, 1764, 4to), based upon vol. iii of the *Sammlung russischer Geschichten,* published at St. Petersburg by G. F. Müller (1705–83), Keeper of the Archives at Moscow, in 1758.
[4] A French translation (Paris, 1767, 2 vols. 12mo), by L. F. G. de Kéralio (1731–93), of *Reisen durch Sibirien* (Göttingen, 1753, 4 vols. 8vo), being the account of his travels through Siberia in 1733–43 by Johann Georg Gmelin (1709–55), of Tübingen, Professor of Chemistry and Natural History in St. Petersburg (1731), and subsequently (1749) Professor of Medicine at Tübingen.
[5] *The Connexion of the Roman, Saxon, and English Coins, deduced from Observations on the Saxon Weights and Money* (London, 1767, 4to); the author was William Clarke (1696–1771), Fellow of St. John's College, Cambridge.
[6] *An Introduction to the Linnæan System of Botany* (London, 1760, 8vo); by James Lee (1715–95), of Selkirk, who came to England, and in 1760 started as a nurseryman at Hammersmith, where he was the means of introducing many exotic plants into cultivation, among them being the fuchsia. Lee was a correspondent of Linnæus, part of whose works he translated into English in his book.   [7] See Letter 330, n. 23.

have forgot. as to Hudson's[8] *Flora Anglica* it is not to be had, being out of print: a new & more correct edition is soon expected. Willughby's[9] book of *fishes* was never publish'd in English, so would not answer your end. that of *Birds* is indeed in English, but not to be had in the shops & sells at auctions from 30 to 40 shillings, so I did not buy it without farther orders. I hope this cargo is safe arrived; & another little one, that I sent to Mifs Wharton & Mifs Peggy, directed to the former, to be left at M[r] Tho: Wilkinson's[10] in Durham: this went by the Newcastle Waggon about 6th of Dec:, & contain'd twelve Flower-roots, viz: 3 Soleil d'or Narcifsus, 2 White Italian d°: (N:B: of the Double white & yellow Italian there are none to be had this year) 2 Pileus Cardinalis, red; 1 Kroon-vogel, 1 Degeraad, double White; 1 Belle Grisdelin. 1 Hermaphrodite, & 1 Incomparable, double blew; Hyacinths. for these you must get glafses from Newcastle. in the same box was a pocket Lens, w[ch] Mifs Wh:[11] (if she pleased) was to give to Aunt Middleton,[12] who wanted such a thing.

I desire to know, what you thought of Mason's plan[13] for your ground (wch makes so pretty a figure on paper); & whether *Summers*[14] came to Old-Park to advise about planting. he is a

[8] William Hudson (*c.* 1730–93), of Kendal, in 1762 published his *Flora Anglica* (London, 8vo). This work, for which it is claimed that it 'marks the establishment of Linnæan principles of botany in England', is said to have been 'composed under the auspices and advice' of Benjamin Stillingfleet (see Letter 311, n. 44).

[9] Francis Willughby (1635–72), of Trinity College, Cambridge; M.A. 1659. He was a friend and collaborator of the naturalist, John Ray (see Letter 58*, n. 9). His two most important works, which were published posthumously under the editorship of Ray, were *Ornithologiæ Libri tres . . .* (London, 1676), and *De Historia Piscium Libri Quatuor . . .* (Oxon., 1686).

[10] No doubt a member of Mrs. Wharton's family.

[11] Mary, born in 1748.

[12] Wharton's mother was a Myddleton (see Letter 373, n. 8).

[13] Mason had made a sketch-plan for 'improvements' of the grounds at Old-Park (see Letter 446). On 9 Nov. of this year Mason wrote to Wharton: 'With this you will receive . . . the Plan, w[ch] if it should tempt you to think of executing (w[ch] (take notice!) I dont desire, for I dont love to lead People into Scrapes.) I would advise you to consult the young Man you saw here who is now at Hornby & who will come over to you on your Letter. . . . He will tell you on seeing the Spot whether the intended Water is feasible; he will also tell you whether Trees will grow with you, w[ch] is a thing I am confident you cannot tell at present. And as he has seen the Plan, he will also explain any difficulties that may occur to you in it. . . . Direct to M[r] Sumner at the E of H Hornby castle, near Bedale.' (*Egerton MS.* 2400.)

[14] A young gardener employed by Lord Holdernesse and Mason, who calls him indifferently Sumner (see n. 13) or Summers (see Letter 484).

very intelligent modest young Man, & might be of great use there. has Mifs Wh: served her time yet as a Bride-maid? I hope it may prove a good omen to her! does Mifs Peggy[15] rival Claude Lorraine yet, & when does she go to York? do Debo[16] & Betty[17] tend their Chrysalises, & their samplers? is Kee's[18] mouth as pretty as ever? does Robin[19] read like a Doctor, dance like a Fairy, & bow like a Courtier? does Dicky[20] kick up his heels, & study Geography? please to answer me as to all these particulars. my Thermometer presents her compliments to her country-sister, & proposes now to open a correspondence with her. she lives against a pale in the garden with her back to the East at 9 o'clock in the morning precisely: at any other hour she is not visible, unlefs upon some great occasion. I was in London from 3 Nov: to 14 Dec:,[21] during wch time the weather was commonly open, damp, & mild, with the wind in the West, veering either to N: or S:. on the last mention'd day I found some Brambles & Feverfew yet flowering in the hedges, & in gardens the double Chrysanthemum, double Chamomile, Borage, Stocks, & single Wall-flowers. these were all cut off on the 24th by an E: wind & hard frost, Therm: at 31. next day & today it was at 30. on the 26th a little snow fell, wch still lies & freezes.

Our Ministry[22] has taken in some odd Coadjutors not much to its credit or strength. it appear'd from the first day the Parliament met, that the Opposition were all to pieces among themselves, & soon after the Duke of Bedf:^d civilly declared to Mr Grenville, that he had the highest opinion of his abilities: but as it was contrary to his principles to keep up a constant opposition to the K:^s measures, he must not wonder, if his Friends should drop the plan they had for sometime been pursu-

---

[15] See Letter 453, n. 8.

[16] Deborah, Wharton's third daughter, born in 1755 (see Letter 294, n. 9).

[17] Elizabeth, the fourth daughter (see Letter 414, n. 4).

[18] Catherine, the youngest, also called Kitty (see Letter 493, n. 2).

[19] Robert the second, born in 1760, Wharton's eldest surviving son (see Letter 313, n. 3).

[20] Richard, the youngest son (see Genealogical Table for details as to these children of Wharton's).

[21] This date (Monday, 14 Dec.) of Gray's return to Cambridge is confirmed by the College records; Walpole, therefore, writing on 19 Dec., was in error in telling Cole (see Letter 458, n. 1) that Gray 'went to Cambridge yesterday se'nnight' (i.e. on Friday, 11 Dec.).

[22] The Chatham–Grafton Ministry, in which Chatham was Lord Privy Seal, and Grafton First Lord of the Treasury.

ing. accordingly he made his terms, four or five of them were directly to be provided for: the rest were to wait till there was room.[23] Ld Shelburne[24] (the Sec:^{y}), & Mr Cook[25] (Joint-Paymaster) were to have gone out, but Ld Chatham insisted on their staying in (it is said) & prevail'd. Mr Conway retires,[26] & is to have the army, when Ld Ligonier dies: this is voluntary, I imagine. Ld Northington[27] goes off with his pension. Ld Weymouth,[28] & Earl Gower[29] supply their places, Mr Thynne[30] is Master of ye Houshold. Ld Sandwich, Joint-Postmaster[31] (Ld Hillsborough[32] being created Secretary of State for America) Rigby[33] is the other, that must come in (to what place I know not) & conduct, I suppose, the House of Commons. how much

23 Walpole wrote to Mann on 14 Dec.: 'I must now prepare you for a new public scene. . . . The Duke of Bedford sent for him [George Grenville], and told him he himself was weary of opposition, and his friends more so; and therefore desired that each squadron might be at liberty *to provide* for themselves. . . . After this *decent* declaration, his Grace sent to lay himself and *his friends* at the Duke of Grafton's feet, begging, as alms, that they might have some of the first and best places under the Government.'

24 See Letter 273, n. 13. He was at this time Secretary of State for the South; he did not resign till Oct. 1768.

25 George Cooke, M.P. for Middlesex from Mar. 1750 till his death in June 1768 (see Walpole to Mann, 9 June 1768). He had been appointed Joint Paymaster-General of the Forces in Nov. 1766, in which place he was succeeded after his death 1768 by Rigby.

26 On 25 Dec. Walpole wrote to Mann: 'Mr Conway will, at the end of next month, quit the Seals, which he has long wished to do, but will remain Cabinet Counsellor, and acting minister in the House of Commons.' He resigned office on 20 Jan. and returned to military life. He ultimately became Commander-in-Chief in 1782.

27 Robert Henley (*c.* 1708–72), M.P. for Bath, 1747–57; Attorney-General, 1756–7; Lord Keeper, 1757–61; Lord Chancellor, 1761–6; Lord President of the Council, 1766–7. In 1760 he was created Baron Henley and in 1764 Earl of Northington.

28 See Letter 292, n. 6. Lord Weymouth succeeded Conway as Secretary of State for the Southern Department in Jan. 1768.

29 See Letter 373, n. 21. He became Lord President on 23 Dec.

30 Second son of Lord Weymouth (see Letter 430, n. 11).

31 He succeeded Hillsborough as Joint Postmaster-General in Jan. 1768.

32 Wills Hill (1718–93), second son of first Viscount Hillsborough in the Peerage of Ireland, whom he succeeded in 1742; he was M.P. for Warwick, 1741–56; he was created a Peer of Great Britain as Baron Harwich, 1756. After holding various offices in Jan. 1768 he was appointed Secretary of State for the Colonies, this third Secretaryship of State having been instituted in consequence of the increase of business with the American colonies (*D.N.B.*).

33 See Letter 236, n. 9. He was appointed Joint Paymaster-General in June 1768 (see n. 25).

better & nobler would it have been to have left all these Beggars in the lurch? indeed what could be said against it, as all that could oppose the Ministry were already broke into three parts,[34] & one of them[35] had declared publickly against the other two? I conclude the Rockingham-party will at last prevail, as they have some character & credit with the People still left.

Adieu, my dear S[r]. you have had, I hope, no returns of your asthma, since you lay in your own bed. my best respects to M[rs] Wharton, & love to all the family. I am ever

Yours

T G:

Dec: 28. 1767. Pemb: Coll:

Shall I write out, & send you, what Leland[36] says of your neighbourhood? it is nothing but short notes taken in his journey: but that journey was towards the end of Henry 8[th's] reign just after the difsolution of Monasteries, w[ch] makes it valuable.

SPECIMEN.

From S[t] Andre's Akeland[37] to Raby Castel[38] 5 miles, part by arable, but more by pastures, & morisch hilly ground, baren of wood. Raby is the largest Castel of Logginges in al the North-cuntery, & is of a strong building: but not set ether on hil, or very strong ground. as I enterid by a causey into it there was a litle stagne on the right hond, and in the first area were but two toures, one at eche end, as Entres, & no other buildid. yn the 2[d] area, as an Entring, was a great Gate of iren with a Tour, & 2 or 3 mo on the right hond. then were al the chief Toures of the 3[d] Court, as in the hart of the castel. The Haul, & al the Houses of Offices be large & stately; & in the haul I saw an incredible great beame of an Hart. the great Chaumber was exceding large, but now it is false-rofid, and devidid into 2 or 3 Partes. I saw ther a litle chaumber, wherein was in windows of colorid glafs al the petigre of y[e] Nevilles, &c:

[34] The Bedford party, the Rockingham party, and the Grenvilles.
[35] The Grenvilles, in the person of George Grenville.
[36] See Letter 186, n. 16.
[37] St. Andrews Auckland, about a mile south-east of Bishop Auckland, in Durham.
[38] See Letter 143, n. 12.

460. GRAY TO NICHOLLS

Dear Nicholls

WRITE by all means forthwith to L^d L:,[1] give a little into his way of thinking, seem to fear you have gone a little too far in communicating so much of T:^{s} letter, wch was not intended for his eye; but say you thought, you saw at bottom so much of respect & affection for him, that you had the lefs scruple to lay open the weaknefses & little suspicions of a Friend, that (you know beyond a doubt) very gratefully & sincerely loves him. remind him [2]*eloquently* (that is, from your heart, & in such exprefsions as that will furnish)[2] how many idle suspicions a sensible mind, naturally disposed to melancholy, & deprefs'd by misfortune, is capable of entertaining, especially if it meets with but a shadow of neglect or contempt from the very (perhaps the only) person, in whose kindnefs it had taken refuge. remind him of his former goodnefs frankly & generously shewn to T:, & beg him not to destroy the natural effects of it by any appearance of pique or resentment, for that even the fancies & chimæras of a worthy heart deserve a little management & even respect. afsure him, as I believe, you safely may, that a few kind words, the slightest testimony of his esteem will brush away all T:^{s} suspicions & gloomy thoughts & that there will need after this no constraint on his own behaviour (no, not so much as to ring a bell)[3] for, when one is secure of people's intentions, all the rest pafses for nothing.

To this purpose (but in my own way) would I write, & mighty respectfully withall. it will come well from you, & you can say without consequence what in T: himself it would be mean to say. L^d L: is rather more piqued than needs, methinks. the truth is, the causes of this quarrel on paper do appear puerile, as to the matter; but the manner is all, & that we do not see. I rather stick by my L^d still, & am set against Madam

---

LETTER 460.—First printed by Mitford (1835–43), vol. v, pp. 69–71; now reprinted from original.

[1] The letter is entirely concerned with the disagreement between Temple and his patron, Lord Lisburne, about which Gray had written to Nicholls on 17 Dec. See Letter 456 and the notes there.

[2]-[2] Mason inserts this sentence in a composite letter, which he dates 26 Jan. 1771. See *Memoirs*, pp. 393–4.

[3] The reference apparently is to Temple's having objected to liberties taken by Lisburne, possibly to his having entered the parsonage-house unannounced.

Minx:[4] yet (as I told you before) the *house* lies hard at my stomach.[5]

There are many letters & things, that I never saw, as that strange one in Wales,[6] & that to Lady Lisb:, now without these how can I judge? you have seen more of the matter, & perhaps may be right: but as yet I do not believe it. what can that *firm & spirited* letter be?[7] I fear it will make matters worse, & yet it was sent away before he had seen T:[s] letter to you. if he had, it would have made it worse still.

You ask, if you should copy L^d L:[s], and send it to T:. I think, rather not. he has now had one from him himself. if you are obliged to do so, it should be only the sense of it, & that abated & mollified, especially all that tastes of contempt.

Adieu! blefs your stars, that you are snug in fat-goose living, without a Minx, & without a Lord. I am faithfully

Yours

Dec: 31. 1767.   T G:

Addressed: To The Revd Mr Nicholls

461. GRAY TO MASON

Dear Mason

I DID not write to you—that's to be sure: but then consider, I had the gout great part of the time, that I pafs'd in Town; & eversince I came hither I have been confined to my room; & besides, you know, you were at Aston, & did not much care. as to Mons:^r de la Harpe[1] he is not to be had at any of the shops, & (they say) never was in England. what I saw & liked of his, must have been in some *Bibliotheque* or *Journal*, that I had borrow'd.

Here are, or have been, or will be all your old & new Friends

---

⁴ Mrs. Temple, see Letter 456, n. 2.

⁵ See Letter 456, n. 5.

⁶ Lord Lisburne had a seat at Crosswood, near Aberystwyth. The strange letter 'in Wales' may be a letter written from there.

⁷ The '*firm & spirited* letter' was presumably Lisburne's reply to Temple. This may be the same as the '*sensible & manly* answer' referred to in Letter 467.

LETTER 461.—First printed by Mitford in *Gray–Mason* (1853), pp. 411–14; now reprinted from original.

¹ Jean François de la Harpe (1739–1803), dramatist and critic. Besides tragedies and other poems, he published in 1765 *Mélanges Littéraires, ou Épîtres et Pièces Philosophiques*. Gray may have seen extracts from this work.

in constant expectation of you at Cambridge, yet Christmas is past, & no Scroddles[2] appears!

Prim *Hurd*[3] attends your call, & *Palgrave* proud,[4]
Stonhewer the lewd, & *Delaval*[5] the loud.
For thee does *Powel*[6] squeeze, & *Marriot*[7] sputter,
And *Glyn*[8] cut phizzes, & Tom *Nevile*[9] stutter.
Brown sees thee sitting on his nose's tip,
The *Widow* feels thee in her aching hip,
For thee fat *Nanny* sighs, & handy *Nelly*,[10]
And *Balguy* with a Bishop in his belly![11]

it is true, of the two Archdeacons,[12] the latter is now here, but goes on Monday: the former comes to take his degree in February. the Rector[13] writes to ask, whether you are come,

[2] Gray addresses Mason as 'Skroddles' in Letter 216, and Mason signs himself 'Scroddles' in Letter 212.

[3] 'Prim Hurd' here, 'Stonhewer' in line 2, and 'Balguy' in line 8 have been heavily scored through in the original, but can be deciphered. For 'Prim Hurd' Mitford printed 'Weddell'. In one of his note-books he has two transcripts, one giving 'Prim Hurd', the other 'Weddell'. It is possible that, when he first copied the verses, he failed to decipher the name correctly.   [4] Mason also talks of 'Proud Palgrave' in Letter 484.

[5] Gray, in Letter 494, says of Delaval: 'he talks as loud as ever.'

[6] See Letter 399, n. 32.   [7] See Letter 397, n. 12.

[8] Robert Glynn (1719–1800) of Eton, where he was three years junior to Gray, and King's College, Cambridge; Scholar, 1737; B.A. 1742; M.A. 1745; Fellow, 1740–1800; M.D. 1752; F.R.C.P. 1763. He was for many years the leading physician at Cambridge ('the loved Iapis on the banks of Cam', as Mathias called him in the *Pursuits of Literature*). He was a friend of Gray, and attended him in his last illness. He is described as having been 'eccentric in manner and dress'. His eccentricity may explain Gray's description of him as 'cutting phizzes'.

[9] Thomas Nevile. Cole described him as having an impediment in his speech (see Letter 237*, n. 2).

[10] From the allusion below these must have been the women at the Coffee-house.

[11] Tovey notes with a reference to Macaulay's *History* (vol. ii, ch. 8): 'When Cartwright, the Popish Bishop of Chester, passed through Westminster Hall, after the acquittal of the seven Bishops (1688), one in the crowd shouted: "Make room for the man with the Pope in his belly."' Another instance of the phrase is quoted in *O.E.D.* from James Howell (1650): 'Some shallow-pated puritan will cry me up to have a Pope in my belly' (*Letters*, vol. i, p. 472). On Warburton's death, in 1781, Balguy (see Letter 234, n. 2) was offered, but declined, the Bishopric of Gloucester.

[12] Hurd and Balguy, Archdeacons of Gloucester and Winchester. 'The former comes to take his degree in February': Hurd graduated D.D. this year.

[13] Palgrave was Rector of Thrandeston and Palgrave in Suffolk (see Letter 273*, n. 1).

that he may do the same. as to Johnny,[14] here he is, divided between the thoughts of fornication & marriage. Delaval only waits for a little intreaty. the Masters,[15] the Doctor,[16] the Poet,[17] & the President,[18] are very prefsing & warm; but none so warm as the Coffee-house and I. come then away: this is no season for planting, & L^d R:^{d}[19] will *grow* as well without your cultivation as with it. at least let us know, what we are to hope for, & when: if it be only for the satisfaction of the Methodist Singing-Man, your Landlord.

You will finish your *Opus magnum*[20] here so clever, & your Series of historical Tragedies[21] with your books (that no body reads) all round you; & your Critick at hand, who never cares a farthing (that I must say for him) whether you follow his opinion or not; & your Hypercriticks, that nobody (not even themselves) understands, tho' you think, you do. I am sorry to tell you, St John's garden is quite at a stand: perhaps you in person may set it going: if not, here is Mr Brown's little garden[22] cries aloud to be laid out (it is in a wretched state to be sure, & without any taste)[23] you shall have unlimited authority over it,

---

[14] Gray's references follow the order of names in the verses, and 'Johnny' must be Richard Stonhewer. His friends seem to have called him 'Jack' or 'Johnny' (see Letter 294, n. 19).

[15] 'The Masters' were Powell, Master of St. John's, and Marriott, Master of Trinity Hall.

[16] Glynn.   [17] Nevile.

[18] James Brown, President (i.e. Vice-Master) of Pembroke.

[19] Lord Richard Cavendish (1752–81), second son of the fourth Duke of Devonshire (see Letter 394, n. 10). Mason was preparing him for Cambridge; in writing to Mason on 24 Oct. 1770 (Letter 535) Gray refers to him as 'your Eléve', and from an unpublished letter of Mason to Alderson of 15 Mar. 1768, it appears that he was then at Aston. He entered Trinity College in Nov. 1768 (see Letter 488). Gray seems to have been chiefly struck by his enormous consumption of beef—he describes him to Nicholls as 'a sensible Boy, aukward & bashful enough all imagination, & eats a buttock of beef at a meal' (Letter 488); and to Mason he speaks of his leaving Cambridge (in Oct. 1770) after 'having digested all the learning and all the beef this place could afford him' (Letter 535).

[20] *The English Garden*, which Mason calls in Letter 450 his 'Opus Magnum sive didacticum'.

[21] Mason's *Argentile and Curan* (see Letter 408, n. 3), which he described when it was first published as 'Written on the old English Model about the year 1766', was probably not yet finished.

[22] A strip of the Fellows' Garden at Pembroke was reserved for the Senior Fellow (see Letter 332, n. 1a).

[23] Mason prided himself on his skill in laying out gardens (see Letters 296, n. 7; 459, n. 13).

& I will take upon me the whole expence. won't you come?
I know, you will. Adieu! I am ever

8 Jan: 1768.   Pemb: Coll:

Yours
T G:

462. GRAY TO HOW

Cambr: Pemb: Coll: Jan: 12. 1768.

S^r

YOU perceive by Mr Brown's letter, that I pafs'd all the sum-
mer in the North of England, went from thence to London,
& did not arrive here till the middle of December, where I
found your parcel.[1] since that time I have been generally
confined to my room, & besides I was willing to go thro' the
eight volumes[2] before I return'd you an answer. this must be
my excuse to you, for only doing now, what in mere civility I
ought to have done long ago. first I must condole with you,
that so neat an edition should swarm in almost every page with
errors of the prefs, not only in notes & citations from Greek,
French, & English authors, but in the Italian text itself, greatly
to the disreputation of the Leghorn Publishers. this is the only
reason (I think) that could make an edition in England necef-
sary:[3] but I doubt you would not find the matter much mended
here, our prefses, as they improve in beauty, declining daily in
accuracy: besides you would find the expence very considerable,
& the sale in no proportion to it, as in reality it is but few people
in England, that read currently & with pleasure the Italian
tongue; & the fine old editions of their capital Writers are sold
at London for a lower price, than they bear in Italy. an
English translation I can by no means advise. the justnefs of
thought & good sense might remain; but the graces of elocution
(wch make a great part of Algarotti's merit) would be entirely

LETTER 462.—First printed in part (in a garbled text) in Mason's *Memoirs*,
pp. 389–91; first printed in full by Mitford (1816), vol. ii, pp. 488–90; now
reprinted from original.
   [1] See Letter 454, n. 3.
   [2] A copy of the first collected edition of Algarotti's works, which How had
sent as a gift to the College library: *Opere del Conte Algarotti, Cavaliere dell'
Ordine del Merito & Ciamberlino di S.M. il Re di Prussia.* (In Livorno, 1764–5.
Presso Marco Cottellini, 8 vols. 8vo.)
   [3] Some years before How had consulted Gray about his design to publish
an edition of Algarotti's works in England or Scotland (see Letters 378, 382).

lost, & that merely from the very different genius & complexion of the two languages.

I rather think these volumes should be handsomely bound, before they are put into the Library: they bind very neatly here; & if you approve it, Mr Brown will order it to be done.[4] doubtlefs there can be no impropriety in making the same present to the University,[5] nor need you at all to fear for the reputation of your Friend: he has merit enough to recommend him in any country, a tincture of various sorts of knowledge; an acquaintance with all the beautiful arts; an easy command, a precision, warmth, & richnefs of exprefsion; & a judgement, that is rarely mistaken, on any subject to wch he applies it. of the Dialogues I have formerly told you my thoughts.[6] the Efsays and Letters (many of them entirely new to me) *on the Arts* are curious & entertaining. those on other subjects (even where the thoughts are not new to me, but borrowed from his various reading & conversation) often better put, & better exprefs'd than in the originals. I rejoice, when I see Machiavel defended or illustrated, who to me appears one of the wisest Men, that any nation in any age has produced. most of the other discourses military or political are well worth reading, tho' that on Kouli-Khan was a mere Jeu d'esprit, a sort of historical exercise. the letters from Rufsia I had read before with pleasure, particularly the narrative of Munich[7] & Lascy's[8] campaigns.

[4] The volumes, which are still in the College library, were duly bound in polished calf, with gilt diapered backs, lettered on green and red labels. On the fly-leaf of the first volume is the following inscription in How's hand:

> Aul: Pemb: Feb: 29. 1768
> Gulielmus Taylor How Socius
> hos libros Bibliothecæ nostræ
> D:D: in memoriam auctoris
> sibi amicissimi.

[5] How sent a similar copy to the University library, which was bound uniformly with the other set. On the fly-leaf of the first volume is the following inscription in his hand:

> Feb: 29. 1768
> Gulielmus Taylor How Aul:
> Pemb: Socius hos libros
> Bibliothecæ publicæ D:D:
> in memoriam Comitis
> Algarotti sibi amicissimi.

[6] See Letters 375, 382.

[7] Burkhard Christoph von Munnich (1683–1767), Russian Field-Marshal (1732) under Peter II.

the detach'd thoughts are often new & just; but there should have been a revisal of them, as they are often to be found in his letters repeated in the very same words. some too of the familiar letters might have been spared. The Congrefs of Cythera[9] I had seen, & liked before, the *Giudicio d'Amore* is an addition rather inferior to it. the verses are not equal to the prose, but they are above mediocrity.

I shall be glad to hear your health is improved, & that you have thoughts of favouring us with your company here. I am S[r] your most obed[t] humble Servant,

Tho: Gray.

Addressed: To William Taylor-How, Esq, at Stondon-Place near Ongar Efsex

463. Gray to Wharton

Pemb: Coll: 17 Jan: 1768.

Dear S[r]

I was much surprised to rèceive a letter superscribed in your hand from London, & am very sorry to see, what occasion'd it. I fear the event the more, because in his best health Mr Wharton[1] had always some complaint in his breast, & now the distemper has fallen upon the weak part.

Whenever you are able to disengage yourself, M[r] Brown & I shall flatter ourselves with the hopes of seeing you at Cambridge for as long a time as you can afford to bestow on us. it is likely you may find Mason too with us, for he talks of setting out about the 20th to come hither.[2] I am ever very sincerely

Yours
T G:

Addressed: To D[r] Wharton at M[r] Wharton's in Boswell-Court, Carey-Street, London   *Postmark:* 18 IA SAFFRON WALDEN

[8] Franz Moritz Lacy (1725–1801), Austrian Field-Marshal (1766), under Maria Theresa and Joseph II.

[9] See Letters 378, 382.

LETTER 463.—First printed by Mitford (1835–43), vol. iv, p. 101; now reprinted from original.

[1] Wharton's brother, Jonathan. He died probably in February (see Letter 475, n. 1).

[2] Mason came on the 20th, 'two days after the fire' (see Letter 464).

464. GRAY TO NICHOLLS

Dear S^r   28 Jan: 1768. P: Coll:

I AND mine are safe, & well, but the chambers opposite to me (Mr. Lyon's)[1] wch were getting ready for Mason, are destroy'd. Mr. Brown[2] was in more immediate danger than I; but he too is well, & has lost nothing. we owe it to Methodism, that any part (at least of that wing) was preserved: for two Saints, who had been till very late at their nocturnal devotions, & were just in bed, gave the first alarm to the college & the town. we had very speedy & excellent afsistance of engines & men, and are quit for the fright, except the damage abovemention'd.[3] I afsure you it is not amusing to be waked between 2 & 3 in the morning & to hear, Don't be frighted, S^r! but the college is all of a fire.

I have not yet return'd the letters[4] you sent me by the fly, not thinking it necefsary to do so immediately; but very soon you

LETTER 464.—First printed by Mitford (1835–43), vol. v, p. 72; now reprinted from original.

[1] Hon. Thomas Lyon (see Letter 332, n. 14); he had recently vacated his Fellowship. His rooms were on the middle floor of the north wing in what was then called the New Court. Gray was lodged in the south wing on the opposite side of the court.

[2] Brown's rooms (which he occupied for more than thirty years) were on the same floor as Lyon's with one set of chambers between them.

[3] The following entries in the College order-book relate to this fire:

'Jan. 26. 1768 ordered that Mr Essex be desired to survey the buildings where the late Fire happened and give us an account in writing what is necessary and proper to be done.

'Ordered at the same time that the Persons who assisted in working the Engines and extinguishing the Fire be rewarded by the Treasurer as we may be able to discover their services.

'Feb. 8. 1768. Woodwork and Mason's work to be done on Mr Essex's plan.'

'Mr Essex' was James Essex (1722–84), builder and architect of Cambridge. He did much important work at Cambridge, as well as on the Cathedrals of Ely and Lincoln. Horace Walpole employed him for his latest additions to Strawberry Hill.

The fire had taken place ten days before Gray wrote. Mitford quotes the following entry in 'one of Gray's MS. Journals' (probably his pocket-diary). 'Fire in the College at half-past two this morning. It was subdued in about an hour and a half. 18 Jan. 1768' (*Walpole–Mason Correspondence*, vol. i, p. 426).

[4] Nicholls had recently sent Gray some of the letters that had passed between Temple and Lord Lisburne, which Gray had not previously seen (see Letter 460). By this time Lisburne had returned to Mamhead, and had met Temple, as Gray says in his postscript.

shall have them. Mason came two days after the fire, & will stay some time. Adieu! I am sincerely

Yours

T G:

I do not see, what you can do: everything depends on their first meeting at Mamhead, & that is now over. I am afraid every thing will go wrong. it is sure, your last letter could do no hurt.

Addressed: To The Revd Mr Nicholls at Augustus Floyer's⁵ Esq in Thrift-Street,⁶ Soho London   *Postmark:* 28 IA [ROYS]TON

465. GRAY TO JAMES DODSLEY¹

[c. Feb. 1 1768]²

LET the Title be only *Poems by Mr Gray* without any mention of notes or additions. you will judge, whether what few notes³ there are should stand at bottom of each page, or be thrown to the end. all I desire is, that the text be accurately

---

⁵ See Letter 425, n. 4.

⁶ A corruption of Frith Street, so called from Richard Frith, who built it *c.* 1680.

LETTER 465.—First printed (with the omission of Gray's notes on the poems and the text of the three new poems) by Arnold Glover in the *Athenæum*, 18 Mar. 1899, p. 388; now printed (with a similar omission) from the original. The manuscript, consisting of 9 folio pages, was acquired by Isaac Reed in 1801; it was afterwards bought by Samuel Rogers, and on his death passed into the possession of his great-nieces, the Misses Sharpe: in 1912 it was presented by Miss Laetitia Sharpe to the British Museum. Gray sent similar instructions, with copy of text and notes, for the printing of his poems by Messrs. Foulis, to James Beattie (see Letter 466). It does not seem necessary, here or in the letter to Beattie, to reproduce the notes to the poems or the text of *The Fatal Sisters, The Descent of Odin,* and *The Triumphs of Owen,* as they were printed correctly by both Dodsley and Foulis.

¹ James Dodsley (1724–97), younger brother of Robert Dodsley (see Letter 144, n. 2), after being employed in his brother's business was, about 1755, taken into partnership, the firm trading as 'R. and J. Dodsley'. In 1759, after Robert Dodsley's retirement, James carried on the business alone.

² Date conjectural. From the close similarity (and for the most part verbal identity) of the instructions sent to Beattie for the Glasgow edition (see Letter 466), it may be concluded that Gray wrote to Dodsley and Beattie at about the same time, possibly on the same day (the letter to Beattie is dated 1 Feb.). In this letter Gray says in the postscript: 'It is Mr Foulis of Glasgow that prints them in Scotland: he has been told, that you are doing the same. I have desired, he would not print a great number, & could wish the same of you.' In his letter to Beattie Gray wrote: 'I can not advise him to print a great number, especially as Dodsley has it in his power to print as many as he pleases, tho' I desire him not to do so.'

³ They were printed as footnotes by Dodsley.

999

printed, & therefore whoever corrects the prefs, should have some acquaintance with the Greek, Latin, & Italian, as well as the English, tongues. let the order stand thus, unlefs you have begun to print already: if so, it is indifferent to me.

1. Ode. (Lo, where the rosy-bosom'd &c:)
2. Ode, on the death of a favourite Cat.
3. Ode, on a distant prospect of Eton-College.
4. Ode, to Adversity.[4]
5. The progrefs of Poësy, a Pindaric Ode.
6. The Bard, a Pindaric Ode.
7. The Fatal Sisters.
8. The Descent of Odin.
9. The Triumphs of Owen, a fragment.
10. Elegy, written in a country church-yard.

You will print the four first & the last from your own large edition (first publish'd with M^r B:^{s} plates)[5] in the 5th & 6th you will do well to follow the edition printed at St:^{y}-hill:[6] I mention this, because there are several little faults of the prefs in your Miscellanies.[7] remember, the *Long Story* must be quite omitted. now for the notes.

[Here follow the notes and the text and notes of Poems 7, 8, 9.]

* * * * * * *

* * * * * * *

I hope, you have not begun to reprint: but if you have, you must throw the notes, &c: to the end, or where you please, omitting the mottoes, wch do not much signify. When you have done, I shall desire you to present in my name a copy to Mr Walpole in Arlington-street, another to Mr Daines Barrington[8]

[4] When Gray transcribed this poem in his Commonplace-book he gave it the title *Ode to Adversity*. When it was first published in 1753 (see n. 5), he called it *Hymn to Adversity* (with which title it appeared in Dodsley's *Collection* in 1755). He now intended to call it *Ode to Adversity*, and it appeared with this title in the Foulis edition. But in Dodsley's the former title *Hymn to Adversity* was retained.

[5] *Designs by Mr. R. Bentley, for Six Poems by Mr. T. Gray* published by Robert Dodsley in 1753.

[6] *Odes by Mr Gray*, published by R. and J. Dodsley in 1757 (see Letter 243, n. 1).

[7] All Gray's poems hitherto printed had appeared in Dodsley's *Collection of Poems by Several Hands* (in vols. ii (1748), iv (1755), and vi (1758)). In his mention of faults of the press he is referring not to the *Odes*, but to the earlier poems printed in the edition with Bentley's plates, the text of which he revised for Bentley's edition (see Letter 170, n. 1a). This is clear from the instructions sent to Beattie (Letter 466).

[8] Hon. Daines Barrington (1727–1800), fourth son of first Viscount

(he is one of the Welch Judges) in the Inner-Temple; & a third to M^r *J: Butler at Andover*:[9] whether this latter Gentleman be living or not, or in that neighbourhood, I am ignorant: but you will oblige me in making the enquiry. if you have no better means of knowing, a line directed to the Post-mistrefs at Andover will bring you information. after this you may (if you please) bestow another copy or two on me.[10] I am

Your obed^t humble Servant

T. GRAY.

P:S: It is Mr *Foulis of Glasgow*, that prints them in Scotland: he has been told, that you are doing the same. I have desired, he would not print a great number, & could wish the same of you.

466. GRAY TO BEATTIE

Feb: 1. 1768.
Pembroke-Hall.

Dear S^r

I AM almost sorry to have raised any degree of impatience in you,[1] because I can by no means satisfy it. the sole reason I

Barrington, and brother of second Viscount, the benefactor of the naturalist, Benjamin Stillingfleet (see Letter 311, n. 44). Having been called to the Bar at the Inner Temple, in 1757 he was appointed Justice of Merioneth, Carnarvon, and Anglesey; and in 1764 Recorder of Bristol; he was second Justice of Chester, 1778–85. He was a Fellow of the Royal Society, and of the Society of Antiquaries, of which he became Vice-President. Besides his legal pursuits he had many interests, including the study of antiquities and natural history, both of which he shared with Gray. In the account of *Cyprinus orsus* in Gray's interleaved copy of Linnæus is the note: 'Specimen a fl. Cherwell allatum apud D. Barrington observavi' (C. E. Norton, *Thomas Gray as a Naturalist*, p. 52). It was to him that Gray was indebted for his knowledge of Evans's *Dissertation on the Bards* (see Appendix M). Barrington was a correspondent of Gilbert White, whose *Natural History of Selborne* was written in the form of letters to Barrington and Pennant (see Letters 508*, n. 6, 541*, n. 3).   9 See Letter 256*, n. 1.

10 A portion of this last paragraph (from 'When you have done') of the letter, which no doubt was placed at his disposal by Rogers, was printed by Mitford as a note to Gray's letter to Wharton of 8 Dec. 1757 (see Mitford (1835–43), vol. iii, pp. 181–2).

LETTER 466.—The letter (exclusive of the instructions for printing the poems) first printed in Mason's *Memoirs*, pp. 329–30; now printed from the original. The instructions for printing the poems (which were sent with the letter, see n. 7) now first printed from the original which was in the possession of the late Mr. A. H. Hallam Murray. The text of the new poems and the notes are not printed (see Letter 465, preliminary note).

1 Beattie's letter (in answer to Gray's letter of 24 Dec. 1767, Letter 457), to which this is the reply, is not extant.

have to publish these few additions[2] now is to make up (in bulk) for the omifsion of that *long story*; & as to the notes, I do it out of spite, because the Publick did not understand the two odes (wch I have call'd Pindaric) tho' the first was not very dark, & the second alluded to a few common facts to be found in any six-penny History of England by way of question & answer for the use of children. the parallel pafsages I insert out of justice to those writers, from whom I happen'd to take the hint of any line, as far as I can recollect.

I rejoice to be in the hands of Mr Foulis, who has the laudable ambition of surpafsing his Predecefsors, the *Etiennes*,[3] & the *Elzeviers*[4] as well in literature, as in the proper art of his profefsion. he surprises me in mentioning Mifs Hepburne,[5] after whom I have been enquiring thcse fourteen years in vain. when the two odes were first publish'd, I sent them to her: but as I was forced to direct them very much at random, probably they never came to her hands. when the present edition comes out, I beg of Mr Foulis to offer her a copy in my name (with my respects, & grateful remembrances). he will send another to you, S^r, & a third to Ld Gray,[6] if he will do me the honour of accepting it. these are all the presents I pretend to make (for I would have it consider'd only as a new edition of an old book) after this if he pleases to send me one or two, I shall think myself obliged to him. I can not advise him to print a great number, especially as Dodsley has it in his power to print as many as he pleases, tho' I desire him not to do so.

---

[2] *The Fatal Sisters, The Descent of Odin,* and *The Triumphs of Owen.*

[3] The French family of Estienne or Étienne (latinized as Stephanus), famous scholars and printers, ten of whom carried on the business, which was founded by Henri Estienne about 1502 and lasted until 1674.

[4] The founder of the Elzevier or Elzevir family of printers was Louis (*c.* 1540–1617), a native of Lorraine, who set up at Leyden and produced his first book in 1583. The Elzeviers subsequently established presses also at Amsterdam and Utrecht. They were famed for the beauty of their 'neat pocket volumes', as Gray calls them in his letter to West of 16 July 1740 (Letter 91), editions of the classics, and other authors, in 12mo, 16mo, and 24mo.   [5] See Letter 244, n. 3.   [6] See Letter 452, n. 5.

[7] The packet contained the instructions for printing, with copy of the new poems and notes to the whole (see preliminary note above). These consist of nine folio pages, closely written, endorsed on p. 9: 'Mr Gray, Cambridge, Materials for the Glasgow Edition of his Poems.' After the preliminary directions there follow notes on the poems with the text of the new poems. In substance the instructions are the same as in the letter to Dodsley (Letter 465), except that in writing to Dodsley Gray lays stress on the

You are very good to me in taking this trouble upon you. all I can say is, that I shall be happy to return it in kind, whenever you will give me the opportunity. believe me,

S^r faithfully Yours
T GRAY.

You will be so obliging to tell me this packet[7] is come to your hands.[8]

Addressed: To Mr Beattie

[*Instructions for printing.*]

The Title (I would wish) should be only *Poems by Mr Gray* without any mention of notes or additions. the size, & disposition of the lines I must leave to Mr Foulis: if he thinks it should be in 4to,[9] the two Odes printed at Str:^y Hill are very well (as you say) as to the form & type,[10] but the paper is rather too thin & transparent. I prescribed nothing to Dodsley, but it appear'd

accuracy of the press; this he omits in writing to Beattie but asks that his punctuation should be corrected (see n. 13).

[8] Beattie received the packet on 9 Feb., but he did not acknowledge it till 16 Feb. (see Letter 469); his letter had not reached Gray when the latter wrote to Walpole on 25 Feb. (Letter 471). On the same date Beattie wrote to Robert Arbuthnot from Aberdeen as follows:

'The writing out a copy of Mr Gray's poems for the press has employed me the last fortnight. They are to be printed at Glasgow by Foulis, with the author's own permission, which I solicited and obtained: and he sent me four folio pages of notes and additions to be inserted in the new edition. The notes are chiefly illustrations of the two Pindaric odes, more copious, indeed, than I should have thought necessary: but, I understand, he is not a little chagrined at the complaints which have been made of their obscurity; and he tells me that he wrote these notes out of spite. . . . I expect the book will be out in a few weeks, if Foulis be diligent, which it is his interest to be, as there is another edition of the same just now printing by Dodsley. I gave him notice of this, by Mr Gray's desire, two months ago; but it did not in the least abate his zeal for the undertaking.' (Forbes's *Life of Beattie,* vol. i, pp. 113–15.)

[9] The book was a quarto with a larger page than that of the *Odes* printed at Strawberry Hill.

[10] The type was considerably larger than that of the *Odes*. It was specially cast for this work by Dr. Alexander Wilson, Professor of Astronomy at Glasgow University, a type-founder, who supplied the Foulis brothers with the types which gave great distinction to their work. The printers in their *Advertisement* to the book stated: 'This is the first work in the Roman character which they have printed with so large a type; and they are obliged to DOCTOR WILSON for preparing so expeditiously, and with so much attention, characters of so beautiful a form.'

to me, that he meant to publish a smaller edition (& consequently a cheaper)[11] than in 4to, but of this I am not certain. M^r F: will also determine, whether the few notes there are shall stand at the bottom of the page (wch is better for the Reader) or be thrown to the end with references (wch improves the beauty of the book).[12] the poems should stand (I think) in this order & with these titles.

1. Ode. Lo! where the rosy &c:
2. Ode, on the death of a favourite Cat.
3. Ode, on a distant prospect of Eton-College.
4. Ode, to Adversity.[12a]
5. The progrefs of Poesy, a Pindaric Ode.
6. The Bard, a Pindaric Odc.
7. The Fatal Sisters (from the Norse-tongue)
8. The Descent of Odin (from the Norse-tongue)
9. The Triumphs of Owen, a fragment (from the Welch)
10. Elegy, written in a country church-yard.

please to observe, that I am entirely unversed in the doctrine of *stops*, whoever therefore shall deign to correct them, will do me a friendly office:[13] I wish I stood in need of no other correction. if M^r F: has the large edition with Mr Bentley's designs, he will do well to print from it (the *long story* being omitted) as it seems the most accurate for in Dodsley's miscellanies there are several blunders of the prefs.[14] the Strawberry-hill edition of the two Pindaricks is also the best. /now for the notes.[15]

[Here follow the notes and the text and notes of Poems 7, 8, 9.]

*   *   *   *   *   *   *
*   *   *   *   *   *   *

[11] Dodsley's edition was a small octavo published at half a crown.

[12] Except for notes on the sources &c. of the Norse and Welsh poems and a few brief notes on *The Triumphs of Owen* the notes are printed at the end of the book, as Beattie recommended to Foulis (see Letter 469).

[12a] See Letter 465, n. 7.

[13] Beattie acted on Gray's suggestion, and the Foulis edition shows considerable variations in punctuation from the other texts of the poems.

[14] See Letter 465, n. 7.

[15] The notes are almost identical with those sent to Dodsley, except that for the motto to be prefixed to the *Ode to Adversity* Gray (who sent Dodsley the quotation from the *Agamemnon* of Aeschylus originally prefixed to the poem) gave Beattie a choice of mottoes. Beattie chose the motto from the *Eumenides*: ξυμφέρει σωφρονεῖν ὑπὸ στένει (misprinted στένου in the Foulis edition).

467. GRAY TO NICHOLLS

Wednesday. 3 Feb: 1768
Pemb: Coll:

Dear S^r

I INTEND to return you the letters[1] by tomorrow's Fly, if nothing hinders. I am never the wiser, nor the more able to account for T:^s letter to Lady L:[2] (wch gave occasion to all the rest) it still looks like the suggestion of his Wife working upon his own natural irritability, & the sort of request made in it for the Berwick-living (at so improper a time) is not any other way to be accounted for. the *sensible & manly* answer[3] to it (I must own) I can not easily digest, especially the end of it: it is plain, as he wrote on, he work'd his temper into a ferment, till at last it absolutely turn'd sower. I can not help his temper, but his heart may (for all that) be right. in the second letter he is conscious, he had gone too far in his exprefsions, & tries to give them a sense they will not bear: but I allow he is throughout too angry & too contemptuous. your last letter to him (tho' I never saw it) I conclude has done no hurt, perhaps has softened him a little. every thing depends upon the manner of their meeting in Devonshire, wch by this time you probably know. I do not yet see, why all this pafsion, why all this trouble of justifying himself to a Man, for whom he never had any kindnefs or regard, & who can be of little use to him in point of interest. Temp: is too precipitate, too rough too in his exprefsions, too much the aggrefsor, if he thinks L^d L: really his Friend; and if he does not, how in the midst of his resentment can he bring himself to shew a desire of accepting farther favours from him? I yet have some little hope, that all may come right again, at least right enough for our purpose; for I am more convinced of T:^s contempt & want of esteem for L:, than I am of L:^s aversion, or neglect of T:.

Mason is here with us, & will stay (I should hope) some time: he is even going to hire a small house opposite to Peter-house, wch he can not inhabit till next winter. Mr. Hutton[4] being dead, he has now a landed estate, the income of which in a few years will be considerable.

LETTER 467.—First printed by Mitford (1835–43), vol. v, pp. 73–4; now reprinted from original.   [1] See Letter 464, n. 4.
[2] For Temple's letter to Lady Lisburne see Letter 456, nn. 2 and 4.
[3] See Letter 460, n. 7.   [4] See Letter 181, n. 3.

old Smith[5] of Trinity is dead, & Dr Hinchliffe[6] will probably succeed him, tho' D[r] Rofs[7] & Brocket[8] are also Competitors for it. are your India-paper,[9] your Axminster-carpets,[10] your Sofas & Pechés-mortels,[11] in great forwardnefs? have you read Mr. Anstey,[12] & the Historical doubts?[13] Adieu! I am sincerely

Yours

T G:

Addressed: To The Rev[d] M[r] Nicholls at Augustus Floyer's Esq in Thrift-Street, Soho London   *Postmark:* CAMBRIDGE 4 FE

468. GRAY TO WALPOLE

Feb. 14, 1768. Pembroke College.

I RECEIVED the book[1] you were so good to send me, and have read it again (indeed I could hardly be said to have read it before) with attention and with pleasure. Your second edition[2] is so rapid in its progrefs, that it will now hardly answer any purpose to tell you either my own objections, or those of other people. Certain it is, that you are universally read here; but what *we* think, is not so easy to come at. We stay as usual to see the succefs, to learn the judgment of the town, to be directed in our opinions by those of more competent judges. If they like you, we shall; if any one of name write against you, we give you up: for we are modest and diffident of ourselves, and not without

---

[5] Robert Smith (1689–1768), LL.D., D.D.; Master of Trinity, 1742–68; Plumian Professor of Astronomy, 1716–60. He was a benefactor of the University and of his College, and founder of the 'Smith's Prizes' in mathematics.

[6] John Hinchliffe (1731–94), of Westminster and Trinity; B.A. 1754; Fellow, 1755; M.A. 1757; D.D. 1764. He succeeded Dr. Smith as Master of Trinity on 16 Feb. 1768; he became Bishop of Peterborough in 1769 and Dean of Durham in 1788, when he resigned the Mastership of Trinity.

[7] Dr. John Ross (see Letter 149, n. 13).

[8] Lawrence Brockett, Professor of Modern History (see Letter 149, n. 7).

[9] As Gray is referring to the furnishing of Nicholls's future home, this was doubtless one of the new-fangled wall-papers, the use of which had recently come into fashion (see Letters 303, 348, 350).

[10] The manufacture of carpets at Axminster, which were woven by hand, like tapestry, was established in 1755. The Axminster industry died out and was transferred to Wilton towards the end of the eighteenth century, though the name survives to this day.   [11] See Letter 231, n. 3.

[12] See Letter 458, n. 4.   [13] By Walpole (see Letter 458, n. 1).

LETTER 468.—First printed in *Works of Lord Orford*, vol. v, pp. 368–70.

[1] Walpole's *Historic Doubts on the Life and Reign of King Richard the Third.*

[2] The second edition was undertaken on the day after the publication of the first and published the next week (see Letter 458, n. 1).

reason. History in particular is not our *fort*; for (the truth is) we read only modern books and the pamphlets of the day. I have heard it objected, that you raise doubts and difficulties, and do not satisfy them by telling us what was *really* the case. I have heard you charged with disrespect to the king of Prufsia;[3] and above all to king William, and the revolution.[4] These are seriously the most sensible things I have heard said, and all that I recollect. If you please to justify yourself, you may.

My own objections are little more efsential: they relate chiefly to inaccuracies of style, which either debase the exprefsion or obscure the meaning. I could point out several small particulars of this kind, and will do so, if you think it can serve any purpose after publication. When I hear you read, they often escape me, partly because I am attending to the subject, and partly because from habit I understand you where a stranger might often be at a lofs.

As to your arguments, most of the principal parts are made out with a clearnefs and evidence that no one would expect where materials are so scarce. Yet I still suspect Richard of the murder of Henry VI. The chronicler of Croyland charges it full on him,[5] though without a name or any mention of circumstances. The interests of Edward were the interests of Richard too, though the throne were not then in view; and that Henry still stood in their way, they might well imagine, because, though deposed and imprisoned once before, he had regained his liberty, and his crown; and was still adored by the people. I should think, from the word *tyranni*, the pafsage was written after Richard had afsumed the crown: but, if it was earlier, does

---

[3] 'To judge impartially, we ought to recall the temper and manners of the times we read of. It is shocking to eat our enemies; but it is not so shocking in an Iroquois, as it would be in the king of Prussia' (*Hist. Doubts*, in *Works of Lord Orford*, vol. ii, pp. 127–8).

[4] 'The great regularity with which the coronation [of Richard III] was prepared and conducted, and the extraordinary concourse of the nobility at it, have not at all the air of an unwelcome revolution, accomplished merely by violence. On the contrary, it bore great resemblance to a much later event, which, being the last of the kind, we term *The Revolution*. . . . Though the partisans of the Stuarts may exult in my comparing king William to Richard the third, it will be no matter of triumph, since it appears that Richard's cause was as good as king William's, and that in both instances it was a free election' (*op. cit.*, p. 135).

[5] 'Parcat Deus, & spatium pœnitentiæ ei donet, *quicunque* sacrilegas manus in christum Domini ausus est immittere. Unde et agens tyranni, patiensque gloriosi martyris titulum mereatur' (quoted by Walpole, *op. cit.*, p. 115).

not the bare imputation imply very early suspicions at least of
Richard's bloody nature, especially in the mouth of a person
that was no enemy to the house of York, nor friend to that of
Beaufort?

That the duchefs of Burgundy, to try the temper of the nation,
should set up a false pretender to the throne (when she had the
true duke of York in her hands), and that the queen-mother
(knowing her son was alive) should countenance that design,[6]
is a piece of policy utterly incomprehensible; being the most
likely means to ruin their own scheme, and throw a just suspicion
of fraud and falsehood on the cause of truth, which Henry could
not fail to seize and turn to his own advantage.

Mr. Hume's first query,[7] as far as relates to the queen-mother,
will still have some weight. Is it probable, she should give her
eldest daughter to Henry, and invite him to claim the crown,
unlefs she had been sure that her sons were then dead? As
to her seeming consent to the match between Elizabeth and
Richard, she and her daughters were in his power, which ap-
peared now well fixed, his enemies' designs within the kingdom
being every where defeated, and Henry unable to raise any
considerable force abroad. She was timorous and hopelefs; or
she might difsemble, in order to cover her secret dealings with
Richmond: and if this were the case, she hazarded little, sup-
posing Richard to difsemble too, and never to have thought
seriously of marrying his niece.

Another unaccountable thing is, that Richard, a prince of the
house of York, undoubtedly brave, clear-sighted, artful, atten-
tive to businefs; of boundlefs generosity, as appears from his
grants; just and merciful, as his laws and his pardons seem to
testify; having subdued the queen and her hated faction, and
been called first to the protectorship and then to the crown by
the body of the nobility and by the parliament; with the com-
mon people to friend (as Carte[8] often afserts), and having
nothing against him but the illegitimate family of his brother
Edward, and the attainted house of Clarence (both of them
within his power);—that such a man should see within a few
months Buckingham, his best friend, and almost all the southern
and western counties on one day in arms against him; that,
having seen all these insurrections come to nothing, he should

---

[6] See *op. cit.*, p. 152.   [7] See *op. cit.*, pp. 162–3.

[8] Thomas Carte (1686–1754), whose *History of England* was published in
four volumes in 1747–55.

march with a gallant army against a handful of needy adventurers, led by a fugitive, who had not the shadow of a title, nor any virtues to recommend him, nor any foreign strength to depend on; that he should be betrayed by almost all his troops, and fall a sacrifice;—all this is to me utterly improbable, and I do not ever expect to see it accounted for.

I take this opportunity to tell you, that Algarotti[9] (as I see in the new edition of his works printed at Leghorn)[10] being employed to buy pictures for the king of Poland,[11] purchased among others the famous Holbein, that was at Venice. It don't appear that he knew any thing of your book: yet he calls it *the consul Meyer and his family*,[12] as if it were then known to be so in that city.

A young man here, who is a diligent reader of books, an antiquary, and a painter,[13] informs me, that at the Red-lion inn at Newmarket is a piece of tapestry containing the very design of your marriage of Henry the sixth,[14] only with several more figures in it, both men and women; that he would have bought it of the people, but they refused to part with it.

Mr. Mason, who is here, desires to present his respects to you. He says, that to efface from our annals the history of any tyrant is to do an efsential injury to mankind: but he forgives it, because you have shown Henry the seventh to be a greater devil than Richard.

Pray do not be out of humour. When you first commenced an author, you exposed yourself to pit, box and gallery. Any coxcomb in the world may come in and hifs, if he pleases; aye, and (what is almost as bad) clap too, and you cannot hinder him. I saw a little squib fired at you in a newspaper by some of the *house of York*, for speaking lightly of chancellors.[15] Adieu!

I am ever yours,
T. GRAY.

[9] See Letter 366, n. 4.　　[10] See Letter 462, n. 2.
[11] Augustus III (1696–1763), by whom he was made a Privy Councillor.
[12] See Walpole's *Anecdotes of Painting*, in *Works of Lord Orford*, vol. iii, pp. 66, 77–8. Algarotti describes the picture in a letter written from Potsdam on 13 Feb. 1751 to Mariette in Paris (see vol. vi, pp. 15 ff., of the Leghorn ed. of Algarotti's works).
[13] Probably Michael Tyson, Fellow of Corpus Christi (see Letter 534, n. 4).
[14] See Letter 186, n. 2.
[15] Walpole 'speaks lightly' of no less than five Chancellors, viz. John Morton, Archbishop of Canterbury, Chancellor, 1473, 1487–1500 (see *Hist. Doubts*, in *Works*, vol. ii, pp. 120–1); Thomas Rotherham, Archbishop of York, Chancellor, 1474–83, whom he calls 'a silly prelate' (*op. cit.*, p. 126); Sir Thomas More, Chancellor, 1529–32, reputed author of *Life of Richard III*,

469. BEATTIE TO GRAY

Dear Sir

I RECEIVED Your most agreable packet[1] a week ago, and have carefully followed all Your instructions. I have written out all the Poems, in the order, and with the titles and mottos and notes, You desired. I never saw but one copy of Bentley's Edition, and that was a great many years ago: I was therefore obliged to transcribe the first second third and fourth Odes and the Elegy in a Country church yard from Dodsley's Collection.[2] Such of the typographical errors as were obvious I have avoided; and I flatter myself that my Manuscript is pretty correct, for Your poems have been deeply imprinted on my memory for many years: however I shall recommend it to Foulis to compare the Manuscript with the folio Edition, if it can be got. The two Pindarick Odes I have taken from the Strawberry hill Edition.

I have wrote out some Directions to the Printer concerning the size of the paper, page, and type;[3] I have made choice of a fair and thick writing paper, and have proposed the Strawberry hill Edition as a pattern for the page and type. I have left it to Mr Foulis to determine, whether the notes shall stand at the foot of each page, or at the end of the book; recommending

whom he accuses of wilful falsehood, of incompetence as a historian, and of egregious absurdity (*op. cit.*, pp. 133–4, 144–5); Sir Francis Bacon, Chancellor, 1618–21, author of *Life of Henry VII* (*op. cit.*, pp. 144–5); and Lord Clarendon, Chancellor, 1658–67, author of the *History of the Rebellion* (*op. cit.*, p. 144 n.). The 'house of York' alluded to by Gray was the Yorke family, to which belonged the Earl of Hardwicke, Lord Chancellor, 1737–56, and his sons, the second Earl and Charles Yorke (see Letter 395, n. 4).

LETTER 469.—Now first printed from original.

[1] See Letter 466, n. 7.

[2] Gray had suggested that for the earlier poems the text of Bentley's edition should be followed (see Letter 466). As Beattie had not a copy of the book, he transcribed these poems from Dodsley's *Collection*, in which they had been printed. Hence in the *Ode to Spring* and the *Ode on the Cat* he missed the corrections which Gray made for Bentley's edition (see Letter 465, n. 7). The text of the *Elegy*, which was printed in vol. iv (1755) of Dodsley's *Collection* was the same as that of the Bentley edition, and Beattie's text was therefore correct. It is to be noted that in line 36 he made (perhaps inadvertently) one variation, printing:

> The path of glory leads but to the grave

in place of

> The paths of glory lead but to the grave.

In the *Elegy* and in some of the other poems Beattie used a free hand in changing spelling, capitals, and punctuation (see Letter 466, n. 13).

[3] See Letter 466, nn. 9, 10.

however the latter,[4] as being most consistent with elegance. In a word, I shall spare no pains to render our Scotch Edition in some measure worthy of the work, and of the Author.

I think You have condescended to Your Readers inattention even more than was necefsary:[5] for my own part, I never found any difficulty in understanding Your poetry. The first of the Pindaric odes is so perspicuous, that I could hardly conceive it pofsible for any person of Common sense to misunderstand it. If there be any obscurity in *the Bard*, it is only in the allusions; for the style and imagery are clear distinct and strong. But readers now-a-days have nothing in view but amusement; and have little relish for a book that requires any degree of attention.

Your new pieces have given me much pleasure: I could expatiate at great length on their beauties. The *Fatal Sisters* exhibits a collection of the most frightful images that ever occupied human imagination: some of them in the hands of an ordinary Poet would have sunk into burlesque (particularly the circumstance of the warriors heads) but You have made every thing magical and dreadful; Your choice of words on this, as on every other occasion, is the happiest that can be. It will (I am persuaded) give very high satisfaction to every Reader of taste, to observe with what exquisite art You have improved this fiction in Your *Bard*: the Norwegian witches excite horror; but the Welch bards do much more—they transport, enrapture, alarm, astonish and confound us.—The descent of Odin is not so interesting throughout, as the Sisters, but it abounds in exquisite images. The picture of the Dog of Darkness has no paralell in antient or modern poetry; I am convinced it owes more to the Imitator than to the Inventor. There are many other fine pafsages in the same poem, such as 'When long of yore to sleep &c.'—It is a pity we have no more of the Welch fragment; what You have given us is excellent, and has, I think, more method and perspicuity, than any other of the poems of that age.

---

[4] See Letter 466, n. 12.

[5] In his instructions Gray had directed that before the *Progress of Poesy* a note should be prefixed: 'When the Author first publish'd this & the following Ode he was advised even by his Friends to subjoin some few explanatory Notes; but had too much respect for the understanding of his Readers to take such liberty.'

This note (duly printed by Dodsley) does not appear in the Foulis edition, but before the notes printed at the end of the book there was this heading:

'NOTES BY THE AUTHOR, Now first published at the desire of Readers, who thought the PROGRESS of POESY, and the WELCH BARDS needed illustration.'

The Public will regret with me, that You have drop'd your design of writing a history of English poetry.[6] Percy in his Diſsertations on Antient Ballads has thrown out some hints on this subject; but much remains to be done; and I shall expect, from what you tell us, that a greater work will make its appearance in due time. I am much obliged to You for ordering a Copy of Your poems to be sent me when published: I will value it much for its own sake, but more for the sake of the Giver. But you owe me no thanks for what I have done in preparing this Edition; it was a most agreable amusement to me; and I think I have done my country a service and even an honour in being the first projector of so good a work.[7]

I write by this Post to Mʳ Foulis to let him know that the Manuscript is ready and will be sent by the first sure hand. None of Your inſtructions will be forgotten. Believe me to be with the truest affection and esteem Dear Sir

Your most faithful humble servant

J BEATTIE.

Aberdeen 16 February 1768.

I can give You no certain information about Miſs Hepburn,[8] but I am much mistaken if I did not hear some years ago that she is dead.

Addressed: To Thomas Gray Esquire— Pembroke Hall Cambridge *Postmark:* FE 19 DUNDEE

[6] In the *Advertisement* prefixed to the *Fatal Sisters* Gray referred to the *History of English Poetry*, which he had once projected: 'He has long since drop'd his design, especially after he had heard, that it was already in the hands of a person well qualified to do it justice both by his taste, and his researches into antiquity.' (See Letter 245*, n. 4.)

[7] The following *Advertisement* was prefixed to the book: 'Some Gentlemen may be surprised to see an edition of Mr. GRAY's POEMS printed at Glasgow, at the same time that they are printed for Mr. Dodsley at London. For their satisfaction the printers mention what follows.

'The property belongs to the Author, and this edition is by his permission. As an expression of their high esteem and gratitude, they have endeavoured to print it in the best manner.

'Mr. BEATTIE, Professor of Philosophy in the University of Aberdeen, first proposed this undertaking. When he found that it was most agreeable to the printers, he procured Mr. Gray's consent, and transcribed the whole with accuracy. His transcription is followed in this Edition.'

The *Advertisement* concludes with a reference to the type used (quoted in Letter 466, n. 10).

[8] Miss Hepburn, about whom Gray had inquired, had died in 1760 or 1761 (see Letter 244, n. 3).

470. WALPOLE TO GRAY

Arlington-street, February 18, 1768.

YOU have sent me a long and very obliging letter,[1] and yet I am extremely out of humour with you. I saw *poems* by *Mr. Gray* advertised:[2] I called directly at Dodsley's to know if this was to be more than a new edition? He was not at home himself, but his foreman told me he thought there were some new pieces, and notes to the whole. It was very unkind, not only to go out of town without mentioning them to me, without showing them to me, but not to say a word of them in this letter. Do you think I am indifferent, or not curious, about what you write? I have ceased to ask you, because you have so long refused to show me any thing. You could not suppose I thought that you never write. No; but I concluded you did not intend, at least yet, to publish what you had written. As you did intend it, I might have expected a month's preference. You will do me the justice to own that I had always rather have seen your writings than have shown you mine; which you know are the most hasty trifles in the world, and which, though I may be fond of the subject when fresh, I constantly forget in a very short time after they are published. This would sound like affectation to others, but will not to you. It would be affected, even to you, to say I am indifferent to fame—I certainly am not, but I am indifferent to almost any thing I have done to acquire it. The greater part are mere compilations; and no wonder they are, as you say, incorrect,[3] when they are commonly written with people in the room, as Richard and the Noble Authors were. But I doubt there is a more intrinsic fault in them; which is, that I cannot correct them. If I write tolerably, it must be at once; I can neither mend nor add. The articles of lord Capel and lord Peterborough, in the second edition of the Noble Authors, cost me more trouble than all the rest together: and you may per-

LETTER 470.—First printed in *Works of Lord Orford*, vol. v, pp. 371–4.
[1] Letter 468.
[2] The following announcement appeared in *The Public Advertiser* for 13 Feb. 1768: '*Speedily will be published*, Elegantly printed in one small Volume, Poems, By Mr Gray. Printed for J. Dodsley, in Pall-mall.' The publication of the volume was announced a month later in *The Public Advertiser* for 12 Mar. 1768: '*This Day are published, Price 2s 6d sewed*, Elegantly printed in one small volume, Poems, By Mr Gray. Printed for J. Dodsley, in Pall-Mall.'
[3] In the letter, to which this is a reply, Gray refers to Walpole's 'inaccuracies of style'.

ceive that the worst part of Richard, in point of ease and style, is what relates to the papers you gave me on Jane Shore, because it was tacked on so long afterwards, and when my impetus was chilled. If some time or other you will take the trouble of pointing out the inaccuracies of it, I shall be much obliged to you: at present I shall meddle no more with it. It has taken its fate: nor did I mean to complain. I found it was condemned indeed beforehand, which was what I alluded to. Since publication (as has happened to me before) the succefs has gone beyond my expectation.

Not only at Cambridge, but here, there have been people wise enough to think me too free with the king of Prufsia![4] A newspaper has talked of my known inveteracy to him.—Truly, I love him as well as I do most kings. The greater offence is my reflection on lord Clarendon.[5] It is forgotten that I had over-praised him before. Pray turn to the new State Papers,[6] from which, *it is said*, he composed his history. You will find they are the papers from which he did *not* compose his history. And yet I admire my lord Clarendon more than these pretended admirers do. But I do not intend to justify myself. I can as little satisfy those who complain that I do not let them know what *really did* happen. If this inquiry can ferret out any truth, I shall be glad. I have picked up a few more circumstances. I now want to know what Perkin Warbeck's proclamation was, which Speed in his history says is preserved by bishop Leslie.[7] If you look in Speed, perhaps you will be able to afsist me.[8]

The duke of Richmond[9] and lord Lyttelton agree with you, that I have not disculpated Richard of the murder of Henry VI. I own to you, it is the crime of which in my own mind I believe him most guiltlefs. Had I thought he committed it, I should never have taken the trouble to apologize for the rest. I am not at all positive or obstinate on your other objections, nor know exactly what I believe on many points of this story. And I am so sincere, that, except a few notes hereafter, I shall leave the matter to be settled or discufsed by others. As you have written much too little, I have written a great deal too much, and think

[4] See Letter 468, n. 3.   [5] See Letter 468, n. 15.
[6] *State Papers collected by Edward Earl of Clarendon*, edited by Dr. Scrope and T. Monkhouse, 3 vols., fol., Oxford, 1767–8.
[7] John Leslie (1527–96), Bishop of Ross, author of a History of Scotland in Latin (*De Origine, Moribus, et Rebus Gestis Scotorum libri decem*), published at Rome in 1578.   [8] See Letter 471.
[9] Charles Lennox (1735–1806), third Duke of Richmond.

only of finishing the two or three other things I have begun—
and of those, nothing but the last volume of painters is designed
for the present public.[10] What has one to do when turned [of]
'fifty,[11] but really think of *finishing*?

I am much obliged and flattered by Mr. Mason's approba-
tion, and particularly by having had almost the same thought
with him. I said, 'People need not be angry at my excusing
Richard; I have not diminished their fund of hatred, I have
only transferred it from Richard to Henry.'—Well, but I have
found you close with Mason—No doubt, cry prating I, some-
thing will come out.[12]—Oh! no—leave us, both of you, to
Annabellas[13] and Epistles to Ferney,[14] that give Voltaire an
account of his own tragedies, to Macarony fables that are more
unintelligible than Pilpay's[15] are in the original, to Mr. Thorn-
ton's hurdy-gurdy poetry,[16] and to Mr. ——, who has imitated
himself worse than any fop in a magazine would have done.[16a]
In truth, if you should abandon us, I could not wonder—When
Garrick's prologues and epilogues, his own Cymons[17] and
farces, and the comedies of the fools that pay court to him, are
the delight of the age, it does not deserve any thing better.

Pray read the new account of Corsica.[18] What relates to

---

[10] Walpole's tragedy *The Mysterious Mother*, begun in 1766, was finished in
March and printed in August of this year. The fourth volume of *Anecdotes
of Painting in England* was printed in 1771, but not published until 1780.

[11] Gray in his reply (Letter 471) quotes 'when turned of fifty' and so
Walpole probably wrote here.

[12]   I found him close with Swift—Indeed?—No doubt,
     (Cries prating Balbus) something will come out.
                   Pope's *Epistle to Arbuthnot. Walpole.*

[13] The reference is obviously to *Amabella*, a poem by Edward Jerningham
(1727–1812), published anonymously in February this year.

[14] *Ferney, an Epistle to M. de Voltaire*, by George Keate (1729–97), pub-
lished in January this year.

[15] *Makarony Fables with the New Fable of the Bees in two cantos addressed to the
Society By Cosmo, Mythogelastick Professor, and F.M.S.*, published early in 1768.
The author was Sterne's friend, John Hall-Stevenson.

[16] Bonnell Thornton (1724–68) published in February this year *The Battle
of the Wigs*. He was the author of a burlesque *Ode on St. Cecilia's Day, adapted
to the Antient British Musick: the Salt Box, the Jew's Harp, the Marrow Bones and
Cleavers, the Hum-Strum or Hurdy-Gurdy*, &c. (London, 1763.) Hence Walpole
talks of his 'hurdy-gurdy poetry'.   [16a] This allusion has not been explained.

[17] Garrick, who had ceased to act, in Jan. 1767, produced at Drury Lane,
Cymon, a Dramatic Romance, which was probably his own composition. Two
farces written by him followed in the same year.

[18] *Account of Corsica*, by James Boswell (1740–95), published this year. Bos-
well sent Walpole a copy of his book, with the following letter: 'Edinburgh,

Paoli[19] will amuse you much. There is a deal about the island and its divisions that one does not care a straw for. The author, Boswell, is a strange being, and, like [——],[20] has a rage of knowing any body that ever was talked of. He forced himself upon me at Paris[21] in spite of my teeth and my doors, and I see has given a foolish account of all he could pick up from me about King Theodore.[22] He then took an antipathy to me on Rouſseau's account, abused me in the newspapers, and exhorted Rouſseau to do so too: but as he came to see me no more, I forgave all the rest. I see he now is a little sick of Rouſseau himself, but I hope it will not cure him of his anger to me. However, his book will I am sure entertain you.

I will add but a word or two more. I am criticized for the expression *tinker up* in the preface.[23] Is this one of those that you object to? I own I think such a low expreſsion, placed to ridicule an absurd instance of wise folly, very forcible. Replace

23 Febry 1768. Sir, I beg your acceptance of a copy of my Account of Corsica to which you have a better claim than you perhaps imagine as I dare say you have forgotten what you said to me at Paris when I had the honour of giving you a few anecdotes of what I had just come from seeing among the brave Islanders. In short Sir your telling me that I ought to publish something in order to shew the Corsicans in a proper light, was my first incitement to undertake the work which has now made its appearance. If it gives any pleasure to Mʳ Horace Walpole, I shall be particularly happy. I shall think that I have been able to make him some small return for the pleasure which his elegant writings have afforded me. I have the honour to be Sir your most obedient humble servant James Boswell.' (*Letters of James Boswell*, vol. i, pp. 146–7.)

[19] Pascal Paoli (1725–1807), leader of the Corsicans in their struggles for independence.

[20] Miss Berry left the name blank. The reference is no doubt to Richard Owen Cambridge (see Letter 27, n. 3).

[21] Boswell gave an account of his visit in his Journal for 22 Jan. 1766: 'Went and found Horace Walpole whom you ['you' is Boswell's mannerism for 'I'] had treated with by cards, lean genteel man. Talked to him of Corsica He said You should give something about them, as there are no authentic accounts. He had seen Theodore, but, whether from pride or stupidity he hardly spoke any.' (*Boswell Papers*, vol. vii, p. 61.)

[22] Theodore, Baron de Neuhoff, a German adventurer, who in return for assistance rendered to the rebellious Corsicans was (in 1736) proclaimed King by them. He was finally expelled by the French, and took refuge in England, where he was imprisoned for debt. He died in London (Dec. 1756). Walpole, who had helped to raise a subscription for him, wrote an epitaph for his grave (in the church of St. Anne, Soho).

[23] 'The want of records, of letters, of printing, of critics; wars, revolutions, factions, and other causes occasioned these defects in ancient history. Chronology and astronomy are forced to tinker up & reconcile as well as they can those uncertainties.'

it with an elevated word or phrase, and to my conception it becomes as flat as pofsible.

George Selwyn says I may, if I please, write historic doubts on the present duke of G—— too. Indeed, they would be doubts, for I know nothing certainly.[24]

Will you be so kind as to look into Leslie de rebus Scotorum, and see if Perkin's proclamation is there, and if there, how authenticated? You will find in Speed my reason for asking this.

I have written in such a hurry, I believe you will scarce be able to read my letter—and as I have just been writing French,[25] perhaps the sense may not be clearer than the writing. Adieu!

Yours ever,
HOR. WALPOLE.

471. GRAY TO WALPOLE

Pembroke-college, Feb. 25, 1768.

To your friendly accusation, I am glad I can plead not guilty with a safe conscience. Dodsley told me in the spring that the plates from Mr. Bentley's designs were worn out,[1] and he wanted to have them copied and reduced to a smaller scale for a new edition. I difsuaded him from so silly an expense, and desired he would put in no ornaments at all. The *Long Story* was to be totally omitted, as its only use (that of explaining the prints) was gone: but to supply the place of it in bulk, lest *my works* should be mistaken for the works of a flea, or a pismire, I promised to send him an equal weight of poetry or prose: so, since my return hither, I put up about two ounces of stuff; viz. The Fatal Sisters, The Descent of Odin (of both which you have copies),[1a] a bit of something from the Welch, and certain

24 Walpole here alludes to the relations of his niece, the Dowager Countess Waldegrave, with the Duke of Gloucester, brother of George III. Lady Waldegrave had in fact been privately married to the Duke on 6 Sept. 1766, but by the Duke's desire, the marriage was not publicly acknowledged until 1772. When the Duke first distinguished Lady Waldegrave by his attentions, Walpole expressed to his niece his strong disapproval of the connexion. This, and his refusal to meet the Duke, caused a breach of Walpole's friendship with Lady Waldegrave until after the public announcement of her marriage.

25 Perhaps to Madame du Deffand, who, in a letter to Walpole of 24 Feb., acknowledges the receipt of one from him on that day.

LETTER 471.—First printed in *Works of Lord Orford*, vol. v, pp. 374–6.

1 Dodsley had reprinted the *Designs* in 1765 and 1766.

1a Walpole had seen them as soon as they were written. On 5 May 1761 he wrote to George Montagu: 'Gray has translated two noble incantations from the Lord knows who, a Danish Gray, who lived the Lord knows when.'

little notes, partly from justice (to acknowledge the debt, where I had borrowed any thing), partly from ill temper,[2] just to tell the gentle reader, that Edward I. was not Oliver Cromwell, nor queen Elizabeth the witch of Endor.[3] This is literally all; and with all this I shall be but a shrimp of an author. I gave leave also to print the same thing at Glasgow;[4] but I doubt my packet has miscarried, for I hear nothing of its arrival as yet. To what you say to me so civilly, that I ought to write more, I reply in your own words (like the pamphleteer,[5] who is going to confute you out of your own mouth), What has one to do, when *turned of fifty*, but really to think of finishing? However, I will be candid (for you seem to be so with me), and avow to you, that till fourscore-and-ten, whenever the humour takes me, I will write, because I like it; and because I like myself better when I do so. If I do not write much, it is because I cannot.[6] As you have not this last plea, I see no reason why you should not continue as long as it is agreeable to yourself, and to all such as have any curiosity of judgment in the subjects you choose to treat. By the way let me tell you (while it is fresh) that lord Sandwich, who was lately dining at Cambridge, speaking (as I am told) handsomely of your book, said, it was pity you did not know that his cousin Manchester[7] had a genealogy of the kings, which came down no lower than to Richard III. and at the end of it were two portraits of Richard and his son, in which that

[2] He wrote to Beattie on 1 Feb.: 'as to the notes I do it out of spite' (see Letter 466 and Letter 469, n. 5).

[3] The volume was published on 12 Mar. this year (see Letter 470, n. 2).

[4] See Letter 466.

[5] The pamphlet in question was *An Answer to Mr Horace Walpole's late Work, entitled, Historic Doubts on the Reign and Life of King Richard the Third; or, an attempt to confute him from his own arguments.* By F. W. G. of the Middle Temple. *Decipimur Specie recti.* (London: Printed for B. White, at Horace's Head, in Fleet-street. M. DCC. LXVIII 4to. pp. 100). The author was not William Guthrie (see Letter 391, n. 3), as Walpole assumed (see Letter 472, n. 5), but the Rev. Frederick William Guydickens (Guidickins), d. 1779.

[6] Gray's conception of his poetical powers was expressed in a letter to Wharton ten years before (Letter 271): 'I by no means pretend to inspiration, but yet I affirm that the faculty in question is by no means voluntary. it is the result (I suppose) of a certain disposition of mind wch does not depend on oneself, & wch I have not felt this long time.' He could only write poetry 'whenever the humour takes me', as he now says to Walpole, or 'just as the maggot bites' as he wrote to Wharton in 1757 (Letter 257). It is noteworthy that after his Imitations of the Norse and Welsh Gray produced nothing but his Installation Ode and some satirical poems.

[7] George Montagu (1737–88), fourth Duke of Manchester (1762).

king appeared to be a handsome man. I tell you it as I heard it: perhaps you may think it worth enquiring into.[8] I have looked into Speed and Leslie.[9] It appears very odd, that Speed in the speech he makes for P. Warbeck, addrefsed to James IV. of Scotland, should three times cite the *manuscript proclamation* of Perkin, then in the hands of Sir Robert Cotton;[10] and yet when he gives us the proclamation afterwards (on occasion of the insurrection in Cornwall) he does not cite any such manuscript. In Casley's Catalogue of the Cotton Library[11] you may see whether this manuscript proclamation still exists or not: if it does, it may be found at the Musæum. Leslie will give you no satisfaction at all: though no subject of England, he could not write freely on this matter, as the title of Mary his mistrefs to the crown of England was derived from that of Henry VII. Accordingly, he every where treats Perkin as an impostor; yet drops several little exprefsions inconsistent with that supposition. He has preserved no proclamation: he only puts a short speech into Perkin's mouth, the substance of which is taken by Speed, and translated in the end of his, which is a good deal longer: the whole matter is treated by Leslie very concisely and superficially. I can easily transcribe it, if you please; but I do not see that it could answer any purpose.

Mr. Boswell's book I was going to recommend to you, when I received your letter: it has pleased and moved me strangely, all (I mean) that relates to Paoli. He is a man born two thousand years after his time! The pamphlet proves what I have always maintained, that any fool may write a most valuable book by chance, if he will only tell us what he heard and saw with veracity. Of Mr. Boswell's truth I have not the least suspicion,

[8] In his *Supplement to the Historic Doubts*, published in 1769, Walpole writes: 'The earl of Sandwich, on reading my Doubts, obligingly acquainted me that the duke of Manchester was possessed of a most curious and original roll, containing the list, portraits & descent of all the earls of Warwick drawn by John Rous himself, the antiquary. This singular manuscript his grace, at my desire, was so good as to lend me; and with his permission I caused ten of the last and most curious portraits to be traced off, and here present them to the public faithfully and exactly engraven.' (*Works of Lord Orford*, vol. ii, p. 216.)

[9] See Letter 470, n. 7.

[10] Sir Robert Bruce Cotton (1571–1631), collector of the famous Cottonian Library, which came into the possession of the nation in 1702, and after being severely damaged by fire (in 1731) was deposited in the British Museum in 1753.

[11] Published in 1734 (see Letter 320, n. 33).

because I am sure he could invent nothing of this kind.[12] The true title of this part of his work is, A Dialogue between a Green-goose and a Hero.

I had been told of a manuscript in Benet-library: the inscription of it is *Itinerarium Fratris Simonis Simeonis*[13] *et Hugonis Illuminatoris*, 1322. Would not one think this should promise something? They were two Franciscan friars that came from Ireland, and pafsed through Wales to London, to Canterbury, to Dover, and so to France in their way to Jerusalem. All that relates to our own country has been transcribed for me, and (sorry am I to say) signifies not a halfpenny: only this little bit might be inserted in your next edition of the Painters:[14] Ad aliud caput civitatis (Londoniæ) est monasterium nigrorum monachorum nomine Westmonasterium, in quo constanter et communiter omnes reges Angliæ sepeliuntur——et eidem monasterio quasi immediatè conjungitur illud famosifsimum palatium regis, in quo est illa vulgata camera, in cujus parietibus sunt omnes historiæ bellicæ totius Bibliæ ineffabiliter depictæ, atque in Gallico completifsimè et perfectifsimè conscriptæ, in non modicâ intuentium admiratione et maximâ regali magnificentiâ.

I have had certain observations on your Royal and Noble Authors given me to send you perhaps about three years ago: last week I found them in a drawer, and (my conscience being troubled) now enclose them to you. I have even forgot whose they are.

I have been also told of a pafsage in Ph. de Comines, which (if you know) ought not to have been pafsed over. The book is not at hand at present, and I must conclude my letter. Adieu!

I am ever yours,

T. GRAY.

[12] In an unpublished letter to William Temple, dated 21 July 1791, Norton Nicholls wrote: 'When the account of Corsica came out, Mr Gray said to me, "I like this book, for one sees the author is too foolish to have invented it" '—a criticism which Nicholls repeats in his *Reminiscences of Gray* written in 1805.

[13] Gray might have heard of the manuscript from Dr. John Sharp (Letter 290, n. 1) or Michael Tyson (Letter 468, n. 13), both Fellows of Corpus. James Nasmith (1740–1808), also a Fellow (1765), who was engaged upon a catalogue of the MSS. bequeathed to the College by Archbishop Parker, which was published in 1777, edited and published in 1778 the MS. from which the passage quoted by Gray was transcribed (*Itineraria Symonis Simeonis et Willelmi de Worcestre, quibus accedit Tractatus de Metro*, Cantab. 8vo).

[14] Walpole did not avail himself of this information.

472. WALPOLE TO GRAY

Arlington-street, Friday night, February 26 [1768].

I PLAGUE you to death, but I must reply a few more words. I shall be very glad to see in print, and to have those that are worthy see your ancient odes; but I was in hopes there were some pieces too that I had not seen. I am sorry there are not. I troubled you about Perkin's proclamation, because Mr. Hume lays great strefs upon it, and insists, that if Perkin affirmed his brother was killed, it must have been true, if he was true duke of York. Mr. Hume would have persuaded me that the proclamation is in Stowe, but I can find no such thing there; nor, what is more, in Casley's catalogue, which I have twice looked over carefully. I wrote to sir David Dalrymple[1] in Scotland, to enquire after it, because I would produce it if I could, though it should make against me: but he, I believe, thinking I enquired with the contrary view, replied very drily, that it was published at York, and was not to be found in Scotland. Whether he is displeased that I have plucked a hair from the trefses of their great historian;[2] or whether, as I suspect, he is offended for king William;[3] this reply was all the notice he took of my letter and book. I only smiled, as I must do when I find one party is angry with me on king William's, and the other on lord Clarendon's[4] account.

The answer advertised is Guthrie's,[5] who is furious that I have taken no notice of *his* History. I shall take as little of his pamphlet; but his end will be answered, if he sells that and one or two copies of his History. Mr. Hume, I am told, has drawn up an answer too, which I shall see, and, if I can, will get him to publish;[6] for, if I should ever choose to say any thing more on

LETTER 472.—First printed in *Works of Lord Orford*, vol. v, pp. 376–8.
[1] That is, Lord Hailes; see Walpole's letter to him of 2 Feb. 1768.
[2] Hume.   [3] See Letter 468, n. 4.   [4] See Letter 468, n. 15.
[5] See Letter 391, n. 3. Walpole wrote to Montagu on 12 Mar.: 'Guthrie has published two criticisms on my *Richard*; one abusive in the *Critical Review*; t'other very civil and even flattering in a pamphlet—both so stupid and contemptible, that I rather prefer the first, as making some attempt at vivacity; but in point of argument . . . both things are below scorn.' The pamphlet, however, was not by Guthrie (see Letter 471, n. 5).
[6] Hume communicated to Walpole what the latter characterized as very unsubstantial arguments, and then handed them to a Swiss writer, Deyverdun, joint-editor with Gibbon of *Mémoires littéraires de la Grande Bretagne*, who published them, together with a review of Walpole's book, in the volume

this subject, I had rather reply to him than to hackney-writers: —to the latter, indeed, I never will reply.[7] A few notes I have to add that will be very material; and I wish to get some account of a book that was once sold at Osborn's,[8] that exists perhaps at Cambridge, and of which I found a memorandum t'other day in my note-book. It is called A paradox, or apology for Richard III. by sir William Cornwallis.[9] If you could discover it, I should be much obliged to you.

Lord Sandwich, with whom I have not exchanged a syllable since the general warrants,[10] very obligingly sent me an account of the roll at Kimbolton;[11] and has since, at my desire, borrowed it for me and sent it to town.[12] It is as long as my lord Lyttelton's History;[13] but by what I can read of it (for it is both ill-written and much decaycd), it is not a roll of kings, but of all that have been pofsefsed of, or been earls of Warwick: or have not—for one of the first earls is Æneas. How, or wherefore, I do not know, but amongst the first is Richard III. in whose reign it was finished, and with whom it concludes. He is there again with his wife and son, and Edward IV. and Clarence[14] and his wife, and Edward their son (who unluckily is a little old man), and Margaret countefs of Salisbury, their daughter—But why do I say with these? There is every body else too—and what is most

for 1768. Walpole deals with them in the *Supplement to the Historic Doubts*, in *Works of Lord Orford*, vol. ii, pp. 192–215 (see also *Short Notes* for 1769). Walpole assumed that the author of the review was Deyverdun, but it was in fact written by Gibbon, and is included among his *Miscellaneous Works* (ed. 1814, vol. iii, pp. 331–49), with Hume's notes printed at the end.

[7] Walpole subsequently did, in fact, devote several pages to Guthrie in the *Supplement to the Historic Doubts*, in *Works*, vol. ii, pp. 187–91.

[8] The book presumably came from the Harleian Library, which was bought by Thomas Osborne, the bookseller (see Letter 322, n. 15).

[9] Sir William Cornwallis, Knight (d. 1614), author of *Essayes of certaine Paradoxes*, one of which is entitled *The Praise of King Richard III* (see Letter 473).

[10] In Feb. 1764 (see Letter 385, n. 9).

[11] Kimbolton Castle, Hunts., seat of the Duke of Manchester, the owner of the roll.

[12] See Letter 471, n. 8. From this roll were taken the two plates of portraits which were engraved to illustrate the *Historic Doubts*, when it was reprinted in *Works of Lord Orford*, vol. ii, pp. 166–7.

[13] *History of the Life of Henry the Second, and of the Age in which he lived*, of which the first two volumes appeared in 1767.

[14] George Plantagenet (1449–78), Duke of Clarence, brother of King Edward IV; m. (1469) Lady Isabel Nevill, eldest daughter of Richard Nevill, Earl of Warwick and Salisbury. Their son was Edward Plantagenet, Earl of Warwick and Salisbury, beheaded in 1499.

meritorious, the habits of all the times are admirably well observed from the most savage ages. Each figure is tricked with a pen, well drawn, but neither coloured nor shaded. Richard is straight, but thinner than my print; his hair short, and exactly curled in the same manner; not so handsome as mine, but what one might really believe intended for the same countenance, as drawn by a different painter, especially when so small; for the figures in general are not so long as one's finger. His queen is ugly, and with just such a square forehead as in my print, but I cannot say like it. Nor, indeed, where forty-five figures out of fifty (I have not counted the number) must have been imaginary, can one lay great strefs on the five. I shall, however, have these figures copied, especially as I know of no other image of the son. Mr. Astle[15] is to come to me to-morrow morning to explain the writing.

I wish you had told me in what age your Franciscan friars lived; and what the pafsage in Comines is.[16] I am very ready to make amende honorable.

Thank you for the notes on the Noble Authors. They shall be inserted when I make a new edition, for the sake of the trouble the person has taken, though they are of little consequence. Dodsley has asked me for a new edition;[17] but I have had little heart to undertake such work, no more than to mend my old linen. It is pity one cannot be born an ancient, and have commentators to do such jobs for one! Adieu!

Yours ever,
Hor. Walpole.

Saturday morning.

On reading over your letter again this morning, I do find the age in which the friars lived—I read and write in such a hurry, that I think I neither know what I read or say.

---

15 Thomas Astle (1735–1803), antiquary and palaeographer; F.S.A. 1763; F.R.S. 1766; author of *Origin and Progress of Writing* (1784).
16 See Letter 471 *ad fin.*
17 Walpole's *Catalogue of the Royal and Noble Authors of England* was originally printed at Strawberry Hill in Apr. 1758; a second edition (dated 1759) was published by Dodsley in December of the same year; a final edition, 'Enlarged with many new Articles, with several Passages restored from the original MS. and with many other Additions', was not published until 1787 and, later, in 1798 in *Works of Lord Orford*, vol. i, pp. [245]–564.

473. GRAY TO WALPOLE

Pembroke-hall, March 6, 1768.

HERE is sir William Cornwallis, entitled Efsayes of certaine Paradoxes.[1] 2d Edit. 1617, Lond.

King Richard III.
The French Pockes
Nothing   }praised.
Good to be in debt
Sadnefse
Julian the Apostate's vertues

The title-page will probably suffice you; but if you would know any more of him, he has read nothing but the common chroniclcs, and those without attention: for example, speaking of Anne the queen, he says, she was *barren*, of which Richard had often complained to Rotheram. He extenuates the murder of Henry VI. and his son: the first, he says, might be a malicious accusation, for that many did suppose he died of mere melancholy and grief: the latter cannot be proved to be the action of Richard (though executed in his presence); and if it were, he did it out of love to his brother Edward. He justifies the death of the lords at Pomfret, from reasons of state, for his own preservation, the safety of the commonwealth, and the ancient nobility. The execution of Hastings he excuses from necefsity, from the dishonesty and sensuality of the man: what was his crime with respect to Richard, he does not say. Dr. Shaw's sermon[2] was not by the king's command, but to be imputed to the preacher's own ambition: but if it was by order, *to charge his mother with adultery was a matter of no such great moment, since it is no wonder in that sex.* Of the murder in the Tower he doubts; but if it were by his order, the offence was to God, not to his people; and *how could he demonstrate his love more amply, than to venture his soul for their quiet?* Have you enough, pray? You see it is an idle declamation, the exercise of a school-boy that is to be bred a statesman.

I have looked in Stowe: to be sure there is no proclamation[3]

LETTER 473.—First printed in *Works of Lord Orford*, vol. v, pp. 379–80.
[1] See Letter 472, n. 9.
[2] Dr. Ralph Shaw (d. 1484), who preached a sermon at St. Paul's Cross on 22 June 1483, impugning the validity of Edward IV's marriage with Elizabeth Woodville (Lady Grey), and claiming that the crown belonged by right to the Protector Richard; he further asserted that Edward IV was himself a bastard, and thus charged Richard's own mother with adultery.
[3] By Perkin Warbeck (see Letter 471).

there. Mr. Hume, I suppose, means *Speed*, where it is given, how truly I know not; but that he had seen the original is sure, and seems to quote the very words of it in the beginning of that speech which Perkin makes to James IV. and also just afterwards, where he treats of the Cornish rebellion.

Guthrie, you see, has vented himself in the Critical Review.[4] His History I never saw, nor is it here, nor do I know any one that ever saw it. He is a rascal, but rascals may chance to meet with curious records; and that commifsion to sir J. Tyrrell[5] (if it be not a lye) is such: so is the order for Henry the sixth's funeral. I would by no means take notice of him, write what he would. I am glad you have seen the Manchester-roll.[6]

It is not I that talk of Phil. de Comines; it was mentioned to me as a thing that looked like a voluntary omifsion: but I see you have taken notice of it in the note to p. 71,[7] though rather too slightly. You have not observed that the same writer says, c. 55, *Richard tua de sa main, ou fit tuer en sa presence, quelque lieu apart, ce bon homme le roi Henry.* Another oversight I think there is at p. 43, where you speak of the *roll of parliament* and the contract with lady Eleanor Boteler,[8] as things newly come to light; whereas Speed has given at large the same roll in his History. Adieu!

I am ever yours,
T. GRAY.

474. WALPOLE TO GRAY

Arlington Street March 8. 1768.

I DONT mean to trouble you with any farther Searches; but I must thank you for your readinefs to oblige me. I will try to return it by keeping the Roll[1] as long as I can, that you may see

---

[4] The article (which was anonymous) was published in the *Critical Review* for Feb. 1768 (vol. xxv, pp. 116–26). Walpole, whose book is contemptuously dismissed by the reviewer as 'historic scribblism', dealt with this article in the *Supplement to the Historic Doubts* (see Letter 472, n. 1).

[5] Sir James Tyrell (d. 1502), the supposed murderer of Edward V and his brother, Richard, Duke of York, in the Tower (1483).

[6] See Letter 471, n. 8.   [7] In *Works*, vol. ii, p. 149 n.

[8] See *Historic Doubts* (in *Works*, vol. ii, p. 133): 'We have the best and most undoubted authorities to assure us, that Edward's precontract or marriage, urged to invalidate his match with the lady Grey, was with the lady Eleanor Talbot, widow of lord Butler of Sudely, and sister of the earl of Shrewsbury; . . . her mother was the lady Katherine Stafford, daughter of Humphrey duke of Buckingham, prince of the blood.'

LETTER 474.—First printed by Toynbee (1915), No. 243.

[1] See Letter 471, n. 8.

it, if you look Londonwards; it is really a great Curiosity, & will furnish one with remarks. Not that I am going to answer such trumpery as Guthrie's,[2] who does not seem to disagree with me (tho I scarce can discover the scope of his jumbled arguments) but is angry I did not declare I agreed with him, tho I vow I never saw his book. It shall rest in peace for me, as all such Writers ever shall. The few Criticisms I have suffered have done more than my own arguments coud: They have strengthened my opinion, seeing how little can be advanced to overturn it. M[r] Hume has shown me an answer he has drawn up. It is nothing but his former arguments enlarged: no one new fact or new light.[3] I am trying to persuade him to publish it, that I may have occasion to add a Short appendix, with some striking particulars; not, to dispute more with him. I propose too to give eight or nine figures from Rous's roll.[4] In the Coronation roll, is this Entry, which you & I overlooked: *Things ordered in haste by My Lord Duke of Buckingham.* Then Immediately follow the Robes for Edward 5th.—proof I think of the Design that He shoud walk.

I shall correct a mistake I find (by Guthrie) I made, about the Duke of Albany.[5] For the Confefsion of the Lady Butler, I take it to be an absolute Lie. The Commifsion of S[r] James Tirrel I have not had time to search for in Rymer,[6] where I suppose it is, if any where. But you did not observe that It is dated in Nov. 1482. Consequently under Edward 4th. & if true, contradicts S[r] T. More, who says Tirrel was kept down. If the Date shoud be 83; it was subsequent by two or three months to the time afsigned for the murder. But enough of all this till I see you.

Have you read the two new volumes of Swift?[7] The Second is the dullest heap of trumpery, flattery, & folly. The first is curious indeed! what a Man! what childish, vulgar Stuff! what grofs language to his Goddefs! what a curious Scene when the Ministry thought themselves ruined! what Cowardice in Such

[2] See Letter 472, n. 7.
[3] See Letter 472, n. 6.
[4] See Letter 471, n. 8.
[5] See *Supplement to the Historic Doubts,* in *Works,* vol. ii, p. 191.
[6] Rymer's *Fœdera,* fifteen volumes of which were published between 1704 and 1713 (and others after Rymer's death).
[7] The last two volumes of Swift's *Letters,* viz. vols. iii and iv (edited by Deane Swift and published this year), of which the former contains the *Journal to Stella.*

a Bully!—then his libels, & his exciting the Ministers to punish libels in the same breath!—the next moment generous & benevolent. But his great Offence with me, is preventing a poor fellow from being pardoned, who was accused of ravishing his own Strumpet.

I think you will like Sterne's sentimental travels,[8] which tho often tiresome, are exceedingly goodnatured & picturesque. Good night!

yrs ever
H W.

P.S.
I this moment hear that the Robbery & setting fire to Mr Conway's House[9] was committed by a Servant belonging to the Duke of Richmond. I know no more yet. They had a great Escape of their lives, tho the lofs & damage is considerable; & they have been most unhappy, as they have none but old & faithfull Servants, & coud not be persuaded any of them were guilty.

475. GRAY TO WHARTON[1]

March 15. 1768.   Pemb: C:

Dear S^r

I AM so totally uninform'd, indeed so helplefs, in matters of law, that there is no one perhaps in the kingdom you could apply to for advice with lefs effect, than to me: this ought to be a sufficient warning to you not to pay more attention to me than I deserve. you may too take into the account my natural indolence & indisposition to act, & a want of alacrity in indulging any distant hopes, however flattering; as you have (I think) from nature the contrary fault, a Medium between us would be pofsibly the best rule of action.

One thing I am persuaded I see clearly, & would advise strongly: it is, that you should never think of separating your

---

[8] *Sentimental Journey through France and Italy*, by Mr. Yorick (2 vols. 12mo, 1768).
[9] See Walpole's letter to Mann, 8 Mar. 1768.
LETTER 475.—First printed by Mitford (1835–43), vol. iv, pp. 116–19; now reprinted from original.
[1] Wharton had been called to London in Jan. 1768 by the serious illness of his brother Jonathan (see Letter 463). Jonathan had died, probably in February; his will was proved on 23 Feb. by Thomas Wharton, who had written to Gray after his return to Old Park.

cause[2] from that of your Nephew.[3] your rights are exactly the same, you must share the profit & the lofs. he is a Minor & under your care: to set up any distinct claim for the private advantage of yourself & family, would surely hurt you in the eye of the world. the slightest apprehension of any such thought will make a total breach between M[r] Ll:[4] & you, whose advice & activity seem of such singular use in all your designs. this will force you to pafs your whole time at London without other afsistance, than what you must hire; & perhaps produce another law-suit between you and your own Nephew. but you speak irresolutely yourself on this head, & as you have had a little time to think, since you wrote your letter, I doubt not, you have already drop'd any such idea. it remains then to communicate immediately to Mr. Ll: the opinions of De Grey,[5] & to advise with him (without reserve) about this application to the Treasury.

Now I am going to talk of what I do not understand: but from what I have lately heard of the D: of Portland[6] & S[r] J: Lowther's[7] case[8] (w[ch] is in some respects similar) if you obtain this Grant[9]

----

[2] The letter gives a general indication of what the cause was, but some legal details lack explanation. Jonathan Wharton had bought tithes: by his will (see n. 1) he had left an annuity of £500 to his wife 'issuing out and charged upon . . . all and every the Tythes of the Rectory of Norton, Storlton, Preston and Hartburn in the County of Durham belonging to me'. After further legacies, he bequeathed the residue of his real and personal estate to his brother Thomas and his nephew Robert Wharton (see n. 3), and appointed Thomas Wharton sole Executor and Administrator. Thomas Wharton and his nephew thus became entitled to the property in the tithes, subject to the charges of the Annuity. There was, however, a claim to the 'extention of the tythes', concerning which apparently Jonathan Wharton had begun a suit, and it was on this question that Wharton had sought Gray's advice.

[3] Robert Wharton, who was under Thomas Wharton's guardianship (see Letter 336, n. 3).

[4] Richard Wharton, the father of Robert, married Ann Lloyd. 'M[r] Ll:' may have been a Mr. Lloyd and a maternal uncle of the boy.

[5] William de Grey (1719–81), at this time Attorney-General.

[6] William Henry Cavendish Bentinck (1738–1809), third Duke of Portland, subsequently Prime Minister.

[7] James Lowther (1736–1802), fifth Baronet; M.P. 1757–84; created Baron Lowther and Viscount and Earl of Lonsdale, 1784.

[8] This case had been decided (in its first stage) only three months before. Of the ground of dispute and the litigation (which went on for some years and was ultimately decided in favour of the Duke of Portland) there is a full account in the *D.N.B.* (James Lowther, Earl of Lonsdale, 1736–1802). In 1767 Sir James Lowther made application to the Treasury, asserting that the

(for wch you must pay too a certain rent to the Crown; & if any one outbids you, they will be prefer'd) your right to it is never the more establish'd, provided any body start up to contest it with you at law, for the Courts are still open to redrefs any injury, that a person pleads he has received by such grant. in this therefore I should be guided by M^r Ll: and Mr Madocks.[10] the application to the Treasury is easy, I believe: St:, or M^r W:[11] will probably acquaint you of the manner: but I could give you good reasons, why the former should not be ask'd to interpose personally in obtaining it, at least why it would be uneasy to him to do so.

There remains then the foundation of all this, the legal right, you & your Nephew have, to this extention of the tythes, about wch your counsel themselves seem dubious enough; & you cannot expect me to be clearer than they, especially as there are two things not at all explained in your letter, viz: What is that Grant to Morrice & Cole, & when made? & who is Rector of the Church, or (if a Vicar) who presents him, for it appears not to be you? all that you seem to me clearly entitled to is a right of continuing the suit,[12] wch your Brother begun, wch contest may beget others to infinity. shall I tell (but without consequence) what I should wish? that you would sell these tythes out of hand, & with them all your expectations & all your lawsuits: if these are worth any thing, Purchasers may be found sanguine enough to give such a price, as Mr Jonathan did, & you will be no loser; if they are not, you may lose a little money, & in my opinion be a great gainer: for this inundation of businefs, of eager hopes, & perhaps more reasonable fears, is the thing in the world the most contrary to your peace, & that

Duke of Portland had no title to certain properties, which he held in Cumberland, and asking that a grant of the Crown interest in these properties should be made to himself 'for three lives or such terms as to their lordships should seem meet'. On 18 Dec. 1767 the grant had been made in Lowther's favour.

⁹ It may be inferred from what Gray says that Wharton had thought that he might establish the right to 'the extention of the tythes' (mentioned in the next paragraph) by laying an information that the possessor's title was bad, and applying to the Treasury for a grant from the Crown to himself (as Sir James Lowther had done: see n. 8).

¹⁰ 'M^r Ll:' (see n. 4) and Mr. Maddocks were perhaps lawyers advising Wharton and his nephew.

¹¹ Stonhewer and Walpole. Stonhewer was private secretary to the Duke of Grafton who was, at this time, First Lord of the Treasury.

¹² This was presumably a suit claiming the 'extention of the tythes', which Jonathan Wharton had started (see n. 2).

of your family. but I determine nothing, we shall hear what the three Referees[13] say, & what M^r Ll: determines upon it.

I have made hast to answer you, considering the difficulty of the case: you will therefore excuse me for my intention's sake. Mason is arrived in London, & lives for the present at Stonhewer's, in Queen-Street. I rejoiced to hear, you got so well over that Monster the Trent.[14] make my best compliments to Mrs Wharton, & your Family. I am sorry to hear Mifs Wharton has been ill:[15] Mr Brown presents his respects to you all, down to Dicky.[16] Adieu! I am ever

Yours,

TG:

Our weather has been mild & fine enough of late. the [next][17] letter will give an account of it. Wilkes (they say) will be chose for the City of London.[18] T. Lyon has lost one of his causes in the house of Lords against Ld Panmure.[19]

476. GRAY TO BROWN

Southampton Row, April 27, 1768.[1]

Dear Sir

BY this time I conclude, you are return'd to Cambridge: tho' I thought it a long time, before I heard of you from Thrandeston,[2] and could have wish'd you had stay'd longer with

---

¹³ This allusion has not been explained.

¹⁴ Wharton, on his return from London to Old Park, would have crossed the Trent at Newark: and the Trent in flood might make a journey difficult (see Letter 443).

¹⁵ Wharton's eldest daughter, now in her twentieth year. From Mar. 1766 Gray refers to her as Miss Wharton; and from this date always in connexion with her ill health.

¹⁶ Wharton's youngest boy (see Letter 459, n. 20).

¹⁷ Supplied conjecturally; MS. damaged.

¹⁸ He was not elected—Walpole wrote to Mann on 1 Apr.: 'The famous Wilkes appeared the moment the Parliament was dissolved. . . . He stood for the City of London, and the last on the poll of seven candidates, none but the mob, and most of them without votes, favouring him.' Having failed in the City, Wilkes then stood for the county of Middlesex, for which he was elected at the head of the poll at the end of March.

¹⁹ See Letter 430, n. 19.

LETTER 476.—First printed by Mitford in *Gray–Mason* (1853), pp. 415–17. Gosse, overlooking the letter in Mitford, claimed to have printed it for the first time, and misdated it by eight years (*Works*, vol. iii, p. 38). The original was formerly in the possession of Mr. Frederick Locker at Rowfant, and from it Gosse presumably made his copy. His text, which is in accordance with Gray's usual practice in the matter of capitals and punctuation, is followed

Palgrave: perhaps you are in Hertfordshire, however I write at a venture. I went to Mr. Mann's,[3] and (tho' he is in Town) not finding him at home, left a note with an account of my businefs with him, and my direction. I have had no mefsage in answer to it: so pofsibly he has written to you, and sent the papers. I know not.

Mr. Precentor is still here, and not in haste to depart, indeed I do not know whether he has not a fit of the Gout: it is certain, he had a pain yesterday in his foot, but whether owing to Bechamel[4] and Claret, or to cutting a corn, was not determined: he is still at Stonhewer's[5] house, and has not made his journey to Eton and to Bath yet, tho' he intends to do it.

We have had no mobs, nor illuminations[6] yet, since I was here. Wilkes's speech[7] you have seen; the Court[8] was so surprised at being contemn'd to its face, and in the face of the World, that the Chief in a manner forgot the matter in hand, and enter'd into an apology for his own past conduct, and so (with the rest of his Afsefsors) shuffled the matter off, and left

here, except in the date, the spelling of Stonhewer, the restoration of lacunae, and the correction of Grenville for Greville.

[1] Gray perhaps omitted the year (as he often did): Mitford printed 1768, which is obviously right: Gosse has 1760.

[2] In the north of Suffolk, about five miles north-west of Eye; it was one of Palgrave's livings (see Letter 273*, n. 1).

[3] There is nothing to show who this was, nor what business Gray and Brown had with him.

[4] A rich white sauce, so named from its inventor, Louis de Béchamel, Marquis de Nointel (d. 1703), surintendant of the household of Philip, Duke of Orleans.

[5] Stonhewer's house was in Queen Street (see Letter 475).

[6] The reference is to the mobs and illuminations at the end of March on the occasion of the Middlesex election, when Wilkes was returned at the head of the poll (see Letter 475, n. 18).

[7] On 23 Apr. Walpole wrote to Mann: 'Wednesday last was the great day of expectation when Mr Wilkes was to, and did, make his appearance in the King's Bench. . . . The Attorney-General moves to commit him. Lord Mansfield and the Judges of the King's Bench tell him the *capias utlegatum* should have been taken out, and, not having been, there was no such person as Mr Wilkes before them; nay, that there was no such person, for, Mr Wilkes being an outlaw, an *utlegatus* does not exist in the eye of the law. However, this *non entity* made a long speech, and abused the Chief Justice [Lord Mansfield] to his face, though they say, with great trembling—and then— why then?—one or two hallooed, and nobody answered, and Mr Wilkes walked away, and the Judges went home to dinner, and a great crowd, for there was a vast crowd, though no mobbing, retired.'

[8] The Court of King's Bench.

the danger to the officers of the Crown, that is indeed, to the Ministry. Nobody had ventured, or would venture to serve the *Capias*[9] upon him. I cannot afsure, it is done yet; tho' yesterday I heard it was, and (if so) he comes again to-day into Court.[10] He profefses himself ready to make any submifsions to the K., but not to give up his pursuit of L$^{d.}$ H$^{x.}$ [11] The Delavals[12] attend very regularly, and take notes of all that pafses. His writ of Error on the Outlawry must come to a decision before the House of Lords.[13]

I was not among the Coal-heavers at Shadwell,[14] tho' seven people lost their lives in the fray: Nor was I in[15] Goodmans Fields[16] where the Bawdy-house was demolish'd. The Ministry (I believe) are but ticklish in their situation: they talk of Grenville[17] and his Brother, again. Lord forbid! it must be dreadful necefsity indeed, that brings them back. Adieu! I am ever yours,

T. G.

If you are at Cambridge, pray let me know.

[9] The *Capias utlegatum*, writ for the arrest of the outlaw.

[10] After a formal arrest Wilkes was committed by Lord Mansfield to the King's Bench prison on that day (27 Apr.).

[11] The reference is to Lord Halifax, by whose orders as Secretary of State under a general warrant Wilkes had been arrested, and his papers seized in Apr. 1763 (see Letter 385, n. 9). Wilkes brought an action against Halifax which was tried in Nov. 1769, and resulted in a verdict for Wilkes, with £4,000 damages.

[12] Sir Francis Blake Delaval, K.B., M.P. for Andover from 1754 till the dissolution in March of this year; and his younger brother, Sir John Hussey Delaval, Bart. (afterwards Lord Delaval), at this time M.P. for Berwick, who had formerly been at Pembroke College, Cambridge (see Letter 127, n. 6).

[13] It was dismissed on 19 Jan. 1769.

[14] On the left bank of the Thames, between Wapping and Limehouse. The fray to which Gray refers is thus reported in the *Public Advertiser* for Friday, 22 Apr. 1768: 'Wednesday night a most terrible Rising happened again [there had been one on the previous Friday] among the Coal-heavers at Shadwell, in which several Houses were pulled down, and the Inhabitants much hurt. Seven or Eight Persons were killed in the fray. . . . A Party of Guards from the Tower were sent for to quell the Disturbance, who fired among the Rioters, and took the Ringleader Prisoner, but were themselves very roughly treated by the Mob.'

[15] The MS. seems to have been damaged since Mitford transcribed it, as Gosse noted that there were lacunae here.

[16] There is a long account of the incident referred to by Gray in the *Public Advertiser* for Monday, 25 Apr. 1768.

[17] The reference is to George Grenville and Lord Temple.

477. GRAY TO NICHOLLS

South:ⁿ Row. 29 May. Sunday. [1768].

ADDIO! You will have the satisfaction of going to Fischer's[1] concert, and hearing Pugnani[2] without me, on Thursday; I don't believe there will be any body one knows there. My respects to Mrs Nicholls,[3] and my cousin, Mifs Floyer,[4] not forgetting the red nightingale.[5] I am gone tomorrow.[6]

Here are a pair of your stray shoes, dancing attendance, till you send for them.

477*. The Duke of Grafton to Gray

[July 27, 1768]

[The Duke of Grafton wrote to Gray, on Wednesday, 27 July, to offer him the Regius Professorship of Modern History at Cambridge, as we know from Gray's letters to Mary Antrobus, Wharton, Mason, and Norton Nicholls (Letters 479, 480, 481, 482). The Duke of Grafton's letter is not extant; but Gray's allusions are sufficient to show what its contents must have been. Certain passages, which Gray underlined in his letters to Mary Antrobus and Wharton, may be taken to contain the actual expressions used by Grafton. As Gray replied in the first person (Letter 478) it is probable that the Duke wrote in the same way. Three passages in the Duke's letter can be traced (the words in italics are those underlined by Gray):

(1) The Duke had the King's commands to *offer* Gray the vacant Professorship (Letters 479, 480, 481, 483).

(2) 'not only as a reward of &c:, but as a credit to &c:' (Letter 482:

LETTER 477.—First printed by Mitford (1835–43), vol. v, p. 75; original missing.

[1] Johann Christian Fischer (1733–1800), oboist and composer, was a native of Freiburg im Breisgau. He came to England and established his reputation by his brilliant playing (see Burney, *History of Music*, vol. iv, pp. 676–7). Fischer's announcement of the concert to which Gray refers appeared in the *Public Advertiser* for Thursday, 2 June 1768: 'For the benefit of Mr Fisher. At the Large Room, Thatch'd House, St. James's-street. This Day, June the 2^d, will be performed a Grand Concert of Vocal and Instrumental Music. First Violin and Concerto by Sig. Pugnani ... Concerto on the Hautbois by Mr Fisher. ... Tickets to be had of Mr Fisher, at Mr Stidman's, Peruke maker in Frith-street, Soho; and at Welcker's Music Shop, Gerrard Street, Soho, at 10s. 6d. each.'

[2] Gaetano Pugnani (1727–1803), celebrated violinist, was for a time leader of the opera band in London. He was a prolific composer. He returned to Italy about 1770.   [3] Nicholls's mother.

[4] Nicholls's cousin Fanny (see Letter 422, n. 11).

[5] This allusion remains unexplained.

[6] Gray went into Kent for a great part of the summer (see Letter 480).

Gray alludes to compliments that he will not repeat in Letters 479, 480, 481).

(3) The Duke added at the end '*that from private as well as publick considerations He must take the warmest part in approving so well judged a measure as he hopes I do not doubt of the real regard & esteem with wch he has the honor to be, &c:*' (Letter 480, cf. Letter 479).]

478. GRAY TO THE DUKE OF GRAFTON[1]

My Lord,   Cambridge,[2] July [27 or 28], 1768.

YOUR Grace has dealt nobly with me; and the same delicacy of mind that induced you to confer this favour on me, unsolicited and unexpected, may perhaps make you averse to receive my sincerest thanks and grateful acknowledgments. Yet your Grace must excuse me, they will have their way: they are indeed but words; yet I know and feel they come from my heart, and therefore are not wholly unworthy of your Grace's acceptance. I even flatter myself (such is my pride) that you have some little satisfaction in your own work. If I did not deceive myself in this, it would compleat the happineſs of,

My Lord,
Your Grace's
Most obliged and devoted servant.

479. GRAY TO MARY ANTROBUS

Dear Mary,   29 July, 1768.

I THANK you for all your intelligence (and the first news I had of poor Brocket's death[1] was from you) and to reward you in

LETTER 478.—First printed in Mason's *Memoirs*, p. 331. Mason may have got a transcript of the letter from Stonhewer or found a draft of the letter among Gray's papers.

[1] Augustus Henry Fitzroy (1735–1811), third Duke of Grafton (1757), styled Earl of Euston 1747–57. In 1751 he entered Peterhouse, where Stonhewer was his private tutor: he graduated M.A. in 1753. After holding various offices in the Government, he became Prime Minister in 1768, and in the same year was elected Chancellor of the University.

[2] Gray at the date was in London (see Letters 480, 481, 482), and there he received Grafton's letter (through Stonhewer) probably on 27 July, the day it was written (see Letter 477*); his reply was written the same day or the next. 'Cambridge' may have been added by Mason, unless Gray was giving his academic address.

part for it, I now shall tell you, that this day, hot as it is, I kifsed the King's hand; that my warrant was signed by him last night; that on Wednesday I received a very honourable letter from the D. of Grafton,[2] acquainting me that his majesty had ordered him to offer me this Profefsorship, and much more, which does me too much credit by half for me to mention it. The Duke adds, *that from private as well as public considerations, he takes the warmest part in approving this measure of the King's.* These are his own words. You see there are princes (or ministers) left in the world, that know how to do things handsomely; for I profefs I never asked for it, nor have I seen his Grace before or after this event.

Dr. R.[3] (not forgetting a certain lady of his) is so good to you, and to me, that you may (if you please) show him my letter. He will not be critical as to the style, and I wish you would send it also to Mr. Brown, for I have not time to write to him by this day's post; they need not mention this circumstance to others, they may learn it as they can. Adieu!

I receive your letter of July 28 (while I am writing), consult your friends over the way, they are as good as I, and better. All I can say is, the Board[4] have been so often used to the name of Antrobus lately, that I fear they may take your petition not in

---

LETTER 479.—First printed by Mitford (1835–43), vol. iv, pp. 121–3. Mitford notes: 'The following letter is found in a curious collection of autographs made by Dr. Clarke in the latter part of his life, and is thus noticed by him: "Gray, whose rising fame, augmenting with every succeeding year of my life, has finally triumphed over false criticism, and the envious assaults of his contemporaries." ' Dr. Edward Daniel Clarke (1769–1822) was a Fellow of Jesus College, Cambridge; first Professor of Mineralogy, 1808; and University Librarian, 1817; a portion of his collection of autographs was sold by Messrs. Evans, of 93 Pall Mall, on 27–8 May 1842 (Catalogue in Brit. Mus. S.C. 680(2)). The letter in question was lot 31.

[1] See Letter 149, n. 7. His death was announced as follows in the *Cambridge Chronicle* for 30 July 1768: 'Cambridge, July 29. On Sunday last died, of the bruises he receiv'd by a fall from his horse the Thursday before, the Rev. Laurence Brockett, B.D., Fellow of Trinity College, Vicar of Over in Cambridgeshire, and Professor of History and Modern Languages in this University: which is in the gift of the King, and worth 400 l. per annum.'

[2] See Letter 477*.

[3] Probably, as Tovey suggests, Dr. Rutherforth, Regius Professor of Divinity (see Letter 135, n. 19); for Mrs. Rutherforth see Letter 364, n. 8.

[4] No doubt at the General Post Office—Mary Antrobus and her sister were anxious to be assured of the reversion of the office of Postmistress at Cambridge on the death of their mother (see Letter 418*, n. 1).

good part. If you are sure of the kindnefs or interest of Mr. A.⁵ the opportunity should not be lost; but I always a little distrust new friends and new lawyers.

I have found a man, who has brought Mr. Eyres (I think) up to my price,⁶ in a hurry; however he defers his final answer till Wednesday next. He shall not have it a shilling lower, I promise; and if he hesitates, I will rise upon him like a fury. Good-night. I am ever yours.

How could you dream that St: or Hinchl:⁷ would ask this for themselves? The only people that ask'd it were Lort,⁸ Marriott,⁹ Delaval,¹⁰ Jebb,¹¹ and Peck—,¹² at least I have heard of no more. Delaval always communicated his thoughts to me, knowing I would make no ill use of that knowledge. Lort is a worthy man, and I wish he could have it, or something as good: the rest are nothing.

⁵ Perhaps Mr. Abdy, and a relative of Mrs. Rutherforth (see n. 3, and Letter 358, n. 4). He was presumably a lawyer.

⁶ The reference is to Gray's interest in the property in Hand Alley, Bishopsgate (see Letter 439, n. 7). 'Mr. Eyres' was Joseph Eyre, the ultimate purchaser (see Letter 439, n. 10, and Appendix U).

⁷ Stonhewer or Hinchliffe (see Letter 467, n. 6).

⁸ Michael Lort (1725–90), the antiquary, of Trinity College, Cambridge; B.A. 1746; M.A. 1750; Fellow, 1750–81; B.D. 1761; D.D. 1780; Regius Professor of Greek, 1759–71. He was a correspondent of Horace Walpole, and published a vindication of Walpole's conduct with regard to Chatterton. See Letter 512* for a letter of Gray to him.

⁹ Dr. James Marriott, Master of Trinity Hall and Vice-Chancellor (see Letter 397, n. 12).

¹⁰ Edward Hussey Delaval (see Letter 163, n. 12); he had been a candidate for the Professorship in 1762 when Brockett was appointed.

¹¹ John Jebb (1736–86), of Peterhouse; B.A. 1757 (second wrangler); M.A. 1760; Fellow, 1761. He was ordained in 1762, and held livings in Norfolk and Suffolk, which he resigned in 1775 on conscientious grounds. Mitford writes: 'Jebb was the great hero of dissent, the head of the latitudinarians of Cambridge, as they were called; a distinguished mathematician and author of great ability and integrity. He gave heretical lectures at his lodgings in the town, and afterwards left the University, and became a physician and politician in London.'

¹² Samuel Peck (1725–91), of Trinity College, Cambridge; Scholar, 1746; B.A. 1747; M.A. 1750; Fellow, 1749; Vicar of Trumpington, Cambs., 1765–79. Mitford records that William Smyth, Fellow of Peterhouse and Professor of Modern History (1807), described Peck, whom he just remembered when an undergraduate, as 'a queer piece of antiquity'. See also Gunning's account of Peck in his *Reminiscences*, vol. ii, pp. 114–17.

480. GRAY TO WHARTON

Jermyn-Street. 1. Aug:

Dear Doctor   (at Mr Roberts's) 1768.

I HAVE been remiſs in answering your last letter, wch was sent me to Ramsgate from Cambridge: for I have paſs'd a good part of the summer in different parts of Kent[1] much to my satisfaction. could I have advised any thing eſsential in poor Mrs Ett:[s2] case, I had certainly replied immediately: but we seem of one mind in it. there was nothing left but to appeal to Delegates[3] (let the trouble & expence be what they will almost) & to punish, if it be practicable, that old Villain, who upon the bench of justice dared to set at nought all common sense & all humanity.

I write to you now chiefly to tell you (and I think you will be pleased, (nay, I expect the whole family will be pleased with it,) that on Sunday se'nnight, Brockett[4] died by a fall from his horse, being (as I hear) drunk, & some say, returning from Hinchinbroke:[5] that on the Wednesday following, I received a letter from the D: of Grafton,[6] saying, He had the K:[s] commands to *offer* me the vacant Profeſsorship, that &c: (but I shall not write all he says) & he adds at the end, *that from private as well as publick considerations He must take the warmest part in approving so well judged a measure as he hopes I do not doubt of the real regard & esteem with wch he has the honor to be,* &c: there's for you. so on Thursday the K: sign'd the warrant, & next day at his Levee I kiſs'd his hand.[7] he made me several gracious speeches, wch I

LETTER 480.—First printed (with omission of postscript) by Mitford (1816), vol. ii, pp. 503–4; first printed in full by Gosse, *Works* (1884), vol. iii, pp. 320–2; now reprinted from original.

[1] A notebook of Gray's (in the possession of Sir John Murray) has entries referring to his visit to Kent in this year. One is dated 'Ramsgate in Kent, 6 June 1768', and another 'Denton, 21 June 1768'. It was on his visit to Denton that he wrote his verses on Lord Holland's Villa (see Letter 489 and Appendix T).

[2] Mrs. Ettrick, Wharton's eldest sister, had a brutal husband, from whom she fled to Wharton for protection (see Letter 401).

[3] The Board of Delegates, appointed by the Crown, heard and determined appeals from the Ecclesiastical Courts. They are referred to again, in the same connexion, in Letter 553.   [4] See Letter 479, n. 1.

[5] Lord Sandwich's seat near Huntingdon.   [6] See Letter 479*.

[7] Mitford (1835–43), vol. i, p. ciii, notes: 'Sir Egerton Brydges informed me, that when Gray went to court to kiss the King's hand for his place, he felt a mixture of shyness and pride which he expressed to some of his intimate friends in terms of strong ill humour.'

shall not report, because every body, who goes to court, does so. by the way I desire, you would say, that all the Cabinet-Council in words of great favour approved the nomination of your humble Serv:ᵗ & this I am bid to say,[8] & was told to leave my name at their several doors. I have told you the outside of the matter & all the manner: for the inside you know enough easily to guefs t, & you will guefs right.[9] as to his Grace I have not seen him before or since.

I shall continue here perhaps a fortnight longer, perishing with heat: I have no Thermometer with me, but I feel it as I did at Naples. next summer (if it be as much in my power, as it is in my wishes) I meet you at the foot of Skiddaw. my respects to Mʳˢ Wharton, & the young Ladies great & small: love to Robin & Richard. Adieu! I am truly

Yours.

At your instance I have kifs'd Mʳˢ Forster,[10] & forgot old quarrels. I went to visit the Daughter, who has been brought to bed of a Boy, & there I met with the Mother.

Addressed: To Thomas Wharton, M:D: of Old-Park near Darlington Durham   *Postmark:* 1 AV

---

[8] This was probably a hint passed to him by Stonhewer.

[9] The allusion here and in the letter to Mason ('the rest you can easily guess', Letter 481) is obviously to the influence of Stonhewer with the Duke of Grafton. It was the general opinion at the time that Gray's appointment as Professor was made at Stonhewer's instance. Cole records: 'On Friday, 29 July 1768, Thomas Gray Esq. Fellow Commoner of Pembroke Hall, kissed his Majesty's hand, on being appointed Professor of Modern History and Languages. It is thought his Friend Mʳ Stonhewer, Secretary to the Duke of Grafton . . . procured it for him' (Brit. Mus. *Add. MS.* 5833, f. 12). Walpole wrote to Conway on 9 Aug. 1768: 'Yes, it is my Gray, Gray the poet, who is made Professor of Modern History. . . . I knew nothing of it till I saw it in the papers; but believe it was Stonhewer that obtained it for him'; and to Thomas Warton on 20 Sept. 1768: 'Mʳ Gray's preferment gave me great pleasure. . . . Mʳ Stonhewer is a great favourite of the Duke of Grafton, and the person that recommended Mʳ Gray' (see also Walpole's letter to Stonhewer of 16 Sept. 1771, in Appendix W). In the edition of *The Poems of Thomas Gray* which Mitford published in 1814 he stated in the preliminary *Advertisement* that he had 'been informed by the very obliging communication of the Duchess-Dowager of Grafton . . . "that Mr. Stonehewer never asked this favour of the Duke; that was his free and unsolicited gift; and that the Duke had himself remarked in some publication, this erroneous statement of the subject".' But in the editions of Gray's *Works* or *Poems*, which Mitford subsequently published, he let the statement stand that it was at Stonhewer's request that the Duke bestowed the Professorship upon Gray.

[10] Gray's first cousin by his father's side: see Letter 163, n. 1.

481. GRAY TO MASON

Jermyn-Street
Aug: [1, 1768]

Dear Mason

WHERE you are, I know not: but before this can reach you, I guefs you will be in residence. it is only to tell you, that I profefs modern history & languages[1] in a little shop of mine at Cambridge, if you will recommend me any customers. on Sunday Brocket died of a fall from his horse, drunk, I believe, & (as some say) returning from Hinchinbroke.[2] on Wednesday the D: of Grafton wrote me a very handsome letter to say, that the King *offer'd* the vacant place to me, with many more speeches too honorable for me to transcribe. on Friday at the Levy I kifs'd his Maj:ˢ hand. what he said, I will not tell you: because every body, that has been at Court, tells what the K: said to them: it was very gracious however. remember you are to say, that the Cabinet-council all approved of the nomination in a particular manner. it is hinted to me, that I should say this publickly, & I have been at their several doors to thank them. now I have told you all the exterior, the rest (the most efsential) you can easily guefs, & how it came about. now are you glad, or sorry, pray? Adieu,

Yours ever

T G. P: M: H: & L:

Postmark: 1 AV DW

482. GRAY TO NICHOLLS

3 Aug: 1768. Jermyn-Street
(Mr Roberts's).

Dear Sr

THAT Mr. Brockett has broke his neck,[1] you will have seen in the News-papers; & also that I (your humble Servant) have

LETTER 481.—First printed by Mitford in *Gray–Mason* (1853), pp. 418–19; now reprinted from original.

1 Gray here, and in his abbreviated signature, implies that he was Professor of Modern History and Languages. Under this title his appointment was announced in the *St. James's Chronicle* (see Letter 483, n. 1). The official title was merely 'Professor of Modern History'. The Professor was required to appoint and to allow proper salaries to two praeceptors in modern languages (see Appendix S).

2 In this letter, as in the letter to Norton Nicholls (Letter 482), Gray repeats much of what he wrote to Wharton, and the notes in that letter (Letter 480) may be consulted.

LETTER 482.—First printed in part (in a garbled text) in Mason's *Memoirs*, p. 332; first printed in full by Mitford (1835–43), vol. v, pp. 75–7; now reprinted from original.   1 See Letter 479, n. 1.

kifs'd the K:ˢ hand for his succefsion. they both are true, but the manner how you know not; only I can afsure you, that I had no hand at all in his fall, & *almost* as little in the second happy event. he died on the Sunday, on Wednesday following, his Gr: of Grafton wrote me a very polite letter to say, that his Maj: had commanded him to *offer* me the vacant Profefsorship, not only as a reward of &c: but as a credit to &c: with much more too high for me to transcribe. *You are to say,* that I owe my nomination to the *whole Cabinet-Council*, & my succefs to the K:ˢ *particular knowledge of me.* this last he told me himself, tho' the day was so hot & the ceremony so embarrafsing to me, that I hardly know what he said.

I am commifsion'd to make you an offer, wᶜʰ, I have told him (not the King) you would not accept, long ago. Mr. Barrett[2] (whom you know) offers to you 100£ a-year with meat, drink, washing, chaise, & lodging, if you will please to accompany him thro' France into Italy. he has taken such a fancy to you, that I can not but do what he desires me, being pleased with him for it. I know, it will never do, tho' before you grew a rich fat Rector, I have often wish'd (ay, & fish'd too) for such an opportunity. no matter! I desire you to write your answer to him yourself as civil, as you think fit, & then let me know the result. that's all. He lives at *Lee near Canterbury.*

Adieu! I am to perish here with heat this fortnight yet, & then to Cambridge.[3] Dʳ M:[4] (Mʳ Vicecan:) came post hither to ask this vacant office on Wednesday last, & went post to carry the news back on Saturday. the rest were Delaval, Lort, Peck, & Jebb.[5] as to Lort, he deserved it, & Delaval is an honest Gentleman: the rest do me no great honor, no more than my Predecefsor did: to be sure, my *Dignity* is a little the worse for wear, but mended & wash'd it will do for me. I am very sincerely

Yours,
T G:

Addressed: To The Revᵈ Mʳ Nicholls at Blundeston near Leostoff Suffolk
     Postmark: 3 AV DW

[2] Thomas Barrett (d. 1803), of Lee Priory, Ickham, near Canterbury; M.P. for Dover, 1773 (see Letter 357, n. 14).

[3] He did not return till quite the end of August (see Letter 485).

[4] Dr. Marriott (see Letter 479, n. 9).

[5] See Letter 479, nn. 8–12.

483. NICHOLLS TO GRAY

Blundeston, Aug. 6, 1768.

MY dear Mr. Profeſsor of history and modern languages, accept my sincerest congratulations; your letter and the St. James's Chronicle[1] brought me the welcome news by the same post yesterday. I read of Brockett's death before, and thought of you the instant, but feared because I wished it of all things, and have been very anxious for information. I am pleased that you have an honourable and profitable office, but more pleased a thousand times that you have it in so honourable a way. The king and his cabinet council are grown into great favour with me, and I believe if I was in parliament I should vote with them right or wrong all the next sefsion. But come and let me tell you how glad I am better than I can write it; you said you would, but now you are grown rich, God knows how you may be altered. I should have written before to invite you, only that I knew not where to direct. Mr. Profeſsor of Arabic[2] has honoured me with his company already for two days in his way to a rich pupil, the son of a Norwich alderman; he says it is *vastly pretty* to have a garden of one's own, with gooseberries and currants, and a field, and a horse, and a cow; in short, he will not be at peace till he has bought a wife[3] and an estate, and then I fear least of all; Lord Fitzwilliam[4] says it will kill him.

And now for Mr. Barrett, to whom I am much obliged, and certainly do not like him the worse for thinking me agreeable; but how I might like him after I had been shut up in a chaise with him for a thousand miles, I know not, especially as I should only be one remove above the valet de chambre with double wages. Besides, I am just settled here at a great expense; and then to desert my cure of souls when I have hardly given them

LETTER 483.—First printed by Mitford (1835–43), vol. v, pp. 77–9.
 [1] 'On Friday last, Thomas Gray, Esq.; kissed his Majesty's Hand on being appointed Professor of History and Modern Languages in the University of Cambridge' (*The St. James's Chronicle; or The British Evening Post. From Saturday, 30 July, to Tuesday, 2 Aug. 1768*). See Letter 481, n. 1.
 [2] Dr. Samuel Hallifax, Fellow of Trinity Hall (see Letter 409, n. 10).
 [3] He married in 1775 a daughter of Dr. William Cooke, Dean of Ely.
 [4] Richard Fitzwilliam (1711–76), sixth Viscount Fitzwilliam (1743), of Meryon, co. Dublin. His eldest son, Hon. Richard Fitzwilliam (1745–1816), afterwards (1776) seventh Viscount, and founder of the Fitzwilliam Museum at Cambridge, was a contemporary of Nicholls at Trinity Hall, whence he graduated M.A. in 1764. Hence no doubt the acquaintance of Lord Fitzwilliam with both Hallifax and Nicholls.

their first drefsing, would not be the part of a good physician. Add to this, that my uncles[5] might not be pleased, and that my mother would be left alone in the land of strangers, and I think I have reason sufficient to write him a very civil refusal, which I mean to do if you have no objection. Neverthelefs, I burn with desire to see Italy, and would give a limb to be in danger of breaking my neck among the Alps, or being buried alive in everlasting snow; but all this I hope to be able to do in my own way, and at my own time. I have just had a letter from Claxton[6] (that man of rueful countenance, whom you, that are without prejudices, cannot bear for that reason) from among the glaciers, which inflames me more than ever. Shall I then ever see a valley of ice which was formed at the creation, or only a day or two afterwards at farthest? mountains of ice that will never melt till the earth difsolves? and crevices through which one might descend to the nursery of earthquakes and volcanoes? not with Mr. Barrett,[7] I believe. At present I live in a country where nature dare not exert herself in this bold way, and thinks she has done very handsomely for me in giving me wood, a pretty lake bordered with it, a hanging meadow on which the house stands, and a dry soil; indeed, two miles from me there is the sea, which does not break into the hollows of rocks, but looks vast, and blue, and beautiful, and roars as it does in other places; I bathe in it, you may admire it, and catch strange fishes, and call them by strange names, and tell me their history and adventures. Then my own lake produces tench, and pike, and eels in abundance. We have no neighbourhood, which you will say (I hear you say it) is a blefsing; but it is a reason de plus why you (if riches have not extinguished every spark of charity in you) should come and comfort our solitude. My mother says you have forgot her, but is enough of a Christian to send you her compliments and congratulations.

N. N.

[5] See Letter 429, n. 7.

[6] John Claxton, a man of means and leisure, a friend of Temple and of Boswell, in whose correspondence with Temple, and in Temple's *Diaries*, his name occurs frequently. In his *Life of Johnson* Boswell records that Claxton was one of the company at a dinner given by the Dilly brothers to Johnson, Goldsmith, Temple, himself, and others on 7 May 1773. Gray in his letter to Nicholls of 20 May 1771 mentions Claxton as a friend of Lieut. John Clarke (see Letter 552).

[7] See Letter 482, n. 2. Nicholls was at Florence with Barrett in the spring of 1772 (see two letters from Nicholls to Barrett in Mitford (1836–43), vol. v, pp. 167–71).

484. MASON TO GRAY

Hornby Castle[1] Aug^st 8th 1768

Dear Mr Profefsor

I WILL not congratulate you, for I would not have you think I am glad. & I take for granted you dont think I am, or at least would not have me so to be, else you would have given me a line[2]—but no matter. I went the other day to Old Park,[3] & read what you had written to the D^r—and he was not so glad neither as to hinder him from making Water[4] wch he did all the time I was with him, & continues still to do & thinks he shall not give over of some months. Dont be afraid the discharge does not come from his vesicatory but his pecuniary Ducts. & I as Physician & Summers[5] as Apothecary hold it to be a most salutary Diabetis.

I have my good luck too I can tell you, for when I was at Hull I met with a Roman Ofsuary of exquisite Sculpture. How I came by it, no matter! tis enough that I am pofsest of it. I send you the inscription wch your Brother Lort[6] or Halifax[7] may perhaps help me to construe, for as to Yourself I take for granted that all Your skill in the learned Languages transpird in the Kifs wch you gave his Majestys little finger, & you rose up a mere

LETTER 484.—First printed by Mitford in *Gray–Mason* (1853), pp. 420–2; now reprinted from original.

[1] See Letter 338, n. 3

[2] Obviously Mason had not received Gray's letter of 1 Aug. (Letter 481).

[3] From the following note from Mason to Dr. Wharton, preserved with the Wharton letters in the British Museum (MS. *Egerton* 2400) it appears that Mason was at Old Park, 6–8 Aug.:

'Hornby Castle Aug.st 5th 1768

Dear D^r

If this finds you at home disengaged, I will come over to you to morrow Evening & stay the Sunday with you. I expect to be made very drunk (as my manner is) in drinking the health of Mr Professor Gray—I shall review your Water but I wont taste a drop.

Y^rs & Mrs Whartons &c.
in great Haste
W. Mason.'

[4] An allusion to the fact that Wharton was making an artificial piece of water in his grounds (see Letter 459, n. 13).

[5] See Letter 459, n. 14.

[6] Regius Professor of Greek (see Letter 479, n. 8).

[7] Dr. Hallifax, Professor of Arabic (see Letter 409, n. 10).

modern Schollar, with nothing left but a little Linæan jargon. Be this as it may heres the Inscription literatim.

PONPONIA PRIMI
.GENIAE
T PONPONIO FELICI
P. ET P. PA.[8]

The first three lines I read Pomponia primigeniae Tito Pomponio Felici. but as to the rest it is all Hebrew Greek to me. Seriously if you can make it out for me I shall be obligd to you.

I go to York on Thursday but I mean to call in my way on M[r] Wedell[9] & Proud Palgrave[10] on Wednesday. Remember me kindly to your Brother M[r] Profefsor Shepherd[11] & the succefsor of M[r] Profefsor Mickleborough[12] & beleive me to be Dear M[r] Profefsor

yours most truly & sincerely
W MASON

Addressed (by Lord Holdernesse): To Thomas Gray Esq[r] at M[r] Roberts Hozier in Jermyn Street London *Franked:* Free Holdernefse *Postmark:* CATTERICK 12 AV *Stamped:* FREE

[8] It seems likely that Mason misread P ET P for F ET F. The inscription would then stand for PONPONIA[E] PRIMIGENIAE TITO PONPONIO FELICI F[ILIAE] ET F[ILIO] PA[RENTES] or PA[TER]. This would be a usual form of funerary dedication.

[9] See Letter 400, n. 13.

[10] A reminiscence of Gray's lines in his letter to Mason of 8 Jan. of this year (see Letter 461). Palgrave no doubt at this time was on a visit to Weddell at Newby Hall.

[11] Antony Shepherd (1721–96), of Christ's College; M.A. 1747; Fellow, 1746–83; Plumian Professor of Astronomy, 1760–96; F.R.S. 1763; D.D. 1766. He had graduated B.A. in 1743 from St. John's, where he was two years senior to Mason.

[12] John Micklebourgh (d. 1756), of Corpus Christi; B.A. 1712; Fellow, 1714; M.A. 1716; B.D. 1724; Professor of Chemistry, 1718–56. His immediate successor was John Hadley, of Queens', a friend of Gray (see Letter 241, n. 19), who died in 1764, and was succeeded by Richard Watson (1737–1816), of Trinity; B.A. 1759; Fellow, 1760; M.A. 1762; D.D. and Regius Professor of Divinity, 1771; Bishop of Llandaff, 1782. He was tutor to Lord Richard Cavendish (who had been Mason's pupil) when he went up to Trinity later in this year (see Letters 461, n. 19, and 488, n. 9).

485. GRAY TO NICHOLLS

Jermyn-Street. Sat:

Dear S^r 27 Aug: 1768.

I HOPE in God, before now you have given Mr Barrett[1] his answer. I always supposed you would refuse,[2] & told him so: yet as he does not write to me, I much doubt whether you have acquainted him of it. why, did not I desire you to do so out of hand? & did not I make my civilities to Mrs. Nicholls? 'tis sure I intended both one & the other: but you never allow for businefs: why, I am selling an estate, & over head & ears in writings.[3] Next week I come to Cambridge. pray let me find a letter from you there, telling me the way to Lovingland:[4] for thither I come, as soon as I have been sworn in,[5] & subscribed, & been at Church. poor Mr Spence[6] was found drown'd in his own garden at Byfield:[7] probably (being paralytic) he fell into the water, & had no one near to help him: so *History* has lost two of her chief supports[8] almost at once. let us pray for their Succefsors![9] his Danish Majesty[10] has had a Diarrhæa, so could not partake of Dr Marriot's[11] collation: if he goes thither at all, I would contrive not to be present at the time. Adieu! I am

Yours

T G:

Addressed: To The Revd Mr Nicholls at Blundeston near Leostoff Suffolk
Postmark: 27 AV

LETTER 485.—First printed by Mitford (1835–43), vol. v, p. 80; now reprinted from original. [1] See Letter 482.
[2] Nicholls in his letter to Gray of 6 Aug. (Letter 483) expressed his intention of writing 'a very civil refusal'.
[3] See Letter 479, n. 6. [4] See Letter 455, n. 3.
[5] The Professor was required to take an oath administered by the Vice-Chancellor. Gray was sworn and admitted at Clare Hall Lodge, 9 Sept. 1768, by Dr. Goddard, Master of Clare Hall, Deputy Vice-Chancellor.
[6] See Letter 131, n. 5. Spence died on 20 Aug.
[7] A mistake for Byfleet, in Surrey.
[8] Spence had been (since 1742) Regius Professor of Modern History at Oxford, as had Brockett at Cambridge.
[9] There seems to have been a delay in appointing a successor to Spence at Oxford. The professorship was offered to John Vivian, of Balliol, on terms that he was not prepared to accept (see Appendix S).
[10] Christian VII (1749–1808), King of Denmark and Norway; he was son of Frederick V, King of Denmark, and Louisa, daughter of George II; he succeeded his father in Jan. 1766, and in Nov. of that year married his first cousin, Caroline Matilda, posthumous daughter of Frederick, Prince of Wales.
[11] See Letter 397, n. 12. He was Master of Trinity Hall, and Vice-

486. GRAY TO MASON

Dear Mason   Pemb: Coll: Sept: 7. 1768.

WHAT can I say more to you about Oddington.[1] you seem engaged to Mr Wood,[2] & in consequence of that to Mr Meller.[3] M^r Br: is not here, & (if he were) I could by no means consult him about it: his view to the Mastership[4] will be affected by it just in the same manner, as if he had accepted of Framlingham,[5] & had it in poſseſsion, wch I little doubt he would accept, if it were vacant & undisputed. as to the dubious title[6] he told me of it himself, & I was surprised at it, as a thing quite new to me. this is all I know, nor (if you were under no previous engagement) could I *direct*, or *determine* your choice: it ought to be entirely your own, as to accept or refuse ought to be entirely his. the only reason I have suggested any thing about it is, that (when we first talk'd on this subject) you ask'd me, whether M^r B: would have it, & I replied, it would hardly be worth his while, as Framl:^{m} was of greater value, in w^{ch} (all things consider'd) I may be mistaken.

Chancellor, in which capacity it fell to him to entertain the King when he came to Cambridge, which he did not do till 29 Aug. (see Letter 486, n. 9). On 24 Aug. Walpole wrote to Mann: 'The poor little King [of Denmark] is fatigued to death, and has got the belly-ache. He was to have set out on Monday [22 Aug.] to hear bad Latin verses at Cambridge, and to see the races at York, but is confined at St. James's.'

LETTER 486.—First printed by Mitford in *Gray–Mason* (1853), pp. 422–5; now reprinted from original.

¹ In Gloucestershire, about two miles from Stow-on-the-Wold. The presentation to the Rectory fell to Mason *ex officio* as Precentor of York. It was vacant by the death in July 1768 of Joseph Atwell, of Exeter College, Oxford; D.D. 1733; Prebendary of York, 1737–68.

² Wood had formerly been Mason's curate (see Letter 263, n. 7). He was now Vicar of Chesterfield.

³ The meaning seems to be that Mason had pledged himself to Wood, to offer the living to him or to Mellor. Joseph Mellor was presented to the living and held it 1768–78. He may have been Wood's curate at this time.

⁴ Mason had, at some time, suggested to Gray that he might offer the living to James Brown. Brown, who was senior Fellow of Pembroke, might expect to be elected Master in the event of Dr. Long's death, if he were a Fellow at the time. But if he were presented to a living, he would (after a year of grace) vacate his Fellowship.

⁵ The living of Framlingham, in Suffolk, is in the gift of Pembroke College. It was held by James Brookes, a former Fellow of Pembroke, from 1734 to 1782.

⁶ Nothing is known to explain the allusion to the 'dubious title' to Framlingham.

I give you joy of your vase: I can not find P. et P. PA. in my Sertorius Ursatus,[7] & consequently do not know their meaning. what shall I do? My learned Brethren are dispersed over the face of the earth. I have lately dug up three small vases, in workmanship at least equal to yours: they were discover'd at a place call'd Burslem in Staffordshire, & are very little impair'd by time. on the larger one is this inscription very legible $\underline{9|}$,[8] & on the two smaller this $\underline{7|}$.[8] you will oblige me with an explanation, for Ursatus here too leaves us in the dark.

I fear the K:[9] of Denmark could not stay, till your hair was drefs'd. he is a genteel lively figure, not made by nature for a Fool: but surrounded by a pack of Knaves, whose interest it is to make him one, if they can. he has overset poor Dr Marriot's[10] head here, who raves of nothing else from morning till night.

Pray make my best compliments to your Brother-Residentiary Mr Cowper,[11] & thank him for his obliging letter of congratulation, wch I did not at all expect: present also my respects & acknowledgements to Mifs Patty. Mr Bedingfield I shall answer soon, both as to his civilities & his reproaches: the latter you might have prevented by telling him, that I gave my *works* to no body, as it was only a new edition. Adieu, & write to me.

I am ever
Yours T G:

[7] From the catalogue of the sale of Gray's books in 1851 it appears that he had the edition published at Paris in 1723: *Explanatio Notarum et Literarum quæ frequentius in antiquis Lapidibus, . . . occurrunt . . . Auctore Sertorio Ursato.*

[8] The figures that Gray pretends were on his vases were presumably potters' marks, such as might be found on ordinary Staffordshire ware. He is scoffing at Mason's find (see Letter 484).

[9] See Letter 485, n. 10. Cooper, *Annals of Cambridge* (vol. iv, pp. 351–2), records: 'On the 29th of August, the King of Denmark came to Cambridge, attended by Comte de Bernstorff his principal Secretary of State, Baron de Schimmelmann Treasurer, . . . &c. The King lodged at the Rose Inn, where the Vicechancellor and Heads waited on him in their robes, and attended him thence to the Senate House, where the whole University and a brilliant company of ladies in the galleries were assembled. He was conducted to a chair of state, where he received the compliments of the Heads, and after a short stay went in procession to the library and to all the principal buildings in the University, where he saw everything that was rare and curious. He expressed the highest satisfaction, and invited the Vicechancellor to supper. Early next morning he proceeded on his journey to York.' See Horace Walpole's account of the King in his letters to Montagu and Mann of 13 Aug.   [10] Master of Trinity Hall and Vice-Chancellor.

[11] Charles Cowper, of St. John's College, Cambridge; B.A. 1718; M.A. 1725. He was Canon of York from 1736 until his death in 1774.

487. GRAY TO BEATTIE

Dear S^r   31 Oct: 1768. Pembroke-Hall, Cambridge.

IT is some time, since I received from Mr Foulis two copies of my poems,[1] one by the hands of M^r T: Pitt,[2] the other by Mr Merrill, a Bookseller of this Town. it is indeed a most beautiful edition, & must certainly do credit both to him, & to me: but I fear, it will be of no other advantage to him; as Dodsley[3] has contrived to glut the Town already with two editions beforehand, one of 1500, & the other of 750, both indeed far inferior to that of Glasgow, but sold at half the price.[4] I must repeat my thanks, S^r, for the trouble you have been pleased to give yourself on my account, & thro' you I must desire leave to convey my acknowledgements to Mr Foulis, for the pains & expence he has been at in this publication.

We live at so great a distance, that perhaps you may not yet have learn'd, what I flatter myself you will not be displeased to hear: the middle of last summer his Majesty was pleased to appoint me Regius Profeſsor of Modern History in this University: it is the best thing the Crown has to bestow (on a Layman) here: the salary is 400£ per ann: but what enhances the value of it to me is, that it was bestowed without being ask'd. the Person, who held it before me, died on the Sunday, & on Tuesday[5] following the Duke of Grafton wrote me a letter to say, that the King offer'd me this Office, with many additional exprefsions of kindnefs on his Grace's part, to whom I am but barely known, & whom I have not seen either before or since he did me this favor. instances of a benefit so nobly confer'd, I believe, are rare, & therefore I tell you of it as a thing that does honor, not only to me, but to the Minister.

LETTER 487.—First printed in Mason's *Memoirs*, pp. 333–4; now printed from original.

[1] The Glasgow edition of Gray's poems (see Letters 457 and 466) had been published six months before. *The Glasgow Journal* for 21–28 April, 1768, announced: 'On Wednesday first [*sc.* 4 May] will be published and sold by R. and A. Foulis, Poems by Mr. Gray in 4to on superfine Royal Paper, Price in Boards, Five Shillings.'

[2] See Letter 250, n. 12. He had presumably returned recently from a visit to Scotland.   [3] See Letter 465.

[4] The price of Dodsley's edition was 2s. 6d. The first issue was published on 12 Mar. The second, which was reset in smaller type, was described on the title-page as 'a new edition'.

[5] A slip on Gray's part; Grafton wrote on the Wednesday (see Letters 479, 480, 481, 482).

As I lived here before from choice, I shall now continue to do so from obligation. if businefs or curiosity should call you south-wards, you will find few Friends, that will see you with more cordial satisfaction, than S^r

Your obliged & very obed:^t Servant
T GRAY

Addressed: To Mr Profefsor Beattie, of the Marischal College Aberdeen
Postmark: CAMBRIDGE

488. GRAY TO NICHOLLS

Nov: 8. 1768. Pemb: Coll:

NOT a single word, since we parted at Norwich,[1] & for ought I know, you may be ignorant, how I fell into the jaws of the King of Denmark at Newmarket, & might have stay'd there till this time, had I not met with Mr Vicechancellor and Mr Orator[2] with their Diplomas & speeches,[3] who on their return to Cambridge sent me a chaise from thence, & deliver'd me out of that den of thieves. however, I pafs'd a night there; & in the next room, divided from me by a thin partition, was a drunken Parson & his party of pleasure singing & swearing & breaking all the ten commandments. all that I saw on my way else was the Abbey-Church at Wyndham,[4] to learned eyes a beautiful remnant of antiquity, part of it in the style of Henry the 1st & part in that of Henry the 6th; the wooden fretwork of the north-ile you may copy, when you build the best room of your new Gothick parsonage. it will cost but a trifle.

So now I am going to Town about my businefs,[5] w^ch (if I dispatch to my mind) will leave me at rest, & with a tolerably

LETTER 488.—First printed by Mitford (1835–43), vol. v, pp. 81–3; now reprinted from original.

[1] Gray had presumably been visiting Nicholls at Blundeston.

[2] Richard Beadon (1737–1824), Fellow of St. John's, had been elected Public Orator in this year (see Letter 399, n. 16).

[3] Cooper, in *Annals of Cambridge* (vol. iv, p. 352), records: 'On the 5th of October, Dr Marriott the Vicechancellor and Mr Beadon the Public Orator waited on the King of Denmark at Newmarket, and in the name of the University presented a letter of address and graces for conferring the same degrees upon the King and his attendants as had been conferred at Oxford' (vol. iv, p. 352).

[4] Wymondham, or Windham, in Norfolk, nine miles south-west of Norwich.

[5] See Letter 479, n. 6.

easy temper for one while. I return hither as soon as I can, & give you notice, what a sweet humor I am in. Mrs Nicholls & you take advantage of it, come & take pofsefsion of the Lodge at Trinity-Hall (by the way I am commifsion'd to offer it to you by Dr Marriott[6] for that purpose, & you have nothing to do but to thank him for his civilities, & say, at what time you intend to make use of them). and so we live in clover, & partake the benefits of a University education together, as of old. Palgrave is return'd from Scotland, & will perhaps be here. Mason too, if he is not married (for such a report there is)[7] may come, & Dr Hallifax is always at your service. Ld Richard Cavendish[8] is come: he is a sensible Boy, aukward & bashful beyond all imagination, & eats a buttock of beef at a meal. I have made him my visit, & we did tolerably well considering. Watson[9] is his publick Tutor, & one Winstanley[10] his private: do you know him?

Marriott has begun a subscription for a Musical Amphitheatre, has appropriated 500£ (Mr. Titley's legacy to the University) to that purpose, & gives 20 Guineas himself.[11] he has drawn a design for the building & has printed an Argument about the Poors-rates, wch he intended to have deliver'd from the Bench, but one of the Parties drop'd the cause. he has spoke at the Quarter-Sefsions two hours together, & moved the Towns-People to tears, & the University to laughter. at laying down his office[12] too he spoke Latin, & said, *Invidiam, &*

6 Master of Trinity Hall.

7 It was a false report.

8 See Letter 461, n. 19.

9 See Letter 484, n. 12. He was at this time Fellow and Tutor of Trinity and Professor of Chemistry.

10 Thomas Winstanley, of Trinity; M.A. 1766.

11 Cooper (*op. cit.*) records: 'Walter Titley, Esq. Fellow of Trinity College, and sometime Envoy Extraordinary to the Court of Denmark, having left £500 to the University to be disposed of as the Vicechancellor should think fit, Dr Marriott the Vicechancellor designed to appropriate it in aid of a subscription for the erection of an amphitheatre for public lectures and musical performances, but this project failed' (vol. iv, p. 352). Cooper quotes several paragraphs relating to this proposal from the *Cambridge Chronicle*, of 5 Nov. 1768, which was evidently Gray's authority.

Walter Titley (1700–68), of Westminster School and Trinity College, Cambridge; B.A. 1722; M.A. 1726; Fellow, 1733. In 1730 he became Envoy Extraordinary at Copenhagen, in which capacity he died there in Feb. 1768. Besides £500 to the University, he left £1,000 each to Westminster School and Trinity College.

12 Of Vice-Chancellor.

opinionum de me commenta delebit dies.[13] he enlarged (wch is never done) on the qualifications of Hinchliffe[14] his Succefsor, *qui Mores hominum multorum vidit & urbes*[15]—*qui cum Magnis vixit & placuit.* next day Hinchliffe made his speech, & said not one word (tho' it is usual) of his Predecefsor. I tell you Cambridge News for want of better. they say, Rigby[16] is to move for the expulsion of Wilkes from the House. my respects to Mamma.[17] I am

Yours
T G:

Tell me about my Uncle & Aunt.[18] direct to Roberts's, Jermyn-Str:

Addressed: To The Revd Mr Nicholls at Blundeston near Leostoff Suffolk By Yarmouth *Postmark:* GREAT YARMOUTH

488*. Gray to Palgrave

[*Dec. 1768*]

[In his letter to Mason of 29 Dec. 1768 (Letter 489) Gray says that he has been forced to write to Palgrave about the secret which Mason had imparted to Palgrave.]

13 A reminiscence of Cicero, *De Nat. Deor.* ii. 2, 5: 'Opinionis commenta delet dies.'
14 See Letter 467, n. 6.
15 Horace, *Ars Poët.* 142.
16 See Letter 236, n. 9. He was at this time Paymaster-General of the Forces. Parliament met on 8 Nov. (the date of this letter), and was almost immediately concerned with what Walpole calls 'the great question of the time, whether Wilkes should be allowed to be a member' (*Memoirs*, vol. iii, p. 172). Rigby's name does not appear in connexion with the motion for his expulsion, which was moved by Lord Barrington, Secretary at War, on 3 Feb. 1769, and carried at three the next morning, by a majority of 82.
17 Nicholls's mother.
18 Nicholls's uncle and aunt. It is probably to these relatives that Nicholls refers in his *Reminiscences of Gray*: 'In one of the visits he made me at Blundeston, I . . . had . . . with me an old relation & his wife, who were so entirely different from anything that could give him pleasure that I thought it impossible he should reconcile himself to their conversation, or endure to stay with me. I think he perceived this, & determined to show me that I had mistaken him; for he made himself so agreable to them that they both talked with pleasure of the time they passed with him as long as they lived.'

489. GRAY TO MASON

29 Dec: 1768.

OH wicked Scroddles![1] there you have gone & told my *Arcanum Arcanorum*[2] to that leaky Mortal Palgrave, who never conceals any thing he is trusted with; & there have I been forced to write to him, & (to bribe him to silence) have told him, how much I confided in his taciturnity, & twenty lies beside, the guilt of wch must fall on you at the last account. seriously you have done very wrong: sure you don't remember the imprudence of D^r G:,[3] who is well-known to that rogue in Pickadilly,[4] & who at any time may be denounced to the Party concern'd, wch five shillings reward may certainly bring about. hitherto luckily nobody has taken any notice of it, nor (I hope) ever will.

Dr Balguy tells me you talk of Cambridge. come away then forthwith, when your Christmas-duties & mince-pies are over: for what can you do at Aston making snowballs all January. here am I just return'd from London: I have seen St:^r[5] whose looks are much mended, & he has leave to break up for a fortnight, & is gone to Bath. poor Dr Hurd has undergone a painful operation: they say, it was not a Fistula, but something very like it. he is now in a way to be well, & by this time goes abroad again. Delaval was confined two months with a like disorder. he suffered three times under the hands of Hawkins,[6] & tho' he is now got out, & walking the streets, does not think himself cured, & still complains of uneasy sensations. nobody but I, & Fraser[7] & Dr Ross (who (it is said) is just made Dean of Ely) are

LETTER 489.—First printed by Mitford in *Gray–Mason* (1853), pp. 425–9; now reprinted from original.

[1] See Letter 212, n. 26.

[2] There can hardly be a doubt that the reference is to Gray's verses on Lord Holland's villa at Kingsgate, which were almost certainly written in the summer of this year (see Appendix T).

[3] No doubt Dr. Gisborne (see Letter 299, n. 10). This may refer to some indiscretion on the part of Gisborne when employed as intermediary to forward an epigram or satire of Mason's to the London journals (see Letter 424, n. 8).

[4] This individual has not been identified. Mitford notes that Lord March (afterwards fourth Duke of Queensberry, known as 'Old Q') was living in Piccadilly at this date, but nothing is known to connect him with Gray's allusion.   [5] See Letter 507, n. 2.

[6] Caesar Hawkins (1711–86), surgeon to Frederick, Prince of Wales, whom he attended in his last illness, and Sergeant-Surgeon to George II and George III.   [7] See Letters 195, 408.

quite well. Dr Thomas of Christ's is B^p of Carlisle.[8] don't you feel a spice of concupiscence? Adieu! I am ever

Yours
T G:

Mr Brown's comp^s. here is Ld Richard:[9] what is come of Foljambe?[10] service to my Curate.[11]

490. GRAY TO NICHOLLS

2 Jan: 1769. Pemb: Coll:

Dear S^r

HERE am I once again, & have sold my estate,[1] & got a thousand guineas, & fourscore pound a year for my old Aunt,[2] & a £20 prize in the lottery,[3] & Lord knows what arrears in the Treasury,[4] & am a rich Fellow enough, go to; & a Fellow, that hath had lofses, & one, that hath two gowns, & every thing

---

[8] It was anticipated in Cambridge (see also Letter 490) that Dr. Hugh Thomas, Master of Christ's College, who was Dean of Ely, would become Bishop of Carlisle in succession to Dr. Charles Lyttelton, who had died on 22 Dec., and that Dr. John Ross, of St. John's College, Cambridge (see Letter 149, n. 13), then Vicar of Frome, would succeed to the Deanery. But these expectations were disappointed (see Letter 491).

[9] See Letters 461, 488.

[10] Francis Ferrand Moore Foljambe (*c.* 1750–1814), son of John Moore, of Hull, and of Anne Foljambe, daughter of Francis Foljambe (d. 1752) of Aldwarke, near Rotheram, Yorks., who in 1758, on succeeding to the Foljambe estates, assumed the surname and arms of Foljambe. He entered St. John's College, Cambridge, as a Fellow-commoner in 1768. Mitford states that he had been a pupil of John Wood, Mason's former curate and from 1768 Vicar of Chesterfield (see Letter 263, n. 7). Aston is within a few miles of Aldwarke. Gray mentions Foljambe again in Letters 527*, 533, 535. In a letter to Horace Walpole, written from Aston on 6 Oct. 1772, asking for introductions to 'persons of fashion' in Paris for Foljambe, Mason describes him as 'a young gentleman of an ancient family and good fortune in this neighbourhood . . . not above three and twenty, . . . a genteel well-behaved young man, with sense and accomplishments sufficient not to make your recommendation improper to any person you may choose to write'. Foljambe was M.P. for York co. for a few months in 1784, High Sheriff in 1787, and later (1802–7) M.P. for Higham Ferrers, Northants.

[11] Mason's curate, Christopher Alderson (see Letter 453).

LETTER 490.—First printed in part (in a garbled text) in Mason's *Memoirs*, pp. 346–7; first printed in full by Mitford (1835–43), vol. v, pp. 86–7; now reprinted from original.

[1] See Letter 479, n. 6, and Appendix U.

[2] Mrs. Olliffe parted with her life interest in the property for an annuity of £80.   [3] See Letter 274, n. 5.

[4] The amount due to him for his stipend as Professor.

handsome about him!⁵ & in a few days I shall have curtains, are you avised of that; ay, & a matterafs to lie upon.

And there's Dʳ Hallifax tells me, there are three or four fellow-commoners got into the lodge.⁶ but they will be out in a week's time, & all ready for Mʳˢ Nicholls's reception & yours. so do your pleasures, I invite nobody. and there's Dʳ Thomas may be Bᵖ of Carlisle,⁷ if he pleases; & (if not) Dr. Powell:⁸ & in the first case Dʳ Rofs will be Dean of Ely and so I am

Yours
T G:

Addressed: To The Revᵈ Mʳ Nicholls at Blundeston near Leostoffe Suffolk By Yarmouth   *Postmark:* CAMBRIDGE

491. GRAY TO NICHOLLS

ARE you not well, or what has happen'd to you? it is better than three weeks since I wrote to you (by Norwich & Yarmouth)¹ to say, I was return'd hither, & hoped to see you; that Trin: Hall Lodge would be vacant, as Hallifax told me, to rèceive Mʳˢ N: & you, & we expected you with impatience. I have had a sore throat, & now am getting well of yᵉ gout. Mason will be here on Tuesday. Palgrave keeps Lent at home & wants to be ask'd to break it. Dʳ Law has bit at the Bishoprick,² &

⁵ Gray is quoting Dogberry in *Much Ado about Nothing*, Act IV, Sc. 2, *ad fin.* Mason, with a literal mind, thought to improve Gray by exchanging 'curtains' to 'new window curtains' and 'matterass' to 'new mattrass'.

⁶ The Master's Lodge at Trinity Hall, the use of which had been offered to Nicholls by the Master (see Letter 488). Dr. Hallifax was a Fellow of Trinity Hall.

⁷ See Letter 489, n. 8. He was not appointed, and consequently Ross did not become Dean of Ely, see Letter 491, n. 2.

⁸ Master of St. John's (see Letter 399, n. 32). But he was not chosen.

LETTER 491.—First printed by Mitford (1835–43), vol. v, p. 87; now reprinted from original.

¹ Letter 490.

² Edmund Law, Master of Peterhouse (see Letter 399, n. 20), was appointed Bishop of Carlisle. The appointment was announced in *Lloyd's Evening Post* of 20–3 Jan. Mitford (*Gray–Mason Correspondence*, p. 428), on the authority of a MS. note given to him by Professor Smyth, explains how it was that Dr. Law and not Dr. Thomas (see Letters 489, 490) was appointed: 'Dʳ Thomas was Master of Christ's College; was offered a bishoprick, and persuaded by Law, formerly of Christ's and Master of Peterhouse, to *decline it, that he himself might be nominated Bishop.* Such was always the representation of Mʳˢ Thomas.'

gives up near 800£ a-year[3] to enjoy it: Dr Rofs has his Prebend of Durham.[4] Adieu, I am

Duty to Mamma.

Pemb: Hall. Jan: 26. 1769.

Yours

T G:

491*. GRAY TO PERCY [?][1]

[c. end Jan. 1769?][2]

P: 339, & 340.[3] The Abbot of Mefx[4]

Look in a Map of the East-riding of Yorkshire, & you will see that at a few miles distance North of *Lekenfield* lies *Watton*; to the South lies *Beverley* (the usual Burying-Place of the Percies); & to the S: East the Abbey of *Meaux*,[5] of which there

3 Which he had received as Canon of Durham.

4 Ross held the Canonry until 1778, when he became Bishop of Exeter.

LETTER 491*.—First printed by Tovey in *Gray and his Friends*, p. 190; now reprinted from original (Brit. Mus. *Add. MS.* 32329). The note is pasted on the same sheet of paper as Letter 340. It was obviously a separate note written on a different occasion (see n. 2).

1 Gray's note was written for Percy's information: it may have been given to Farmer or some other friend of Percy, and not sent to Percy direct (see Appendix N).

2 Date conjectural. Gray's note is a correction of a note printed at the foot of the text on p. 340 of Percy's *Northumberland Houshold Book*. The correction appears in the additional notes at the end of the volume. Gray must have written it after the text of the book was printed, and before the final notes were written. Percy printed the text in the course of 1767 and 1768. He sent a copy of it to Farmer on 22 Aug. 1768 (see Brit. Mus. *Add. MS.* 28224, f. 90). It may have been Farmer who showed it to Gray, and at some time when Mason was with Gray (Gray says 'Mr Mason dictates this note') Gray's note was written. Gray does not seem to have seen Mason in the latter part of 1768, but Mason was expected in Cambridge towards the end of Jan. 1769 (see Letter 491). This is the most likely occasion for the note to have been written.

3 The numbers are those of the pages of the *Northumberland Houshold Book*: the mention of 'Th' abbot of Mesx' is at the turn of p. 339.

4 Percy gave a footnote to 'Mesx': 'This word is obscurely written in the MS. It may perhaps be "Mefr", i.e. "Mifrule". See below, p. 344.' This note he corrected by an additional note at the end of the volume (p. 438): ' "The Abbot of Mefx, &c" This I find to be the real name of an Abbey in the East-riding of Yorkshire. A few miles distance North of Leckingfield lies Watton etc.' (he then gives, almost verbatim but without acknowledgement of the source, the note written by Gray). For Percy's correspondence with Mason on the same subject see Appendix N, n. 9.

5 The Abbey of Meaux was a few miles east of Beverley, in a part of Yorkshire which Mason, who passed his early life at Hull, would be likely to know.

are still some remains visible: the name is pronounced *Meuſs*.
(Mr Mason dictates this note)
Mr Percy's note therefore is wrong.

492. GRAY TO WALPOLE

MR. GRAY (upon the information of Mr Palgrave[1]) lets
Mr Walpole know, that there is at *Luton* a Chappel[2] built
in Henry 7th's time by a Lord Hoo & Hastings[3] & lined through-
out with most beautiful Gothick woodwork: this is going to be
demolish'd, & he imagines, Mr Walpole may have its inside for
a song.

Friday. [April, 1769][4] Jermyn-Street.

Folded as a note, and addressed: To the Hon. Horace Walpole

493. GRAY TO WHARTON

London. 20 April. 1769.

Dear Doctor

YOU have reason to call me negligent, nor have I any thing
to alledge in my own defence, but two succeſsive fits of the
gout, wch tho' weakly & not severe, were at least dispiriting, &
lasted a long time. I rejoiced to hear your alarms for Robin[1] &
Kitty[2] ended so happily, & with them (I hope), are fled a great
part of your future inquietudes on their account. in the summer
I flatter myself we may all meet in health once more at Old-

LETTER 492.—First printed by Toynbee (1915), No. 244.

[1] Both Palgrave and Gray were in London at the date assigned to this
note, as appears from Gray's letter to Brown of 20 Apr. 1769 (Letter 494).

[2] This was no doubt the private chapel at Luton Hoo, in Bedfordshire,
the seat of the Marquess of Bute, in which, according to Lewis (*Topog. Dict.*,
vol. iii, p. 175), there was 'some fine carved screen work, in the later English
style, which originally formed the interior decoration of a chapel erected at
Tittenhanger by Sir Thomas Pope in the middle of the sixteenth century'.
In a letter to Lord Strafford of 3 July of this year (1769) Walpole writes:
'I hear the chapel of Luton is to be preserved; and am glad of it, though I
might have been the better for its ruins'—obviously a reference to Gray's
suggestion as to his acquisition of the 'Gothick woodwork'.

[3] Sir Thomas Hoo (*c.* 1400–55), created (1447) Baron of Hoo and
Hastings.

[4] Date conjectural, but fixed approximately by the references to Mr.
Palgrave and to the chapel at Luton (see nn. 1, 2).

LETTER 493.—First printed by Mitford (1816), vol. ii, pp. 509–10; now
reprinted from original.   [1] See Letter 313, n. 3.

[2] Wharton's youngest daughter (see Letter 459, n. 18).

Park, & a part of us perhaps at the foot of Skiddaw. I am to call Mason in my way, & bring him with me to visit his own works.[3] M[r] Brown admitted your Nephew[4] according to your orders, & will provide him with a room against October. I do not guefs, what intelligence St: gave you about my employments: but the worst employment I have had has been to write something for musick against the D: of G:[5] comes to Cambridge. I must comfort myself with the intention: for I know it will bring abuse enough on me. however it is done, & given to the V: Chancellor,[6] & there is an end. I am come to Town for a fortnight, & find every thing in extreme confusion,[7] as you may guefs from your news-papers: nothing but force threaten'd on both sides, & the Law (as usual) watching the event & ready to side with the strongest. the only good thing

[3] The improvements he had planned for the grounds of Old Park (see Letters 459, 484).   [4] See Letter 336, n. 3.

[5] On 1 July 1769 the Duke of Grafton, who had been elected Chancellor on 29 Nov. 1768, was to be installed. Following the precedent of the Duke of Newcastle's installation (when Mason wrote the Ode, see Letter 150), an ode, set to music, was to be performed in the Senate House. Motives of gratitude (Letter 497) caused Gray to offer 'unasked' (Letter 501) to write it. Norton Nicholls in his *Reminiscences of Gray* says: 'After I had quitted the University I always paid M[r] Gray an annual visit; during one of these visits it was he determined as he said to offer with a good grace what he could not have refused if it had been asked of him viz. to write the Installation Ode for the Duke of Grafton. This however he considered as a sort of task to which he submitted with great reluctance; & it was long after he first mentioned it to me, before he could prevail with himself to begin the composition. One morning when I went to him as usual after breakfast, I knocked at his door, which he threw open, & exclaimed with a loud voice,

"Hence! avaunt, 'tis holy ground."

I was so astonished, that I almost feared he was out of his senses; but this was the beginning of the Ode which he had just composed.'

John Sharp, Fellow of Corpus Christi College, Cambridge (see Letter 290, n. 1), wrote to Garrick on 28 Mar. 1769: 'As to yours, I will say as we now say of M[r] Gray,—no man can write so well when he is bid: he cannot make the Installation Ode for the Duke of Grafton, his friend and patron; Mason must *preach* one on the occasion, for he is

"Ordain'd, you know, and made divine".'

And on 26 May 1769: 'I can tell you that M[r] Gray makes the Ode at last, and our professor has already got a part of it, to set to music. I met M[r] G. here at dinner last Sunday; he spoke handsomely of your happy knack at epilogues: but he calls the Stratford Jubilee, Vanity Fair.' (*Private Correspondence of David Garrick*, vol. i, pp. 337, 349.)

[6] Dr. John Hinchliffe, Master of Trinity.

[7] In connexion with the election of Wilkes for Middlesex (see Letter 494, n. 6).

I hear is, that France is on the brink of a general bankrupcy, & their fleet (the only thing they have laid out money on of late) in no condition of service.

The Spring is come in all its beauty, & for two or three days I am going to meet it at Windsor. Adieu & let us pray it may continue till July. remember me to Mrs Wharton & all the family. I am ever

Yours

Mason has just left us & is gone to Aston.   T G:

Addressed: To Thomas Wharton Esq at Old-Park near Darlington Durham to be left at Sunderland bridge *Postmark:* 20 [A]P

494. GRAY TO BROWN

Dear Sir   [c. April 20, 1769.]¹

I AM sorry to think you are coming to town at a time when I am ready to leave it;² but so it must be, for here is a son born unto us,³ and he must die a heathen without your afsistance; Old Pa. is in waiting ready to receive you at your landing. Mason set out for Yorkshire this morning. Delaval is by no means well, and looks sadly, yet he goes about and talks as loud as ever;⁴ he fell upon me tooth and nail (but in a very friendly manner) only on the credit of the newspaper, for he knows nothing further; told me of the obloquy that waits for me; and said everything to deter me from doing a thing that is already done. Mason⁵ sat by and heard it all with a world of complacency.

LETTER 494.—First printed by Mitford in *Gray–Mason* (1853), pp. 454–6. Mitford, who is the sole authority for the text, seems to have made mistakes in transcribing it (see nn. 10, 12).

¹ The letter must have been written about the same date as the letter to Wharton of 20 Apr. It was written after the proceedings in the House of Commons on 15 Apr. (see n. 6), and in both letters there are similar references to Mason's departure for Yorkshire.

² Brown left Cambridge at the beginning of May. Gray was going to Windsor for two or three days (Letter 493). There is nothing to show where he went from Windsor. He did not return to Cambridge until about 16 May.

³ This is apparently an allusion to the *Installation Ode*, which he had recently finished.

⁴ 'Delaval the loud' (see Letter 461, n. 5). In Letter 489 Gray refers to his illness.

⁵ Mason had written the Ode for the Installation of the Duke of Newcastle in 1749. He was probably not proud of it, and did not include it in his *Collected Poems* until the edition of 1797.

Edward Hussey Delaval

from a painting, attributed to Nathaniel Dance,
at Doddington Hall, Lincoln

You see the determination of a majority of fifty-four,[6] only two members for counties among them. It is true that Luttrell was insulted, and even struck with a flambeau, at the door of the House of Commons on Friday night;[7] but he made no disturbance, and got away. How he will appear in public I do not conceive. Great disturbances are expected, and I think with more reason than ever. Petitions to Parliament, well-attended, will (I suppose) be the first step, and next, to the King to difsolve the present Parliament. I own I apprehend the event whether the mob or the army are to get the better.

You will wish to know what was the real state of things on the *hearse-day*:[8] the driver, I hear, was one Stevenson, a man who lets out carriages to Wilkes's party, and is worth money. Lord Talbot[9] was not rolled in the dirt, nor struck, nor his staff broken, but made the people a speech, and said he would down on his knees to them if they would but disperse and be quiet. They asked him whether he would stand on his head for them, and begun to shoulder him, but he retired among the soldiers. Sir Ar. Gilmour[10] received a blow, and seized the man who

---

[6] Wilkes had been returned for Middlesex on 13 Apr. by a large majority over Luttrell, but as Walpole relates, the Ministers declared their intention 'to substitute Luttrell on the poll, as being the legal candidate who had had the greatest number of voices. . . . The next day [15 Apr.], though Saturday, the House sat, and the debate lasted till two o'clock on Sunday morning, when it was carried to admit Luttrell by only 197 voices to 143—so little was the Court sure of their majority on so violent a measure!' (*Memoirs*, vol. iii, p. 237).

[7] Walpole writes: 'Luttrell, the preceding night [14 Apr.], had been assaulted by persons unknown, as he quitted the House; and, for some months, did not dare to appear in the streets, or scarce quit his lodging' (*op. cit.*, vol. iii, p. 239).

[8] Gray refers to the riots which had taken place on 22 Mar. and of which Walpole gave an account in his letter to Mann of 23 Mar. It was intended that a loyal address should be presented at St. James's by six hundred merchants and others: 'This imposing cavalcade no sooner set forth than they were hissed and pelted; . . . Not a third part reached St. James's, and they were overtaken by a prodigious concourse, attending a hearse drawn by four horses . . . This procession drove to St. James's Gate, where Grenadiers were fixed to prevent their entrance. . . . Here the King, ministers, and foreign ministers were besieged till past four, though the Riot Act was read, and Lord Talbot came down, and seized one man, while the mob broke the Steward's wand in his hand. It was near five before they could recover and present the address, which the mob had tried to seize.'

[9] He was Lord Steward of the Household (see Letter 345, n. 13).

[10] Gray probably wrote 'A^r' as an abbreviation of Alexander. Alexander Gilmour (*c.* 1735–92), third and last Baronet, of Craigmillar, co. Edinburgh

struck him, but the fellow fell down and was hustled away among the legs of the mob. At Bath House[11] a page came in to his mistreſs, and said, he was afraid Lord Bath[12] did not know what a disturbance there was below; she asked him if 'the house was on fire?' he said 'No; but the mob were forcing into the court:' she said 'Is that all; well I will go and look at them:' and actually did so from some obscure window. When she was satisfied, she said, 'When they are tired of bawling I suppose they will go home.'

Mr. Roſs, a merchant, was very near murdered, as the advertisement sets forth, by a man with a hammer, who is not yet discovered, in spite of the £600 reward.[13] I stay a week longer. Adieu: I am ever yours,

T. G.

495. GRAY TO WALPOLE

Pembroke-Hall. 26 May. 1769

OLD Cole lives at *Water-Beach*[1] near the road from Cambridge to Ely: but I believe, you had best send the book[2] to me, &

(1750); he was an officer in the Foot Guards; a Clerk Comptroller of the Household, 1765; M.P. for co. Edinburgh in three Parliaments, 1761–74.

[11] The text is probably corrupt (see n. 12).

[12] The text must be corrupt. Gosse, perhaps inadvertently, substituted 'Lady Bath' for 'Lord Bath', which Mitford printed. But there was no Lord Bath or Lady Bath at this time. The Earl of Bath had died in 1764, and his wife had predeceased him in 1758. Bath House, at the date of this letter, was owned by Frances Pulteney, daughter of Daniel Pulteney, cousin of the Earl, whose estates she inherited in 1767. (She had married William Johnstone, who had taken the name of Pulteney.) It may reasonably be assumed that there were obliterations in the manuscript (Brown seems to have made a practice of obliterating names in the letters of Gray, which he kept) and that 'Bath House' and 'Lord Bath' were mistaken restorations made by Mitford. It may even be conjectured that Gray wrote 'Bedford House' and 'the Duke'. The Duke of Bedford was unpopular and Walpole's narrative (quoted in n. 6) proceeds to tell how the Duke of Kingston, coming from Bedford House, was 'taken for the Duke of Bedford and had his new wedding-coach, favours and liveries covered with mud'.

[13] 'The Treasury offered a reward of £500 for discovering the person who, at the procession of the merchants, had, with a hammer, broke the chariot of one Ross, an aged merchant, and wounded him in several places' (Walpole, *Memoirs*, vol. iii, p. 235).

LETTER 495.—First printed by Toynbee (1915), No. 245.

[1] Rev. William Cole (see Letter 26, n. 17) resided at Waterbeach, five miles from Cambridge, from 1768 to 1770, when he removed to Milton in the same neighbourhood.

[2] This was the *Biographical History of England, from Egbert the Great to the*

I will take care it shall be deliver'd to him. I have not seen it yet, but propose to buy it on your recommendation. if it has a hundrdth part of Linnæus's³ merit, it must be divine! what the title means, I do not conceive.

Addressed: To The Honble Horace Walpole in Arlington Street London
Postmark: 27 MA

496. [?] AND GRAY TO NICHOLLS

Pembroke Wednesday June 7th.

I HAVE just recollected that Mr Boycot¹ may pofsibly be able to give you some afsistance.

P:S: Well! why, you don't say any thing to me. here am I; & as soon as our ceremonies² are over, look with your telescope at the top of Skiddaw,³ & you will see me.

Revolution, consisting of Characters dispersed in different Classes, and adapted to a Methodical Catalogue of Engraved British Heads (Lond. 1769, 2 vols. 4to), by James Granger (1723–76), Vicar of Shiplake, as appears from Walpole's letter to Cole of 27 May: 'Mr Gray tells me you are still at Waterbeach. Mr Granger has published his Catalogue of Prints and Lives down to the Revolution, and, as the work sells well, I believe, nay, do not doubt but we shall have the rest. There are a few copies printed but on one side of the leaf. As I know you love scribbling in such books as well as I do, I beg you will give me leave to make you a present of one set. I shall send it in about a week to Mr Gray, and have desired him, as soon as he has turned it over, to convey it to you.'

³ As Mason says (*Memoirs*, p. 341) Gray's favourite study for the last ten years of his life was Natural History. He had his own copy of Linnæus' *Systema Naturæ* interleaved, and enriched it with copious notes and delicately executed drawings of birds, insects, and shells. The volumes are now in Harvard University Library (see *The Poet Gray as a Naturalist*, by Charles Eliot Norton). Gray's allusion to Linnæus here may have been induced by Walpole's having twitted him with absorption in the study. In a letter to the Countess of Upper Ossory, of 8 Sept. 1791, Walpole wrote: 'Mr Gray often vexed me by finding him heaping notes on an interleaved *Linnæus*, instead of pranking with his lyre.'

LETTER 496.—First printed by Mitford (1835–43), vol. v, p. 95; now reprinted from original. This note is written on a narrow slip of paper, without any address; only the postscript is in Gray's hand, the other part is in a round hand which has not been identified.

¹ There is nothing to show who Boycot was, nor for what purpose his assistance was required.

² The installation of the Duke of Grafton as Chancellor of the University on 1 July.

³ See Letter 493.

497. GRAY TO STONHEWER

[June 12, 1769.]

*   *   *   *   *

*   *   *   *   *

I DID not intend the Duke should have heard me till he could not help it.[1] You are desired to make the best excuses you can to his Grace for the liberty I have taken of praising him to his face; but as somebody was necefsarily to do this, I did not see why Gratitude[2] should sit silent and leave it to Expectation[3] to sing, who certainly would have sung, and that *à gorge deployée* upon such an occasion.

*   *   *   *   *

*   *   *   *   *

498. NICHOLLS TO GRAY

June 14, 1769.

I KNOW you think that I have entirely neglected botany, or you would have had twenty troublesome letters before now; but this is not entirely the case, as my journal will witnefs for me when you see it. I have indeed met with severe rebuffs and discouragements, and difficulties that almost reduced me to despair; but I believe it is because I ventured beyond my strength, and expected to make out readily every wild flower I found, instead of condescending to take my garden for a master, and learn gradually the botanical characters from flowers I know; which seems more reasonable than endeavouring to discover the others by characters I have not yet learnt. I have not writ to ask questions, because there would be no end of it, and I am sure I should never make you understand me except I enclosed the plant. But I have had innumerable to ask

LETTER 497.—Part of letter, first printed by Mason in *Memoirs*, p. 349, n.

[1] Mason states that this note was written to Stonhewer on 12 June, when, at his request, Gray sent him the *Installation Ode* in manuscript for the Duke of Grafton's perusal.

[2] In stanza v of the Ode Gray dwells on the sweetness of 'The still small voice of Gratitude'.

[3] Gray may have had in mind a passage in Pope's letter to Lord Halifax of 1 Dec. 1714: 'I am obliged to you, both for the favours you have done me, and those you intend me . . . if I ever become troublesome or solicitous, it must not be out of expectation, but out of gratitude' (see Mitford, *Works of Gray* (1835–43), vol. i, p. lii, n.).

LETTER 498.—First printed by Mitford (1835–43), vol. v, pp. 88–91.

if you had been at my elbow. Having nothing to say myself, I waited for some time rather in expectation of hearing some news of the Ode,[1] which I long most impatiently to see; Oh! whilst I remember it, (to set my conscience at ease) I must tell you that some time ago I received a letter from Woodyer[2] the bookseller, (to acknowledge the receipt of some money I sent him) in which there was a postscript longer than the letter itself, to say how much obliged &c. he should be if, by my interposition, he (Woodyer) might be admitted to a share in the sale of the Ode said to be yours, if it should be printed, for that it would sell prodigiously. Unto which, his most humble request, I have so far graciously condescended as (not answering his letter, because that would divulge the secret which is already public) to make it known to you. Thus much I have done, because as he did me the honour of preferring me, I was not certain whether in justice I could supprefs it entirely; how just or reasonable the request itself may be I know not, and so I wash my hands of him and ask pardon.

Why will you mention Skiddaw[3] or any such insolent mountain to me who live within two miles of the sea and cannot see it till I come within two yards of it? think of me when you listen to the sound of Lawdoor[4] waterfall, or wander among the rocks of Borrowdale, and send an eagle to fetch me from Dorsetshire and deliver me from the naked downs. Alas! alas! when shall we live among the Grisons? visit the Bishop of Coire? or pafs a summer at Chiavenna?

I have been very idle (that you will not be surprised to hear) except in my garden, and there very diligent, very much amused, very much interested, and perfectly dirty with planting, transplanting &c. and with tolerable succefs.[5] Besides I have now free accefs, and an open firm descent to my lake, and a very shady little walk that winds a little way close on its bank; and have planted weeping willows, and poplars, and alders, and

---

[1] Gray's *Installation Ode*.
[2] A Cambridge bookseller. Gray seems to have made a pretence of keeping his authorship of the Ode a secret: it was obviously well known by this time.   [3] See Letter 496.
[4] Nicholls perhaps wrote 'Lowdoor': the reference is obviously to the falls of Lodore at the upper end of Derwentwater.
[5] Mathias in his *Letter on the death of the Rev. Norton Nicholls* (in Mitford (1835–43), vol. v, p. 9) refers to the skill and taste with which Nicholls made his villa at Blundeston 'one of the most finished scenes of cultivated sylvan delight'.

sallows; and shall expect you next summer to come and find fault, and sit in the shade.

I am just reading Mémoires de Sully,[6] which please me extremely, more than almost any thing; and particularly what I read a few minutes ago, the surprise of the fortrefs of Fescamp by Bois Rosé.[7] You remember the fifty men hanging by a rope midway of a perpendicular rock six hundred feet high, and the sea at bottom rising till it set the boats that brought them adrift, and prevented the pofsibility of their returning. Fear seizing the foremost man, and Bois Rosé (who was last of the train) climbing over the backs of the fifty to lead them on. It is told with all its circumstances more like the surprise of Platæa or other such descriptions in Thucydides, than a French writer.

Dr. Marriott has not writ, and is, I hear, to have his house full of foreign ambafsadors; so our Cambridge journey is at an end. We shall set out from hence about the middle of July for the west; but I beseech you let me hear first from you; and....[8] from Keswick it would really be cruel to refuse me a line, though you will not write from .....[8] or Cambridge.

I should be extremely obliged to you if you would once more lend me your book of Wilton,[9] if you could send it by the fly, to be left at Payne's[10] at the Meuse Gate[11] for me till I call; and add necefsary instructions for the country about Southampton, for that must be my Keswick this year.

Adieu! I really want to hear a little oftener from you; if I thought writing about nothing, on my part, would have any effect, that should not stand in the way. I am most faithfully and affectionately yours,

N. N.

Blundeston, 14th June, 1769. My mother's compliments.

[6] See Letter 214, n. 14.

[7] This feat of Charles Goustimenil de Boisrozé, a captain of the League against Henri IV, was performed on the night of 10 Nov. 1592. The action is described in vol. i, pp. 300 ff., of *Mémoires du Duc de Sully*, 3 vols. 4to, Londres, 1747.   [8] Mitford leaves gaps here.

[9] Probably *A New Description of the Curiosities in Wilton House*, by James Kennedy (8vo, 1764), Gray's copy of which, 'with numerous MS. critical remarks' by him, was sold by Evans in Nov. 1845. Mitford's transcript of Gray's notes in this volume is in the British Museum (*Add. MS.* 32561).

[10] Thomas Payne (1719–99), the London bookseller, commonly known as 'honest Tom Payne'.

[11] Payne's shop was in Castle Street, next the Mewsgate, the entrance by St. Martin's Church to the King's Mews, Charing Cross, which stood on the site of Trafalgar Square.

499. GRAY TO NICHOLLS

Pemb: Coll: 24 June. 1769.

AND SO you have a garden of your own, & you plant & transplant & are dirty & amused! are not you ashamed of yourself? why, I have no so such thing, you monster; nor ever shall be either dirty or amused as long as I live! my gardens are in the window,[1] like those of a Lodger up three pair of stairs in Petticoat-lane[2] or Camomile-street,[3] & they go to bed regularly under the same roof that I do. dear, how charming it must be to walk out in one's own garding, & sit on a bench in the open air with a fountain, & a leaden statue, & a rolling stone,[4] & an arbour! have a care of sore-throats tho', & the *agoe*.

Odicle[5] has been rehearsed again & again, & the boys have got scraps by heart: I expect to see it torn piece-meal in the North-Briton, before it is born. the musick is as good as the words: the former might be taken for mine, & the latter for Dr. Randal's.[6] if you will come, you shall see it & sing in it with Mr Norris,[7] & Mr Clerke,[8] the Clergyman, and Mr Reinholt,[9] & Mifs Thomas,[10] great names at Salisbury & Gloster musick-meeting, and well-versed in Judas-Maccabæus.[11] Dr Marriott

LETTER 499.—First printed in part (in a garbled text) in Mason's *Memoirs*, pp. 346–8; first printed in full (save for first PS.) by Mitford, *Works* (1835–43), vol. v, pp. 91–4; now reprinted from original.

[1] Cole wrote the following note on this passage: 'Mr Gray's chamber windows were ever ornamented with Mignionette, or other sweet herbs and flowers, elegantly planted in China vases.' Quoted by Mitford (1835–43), vol. i, p. cix.

[2] Formerly Hog Lane, now Middlesex Street, Whitechapel.

[3] In Bishopsgate, from opposite Wormwood Street to St. Mary Axe.

[4] That is, a stone roller.

[5] *The Installation Ode*. Gray applied the same nickname to *The Bard* (see Letter 238). As Gray anticipated, the *Ode* did not escape attack (see Letter 501, n. 5).

[6] John Randall (1715–99), organist of King's College, Cambridge, 1745–99; Mus. Bac. 1744; Mus. Doc. 1756; Professor of Music, 1755–99. He acted in Smart's play in 1747 (see Letter 135, n. 10).

[7] Thomas Norris (1741–90), originally a chorister in Salisbury Cathedral. In 1765 he was appointed organist at Christ Church and at St. John's College, Oxford, where he graduated Mus. Bac. in the same year.

[8] Nothing appears to be known of this singer.

[9] Charles Frederick Reinhold (1737–1815), originally a chorister of St. Paul's and the Chapel Royal. For many years he was the popular bass singer at Marylebone Gardens.

[10] Nothing appears to be known of this singer.

[11] First produced by Handel as the Lent oratorio at Covent Garden in

is to have Ld Sandwich[12] & the Attorney-General[13] at his Lodge, not to mention foreign Ministers, who are to lie with Dr Hallifax, or in the stables. Ld North[14] is at King's, Ld Weymouth[15] at Mrs Arbuthnot's, they talk of the D: of Bedford, who (I suppose), has a bed in King's-Chappel. the Archbishop[16] is to be at Christ's, B^{ps} of London[17] at Clare-Hall, of Lincoln[18] at Dr Gordon's,[19] of Chester[20] at Peter-House, of Norwich[21] at Jesus, of St David's[22] at Caius, of Bangor,[23] at the Dog & Porridge-pot, Marq: of Granby[24] at Woodyer's.[25] the Yorkes & Townshends will not come. Soulsby the Taylor lets his room for 11 guineas the 3 days, Woodyer aforesaid for 15. Brotherton asks 20. I have a bed over the way offer'd me at 3 half-crowns a night, but it may be gone, before you come. I believe, all that are unlett will be cheap, as the time approaches. I wish it were once over, & immediately I go for a few days to London, & so (with Mr Brown) to Aston, tho' I fear it will rain the whole summer, & Skiddaw will be invisible & inaccefsible to mortals. I forgot to tell you, that on the Monday (after his Grace has

1747. Presumably it had been performed recently at the Gloucester festival.

12 At this time Joint Postmaster-General; Sandwich, North, Weymouth, and Granby were among the recipients of honorary degrees on the Monday after the Installation.

13 William De Grey (see Letter 475, n. 5).

14 Frederick North (1732–92), at this time Chancellor of the Exchequer, eldest son of first Earl of Guilford; styled Lord North, 1752–90, succeeded to the earldom in 1790; First Lord of the Treasury (Prime Minister), 1770–82.

15 Secretary of State for the Southern Department (see Letter 292, n. 6).

16 Hon. Frederick Cornwallis (see Letter 16, n. 5); he had been appointed Archbishop of Canterbury in 1768.

17 Dr. Richard Terrick (see Letter 401, n. 12); he had been a Fellow of Clare Hall.   18 Dr. John Green (see Letter 241, n. 12).

19 Archdeacon of Lincoln (see Letter 372, n. 6).

20 Dr. Edmund Keene, formerly Master of Peterhouse (see Letter 143, n. 3).

21 Dr. Philip Yonge, formerly Master of Jesus (see Letter 272, n. 7).

22 Dr. Charles Moss (1711–1802), of Caius College; B.A. 1731; M.A. and Fellow, 1735; D.D. 1747; Bishop of St. David's, 1766–74; of Bath and Wells, 1774–1802.

23 Dr. John Ewer (d. 1774), of Eton and King's College; B.A. 1728; M.A. 1732; Fellow, 1727–36; D.D. 1756; Bishop of Llandaff, 1761–8; of Bangor, 1768–74. He was for a time assistant master at Eton, and travelling tutor to the Marquess of Granby.

24 Commander-in-Chief (see Letter 279, n. 5).

25 See Letter 498, n. 2.

breakfasted on a Divinity-act) twelve Noblemen & Fellow-commoners are to settle his stomach with verses made & repeated by themselves. Saturday next[26] (you know) is the great day, & he goes away on Monday after this repast. I have got *De la Lande's*[27] Voyage thro' Italy in 8 vol:ˢ. he is a Member of the Acad: of Sciences, & pretty good to read. I have read an 8ᵛᵒ volume of Shenstone's letters.[28] poor Man! he was always wishing for money, for fame, & other distinctions, & his whole philosophy consisted in living against his will in retirement, & in a place,[29] wᶜʰ his taste had adorn'd; but wᶜʰ he only enjoy'd, when People of note came to see & commend it. his correspondence is about nothing else but this place & his own writings with two or three neighbouring Clergymen, who wrote verses too. I will send the Wilton-book[30] directed to Payne for you, tho' I know it will be lost, & then you will say, it was not worth above a shilling, wᶜʰ is a great comfort to me. I have just found the beginning of a letter, wᶜʰ somebody had drop'd: I should rather call it first thoughts for the beginning of a letter, for there are many scratches & corrections. as I can not use it myself (having got a beginning already of my own) I send it for your use upon some great occasion.

Dear Sʳ

After so long silence the hopes of pardon & prospect of for-givenefs might seem entirely extinct or at least very remote, was I not truly sensible of your goodnefs & candour, wᶜʰ is the only Asylum that my negligence can fly to: since every apology would prove insufficient to counterballance it, or alleviate my

---

[26] 1 July.

[27] *Voyage d'un François en Italie, dans les années 1765 et 1766* (Paris, 1769, 8 vols. 12mo), by the celebrated astronomer, Joseph Jérôme le François de Lalande (1732–1807). He was elected to the Académie des Sciences in 1753, and in 1761 succeeded Delisle as Professor of Astronomy in the Collège de France.

[28] See Letter 248, n. 9. Dodsley had published in 1764 *The Works in Verse and Prose of William Shenstone Esq.* in two volumes. In 1769 he published a third volume 'containing Letters to particular Friends'.

[29] The Leesowes, a property near Halesowen, in Worcestershire, Shenstone's birthplace, which he inherited. Walpole wrote to Cole on 14 June: 'I have been eagerly reading Mʳ Shenstone's *Letters*, which, though containing nothing but trifles, amused me extremely. . . . Poor man! he wanted to have all the world talk of him for the pretty place he had made, and which he seems to have made only that it might be talked of.'

[30] See Letter 498, n. 9.

fault. how then shall my deficiency presume to make so bold an attempt, or be able to suffer the hardships of so rough a campaign? &c: &c: &c:

And am, Dear S^r

        Kindly Yours

           T: G:

[My][31] respects to Mrs Nicholls.

I do not publish at all,[32] but Alma Mater prints 5 or 600 for the company.[33]

I have nothing more to add about Southampton, than what you have transcribed already in your map-book.[34]

Addressed: To The Revd Mr Nicholls at Blundeston near Leostoff, Suffolk By Norwich *Postmark:* CAMBRIDGE

500. NICHOLLS TO GRAY

Blundeston, Monday, July 3, 1769.

ALL, alas! is over, and I have been compelled by cruel necefsity to figure to myself all the splendours and glories; how the Ode was sung, and played, and applauded (all but) as it deserves (the first glimpse I shall see of it will be I suppose in the critical review[1]). How thoroughly sensible of the honour the duke was. How he was prefsed to death by people who never saw a duke before; and thought themselves in heaven if a chance word dropped on them in the crowd. How Dr. Gordon[2] clapped with both his hands, and grinned with all his teeth when his Grace but looked as if he would speak, and bowed lower than even clergymen are used to bow. I should have been glad to

[31] MS. torn.

[32] Gray contrived that his name should not appear on the title-page. The omission was an affectation as his authorship was known to everybody.

[33] The Ode was printed in eight pages 4to, with the title: 'Ode performed in the Senate-House at Cambridge, July 1, 1769, at the installation of His Grace Augustus-Henry Fitzroy, Duke of Grafton, Chancellor of the University. Set to music by Dr Randal, Professor of Music. Cambridge, Printed by J. Archdeacon Printer to the University. M.DCC.LXIX.' A second edition was issued in the same year.

[34] It may be suggested that Gray had lent Nicholls the atlas which he had annotated with a list of Antiquities, Houses, &c., in England and Wales (see Letter 267, n. 4), and that Nicholls had copied the list. When Mason printed Gray's *Catalogue of Antiquities etc.*, he stated in the *Advertisement* that 'many of his friends had transcribed it in his life-time'.

LETTER 500.—First printed by Mitford (1835–43), vol. v, pp. 95–7.

[1] Brief extracts from it were printed in the *Critical Review* for Sept. 1769; it was printed in full in the *London Chronicle* of 1–4 July 1769; and in the *Gentleman's Magazine* for July.   [2] See Letter 499, n. 19.

have heard the Ode, and very glad to have seen you; but I suspect that I shall like it as well without Dr. Randal's music. And as for you, you would have been so beset with ministers of state that I should have seen nothing of you; so I thought it best to remain in quiet here, rather than to put myself to a great deal of inconvenience, expense, and trouble, to get into the midst of a bustle which I hate, and be disappointed at last.

We shall depart, I suppose, the middle of this month, so, if after that time you direct to me at Augustus Floyer's,[3] Esq. at Upwey, near Dorchester, Dorsetshire, I shall be very glad to hear news from Yorkshire, or Cumberland, or Westmoreland, or no news at all provided I hear.

Many thanks for the Wilton book![4]

I have read the first volume of Robertson.[5] It may be all vastly right, but it certainly is a little tiresome to have five hundred pages of disquisitions on feudal tenures, &c. such a pile of gothic learning in your way, when you are all impatience to begin an interesting history; and surely, it is not good policy in the author to tire you to death in order to interest you the more. All that I know is, that it is not at all like Mémoires de Sully. But then Robertson is a grave historian, and the other only a writer of memoirs. Why then a writer of memoirs is a better thing than an historian.

And so my mother waits to carry my letter to the post, and desires her compliments.

I am at the moment *inebriated* with gales of mignonette of my own sowing. 'Oh the pleasures of the plain', &c. For God's sake leave Pembroke (at least when there are leaves on the trees) and get a house in Wales, and let me come and paſs a summer with you. Adieu! do not despise me when you come among the mountains.

Yours most sincerely,
N. N.

P.S. My service to *creeping Gain*,[6] (I do not mean Mr Gould[7]) I hope it has conceived vast hopes from the smiles of his Grace.

---

[3] His cousin (see Letter 508, n. 8) at this time lived at Upwey.

[4] See Letter 498, n. 9.

[5] See Letter 292, n. 17. His *History of Charles V* (Lond. 3 vols. 4to) had just been published.

[6] A reference to the Chorus in Gray's *Installation Ode*:

> Nor Envy base, nor creeping Gain
> Dare the Muse's walk to stain.

[7] See Letter 392, n. 11.

501. GRAY TO BEATTIE

[Cambridge, July 16, 1769.]¹

Dear Sʳ

I HAVE been so unfortunate as to lose the pleasure of seeing your two Friends Dʳ Gerard² & Mʳ Duncan. when they pafs'd thro' this place, I was at London; & tho' Lᵈ Strathmore told me, there was a Gentleman, who had letters for me, he coud not tell me where he was lodged. after my return hither,³ when they (I suppose) were leaving London, I received your letter by the post.

The late ceremony of the D: of Grafton's Installation⁴ has hinder'd me from acknowledging sooner the satisfaction your friendly compliment gave me. I thought myself bound in gratitude to his Grace unasked to take upon me the task of writing those verses, that are usually set to musick on this occasion. I do not think them worth sending you, because they are by nature doom'd to live but a single day, or if their existence is prolong'd beyond that date, it is only by means of news-paper parodies,⁵ & witlefs criticism.⁶ this sort of abuse I had reason to expect, but did not think it worth while to avoid it.

LETTER 501.—First printed in part (in a garbled text) in Mason's *Memoirs*, pp. 348–50; now first printed in full from original.

¹ Date inserted by Mason.

² Alexander Gerard (1727–95), Professor of Moral Philosophy, and subsequently (1760–71) of Divinity at Marischal College, Aberdeen: from 1771 Professor of Divinity at King's College, Aberdeen; author of *Essay on Taste* (1759), *Essay on Genius* (1774). Beattie was his pupil and succeeded him in the Chair of Moral Philosophy.

³ Gray returned to Cambridge about the middle of May.

⁴ A letter of Richard Gough to the Rev. Benjamin Forster, dated 6 July 1769 (published in Nichols, *Illustrations*, vol. v, p. 315, and in Cooper's *Annals of Cambridge*, vol. iv, p. 360), gives an account of the proceedings at the Installation. After a speech from the Public Orator and the Chancellor's reply 'followed the Ode, well set and performed, but charged with obscurity'. There was a great banquet in the hall of Trinity College, and a performance of *Acis and Galatea* in the Senate House. On the Monday following (3 July) fourteen Noblemen, &c., were admitted to Doctors' degrees. The Duke's expenses were said to be about £2,000.

⁵ Two parodies of Gray's *Ode* appeared, one in the *St. James's Chronicle* 1–4 July, beginning:

         Hence! avaunt! 'tis venal ground,

and an *Ode to Liberty* in the *London Chronicle* of 14–16 Sept. beginning:

         Hence! avaunt! 'tis sacred ground,
         Let pallid Freedom ever fly. . . .

A more direct attack on Gray was made in a parody of the 'Epitaph' of

Mr Foulis is magnificent in his gratitude:[7] I can not figure to myself, how it can be worth his while to offer me such a present. you can judge better of this than I, & if he does not hurt himself by it, I would accept the *Homer*[8] with many thanks. I have not got, nor even seen it.

Gray's *Elegy*, which was published in the *London Chronicle* of 27–9 July with a prefatory note:

'As a certain Church-yard Poet has deviated from the principles he once profest, it is very fitting that the necessary alterations should be made in his epitaph.—*Marcus.*'

EPITAPH

Here rests his head upon the lap of earth,
    One nor to fortune nor to fame unknown;
Fair science frown'd not on his humble birth,
    And smooth-tongued flatt'ry mark'd him for her own.

Large was his wish—in this he was sincere—
    Fate did a recompence as largely send,
Gave the poor C . . r four hundred pounds a year,
    And made a d . . . y Minister his friend.

No further seek his deeds to bring to light,
    For, ah! he offer'd at Corruption's shrine;
And basely strove to wash an Ethiop white,
    While Truth and Honour bled in ev'ry line.

⁶ A week before Junius had published his fifth letter to the Duke of Grafton, dated 8 July, in which he contemplated the time when the Duke would be dismissed from office, and retreat to Cambridge: 'You will have reason to be thankful if you are permitted to retire to that seat of learning, which . . . has chosen you to encourage the growing virtue of their youth, and to preside [as Chancellor of the University] over their education. Whenever the spirit of distributing Prebends and Bishopricks shall have departed from you, you will find that learned seminary perfectly recovered from the delirium of an installation, and, what in truth it ought to be, once more a peaceful scene of slumber and thoughtless meditation. The venerable tutors of the University will no longer distresss your modesty by proposing you for a pattern for their pupils. The learned dulness of declamation will be silent; and even the venal Muse, though happiest in fiction, will forget your virtues.' The letter of Junius and the Ode from the *St. James's Chronicle* were reprinted in the *London Magazine* for July 1769.

⁷ This is explained by a letter of Robert Foulis to Beattie dated 25 March 1769 (printed in Miss Forbes's *Beattie and his Friends*, pp. 36–7): 'As we had more at heart doing justice to the merits of the poems, than procuring profit, we printed no more copies than what we thought we could be able to sell in our own shop . . . we can, however, from the agreeable reception they met with in Glasgow, afford a little present for Mr. Gray, which shall be either a copy of our folio edition of Homer or a set of our new edition of the Greek Historians, in twenty-nine volumes, as you shall judge most proper or most agreeable to him.'

⁸ *Homeri Opera, Græce*, ex edit. Sam. Clarke (Glasguæ, 1756–8. fol. 4 vols.).

I could wish to subscribe to his new edition of Milton,[9] & desire to be set down for two copies of ye large paper: but you must inform me where & when I may pay the money.

You have taught me to long for a second letter, & particularly for what you say will make the contents of it:[10] I have nothing to requite it with, but plain & friendly truth, & that you shall have, join'd to a zeal for your fame, & a pleasure in your succefs.

I am now setting forward on a journey towards the North of England, but it will not reach so far as I should wish, as I must return hither before Michaelmas, & shall barely have time to visit a few places & a few Friends.

I am, S^r, faithfully & sincerely

Yours
T GRAY.

If you favor me with a letter soon, be pleased to direct *at Tho: Wharton's Esq* of Old-Park near Darlington, Durham. To be left at Sunderland-Bridge.

502. GRAY TO WHARTON

17 July 1769. Pemb: Coll:

Dear Doctor

MASON being in residence at York, I lay aside my first design of going obliquely to Aston, & thence to Keswick; & set out with Mr Brown[1] tomorrow the common northern road. we shall probably pafs two or three days at York, & then come to Old-Park. about the end of August we may crofs the Apennine, & visit M: Skiddaw, when Mason may accompany or meet us

Gray's copy is now owned by Mr. Ronald Syme of Trinity College, Oxford. It has an inscription stating that it 'passed successively by gift from the Poets Gray and Mason to the Rev^{ds} Christopher and William Alderson, Rectors of Aston'. In 1843 it was given by William Alderson to the Rev. Alleyne Fitzherbert.

[9] This was published in one vol. folio in 1770.

[10] Mason notes: 'His correspondent had intimated to him his intention of sending him his first book of the Minstrel.' Beattie's answer to this letter, containing specimens of the *Minstrel*, was written in November of this year (Letter 507*).

LETTER 502.—First printed by Mitford (1816), vol. ii, p. 518; now reprinted from original.

[1] Brown was absent from Cambridge for about two months from the middle of July. There is nothing to show where he went after leaving Old Park, but in Letter 504 there is an allusion to his having 'deviated a little from the common track'.

on our way, & so you drop me there to find my way thro' the deserts of Lancashire in my return homewards.

I am so fat, that I have suffer'd more from heat this last fort-night, than ever I did in Italy. the Thermom: usually at 75, & (in the sun) at 116. my respects to M^{rs} Wh: & the family. I am ever

Yours
T G:

Addressed: To Thomas Wharton Esq of Old-Park near Darlington Durham to be left at Sunderland-Bridge *Postmark:* CAMBRIDGE

503. GRAY AND WHARTON TO MASON

Old-Park. Aug: 26. 1769. Saturday.

Dear Mason

I RECEIVED last night your letter big with another a week older than itself. you might as well have wrote to me from the deserts of Arabia, & desired me to step over & drink a dish of tea with you.[1] this morning I sent to Aukland[2] for a chaise: the Man's answer is, that he had a chaise with four horses return'd yesterday from Hartlepool, that the road was next to impafsable, & so dangerous, that he does not think of sending out any other that way, unlefs the season should change to a long drought. I would have gone by Durham, but am afsured, that road is rather worse. what can I do? you speak so jauntily, & enter so little into any detail of your own journey, that I conclude you came on horseback from Stockton (wch road however is little better for carriages) if so, we hope you will ride over to Old-Park with Mr Alderston:[3] there is room for you both, & hearty welcome. the Doctor even talks of coming (for he can ride) to invite you on Monday. I wonder how you are accommodated, where you are; & what you are doing with Gen: Carey: I would give my ears to get thither, but all depends on the sun. Adieu!

It is twenty miles to Old-Park, & the way is by *Hart,* over Sherraton-moor & through Trimden there is no village else that has a name. pray, write a line by the bearer.

LETTER 503.—First printed by Mitford in *Gray–Mason* (1853), pp. 430–1; now reprinted from original.

[1] Mason was at Hartlepool and had evidently asked Gray to come over from Old Park.

[2] Bishop Auckland is about four miles from Old Park.

[3] See Letter 453, n. 7.

we have a confirmation of the above accou[n]t of the state of the roads from other evidences—neverthelefs I shall certainly come on horseback on Monday to inquire after your proceedings and designs and to preveil upon You and Mr Aldeston to return with me to Old Park—a rainy morning perhaps may stop me a few hours but when it clears up I shall set forward. Adieu—accept all our Complimts.

Yrs ever
T. W.

Addressed (by Gray): To The Revd Mr Mason at Hartlepool

504. GRAY TO BROWN

Dear Sir   Lancaster, 10 Oct. 1769.

I SET out on the 29th September, with poor Doctor Wharton, and lay at Brough,[1] but he was seized with a fit of the asthma the same night, and obliged in the morning to return home. I went by Penrith to Keswick, and pafsed six days there lap'd in Elysium;[2] then came slowly by Ambleside to Kendal, and this day arrived here. I now am projecting to strike acrofs the hills into Yorkshire, by Settle, and so get to Mason's; then, after a few days, I shall move gently towards Cambridge.[3] The weather has favoured all my motions just as I could wish.

I received your letter of 23 Sept.; was glad you deviated a little from the common track, and rejoiced you got well and safe home.

I am, ever yours
T. G.

505. GRAY TO WHARTON

Journal.[1] 30 Sept: 1769.

WD at N:W. clouds & sunshine. a mile & ½ from Brough[2] on a hill lay a great army encamp'd.[3] to the left open'd a fine valley with green meadows & hedge-rows, a Gentleman's house

LETTER 504.—First printed by Mitford in *Gray–Mason* (1853), p. 432.
   [1] Brough under Stainmoor, in Westmorland, eight miles south-east of Appleby (see Letter 453).
   [2] In his *Journal* for 2 Oct. (Letter 506) Gray describes the Keswick valley as 'the Vale of Elysium'.
   [3] He returned to Cambridge on 22 Oct.—see his letter to Wharton of 18 Apr. 1770 (Letter 519).
   LETTER 505.—First printed (in a garbled text) in Mason's *Memoirs*, pp. 350–4; now reprinted from original (see n. 1).
   [1] This letter contains the beginning of Gray's *Journal*, written during his

peeping forth from a grove of old trees. on a nearer approach appear'd myriads of horses & cattle in the road itself & in all

tour in the Lakes and Yorkshire. For the first time since he went with Walpole to France and Italy in 1739 Gray wrote a continuous and detailed account of his travels and doings day by day. Mason explains its purpose in a note: 'Dr. Wharton, who had intended to accompany Mr. Gray to Keswick, was seized at Brough with a violent fit of his asthma, which obliged him to return home. This was the reason that Mr Gray undertook to write the following journal of his tour for his friend's amusement. He sent it under different covers.'

It is obvious from many passages throughout the *Journal*, that it was written for Wharton (see under date 3 Oct.: 'oh Doctor! I never wish'd more for you', and 7 Oct.: 'Rec:^{t} to dress Perch (for Mrs Wharton)' etc.). He wrote the *Journal* in pocket note-books, and sent parts of it, as he transcribed them, in letters to Wharton. But it was not until he had finished the tour and was on his way to Cambridge that he sent the first part; three other parts followed during the next three months, but the last part (about half of the whole *Journal*) Gray never sent to Wharton. It was copied by Alderson, Mason's curate, and sent by Mason to Wharton with a letter of 24 July 1770, in which Mason wrote (British Museum *Egerton MS.* 2400): 'I inclose the fragment of the Journal wch Alderson copyd and desird me to forward you with his compliments' (see Letter 511 A).

The dates at which the parts were sent to Wharton are as follows:

Letter 505.	18 Oct. 1769	from Aston.	*Journal* 30 Sept.–1 Oct.
506.	29 Oct.	from Cambridge.	,, 1–3 Oct.
508*.	[Nov.	from Cambridge.]	,, 3–4 ,,
511.	3 Jan. 1770	from Cambridge.	,, 5–8 ,,
511 A.	24 July 1770	(Alderson's copy sent by Mason.)	,, 8–14 ,,

The authorities for the text of the *Journal* are: (*a*) two of Gray's note-books (in the possession of Sir John Murray), which contain the whole as originally written by Gray; (*b*) Gray's own transcript of the first half (from 30 Sept. to part of 8 Oct.); (*c*) Alderson's transcript of the second half (from part of 8 to 14 Oct.): Both transcripts (which are with the manuscripts of Gray's letters to Wharton) have slight variations from the text of the note-books, some of which were probably mere errors in copying.

Mason printed the text continuously (prefixing the note which Gray added at the end of Letter 505, and omitting the postscripts appended to Letters 506, 508*, 511). He exercised his usual licence of omitting, inserting, and transposing passages with occasional alterations of what Gray had written. Mitford printed from Gray's and Alderson's transcripts sent to Wharton, which, by a strange error, he described as 'in the handwriting of Dr. Wharton' (Mitford, 1816, vol. ii, p. 519, n.).

The text now printed follows, for the first four parts of the *Journal*, Gray's own transcript, which he sent to Wharton, and includes the postscripts, which Gray appended to each. The last part (Letter 511 A) is printed from Gray's holograph in the second of the Murray note-books.

² Where Wharton left him (Letter 504, n. 1).

³ There is a great fair for cattle kept on the hill near Brough, on this day and the preceding. *Mason.*

the fields round me, a brisk stream hurrying crofs the way, thousands of clean healthy People in their best party-color'd apparel, Farmers & their families, Esquires & their daughters, hastening up from the dales & down the fells on every side, glittering in the sun & prefsing forward to join the throng: while the dark hills, on many of whose tops the mists were yet hanging, served as a contrast to this gay & moving scene, wch continued for near two miles more along the road, and the crowd (coming towards it) reach'd on as far as Appleby.

On the ascent of the hill above Appleby the thick hanging wood & the long reaches of the Eden (rapid, clear, & full as ever) winding below with views of the Castle & Town gave much employment to the mirror:[4] but the sun was wanting & the sky overcast. oats & barley cut every where, but not carried in. pafsed Kirby-thore, S^r W: Dalston's[5] house at Acorn-bank, Whinfield-park, Harthorn-oaks, Countefs-pillar, Brougham-Castle, Mr Brown (one of ye six Clerks)[6] his large new house, crofs'd the Eden & the Eimot[7] (pronounce *Eeman*) with its green vale, & at 3 o'clock dined with Mrs Buchanan, at *Penrith* on trout & partridge. in the afternoon walk'd up the *Beacon-hill* a mile to the top, saw Whinfield and Lowther-parks, & thro' an opening in the bosom of that cluster of mountains, wch the Doctor well remembers, the Lake of Ulz-water, with the craggy tops of a hundred namelefs hills. these to W: & S:, to the N: a great extent of black & dreary plains, to E: *Crofs-fell* just visible thro' mists & vapours hovering round it.

Oct: 1. W^d at S:W: a grey autumnal day, air perfectly calm & gentle. went to see *Ulz-water* 5 miles distant. soon left the Keswick-road & turn'd to the left thro' shady lanes along the Vale of *Eeman*, wch runs rapidly on near the way, ripling over the stones. to the right is *Delmaine*, a large fabrick of pale red

---

[4] Mr Gray carried usually with him on these tours a Plano-convex Mirror of about four inches diameter on a black foil, and bound up like a pocket-book. A glass of this sort is perhaps the best and most convenient substitute for a Camera Obscura, of any thing that has hitherto been invented. *Mason.*

[5] In the Annual Register for 1771 the death is recorded on 1 Oct. of 'Sir William Dalton [*sic*], Bart. at his seat at Acorn Bank in Westmoreland'. This must be Gray's 'Sir William Dalston'; according to G. E. C.'s *Complete Baronetage*, vol. ii, p. 82, he was not in the succession to the Baronetcy, which ran in another branch of the Dalston family and became extinct in 1765.

[6] The six official clerks formerly connected with the Court of Chancery; their office was abolished in 1843.

[7] The Eamont, which flows out of the north end of Ullswater, forming the boundary between Westmorland and Cumberland.

stone with 9 windows in front & 7 on the side built by Mr Hafsel,[8] behind it a fine lawn surrounded by woods & a long rocky eminence rising over them. a clear & brisk rivulet runs by the house to join the Eeman, whose course is in sight & at a small distance.

Farther on appears *Hatton St John*,[9] a castle-like old mansion of Mr Huddleston. approach'd *Dunmallert*, a fine pointed hill, cover'd with wood planted by old Mr Hafsle beforemention'd, who lives always at home & delights in planting. walk'd over a spungy meadow or two & began to mount this hill thro' a broad & strait green alley among the trees, & with some toil gain'd the summit. from hence saw the Lake opening directly at my feet majestic in its calmnefs, clear & smooth as a blew mirror with winding shores & low points of land cover'd with green inclosures, white farm-houses looking out among the trees, & cattle feeding. the water is almost every where border'd with cultivated lands gently sloping upwards till they reach the feet of the mountains, wch rise very rude & aweful with their broken tops on either hand. directly in front at better than 3 mile's distance, *Place-Fell*,[10] one of the bravest among them, pushes its bold broad breast into the midst of the Lake & forces it to alter it's course, forming first a large bay to the left & then bending to the right.

I descended *Dunmallert* again by a side avenue, that was only not perpendicular, & came to *Barton*-bridge over the *Eeman*, then walking thro' a path in the wood round the bottom of the hill came forth, where the *Eeman* ifsues out of the lake, & continued my way along it's western shore close to the water, & generally on a level with it. Saw a cormorant flying over it & fishing. . . . (to be continued)

Dear D^r   Aston. 18 Oct: 1769.[11]

I hope you got safe and well home after that troublesome night: I long to hear you say so. for me I have continued well, been so favour'd by the weather, that my walks have never once been hinder'd till yesterday, (that is during a fortnight & 3 or 4 days, & a journey of 300 miles, & more) & am now at Aston

---

[8] Probably Edward Hasell (b. 1706) of Dalemain, who married a daughter of Sir Christopher Musgrave (d. 1736), fifth Baronet, of Edenhall. Gray spells the name 'Hassle' below.   [9] Hutton St. John.
[10] On the Westmorland side of the lake (see Letter 506 *ad init.*).
[11] The note follows the first instalment of the *Journal* on the same page.

for two days. tomorrow I go towards Cambridge: Mason is not here, but Mr Alderson receives me. my best respects to the family! Adieu! I am ever

Yours (pray, tell me about Stonhewer).¹²

Addressed: To Thomas Wharton Esq. of Old-Park near Darlington Durham
Postmark: SHEFFIELD

506. GRAY TO WHARTON

Journal continued. 1 Oct: 1769.

THE figure of *Ulz-water* nothing resembles that laid down in our maps: it is 9 miles long, & (at widest) under a mile in breadth. after extending itself 3 m: & ½ in a line to S: W: it turns at the foot of *Place-Fell*, almost due West, and is here not twice the breadth of the Thames at London. it is soon again interrupted by the roots of *Helvellyn*, a lofty & very rugged mountain, & spreading again turns off to S: E:, & is lost among the deep recefses of the hills. to this second turning I pursued my way about four miles along its borders beyond a village scatter'd among trees & call'd *Water-malloch*,¹ in a pleasant grave day, perfectly calm & warm, but without a gleam of sunshine: then the sky seeming to thicken, the valley to grow more desolate, & evening drawing on, I return'd by the way I came to *Penrith*.

Oct: 2. W^d at S: E:, sky clearing, *Crofs-fell* misty, but the outline of the other hills very distinct. set out at 10 for *Keswick*, by the road we went in 1767.² saw *Greystock*-town & castle to the right, wch lie only 3 miles (over the Fells) from *Ulz-water*. pafs'd through *Penradock*³ & *Threlcot*⁴ at the feet of *Saddleback*, whose furrow'd sides were gilt by the noon-day Sun, while its brow appear'd of a sad purple from the shadow of the clouds, as they sail'd slowly by it. the broad & green valley of *Gardies* and *Low-side*, with a swift stream glittering among the cottages & meadows lay to the left; & the much finer (but narrower) valley of St *John's* opening into it: *Hill-top* the large, tho' low, mansion of the Gaskarths,⁵ now a Farm-house, seated on an

¹² Stonhewer's father was on his death-bed (see Letter 507, n. 1).
LETTER 506.—First printed (in a garbled text) in Mason's *Memoirs*, pp. 354–7; now reprinted from original.
¹ Watermillock, seven miles south-west from Penrith.
² When Gray and Wharton went to Keswick, and had to give up their tour because of Wharton's asthma (Letter 453).
³ Penruddock.   ⁴ Threlkeld.
⁵ The home of Joseph Gaskarth, Fellow of Pembroke (see Letter 148, n. 17).

eminence among woods under a steep fell, was what appear'd the most conspicuous, & beside it a great rock like some antient tower nodding to its fall.[6] pafs'd by the side of *Skiddaw* & its cub call'd *Latter-rig*,[7] & saw from an eminence at two miles distance the Vale of Elysium in all its verdure, the sun then playing on the bosom of the lake, & lighting up all the mountains with its lustre.

Dined by two o'clock at the Queen's Head, & then straggled out alone to the *Parsonage*, fell down on my back acrofs a dirty lane with my glafs open in one hand, but broke only my knuckles: stay'd neverthelefs, & saw the sun set in all its glory.

Oct: 3. W[d] at S: E:, a heavenly day. rose at seven, & walk'd out under the conduct of my Landlord[8] to *Borrodale*. the grafs was cover'd with a hoar-frost, w[ch] soon melted, & exhaled in a thin blewish smoke. crofs'd the meadows obliquely, catching a diversity of views among the hills over the lake & islands, & changing prospect at every ten paces, left *Cockshut* & Castle-hill (w[ch] we formerly mounted) behind me, & drew near the foot of *Walla-crag*, whose bare & rocky brow, cut perpendicularly down above 400 feet, as I guefs, awefully overlooks the way: our path here tends to the left, & the ground gently rising, & cover'd with a glade of scattering trees & bushes on the very margin of the water, opens both ways the most delicious view, that my eyes ever beheld. behind you are the magnificent heights of *Walla*-crag; opposite lie the thick hanging woods of L[d] Egremont,[9] & *Newland*-valley with green & smiling fields embosom'd in the dark cliffs; to the left the jaws of *Borodale*, with that turbulent Chaos of mountain behind mountain roll'd in confusion; beneath you, & stretching far away to the right, the shining purity of the *Lake*, just ruffled by the breeze enough to shew it is alive, reflecting rocks, woods, fields, & inverted tops of moun-

---

[6] Gray must have had in mind his own line,

Turrets and arches nodding to their fall

(from his verses on Lord Holland's villa), which was itself a reminiscence of Pope, *Essay on Man*, Ep. iv, l. 129.

[7] Latrigg.

[8] Samuel Rogers, in his Journal, dated Edinburgh 15 July 1789, records that Dr. Robertson 'said M[r] Gray devoted a month to the Lakes; that his cicerone, Hodgkins, who was a sensible fellow, described him as difficult to be pleased, and peevish from ill-health; that he could not ride on horseback, and would not go on the water' (P. W. Clayden, *Early Life of Samuel Rogers*, p. 92). Gray's 'cicerone' may have been his landlord at Keswick.

[9] George O'Brien Wyndham (1751–1837), third Earl of Egremont.

tains, with the white buildings of *Keswick, Crosthwait*-church, & *Skiddaw* for a back-ground at distance. oh Doctor! I never wish'd more for you; & pray think, how the glaſs played its part in such a spot, wch is called *Carf-close-reeds*: I chuse to set down these barbarous names, that any body may enquire on the place, & easily find the particular station, that I mean. this scene continues to *Barrow-gate*, & a little farther, paſsing a brook called *Barrow-beck*, we enter'd *Borodale*. the crags, named *Lodoor-banks* now begin to impend terribly over your way; & more terribly, when you hear, that three years since an immense maſs of rock tumbled at once from the brow, & bar'd all acceſs to the dale (for this is the only road) till they could work their way thro' it. luckily no one was paſsing at the time of this fall; but down the side of the mountain & far into the lake lie dispersed the huge fragments of this ruin in all shapes & in all directions. something farther we turn'd aside into a coppice, ascending a little in front of *Lodoor* water-fall. the height appears to be about 200 feet, the quantity of water not great, tho' (these three days excepted) it had rain'd daily in the hills for near two months before: but then the stream was nobly broken, leaping from rock to rock, & foaming with fury. on one side a towering crag, that spired up to equal, if not overtop, the neighbouring cliffs (this lay all in shade & darkneſs) on the other hand a rounder broader projecting hill shag'd[9a] with wood & illumined by the sun, wch glanced sideways on the upper part of the cataract. the force of the water wearing a deep channel in the ground hurries away to join the lake. we descended again, & paſsed the stream over a rude bridge. soon after we came under *Gowder-crag*, a hill more formidable to the eye & to the apprehension than that of *Lodoor*; the rocks atop, deep-cloven perpendicularly by the rains, hanging loose & nodding forwards, seem just starting from their base in shivers: the whole way down & the road on both sides is strew'd with piles of the fragments strangely thrown acroſs each other & of a dreadful bulk. the place reminds one of those paſses in the Alps, where the Guides tell you to move on with speed, & say nothing, lest the agitation of the air should loosen the snows above, & bring down a maſs, that would overwhelm a caravan. I took their counsel here and hasten'd on in silence.

Non ragioniam di lor; ma guarda, e paſsa![10]

9a *Comus*, 428.   (to be continued)

Richard Stonhewer

from a photograph of the painting by Sir Joshua Reynolds

Dear D^r

Have you lost the former part of my journal? it was dated from *Aston*, 18 Oct:. How does Stonhewer[11] doe? will his Father's condition allow him to return as yet? I beg my respects to all the family at Old-Park, & am ever

Yours

29 Oct: 1769. Cambridge. T G:

507. GRAY TO STONHEWER

My dear Sr Nov: 2. 1769. Camb:^{ge}

I AM sincerely pleased with every mark of your kindnefs, & as such I look upon your last letter in particular. I feel for the sorrow you have felt, & yet I can not wish to lefsen it: that would be to rob you of the best part of your nature, to efface from your mind the tender memory of a Father's[1] love, & deprive the Dead of that just & grateful tribute wch his goodnefs demanded from you.

I must however remind you, how happy it was for him, that you were with him to the last; that he was sensible perhaps of your care, when every other sense was vanishing—he might have lost you last year,[2] might have seen you go before him at a time, when all the ills of helplefs old-age were coming upon him, & (tho' not destitute of the attention & tendernefs of others) yet destitute of *your* attention & *your* tendernefs. May God preserve you my best Friend! & (Long after my eyes are closed) give you that last satisfaction in the gratitude & affection of a Son,[3] wch you have given your Father.

I am ever
Most truly & entirely
Yours
T G:

Addressed: To Richard Stonhewer, Esq. at Durham By Caxton-bag *Postmark:* CAMBRIDGE

<hr>

[10] Dante, *Inferno*, iii. 51: 'Let us not speak of them; but look, and pass on.'

[11] Stonhewer's father died on the date of this letter (see Letter 507, n. 1).

LETTER 507.—First printed by Mitford in *Gray–Mason* (1853), pp. 433–4; now reprinted from original.

[1] His father, who died on 29 Oct., was Rector of Houghton-le-Spring, Durham, 1727–69.

[2] Stonhewer has added the note: 'I had been very ill at the time alluded to.' He has docketed the letter: 'Novr. 2^d 1769 On my father's Death.' Gray alludes to Stonhewer's health in a letter to Mason of 29 Dec. 1768 (Letter 489).   [3] Stonhewer died unmarried.

507*. BEATTIE TO GRAY

[Aberdeen, Nov. 1769][1]

Dear Sir

FOR these three or four months past I have been in a state of dissipation and idleness, endeavouring if possible to rid myself of a vertigo which has troubled me much of late years, and which while it lasts disqualifies me entirely for reading and writing. If it had not been for this, I should long ere now have answered the very obliging letter I had the honour to receive from You in August[2] last. Soon after I received it I wrote to Mr Foulis, telling him that You had made choice of the Glasgow Homer, and desired to subscribe for two copies of the large paper of his Milton. That work is now begun;[3] and is said by those who have seen a specimen to be one of the most magnificent books ever published in this country.

I wonder You can bring Yourself to think so meanly of the Installation-Ode; for You say it can only live a few days. I am quite certain this is a mistake; it will make the name of the Duke of Grafton known as long as the English language is understood; which is an honour, no other great man of this age has any chance of obtaining at the hands of the muses. I will not say that this Ode is equal to some of Your other poems; but I will venture to affirm that it is the finest panegyrical poem in the world. The whole is contrived and executed in the highest Dithyrambick taste. The beginning and end peculiarly excellent. The figure of Newton[4] is exceeded by nothing in descriptive poetry. When You adopt the *liquid language of the skies*, Your sentiments words and numbers are perfectly Elysian. That happiness of expression for which You are so very remarkable, appears throughout.—'And bid it round heaven's altars shed The fragrance of its blushing head'[5] is only one instance, but it is a signal one. I known not whether I most admire the propriety of the metaphor, the beauty of the image, or the

LETTER 507*.—Now first printed from original.

[1] Date conjectural; as Beattie speaks of its being 'three or four months' since he received Gray's last letter, which was written in July (not August, as he says), this reply was perhaps written in November.

[2] Gray's letter was written on 16 July (see Letter 501).

[3] See Letter 501.

[4]   Meek Newton's self bends from his state sublime,
       And nods his hoary head (ll. 25–6).

[5] Lines 73–4.

delicacy of the exprefsion: all the three are in perfection. Your imitation of Milton is delightful.[6] The poetry is exquisite, and the imitation exact: but it has another claim to my approbation. I have always thought the hymn on the nativity, notwithstanding its faults, to be one of the finest poems in the world; I think I am intoxicated, or rather bewitched with it: and Your making choice of it for an object of Your imitation seems to justify my opinion of it.—But I cannot within the compafs of a letter say one half of what I have to say in praise of Your poem. I have heard some people object to its obscurity; but sure their attention must be very superficial, or their apprehension very weak, who do so. I understood every word of it at the first reading, except one pafsage (which however I made out at the second) where the printer had made nonsense, by placing a full point at the end of a line where there ought to have been no point at all.[7] Do, Sir, permit us to hope, now when Your hand is in again, that You will not abandon the muses. This age is indeed nowise remarkable for good qualities of any kind: taste and learning were never I believe lefs attended to in any period since the revival of letters; but still there are a few honest and sensible folks among us, whom it is certainly worth while to do something to please. My attention was never more awakened than when I found by the newspapers that You was to compose this Installation-ode; if You knew half the pleasure I received from it, You would not wonder that I am so very anxious to see more of Your works. I hope You have no vertigo's or headachs to excuse You: God forbid. May You long, very long, live healthy and happy.

It is a strange transition, and yet I must now speak a little of my own works. I told You in my last,[8] that I had begun a kind of poem, and I promised to send a specimen, which accordingly I have enclosed.[9] The piece will consist of three books of which near two are finished; but bad health and necefsary businefs have prevented my making any additions these six months. However I am in no hurry. As this will probably be the last of my poetical compositions I propose to finish it at great leisure. It is indeed the only one of them for which I have any esteem;

[6] In lines 27–34.
[7] There is nothing in the text of the first edition to suggest that the printer was at fault.   [8] See Letter 501, n. 10.
[9] This specimen of the *Minstrel* is no longer with the letter. Gray did not send his criticisms until July 1770 (Letter 529).

which perhaps is owing to its being the latest. Whether it will have any merit or not I cannot say; I am sure my other things have very little. The title of this piece is *The Minstrel.* The first hint of it was suggested by Mr Percy's Efsay on the English Minstrels.[10] There was something in the character of the Minstrel there described, which struck me and pleased me. I suppose my Hero born in a solitary and mountainous country; by trade a shepherd. His imagination is wild and romantick; but in the first part of his life he has hardly any opportunity of acquiring knowledge, except from that part of the book of nature which is open before him. The first Canto is a kind of poetical or sentimental history of this period. In the second he meets with a Hermit, who in his youth had been a man of the world, and who instructs Edwin (the young Minstrel) in history, philosophy, musick, &c. The young man, agreably to that character which he bears from the beginning, shows a strong attachment to poetry, which the old hermit endeavours by all pofsible means to discourage. Edwin seems disposed to follow his advice, and abandon the muses; when an irruption of Danes or robbers (I have not as yet determined which) strips him of his little all, and obliges him through necefsity to take his harp on his shoulder, and go abroad into the world in the character of a Minstrel. And here the poem is to end.—The measure is the same with that of Spenser in the fairy queen; but I have avoided all antiquated exprefsions. I chose this measure, partly because it seemed to suit my Gothick subject; but chiefly because it is extremely agreable to my ear, and seems to admit greater varieties in the composition than any other English stanza. The pafsage I have sent you for a specimen is in my judgment neither one of the best nor one of the worst. It is taken from the first book, which describes the hero's pursuits and amusements in the first years of his life. I beg Your pardon for sending it in so bad order. I cut it out of a book to save the labour of transcribing, which the present state of my health would render a very uneasy work. The numbers of the stanza's will direct to the order in which they are to be read. You need not return them as I have another copy.[11]

[10] *An Essay on the Ancient Minstrels in England,* prefixed to Percy's *Reliques of Ancient English Poetry,* first published in 1765.
[11] The conclusion of the letter, which was perhaps attached to the extract from Beattie's *Minstrel,* is apparently missing.

508. NICHOLLS TO GRAY

Bath, Nov. 27, 1769.

I HAVE two reasons for writing, one because it seems an age to me since I heard of you, the other to mention that I have taken the liberty of recommending to your notice Mr. de Bonstetten.[1] I have given him a letter to you, but yet I thought it best to apprise you of it, that he might not come an entire stranger. I picked him out from among the mob in the rooms here,[2] and like him very much; I shall be a little disappointed if you do not think him better than common for his age, and very little spoiled considering that he is the only son of the treasurer of Berne, and of one of the six noble families which bear the chief sway in the aristocracy. He was first at the university of Lausanne; afterwards his father sent for him home; then he went to Leyden, but thought Holland a most triste pays, and begged to be released, so he had leave to crofs over to

LETTER 508.—First printed by Mitford (1835–43), vol. v, pp. 97–100.

[1] Charles Victor de Bonstetten (1745–1832), whose birth and early history Nicholls relates, came to England in Aug. 1767, and after a brief stay in London went to live in the family of a clergyman, whom he called 'Mr Schmidith', at South Moreton in Berkshire, that he might learn English. Early in Nov. 1769 he went to Bath, where he made the acquaintance of Nicholls (see n. 2), with the result described in this letter. From Bath, armed with letters of introduction, he went to London, where he was presented to the King, and lived in the fashionable world. (For an account of his stay at South Moreton, at Bath, and in London see de Bonstetten's letter of 30 Dec. 1827 to Heinrich Zchokke in *Prometheus*, Zweiter Theil, pp. 173 ff., Aarau, 1832.) Early in December, soon after he received the letter from Nicholls, Gray went to London, and made a stay there of two or three weeks, during which he introduced himself to Bonstetten, whom he took back with him to Cambridge before the end of the month. It was probably on this occasion that, as is related by Sir Egerton Brydges in his *Autobiography* (vol. ii, p. 111), Gray pointed out Dr. Johnson to Bonstetten, with the exclamation, 'Look! look! Bonstetten! the great bear—there goes *Ursa Major!*' (For Bonstetten's stay at Cambridge see Letter 512.)

[2] The incident which led to their becoming acquainted was described in his letter to Zchokke (see n. 1), which is quoted (in a French translation) by Dr. Marie L. Herking in *Charles Victor de Bonstetten, Sa Vie, Ses Œuvres*, Lausanne (1921): 'Je n'ai jamais trouvé autant de qualités de cœur qu'en Angleterre. . . . J'arrivais à Bath absolument inconnu, sans recommandation. . . . Dans ma pension j'avais fait la connaissance de quelques familles anglaises et irlandaises qui m'accueillirent comme un ami. A un grand bal, je montai sur une table pour mieux voir danser. Un jeune Anglais s'y était déjà installé. Pour ne pas tomber nous nous jetâmes dans les bras l'un de l'autre. Cet homme était Nicholls, l'ami et le confidant de Gray. . . . Nicholls resta mon ami jusqu'à sa fin, il se souvint même de moi dans son testament.'

England; he seems to have read, and to be unwilling now to waste his time if he knew how to employ it; I think he is vastly better than any thing English (of the same age) I ever saw; and then, I have a partiality to him because he was born among mountains; and talks of them with enthusiasm—of the forests of pines which grow darker and darker as you ascend, till the *nemorum nox*[3] is completed, and you are forced to grope your way; of the cries of eagles and other birds of prey adding to the horror; in short, of all the wonders of his country, which disturb my slumbers in Lovingland.[4] I made Wheeler[5] acquainted with him, who likes him as well as I, and has given him letters to Mr. Pitt[6] and to Mrs. Hay,[7] which have succeeded very well. When I go into Switzerland I am to be so directed! so recommended! and to travel with such advantages! but it is absolutely necefsary to pafs a month at Zurich to learn German; and the mountains must be traversed on foot; avec des Grimpons aux mains, and shoes of a peculiar construction. I'd give my ears to try.

So, because it would have given me infinite pleasure to have heard from the banks of Derwent Water, and because I gave you my direction, I was not to have a single line! for my part I would have told you long ago how I was pleased with the country about Southampton, delighted with Nettley Abbey, enchanted with the Isle of Wight, (where I pafsed three days alone searching every corner) how from thence I went to my cousin's in Dorsetshire,[8] stayed six weeks, and came hither on my cousin Fanny's[9] account; how pleased we were with Stour Head![10] how much more than pleased with Mr. Morrif's[11] (which we saw just when Autumn had begun to tinge the woods with a thousand beautiful varieties of colour) and with other

---

[3] Nicholls is quoting from Gray's *Alcaic Ode* (written in the Album of the Grande Chartreuse):

Inter aquas nemorumque noctem.

[4] See Letter 455, n. 3.   [5] See Letter 421, n. 18.

[6] Thomas Pitt of Boconnoc (see Letter 250, n. 12).

[7] This lady was perhaps a connexion of the Earl of Kinnoull (whose name was Hay), whom Pitt accompanied on his visit to Lisbon in 1760 (see Letter 308, n. 24).

[8] At Upwey (see Letter 500, n. 4).   [9] See Letter 422, n. 11.

[10] In Wiltshire, near Stourton, the seat of Richard Hoare, afterwards (1786) first Baronet of Stourhead.

[11] No doubt the Mr. Morris whose seat and the fine gardens made by him at Piercefield, near Chepstow, Nicholls visited again, in company with Gray, in 1770 (see Letter 530).

scenes on the Severn. All this and more I would have told you; and if I had been as tedious as an Emperor, I could have found in my heart to have bestowed it all upon you, only you took care to secure yourself by leaving me without a direction.

We leave this place on Wednesday se'nnight and shall be in town the Saturday after. God knows where you are, but if in town I shall have a chance of seeing you. We shall depart for Blundeston the Wednesday after.

This place (Bath) surprised and pleased me extremely at first. It was so new a sight to see a town built of hewn stone, instead of ragged and dirty brick, and streets and parades on a regular plan, and above all the circus, instead of the confused heap of buildings of all shapes and sizes which compose every other town in England. The neighbouring country is very pretty— hills of some height with cultivated valleys running among them, the principal one (which leads to Bristol) watered by the Avon. There are many fine trees in the hedge-rows; and some woods clothing the sides of the hills. I have seen Mr. Mason's monument for his wife,[12] and like it; but the medallion is I think too small; and the sculpture so small and delicate that it is seen to disadvantage at the height where it is placed.

Perhaps you will believe me if I say I long to see or hear from you! indeed I do most devoutly. I have a heart that would be much more at home at Pembroke Hall than it is at Bath. Adieu! my dear Sir, I am ever most faithfully yours,

N. N.

My mother and cousin send their compliments to you.

508*. GRAY TO WHARTON
(Journal continued).

OCT: 3. The hills here are cloth'd all up their steep sides with oak, ash, birch, holly, &c: some of it has been cut 40 years ago, some within these 8 years, yet all is sprung again green, flourishing, & tall for its age, in a place where no soil appears but the staring rock, & where a man could scarce stand upright.

Met a civil young Farmer overseeing his reapers (for it is oat-harvest here) who conducted us to a neat white house in the village of Grange, wch is built on a rising ground in the midst of

---

[12] In Bristol cathedral (see Letters 440, 444).

LETTER 508*.—First printed (in a garbled text) in Mason's *Memoirs*, pp. 357–60; now reprinted from original.

a valley. round it the mountains form an aweful amphitheatre, & thro' it obliquely runs the Darwent clear as glafs, & shewing under it's bridge every trout, that pafses. beside the village rises a round eminence of rock cover'd entirely with old trees, & over that more proudly towers *Castle-crag*, invested also with wood on its sides, & bearing on its naked top some traces of a fort said to be Roman. by the side of this hill, wch almost blocks up the way, the valley turns to the left & contracts its dimensions, till there is hardly any road but the rocky bed of the river. the wood of the mountains increases & their summits grow loftier to the eye, & of more fantastic forms: among them appear *Eagle's-cliff, Dove's-nest, Whitedale-pike,* &c: celebrated names in the annals of Keswick. the dale opens about four miles higher till you come to *Sea-Whaite* (where lies the way mounting the hills to the right, that leads to the *Wadd-mines*[1]) all farther accefs is here barr'd to prying Mortals, only there is a little path winding over the Fells, & for some weeks in the year pafsable to the Dale's-men; but the Mountains know well, that these innocent people will not reveal the mysteries of their ancient kingdom, the reign of Chaos & old Night.[2] only I learn'd, that this dreadful road dividing again leads one branch to *Ravenglas,*[3] & the other to *Hawkshead.*[4]

For me I went no farther than the Farmer's (better than 4 m: from Keswick) at *Grange*: his Mother & he brought us butter, that Siserah would have jump'd at, tho' not in a lordly dish, bowls of milk, thin oaten-cakes, & ale; & we had carried a cold tongue thither with us. our Farmer was himself the Man, that last year plunder'd the Eagle's eirie: all the dale are up in arms on such an occasion, for they lose abundance of lambs yearly, not to mention hares, partridge, grous, &c: he was let down from the cliff in ropes to the shelf of rock, on wch the nest was built, the people above shouting & hollowing to fright the old birds, wch flew screaming round, but did not dare to attack him. he brought off the eaglet (for there is rarely more than one) & an addle egg. the nest was roundish & more than a yard over, made of twigs twisted together. seldom a year pafses but they take the brood or eggs, & sometimes they shoot one, sometimes

---

[1] Wadd, or Wad, is the local name for plumbago or graphite, commonly known as blacklead.   [2] Milton, *Par. Lost,* i. 543.

[3] Ravenglass, on the Cumberland coast, about five miles north of Bootle.

[4] In Lancashire, about two miles west from Windermere, and about seven south from Ambleside.

the other Parent, but the surviver has always found a mate (probably in Ireland) & they breed near the old place. by his description I learn, that this species is the *Erne* (the Vultur *Albicilla* of Linnæus in his last edition,[5] but in yours *Falco Albicilla*) so consult him & Pennant[6] about it.

Walk'd leisurely home the way we came, but saw a new landscape: the features indeed were the same in part, but many new ones were disclosed by the mid-day Sun, & the tints were entirely changed. take notice this was the best or perhaps the only day for going up Skiddaw, but I thought it better employ'd: it was perfectly serene, & hot as midsummer.

In the evening walk'd alone down to the Lake by the side of *Crow-Park* after sunset & saw the solemn colouring of night draw on, the last gleam of sunshine fading away on the hill-tops, the deep serene of the waters, & the long shadows of the mountains thrown acrofs them, till they nearly touch'd the hithermost shore. at distance heard the murmur of many waterfalls not audible in the day-time.[7] wish'd for the Moon, but she was *dark to me & silent, hid in her vacant interlunar cave.*[8]

Oct: 4. W[d] E:, clouds & sunshine, & in the course of the day a few drops of rain. Walk'd to *Crow-park*, now a rough pasture, once a glade of ancient oaks, whose large roots still remain on the ground, but nothing has sprung from them. if one single tree had remain'd, this would have been an unparallel'd spot, & Smith[9] judged right, when he took his print of the Lake from

---

[5] The twelfth edition of his *Systema Naturæ* had been published at Stockholm in 1766–8.

[6] Thomas Pennant (1726–98), the well-known traveller and naturalist, a friend of Gilbert White (see Letter 465, n. 8). The work in question here was his *British Zoology* (Lond., fol., 1766; and 2 vols. 8vo., 1768).

[7] Wordsworth's lines in the *White Doe of Rylstone* (quoted by Mitford):

> A soft and lulling sound is heard
> Of streams inaudible by day (*Canto* IV)—

may have been suggested by this passage.

[8] Milton, *Samson Agonistes*:

> The Sun to me is dark
> And silent as the Moon
> When she deserts the night,
> Hid in her vacant interlunar cave
> (ll. 86–9).

[9] The landscape painter, Thomas Smith (d. 1767), known from his birthplace as 'Smith of Derby', was one of the earliest delineators of the beauties of English scenery, and had a great reputation in his day. Many of his drawings were engraved by Vivares (see 511A, n. 25) and others; he himself

hence, for it is a gentle eminence, not too high, on the very margin of the water & commanding it from end to end, looking full into the *gorge* of *Borodale*. I prefer it even to *Cockshut*-hill, wch lies beside it, & to wch I walk'd in the afternoon: it is cover'd with young trees both sown & planted, oak, spruce, scotch-fir, &c: all wch thrive wonderfully. there is an easy ascent to the top, & the view far preferable to that on Castle-hill (wch you remember) because this is lower & nearer to the Lake: for I find all points, that are much elevated, spoil the beauty of the valley, & make its parts (wch are not large) look poor & diminutive.[10] while I was here, a little shower fell, red clouds came marching up the hills from the east,[11] & part of a bright rainbow seem'd to rise along the side of Castle-hill.

From hence I got to the *Parsonage* a little before Sunset, & saw in my glafs a picture, that if I could transmitt to you, & fix it in all the softnefs of its living colours, would fairly sell for a thousand pounds. this is the sweetest scene I can yet discover in point of pastoral beauty. the rest are in a sublimer style.

(to be continued *without end.*)

P:S: I beg your pardon, but I have no franks. the quill arrived very safe, & doubtlefs is a very snug and commodious method of travelling, for one of the rarities was alive & hearty, & was three times plunged in spirits, before I could get it to die. you are much improved in observation, for a common eye would certainly take it for a pismire. the place of its birth, form of ye antennae, & abdomen, particularly the long *aculeus* under it, shew it to be a *Cynips* (look among the *Hymenoptera*) not yet compleat, for the 4 wings do not yet appear, that I see. it is not a species described by Linnæus, tho' he mentions others, that breed on the leaves, footstalks, buds, flowers & bark of the Oak.

engraved in 1767 from his own pictures a set of four views of the lakes of Cumberland, one of which doubtless was the print to which Gray here refers.

[10] Mason notes here: 'The *Picturesque Point* is always thus low in all prospects: A truth, which though the Landscape Painter knows, he cannot always observe; since the Patron who employs him to take a view of his place, usually carries him to some elevation for that purpose.'

[11] A reminiscence of Cowley, as appears from Gray's own note on l. 52 of his *Progress of Poesy*:

> Or seen the Morning's well-appointed Star
> Come marching up the eastern hills afar. *Cowley*—

which is a quotation (slightly altered) from stanza iv of Cowley's *Brutus, An Ode.*

remember me to Mrs Wharton & the family. my love to S^tr, if he has not left Durham. Adieu!

[Cambridge, Nov. 1769]¹²

509. GRAY TO MASON

Dear S^r   Dec: 2. 1769. Pemb: Coll:

I AM afraid something is the matter with you, that I hear nothing from you, since I pafs'd two days with you *in your absence*.¹ I am not in Ireland, as you perhaps might imagine by this natural sentence: but shall be as glad to hear from you, as if I were.

A week ago I saw something in the Newspaper sign'd *An Enemy to brick-walls in improper places.* while I was studying how (for brevity's sake) to translate this into Greek, Mr Brown did it in one word, Μασονίδης. I hope, it is not that complaint, hard (I must own) to digest, that sticks in your stomach, & makes you thus silent.

I am sorry to tell you, that I hear a very bad account of Dr Hurd: he was taken very ill at Thurcaston,² & obliged with difficulty to be carried in a chaise to Leicester. he remained there confined some time, before he could be convey'd on to London. as they do not mention, what his malady is, I am much afraid, it is a return of ye same disorder that he had last year in Town.³

I am going thither for a few days myself, & shall soon be able to tell you more of him.

Wyatt⁴ is return'd hither very calm, but melancholy, & looking dreadfully pale: he thinks of orders, I am told. Adieu! I am ever

Yours
T G:

¹² The letter is not dated: the reference at the end to Stonhewer being possibly still at Durham suggests that it was written not very long after his father's death (see Letter 507).

LETTER 509.—First printed by Mitford in *Gray–Mason* (1853), pp. 434–5; now reprinted from original.

¹ Gray is referring to the two days he spent at Mason's rectory at Aston in October, when he was received in Mason's absence by his curate, Alderson (see Letter 505 *ad fin.*).

² Hurd's rectory in Leicestershire (see Letter 231*, n. 1).

³ See Letter 489.

⁴ William Wyatt (d. 1813), of Pembroke College, Cambridge; B.A. 1762; Fellow, 1763; M.A. 1765. Cole's reference to him (*Add. MS.* 5876, f. 30) as

509*. H<small>URD TO</small> G<small>RAY</small>
Dear Sir

I TROUBLED you some time ago, by Mr Mason, with a petition on behalf of Mr T. Warton,[1] who is digesting his history of E. Poetry, and wishes very much to know what your idea was for the scheme of such a work.[2] I told him, I did not know what progre∫s you had made in that design, or whether you had drawn out a plan of it, but that, if you had, I believed you would readily acquaint him with it. This pa∫sed in the Summer, & since that I have heard nothing of him. But as I suppose you are now in college, after your various wanderings by sea and land, you will give me a pleasure to let me know what I shall

'one who has been deranged in his intellect' may explain Gray's allusion. In November of this year he was so heavily in debt that there was a College order sequestrating his dividends to pay his debts to Fellows and College servants. He did not take orders until 1782, when he was presented to the College living of Framlingham.

L<small>ETTER</small> 509*.—First printed in *Hurd–Mason Correspondence*, pp. 68–9.

[1] Thomas Warton (1728–90), younger son of Thomas Warton, the elder, and brother of Dr. Joseph Warton, Head Master of Winchester (see Letter 129, n. 18), entered Trinity College, Oxford, in 1744; B.A. 1747; M.A. 1750; Fellow, 1751; Professor of Poetry at Oxford, 1757–67; Camden Professor of Ancient History at Oxford, 1785–90; Poet Laureate, 1785–90; author of the *History of English Poetry* (1774–81).

[2] Hurd's request is explained by letters from Warton to Hurd (now at Hartlebury Castle, printed in *The Bodleian Quarterly Record*, Part VI, no. 72, 1931, pp. 303 ff.). Warton had for many years projected a history of English Poetry, and alludes to his scheme in Letters to Hurd of 1762, 1763, 1764. Gray had intended to collaborate with Mason in a work on the same subject, but when he published his *Poems* in 1768 announced that he had 'long since drop'd the design' (see Letter 245*, n. 4). On 26 July 1769 Warton wrote to Hurd from Winchester: 'When I had the pleasure of seeing you at Oxford, you very obligingly offered to ask Mr Gray for the plan he had formed of *The History of English Poetry*. I then told you my Resolutions of prosecuting that Subject: and am now retired into the Country on purpose to throw my materials into form, to finish a work to which my Studies have been long directed, under your kind encouragement & the flattering hopes of your Approbation.' Hurd, as he says, had sent Warton's request to Mason to be forwarded to Gray: on 25 Sept. Hurd wrote to Balguy giving a message for Thomas Warton, who was still at Winchester: 'I could not yet procure an answer from Mr Gray, who has been from Cambridge since the Commencement, and as Mason informs me is now rambling in the North . . . I dare say I shall easily prevail to have a copy of it (the scheme he had projected for himself in writing the History of English poetry) sent to Oxford' (Kilvert's *Memoirs of Hurd*, p. 105). Hurd now renewed his request, and within a few days after this letter saw Gray in London (Letter 510). Gray did not write to Warton until 15 April 1770 (Letter 518).

further say on this subject to Mr Warton. If you have any papers to communicate to him, & will send them to me, I will take care they shall be transmitted safely to Oxford. I believe I may answer to you for him, that he will make no improper use of your favours.

Of Mr Mason I hear nothing, except, by Dr Gisburne,[3] that he is now at Aston. He complains, that you and I are hypercritical, or rather hyper-political: But in this he is mistaken: We only wish to see his Georgic,[4] truly Virgilian.

Mr Nevile has sent me his *Imitations.*[5] They are not to be considered, as *Satires*, for popular reading; but as *clafsical amusements*, sometimes copying the sense, & sometimes the manner, of his originals. And in this light, they have frequently great merit.

You did not send me a copy of the Installation Ode; which piqued me, so much, that I was greatly disappointed when, with so good a disposition to find fault, I was obliged, with all the world, to commend & admire it

> I am very truly, Dear Sir,
> Your affectionate humble
> Servant

Lincoln's Inn,[6] Dec. 4, 1769　　　　　　R. HURD

Addressed: To Thomas Gray Esqr at Pembroke Hall, Cambridge; *readdressed:* Mr Roberts,[7] Hosier and Hatter, at the three Squirrels in Jermyn Street, London

510. GRAY TO MASON

Dear S^r　　　　　　　14 Dec: 1769. Jermyn-Street.

I HAVE seen Dr Hurd, & find the story I told you[1] is not true, tho' (I thought) I had it on very good authority. he was indeed

---

[3] See Letter 299, n. 10.

[4] Mason was at this time engaged upon his poem, *The English Garden*, the first book of which was published in 1772. In a note to his preface he speaks of it as being of 'that species of composition which has the *Georgics of Virgil* for its original'. He had, *more suo*, submitted it to Gray and Hurd for their criticism. Gray's opinion was not favourable. Nicholls in his *Reminiscences* says: 'Gray mentioned the Poem of the Garden to me with disapprobation, & said it should not be published if he could prevent it.'

[5] (See Letter 237*, n. 2.) His *Imitations of Juvenal and Persius* were published this year. He had published *Imitations of Horace* in 1758.

[6] Hurd had been appointed preacher at Lincoln's Inn in Nov. 1765.

[7] See Letter 176, n. 3.

LETTER 510.—First printed by Mitford in *Gray–Mason* (1853), p. 436; now reprinted from original.　　　　　　[1] See Letter 509.

ill at Thurcaston, but not so since, & walk'd an hour in Lincoln's-Inn walks with me very hearty, tho' his complexion presages no good. St: is come to town, & in good health. the weather & *the times* look very gloomy, & hang on my spirits, tho' I go to the Italian Puppet-Shew[2] (the reigning diversion) to exhilarate them. I return to Camb: on Tuesday next, where I desire you would send me a more exhilarating letter. Adieu, I am ever

Yours
T G:

All your acquaintances here are well: Ld Newnham[3] & Mr Ramsden,[4] & all.

511. GRAY TO WHARTON
Journal continued.

3 Jan: 1770. Pemb: C:

OCT: 5. W^d N:E: Clouds & sunshine. Walk'd thro' the meadows & corn-fields to the Derwent & crofsing it went up *How-hill*. it looks along Bafsinthwaite[1]-water & sees at the same time the course of the river & a part of the Upper-Lake with a full view of Skiddaw. then I took my way through Portingskall[2] village to the *Park*, a hill so call'd cover'd entirely with wood: it is all a mafs of crumbling slate. pafs'd round its foot between the trees & the edge of the water, & came to a Peninsula that juts out into the lake & looks along it both ways. in front rises Walla-crag, & Castle-hill, the Town, the road to

---

2 There was an exhibition of 'Italian Fantoccini' at Hickford's Room in Panton Street about 1770 (see *Notes and Queries*, 3rd series, vol. v, p. 32).

3 Viscount Nuneham (see Letter 197, n. 10).

4 Jesse Ramsden (1735–1800), famous optician and mechanician, born near Halifax, Yorks.; in 1758 he became apprentice to a mathematical instrument maker in London. Having married a daughter of John Dollond, F.R.S., the founder of the celebrated firm of opticians, about 1766 he opened a shop in the Haymarket. He took out patents for important improvements in astronomical instruments, and became renowned as an instrument maker throughout Europe. According to Gray, who complained of his dilatoriness, he was a favourite of Mason (see Letter 524 *ad fin.*).

LETTER 511.—First printed (in a garbled text) in Mason's *Memoirs*, pp. 360–4; now reprinted from original. The text, which is printed from Gray's transcript, which he sent to Wharton (see Letter 505, n. 1), deviates in some passages from that of the Murray note-books, chiefly in the omission of details. The more important omissions are recorded in the notes.

1 Bassenthwaite, out of the north end of which the Derwent flows.

2 Portinscale.

Penrith, Skiddaw & Saddleback. returning met a brisk and cold N: Eastern blast, that ruffled all the surface of ye lake and made it rise in little waves that broke at the foot of the wood. After dinner walked up the Penrith-road 2 miles or more & turning into a corn-field to the right, call'd Castle-Rigg, saw a Druid-Circle of large stones 108 feet in diameter, the biggest not 8 feet high, but most of them still erect: they are 50 in number. the valley of St John's appear'd in sight, & the summits[3] of *Catchidecam* (called by Camden, *Casticand*) & *Helvellyn*, said to be as high as *Skiddaw*, & to rise from a much higher base. a shower came on, & I return'd.

Oct: 6. W^d E: Clouds & sun. went in a chaise 8 miles along the east-side[4] of Bassingth: Water to *Ouse-Bridge* (pronounce *Ews-bridge*) the road in some part made & very good, the rest slippery & dangerous cart-road, or narrow rugged lanes but no precipices: it runs directly along the foot of Skiddaw. opposite to *Widhope-Brows*[5] (cloth'd to the top with wood) a very beautiful view opens down the Lake, wch is narrower & longer than that of Keswick, less broken into bays & without islands. at the foot of it a few paces from the brink gently sloping upward stands *Armathwate* in a thick grove of Scotch firs,[6] commanding a noble view directly up the lake. at a small distance behind the house is a large extent of wood, & still behind this a ridge of cultivated hills, on w^ch (according to the Keswick-proverb) *the Sun always shines.* the inhabitants here on the contrary call the vale of Derwent-water *the Devil's Chamber-pot*, & pronounce the name of *Skiddaw-fell* (wch terminates here) with a sort of terror & aversion. *Armathwate-House* is a modern fabrick, not large, & built of dark-red stone, belonging to Mr *Spedding*, whose Gr:father was Steward to old S^r *Ja: Lowther*,[7] & bought this estate of the *Himers.* so you must look for Mr Michell in some

---

[3] Murray MS.: 'the valley of *Naddle* appear'd in sight, and the fells of *St. John's*, particularly the summits etc.'

[4] The Murray MS. has 'W: side'—an obvious slip, Skiddaw being on the east side of the lake.

[5] Murray MS.: 'opposite to Thornthwait-fells and the brows of Widhope.'

[6] Murray MS: 'Scotch firs round it, & a large wood behind it. it looks directly up the whole length of the Lake almost to Keswick & beyond this a ridge of cultivated hills.'

[7] James Lowther (*c.* 1673–1755), fourth and last Baronet of Whitehaven (1731). On his death in 1755 his estates and a fortune estimated at two millions passed to his cousin, Sir James Lowther, fifth Baronet of Lowther (1751) (see Letter 475, n. 7).

other country. the sky was overcast & the wind cool, so after dining at a publick house, wch stands here near the bridge (that crofses the Derwent just where it ifsues from the lake) & sauntering a little by the water-side I came home again. the turnpike is finish'd from Cockermouth hither (5 miles) & is carrying on to Penrith. several little showers to-day. A Man came in, who said there was snow on *Crofs-fell* this morning.

Oct: 7. Market-day here. W^d N:E: Clouds & Sunshine. little showers at intervals all day. yet walk'd in the morning to Crow-park, & in the evening up Penrith-road. the clouds came rolling up the mountains all round very [unpromising];[8] yet the moon shone at intervals. it was too damp to go towards the lake. tomorrow mean to bid farewell to Keswick.

Botany might be studied here to great advantage at another season because of the great variety of soils & elevations all lieing within a small compafs. I observed nothing but several curious Lichens, & plenty of gale or Dutch myrtle perfuming the borders of ye lake. this year the Wadd[9] mine had been open'd (which is done once in 5 years) it is taken out in lumps sometimes as big as a man's fist, & will undergo no preparation by fire, not being fusible. when it is pure soft, black, & close-grain'd, it is worth sometimes 30 shillings a pound.[10] there are no Charr ever taken in these lakes, but plenty in Butter-mere-water, which lies a little way N: of Borrodale, about Martlemas,[11] wch are potted here. they sow chiefly oats & bigg[12] here, wch are now cutting, & still on the ground.[13] the rains have done much hurt; yet observe, the soil is so thin & light, that no day has pafs'd, in wch I could not walk out with ease, & you know, I am no lover of dirt.[14] Fell-mutton is now in season for about six weeks; it grows fat on ye mountains, & nearly resembles venison: excellent Pike & Perch (here called *Bafs*)[15] trout is out of season. partridge in great plenty.

[8] Supplied from the Murray MS. 'Very' comes at the end of a page in Gray's transcript, and he omitted to write the word he had in mind when he began the next page.

[9] See Letter 508*, n. 1.

[10] The Murray MS. has here: 'the mine lies about a mile up the Fells, near *See-wait* at the head of Borrodale.'

[11] Martinmas, 11 Nov.   [12] Four-rowed barley.

[13] The Murray MS. has here: 'there is some hay not yet got in.'

[14] The Murray MS. has here: 'their wheat comes from Cockermouth or Penrith.'

[15] Gray omitted the stop after 'Bass)'; 'trout' begins a new line.

Rec:ᵗ to drefs Perch (for Mʳˢ Wharton)

Wash, but neither scale, nor gut them. broil till enough; then pull out the fins, & open them along yᵉ back, take out the bone & all the inwards without breaking them. put in a large lump of butter & salt, clap thè sides together, till it melts, & serve very hot. it it excellent. the skin must not be eaten.[16]

Oct: 8. Left Keswick & took the Ambleside-road in a gloomy morning. Wᵈ E: & afterwᵈˢ N:E:. about 2 m: from the Town mounted an eminence call'd *Castle-rigg*, & the sun breaking out discover'd the most enchanting view I have yet seen of the whole valley behind me, the two lakes, the river, the mountains all in their glory! had almost a mind to have gone back again. the road in some few parts is not compleated, but good country-road thro' sound, but narrow & stony lanes, very safe in broad day-light. this is the case about *Causeway-foot* & among Naddle-Fells to *Lanewaite*. the vale you go in has little breadth, the mountains are vast & rocky, the fields little & poor, & the inhabitants are now making hay, & see not the sun by two hours in a day so long as at Keswick. came to the foot of Helvellyn along wᶜʰ runs an excellent road, looking down from a little height on *Lee's-water*[17] (call'd also Thirl-meer, or Wiborn[18]-water) & soon descending on its margin. the lake from its depth looks black (tho' really clear as glafs) & from the gloom of the vast crags, that scowl over it: it is narrow & about 3 miles long, resembling a river in its course. little shining torrents hurry down the rocks to join it, with not a bush to overshadow them, or cover their march. all is rock & loose stones up to the very brow, wᶜʰ lies so near your way, that not half the height of Helvellyn can be seen. . (to be continued, but now we have got franks)

Happy new year & many to you all. Hepatica & Mezereon[19] now in flower! I saw Mʳˢ Jonathan,[20] who is much fallen away, & was all in tears for the lofs of her Brother's child: she & Mifs

[16] At this point the first of the Murray note-books came to an end. At the beginning of the second one Gray wrote two pages of notes on the roads from Keswick, Kendal, &c., before continuing the *Journal*. These notes are printed by Tovey as if they were part of the *Journal* (vol. iii, pp. 247–8).

[17] Leatheswater (so called from the former owners) was, as Gray says below, one of the three names of Thirlmere.

[18] Wythburn.

[19] *Daphne mezereon*, also called *Dutch mezereon*.

[20] Wharton's sister-in-law (see Letter 116, n. 15).

Wilson[21] desired their compliments. your nephew[22] is here & very well. so is Mr Brown, who presents his best wishes.

Addressed (by Fraser): To Thos Wharton Es^q of Old Park near Darlington Durham   *Franked :* Free Wm Fraser   *Postmark :* CAMBRIDGE

511 A. [Continuation of Journal]

PAST by the little Chappel of Wiborn,[1] out of wch the Sunday-congregation were then ifsuing.

Past a beck near *Dunmail-raise*, & enter'd *Westmoreland* a second time. now begin to see *Helm-Crag* distinguish'd from its rugged neighbours not so much by its height, as by the strange broken outline of its top, like some gigantic building demolish'd, & the stones that composed it, flung crofs each other in wild confusion. just beyond it opens one of the sweetest landscapes, that art ever attempted to imitate. (the bosom of ye mountains spreading here into a broad bason) discovers in the midst Grasmere-water. its margin is hollow'd into small bays with bold eminences some of rock, some of soft turf, that half conceal, and vary the figure of the little lake they command, from the shore a low promon-

[21] Probably a sister of Mrs. Jonathan Wharton, whose maiden name was Wilson.

[22] Robert Wharton, at this time an undergraduate at Pembroke College (see Letter 336, n. 3).

LETTER 511 A.—First printed (in a garbled text) in Mason's *Memoirs*, pp. 364–79; now reprinted from Gray's original version in his note-book. This portion of the *Journal* in the Egerton MS. is not in Gray's hand, but is represented by the transcript which was made by Mason's curate, Alderson, and was sent to Wharton by Mason on 24 July 1770 (see Letter 505, n. 1). It is clear that Gray did not himself transcribe and send to Wharton this portion of the *Journal*, as he had done in the case of the preceding portions. He seems not to have written to Wharton again until 18 Apr. (Letter 519). In that letter he says: 'I have utterly forgot, where my journal left off, but (I think) it was after the account of Gordale near Settle. if so, there was little more worth your notice.' He then gives a summary of his journey from Skipton to Ottley (where the *Journal* ended) and on to Leeds, Aston, and Cambridge. His memory was at fault, if, as is assumed, he had not sent any part of his *Journal* after his account of the journey from Keswick to Wythburn. In June 1770 he met Wharton at Mason's house (Letter 514*) and may have then arranged for the transcript to be made. This concluding part of the *Journal* is here printed from the Murray note-book (see Letter 505, n. 1) with certain necessary corrections, which are noted. It does not, strictly speaking, form part of Gray's Correspondence, but it is included in order that the *Journal* may be given in its entirety.

[1] Wythburn, a village at the southern end of Thirlmere (see Letter 511, n. 18) close to where the Wyth Burn issues from the lake.

tory pushes itself far into the water, & on it stands a white
village with the parish-church rising in the midst of it, hanging
enclosures, corn-fields, & meadows green as an emerald with
their trees & hedges & cattle fill up the whole space from the
edge of the water & just opposite to you is a large farm-house
at the bottom of a steep smooth lawn embosom'd in old woods,
wch climb half way up the mountain's side, & discover above
them a broken line of crags, that crown the scene. not a single
red tile, no flaring Gentleman's house, or garden-walls, break
in upon the repose of this little unsuspected paradise, but all is
peace, rusticity, & happy poverty in its neatest most becoming
attire.

The road winds here over *Grasmere*-hill, whose rocks soon
conceal the water from your sight, yet it is continued along
behind them, & contracting itself to a river communicates with
Ridale-water, another small lake, but of inferior size & beauty.
it seems shallow too, for large patches of reeds appear pretty
far within it. into this vale the road descends. on the opposite
banks large & ancient woods mount up the hills, & just to the
left of our way stands *Rydale*-hall, the family-seat of Sr Mic:
Fleming,[2] but now a farm-house, a large old-fashion'd fabrick
surrounded with wood & not much too good for its present
destination. Sr Michael is now on his travels, & all this timber
far & wide belongs to him. I tremble for it, when he returns.
near the house rises a huge crag call'd *Rydale-head*, wch is said
to command a full view of Wynander-mere, & I doubt it not,
for within a mile that great Lake is visible even from the road.
as to going up the crag one might as well go up Skiddaw.

Came to Ambleside, 18 m: from Keswick meaning to lie
there, but on looking into the best bed-chamber dark & damp
as a cellar grew delicate, gave up Winandermere in despair &
resolved I would go on to *Kendal* directly, 14 m: farther. the
road in general fine turnpike, but some parts (about 3 m: in all)
not made, yet without danger.

Unexpectedly was well-rewarded for my determination. the
afternoon was fine, & the road for full 5 m: runs along the side
of Winder-mere with delicious views acrofs it & almost from one
end to the other. it is ten miles in length, & at most a mile over,
resembling the course of some vast & magnificent river, but
no flat marshy grounds, no osier-beds, or patches of scrubby
plantation on its banks. at the head two vallies open among the

---

[1] Sir Michael le Fleming, fourth Baronet of Rydal (1757–1806).

mountains, one that by wch we came down, the other *Langsledale*,[3] in w^{ch} *Wreenose*[4] & *Hard-Knot*, two great mountains, rise above the rest. from thence the fells visibly sink & soften along its sides, sometimes they run into it (but with a gentle declivity) in their own dark & natural complexion, oftener they are green & cultivated with farms interspersed & round eminences on the border cover'd with trees: towards the South it seem'd to break into larger bays with several islands & a wider extent of cultivation. the way rises continually till at a place call'd *Orrest-head* it turns to S:E: losing sight of the water.

Pafs'd by *Ings-Chappel*, & *Staveley*, but I can say no farther, for the dusk of evening coming on I enter'd *Kendal* almost in the dark, & could distinguish only a shadow of the Castle on a hill, & tenter-grounds[5] spread far & wide round the Town, wch I mistook for houses. my inn promised sadly having two wooden galleries (like Scotland) in front of it. it was indeed an old ill-contrived house, but kept by civil sensible people, so I stay'd two nights with them & fared & slept very comfortably.

Oct: 9. W^d N:W: clouds & sun. air mild as summer. all corn off the ground, sky-larks singing aloud (by the way I saw not one at Keswick, perhaps because the place abounds in birds of prey). went up the Castle-hill. the Town consists chiefly of three nearly parallel streets almost a mile long. except these all the other houses seem as if they had been dancing a country-dance & were out: there they stand back to back, corner to corner, some up hill, some down without intent or meaning. along by their side runs a fine brisk stream, over which are 3 stone-bridges. the buildings (a few comfortable houses excepted) are mean, of stone & cover'd with a bad rough-cast. near the end of the Town stands a handsome house of Col: Wilson's, & adjoining to it the Church, a very large Gothick fabrick with a square Tower. it has no particular ornaments but double isles, & at the east-end 4 chappels, or choirs. one of the *Pars*, another of the *Stricklands*, the 3^d is the proper choir of ye church, & the 4th of y^e *Bellingcams*, a family now extinct. [6]there

---

[3] A mistake for Langdale. Longsleddale is in a different part of the district.   [4] Corrected in the Alderson transcript to 'Wrynose'.

[5] A 'tenter' is a wooden framework on which cloth is stretched after being milled, so that it may dry evenly; rows of these, of the length of a web of cloth, formerly used to stand in open spaces, hence known as 'tenter-grounds', outside the town where the cloth was manufactured.

[6] The passage referring to the altar tombs (the next seventeen lines) was omitted in the transcript.

is an altar-tomb of one of them dated 1577 with a flat brafs, arms & quarterings. & in the window their arms alone, Arg: a hunting-horn, sab: strung Gules. in the *Strickland's* chappel several modern monuments, & another old altar-tomb, not belonging to the family: on the side of it, a Fefs dancetty between 10 Billets (Deincourt?)[7] in the *Parr*-chappel is a third altar-tomb in the corner, no fig: or inscription, but on the side cut in stone an escutcheon of *Roos* of Kendal (3 Water-Budgets) quartering *Parr* (2 bars in a bordure engrail'd). 2dly an escutcheon, Vaire, a Fefs (for Marmion). 3dly. an escutcheon. three Chevronels braced & a Chief (wch I take for Fitzhugh) at the foot is an escutcheon surrounded with the Garter, bearing *Roos* & *Parr* quarterly, quartering the other two beforemention'd. I have no books to look in, therefore can not say, whether this is the Ld *Parr of Kendal* (Queen Catharine's Father) or her Brother, the Marquis of *Northampton*. it is a Cenotaph for the latter, who was buried at Warwick in 1571.[8] the remains of the Castle are seated on a fine hill on the side of the river opposite to the Town. almost the whole enclosure of walls remains with 4 towers, 2 square & 2 or 3 round, but their upper part & embattlements are demolished. it is of rough stone & cement, without any ornament or arms, round enclosing a court of like form & surrounded by a mote, nor ever could have been larger than it is, for there are no traces of outworks. there is a

[7] Thomas West (1720–79) in his *Guide to the Lakes in Cumberland, Westmorland and Lancashire* (4th ed. 1789, p. 176), after quoting Gray's account explains: 'This Tomb is probably of Ralph D'Aincourt, who in the reign of King John married Helen, daughter of Anselm de Furness, whose daughter and sole heir, Elizabeth, married William, son of Sir Robert de Strickland, of Great Strickland, knight, 23 of Henry iii. The son and heir was Walter de Strickland, who lived in the reign of Edward i, . . . erected the above tomb to the memory of his grandfather Ralph d'Aincourt. The descendants of the said Walter de Strickland have lived at Sizergh, in this neighbourhood ever since, and this chapel is the family burying place.' (West's note is quoted (with some variations) by Mitford (1835–43), vol. iv, p. 176, from a MS. note of T. D. Whitaker (see Letter 412, n. 5).)

[8] Mitford here quotes the following MS. note of Whitaker: 'Mr Gray's mistake is very excusable; but 1st, it is highly improbable that it should be a cenotaph for William Parr, Marquis of Northampton [1513–71], as there is no quartering of Bourchier Earl of Essex. 2nd. It is not the tomb of Sir Thomas Parr, father of Queen Catherine (by the way he was not Lord Parr of Kendal), for he was never Knight of the Garter; but in all probability it belongs to Sir William Parr, father of Sir Thomas, who was installed Knight of the Garter, An. [13], Edw. IV. and married Elizabeth, daughter of Richard Lord Fitzhugh.'

good view of the town & river with a fertile open valley, thro wch it winds.

After dinner went along the Milthrop[9]-turnpike 4 m: to see the falls (or force) of the river *Kent.* came to *Siserge* (pronounce Siser) & turn'd down a lane to the left. Siser, the seat of the *Stricklands*[10] an old Catholick family, is an ancient Hall-house, with a very large tower embattled: the rest of the buildings added to this are of later date, but all is white & seen to advantage on a back ground of old trees: there is a small park also wellwooded. opposite to this turn'd to the left & soon came to the river. it works its way in a narrow & deep rocky channel o'erhung with trees. the calmnefs & brightnefs of ye evening, the roar of the waters, & the thumping of huge hammers at an iron-forge not far distant made it a singular walk, but as to the falls (for there are two) they are not 4 feet high. I went on down to the forge & saw the Dæmons at work by the light of their own fires: the iron is brought in pigs to Milthrop by sea from Scotland &c. & is here beat into bars & plates. two miles farther at *Levens* is the seat of Ld Suffolk,[11] where he sometimes pafses the summer. it was a favourite place of his late Countefs: but this I did not see.

Oct: 10. went by *Burton* to Lancaster. W^d N:W: clouds & sun. 22 m: very good country well enclosed & wooded with some common interspersed. pafs'd at the foot of *Farlton-Knot,* a high fell. 4 m: N: of Lancaster on a rising ground call'd *Bolton* (pron: *Bouton*)-*Wait* had a full view of *Cartmell-sands* with here and there a Pafsenger riding over them (it being low water) the points of Furnefs shooting far into the sea, & lofty mountains partly cover'd with clouds extending North of them. Lancaster also appear'd very conspicuous & fine, for its most distinguish'd features the Castle & Church, mounted on a green eminence, were all, that could be seen. woe is me! when I got thither, it was the second day of their fair. the Inn (in the principal street) was a great old gloomy house full of people, but I found tolerable quarters, & even slept two nights in peace.

Ascended the Castle-hill in a fine afternoon. it takes up the higher top of the eminence on wch it stands, & is irregularly

---

[9] Milnthorpe.   [10] See n. 7.
[11] Thomas Howard (1721–83), fourteenth Earl of Suffolk. 'His Countess' was Elizabeth, daughter of William Kingscote, of Kingscote, Gloucestershire, who died in 1769. Their daughter Diana married Sir Michael le Fleming (see n. 2).

round, encompafsed with a deep mote. in front towards the Town is a magnificent Gothick Gateway, lofty & huge, the overhanging battlements are supported by a triple range of corbels, the intervals pierced thro' & shewing the day from above. on its top rise light watchtowers of small height. it opens below with a grand pointed arch: over this is a wrought tabernacle, doubtlefs once containing the Founders figure, on one side a shield of France semy quarter'd with England, on the other the same with a label ermine for John of Gant D: of Lancaster. this opens to a court within, wch I did not much care to enter, being the County Gaol & full of Prisoners, both Criminals & Debtors. from this gateway the walls continue & join it to a vast square tower of great height, the lower part at least of remote antiquity, for it has small round-headed lights with plain short pillars on each side of them, there is a third tower also square & of lefs dimensions. this is all the castle, near it & but little lower stands the Church, a large & plain Gothic fabrick, the high square Tower at the West-end has been rebuilt of late years, but nearly in the same style. there are no ornaments of arms, &c: any where to be seen. within it is light-some & spacious, but not one monument of antiquity, or piece of painted glafs is left. from the Church-yard there is an exten-sive sea-view (for now the tide had almost cover'd the sands, & fill'd the river) & besides greatest part of Furnefs I could dis-tinguish *Peel*-Castle on the isle of Fowdrey,[12] wch lies off its southern extremity. the Town is built on the slope & at the feet of the Castle-hill more than twice the bignefs of Aukland with many neat buildings of white stone, but a little disorderly in their position ad libitum like Kendal. many also extend below on the keys by the river-side, where a number of ships were moor'd, some of them three-mast vefsels deck'd out with their colours in honor of the Fair. here is a good bridge of 4 arches over the *Lune*, wch runs (when the tide is out) in two streams divided by a bed of gravel, wch is not cover'd but in spring-tides. below the town it widens to near the breadth of ye Thames at London, & meets the sea at 5 or 6 m: distance to S:W:

Oct: 11. W^d S:W: clouds & sun. warm & a fine dappled sky. crofs'd the river & walk'd over a peninsula 3 miles to the village of *Pooton* wch stands on the beach. an old Fisherman mending his nets (while I enquired about the danger of pafsing those

12 Foulney.

sands) told me in his dialect a moving story, how a brother of the trade, a *Cockler* (as he styled him) driving a little cart with two daughters (women grown) in it, & his Wife on horseback following, set out one day to pafs the 7 mile sands, as they had frequently been used to do, for nobody in the village knew them better than the old Man did. when they were about half way over, a thick fog rose, & as they advanced, they found the water much deeper than they expected. the old man was puzzled, he stop'd, & said he would go a little way to find some mark he was acquainted with. they staid a little while for him, but in vain. they call'd aloud, but no reply. at last the young women prefs'd their mother to think, where they were, & go on. she would not leave the place, she wander'd about forlorn & amazed, she would not quit her horse, & get into the cart with them. they determined after much time wasted to turn back, & give themselves up to the guidance of their horses. the old Woman was soon wash'd off and perish'd. the poor Girls clung close to their cart, & the horse sometimes wading & sometimes swimming brought them back to land alive, but senselefs with terror & distrefs & unable for many days to give any account of themselves. the bodies of their parents were found soon after;[13] that of the Father a very few paces distant from the spot, where he had left them.[14]

In the afternoon wander'd about the town & by the key till it grew dark. a little rain fell.

Oct: 11 [12][15] W^d N:E: sky gloomy, then gleams of sunshine. set out for *Settle* by a fine turnpike road, 29 miles.

Rich & beautiful enclosed country diversified with frequent villages & churches, very unequal ground, & on the left the river Lune winding in a deep valley, its hanging banks clothed with fine woods, thro' wch you catch long reaches of the water, as the road winds about at a considerable height above it. pafs'd the *Park* (Hon: Mr Clifford's, a catholick) in the most picturesque part of the way. the grounds between him & the

13 The MS. has 'next ebb' written above the line as an explanation of 'soon after'.

14 In the MS. there followed: '& all the village mourned over them', which was scored through.

15 The MS. has '11', an obvious error, which is corrected in the transcript. Gray stayed two nights at Lancaster as he says above. The events of two days are entered as 'Oct 11'. The error affects the dates of the three days following, 11, 12, 13. The dates are ultimately corrected, by a duplicated entry for 14 Oct. (see n. 30).

river are indeed charming: the house is ordinary, & the park nothing but a rocky fell scatter'd over with ancient hawthorns. came to *Hornby* a little Town on the river Wanning, over wch a handsome bridge is now in building. the Castle in a lordly situation attracted me, so I walkd up the hill to it. first presents itself a large but ordinary white Gentleman's house sash'd. behind it rises the ancient Keep built by Edward Stanley, Lord Mounteagle[16] (inscribed Helas et quand?) he died about 1524 in Henry the 8th's time. it is now a shell only, tho' rafters are laid within it as for flooring. I went up a winding stone-staircase in one corner to the leads, & at the angle is a single hexagon watch-tower rising some feet higher, fitted up in the tast of a modern *Toot*[17] with sash-windows in gilt frames, & a stucco cupola, & on the top a vast gilt eagle by Mr *Charteris*,[18] the present Pofsefsor. but he has not lived here since the year 1745, when the people of Lancaster insulted him, threw stones into his coach, & almost made his Wife (Lády Katherine Gordon) miscarry. since that he has built a great ugly house of red stone (thank God it is not in England) near Haddington, wch I remember to have pafs'd by.[19] he is the 2^d Son of the Earl of Wemyfs, & brother to the Ld Elcho, Grandson to Col: Charteris,[20] whose name he bears.

From the leads of the Tower there is a fine view of the country round, & much wood near the castle. Ingleborough, wch I had

---

[16] Gray wrote originally 'one of the Stanleys: Lords Morley and Mounteagle'. It was so transcribed by Alderson, but the MS. is there corrected (apparently in Mason's hand) to 'Edward Stanley: Lord Mounteagle'. Edward Stanley, the Stanley of Scott's *Marmion*, distinguished himself at the battle of Flodden in 1513; he was created K.G. and Lord Monteagle in the following year, and died in 1523.

[17] A look-out, belvedere.

[18] Hon. Francis Charteris (formerly Wemyss) (1723–1808), second son of James Wemyss (1699–1756), fifth Earl of Wemyss (1720), and Janet, only daughter and heiress of Colonel Francis Charteris (see n. 20). On the death, in 1732, of his maternal grandfather, Colonel Francis Charteris (see n. 20), he inherited his estates, and assumed the name of Charteris. His elder brother, Lord Elcho, joined in the Jacobite rising in 1745, but escaped abroad after the battle of Culloden, and was attainted, the peerage which devolved upon him at the death of his father becoming thereby forfeited. On the death of Lord Elcho in Paris in 1787, Francis Charteris, who in 1745 married Lady Catherine Gordon, daughter of the second Duke of Gordon, became *de jure* Earl of Wemyss, and assumed the title.

[19] Gray saw it on his Scotch tour (see Appendix Q, n. 3).

[20] Colonel Francis Charteris (1675–1732) the notorious profligate of Arbuthnot, Pope, and Hogarth.

seen before distinctly at Lancaster to N:E: was now compleatly wrap'd in clouds all but its summit, wch might have been easily mistaken for a long black cloud too, fraught with an approaching storm. now our road begun gradually to mount towards the *Apennine*, the trees growing lefs, and thinner of leaves, till we came to Ingleton 18 m: it is a pretty village situated very high & yet in a valley at the foot of that huge creature of God *Ingleborough*. two torrents crofs it with great stones roll'd along their bed instead of water: over them are two handsome arches flung. here at a little ale-house were Sr Bellingcam Graham[21] & Mr Parker, L^d of ye Manour (one of them 6 feet ½ high, & the other as much in breadth) come to dine.

The nipping air (tho' the afternoon was growing very bright) now taught us, we were in Craven. the road was all up & down (tho' no where very steep). to the left were mountain-tops (Weryside),[22] to the right a wide valley (all inclosed ground) & beyond it high hills again. in approaching Settle the crags on the left drew nearer to our way, till we ascended *Brunton-brow*, into a chearful valley (tho' thin of trees) to *Giggleswick* a village with a small piece of water by its side cover'd over with coots. near it a Church, wch belongs also to *Settle* & half a mile farther having pafsed the *Ribble* over a bridge arrived at *Settle*. it is a small market-town standing directly under a rocky fell. there are not a dozen good-looking houses, the rest are old & low with little wooden portico's in front. my inn pleased me much (tho' small) for the neatnefs & civility of the good Woman that kept it, so I lay there two nights, & went

Oct: 12 [13][23] to visit *Gordale-Scar*. W^d N:E: day gloomy & cold. it lay but 6 m: from Settle, but that way was directly over a Fell, & it might rain, so I went round in a chaise the only way one could get near it in a carriage, wch made it full 13 m: & half of it such a road! but I got safe over it, so there's an end, & came to *Malham* (pronounce *Maum*) a village in the bosom of the mountains seated in a wild & dreary valley. from thence I was to walk a mile over very rough ground, a torrent rattling along on the left hand. on the cliffs above hung a few goats:

[21] The MS. has 'Bellingcam'.

[22] Gray inserted 'Weryside' above the line in explanation of 'mountain-tops'. The mountain-group in question is obviously Whernside, the situation of which exactly answers to Gray's description of his route from Ingleton to Giggleswick and Settle. Gray presumably wrote the name according to the local pronunciation, or what he took to be such.

[23] See n. 15.

one of them danced & scratched an ear with its hind-foot in a
place where I would not have stood stock-still

for all beneath the moon.[24]

as I advanced the crags seem'd to close in, but discover'd
a narrow entrance turning to the left between them. I followed
my guide a few paces, & lo, the hills open'd again into no large
space, & then all farther way is bar'd by a stream, that at the
height of about 50 feet gushes from a hole in the rock, & spread-
ing in large sheets over its broken front dashes from steep to
steep, & then rattles away in a torrent down the valley. the
rock on the left rises perpendicular with stubbed yew-trees &
shrubs, staring from its side to the height of at least 300 feet.
but these are not the thing! it is that to the right, under wch you
stand to see the fall, that forms the principal horror of the
place. from its very base it begins to slope forwards over you
in one black & solid mafs without any crevice in its surface,
& overshadows half the area below with its dreadful canopy.
when I stood at (I believe) full 4 yards distance from its foot,
the drops wch perpetually distill from its brow, fell on my head,
& in one part of the top more exposed to the weather there
are loose stones that hang in air, & threaten visibly some idle
Spectator with instant destruction. it is safer to shelter yourself
close to its bottom, & trust the mercy of that enormous mafs,
wch nothing but an earthquake can stir. the gloomy uncomfort-
able day well suited the savage aspect of the place, & made it
still more formidable. I stay'd there (not without shuddering) a
quarter of an hour, & thought my trouble richly paid, for the
imprefsion will last for life. at the alehouse where I dined, in
Malham, Vivares,[25] the landscape-painter, had lodged for a
week or more. Smith[26] & Bellers[27] had also been there, & two
prints of Gordale have been engraved by them. return'd to my
comfortable inn. night fine, but windy & frosty.

Oct: 13 [14].[28] Went to Skipton, 16 miles. W^d N:E: gloomy,

---

[24] *King Lear*, iv. 6:
                    For all beneath the moon
        Would I not leap upright.

[25] François Vivares (1709–80), who made a great reputation by his
engravings of English scenery.

[26] Smith of Derby (see Letter 508*, n. 9).

[27] William Bellers (*fl.* 1761–74), landscape painter; eight views of the
Cumberland and Westmorland lakes were engraved after paintings by him.

[28] MS. '13' (see n. 15).

at one o'clock a little sleet falls. from several parts of the road, & in many places about Settle I saw at once the three famous hills of this country, Ingleborough, Penigent, & Pendle, the first is esteem'd the highest. their features are hard to describe, but I could trace their outline with a pencil.[29]

Craven after all is an unpleasing country, when seen from a height. its valleys are chiefly wide & either marshy, or enclosed pasture with a few trees. numbers of black Cattle are fatted here, both of the Scotch breed, & a larger sort of oxen with great horns. there is little cultivated ground, except a few oats.

[[Oct: 14. W^d N:E: gloomy. at noon a few grains of sleet fell, then bright & clear. Went thro' Long-Preston & Gargrave to]]^30 *Skipton* [[16 miles. it]]^30 is a pretty large Market-Town in a valley with one very broad street gently sloping downwards from the Castle, wch stands at the head of it. this is one of our

---

29 The sketch is reproduced from the Murray MS.

30 The words in double brackets should be omitted. Gray by an oversight recorded in the Murray MS. his journey to Skipton under two dates, 13 Oct. and 14 Oct. The error may have been induced by the fact that he had entered the events of 12, 13, 14 Oct. under the dates of 11, 12, 13 Oct. (see n. 15). After beginning his account of the journey to Skipton under 13 Oct. (which should have been 14 Oct.) he must have broken off: when he resumed, he was probably conscious that he did not go to Skipton till 14 Oct., and without reading what he had already written under 'Oct. 13' entered his journey to Skipton again, this time with the right date. This had the effect of correcting, for the journey to Skipton, the error of date which he had made in the three previous days. In the Alderson transcript the dates of the Murray MS. of 11, 12, 13 Oct. were corrected to 12, 13, 14 Oct., but the repetition of the journey to Skipton was left uncorrected and entered on two days, 14, 15 Oct. Mason in his version corrected both sets of errors. Later editors have overlooked the duplication of the entry for the journey to Skipton under two dates.

good Countefse's[31] buildings, but on old foundations: it is not very large, but of a handsome antique appearance with round towers, a grand Gateway, bridge & mote, & many old trees about it, in good repair, & kept up, as a habitation of the Earl of Thanet,[32] tho' he rarely comes thither. what with the sleet & a foolish dispute about chaises, that delay'd me, I did not see the inside of it, but went on 15 miles to *Ottley*. first up *Shode-bank*, the steepest hill I ever saw a road carried over in England, for it mounts in a strait line (without any other repose for the horses, than by placing stones every now & then behind the wheels) for a full mile. then the road goes on a level along the brow of this high hill over Rumbald-moor, till it gently descends into *Wharldale*: so they call the Vale of the Wharf, & a beautiful vale it is, well-wooded, well-cultivated, well-inhabited, but with high crags at distance, that border the green country on either hand. thro' the midst of it deep, clear, full to the brink, & of no inconsiderable breadth runs in long windings the river. how it comes to pafs that it should be so fine & copious a stream here, & at Tadcaster (so much lower) should have nothing but a wide stony channel without water, I can not tell you. I pafs'd through *Long-Addingham*, *Ilkeley* (pronounce *Eecla*) distinguish'd by a lofty brow of loose rocks to the right, *Burley*, a neat & pretty village among trees. on the opposite side of the river lay *Middleton*-Lodge, belonging to a Catholick Gentleman of that name; *Weston*, a venerable stone-fabrick with large offices, of Mr Vavasor, the meadows in front gently descending to the water, & behind a great & shady wood. Farnley (Mr Fawke's)[33]

[31] This was Anne Clifford (1590–1676), *suo jure* Baroness Clifford, only daughter and heiress of George Clifford, third Earl of Cumberland; she married, (1) in 1609, Richard Sackville, third Earl of Dorset (d. 1624); (2) in 1630, Philip Herbert, fourth Earl of Pembroke and Montgomery (d. 1650). She died at Brougham Castle in 1676, in her eighty-seventh year, and was buried in the Church of St. Lawrence, Appleby. She resided at fixed times at each one of her six castles, Skipton, Appleby, Brougham, Brough, Pendragon, and Bardon Tower, all of which (besides several churches connected with her estates) she repaired. In her sixty-third year she compiled her autobiography, of which there is a transcript in the British Museum (*D.N.B.*). Gray calls her 'our good Countess', because, when he and Wharton were at Appleby together in 1767, he had written a burlesque epitaph on her (see Letter 453, n. 3).

[32] Sackville Tufton (1733–86), eighth Earl of Thanet (1753); his father, the seventh Earl, was nephew of the sixth Earl, who was Lord Clifford, in right of his descent from Anne, Countess of Dorset and of Pembroke and Montgomery, who was Baroness Clifford in her own right (see n. 31).

[33] The representative of the family at this date appears to have been

a place like the last, but larger, & rising higher on the side of the hill. *Ottley* is a large airy Town, with clean but low rustick buildings, & a bridge over the Wharf. I went into its spatious Gothic Church, wch has been new-roof'd with a flat stucco ceiling. in a corner of it is the monument of Tho: Ld Fairfax,[34] & Helen Aske, his Lady, descended from the Cliffords & Latimers, as her epitaph says. the figures not ill-cut particularly his in armour, but bare-headed, lie on the tomb. I take them for the Grand Parents[35] of the famous Sr Tho: Fairfax.[36]

512. BONSTETTEN[1] AND GRAY TO NICHOLLS
Cambridge the 6. Jan. 1770.

H ENCE vain deluding Joys[2] is our motto hier, written on every feature, and ourly spoken by every solitary Chapel bel; So that decently you cant expect no other but a very grave letter.

Walter Ramsden Beaumont Fawkes, who took the name and arms of Fawkes in lieu of Hawkesworth, in compliance with the will of his cousin, Francis Fawkes of Farnley.

³⁴ Thomas Fairfax (1560–1640); first Lord Fairfax of Cameron, 1627; he married in 1562 Ellen, daughter of Robert Aske, of Aughton, co. York, who died in 1620.

³⁵ In the transcript and in Mason's printed version 'Parents' (an obvious error).

³⁶ Thomas Fairfax (1612–71), third Lord Fairfax of Cameron (1648), the famous Parliamentary General; he was the son of Ferdinando Fairfax, second Lord Fairfax (d. 1648), who was the eldest son of the first Lord mentioned above.

At this point both the Murray MS. and the Egerton transcript come to an end. A brief summary of the rest of his journey Gray sent to Wharton on 18 Apr. 1770 (Letter 519).

LETTER 512.—First printed by Mitford (1835–43), vol. v, pp. 101–3; now reprinted from original.

¹ After Gray had made Bonstetten's acquaintance in London (see Letter 508, n. 1) Bonstetten went with him to Cambridge about 21 Dec. 1769 and stayed there (except for a brief absence, see Letter 512**) for the next three months. Of his life in Cambridge, of which this letter gives a lively account, we have information in his letter to his mother of 6 Feb. (printed in Appendix V), in *Erinnerungen aus Bonstetten's Jugendleben von ihm selbst geschrieben* (Zürich, 1826), and in *Souvenirs de Ch. Victor de Bonstetten écrites en 1831* (Paris, 1831). While in Cambridge he lodged in a coffee-house near Pembroke College, where at first he had his meals and pursued his studies, visiting Gray 'de cinq heures à minuit', as he says in his *Souvenirs*. After a time he seems to have spent more time with Gray, for in his letter to his mother he writes: 'Je mange tous les jours chez lui, je vais chez lui à toute heure, il lit avec moi ce que je veux, je travaille dans sa chambre.' In a passage in his *Souvenirs*, p. 116, he records the impression which Cambridge had left on his mind

I realy beg you pardon to wrap up my thoughts in so smart a drefs as an in quarto sheet. I know they should apear in a folio leave, but the Ideas themselves shall look so solemn as to belie their drefs.—Tho' I wear not yet the black gown, and am only an inferior Priest in the temple of Meditation, yet my countenance is already consecrated. I never walk but with even steps and musing gate, and looks comercing with the skyes; and unfold my wrinkles only when I see mr. Gray, or think of you. Then nothwithstanding all your learnings and knowledge, I feel in such occasions that I have a heart, which you know is as some others a quite prophane thing to carry under a black gown. I am in a hurry from morning till evening.[3] At 8 o Clock I am roused by a young square Cap, with whom I follow Satan through Chaos and night. He explaind me in Greek and latin, the *sweet reluctant amorous Delays* of our Grandmother Eve. We finish our travels in a copious breakfeast of muffins and tea. Then apears Shakespair and old Lineus[4] struling together as

sixty years later: 'Gray y vivait enseveli dans une espèce de cloître, d'où le quinzième siècle n'avait pas encore déménagé. La ville de Cambridge, avec ses colléges solitaires, n'était qu'une réunion de couvens, où les mathé-matiques, et quelques sciences, ont pris la forme et le costume de la théo-logie du moyen âge. De beaux couvens à longs et silencieux corridors, des solitaires en robe noire, de jeunes seigneurs travestis en moines à bonnets carrés, partout des souvenirs de moines à côté de la gloire de Newton.' Of Gray himself he wrote: 'Je racontais à Gray ma vie et mon pays, mais toute sa vie à lui était fermeé pour moi; jamais il ne me parlait de lui. Il y avait chez Gray entre le présent et le passé un abîme infranchissable. Quand je voulais en approcher, de sombres nuées venaient le couvrir. Je crois que Gray n'avait jamais aimé, c'était le mot de l'énigme; il en était résulté une misère de cœur, qui faisait contraste avec son imagination ardente et pro-fonde qui, au lieu de faire le bonheur de sa vie, n'était que le tourment. Gray avait de la gaieté dans l'esprit et de la mélancolie dans le caractère. Mais cette mélancolie n'est qu'un besoin non satisfait de la sensibilité. Chez Gray elle tenait au genre de vie de son âme ardente, reléguée sous le pôle arctique de Cambridge.'

[2] Bonstetten's study of Milton is reflected in his quotations from *Il Penseroso* here, and below: 'looks commercing with the skies' (ll. 38–9); and from *Paradise Lost*: 'Chaos and night' ('the reign of Chaos and old Night', i. 543) and 'sweet amorous delays' ('sweet, reluctant, amorous delays'. iv. 311).

[3] Some evidence of his labours is given by the Pembroke College Library Register, which records the loan to Mr. Bonstetten of Johnson's *Dictionary* and *Biographica Britannica*.

[4] Mitford, *Gray–Mason* (1853), p. 481, quotes Cole: 'Mr Miller, who was curator of the physic garden at Cambridge, gave lectures on botany and on Linnæus to a Mons. Bonstetten, who studied at Cambridge for some months. . . . He was a most studious young gentleman, of a most amiable figure. . . . Mr Miller read lectures to him to the very last day of his being at

two ghost would do for a damned Soul. Sometimes the one get the better sometimes the other. Mr Gray, whose acquaintance is my greatest debt to you, is so good as to shew me Macbeth, and all witches Beldams, Ghost and Spirits, whose language I never could have understood without his Interpretation. I am now endeavouring to drefs all those people in a french drefs, which is a very hard labour.

I am afraid to take a room, which Mr. Gray shall keep still much better. So I stop hier my everrambling pen. My respectful Compliments to M.ᵈ Nichole. Only remember that you have no where a better or more grateful friend than your de Bonstetten.—I loosd Mr. Wheeler⁵ letter and his direction.

⁶I never saw such a boy: our breed is not made on this model. he is busy from morn[ing] to night, has no other amusement, than tha[t] of changing one study for another, like[s] nobody, that he sees here, & yet wishes to stay longer, tho' he has pafs'd a whole fortnight with us already. his letter has had no correction whatever, & is prettier by half than English.

Would not you hazard your journal: I want to see, what you have done this summer tho' it would be safer & better to bring it yourself, methinks!

Complimens respectueux à Mad: Nichole, & à notre aimable Cousine, la *Sposa*.⁷

Addressed (by Gray): To The Revᵈ Mʳ Nicholls at Blundeston near Leostoff Suffolk by Yarmouth   *Postmark:* CAMBRIDGE

512*. GRAY TO LORT¹

Mʳ GRAY presents his humble services to Prof.ʳ Lort, is much obliged to him for his politenefs in inviting Mʳ Bonstetten, but the day is so bad that Gentleman desires to be excused at

Cambridge.' Gray in his letter to Nicholls of 14 Apr. (Letter 517) refers to the 'five lessons from Miller' that Bonstetten had.

⁵ See Letter 508, n. 5.

⁶ Gray wrote the postscript and the address.

⁷ No doubt a reference to the engagement of Nicholls's 'cousin Fanny' (see Letters 422 and 477), whose marriage took place on 17 Mar. following (see Letter 533, n. 9).

LETTER 512*.—First printed in Messrs. Sotheby's catalogue of 18 Nov. 1929 (Lot 170).

¹ Michael Lort, Professor of Greek at Cambridge (see Letter 479, n. 8).

Charles Victor de Bonstetten, as Hamlet,
from a painting in the possession of M. Wolfgang de Reding-Biberegg,
Schwyt, Switzerland

present. Mr Gray himself intends to dine at Trinity, & will call on the Profeſsor before one.

Saturday, Pem Coll [Feb. or March, 1770]²

512**. Bonstetten to Gray

[London, Feb. or March, 1770]

[In his letter to Bonstetten of 9 May 1770 (Letter 523), Gray writes: 'As often as I read over your truly kind letter, written long since from London, I stop at these words: "La mort qui peut glacer nos bras avant qu'ils soient entrelacés".' In a letter to his mother, written from Cambridge on 6 Feb. 1770 (see Appendix V), Bonstetten says, in reference to his approaching departure from England: 'Je ne m'arrêterai à Londres que pour aller au Parlement avec Mr. Pitt et chez quelques seigneurs qui ont eu des bontés pour moi. . . . Je partirai Lundi [12 Feb.] de Cambridge et serai peut-être dans 15 jours à Paris.' He did not, however, start for Paris when he intended, but returned once more to Cambridge, as appears from Gray's letter to Norton Nicholls of 20 Mar. (Letter 513) in which he says: 'On Wednesday next [21 Mar.], I go (for a few days) with Mons: de B: to London. . . . He goes for Dover on Friday.' Bonstetten's letter from London, which apparently, like the rest of the letters written by him to Gray, has not been preserved, was probably written some time between 12 Feb., the date on which he proposed to go to London, and the date (unknown) of his return to Cambridge for the last time.]

513. GRAY TO NICHOLLS

March 20. 1770.

Dear S^r

I AM sorry for your disappointments & my own. do not believe, that I am cold to M^r Cl:^{s1} translation: on the contrary I long to see it, & wonder you should hesitate for want of Franks (wch here I have no means of getting) do I care about postage, do you think?

² The date of the year is determined by the fact that Bonstetten was in Cambridge in that year; the month is conjectural.

LETTER 513.—First printed by Mitford (1835–43), vol. v, pp. 103–4; now reprinted from original.

¹ Mitford printed 'Clarke's'—and in a note assumed, no doubt rightly, that the work to which Gray alludes was *Military Institutions of Vegetius, in Five Books, Translated from the Original Latin. With a Preface and Notes.* By Lieutenant John Clarke. (London: Printed for the Author. MDCCLXVII. 8vo.) In the Army List for 1767 John Clarke appears as 1st Lieut. of Marines (half-pay). Clarke was one of a circle of friends, which comprised Nicholls,

On Wednesday next[2] I go (for a few days) with Mons: de B: to London. his cursed F:[r3] will have him home in the autumn, & he must pafs thro France to improve his talents & morals. he goes for Dover on Friday. I have seen (I own) with pleasure the efforts you have made to recommend me to him, *sed non ego credulus illis*,[4] nor I fear, he neither. he gives me too much pleasure, & at least *an equal share* of inquietude. you do not understand him so well as I do, but I leave my meaning imperfect, till we meet. I have never met with so extraordinary a Person. God blefs him! I am unable to talk to you about any thing else, I think.

I wonder'd, you should think of Paris at the time of the Dauphin's marriage:[5] it will be a frippery spectacle, & the expence of every thing triple. as to *Wales*,[6] doubtlefs I should wish it this summer, but [7]I can answer for nothing, my own employment[8] so sticks in my stomach, & troubles my conscience.[7] when I return hither, I will write to you better & more fully. Adieu! I am very sincerely yours

Addressed: To The Revᵈ Mʳ Nicholls at Blundeston near Leostoff Suffolk By Yarmouth *Postmark:* CAMBRIDGE

513*. Bonstetten to Gray

[In Gray's letters to Bonstetten and to Norton Nicholls in 1770 and 1771 he mentions many letters, which he had received from Bonstetten after he left England. None of these letters is extant. The letters, with their approximate dates and with references to the letters of Gray in which they are mentioned are as follows: 31 Mar.

Temple (see Letter 422), Boswell, and Claxton (see Letter 483). It was probably through Nicholls that Gray became acquainted with him. He paid Gray a visit in his lodgings in Jermyn Street just a month before Gray died (see Letter 556, n. 5).

[2] 'Wednesday next' was in fact the next day, 21 Mar., unless Gray misdated his letter. That the 'Friday' was 23 Mar. is explicitly stated by Gray in his next letter.   [3] Father.   [4] Virgil, *Ecl.* ix. 34.

[5] The marriage of the Dauphin, afterwards (1774) Louis XVI, to the Austrian Archduchess, Marie Antoinette, daughter of the Empress Maria Theresa, took place at Versailles on 16 May 1770, he being sixteen and his bride fifteen.

[6] Gray made a tour with Nicholls, but not to Wales (see Letter 530).

[7-7] This sentence, detached from its context, is foisted by Mason into a composite and garbled letter, which he prints, with the date 24 May 1771, as addressed to Wharton.

[8] His duties as Regius Professor of History (see Appendix S).

1770, from Abbeville (Letter 514); 5 Apr., from Paris (Letter 517); 30 Apr., from Paris (Letter 524); 16 May, from Paris (Letters 524, 525); 5 Sept., from Paris (Letter 533); Nov., from Aubonne (Letter 536); 'several letters from Berne' of Dec. 1770 and Jan. 1771 (Letter 540); 15 Feb. 1771, from Berne (Letter 543); 22 Apr., from Berne (Letter 550).]

514. Gray to Nicholls

4 April. 1770. P: Hall:

A<small>T</small> length, my dear S^r, we have lost our poor de B:ⁿ I pack'd him up with my own hands in the Dover-machine at 4 o'clock in the morning on Friday, 23 March,[1] the next day at 7 he sail'd & reach'd *Calais* by noon, & *Boulogne* at night. the next night he reach'd *Abbeville*, where he had letters to Mad: Vanrobais, to whom belongs the famous manufacture of cloth there. from thence he wrote to me,[2] & here am I again to paſs my solitary evenings, wch hung much lighter on my hands, before I knew him. this is your fault! pray let the next you send me, be halt & blind, dull, unapprehensive & wrong-headed. for this (as Lady Constance says) *Was never such a gracious Creature born!*[3] & yet—but no matter! burn my letter[4] that I wrote you, for I am very much out of humour with myself & will not believe a word of it. you will think, I have caught madneſs from him (for he is certainly mad) & perhaps you will be right. oh! what things are Fathers & Mothers! I thought they were to be found only in England, but you see.

Where is Capt: Clarke's Translation?[5] where is your journal?[6] do you still haggle for me to save sixpence, you Niggard? why now I have been in Town & brought no franks with me yet. the translation of *Gruner*[7] can not be had this month or six weeks,

L<small>ETTER</small> 514.—First printed by Mitford (1835–43), vol. v, pp. 104–6; now reprinted from original.

[1] Gray lent Bonstetten £20 on the day of his departure, a memorandum of which James Brown found in Gray's pocket-book for 1770 after his death (see Brown's letter to Nicholls of 29 June 1773, n. 6, in Appendix W).

[2] On 31 Mar. (see Letter 517).

[3] *King John*, iii. 4:

Since the birth of Cain, the first male child,
To him that did but yesterday suspire
There was not such a gracious creature born.

[4] Letter 513.   [5] See Letter 513, n. 1.
[6] See PS. to Letter 512.
[7] Gottlieb Sigmund Gruner, Swiss lawyer and naturalist (d. 1778). He was the author of *Die Eisgebirge des Schweizerlandes* (Berne, 1760–2, 3 vol. 8vo),

so I am destitute of all things. this place never appear'd so horrible to me, as it does now. could not you come for a week or fortnight? it would be sunshine to me in a dark night! even Dr Hallifax[8] wishes, you would come. at least write to me out of hand, for I am truly & faithfully

Yours
T G:

'Vous ne voyez plus que de la misere & de la gayeté. les villages sont plus rares, plus petits: le silence dans ces deserts annonce par tout un Maitre. il me sembloit, que je devois demander a ces hommes en guenilles, qui leur avoit pris leurs habits, leurs maisons; quelle peste avoit ravagé la nation. mais ils ont le bonheur de ne penser point, & de jouer jusqu'au moment qu'on les egorge.

'Mais gardons notre indignation pour çeux qui sont si stupides, qu'ils prennent de pareilles mœurs pour modeles.'[9]

Addressed: To The Revd Mr Nicholls at Blundeston near Leostoff Suffolk By Yarmouth *Postmark:* CAMBRIDGE

514*. Gray to Mason and Mason to Gray

[Missing letters that passed between Gray and Mason in Apr. and May 1770 can be traced on the evidence of three letters of Mason to Wharton, which are preserved in the Wharton Correspondence (Brit. Mus. *Egerton* 2400). They refer to an intended visit of Gray to Mason at Aston, where he was to meet Wharton. Gray had not seen Wharton or Mason since his tour to the Lakes, and some stress was laid on the engagement. Brown was invited also, but he did not leave Cambridge. The first mention is in a letter of Mason to Wharton dated from Aston, 8 Apr.: 'I must tell you at present that altho my house is down in part, I have a tolerable room to give you a tolerable dinner in at Aston and I can lodge you with great conveniency at the Hall wch is only just cross the Church Yard, & who knows but *en passant* this may produce a second Elegy from Mr Gray. I have written to him by this post to tell him that in the middle of May the coast will be clear (for I know he will not come

---

of which a French translation, *Histoire Naturelle des Glaciers de Suisse, traduction libre de l'allemand de* M. Grouner, par M. de Kéralio (Paris, 4to) was published in 1770. The work contains two maps and 18 plates. Gray's copy of the translation, with numerous annotations by him, is now in the library of Pembroke College, Cambridge.

8 See Letter 409, n. 10.

9 This was obviously an extract from Bonstetten's letter.

unless he is sure of that) and I have said all I could to press him &
the President to give you the meeting.' (The reference to 'the coast
being clear' means that Lord Holdernesse would have left Aston.)
Gray refers to his intended visit to Aston 'the last week of May',
in writing to Nicholls on 14 Apr. and to Wharton on 18 Apr.
(Letters 517, 519). On 15 May Mason wrote to Wharton from
Aston: 'I have written to Mr Gray by this post to let him know that
Lord H is gone to Town & therefore he may keep his own time the
last week of the month if he pleases. I have desird him to fix the
day of his coming both to You & Me by the same post, wch I thought
would save time; as by that means you would have quicker intelli-
gence of his motions.' After the receipt of Mason's letter Gray wrote
to Nicholls on 22 May (Letter 524), suggesting as he had done before
(Letter 517) that Nicholls should go with him to Aston, and that
they should begin their tour together from there (see also Letter 527).
About 24 May he wrote to Mason, as Mason reported to Wharton
in a letter of 27 May: 'I rec^d a Letter from Mr Gray only last night
in wch he tells me he shall be at Aston either on Saturday or Sunday
next [2 or 3 June] and bids me acquaint you with his intention.'
Gray left Cambridge about 3 June, and seems to have stayed a
fortnight at Aston. He returned to Cambridge before starting with
Nicholls for their journey to the west.]

515. GRAY TO BONSTETTEN

Cambridge, April 12, 1770.

NEVER did I feel, my dear Bonstetten, to what a tedious length
the few short moments of our life may be extended by
impatience and expectation, till you had left me: nor ever knew
before with so strong a conviction how much this frail body
sympathizes with the inquietude of the mind. I am grown old
in the compafs of lefs than three weeks, like the Sultan in the
Turkish Tales, that did but plunge his head into a vefsel of

LETTER 515.—Three letters of Gray to Bonstetten (Letters 515, 520, 523)
were first printed in Friedrich Matthisson's *Auserlesene Gedichte, heraus-
gegeben von J. H. Füssli* (Zürich, 1791), pp. 96–8; they were reprinted (with
errors of spelling corrected) by Anne Plumptre, in *Letters written from various
parts of the Continent, between the years 1785 and 1794. . . . Translated from the
German of Frederick Matthisson* (Lond. 1799), pp. 533–5; they are now re-
printed (with mis-spellings corrected) from the Tübingen (1811) reprint of
the Zürich text (which was not available).

According to Miss Plumptre (*op. cit.*, p. v), Mason applied to Bonstetten
for leave to publish Gray's letters, which he refused; afterwards permitting
them to be printed, by his friend Matthisson, in the notes to a poem on the
Lake of Geneva, in which Gray is introduced.

water and take it out again (as the standers-by affirm'd) at the command of a Dervish, and found he had pafs'd many years in captivity and begot a large family of children.[1] The strength and spirits that now enable me to write to you, are only owing to your last letter, a temporary gleam of sunshine. Heaven knows, when it may shine again! I did not conceive till now (I own) what it was to lose you, nor felt the solitude and insipidity of my own condition, before I pofsefs'd the happinefs of your friendship.

I must cite another Greek writer[2] to you, because it is very much to my purpose. He is describing the character of a Genius truly inclined to Philosophy. It includes (he says) qualifications rarely united in one single mind, quicknefs of apprehension and a retentive memory; vivacity and application, gentlenefs and magnanimity: to these he adds an invincible love of truth, and consequently of probity and justice. Such a soul (continues he) will be little inclined to sensual pleasures, and consequently temperate; a stranger to illiberality and avarice being accustom'd to the most extensive views of things and sublimest contemplations, it will contract an habitual greatnefs, will look down with a kind of disregard on human life and on death, consequently will pofsefs the truest fortitude. Such (says he) is the Mind born to govern the rest of Mankind. But these very endowments so necefsary to a soul form'd for philosophy are often the ruin of it (especially when join'd to the external advantages of wealth, nobility, strength and beauty) that is, if it light on a bad soil; and want its proper nurture, which nothing but an excellent education can bestow. In this case he is depraved by the publick example, the afsemblies of the people, the courts of justice, the theatres, that inspire it with false opinions, terrify it with false infamy, or elevate it with false applause: and remember, that extraordinary vices and extra-

---

[1] Walpole refers to this same Oriental tale in his letter to Lord Strafford of 8 Sept. 1761: 'Lady Betty Mackenzie is the individual woman she was—she seems to have been gone three years, like the Sultan in the Persian tales, who popped his head into a tub of water, pulled it up again, and fancied he had been a dozen years in bondage in the interim. She is not altered in a tittle.' This tale, which is described by Addison as 'a very pretty story in the Turkish Tales', is given by him in No. 94 of the *Spectator*. He no doubt took it from the *Turkish Tales* published by Tonson in 1708.

[2] The quotations (epitomized from the sixth book of Plato's *Republic*, 485–92) Gray transcribed almost verbatim from his notes on Plato in his Commonplace-book (printed in Mathias, *Works*, vol. ii, pp. 441 ff.).

ordinary virtues are alike the produce of a vigorous Mind: little souls are alike incapable of the one or the other.

If you have ever met with the portrait sketch'd out by Plato, you will know it again: for my part (to my sorrow) I have had that happinefs: I see the principal features, and I foresee the dangers with a trembling anxiety. But enough of this, I return to your letter: it proves at least, that in the midst of your new gaieties, I still hold some place in your memory, and (what pleases me above all) it has an air of undifsembled sincerity. Go on, my best and amiable Friend, to shew me your heart simply and without the shadow of disguise, and leave me to weep over it (as I now do) no matter whether from joy or sorrow.

516. GRAY TO FARMER[1]

M[r] GRAY returns M[r] Farmer's Books, with many Thanks. The MS. Letters would be of some Value, if the Transcriber had better understood what he was about: but there are so

LETTER 516.—First printed in the sale catalogue of Farmer's library, *Bibliotheca Farmeriana* (Lond. 1798), where it formed part of Lot 8102: 'The negotiations of Thomas Wolsey, Cardinal. This MS. D[r] Farmer sent to M[r] Gray, who returned it with the following note.'

Cole was shown Gray's note by Farmer on 31 Oct. 1780, and made a copy of it; he added, 'This Note is written on a small Bit of Paper & has no Direction: probably sent under Cover of the Parcel returned to D[r] Farmer' (Brit. Mus. *Add. MS.* 5860, f. 57).

[1] Richard Farmer (1735–97), B.A. 1757; M.A. 1760; D.D. 1775; Fellow and Tutor of Emmanuel College, of which he subsequently became Master (1775), author of an *Essay on the Learning of Shakespeare* (his only published work). He was a friend and correspondent of Thomas Percy, who in the Preface to his *Reliques of Ancient English Poetry* (1765) paid a tribute to Farmer's 'extensive knowledge of ancient English Literature' (see Letter 340, n. 3).

Cole, in his note of 31 Oct. 1780 mentioned above, adds the following account of the relations between Gray and Farmer: 'it must have been about the Year 1770; as the first Time they ever met to be acquainted together, was about that Time, I met them at M[r] Oldham's Chambers in Peter House to Dinner. Before, they had been shy of each other: and tho' M[r] Farmer was then esteemed one of the most ingenious men in the University, yet M[r] Gray's singular Niceness in the Choice of his Acquaintance made him appear fastidious to a great Degree to all who was not acquainted with his Manner. Indeed there did not seem to be any Probability of any great Intimacy, from the Style & Manner of each of them: the one a chearful, companionable, hearty, open, downright Man, of no great Regard to Dress or comon Forms of Behaviour: the other, of a most fastidious & recluse Distance of Carriage, rather averse to all Sociability, but of the graver Turn: nice & elegant in his

many words mistaken, so many omitted, that the Sense can often only be made out by Conjecture.

Does not recollect that they have been printed in any of the Collections: but thinks he has seen several of them (the Originals) in the Harleian Library.[2] Lord Herbert[3] plainly had seen them, & (as far as they goe) has made them the Foundation of his History.[4] They serve to shew, as he says, That the Cardinal,[5] in his Dispatches was more copious than eloquent.

The Instructions to Tunstall[6] & Wingfield,[7] after the Battle of Pavia, & the King's Directions after he had signed the Peace with Francis,[8] are most remarkable.

Pemb: Hall. 12 April. [1770][9]

Person, Dress & Behaviour, even to a Degree of Finicalness & Effeminacy. So that Nothing but their extensive Learning & Abilities could ever have coalesced two such different Men: & both of great Value in their own Line & Walk. They were ever after great Friends, & Dr Farmer & all of his Acquaintance had soon after too much Reason to lament his Loss, & the Shortness of their Acquaintance.'

Cole's statement that it must have been about the Year 1770 that Dr Farmer and Mr Gray ever met to be acquainted together needs examination. It would have been scarcely possible for Gray and Farmer to have lived for so many years in Cambridge without being known to one another, and in Percy's letters to Farmer there are references which can only be explained on the assumption that Farmer could consult Gray about questions raised by Percy and ask for his help (see Appendix N). It seems reasonable to conclude that Cole's meaning is that, while Gray and Farmer had known each other before, it was not until they dined together at Mr. Oldham's chambers that they became on friendly terms.

　[2] In the British Museum, where in Sept. 1759, as he tells Wharton, Gray transcribed 'volumes of antiquity' (see Letter 303).

　[3] Lord Herbert of Cherbury (see Letter 376).

　[4] His *Life and Reign of King Henry VIII*, first published in 1649.

　[5] Wolsey.

　[6] Cuthbert Tunstall (1474–1559), Bishop of London, 1522–30; after the defeat and capture of Francis I at the battle of Pavia (24 Feb. 1525), he and Sir Richard Wingfield were sent on an embassy to Charles V in Spain, which proved abortive.

　[7] Sir Richard Wingfield (c. 1469–1525); he died at Toledo during the embassy to Spain.

　[8] The peace in question was presumably that concluded in Aug. 1525 between Henry VIII and Louise of Savoy, Regent of France during the captivity of her son Francis I.

　[9] The date of the year, which is conjectural, is suggested by Coles's statement. An earlier year is perhaps possible (n. 1). It should be noted that on 12 Apr. in 1770 Gray was in residence, but not in 1768 or 1769.

517. GRAY TO NICHOLLS

Camb: 14 Apr: 1770.

I THOUGHT my mysteries[1] were but too easy to explain, however you must have a little patience, for I can hazard only word of mouth. what you say of poor B: is so true, & (let me add) exprefses so well my own feelings, that I shall transcribe your words, & send them to him:[2] were I in his place, I should be grateful for them! by this time I should think, you may have received a letter from him yourself, for in that I received from Abbeville, 31 March, he spoke of his intention to write to you. I wrote to you myself as soon as I return'd from London, the 1st (I think) of April.[3]

I am coming to see you, my good Friend, that is, on Monday se'nnight I mean to call on Palgrave[4] for a few days in my way to Blundeston. as to Wales you may do with me, what you please, I care not. there is this inconvenience in our way, that I must call on Mason at Aston (& so may you too) for a little while, the last week in May:[5] from thence we strike acrofs to Chester, & enter Wales.[6] for the summer of next year (tho' I shall be dead first) I am your Man, only I desire it may be a secret between ourselves, till the time comes, as you love your life.

I rejoice to see, you are so great a Gardiner & Botanist: my instructions will be very poor: De B: with five lefsons from Miller[7] (before he departed for Sumatra) & his own matchlefs industry, could have told you much more than I can. it would be strange if I should blame you for reading Isocrates. I did so myself 20 years ago, & in an edition at least as bad as yours. the *Panegyrick*, the *De Pace*, *Areopagitic*, & *Advice to Philip*, are by far the noblest remains we have of this Writer, & equal to most things extant in the Greek tongue: but it depends on your

LETTER 517.—First printed in part (in a garbled text) in Mason's *Memoirs*, p. 393; first printed in full by Mitford (1835), vol. v, pp. 106–8; now reprinted from original.

[1] See the letter to Nicholls of 4 Apr. 1770 (Letter 514). Nicholls had replied in a letter which is not extant. The contents are indicated by what Gray says in this letter.

[2] As he did in his next letter to Bonstetten (Letter 520).

[3] It was on the 4th (see n. 1).

[4] At Palgrave or Thrandeston in Suffolk, of which parishes Palgrave was Rector (see Letter 273*, n. 1).   [5] See Letter 514*.

[6] This tour took place in July and August of this year (see Letters 530, 531).   [7] See Letter 512, n. 4.

judgement to distinguish between his real & occasional opinion of things, as he directly contradicts in one place what he has advanced in another, for example in the *Panathenaic* & the *De Pace*, &c: on the naval power of Athens: the latter of the two is undoubtedly his own undisguised sentiment.

Talk your fill to me, & spare not. it would perhaps be more flattering, if you lived in the midst of an agreable society: but even as it is, I take it in good part, & heartily thank you, for you have given me a late instance of your partiality & kindnefs, that I shall ever remember.

I received on yᵉ 10ᵗʰ of this month a long letter from Paris lively & sensible as usual: but you will see it, & I shall hope for a sight of such as you have got by you. there are two different directions. A Mons: M:ʳ B: *a l'hotel de Luxembourg, rue des Petits Augustins, Fauxbourg Sᵗ Germain, Paris.* the other, to the same, *chez Mefsʳˢ Lullin, Freres, & Rittiel, rue Thevenot, Paris.*8 the latter seems the safer, but then I am uncertain, whether I read it right. what shall I do? I have tried both ways, but do not know yet with what succefs. Adieu, Dear Sʳ, I am very faithfully

Yours
T G:

Addressed: To The Revᵈ Mʳ Nicholls at Blundeston near Leostoff Suffolk By Yarmouth *Postmark:* CAMBRIDGE

518. GRAY TO WARTON[1]

15 April. 1770
Sʳ   Pembroke Hall.

OUR Friend Dr. Hurd[2] having long ago desired me in your name to communicate any fragments, or sketches of a design, I once had to give a history of English poetry,[3] you may well

8 A different form of this address is given in Letter 527.

LETTER 518.—First printed in *Gentleman's Magazine* for Feb. 1783 (vol. liii, p. 100), where it is described as 'Copy of an original Letter from Mʳ Gray to Mʳ T. Warton, on the History of English Poetry. [Communicated by a Gentleman of Oxford.]'; now collated with the text printed in 1810 by Alexander Chalmers (at that time owner of the original) in his *Works of the English Poets*, vol. xviii, pp. 79–80; and with an eighteenth-century transcript (made apparently from the original, as it reproduces most of Gray's peculiarities of abbreviation, punctuation, &c.) found recently among the Warton papers formerly belonging to Sir John Murray and now in the British Museum. The text now printed is based on this transcript, with a few omissions supplied from other versions, and small corrections, chiefly in the spelling of proper names.

Among the Gray manuscripts in the Loyd collection are two drafts in

think me rude or negligent, when you see me hesitating for so many months, before I comply with your request, and yet (believe me) few of your friends have been better pleased than I to find this subject (surely neither unentertaining, nor unuseful) had fallen into hands so likely to do it justice, few have felt a higher esteem for your talents, your taste, & industry. in truth the only cause of my delay has been a sort of diffidence, that would not let me send you any thing so short, so slight, & so imperfect, as the few materials I had begun to collect, or the observations I had made on them. a sketch of the division & arrangement of the subject however I venture to transcribe, and would wish to know, whether it corresponds in any thing with your own plan, for I am told your first volume is already in the prefs.

INTRODUCTION

On the poetry of the *Galic* (or Celtic) nations, as far back as it can be traced.

On that of the Goths: its introduction into these islands by the Saxons & Danes, & its duration. on the origin of rhyme among the Franks, the Saxons, & Provençaux. some account of the Latin rhyming poetry from its early origin down to the 15th Century.

P: 1

On the School of Provence, wch rose about the year 1100, & was soon followed by the French & Italians. their heroic poetry, or romances in verse, Allegories, fabliaux, syrvientes, comedies, farces, canzoni, sonnets, balades, madrigals, sestines, &c:

Of their imitators the *French*, & of the first *Italian* School (commonly call'd the Sicilian) about the year 1200 brought to perfection by Dante, Petrarch, Boccace, & others.

State of Poetry in England from the Conquest (1066) or rather from Henry 2^{d's} time (1154) to the reign of Edward the 3^d (1327).

P: 2

On *Chaucer* who first introduced the manner of the Provençaux improved by the Italians into our country. his character

Gray's hand of a 'Scheme for a History of English Poetry', from one of which the sketch sent to Warton was, in great part, verbally transcribed.
[1] See Letter 509*, n. 1.   [2] Letter 509*.
[3] See Gray's *Advertisement* prefixed to the Imitations of the Norse and Welsh Odes in the 1768 edition of his *Poems*, and Letter 245*, n. 4.

& merits at large; the different kinds in wch he excell'd.
Gower, Occleve, Lydgate, Hawes, G: Douglas, Lindsay, Bellenden, Dunbar, &c:

P: 3

Second Italian School (of Ariosto, Taſso, &c:) an improvement on the first, occasion'd by the revival of letters the end of the 15th century. The lyric poetry of this & the former age introduced from Italy by Ld Surrey, Sr T. Wyat, Bryan, Ld Vaux, &c: in the beginning of the 16th century. *Spenser*, his character. Subject of his poem allegoric & romantic, of Provençal invention: but his manner of [treating]⁴ it borrow'd from the Second Italian School. Drayton, Fairfax, Phin: Fletcher, Golding, Phaer, &c: this school ends in Milton.

A *third Italian* School, full of conceit, begun in Q: Elizabeths reign, continued under James, & Charles the first by *Donne*, Crashaw, Cleveland; carried to its height by Cowley, & ending perhaps in *Sprat*.

P: 4

School of France, introduced after the Restoration. Waller, Dryden, Addison, Prior, & Pope, wch has continued down to our own times.

You will observe, that my idea was in some measure taken from a scribbled paper of *Pope*,⁵ of w^{ch} (I believe) you have a

---

⁴ The text in the *Gentleman's Magazine* has 'tracing'; the transcript 'creating': it is evident from Gray's draft of the scheme (see preliminary note) that he wrote 'treating'.

⁵ Pope's 'scribbled paper' was unearthed by Warburton, his literary executor, who on 18 July 1752 wrote to Hurd: 'The inclosed scrap of paper is for our friend Mr Mason. I promised it to him. It seems to be the heads of a discourse on the birth and genealogy of English poetry. It is in Mr Pope's hand' (*Letters from a late eminent Prelate to one of his Friends*, p. 89). A copy was given to Warton by Mason in 1763 (Warton's letter to Hurd of 25 Dec. 1763; see Letter 509*, n. 2). Warton refers to the gift and to Gray's help in the preface to the first volume of his *History of English Poetry*: 'A few years ago Mr Mason . . . gave me an authentic copy of Mr Pope's scheme of a History of English Poetry, in which our poets were classed under their supposed respective schools. The late lamented Mr Gray had also projected a work of this kind, and translated some Runic odes for its illustration, now published; but soon relinquishing the prosecution of a design, which would have detained him from his own noble inventions, he most obligingly condescended to favour me with the substance of his plan, which I found to be that of Mr Pope, considerably enlarged, extended, and improved.' This draft plan of Pope's was first printed (in a corrupt text) in 1769 by Owen Ruffhead in his *Life of Pope*, pp. 424–5. Mathias reprinted

copy. you will also see that I have excluded *dramatic* Poetry entirely wch if you have taken in, it will at least double the bulk & labour of your book.⁶

*　*　*　*　*　*　*　*　*　*　*
*　*　*　*　*　*　*　*　*　*　*

I am, sir, with great esteem, your most humble and obedient servant,

THOMAS GRAY.

519. GRAY TO WHARTON

18 April 1770.

My dear S^r

I HAVE been sincerely anxious for Mifs Wharton, whose illnefs must have been indeed severe, if she is only now recovering. let us hope everything from the spring, wch begins (tho' slowly) to give new life to all things, & pray give my best respects to her, & thanks for remembring me & my dictionary at a time, when she well may be excused for thinking of nothing but herself.

I have utterly forgot, where my journal¹ left off, but (I think) it was after the account of *Gordale* near Settle. if so, there was little more worth your notice: the principal things were *Wharldale* in the way from Skipton to Ottley, & *Kirstall-Abbey* 3 mile from Leedes. the first is the valley form'd by the River Wharf, well-cultivated, well-inhabited, well-wooded, but with high rocky crags at distance, that border the green country on either hand: thro' the midst of it runs the river in long windings deep, clear, & full to the brink, and of no inconsiderable breadth. how it comes to be so fine & copious a stream here, & at Tadcaster (so much lower) should have nothing but a wide stony

it (in *Works of Gray*, vol. ii, pp. v–vi) from a transcript by Gray in his Commonplace-book, headed: 'The following is an exact transcript from a paper in Mr Pope's own hand-writing, which was given by Mr Warburton to Mr Mason, in 1752. It is a *slight* sketch for a History of English Poetry.'

⁶ Chalmers's text and that of the Warton transcript end here. Chalmers adds in a note: 'This letter concludes with requesting the favour of some attention to a foreign young gentleman, then entered of one of the colleges.' See Letter 521, n. 5.

LETTER 519.—First printed in part (in a garbled text) in Mason's *Memoirs*, pp. 379–80; first printed in full by Mitford (1816), vol. ii, pp. 552–4; now reprinted from original.

¹ Gray had apparently not sent Wharton any part of his *Journal* after the instalment sent on 3 Jan. 1770, which stopped in the middle of his account of his journey on 8 Oct. 1769 (see Letter 511A, preliminary note).

channel with little or no water, I cannot tell you. *Kirstall*[2] is a noble ruin in the Semi-Saxon style of building, as old as K: Stephen toward the end of his reign, 1152. the whole Church is still standing (the roof excepted) seated in a delicious quiet valley on the banks of the river *Are*,[3] & preserved with religious reverence by the Duke of Montagu.[4] adjoining to the church between that & the river are variety of chappels & remnants of the abbey, shatter'd by the encroachments of the ivy, & surmounted by many a sturdy tree, whose twisted roots break thro' the fret of the vaulting, & hang streaming from the roofs. the gloom of these ancient cells, the shade & verdure of the landscape, the glittering & murmur of the stream, the lofty towers & long perspectives of the Church, in the midst of a clear bright day, detain'd me for many hours & were the truest subjects for my glafs[5] I have yet met with any where. as I lay at that smoky ugly busy town of Leedes, I drop'd all farther thoughts of my journal, & after pafsing two days at Mason's (tho' he was absent)[6] pursued my way by Nottingham, Leicester, Harborough, Kettering, Thrapston, & Huntington to Cambridge, where I arrived, 22 Oct:, having met with no rain to signify, till this last day of my journey. there's luck for you!

I do think of seeing Wales this summer,[7] having never found my spirits lower than at present, & feeling that motion & change of the scene is absolutely necefsary to me. I will make Aston in my way to Chester, & shall rejoice to meet you there the *last week in May*;[8] Mason writes me word, that he wishes it, & tho' his old house is down & his new one not up, proposes to receive us like Princes in grain. Adieu, my dear S^r & believe me most faithfully yours,   T G:

My best compliments to Mrs Wharton & the family. our weather till Christmas continued mild & open. 28 Dec: some snow fell but did not lie. the 4th of Jan: was stormy & snowy, wch was often repeated during that month, yet the latter half of it was warm & gentle. 18 Feb: was snow again, the rest of

---

2 See Letter 363, n. 5.   3 The Aire.

4 George Brudenell (1712–90), fourth Earl of Cardigan (1732); he married the daughter of John Montagu, second Duke of Montagu, upon whose death in 1749, without heir male, he assumed the name of Montagu; in 1766 he was created Duke of Montagu, which title became extinct at his death in 1790.

5 See Letter 505, n. 4.   6 See Letter 505 (postscript).

7 See Letter 517, n. 6.   8 See Letter 514*.

it mostly fine. snow again on 15th March, from 23 to 30 March was cold & dry, W^d E: or N:E:. on ye 31st rain. from thence till within a week past, W^d N:W: or N:E: with much hail & sleet; & on 4 Apr: a thunder-storm. it is now fine spring-weather.

1 March.	first violet appear'd. frogs abroad.
4 ——	Almond blow'd, & Gooseberry spread its leaves.
9 ——	Apricot blow'd.
1 April.	Violets in full bloom, & double Daffodils.
5 ——	Wren singing. double Jonquils.

Addressed: To Thomas Wharton Esq of Old Park near Darlington Durham
Postmark: CAMBRIDGE

520. GRAY TO BONSTETTEN

19 April 1770.

ALAS! how do I every moment feel the truth of what I have somewhere read: *Ce n'est pas le voir que de s'en souvenir*, and yet that remembrance is the only satisfaction I have left. My life now is but a perpetual conversation with your shadow.—The known sound of your voice still rings in my ears.—There, on the corner of the fender you are standing, or tinkling on the Pianoforte, or stretch'd at length on the sofa.—Do you reflect, my dearest Friend, that it is a week or eight days, before I can receive a letter from you and as much more before you can have my answer, that all that time (with more than Herculean toil) I am employ'd in pushing the tedious hours along, and wishing to annihilate them; the more I strive, the heavier they move and the longer they grow. I can not bear this place, where I have spent many tedious years within lefs than a month, since you left me. I am going for a few days to see poor Nicholls invited by a letter, wherein he mentions you in such terms, as add to my regard for him, and exprefs my own sentiments better than I can do myself.[1] 'I am concern'd (says he) that I can not pafs my life with him, I never met with any one that pleased and

LETTER 520.—First printed in the Zürich (1791) edition of Matthisson's *Auserlesene Gedichte*, pp. 99–101; now reprinted (with mis-spellings corrected) from the Tübingen (1811) reprint of the Zürich text (see Letter 515, preliminary note).

[1] In Gray's letter to Nicholls of 14 Apr. (Letter 517) he says he shall transcribe what Nicholls has written of Bonstetten. The letter from Nicholls is not extant.

suited me so well: the miracle to me is, how he comes to be so little spoil'd, and the miracle of miracles will be, if he continues so in the midst of every danger and seduction, and without any advantages, but from his own excellent nature and understanding. I own, I am very anxious for him on this account, and perhaps your inquietude may have proceeded from the same cause. I hope, I am to hear, when he has pafs'd that cursed sea, or will he forget me thus *in insulam relegatum?* If he should, it is out of my power to retaliate.'

Sure you have wrote to him, my dear Bonstetten, or sure you will! he has moved me with these gentle and sensible exprefsions of his kindnefs for you. Are you untouch'd by them?

You do me the credit (and false or true, it goes to my heart) of ascribing to me your love for many virtues of the highest rank. Would to heaven it were so; but they are indeed the fruits of your own noble and generous understanding, that has hitherto struggled against the stream of custom, pafsion, and ill company, even when you were but a Child, and will you now give way to that stream, when your strength is increased? Shall the Jargon of French Sophists, the allurements of painted women *comme il faut,* or the vulgar carefses of prostitute beauty, the property of all, that can afford to purchase it, induce you to give up a mind and body by Nature diftinguish'd from all others to folly, idlenefs, disease, and vain remorse? Have a care, my ever-amiable Friend, *of loving, what you do not approve,* and know me for your most faithful and most humble Despote.

521. Warton to Gray

Sir,

I AM infinitely obliged to you for the Favour of your Letter.[1] Your Plan for the *History of English Poetry* is admirably constructed; and much improved from an Idea of Pope,[2] which Mr Mason obligingly sent me by Application from our Friend Dr Hurd. I regrett that a writer of your consummate Taste should not have executed it.

Although I have not followed this Plan, yet it is of great service to me, and throws much light on many of my Periods, by giving connected views and Details. I begin with such an

LETTER 521.—First printed in part by A. Chalmers (who owned the original both of Gray's letter to Warton and of this reply) in his *Works of the English Poets* (Lond. 1810), vol. xviii, p. 81. Now printed in full from original.

[1] That of 15 Apr. (Letter 518).   [2] See Letter 518, n. 5.

introduction, or general Difsertation, as you had intended:
viz. on the Northern Poetry with its introduction into England
by the Danes and Saxons, & its duration. I then begin my
History at the conquest which I write chronologically in Sec-
tions; and continue, as matter succefsively offers itself, in a
series of regular Annals, down to & beyond the Restoration. I
think with you, that Dramatic poetry is detached from the idea
of my work,[3] that it requires a separate consideration, & will
swell the size of my book beyond all bounds. One of my Sec-
tions, a very large one, is entirely on Chaucer, and exactly fills
your Title of *Part Second*. In the course of my Annals I consider
collaterally the Poetry of different Nations as influencing our
own. What I have at present finished ends with the section
on Chaucer, & will almost make my first Volume; for I design
two Volumes in quarto. This first Volume will soon be in the
prefs.[4] I should have said before, that although I proceed
chronologically, yet I often stand still to give some general view,
as perhaps of a *particular species* of poetry, &c. and even *anticipate*
sometimes for this purpose. These *views* often form *one* Section;
yet are interwoven into the Tenor of the work without inter-
rupting my historical series. In this respect, some of my Sections
have the effect of your *Parts* or *Divisions*.

You do me a favour in requesting me to pay an attention to
Mr Stiguer.[5] I return to Oxford in a few Days, when I will
make it my businefs to find him out, and to introduce him

---

[3] Warton afterwards changed his mind, as appears from the following
passage in the preface to his first volume: 'It was recommended to me, by a
person eminent in the republic of letters [i.e. Gray], totally to exclude from
these volumes any mention of the English drama. I am very sensible that
a just history of our Stage is alone sufficient to form an entire and extensive
work; and this argument, which is by no means precluded by the attempt
here offered to the public, still remains separately to be discussed, at large,
and in form. But as it was professedly my intention to comprise every species
of English Poetry, this, among the rest, of course claimed a place in these
annals, and necessarily fell into my general design.'

[4] The first volume was published in 1774; a second in 1778; and a third
in 1781.

[5] Warton seems to have misread the name. The young foreigner recom-
mended by Gray (see Letter 518, n. 6) must have been Christopher Steiger,
of Thun, Switzerland, who matriculated from University College on 8 May
1771, aged 17. His family ranked as belonging to the patriciate of Berne
(see Dr. Herking's *Charles Victor de Bonstetten*, p. 21). Christopher Steiger
had no doubt been recommended to Gray by Bonstetten. If he was at
Oxford at the time when Gray wrote, he must have come up a year before
he matriculated.

according to your wishes. I do not know his College, nor have I heard of his name. But he will easily be found out.

I cannot take my Leave without declaring, that my strongest incitement to prosecute the *History of English Poetry* is the pleasing hope of being approved by you; whose *true genius* I so justly venerate, and whose *genuine Poetry* has ever given me such sincere pleasure. I am, Sir, with the greatest Esteem, your most obedient humble Servant

T. Warton

Winchester-College,[6] April 20, 1770.

522. BEATTIE TO GRAY

Dear Sir

I TROUBLED You with a letter some months ago,[1] enclosing a specimen of a Poem,[2] which I have some thoughts of finishing when I find myself at leisure.—The design of this, is to solicit Your acceptance of a Book called An Eſsay on Truth[3] which Mr Dilly[4] Bookseller in London sends You by my desire. It is not such a present as I wish to make, but it is the best that is now in my power. You will think perhaps that I am very anxious to become a voluminous Author; but that is not the case. The present publication is the consequence of neceſsity rather than choice. I expect neither praise nor profit from it; nay, though it were to be succesful, which I am confident cannot happen, my vanity would not be flattered in the least; for I set no value on such performances. The occasion of my writing it was this. The buſineſs of my profeſsion obliged me, when I first entered upon it, to be more conversant than I could have wished

---

[6] Warton's brother, Dr. Joseph Warton, was at this time head master of Winchester.

LETTER 522.—Now first printed from original.

[1] In Nov. 1769 (see Letter 507*, n. 1).

[2] *The Minstrel* (see Letter 507*, n. 9).

[3] This work, the full title of which was *An Essay on the Nature and Immutability of Truth, in opposition to Sophistry and Scepticism* (8vo, 6s.), was published by Dilly in this month (May).

[4] Charles Dilly (1739–1807), bookseller in the Poultry, at first in partnership with his elder brother, Edward, and after his death (1779) alone. He published Boswell's *Tour to the Hebrides* (1785) and his *Life of Johnson* (1791). The brothers were famous for their dinners, at which Johnson and Boswell were frequent guests. It was at their table (15 May 1776) that Johnson met Wilkes.

with our modern moral & metaphysical writers. I had little relish for them from the first, and as I began to understand them better, I hated and despised them the more. Their principles and method of investigation seemed to me to be equally unfavourable to Science virtue and good taste. I saw with concern, that the Publick in general, and the people of this country in particular, were every day growing more and more attached to them; and I also saw, or thought I saw, that those who admired them most, understood them the least. I used to exprefs myself on this subject with so little reserve in my Publick Lectures, that some degree of curiosity was excited in the small circle where I am known; and I found it was become necefsary for me, if I would clear myself of the imputation of being a mere Declaimer and retailer of paradoxes, to publish my sentiments at large, with the grounds of them. This is what I have endeavoured to do in the book which now craves the honour of Your acceptance; I have not the face to add—and of Your perusal, for I should really be sorry to see You so ill employed, as in the study of a metaphysical controversy. Besides I know, that in England Metaphysick has not got such a footing as with us. Whether it be owing to the attachment which many among us have to a Countryman,[5] or to something of a minute and sophistical spirit in the genius of our people, I know not; but certain it is, that we Scots are at present much inclined to be scepticks and metaphysicians. Every body here who can read, reads metaphysick, our writers write it, and our parsons preach it.—If You should at any time do my book the honour to look into it, may I hope that You will favour me with Your opinion of the Style: As to the doctrine, I dare say we are of the same mind. The style falls far short of my idea of good English: it is often stiff and pedantick in spite of all my endeavours to the contrary. I have indeed studied perspicuity more than elegance; because I know that my doctrine will be most favourably received by those who understand it best. I have frequently given a little into declamation, and something of a flippant drollery, both which I know are unsuitable to a philosophical enquiry. I did this, partly to amuse myself, and partly to [render m]y[6] subject not altogether unentertaining.

[In my l]ast[6] I complained of bad health; I am no[w][6] much

---

[5] The reference is to Hume, whose philosophical principles were directly attacked in Beattie's book.

[6] MS. damaged.

[better],[6] and should be glad to hear that You a[re][6] well and happy.   For I am, with the most perfect regard and esteem Dear Sir

Your affectionate & most
humble servant
J BEATTIE

Aberdeen 1st May 1770

I know not what Mr Foulis has done with his Milton.   I thought it would have been finished long before now. I hope he has not neglected to send Your Homer.[7]

Addressed: To Thomas Gray Esquire Regius Profefsor of Modern History Cambridge with a Book—To be forwarded by Mr Dilly

523. GRAY TO BONSTETTEN

9 May 1770.

I AM return'd, my dear B., from the little journey I had made into Suffolk[1] without answering the end proposed. The thought, that you might have been with me there, has embitter'd all my hours. Your letter has made me happy; as happy as so gloomy, so solitary a Being as I am is capable of being. I know and have too often felt the disadvantages I lay myself under, how much I hurt the little interest I have in you, by this air of sadnefs so contrary to your nature and present enjoyments: but sure you will forgive, tho' you can not sympathize with me. It is impofsible with me to difsemble with you. Such as I am, I expose my heart to your view, nor wish to conceal a single thought from your penetrating eyes.—All that you say to me, especially on the subject of Switzerland, is infinitely acceptable. It feels too pleasing ever to be fulfill'd, and as often as I read over your truly kind letter, written long since from London, I stop at these words: *La mort qui peut glacer nos bras avant qu'ils soient entrelacés.*[2]

---

[7] See Letter 501, n. 8.

LETTER 523.—First printed in the Zürich (1791) edition of F. Matthisson's *Auserlesene Gedichte*, pp. 101–2; now reprinted (with mis-spellings corrected) from the Tübingen (1811) reprint of the Zürich text (see Letter 515, preliminary note).

[1] Gray refers to his visit to Nicholls at Blundeston (see Letter 520).

[2] See Letter 512**.

524. GRAY TO NICHOLLS

Dear S^r

22 May. 1770. Jermyn-Str:^t .

WHEN I return'd to Cambridge, I found a long letter from De B:[1] exprefsing much kindnefs, but in a style *un peu trop alambiqué*,[2] & yesterday I had another shorter,[3] & making bad excuses for not writing oftener: he seems at present to give into all the French nonsense & to be employ'd much like an English boy broke loose from his Governor. I want much to know, whether he has wrote to you yet: if not, I am seriously angry, tho' to little purpose. A *Marquis de Villevielle*,[4] who is here with the French Embafsador,[5] has found me out, & seems a quiet good sort of young Man. he knows & tries to speak English, & has *translated me* by way of exercise. that is our bond of union, but I have seen no specimen yet. he returns home soon with Mr de Chatelet; but means to return & acquaint himself better with this country.

On Monday or Tuesday[6] I mean to leave this place & after pafsing two or three days at Cambridge proceed to Aston,[7] where Mason expects me. now if you like to accompany me, you will meet me at Camb: & we pursue our way together, trees blooming & nightingales singing all round us. let me know your mind & direct to me at Camb:^{ge}.

I have not forgot your microscope, but my Mr Ramsden[8] (Mason's Favourite) is such a Lyar & a Fool, that ten to one it is not finish'd this month or two. my respects to Mrs. Nicholls!

LETTER 524.—First printed by Mitford (1835–43), vol. v, pp. 108–9; now reprinted from original.

[1] Gray returned to Cambridge about 7 May: the first-mentioned letter of Bonstetten (from Paris) would have been written about 30 Apr.

[2] Term used by Voltaire of Corneille in the sense of 'over-subtle', 'over-refined'.

[3] Written probably about 16 May.

[4] Correctly, Villevieille, the title of the family of Gai, of Italian origin from Gaeta, who settled in Provence in the fifteenth century.

[5] This was Louis Marie Florent (1727–93), Comte (afterwards Duc) du Châtelet; he was ambassador in London from 1767 to 1770 (June) in succession to the Comte de Guerchy.

[6] 28 or 29 May; he did not, however, leave till the 31st (see Letter 527).

[7] Gray appears to have reached Aston in the first week of June (see Letter 514*).

[8] See Letter 510, n. 4.

I hope the sermon[9] is compleated[10] between you. Adieu! I am faithfully yours

T G:

I have got *Gruner's*[11] book.

Addressed: To The Revd Mr Nicholls at Blundeston near Leostoff Suffolk
Postmark: 22 MA

525. GRAY TO BROWN

22 May. 1770   Jermyn Street

Dear S^r

I HAVE received two letters from you with one enclosed from Paris,[1] & one from Mason.[2] I met poor Baker[3] two or three days after the fire[4] with evident marks of terror in his countenance: he has moved his quarters (I am told) somewhere into Gray's-inn Lane near the fields.[5]

I do not apprehend any thing more than usual from the City-remonstrance,[6] & the Party principally concern'd I hear does not in the least regard it. the conversation you mention in the house of Lords is very true: it happen'd about a fortnight since,

[9] See Letter 526, n. 4.

[10] Substituted for 'finish'd', which is scored through, no doubt to avoid the repetition.

[11] See Letter 514, n. 7.

LETTER 525.—First printed by Mitford in *Gray–Mason* (1853), pp. 439–42; now reprinted from original.

[1] No doubt the shorter letter from Bonstetten referred to by Gray in his letter to Nicholls of this same date (see Letter 524, n. 3).

[2] See Letter 514*.

[3] This may have been Richard Baker, Fellow of Pembroke; B.A. 1762; M.A. 1765; D.D. 1788. He was one of the three Fellows of Pembroke who witnessed Gray's will on 2 July of this year.

[4] The *Annual Register* for 1770, under 16 May, records: 'This morning between three and four o'clock, a fire broke out at the house of Mr Pool in Palsgrave-head-court without Temple-bar, which consumed the same with all the furniture.' Besides other houses 'part of Mr Twining's tea warehouse is burnt down; not one house in the court on either side escaped the fury of the flames' (p. 106). The *Gentleman's Magazine* for the same date describes it as 'a terrible fire', and states that one woman was burnt to death.

[5] North of the garden wall of Gray's Inn were formerly open fields, known as Gray's Inn Fields.

[6] It was the right of the Common Council and the Court of Aldermen to present Addresses to the King in person. After a Remonstrance in Mar. 1770 had been answered by the King in terms of high displeasure, a second Remonstrance was presented at St. James's on 23 May by Lord Mayor Beckford, attended by the Aldermen and Common Councillors.

& the A:ᴾ7 replied, it was not any concern of his, as he had received no complaint from the Un:7 on that head.8 it begins to be doubted, whether Lᵈ Anglesey9 will carry his point, his witnefses being so very Irish10 in their understandings & consciences, that they puzzle the cause they came to prove: but this can not be clear'd up till another sefsion. Pa: & I have often visited, but never met: I saw my Lᵈ & Tom11 the other day at breakfast in good health, & Lady Maria12 did not beat me, but giggled a little. Mons:ʳ de Villevielle13 has found me out, & seems a sensible quiet young Man. he returns soon to France with the Embafsador,14 but means to revisit England, & see it better. I dined at Hampton-court on Sunday all alone with St:, who enquired after you, & the next day with the same & a good deal of company in Town. I have not seen him so well this long time. I am myself indifferent, the head-ach returns

This second Remonstrance, to which Gray here refers, was marked by a departure from the established etiquette on the part of Beckford, 'who, contrary to all form and precedent, tacked a volunteer speech to the Remonstrance . . . being an innovation, it much discomposed the solemnity. It is always usual to furnish a copy of what is to be said to the King, that he may be prepared with his answer' (Walpole to Mann, 24 May 1770).

7 See Letter 499, n. 16.

8 It is possible that this refers to the agitation in the University for the abolition of the compulsory subscription to the 39 articles, which came to a head in the following year, when graces were proposed (on 11 June and 6 Dec.) 'that subscription to the 39 articles should not be necessary as a qualification for any degree', and 'that Bachelors of Arts should be exempt from subscription to the 39 articles', both of which were rejected (see Cooper's *Annals of Cambridge*, vol. iv, pp. 362–3).

9 Richard Annesley, sixth Earl of Anglesey (1737), married (it is believed bigamously) Juliana Donovan, by whom he had a son Arthur, born in 1744. On the death of the Earl in 1761 this son, though opposed by the next heir, was held in Ireland to have succeeded to the Irish honours, and took his seat in the Irish House of Lords as Viscount Valentia on attaining his majority in 1765. On his petitioning, however, for a writ of summons to the Parliament of Great Britain as Earl of Anglesey, &c., the House of Lords for that kingdom (to whom it had been referred) decided (22 Apr. 1771) that he 'had no right to the titles, honours, and dignities claimed by his petition'.

10 The word is legible under its obliteration.

11 The Earl of Strathmore and his brother Hon. Thomas Lyon.

12 Lady Maria was the infant daughter and eldest child (born 23 Apr. 1768) of Lord Strathmore, who had been married in Feb. 1767 (see Letter 431). Mitford was mistaken in assuming that Lady Maria was Tom Lyon's wife.

13 See Letter 524, n. 4.

14 The Comte du Châtelet (see Letter 524, n. 5).

now & then, & a little grumbling of the gout, but I mean to see you on Monday or Tuesday next.[15] Adieu! I am ever Yours

T G:

P:S: Pray, is Mrs Olliffe[16] come to Cambridge.

Addressed: To The Revd Mr Brown President of Pembroke-Hall Cambridge
Postmark: 22 MA

525*. Gray to Mason

[*c. 24 May 1770*]

[On 26 May Mason received a letter from Gray (which is not extant), in which he wrote that he would be at Aston on 2 or 3 June. See Letter 514*.]

526. NICHOLLS TO GRAY

May 26th. [1770]

WHY you will not write I can't guefs,[1] because if you recollect I was to wait your more certain direction before I wrote to Bonstetten.[2] I have not heard from him, but that only serves to make me obstinate; I do not so easily give up, or suffer myself to be given up by a person whom I think worth my esteem. I have had an answer from the bishop[3] (for he is determined to shew me that he thinks a gentleman entitled to an answer) most civil in terms, but most uncivil in fact, for preach[4] I must; indeed I had no other expectation. It is not however about my own foolish concerns that I write now. I have this moment received the enclosed from poor Temple, and have been as irresolute and full of doubts whether to send it all, or transcribe from it, as I am every day about the Genera of Linnæus. You will see best from his own words what he wants, and I am sure you will feel his situation; any instance of attention and kindnefs from you will be a medicine to his distrefs; his spirits require to be raised, and I know nothing so likely to raise them; if you should write yourself it would be an act of charity indeed! he has no other refuge or consolation than his books, when his mind is unbent from that attention it sinks into despair. In

---

[15] See Letter 524, n. 6.   [16] See Letter 271, n. 3.

LETTER 526.—First printed by Mitford (1835–43), vol. v, pp. 109–11.

[1] Gray's letter of 22 May (Letter 524) had evidently not yet reached Nicholls.   [2] See Letter 517 *ad fin.*

[3] Dr. Philip Yonge, Bishop of Norwich since 1761.

[4] It was no doubt the sermon which the Bishop required Nicholls to preach to which Gray refers at the end of his letters to Nicholls of 22 May and 24 June (Letters 524, 528).

short his letter is too faithful a portrait of his mind, and I send it you because I think you are interested in his fate. What must I say to him about that resolution of separating which he seems to speak of seriously?⁵ Will it pafs off of itself? or should I difsuade it? or what can it mean? separating only from her bed? that will be a source of perpetual ill-humours and misery, if not impofsible. as for any other separation how can he pofsibly afford that? I should scruple to have sent you the letter if I were not conscious to myself of acting from motives of the truest friendship. I would do the best, but am quite at a lofs. I am sure your heart will prompt you to advise me.

I fear you are on your journey to Yorkshire,⁶ but I trust this will be safely conveyed to you. I shall however for fear of accidents blot out names—the direction, if you will write yourself, is near Chudleigh.⁷

I live in hopes of the first week in July.⁸ Adieu!

N. N.

527. GRAY TO NICHOLLS

[c. 2 June 1770]¹

[Dear]² Nicholls

I WROTE to you from London lately not knowing but you might care to go with me into Yorkshire tomorrow, but as I neither find you here,³ nor any letter from you, I conclude that is not to be. I would wish by all means to oblige & serve T:⁴ in any way I am able, but it can not be *in his way* at present. he & you

⁵ The unfortunate Temple (see Letter 456) was again beset with troubles, real or imaginary. He wrote of them to Boswell also, and to him had mentioned a 'strange scheme' of changing his profession (*Letters of James Boswell*, edited by C. B. Tinker, p. 175). To Nicholls he had written of his resolution of separating from his wife. Meanwhile he wished to console himself by the reading of history, and sought direction from Gray and Boswell (Boswell sent him advice from Hume). His troubles and his desire of advice for reading history were repeated in 1771 (Letters 545, 549, 550).

⁶ To visit Mason at Aston (see Letter 524).

⁷ The post-town for Mamhead, where Temple's rectory was.

⁸ When he and Gray were to start on their projected tour in Wales.

LETTER 527.—First printed by Mitford (1835–43), vol. v, pp. 85–6; now reprinted from original. The letter was overlooked by Tovey.

¹ This letter, which is not dated, was obviously written from Cambridge during Gray's brief stay there ('only two days', as he says in this letter) after his return from London, and before he set out for his journey to Yorkshire to visit Mason, on which he had suggested that Nicholls might accompany him (see Letter 524).   ² MS. torn.

³ At Cambridge (see n. 1).   ⁴ Temple (see Letter 526).

seem to think, that I have nothing else to do but to transcribe a page from some common-place-book on this head: if it were so, I should not hesitate a minute about it. but as I came from Town only on Thursday last,[5] have only two days to pafs here, & must fetch all the materials from my own recollection, he must excuse me for the present. let him begin with Ld Bacon's Henry 7th,[6] & Ld Herbert's Henry 8th,[7] & by that time I return from Aston (wch will be in 3 weeks or lefs) perhaps I may be able to help him onwards a little. I keep the letter till we meet, least it be lost. I would reply nothing to the article of *separation* ([8]

*　*　*　*　*　*　*　*　*　*　*

*　*　*　*　*　*　*　*　*[9] for himself.[10]

*　*　*　*　*[11] point.[12] Adieu!

Direct, *à* Mons:^{r} Mons: de B: *chez* Mefs:^{rs} *Lullin*, Freres, Banquiers, rue Thevenot, Paris.[13]

Addressed: To the Revd Mr Nicholls

527*. GRAY TO ALDERSON[1]

23 June. 1770. Cambridge

Dear S^r

A CERTAIN letter[2] was sent me from hence to Aston on this day (Saturday) se'nnight, wch probably reach'd Sheffield on Tuesday last (19 June). as it has not yet reach'd my hands, & I should be very sorry to lose it, I must beg you to make enquiry about it, to pay whatever it is charged (a double & perhaps

---

[5] May 31.

[6] *History of the Reign of King Henry VII*, first published in 1622.

[7] See Letter 516, n. 4.

[8] The preceding nine words have been scored through, but are still legible.

[9] A passage here has been heavily scored through, and is undecipherable.

[10] These two words have been scored through, but are still legible.

[11] Several words here have been heavily scored through, and are undecipherable.

[12] Scored through, but still legible. In the suppressed passage Gray evidently referred to Temple's unhappy relations with his wife, as to which Nicholls had asked his advice (see Letter 526, n. 5).

[13] This was one of the alternative addresses which Gray sent to Nicholls on 14 Apr. (see Letter 517).

LETTER 527*.—Now first printed from original.

[1] The Rev. Christopher Alderson, Mason's curate; see Letter 453, n. 7.

[2] This may have been a letter from Bonstetten, who at this time was in Paris.

triple postage) & new direct it back to me *at Pembroke-Hall, Cambridge.* Mʳ Mason will repay you for me. Forgive me this trouble, as I know not to whom else I could write about it, & believe me.

Your very humble Servant
THO: GRAY

Mʳ Brown & Mʳ Foljambe³ desire their compliments.

Addressed: To The Revᵈ Mʳ Alderson of Aston near Sheffield Yorkshire
Postmark: CAMBRIDGE

528. GRAY TO NICHOLLS

Pemb: Coll: 24 June. 1770.

Dear Sʳ

I AM return'd from Aston, & now wait your commands. my idea is, that we might meet on the first or second of July at Huntingdon or at the Wheat-Sheaf,¹ 5 miles further on the Northern road (for I do not like to be here at the Commencement)² & thence find our way crofs by Thrapston³ into Warwickshire, so thro' Worcestershire, Shropshire, & other of the midland counties for about three weeks; but the particular route & objects we are to see I leave to be determined on joint consultation. the Wheat-sheaf I only mention as a very good Inn (tho' a little out of our way) where I pofsibly may go, & wait a day or two for you. send me word, whether it suits you, & precisely tell me the day you can come. my compliments to Mʳˢ Nicholls. I am sincerely

Yours
T G:

I wish you a good delivery.⁴

Addressed: To The Revᵈ Mʳ Nicholls at Blundeston near Leostoff Suffolk
By Yarmouth *Postmark:* CAMBRIDGE

³ See Letter 489, n. 10.
LETTER 528.—First printed by Mitford (1835–43), vol. v, pp. 111–12; now reprinted from original.
¹ At Alconbury Hill on the Great North Road, 5¼ miles from Huntingdon.
² As Commencement was on the first Tuesday in July (see Letter 129, n. 17), it would fall this year on 3 July.
³ In Northants., 16½ miles from Huntingdon.
⁴ No doubt a jesting reference to the sermon mentioned in Gray's letter to Nicholls of 22 May (Letter 524); as Tovey remarks, the period of gestation had been somewhat long.

529. GRAY TO BEATTIE

Pembroke Hall, July 2,[1] 1770.

I REJOICE to hear that you are restored to a better state of health, to your books, and to your muse once again.[2] That forced difsipation and exercise we are obliged to fly to as a remedy, when this frail machine goes wrong, is often almost as bad as the distemper we would cure; yet I too have been constrained of late to pursue a like regimen, on account of certain pains in the head (a sensation unknown to me before), and of great dejection of spirits. This, Sir, is the only excuse I have to make you for my long silence, and not (as perhaps you may have figured to yourself) any secret reluctance I had to tell you my mind concerning the specimen you so kindly sent me of your new Poem.[3] On the contrary, if I had seen anything of importance to disapprove, I should have hastened to inform you, and never doubted of being forgiven. The truth is, I greatly like all I have seen, and wish to see more. The design is simple, and pregnant with poetical ideas of various kinds, yet seems somehow imperfect at the end. Why may not young Edwin, when necefsity has driven him to take up the harp, and afsume the profefsion of a Minstrel, do some great and singular service to his country? (what service I must leave to your invention) such as no General, no Statesman, no Moralist could do without the aid of music, inspiration, and poetry. This will not appear an improbability in those early times, and in a character then held sacred, and respected by all nations. Besides, it will be a full answer to all the Hermit has said, when he difsuaded him from cultivating these pleasing arts; it will shew their use, and make the best panegyrick of our favourite and celestial science. And lastly, (what weighs most with me) it will throw more of action, pathos, and interest into your design, which already abounds in reflection and sentiment. As to description, I have always thought that it made the most graceful ornament of poetry, but never ought to make the subject. Your ideas are new, and

LETTER 529.—First printed in Mason's *Memoirs*, pp. 383–5.
[1] On this day Gray signed his will, with three Fellows of Pembroke as witnesses, Richard Baker, M.A. 1765 (see Letter 525); Thomas Wilson, M.A. 1769 (see Letter 535); Joseph Turner, M.A. 1770 (subsequently Master of Pembroke, 1784–1828).
[2] This letter is Gray's reply to Beattie's letters of Nov. 1769 (Letter 507*), and 1 May 1770 (Letter 522).
[3] Part of the first book of *The Minstrel* (see Letter 507*, n. 9).

borrowed from a mountainous country, the only one that can furnish truly picturesque scenery. Some trifles in the language or versification you will permit me to remark.

*   *   *   *   *   *   *   *   *   *   *

*   *   *   *   *   *   *   *   *   *   *4

I will not enter at present into the merits of your *Eſsay on Truth*, because I have not yet given it all the attention it deserves, though I have read it through with pleasure; besides I am partial; for I have always thought David Hume[5] a pernicious writer, and believe he has done as much mischief here as he has in his own country. A turbid and shallow stream often appears to our apprehensions very deep. A profeſsed sceptic can be guided by nothing but his present paſsions (if he has any) and interests; and to be masters of his philosophy we need not his books or advice, for every child is capable of the same thing, without any study at all. Is not that *naiveté* and good humour, which his admirers celebrate in him, owing to this, that he has continued all his days an infant, but one that unhappily has been taught to read and write? That childish nation, the French, have given him vogue and fashion, and we, as usual, have learned from them to admire him at second hand.

530. GRAY TO WHARTON

My dear Doctor

IT happen'd, that I was in London at the time, when St:[1] received your letter relating to Mr. L:[s] request. as my name was mention'd in it, I ought to make my excuses to you as well as he, wᶜʰ it is indeed easy to do, as I could by no means ask any thing but thro' him, & (tho' this had been in my power) it would have been a very bad plea to say, my Lᵈ, you have done me a very unexpected favour not long since; & therefore I must beg you to do another at my desire for a Friend of mine. but the truth is, at this time our application could not have had any succeſs, as our Principal would certainly never apply to three different Persons, with whom he has no connection; nor care

---

4 A few paragraphs of particular criticism are here omitted. *Mason.*

5 Beattie had attacked Hume in his *Essay* (see Letter 522, n. 5): Hume is said to have complained that he had not been used like a gentleman.

LETTER 530.—First printed in part (in a garbled text) in Mason's *Memoirs*, pp. 394–5; first printed in full by Mitford (1816), vol. ii, pp. 560–1; now reprinted from original.   1 Stonhewer.

to be refused, or even obliged by them. the inside of things can not be well explain'd by letters; but if you saw it, you would immediately see in its full light the impracticability of the thing.[2]

I am lately return'd[3] from a six weeks ramble thro' Worcestershire, Gloucestershire, Monmouthsh:[re] Herefordsh:[re] & Shropshire, five of the most beautiful counties in the kingdom. the very light, & principal feature in my journey was the river *Wye*, w[ch] I descended in a boat for near 40 miles from Rofs to Chepstow: its banks are a succefsion of namelefs wonders: one out of many you may see not ill described by Mr. Whateley[4] in his *Observations on Gardening* under the name of the *New-Weir*: he has also touch'd upon two others, *Tinterne-Abbey*, and *Persfield* (M[r] Morris's).[5] both of them famous scenes; & both on the Wye. Monmouth, a town I never heard mention'd, lies on the same river in a vale, that is the delight of my eyes, & the very seat of pleasure. the vale of Abergavenny, Ragland & Chepstow-Castles, Ludlow, Malvern-hills, Hampton Court near Lemster,[6] the Leasowes,[7] Hagley,[8] the three Cities & their Cathedrals,[9] & lastly Oxford[10] (where I past two days in my return with great satisfaction), are the rest of my acquisitions, & no bad harvest to my thinking. I have a journal written by the companion[11] of my travels, that serves to recall & fix the fading images of these things.[12]

[2] Gray had evidently been asked to use his interest with the Duke of Grafton on behalf of some third party. Nothing is known as to the identity of Mr. L., nor as to the nature of his request.

[3] The College books show that he returned to Cambridge in the previous week after an absence of less than seven weeks. If he stayed a fortnight in London (as he told Mason in Letter 531) his 'ramble' cannot have taken six weeks. On this tour see Nicholl's *Reminiscences* in Appendix Z.

[4] Thomas Whately (d. 1772), uncle of Archbishop Whately, was M.P. for Ludgershall, 1761–8, and for Castle Rising, 1768–72; Secretary to the Treasury, 1764–5; and Under-Secretary of State, 1771–2. He published anonymously *Observations on Modern Gardening, Illustrated by Descriptions* (Lond. 1770). For his remarks on the New Weir on the Wye ('near a place called Symond's Gate, between Ross and Monmouth'), see pp. 108–9; for his description of Tintern Abbey, pp. 133–5; and of Persfield, pp. 236–7.

[5] See Letter 508, n. 11.

[6] Leominster, in Herefordshire; Hampton Court, formerly the seat of the Coningsbys, was at this time in the possession of their representative, Lady Frances Hanbury-Williams (widow of Sir Charles Hanbury-Williams), daughter and sole heir of Thomas Coningsby, Earl of Coningsby (d. 1729).

[7] In Worcestershire, the residence of Shenstone (see Letter 499, n. 29).

[8] In Worcestershire, the seat of the Lytteltons.

[9] Worcester, Gloucester, and Hereford.

[10] This appears to have been Gray's first and only visit to Oxford.

I desire to hear of your health, & that of your family. are Mifs Wh:ⁿ & Mifs Peggy quite recover'd? my respects to M^{rs}. Wharton & them. I am ever

Yours
T G:

Pemb: Coll: Aug: 24. 1770.

Addressed: To Thomas Wharton Esq of Old Park near Darlington Durham
Postmark: CAMBRIDGE

531. GRAY TO MASON

Dear Mason   [Sept. 7, 1770][1]

I AM very well at present, the usual effect of my summer-expeditions, & *much obliged t'ye Gentlemēn,*[2] for your kind enquiry after me. I have seen Worcestershire, Gloucest:^{re}, Monmouthsh:^{re}, Herefordshire, Shropshire, five of the best counties this kingdom has to produce.[3] the chief grace & ornament of my journey was the river Wye, wch I descended in

[11] Norton Nicholls.

[12] In the same summer William Gilpin (1724–1804), a friend of Mason (see Letter 318, n. 1), made a tour of the Wye of which he published an account in 1782, under the title *Observations on the River Wye and several parts of South Wales, &c., relating chiefly to Picturesque Beauty made in the Summer of the Year 1770.* The Preface to the book is in the form of a letter to the Rev. William Mason and has the following reference to Gray: 'In the same year in which this little journey was made, Mr Gray made it likewise; and hearing that I had put on paper a few remarks on the scenes, which he had so lately visited, he desired a sight of them. They were then only in a rude state; but the handsome things he said of them to a friend of his [William Fraser, Esq., Under-Secretary of State, as Gilpin explains in a note], who obligingly repeated them to me, gave me, I own, some little degree of credit in my own opinion; and made me somewhat less apprehensive in risking them before the public. If this work afforded any amusement to Mr Gray, it was the amusement of a very late period of his life. He saw it in London, about the beginning of June, 1771; and he died . . . at the end of the July following. Had he lived, it is possible he might have been induced to have assisted me with a few of his own remarks on scenes which he had so accurately examined; the slightest touches of such a master would have had their effect. No man was a greater admirer of nature than Mr Gray, nor admired it with better taste.'

LETTER 531.—First printed by Mitford in *Gray–Mason* (1853), pp. 437–8; now reprinted from original.

[1] This is the date endorsed on the letter by Mason.

[2] From Gray's underlining the words and marking the *ē*, it may be assumed that he was repeating some expression familiar to Mason and himself.

[3] See notes to Letter 530.

a boat from Rofs to Chepstow (near 40 miles) surrounded with ever-new delights, among wch were the New-Weir (see Whateley) Tinterne-Abbey, & Persfield. I say nothing of the vale of Abergavenny, Ragland-Castle, Ludlow, Malvern-hills, the Leasowes, & Hagley, &c: nor how I past two days at Oxford very agreeably. the weather was very hot, & generally serene. I envy not your Greffiers,[4] nor your Wensle-dale & Aisgarth-forces,[5] but did you see Winander-mere, & Grafsmere, did you get to Keswick?[6] & what do you think of the matter? I stay'd a fortnight stewing in London, & now am in the midst of this dead quiet[7] with no body but Mr President[8] near me, & he is not dead, but sleepeth.

The politicks of the place are that B^p Warburton[9] will chouse B^p Keene[10] out of Ely by the help of Ld Mansfield,[11] who can

[4] Mason wrote to Wharton from Hornby Castle (a seat of Lord Holdernesse) on 24 July 1770: 'I was to have accompanied this with an invitation from Lord Holdernesse to see you at the Castle while I am here; but as The Dutch Greffier Fagel & another foreigner are daily expected His Lordship thinks that such a visit at present will not be so agreeable to you as in September; when his Lordship will return here from Aston. . . . I have been here about a week & want greatly to proceed forward to Keswick. But I fear I shall not be able to get off till my York residence calls me away on the 12th of next Month. However when the Greffier arrives I mean to make a strong push for my Liberty' (Brit. Mus. *Egerton* 2400). The important office of Greffier of the States-General of Holland had been held by members of the Fagel family since 1670. The Greffier here in question was Hendrik Fagel, who was born at The Hague in 1706, was appointed Greffier in 1744, and died in 1790. He was a man of letters, and is said to have been one of the authors of the French translation of the letters of Lady Mary Wortley Montagu which was published at Amsterdam in 1764. According to Mitford (who refers to mentions of him in Mrs. Elizabeth Carter's *Memoirs*, vol. i, p. 345; and *Letters*, vol. iii, p. 277) (see *Gray–Mason Correspondence*, 2nd ed., p. 534), he was nearly related to Lady Holdernesse, who was Dutch (see Letter 206, n. 8).

[5] Aysgarth, in Wensleydale, in North Riding of Yorks., about eight miles west of Middleham.

[6] See n. 4. In the foregoing paragraph Gray is evidently referring to a letter of Mason's which is not extant.   [7] He writes from Cambridge.

[8] James Brown, President of Pembroke.

[9] Bishop of Gloucester since Dec. 1759.

[10] Bishop of Chester since Mar. 1752 (see Letter 143, n. 3). The Bishop of Ely was Dr. Matthias Mawson (1683–1770), formerly Master of Corpus Christi College, Cambridge (1724–44), and successively Bishop of Llandaff, and of Chichester. He had been translated to Ely in 1754, and was now in his eighty-eighth year, and very infirm. Consequently a vacancy in the see was imminent. He died on 23 Nov. following, and was succeeded by Keene (see Letter 540, n. 6).

[11] Lord Chief Justice (see Letter 120, n. 25). There had been a long-

be refused nothing at present. every one is frighted, except Tom Neville.[12]

Palgrave, I suppose, is at Mr Weddel's,[13] & has told you the strange casualties of his household. Adieu! I am ever

Yours
T G:

The letter in question[14] was duely received.

532. GRAY TO WALPOLE

I AM ashamed to excuse myself to you, tho it was not negligence, but forgetfulnefs. the other day going into the publick Library I first recollected your commifsion, & consulted the chronicle of Croyland.[1] the only edition I find of it, has certainly these words—sed quo genere *violenti* interitûs, ignoratur. either you have made use of some edition, where that efsential word is omitted,[2] or cited after *Buck*[3] without suspecting his fidelity.

I am ever
Yours

Pemb: Hall. 12 Sept: 1770.   THO: GRAY.

Addressed: To The Honble Horace Walpole in Arlington Street London
Postmark: ROYSTON 13 SE

standing friendship between Warburton and Mansfield. The latter (as Murray), when Solicitor-General, had procured Warburton's election as Preacher at Lincoln's Inn in 1746; and Warburton in 1758 had dedicated to him, as Lord Chief Justice, the third edition of the second volume of his *Divine Legation*. Lord Mansfield was at this time Speaker of the House of Lords (while the Great Seal was in commission), where he had successfully opposed Lord Chatham's attempt to involve the Lords in the struggle between Wilkes and the House of Commons.

[12] See Letter 237*, n. 2.   [13] See Letter 400, n. 13.

[14] This may be the letter about which Gray wrote to Alderson on 23 June (see Letter 527*).

LETTER 532.—First printed by Toynbee (1915), No. 246.

[1] This was one of the authorities cited by Walpole in his *Historic Doubts on Richard III* (see Letter 458, n. 1).

[2] In the *Historic Doubts* (in *Works*, vol. ii, p. 148, note) Walpole quotes the chronicler as saying: 'Vulgatum est regis Edwardi pueros concessisse in fata, sed quo genere interitus ignoratur.' The omission of *violenti* was charged against Walpole by Dr. Milles, Dean of Exeter, and President of the Society of Antiquaries, in some *Observations* published by the Society in 1770. Walpole published a *Reply* (dated 28 Aug. 1770) in which he dealt with the question (see *Works*, vol. ii, pp. 227*–9*).

[3] Sir George Buck (d. 1623), author of the *History of the Life and Reign of Richard the Third* (published in 1646), which is frequently quoted by Walpole in the *Historic Doubts*.

Dear S^r   533. GRAY TO NICHOLLS

VENGA, venga, V: S: si serva!¹ I shall be proud to see you both. the lodgings over the way will be empty, but such an entry, such a staircase! how will M^{rs} N: be able to crowd thro' it? with what grace, when she gets out of her chair, can she conduct her hoop-petticoat thro' this augre-hole, and up the dark windings of the *grand escalier*, that leads to her chamber? it is past my finding out. so I delay, till I hear from you again, before I engage them. I believe, there may be a bed for *you*, but is there room for Mrs Kipiffe, Mamma's Maid? I am sure, I know not.

I was very ill, when I received your letter, with a feverish disorder; but have cured it merely by dint of *sage-tea*, the beverage of life. it is a polydynamious plant, take my word: tho' your Linnæus would persuade us, it is merely *diandrious*.² I applaud your industry; it will do you a power of good one way or another, only don't mistake a Carabus³ for an Orchis, nor a Lepisma⁴ for an Adenanthera.⁵ here is Mr Foljambe⁶ has got a *Flying* Hobgoblin from the E: Indies, & a power of rarities; & then he has given me such a *Phalæna*⁷ with looking-glaſses in its wings; & a Queen of the *White Ants*,⁸ whose belly alone is as big as many hundred of her subjects, I do not mean their bellies only, but their whole persons: and yet her head & her *tetons* & her legs are no bigger than other people's. oh, she is a jewel of a pismire!

I hear the triumphs & see the illuminations of Alloa hither, but did M^{rs} E:⁹ lie a night at Edinburgh in her way thither?

LETTER 533.—First printed by Mitford (1835–43), vol. v, pp. 112–13; now reprinted from original.

¹ 'Make yourself at home!' (literally, 'help yourself'). Nicholls came (see Letter 536 *ad init.*).

² The usual form is 'diandrous'.   ³ A genus of beetles.

⁴ The generic name for the insects popularly known as 'silver-fish'.

⁵ A genus of leguminous shrubs with bright-red seeds.

⁶ See Letter 489, n. 10.

⁷ A term used by Linnæus as a generic name for all moths.

⁸ At the end of Gray's note-book, which contains the *Journal* of his tour to the Lakes (see Letter 505, n. 1), is a description in English, followed by a technical description in Latin, of 'The White Ant from Bengal. March 1770. given by Mr Ingham, Surgeon to Lord Clive, to Mr Foljambe, & by him to me'.

⁹ The identity of 'Mrs. E:' is revealed by the following entry in Boswell's *Journal* for 15 Oct. 1774: 'Captain James Erskine of Alloa had been with us at Inverkeithing. He . . . insisted that we should go for a night or two to

does she meet with no signs of mortality about her castle? are
her subjects all civet-cats & musk-deer? My respects to your Mother. Adieu! I have had an infinite
letter from Bonst:[n],[10] he goes in October to *Rocheguion*[11] on the
Loire, with the Dutchess d'Enville.[12] the people in several
provinces are starving to death on the highways. the King (in
spite to his parliaments & nation) it is thought, will make the
Duke d'Aiguillon[13] his chief Minister.

Sept: 14. 1770.

Addressed: To The Revd Mr Nicholls, at William Turner's[14] Esq at Richmond
Surrey *Postmark:* 15 SE

Alloa. . . . At night we went to Alloa. It was pleasing to me to come at last
to this ancient seat of which I had so often heard. I was glad to see my old
class fellow Johnnie Erskine in his own house, and his Lady, formerly Miss
Floyer, whom I had seen in London in the year 1763 when my friend Temple
admired her much' (Private Papers of James Boswell, vol. x, p. 28).
   The Erskines of Alloa were of the family of the Earl of Mar. Boswell's
old class fellow was John Francis (1741–1825), grandson and lineal repre-
sentative of the eleventh Earl, the Jacobite Earl, who was attainted for tak-
ing part in the rising on behalf of the Pretender in 1715. Erskine joined the
Army in 1757, and retired from it as Captain in 1770, on 17 Mar. of which
year he married at Upwey, in Dorsetshire (see Letter 500), Frances, only
daughter of Charles Floyer, Governor of Madras. 'Mrs. E:', therefore, was
Mrs. John Erskine, who was none other than Nicholls's cousin Fanny (see
Letters 422, n. 11; 425, n. 4; 477, n. 4); and the 'triumphs and illuminations'
at Alloa were evidently in honour of the home-coming of the newly married
couple. In 1776, on the death of his mother, Erskine succeeded to the family
estate of Alloa; and in 1824, the year before his death, at the age of 83, he
was restored Earl of Mar. Boswell's friend, Captain Andrew Erskine, was
the younger brother of John Erskine.
   [10] The letter in question was no doubt written from Paris.
   [11] La Roche Guyon, not on the Loire, but on the Seine, midway between
Paris and Rouen, in what is now the Department of Seine et Oise.
   [12] Marie Louise Nicole de la Rochefoucauld (b. 1716), cousin and wife
(1732) of Jean Baptiste Louis Frédéric de la Rochefoucauld de Roye, Duc
d'Anville (d. 1746). The country-seat of the Duchesse, who was an intimate
friend of Mme du Deffand, was at La Roche Guyon. Bonstetten had made the
acquaintance of the Duchesse, and of her daughter-in-law, at Geneva in 1765.
   [13] Emmanuel Armand du Plessis-Richelieu (1720–80), Duc d'Aiguillon;
he intrigued with Mme du Barry against the Duc de Choiseul, the first
minister, and after the disgrace of the latter (Dec. 1770) was appointed in
his place (June 1771). He was execrated on account of his persecution, as
Governor of Brittany, of La Chalotais in 1765 (see Letter 431, n. 4).
   [14] An uncle of Nicholls (see Letter 429, n. 7). Horace Walpole wrote to
Miss Berry on 27 Nov. 1790: 'The very old uncle of the Abbé Nichols is
dead, and, as he tells me, has left well to his mother and him, and he is come
to live [at Richmond] with her, and I shall hear him sing, I conclude, at the
Duke [of Queensberry]'s concerts.'

534. GRAY TO WALPOLE

Sept: 17. 1770. Pemb: Coll:

I WRITE, having nothing efsential to say, merely because you are ill,[1] & have but too much time to read me. I plead no merit in my sympathy, because I have the same enemy, & am daily expecting her attacks, the more violent perhaps for having been now for some years suspended.[2] talk not of round windows, nor of dying in them: our distemper (remember) is the means of health & *long life*,[3] now this latter is only the name of another distemper, of wch I know enough already to say, when the gout pinches me, *'tis well, it is nothing worse.* I do not understand, why (with your temperance) you are treated so severely; but suspect, it is owing to a little indolence & want of motion between the fits, as I have lately heard you complain of a tendernefs in your feet, that would not let you walk as usual. Man is a creature made to be jumbled, & no matter whether he goes on his head or heels, move or be moved he must. I am convinced, I owe my late & present ease to the little expeditions I always make in summer. the smartnefs of the pain you undergo, is an undoubted sign of strength & *youth*, & the sooner it will be over. I know, this is poor comfort: but I flatter myself, that in some few days you will be at ease, & will have the good nature to tell me so.

I have neither seen Tyson,[4] nor Cole of late, but will take care they shall know, what you say. the latter lives at Milton[5] near the Ely road. for myself I shall hardly be in Town before the end of November. Adieu! I am

Yours ever

T G:

Addressed: To The Honble Horace Walpole in Arlington Street London
Postmark: ROYSTON 18 SE

LETTER 534.—First printed by Toynbee (1915), No. 247.

[1] Walpole had been seized with a very severe fit of gout, which laid him up for many weeks (see letters to Lady Ossory of 15 Sept., and to Montagu of 16 Oct., 1770).

[2] He had not long to wait; see next letter.

[3] Writing to Mann on 20 Sept., just after the receipt of this letter, Walpole, speaking of his illness, says: 'I taste very little comfort in that usual compliment, of the gout being an earnest of long life.'

[4] Michael Tyson (1740–80), antiquary and artist, Fellow of Corpus Christi College, Cambridge; B.A. 1764; M.A. 1767; B.D. 1775; he was a friend of Walpole, Gray, Cole, and Mason (see Letter 144, n. 50).

[5] See Letter 495, n. 1.

535. GRAY TO MASON

24 Oct: 1770. Pemb: Hall.

Dear Mason

I HAVE been for these three weeks & more confined to my room by a fit of the gout, & am now only beginning to walk alone again. I should not mention the thing, but that I am well-persuaded, it will soon be your own case, as you have so soon laid aside your horse, & talk so relishingly of your old Port. I can not see any objection to your design for M^r P:,[1] as to Wilson[2] we know him much alike. he seems a good honest Lad, & (I believe) is scholar enough for your purpose.[3] perhaps this connection may make (or marr) his fortune. our friend Foljambe[4] has resided in college & persevered in the ways of godlinefs till about ten days ago, when he disappear'd, & no one knows, whether he is gone a hunting or a fornicating. the little Fitz-herbert[5] is come a Pensioner to St John's, & seems to have all his wits about him. your Eléve Ld Richard Cav:^sh[6] having digested all the learning and all the beef this place could afford him in a two month's residence[7] is about to leave us, & his little

LETTER 535.—First printed by Mitford in *Gray–Mason* (1853), pp. 442–5; now reprinted from original.

[1] The name is supplied by Mason as 'Pierse' in his letter to Gray of 27 Mar. 1771 (Letter 547). Henry Peirse of Bedale, Yorks., was admitted to Pembroke as a Fellow-commoner in July 1771.

[2] Thomas Wilson, of Pembroke College; B.A. 1766; Fellow, 1767; M.A. 1769; Vicar of Soham, Cambs. (a College living), 1769; d. 1797.

[3] Obviously as tutor to Peirse.   [4] See Letter 489, n. 10.

[5] Alleyne Fitzherbert (1753–1839), fifth and youngest son of William Fitzherbert of Tissington, Derbyshire (see Letter 444, n. 6); he matriculated as a pensioner at St. John's College in July 1770. After a distinguished University career, in 1777 he entered the diplomatic service; he was created an Irish peer as Baron St. Helens, in 1791. While in his first year at College he was called upon by Gray, as he informed Rogers, to whom he gave the following account, which Rogers communicated to Mitford: 'I came to St. John's College, Cambridge, in 1770, and that year received a visit from Gray, having a letter of introduction to him. He was accompanied by Dr Gisborne, Mr Stonhewer, and Mr Palgrave, and they walked one after one, in Indian file. When they withdrew, every College man took off his cap as he passed, a considerable number having assembled in the quadrangle to see Mr Gray, who was seldom seen. I asked Mr Gray, to the great dismay of his companions, what he thought of Mr Garricks Jubilee Ode, just published? He answered, He was easily pleased.'   [6] See Letter 461, n. 19.

[7] Lord Richard had matriculated in 1768 (Letter 488), and he received the M.A. degree on 2 Nov. 1770. A nobleman taking his degree *jure nobilitatis* had to be of two years standing, but no length of residence was prescribed. See Addendum, vol. i, p. lx above.

Brother George[8] succeeds him. B[p] Keene has brought a Son[9] from Eton to Peterhouse, & D[r] Heberden[10] another[11] to S[t] John's, who is enter'd Pensioner, & destined to the Church. this is all my University-news, but why do I tell you? come yourself & see, for I hope you remember your promise at Aston, & will make us in your way, as you go to your town-residence. You have seen Stonh:[r] (I imagine) who went northwards on Saturday last. pray tell me how he is, for I think him not quite well. tell me this & tell me when I may expect to see you here. I am ever

Yours
T G:

536. GRAY TO NICHOLLS

25 Nov: 1770.

I DO not see, why you should suppose that *you* only are to have the privilege of being ill. for me, from the time you left me (till within these three days) I have been only one day out of the walls of this college. that day was employ'd in going to the Hills[1] by way of airing after the gout, & in catching such a cold & cough as has given me no rest night or day, & has only now taken its leave of me. I sent away your letter to B: directly: I saw no reason against it. he was then at Aubonne near Geneva with his Brother, & is now at Berne. the picture[2] is not arrived, nor (I suppose) ever will; tho' he says, he has sent it, but by what conveyance, or by what hand he does not say.

You do me wrong: I have thought very frequently of you, & especially since S[r] A: Allen's[3] death. I am rather glad his

---

[8] Lord George Augustus Henry Cavendish (1754–1834), third and youngest son of fourth Duke of Devonshire; afterwards created Earl of Burlington in 1831; entered Trinity College in 1770. He is said to have been, save for Fitzherbert (see n. 5), the last survivor of those who had known Gray.

[9] Benjamin Keene, M.A. 1774.   [10] See Letter 135, n. 20.

[11] Thomas Heberden, B.A. 1775; M.A. 1778; he became a Fellow of St. John's, and was Prebendary successively of Exeter (1778), Chichester (1784), and Bath and Wells (1786); he died at the age of 90 in 1843.

LETTER 536.—First printed by Mitford (1835–43), vol. v, pp. 114–15; now reprinted from original.

[1] The Gog Magog hills to south-east of Cambridge.

[2] A portrait of Bonstetten (see Letter 540, n. 7).

[3] Sir Ashurst Allin (*c.* 1720–70), third Baronet (1765), of Somerleyton, Suffolk; he was at Emmanuel College, Cambridge (M.A. 1739), was ordained, and became Rector of Blundeston cum Flixton; he died on 6 Nov. 1770,

family were about him, tho' I know not well why, for he perhaps was insensible to it. these sort of deaths are alarming to the Spectator; but perhaps the best for the Sufferer. I have now every day before my eyes a Woman of ninety, my Aunt,[4] who has for many years been gradually turning into chalk-stones: they are making their way out of the joints of both feet, & the Surgeon twice a day comes to increase the torture. she is just as sensible & as impatient of pain, & as intractable as she was 60 years ago. she thinks not at all of death, & if a mortification does not come to release her, may lie in this agony for months (at least) helplefs & bed-rid. this is what you call a *natural* death!

It is well, you live in a dry country, but do not your lakes[5] overflow? can any thing get from Norwich[6] to Blundeston? 200,000 acres are drown'd in the Fens here & cattle innumerable. our Friends at Worcester, Gloucester, &c: are sailing thro' the streets from house to house.[7] Adieu! the Post is impatient. my respects to M^rs N:, I am

Faithfully Yours
T G:

Addressed: To The Revd Mr Nicholls at Blundeston near Leostoff Suffolk by Norwich *Postmark:* CAMBRIDGE

537. NICHOLLS TO GRAY

Blundeston, Nov. 28, 1770.

GOD forbid that I should claim to myself the privilege you mention. That fool, young S——, at his return from Cambridge, told me that you had been perfectly well some time,

leaving a daughter, Frances, and a son, Thomas, who succeeded him in the baronetcy, and died unmarried in 1794, when the baronetcy became extinct.
    4 Mrs. Olliffe (see Letter 525, n. 16). She died a few weeks before Gray.
    5 See Letter 455, n. 3.   6 Substituted for Yarmouth.
    7 See Letter 537. The *Gentleman's Magazine* for Nov. 1770 gives the following reports of the floods: 'The accounts that have been received during the course of the present month, of the melancholy effects of the floods in several parts of the kingdom, exceed anything of the kind that has happened in the memory of man. The cities and towns situated on the banks of the Severn have suffered very great distress; those on the Trent have suffered still more; the great Bedford Level is now under water. . . . But the most affecting scene of all happened at Coventry, where the waters in the middle of the night came rolling into the lowermost street of the town. . . . More than seventy persons have been taken up drowned in this city only' (vol. xl, p. 541).
    LETTER 537.—First printed by Mitford (1835–43), vol. v, pp. 115–19. Misprints in Mitford's text, 'prima ætatis Christiana' (for primæ ætatis Christianæ) and 'joumées' (for journées), have been corrected.

which, of course, relieved me from all anxiety on that account. What a blefsing it is to have a galloping imagination: I fancied you in town, with people whom you loved better, or who at least engrofsed you for the time, hearing news, or bad operas, amused, in short, and quite thoughtlefs of me in my hermitage. But you was in flannel too, so I beg your pardon.

I have returned to reading a little since my pain left me; I have run through eight centuries of Christianity in Mosheim.[1] I am pleased with the good sense, judgment, and impartiality of the author, and with his plain manly stile; but that this should be a history of religion, that Monothelites, and Monophysites, and Stylites should think they were doing God service is wonderful! Simeon,[2] a Syrian, was founder of the last sect, he was first a shepherd and then a monk, and built himself five columns, one of six cubits high, the next twelve, the next twenty-two, another thirty-six, and the last forty; and on these he pafsed thirty-seven years of his life, advancing in a progrefsive state upwards towards heaven. Then the pride and power of bishops, growing out of an humble and laborious office, totally different in its nature and intention! Patriarchs lording it over these, and the 'gran verme'[3] at last devouring all. New doctrines invented every day, and propagated like the religion of Mahomet. The pafsions of men hurrying them out of sight of the true object of contention. All this, and thousand times more that I forget (thank Heaven) as fast as I read it, makes me wish myself at the last page; when the Reformation *commence à éclore*, I shall apply myself to Burnet,[4] in hopes of learning a little profane history to mix with my divine, which is really a bad mefs by itself. I think that there is lefs inconvenience, after all, in believing as one's nurse bids one, than in resolving to understand and explain to all the world what reason was never meant to meddle with. 'Illa enim (says Mosheim, speaking of the fifth century,) primæ ætatis Christianæ sancta et veneranda simplicitas, quæ Deo loquenti credere, et mandanti obedire jubebat, præcipuis horum temporum doctoribus agrestis vide-

---

[1] Johann Lorenz von Mosheim (see Letter 299, n. 8). The work which Nicholls was reading was the *Institutiones Historiae Ecclesiasticae Antiquae et Recentioris*, in four books, first published at Helmstädt in 1726; a new edition appeared in 1755. As appears from the passage he quotes below, Nicholls was reading it in the original Latin.

[2] St. Simeon Stylites.

[3] No doubt a reminiscence of Dante, who calls Cerberus, at the mouth of Hell, 'il gran vermo' (*Inf.* vi. 22).   [4] See Letter 19, n. 3.

batur.' But Mosheim and Homer and all is at a stand now, or obliged at least to make room for Froifsart.[5] In the evening I read Rapin[6] to my mother; so being come to Edward the Third, I took up Froifsart, to keep pace with the other, and am so delighted that I read nothing else, 'et ay-je tant chevauché par mes journées,' that I am arrived at the peace of Bretigny.[7] He is my historian, for he tells me all that he knows, and tells for the sake of telling, and forgets himself to talk of other people; which I believe is never the case for a single moment with our modern historians, who all write for vanity or profit, and betray their design; there is something so very apprêté in all of them, and so very much the contrary in him. If it is owing to the simplicity of the age, and if it would not suit with the present times, I am sorry for it, for I like it much better. What a miserable state was France in when their king[8] was a prisoner in England, when English garrisons lived at discretion in all parts of the kingdom, English armies spread desolation through every part of it, and the Jaquerie,[9] to complete their misery, raged everywhere without control! I want to know whether you do not think Edward the First and Edward the Third's pretensions to Scotland very unjust, and a stain to their characters, when one considers the mischiefs they caused? and whether you think Edward the Third's pretensions to the crown of France, and the torrents of blood that were shed to support them, give a real lustre to his reign? and whether it was a worthy action to protest in private against the King of France and his title, and yet do him public homage? My brave Lord Herbert of Cherbury[10] would have   *   *   *[11]

[5] Froissart's *Chroniques* cover the period from 1326 to 1400 (see Letter 308, n. 1; and Letter 543).
[6] Paul Rapin de Thoyras (1661–1725), author of *L'Histoire d'Angleterre*, printed at The Hague, 1724–36 (13 vols. 4to); the work covers the period from the invasion of the Romans to the death of Charles I. An English translation, with notes by Nicholas Tindal, was published in 1725–31 (2 vols. fol.). Nicholls in his *Reminiscences* (Appendix Z) quoted Gray's opinion: 'Rapin's he looked on as the only general history of England.'
[7] The treaty, disastrous to France, signed on 8 May 1360.
[8] King John II, who had been taken prisoner at the battle of Poitiers in 1356.
[9] The insurrection of the peasants in the Île-de-France in the summer of 1358, in the suppression of which some 10,000 were massacred.
[10] See Letter 376, preliminary note.
[11] Presumably some expression considered unseemly by Mitford has been suppressed here.

My friend Dr. Warner,[12] and his very amiable wife, with Mifs Allin,[13] are gone this day to attempt the London road. The Dr. is prudent, and will not willingly drown himself and them; but the Yarmouth coach, when it has gone at all, has gone with eight horses and four postilions. A waggon and coach were overset in the water at Ixworth[14] near Bury, but no mischief done. The marshes which I see from my bedchamber window are become an ocean. I have heard from Clarke,[15] who has been these five months at Kylmarnock in Ayrshire, and stays five more: from Wheeler,[16] who has been at Bath with his old haridan again. I have besides received a silly letter from Mr. Wilson, and a polite one from Dr. Gisburne,[17] apologizing for not seeing me before he left Richmond, &c. I have heard of Temple, who has sold some of his estate, got rid of some vexation,[18] met with more, and is now returned to Mamhead. Adieu! accept my mother's best compliments, and believe me always sincerely yours,

N. N.

538. Cole to Gray.

[*22 Dec. 1770*]

[It appears from Cole's MS. *Athenae Cantabrigienses* (Brit. Mus. *Add. MS.* 5875) that on 22 Dec. 1770 he wrote a letter[1] to Gray commenting on the funeral of Dr. Roger Long, Master of Pembroke, who died on 16 Dec. 1770, and was buried on 21 Dec. in a vault of the College Chapel. Cole writes: 'That very Day I received a L^r on my getting Home[2] from Mr Horace Walpole,[3] to desire me to call on M^r

---

[12] Nothing is known of this friend of Nicholls. Nicholls mentions him again in Letter 541.

[13] See Letter 536, n. 3. According to Mitford (1835–43, vol. v, p. 179) the house at Blundeston, which had been bequeathed to Miss Allin by her father, was rented from her by Nicholls (see Letters 545, n. 10, and 554, n. 6).

[14] About three miles north-east of Bury St. Edmunds.

[15] See Letter 513, n. 1.   [16] See Letter 421, n. 18.

[17] See Letter 299, n. 10.

[18] His troubles culminated before very long (see Letter 551, n. 1).

LETTER 538.—[1] Cole referred to this letter also in a MS. note in his copy of Mason's *Memoirs* (quoted by Mitford (1835–43), vol. i, p. cvi): 'The last time I saw him [Mr. Gray] was at the funeral of Dr Long, master of his college, in Dec. 1770. [The day after], I had occasion to write to him, and in my letter, partly in joke, partly in earnest, I took notice of the slovenliness, and want of proper decency and solemnity at such an occasion. His answer, dated Sat. Dec. 22, 1770, was as below.' He then gave Gray's reply (see Letter 539). 'The day after' is a necessary correction of Mitford's misreading, 'Thursday after' (which would have been Dec. 27).

[2] Cole was then living at Milton, a village on the Ely road, about three miles from Cambridge.

GULIELMUS COLE, A.M. A.S. Soc.

William Cole
from an engraving by Facius after a painting by Thomas Kerrich

Gray, Fellow Com̃oner of Pembroke & who was at the Funeral, but being in the Combination I would not call him from his Company, tho' had been at his Chambers: I wrote the next Day a Note to him, of the unceremonious & indecent Manner of the Funeral, & concluded by saying, that after what passed in the Chapel to compleat all, they had taken the poor M.ʳ from a warm Hall & a noble Fire & flung him into a Well or Ditch half full of Water.[4] Mʳ Gray's Answer to my Servant was: . . ' (Here Cole quoted Gray's letter.[5])]

539. GRAY TO COLE[1]

How did we know, pray? No Body here remember'd another Burying of the Kind:[2] shall be proud of your Advice the next opportunity, which (we hope) will be some Forty years hence.[3] I am sorry you would not send for me last Night. I shall not be able to wait on you chez vous, so soon as I would wish, for I go in a few Days to Town, when I shall see Mʳ Walpole.

Adieu! at my Return we shall meet.

Sat: 22. Dec: 1770.

[3] On 20 Dec. Walpole wrote to Cole from Arlington Street: 'If you go over to Cambridge, be so good as to ask Mʳ Gray when he proposes being in town: he talked of last month.'

[4] In the same passage of his MS. *Athenae Cantabrigienses* Cole has the following note on the funeral: 'Dining at Mʳ Coleman's the President of Benet College, on Friday Dec: 21. [1770] & hearing there that Dʳ Long was to be buried that Evening at 6 o'Clock, Mʳ Tyson & I went thither to see the Vault in which Bp. Wren was interred.' [Matthew Wren (1585–1667), Fellow of Pembroke College 1605–23, afterwards Master of Peterhouse, and Bishop successively of Hereford, Norwich, and Ely, built the Chapel at Pembroke in 1763 to the design of his nephew, Christopher, then beginning his career as an architect.] Cole proceeds to give a somewhat confused account of the vault, in which there was a foot of water, and of the arrangements for putting the wooden coffin in a stone coffin, which had been prepared to enclose it. He continues: 'When we went to Pembroke, we found the Coffin in the Middle of the Hall, with a Pall & Verses by the Society, pinned on it: the Fellows were in the Combination Room, & Scholars in the Hall by the Fire: the Fellows supported the Pall & one in a Surplise [*sic*], Mʳ Baker, I think his Name is, & one Scholar in another Surplice, the one to read the Evening Service & the other the first Lesson out of the Proverbs, which was probably the right one for the Day, but wrong for the Occasion.'

[5] Letter 539.

LETTER 539.—First printed by Mitford (1835–43), vol. iv, p. 194; now eprinted from Cole's transcript (Brit. Mus. *Add. MS.* 5875, f. 65).

[1] See Letter 538, to which this is the reply.

[2] Dr. John Hawkins, Dr. Long's predecessor, died in 1736, three years after his resignation.

[3] James Brown, Long's successor, died at the age of 80 in 1784.

540. GRAY TO NICHOLLS

26 Jan: 1771
Pemb: Coll:

Dear S^r

I WANT to know a hundred things about you. are you fix'd in
your house, for I hear many vague reports of Mifs A:[1]
inclination to part with the estate, & that the *Loves* are desirous
of the purchase, & would bid high? what part of the mansion
(where I used to tremble at a breath of air) was blown down in
the high wind? did not you blefs your stars for that dreary flat,
that lay between you & Corton,[2] & bar'd all sight of the sea in
its fury, & of the numberlefs wrecks, that strew'd all your coast?
as to our little & unpicturesque events you know them, I find,
& have congratulated Mr Presendent,[3] who is now our Master,[4]
in due form: but you do not know, that it never rains but
it pours: he goes to Town on Monday for institution to the
Living of Streatham[5] in the Isle of Ely worth from two to three
hundred pound a-year & given him by the King's Majesty.
the detail is infinite, the attacks, the defences, the evasions, the
circumventions, the sacrifices, the perjuries, are only to be told
by word of mouth: suffice it to say, that it is carried swimmingly
& triumphantly against two Lords temporal & one spiritual,[6]

LETTER 540.—First printed (in a garbled text) in Mason's *Memoirs*,
pp. 392–3; first printed in full by Mitford (1835–43), vol. v, pp. 119–21;
now reprinted from the original.

1 For Miss Allin see Letter 536, n. 3.

2 On the coast two miles north of Lowestoft.

3 As Tovey notes, this is probably what the gyps and bed-makers called
Brown.

4 He was elected on 21 Dec. 1770, the day of Dr. Long's funeral (see
Letter 538).

5 Stretham, about four miles south-west of Ely. The previous Rector,
the Rev. Mr. Thomas, died on 6 Jan. 1771 (*Public Advertiser*, 22 Jan.), and
on 26 Jan. (the day on which Gray wrote this letter) the following notice
appeared in the *London Gazette*: 'St James's, 26 Jan. The King has been
pleased to present James Brown, Master of Arts, and Master of Pembroke
College, Cambridge, to the Rectory of Stretham in the County of Cambridge,
and Diocese of Ely, and in his Majesty's gift for this Turn, by Lapse' (see
n. 6).

6 The spiritual Lord was Keene. On 25 Dec. 1770 the King had 'recom-
mended' to the Dean and Chapter of Ely Dr. Edmund Keene, Bishop of
Chester, to be elected Bishop, and 9 Jan. 1771 he was duly elected. But his
'temporalities' were not restored to him until 18 Feb., and until that date
the right of presentation lapsed to the Crown. It was between the vacancy
in the Rectory on 6 Jan. and the presentation of Brown on 26 Jan. (see n. 5)

who sollicited for their several Protegés in vain: so our good Uncle Toby will have about 400£ a-year, no uncomfortable pittance! I have had several capricious letters from Berne. he has sent me some pretty views of his native country, & its inhabitants. the portrait[7] too is arrived done at Paris, but no more like *than I to Hercules*:[8] you would think, it was intended for his Father, so grave & so composed: doubtlefs he meant to look, like an Englishman or an owl. pray send me the letter,[9] & do not suppose I grudge postage.

I rejoice you have met with Froifsart:[10] he is the Herodotus of a barbarous age. had he but had the luck of writing in as good a language, he might have been immortal! his locomotive disposition (for then there was no other way of learning things) his simple curiosity, his religious credulity, were much like those

that Keene carried on the intrigues, to which Gray alludes here and which he relates in more detail in his letter to Wharton (Letter 542). There is a lively account of the proceedings in a letter of Mason's to his friend Benjamin Forster (1736–1805), Fellow of Corpus Christi College, Cambridge. Mason wrote on 3 Feb. 1771 from Curzon Street (where he was staying with Ston-hewer): 'I am not conscious of any superlative degree of spirits. Frisky indeed I have been, and frisky in a good cause; for by the friskiness of myself, and some of my friends, my new Lord of Ely has been prevented from succeeding in an act of rascally rapaciousness, which outdoes every instance that has ever occurred in the annals of Episcopacy since the Reformation. *Longa est fabula*; and it must be deferred till we meet: in the meanwhile take the sum of it. The living of Stretham, in the Isle of Ely, became vacant during the vacancy of the see. The Duke of Grafton procured it from the King in the handsomest way for Mr. Brown. Notwithstanding this, the Bp set every engine at Work to stop the Business that he might give it to his Nephew, & even got Mr. Brown to resign his pretentions on a promise of putting him on his list for some other preferment that might afterwards fall. But by our getting the King's hand hastily to the Presentation, and passing it briskly thro all the offices up to the great Seal, the Bp was forced to submit, tho with the worst grace possible. And now Our honest friend is actually in possession of a Living worth near 300l. within ten miles of Cambridge wᶜʰ added to his Mastership (that without it would have hardly been a maintenance), will make him happier than the Bishop as he is better than all the Bench put together.' (Nichols's *Illustrations of the Literary History of the Eighteenth Century*, vol. viii, pp. 635–6, the latter part of the text corrected by the facsimile of the original in Professor Draper's *William Mason*, p. 78.)

[7] The portrait of Bonstetten. After Gray's death this portrait was presented to Nicholls by Brown and Mason, as Gray's executors (see Brown's letter to Nicholls of 29 June 1773, in Appendix W).

[8] *Hamlet* i. 2: 'My father's brother, but no more like my father Than I to Hercules.'

[9] This was a letter from Bonstetten to Nicholls (see Letter 541, n. 1).

[10] See Letter 537.

of the old Grecian.   our Ancestors used to read the Mort
d'Arthur,[11] Amadis de Gaul,[12] & Froifsart, all alike, that is,
they no more suspected the good faith of the former than they
did of the latter, but took it all for history.   when you have *tant
chevauché*[13] as to get to the end of him, there is Monstrelet[14] waits
to take you up, & will set you down at *Philip de Comines*.[15] but
previous to all these you should have read *Villehardouin*,[16] &
Joinville.[17] I do not think myself bound to defend the character
of even the best of Kings.   pray slash them, & spare not.   my
best compliments to M[rs] Nicholls.   I am very sincerely,
                                                    Yours
                                                    T G:
Your friend M[r] Crofts[18] has just left me.   he is a candidate
for the University & will succeed in the room of De Grey, now
Chief-Justice of y[e] Common-Pleas.

Addressed: To The Rev[d] M[r] Nicholls at Blundeston near Leostoff Suffolk
By Norwich *Postmark:* CAMBRIDGE

541. NICHOLLS TO GRAY

Blundeston, Jan. 31, 1771.

IF you knew the pleasure your letters give me, I think you
would not be quite so stingy of them, in four months I have
only been able to squeeze two from you, and I suspect that I

[11] In writing to Wharton in 1760 (Letter 308) Gray associates the *Mort
d'Arthur* with Froissart's Chronicles.
[12] See Letter 330, n. 13.
[13] Nicholls had written (Letter 537) 'et ay-je tant chevauché par mes
journées'.
[14] See Letter 543, nn. 8, 10.
[15] See Letter 112, n. 24; his *Mémoires*, which cover the years 1464–83,
1494–8, were first printed in 1524–5.
[16] Geoffroi de Villehardouin (*c.* 1165–1215), author of *La Conquête de
Constantinople*, a history of the Fourth Crusade, 1202–4; first printed in 1585.
[17] Jean de Joinville (1224–1319), author of the *Histoire de Saint Louis*,
dealing with the Crusade of Louis IX in 1248, on which Joinville accom-
panied him. The work was first printed in 1547.
[18] Richard Croftes, of St. John's College, Cambridge, M.A. 1761; he was
elected Burgess for the University on 4 Feb. 1771, in succession to William De
Grey, the Attorney-General. De Grey had been elected Burgess on 1 Feb.
1770, and now vacated the seat on being appointed (28 Jan. 1771) Lord
Chief Justice of the Common Pleas.
LETTER 541.—First printed by Mitford (1835–43), vol. v, pp. 121–6. The
following obvious misprints in Mitford's text have been corrected: Courte
(for Comte), quères (for guères), Lindesins, Vulterus, valerat, Guiaciardini.

owe this last in some degree to your desire of seeing De Bon-
stetten's to me;[1] if that is the case the end is answered, for I
received yours yesterday and send it enclosed to day. I answered
it only yesterday; I told him 'that I believed what he said,
because he said it, and because in such a case I had infinitely
rather be a dupe than too mistrustful.' I said not a word about
Berne,[2] for I am entirely ignorant of your intentions, I only
know that it will be impofsible for me to get either money or
a curate at a moment's warning. What may be my situation too
at the time I am uncertain; at present the matter stands thus.
Mifs Allin has, whether she lets or sells this house and estate,
promised me the refusal. Mr. Love however, I hear from com-
mon report only, (but it is very likely) is trying to make a
bargain for himself; that this will have no other effect than
perhaps raising the price I am clear, for Mifs Allin has honour
enough, and I believe regard enough for me as a neighbour and
friend of her father's, to use me at least fairly, but this you'll say
will not prevent her agents from consulting her interest by
selling her estate for as much as they can get. I suppose not,
and therefore, if they ask any extravagant price, and I had the
money to give, Mr. Love should have it. As for the house, it is
worth little, I question even its safety; so that, if I bought it dear,
and then had to pull down and rebuild, to add or alter, or at
least to make great repairs, I should soon have spent all I have,
and all I expect, and be condemned for want of sixpence in my
pocket to live in this desert all the days of my life. If it were to
be bought cheap, and I was sure that the house would stand as
it does or require but little expense in repairs or alteration, and
my uncles[3] would advance the purchase money, it would be
worth having. Or if Mifs Allin would let me a lease of it not
for a very long term. Hitherto all I have done is to obtain Mifs
Allin's promise,[4] through Dr. Warner (for she was incapable of
seeing any one when she left Somerly)[5] that as soon as any thing
is determined with respect to this estate I shall have the first
notice. I wrote to my eldest uncle to say so, and remain now at
quiet, and leave Mr. Love to use his little arts as he pleases.

[1] See Letter 540, n. 9.
[2] This refers to a proposal of Bonstetten that Gray and Nicholls should
pay him a visit.
[3] See Letter 429, n. 7.
[4] See Letter 537, n. 13.
[5] That is, Somerleyton, where was the seat of the Allin family (see Letter
536, n. 3).

There's an end of my tiresome story! but you asked me, and I have bestowed it all on you.

I am so glad that you speak so handsomely of my Beaumaistre Mefsire Jehan. He is indeed the Herodotus of a barbarous age.[5a] I beg, if you will not allow him to be immortal, that you will grant him yet many a good century to come of life and fame. I want to know who he was, I design to gather together all that is scattered about his book relating to himself; viz. at whose request he wrote the different parts of his work, where he travelled, by whom he was patronized, and how he got his information, &c. but after all, who was he? He seems to have been of some considerable rank, and much considered, whether on that account or on account of 'çeste noble et haute histoire,' I know not. When Mefsire Espaing de Lyon and he travelled together from Carcafsonne to the E. of Foix's court at Ortais[6] in Bearn, they appear to be on terms of equality and familiarity, and Mefsire Espaing de Lyon was I find on all occasions one of the principal Chevaliers belonging to the Comte de Foix, who was celebrated for the state and grandeur in which he lived; by the Earl himself he was very well received, and kept his Christmas at Ortais as his guest, when prelates and hauts Barons en grande Foison were there too; from thence he went in the train of the E—'s young niece,[7] who was going to be married to the old D. of Berri. In the title page of my (Preston's) book is written in a bad French hand after his name, tresorier et chanoine degimay[8] et delisle, does that imply an ecclesiastic or secular person? or what was a chanoine? I have more questions to ask if you will take the trouble of answering them. What were men at arms? were they always persons of superior rank, as they seem generally to have been? were they better armed than the rest? had they a stated number of attendants, or did it vary, which I rather think? were those attendants armed and ranked in the army, and so reckoned as part of its strength, or only followers for pomp and convenience? I dont know exactly what an escuyer was, but at least a gentleman he must have been, for I find them encountering with knights at justs.

It is astonishing how much better I understand French of the

[5a] As Gray had called him (see Letter 540).   [6] Orthez.

[7] Jeanne, daughter of the Comte d'Auvergne et de Boulogne, married in 1389, as his second wife, Jean de France (1340–1416), Duc de Berry (1360), third son of King John II of France, and brother of Charles V.

[8] De Chimay (see Letter 543).

fourteenth than English of the sixteenth century; I want you every moment for an interpreter in reading Hall's[9] account of the Camp of the Cloth of Gold.

I think nothing can be a stronger instance of the advantage the simple style of a cotemporary has over the polished periods of a later writer, than the dying words of Douglas,[10] who was killed in a battle near Newcastle, between the Scotch and English, anno 1388, related by Froifsart, and translated by Buchanan.[11] As he lay pierced with many mortal wounds; 'Mefsire Jehan de Sainct Cler[12] demanda au Comte, Cousin comment vous va? Petitement, dit le Comte. Loué en soit Dieu. Il n'est guères de mes ancesseurs qui soient morts en chambres ne sur licts. Je vous dy, Pensez de moi vanger: car je me compte pour mort. Le cueur me faut trop souvent, redrecez ma bannière, et criez Douglas: mais ne dites à amy, nà ennemy que je soye au party ou vous me voyez: car mes ennemis (s'ils le scavoient) s'en reconforteroient.' Froifsart, vol. iii. c. 127.

In hoc statu propinqui ejus, Joannes Lindesius,[13] Joannes et Valterus Sinclari, de eo cum rogafsent ecquid valeret? 'Ego, inquit, recte valeo: morior enim non in lecto segni fato, sed quemadmodum omnes prope majores mei: illa vero a vobis postrema peto: primum ut mortem meam et nostros et hostes celetis: deinde ne vexillum meum dejectum sinatis: deinde[14] ut meam cædem ulciscamini. Hæc si sperem ita fore, cætera æquo animo feram.' Buch. lib. 9.

This last is certainly more like a Roman hero, but is it not lefs like James Douglas? and after this I must tell you that I have just read Comines in a bad translation,[15] but as the

[9] See Letter 186, n. 6.

[10] James Douglas (*c.* 1358–88), second Earl Douglas (1384); he was killed on the eve of victory in Aug. 1388 in the battle of Otterburn (celebrated in the ballad of 'Chevy Chase') against Percy (Hotspur), son of the Duke of Northumberland, who was taken prisoner.

[11] George Buchanan (1506–82), author of *Rerum Scoticarum Historia*, in nine books, first printed at Edinburgh in 1582 (fol.).

[12] Sir John St. Clair and his brother, Sir Walter St. Clair, were the sons of Sir John St. Clair of Herdmanston, who was taken prisoner at the Battle of Neville's Cross (1346).

[13] This was Sir James (not John) Lindsay (d. 1396), ninth Baron Lindsay (1357).

[14] Mitford prints 'deinde', which Nicholls may have written; the correct reading appears to be 'demum'.

[15] An English translation of Thomas Danett was published in 1596 (Lond.

Spanish Ambaſsador has signed the convention, with a reserva-
tion of my former rights,[16] and determining to do better as soon
as I shall have it in my power. Temple begs your aſsistance.[17]
Adieu!

N. N.

I live not, alas! in the midst of libraries, consequently cannot
get one of the books you are so kind to mention. I found the
gap between Froiſsart and Comines, and longed for Monstrelet,
which I found quoted so often by Rapin and Hainault,[18] whom
I have read as far as the period I am arrived at in English
history, and shall continue. His outline seems that of a master,
and he has contrived to put more than one could expect in an
abridgment.

My mother desires me to make her compliments to you. We
both congratulate Mr. Brown on his additional good fortune.[19]
I am reading Guicciardini[20] with delight, though he is a polished
historian, and Burnet's History of the Reformation. My mother
and I have read since November, Rapin from William the
Conqueror to the end of Henry VIII. Bacon's Henry VII. and
are now beginning Lord Herbert.[21] Have you received my
herrings?

fol.), of which a fourth edition was issued in 1674. Another, by Thomas
Uvedale, was published in 1712 (Lond. 2 vols. 8vo); second edition, 1723.

[16] This refers to the convention for settling the dispute between England
and Spain for the possession of the Falkland Islands. These had been occu-
pied by Captain Byron in 1765 without protest on the part of Spain. In
1769, however, the English garrison was forcibly expelled by a Spanish
expedition, whose commander claimed for Spain the whole of the islands.
In a Declaration signed in London on 22 Jan. 1771 the Spanish Government
disavowed the action of the Spanish commander, and engaged to restore the
fort and all property that had been taken possession of. But the Spanish
Ambassador Extraordinary, the Prince of Maserano, subjoined a reserva-
tion to the effect that the above engagement did not in any wise affect the
question of the prior right of sovereignty to the Falkland Islands.

[17] See Letter 545, n. 9.
[18] No doubt Nicholls means the Président Charles Jean François Hénault
(see Letter 129, n. 4). Hénault had died in the previous November.
[19] See Letter 540, n. 5.
[20] Francesco Guicciardini (1483–1540), author of *Storia d'Italia*, in twenty
books, covering the period between 1494 and 1532; first published at
Florence in 1561 (fol.).
[21] See Letter 527, nn. 6, 7.

541*. GRAY TO ASHBY[1]

[Cambridge. c. Jan.–Feb. 1771?][2]

THE bird you send me is the *Bohemian Chatterer*, or Silk-tail (see Pennant, V: 1. p: 173)[3] the *Lanius Garrulus* of Linnæus,[4] but in his last edition[5] removed to the Genus *Ampelis*. it is no native of our island, but sometimes comes over in little flocks during a hard winter. this is a young one, varying in some particulars, especially in the *remiges*,[6] where the scarlet points (ye character of ye species) do but begin to appear. &c:[7]

Folded as a note and addressed: To the President of St Johns

LETTER 541*.—Now first printed from original.

[1] Within the possible limits of date for this letter (see n. 2) the President of St. John's was the Rev. George Ashby (1724–1808); admitted to St. John's 1740; B.A. 1744; M.A. and Fellow, 1748; President of the College, 1767–75. Subsequently Rector of Barrow in Suffolk. He was an antiquarian of varied learning. There is evidence of his interest in natural history and of his receiving help on the subject from Gray in a note-book now at Harvard University (bought by Mitford at the sale of Ashby's books in 1808). This contains notes based on the tenth edition of Linnæus, which are, at least in great part, in Ashby's hand. There are references to Gray in some passages. (Mitford was probably mistaken in attributing entries to Gray; and a confused note in his *Works of Gray* (1835–43), vol. i, p. lxxiii, is also open to question.)

[2] The date is conjectural. From the reference to the second edition of Pennant's book published in 1768 (see n. 3) it is clear that the letter could not have been written before 1768, and Gray's statement that the bird 'sometimes comes over during a hard winter' would fit the severe spell of cold at the beginning of 1771 (see Letter 542).

[3] The reference is to the second edition (1768) of Pennant's *British Zoology* (see Letter 508*, n. 6). Under the heading, 'The Chatterer-Garrulus Bohemicus, Bohemian Chatterer. . . . Ampelis garrulus', Pennant writes: 'The critical *Faunist* may possibly censure us for admitting a native of *Germany* into a *British* zoology; but as we can plead the extreme beauty of this bird, and that it does sometimes (though very rarely) visit the northern parts of *England* in large flocks, we hope to be excused for admitting it here.' On 4 Nov. 1767 Gilbert White wrote to Pennant of his having seen a specimen of this bird, which had been shot in the severe weather of the preceding winter, and he mentioned 'the five peculiar crimson tags or points which it carries at the ends of five of the short remiges' (*Natural History of Selborne*, Letter xii).

[4] Gray in his interleaved copy of the tenth edition (1758) of Linnæus' *Systema Naturae* (see Letter 495, n. 3) wrote a 'List of all the Birds found in Great Britain', in which under the heading 'Lanii' is: '20 The Bohemia-Chatterer** *Garrulus*' (the two asterisks indicating that the bird was 'extremely rare'). (See C. E. Norton, *The Poet Gray as a Naturalist*, p. 27.)

[5] The reference is to vol. i, p. 297, of the twelfth edition of Linnæus (1766–8).

[6] The primary and secondary wing feathers (see Gilbert White, quoted in n. 3).

[7] On the bottom margin of the note is written 'Mr Gray now Ampelis

542. GRAY TO WHARTON

2 Feb: 1771. Pemb: Coll:

IT never rains, but it pours, my dear Doctor. you will be glad to hear, that M^r Br: has added to his Mastership (wch is better than 150£ a-year) a Living hard by Cambridge, Stretham[1] in the isle of Ely, worth, as it was lett above 40 years ago, at least 240£ more. it was in the gift of the Crown during the vacancy of the See of Ely, & that its value is really more than I have said, you will hardly doubt, when you hear, it was carried against an Earl, a Baron, & a Bishop,[2] the latter of the three so strenuous a Suitor, that he still persisted above a week after I had seen the Presentation sign'd to M^r B: by the King's own hand, nay, he still persisted a day, after the K: had publickly declared in the Drawing-room, that he had given it M^r B: by name. and who was this bishop? no other than your Friend, who wanted it for a Nephew of his, a *poor unfortunate* Nephew, that had been so imprudent[3] many a year ago to marry a Farmer's daughter, where he boarded, when Curate; & continued ever since under a cloud, because his uncle would give him nothing. as to us, we had a Duke,[4] an Earl, a Viscount, & a Bishop on our side, & carried it so swimmingly you would stare again. there was a prologue & an exegesis & a peripeteia, & all the parts of a regular drama; & the Heroe is gone to London, was instituted yesterday, & today is gone to Lambeth, for the Archbishop[5] too spoke a good word for us & at a very critical time. the old Lodge[6] has got rid of all its harpsichords[7] & begins to brighten up: its inhabitant is lost like a Mouse in an old cheese. he has

Garrulus', and above the word *Ampelis* in the text of the letter 'p. 297' has been inserted. The additions were presumably made by Ashby, and in his note-book (see n. 1) Ashby added to his account of '*The Bohemian Jay or Chatterer*' the words: 'now Ampelis Garrulus, p. 297'.

LETTER 542.—First printed by Mitford (1816), vol. ii, pp. 564–6; now reprinted from original.
   [1] See Letter 540, n. 5.
   [2] See Letter 540, n. 6.
   [3] Substituted for 'unfortunate' scored through.
   [4] The Duke of Grafton (see Letter 540, n. 6).
   [5] Cornwallis (see Letter 16, n. 5).
   [6] The Master's Lodge, at Pembroke.
   [7] An allusion to the musical tastes of Dr. Long, the late Master (see Letter 39, n. 2).

received your generous offer of a benefaction to the common good, but it is too much to tax yourself: however we all intend to bring in our mites, & shew the way to the high & mighty: when a fund[8] is once on foot, they will bestirr themselves.
I am sincerely concern'd to find Mifs Wharton is still an Invalide. I believe, you must send her into the milder regions of the South, where the sun dispells all maladies. we ourselves have had an untoward season enough: vast quantities of rain instead of winter, the Thermom:^{r} never below 40 deg:, often above 50, before Christmas; unusual high winds (wch still continue) particularly the 19th of Dec: at night it blew a dreadful storm. the first grain of snow was seen on X^{mas} Day, of wch we have had a good deal since, but never deep or lasting. the 2^d week in Jan: was really severe cold at London, & the Thames frozen over. one morning that week the glafs stood here (at 8 in the morning) at 16 degrees, wch is the lowest I ever knew it at Cambridge. at London it never has been observed lower than 13 (understand me right: I mean, 13 above Zero of Farenheit) & that was 5 Jan, 1739.[9] now it is very mild again, but with very high winds at N:W:.
I give you joy of our awkward peace with Spain.[10] Mason is in Town[11] taking his swing, like a Boy in breaking-up-time. remember me kindly to Mrs Wharton, & all the good family. did I tell you of my breaking up in summer in the midland counties, & so as far as Abergavenny one way, & Ludlow the other?[12] I have another journal[13] for you, in several volumes. I have

---

[8] The College accounts for this year show considerable expenditure on the Lodge (and other College buildings), but no entry relating to a subscription has been traced (see Letter 547, n. 12).
[9] The winter of 1739–40 was very severe and the Thames was frozen over for nearly eight weeks. West wrote a Latin poem on the subject, a copy of which is in Gray's Commonplace-book (see Letter 131, n. 15).
[10] See Letter 541, n. 16.
[11] Gray had been in town from the end of the year until about 17 Jan. He had seen Walpole (see Walpole's letter to Cole of 10 Jan. 1771) and Mason. Mason had thoughts of visiting Cambridge; in his letter to Forster (quoted in Letter 540, n. 6) he wrote: 'If I can learn when Pa intends to be at Cambridge I have some thought of going down there for a week or so before my waiting in March commences; but I dare not go there unless Pa meets me, for the Professor is so touchy that I am afraid of being alone with him.'
[12] He had done so in his letter of 24 Aug. 1770 (Letter 530).
[13] This was no doubt Nicholls's journal of their tour (see Letter 530, n. 11).

had a cough for above 3 months upon me, wch is incurable.[14]
Adieu!

I am ever
Yours
T G:

Addressed: To Thomas Wharton Esq of Old-Park near Darlington Durham
   Postmark: CAMBRIDGE

543. GRAY TO NICHOLLS

Dear S^r

YOUR Friend *Jean Froifsart*, Son of Thomas by profefsion a
Herald-painter, was born at Valenciennes in Haynault
about the year 1337. was by nature fond of every *noble* diversion,
as hunting, hawking, drefs, good-cheer, wine, & women (this
latter pafsion commenced at 12 years old) and was in his own
time no lefs distinguish'd by his gallant poesies (still preserved
in Mfs) than by his historical writings, wch he begun at the
desire of *Robert de Namur*, Seigneur de Beaufort, when he was
barely 20 years of age. at 24 he made his first voyage into
England, & presented the first part of his history to Edw: the
3^d's Queen, Philippa of Haynault, who appointed him *Clerk of
her chamber*, that is, Secretary, by wch he became one of the
Houshold in that Court. after the death of this Queen in 1369
he had the Living of *Lefsines* in his own country given him, &
must then consequently be a Priest. he attach'd himself to
Wenceslaus of Luxemburg, Duke of Brabant, who dying in
1384, he became Clerk of the Chappel to Guy Comte de Blois,
who probably gave him a canonry in the collegiate Church of
Chimay near Marienbourg in the county of Haynault.[1] he also
had obtain'd of the Pope a reversion of another canonry in the
Church of Lisle; but of this he never could get pofsefsion. after
27 years absence from England he made a third voyage thither
in 1395, & stay'd in it only 3 months. his Patron Guy de Blois
died in 1397, & Froifsart survived him certainly 4 years, but
how much more is uncertain. these & many more particulars

---

[14] Mason foists this last sentence, in a garbled form, into a patchwork
letter which he prints, with the date 24 May 1771, as Gray's last letter to
Wharton.
   LETTER 543.—First printed by Mitford (1835–43), vol. v, pp. 127–9; now
reprinted from original.
[1] Substituted for 'Flanders' scored through.

are taken from the account of his life & writings collected by Mons: *de la Curne* de St Palaye,[2] in 10 Tome of the *Mem: de l'Acad: des Inscript:^{ns}* &c: where you may see much more about him. the same Author defends him strongly against the suspicions, that have been entertain'd, of his partiality to the English Nation.

A Man at arms was a complicated machine, consisting of about seven Men, i:e: the Knight or Gentleman himself compleatly & heavily arm'd & mounted on his great war-horse caparison'd & arm'd as strongly as the Rider: the rest were his Esquires rather meant to afsist him & watch his motions in the combat, than to engage in action themselves. all of them were (as I apprehend) on horseback, & thus taken together, made the principal strength & principal expence of armies in those days. *Ecuyers* were the sons of Gentleman,[3] train'd up in quality of *Pages* till 12 years old (commonly not in their Father's Castle, but in that of some famous Knight, his Friend) after wch age they afsumed the title of *Esquires*, were exercised daily in feats of arms & curtesy, attended the person of their Lord at home & abroad, and at 21 were qualified to receive themselves the order of knighthood. read the same St Palaye's *Mem: de l'ancienne Chevalerie*, 2 v: 8vo 1759, Paris. if you would have me say any thing to T:[4] you must remind me, what period of time he enquired about, for my memory fails me.

You may be sure of a month's notice from me, if I undertake the voyage,[5] wch seems to me next to impofsible. I received a letter from B:^{n} last night, wch mentions you kindly, & seems very desirous, we should come this summer. what you m[entio]n[6] of herrings[7] I know not: I have never seen or heard of them!

Monstrelet[8] reaches from A:D: 1400 to 1467,[9] & there are additions at the end of him, that come down to 1516. it is a

[2] Jean Baptiste de la Curne de Sainte-Palaye (1697–1781); he was elected an associate of the Académie des Inscriptions et Belles Lettres in 1724, for which he wrote a series of studies on the chroniclers of the Middle Ages; and a member of the Académie Française in 1758. In 1759 he published his *Mémoires sur l'ancienne Chevalerie*.

[3] A slip for 'Gentlemen'.

[4] Temple. See Letter 545, n. 9.

[5] See Letter 541, n. 2.

[6] MS. torn.

[7] Nicholls in the postscript to his letter of 31 Jan. (Letter 541) asks: 'Have you received my herrings?'

[8] See Letter 186, n. 21.

[9] Not 1467, but 1444.

splendid & very substantial Folio, publ:ᵈ in 1572.¹⁰ Adieu!
my respects to Mrs. Nicholls.

24 Feb: 1771¹¹

Addressed: To The Revᵈ Mʳ Nicholls at Blundeston near Leostoff Suffolk by
Norwich *Postmark:* CAMBRIDGE

544. GRAY TO BEATTIE
Cambridge, 8ᵗʰ March, 1771.

THE *Minstrel*¹ came safe to my hands, and I return you my
sincere thanks for so acceptable a present. In return, I shall
give you my undisguised opinion of him, as he proceeds, without
considering to whom he owes his birth, and sometimes without
specifying my reasons; either because they would lead me too
far, or because I may not always know what they are myself.
    I think we should wholly adopt the language of Spenser's
time, or wholly renounce it.² You say, you have done the latter;
but, in effect, you retain *fared, forth, meed, wight, ween, gaude,
shene, in sooth, aye, eschew,* &c.; obsolete words, at least in these

¹⁰ *Les Chroniques de France, d'Angleterre et de Bourgogne* . . . (*avec les continua-
tions jusqu'en 1516*) (Paris, 1572, 3 vols. fol.).
    ¹¹ On a blank space in Gray's letter Nicholls wrote (in a hand very like
Gray's) the following notes:
    'Rapin says every man at arms had with him three or four & sometimes
5 knights.
    'But there were Esquires past the age of 21. for Henri Castede who told
Froissart the State of Ireland when he was last in Engᵈ was 50.
    'What were Heralds who seem to have been so liberally rewarded, & called
in with the Minstrels at great entertainments as well as employ'd in denounc-
ing war &c? Difference between Bannière & Pennon?'
    Nicholls puts the questions to Gray in his letter of 16 Mar. (Letter 545).
    LETTER 544.—First printed (with Beattie's comments) in *An Account of
the Life and Writings of James Beattie, LL.D.*, by Sir William Forbes, vol. i,
pp. 196 ff. Sir William Forbes printed as notes to Gray's letter Beattie's
'own remarks on these criticisms of Mr. Gray', which he found in a paper in
Beattie's handwriting. These notes are printed below.
    ¹ *The Public Advertiser* for 23 Feb. 1771 records the publication of '*The
Minstrel; or, The Progress of Genius: a Poem.* Book the First'. The publication
was anonymous.
    ² As Tovey points out, Gray and West had discussed the same question
in Apr. 1742. West wrote of Gray's *Agrippina*: 'the style appears too anti-
quated' (Letter 102). Gray replied: 'The language of the age is never the
language of poetry; except among the French. . . . Our poetry on the
contrary, has a language peculiar to itself' (Letter 103). Gray now takes the
other side, and Beattie's notes are in accord with Gray's earlier principles.

parts of the island, and only known to those that read our ancient authors, or such as imitate them.³

St. 2. v. 5. The *obstreperous* trump of fame hurts my ear, though meant to exprefs a jarring sound.

St. 3. v. 6. *And from his bending*, &c., the grammar seems deficient: yet as the mind easily fills up the ellipsis, perhaps it is an atticism, and not inelegant.

St. 4. and ult. *Pensions, posts, and praise.* I cannot reconcile myself to this, nor to the whole following stanza; especially *the plaister of thy hair.*⁴

Surely the female heart, &c., St. 6. The thought is not just. We cannot justify the sex from the conduct of the Muses, who are only females by the help of Greek mythology; and then, again, how should they bow the knee in the fane of a Hebrew or Philistine devil? Besides, I am the more severe, because it serves to introduce what I most admire.⁵

St. 7. *Rise, sons of harmony*, &c. This is charming; the thought and the exprefsion. I will not be so hypercritical as to add, but it is *lyrical*, and therefore belongs to a different species of poetry. Rules are but chains, good for little, except when one can break through them; and what is fine gives me so much pleasure, that I never regard what place it is in.

St. 8, 9, 10. All this thought is well and freely handled, particularly, *Here peaceful are the vales*, &c. *Know thine own worth*, &c. *Canst thou forego*, &c.

St. 11. *O, how canst thou renounce*, &c. But this, of all others, is my favourite stanza. It is true poetry; it is inspiration; only (to show it is mortal) there is one blemish; the word *garniture* suggesting an idea of drefs, and, what is worse, of French drefs.⁶

St. 12. Very well. *Prompting th' ungenerous wish*, &c. But do not say *rambling muse; wandering*, or *devious*, if you please.⁷

³ *To fare*, i.e. *to go*, is used in Pope's *Odyssey*, and so is *meed*; *wight* (in a serious sense) is used by Milton and Dryden. *Ween* is used by Milton; *gaude* by Dryden; *shene* by Milton; *eschew* by Atterbury; *aye* by Milton. The poetical style in every nation (where there is a poetical style) abounds in old words. *Beattie.*

⁴ I did not intend a poem uniformly epical and solemn; but one rather that might be lyrical, or even satirical, upon occasion. *Beattie.*

⁵ I meant here an ironical argument. Perhaps, however, the irony is wrong placed. Mammon has now come to signify *wealth* or *riches*, without any regard to its original meaning. *Beattie.*

⁶ I have often wished to alter this same word, but have not yet been able to hit upon a better. *Beattie.*

⁷ *Wandering* happens to be in the last line of the next stanza save one, otherwise it would certainly have been here. *Beattie.*

St. 13. *A nation fam'd*, &c. I like this compliment to your country; the simplicity, too, of the following narrative; only in st. 17 the words *artlefs* and *simple* are too synonymous to come so near each other.

St. 18. *And yet poor Edwin*, &c. This is all excellent, and comes very near the level of st. 11 in my esteem; only, perhaps, *And some believed him mad*, falls a little too flat, and rather below simplicity.

St. 21. *Ah, no!* By the way, this sort of interjection is rather too frequent with you, and will grow characteristic, if you do not avoid it.

In that part of the poem which you sent me before, you have altered several little particulars much for the better.[8]

St. 34. I believe I took notice before of this excefs of alliteration. *Long, loaded, loud,* lament, *lonely,* lighted, *lingering, listening;* though the verses are otherwise very good, it looks like affectation.[9]

St. 36, 37, 38. Sure you go too far in lengthening a stroke of Edwin's character and disposition into a direct narrative, as of a fact. In the mean time, the poem stands still, and the reader grows impatient. Do you not, in general, indulge a little too much in *description* and *reflection?* This is not my remark only, I have heard it observed by others; and I take notice of it here, because *these* are among the stanzas that might be spared; they are good, nevertheless, and might be laid by, and employed elsewhere to advantage.[10]

St. 42. Spite of what I have just now said, this digrefsion pleases me so well, that I cannot spare it.

St. 46, v. ult. The *infuriate* flood. I would not make new words without great necefsity; it is very hazardous at best.[11]

---

[8] I had sent Mr. Gray from st. 23 to st. 39 by way of specimen. *Beattie.*— See Letter 507*.

[9] It does so, and yet it is not affected. I have endeavoured once and again to clear this passage of those obnoxious letters, but I never could please myself. Alliteration has great authorities on its side, but I would never seek for it; nay, except on some very particular occasions, I would rather avoid it. When Mr. Gray, once before, told me of my propensity to alliteration, I repeated to him one of his own lines, which is indeed one of the finest in poetry—

Nor cast one longing lingering look behind.
                                        Beattie.

[10] This remark is perfectly just. All I can say is, that I meant, from the beginning, to take some latitude in the composition of this poem, and not confine myself to the epical rules for narrative. In an epic poem these digressions and reflections, &c., would be unpardonable. *Beattie.*

[11] I would as soon make new coin, as knowingly make a new word,

St. 49, 50, 51, 52. All this is very good; but *medium* and *incongruous*, being words of art, lose their dignity in my eyes, and savour too much of prose. I would have read the last line—'Presumptuous child of dust, be humble and be wise.' But, on second thoughts, perhaps—'*For thou art but of dust*'—is better and more solemn, from its simplicity.

St. 53. *Where dark*, &c. You return again to the charge. Had you not said enough before?[12]

St. 54. *Nor was this ancient dame*, &c. Consider, she has not been mentioned for these six stanzas backward.

St. 56, v. 5. *The vernal day*. With us it rarely thunders in the spring, but in the summer frequently.[13]

St. 57, 58. Very pleasing, and has much the rhythm and exprefsion of Milton in his youth. The last four lines strike me lefs by far.

St. 59. The first five lines charming. Might not the mind of your conqueror be checked and softened in the mid-career of his succefses by some domestic misfortune (introduced by way of episode, interesting and new, but not too long), that Edwin's music and its triumphs may be a little prepared, and more consistent with probability?[14]

I am happy to hear of your succefses in another way, because I think you are serving the cause of human nature, and the true interest of mankind. Your book is read here too, and with just applause.[15]

except I were to invent any art or science where they would be necessary. *Infuriate* is used by Thomson, *Summer*, 1096; and, which is much better authority, by Milton, *Par. Lost*, book vi, v. 487. *Beattie.*

[12] What I said before referred only to sophists perverting the truth; this alludes to the method by which they pervert it. *Beattie.*

[13] It sometimes thunders in the latter part of spring. *Sultry day* would be an improvement perhaps. *Beattie.*

[14] This is an excellent hint; it refers to something I had been saying in my last letter to Mr. Gray, respecting the plan of what remains of the *Minstrel*. *Beattie.*—See Letter 507*.

[15] Mr. Gray has been very particular. I am greatly obliged to him for the freedom of his remarks, and think myself as much so for his objections as for his commendations. *Beattie.*—The book referred to is his *Essay on the Immutability of Truth* (see Letter 529).

545. NICHOLLS TO GRAY

Blundeston, March 16, 1771.

YESTERDAY I received a letter from De Bonstetten, crammed fuller than it could hold, and containing besides two little after-thoughts, one three inches by two, the other two by one, which flew out when I opened the letter like the oracles of the Sybil. But I like this much better than any I have received; he intreats us a deux genoux to come, and I you in the same posture and with equal earnestnefs; if he does not esteem me he is an idiot to take so much pains to persuade me to believe it, because, if he were false, I see no end that it could answer to make a dupe of me at the expense of so much labour and unnecefsary difsimulation. He promises, if we come, that he will visit us in England the summer following. Let us go then, my dear Mr. Gray, and leave low thoughted care[1] at the foot of the mountains, for the air above is too pure for it. During the winter, my wandering inclinations are quiet in their hybernacula; but these two or three last glorious days succeeding the rigour of such an unusual season, have awakened them; the animal and vegetable world rejoice, and every thing that has life in it begins to shew it. I have lived in the air (being fortunately compelled to attend my garden myself) except during dinner, &c. The effect of this and De Bonstetten's letter is, that I find something 'che mi sprona'[2] invincibly to go to Switzerland this summer. A deux genoux, I again intreat you to go with me. To-day, as I sat at breakfast in a room without sun, I felt myself in prison, and the world abroad appeared to me not a reality, but some golden vision raised by enchantment. The moment the windows were flung up, an earthly smell came in, exhaled by the sun from the loose and fermenting mould of the garden and fields. 'In those vernal seasons of the year, when the air is calm and pleasant, it were an injury and sullennefs against nature not to go out and see her riches, and partake in her rejoicing with heaven and earth.'[3] I am not so sullen; I do

LETTER 545.—First printed by Mitford (1835–43), vol. v, pp. 130–4. Mitford printed (see p. 1174) 'Frendensick' as the name of Bonstetten's friend. From Bonstetten's letter to his mother (see Appendix V) the name appears to be 'Freundenrich', and Mitford's text has been corrected accordingly.

[1] Milton, *Comus*: 'With low-thoughted care, Confined and pestered in this pinfold here.'

[2] 'Which spurs me'—doubtless a reminiscence of Dante, *Purg.* xxix. 39.

[3] Milton, *On Education* (in *Works*, 1848, vol. iii, p. 477).

partake with her, and feel that this is a natural joy, which confeſses its origin by being sincere and unmixed, and by leaving no bitternefs on the palate behind it; but, on the contrary, opens, dilates, and warms the heart. I really find myself as inclined to pray, in such a day as this, as Petrarch was on the summit of the mountain.[4] Pardon this rant, which, though I felt, I ought perhaps to have reprefsed. The burthen of the song is, 'Go to Switzerland with me, I beseech you.' In the mean time, for I have not a moment to lose, I shall venture to bespeak a curate from the first of June to the last of October, and consider of ways and means for a supply adequate to my great occasions: but I will go, though twenty St. Gothards were in the way. The geometra fasciaria, I think (ignorant, alas! that I was an enemy of the Linnæan faction) flew against me in the twilight yesterday evening; otherwise I have found but few insects yet. I have some larvæ in boxes, that I met with under the roots of plants. The moſses require too painful an attention without an instructor, so I shall wait for one. I have looked at a few common birds, and this is all. The rest of my time has been taken up with Froifsart, Guicciardini, &c. I am still reading the latter, and extracting from the former. A thousand thanks for your letter, full of information, but giving me a curiosity to see books that I cannot get here. Pray what were the heralds, who seem to have been so liberally rewarded, and called in with the minstrels at great entertainments, as well as employed in carrying defiances, &c. What is the difference between bannière and pennon?[5] each principal commander (but these are vague words) seems to have marched with a bannière peculiar to him, on which his arms were painted, and a pennon seems inferior. I have put the story of the Irish Kings,[6] from Froifsart, into English; and am now gathering many scattered curiosities relating to the manners of the Scotch in that age. I am besides reading at odd times Hall's Chronicle,[7] and my mother and I have just begun the second volume of Robertson's Charles the Fifth, because we know something about him already from Rapin and Lord Herbert, and I from Guicciardin. I long for

[4] On 26 Apr. 1336 Petrarch and his brother Gherardo started from the village of Malaucène, about twenty miles north-east of Avignon, and climbed Mont Ventoux (6,270 ft.), an isolated peak in the Department of Vaucluse. When at the summit Petrarch relates, not that he prayed, but that he read the *Confessions* of St. Augustine, which he had taken with him.

[5] See Letter 543, n. 11.

[6] See Letter 308, n. 5.   [7] See Letter 541, n. 9.

a book often quoted by Lord Herbert, and that should be curious; Sandoval[8] especially, as I can now read Spanish pretty easily, for I have finished Don Quixote. Temple desires a plan for modern history,[9] not confined to any particular period, but beginning as early as you think proper, and continued as late;— if you think this an immodest request, you may do as much or as little of it as you please; but whatever you may do will be a kindnefs to him (whose only consolation consists in his books and a few friends who wish him well, without being able to do more) and received with great joy and gratitude. I believe my house will be continued to me on the present footing.[10] De Bonstetten in one of the flying scraps says, 'M. Freundenrich[11] mon ami qui est dans votre pays cherche quelque homme de Lettres qui veuille le prendre en pension pour cet Eté.—Vous ferez quelque chose de ce pauvre homme, il a des talens, son education a été négligé. Je vous supplie de vous interefser à cette affaire.' But by what means? For he has not told me where he is to be found; nor do I perfectly understand what le prendre en pension means. Is it that he would board with some one who would instruct him in English and other matters? Perhaps M. Freundenrich is a person that he has mentioned to you, and thinks I know him of course. Do you know a book that De Bonstetten recommends to me, Danielis Eremitæ Vita,[12] &c. with a voyage to Switzerland at the end? Pray let me hear soon. My mother's compliments. The post is forbid to send letters crofs.[13]

N. N.

---

[8] Prudencio de Sandoval (d. 1620), author of *La Vida y Hechos del Emperador Carlos V* (Pamplona, 1618, 2 vol. fol.), which was one of Robertson's authorities.

[9] Temple was repeating the request he had made a year before (see Letter 526, n. 5) for direction in reading history.

[10] See Letter 537, n. 13; and Letters 541 and 554.

[11] In his letter to his mother (Appendix V) Bonstetten refers to Freundenrich.

[12] *Danielis Eremitae Nobilis Belgae de Helvetiorum, Rætorum, Sedunensium situ, republica, moribus, Epistola, ad D. Ferd. Gonzagam, Mantuae Ducis Filium*, being pp. 399–427 of *Dan. Eremitae Aulicae Vitae ac Civilis Libri IV. Ejusdem Opuscula Varia* (Utrecht, 1701), edited, with a preface, by Joannes Georgius Graevius (Greffe). According to Mitford Daniel Eremita (1564–1615) was Secretary to the Duke of Florence.

[13] Roads were divided into 'great' or 'direct roads' and 'cross' roads. Presumably some recent post-office regulation had required letters to be sent by the great roads, and not by the shorter routes on the cross roads.

545*. GRAY TO WALPOLE

[Cambridge], March 17, 1771.

*   *   *   *   *

*   *   *   *   *

HE must have a very good stomach that can digest the *Crambe recocta*[1] of Voltaire. Atheism is a vile dish, tho' all the cooks of France combine to make new sauces to it. As to the Soul, perhaps they may have none on the Continent; but I do think we have such things in England. Shakespear, for example, I believe had several to his own share. As to the Jews (tho' they do not eat pork) I like them because they are better Christians than Voltaire.

*   *   *   *   *

*   *   *   *   *

545**. Gray to Walpole

[*c. 23 Mar. 1771*]

[In his letter to Gray of 25 Mar. (Letter 546) Walpole says in a post-script: 'I have this minute received yours.' Gray's letter, which must have been written from Cambridge on 23 or 24 Mar., is not extant.]

546. WALPOLE TO GRAY

Arlington Street

March 25. 1771.

I AM very much pleased with the head of Richardson,[1] and very angry with Bannerman,[2] who shall do nothing for me, since he will not do any thing for me. I only suspend the Bull of

LETTER 545*.—Part of letter, reprinted from Mason's *Memoirs*, p. 385, note. The extract is probably from a missing letter of Gray's to which Walpole's letter of 25 Mar. is a reply (Letter 546).

[1] 'Crambe repetita', *Juvenal*, vii. 154.

LETTER 546.—First printed by Toynbee (1915), No. 248.

[1] Jonathan Richardson, the elder (1665–1745), the portrait-painter. He painted portraits both of Walpole and Gray in their youth. The engraving to which Walpole refers is by Charles Bretherton (see *Works of Lord Orford*, vol. iii, p. 413).

[2] Alexander Bannerman, an engraver, native of Cambridge, where he was resident at this time. Walpole employed him to engrave some of the heads in his *Anecdotes of Painting*, and had offered to employ him again for the fourth and last volume, which was now preparing (see Walpole to Cole, 15 Nov. 1770), but which was not published till 19 Oct. 1780, though the printing was completed on 13 Apr. of this year (1771), as is recorded in Walpole's *Journal of the Printing-Office at Strawberry hill*.

Excommunication, till I am sure I shall not want Him. If the young Man copies Mezzotinto, as well as he does etching, which is not probable, I shall beg you to seize the prints in Bannerman's hands, if it is not inconsistent with the Charters of the City of Cambridge, & deliver them to Mr Tyson's Engraver.[3] But as you talked of being in town in March, I hope to settle this with you by a verbal negotiation.

I have had my House in town broken open, & every thing broken open in my House, & I have not lost to the Value of sixpence.[4] The Story is so long, that if I began to tell it you, you woud be here before it was finished, tho you shoud not arrive till Christmas. It is talked of more than My Lord Mayor,[5] & My Lord Mayor knows as much what to make of it, as any Body does. If you know any Saint that dragged a beautifull young Woman into a Wood to ravish her, & after throwing her on her back, & spreading open her Legs, walked quietly away without touching her, to show his continence, you have a faint Idea of my House-breakers. Some people have confounded me with my cousin[6] just arrived from France, & imagine they sought for French papers; others say I am Junius— but Lord help me! I am no such great Man, nor keep Treason in my glafs-case of China. My Miniatures, thank you, are very safe, & so is Queen Elizabeth's old face,[7] & all my coins & medals, tho the doors of the Cabinets were broken to pieces. you never saw such a Scene of havoc as my first floor was, & yet five pounds will repair all the damage. I have a suspicion about the person, whom we are watching, but not the least guess at his Selfdenial. He burst a great hole in the door of the Area, & must have had an Iron crow to force open the Chest, for the brafs flapper is bent & shivered into seven pieces, but contented himself with tumbling the prints & tapestry chairs. Silver

---

3 See Walpole to Cole, 20 Dec. 1770.

4 See the detailed account in Walpole's letter to Mann of 22–6 Mar. 1771.

5 Brass Crosby (1725–93), M.P. for Honiton. He had defied the House of Commons in the matter of the arrest of a printer under a general warrant, and two days after the date of this letter was committed to the Tower, where he remained until the end of the session (see Walpole to Mann, 22 and 30 Mar.).

6 Hon. Robert Walpole (1736–1810), youngest son of Lord Walpole of Wolterton, Sir Robert Walpole's younger brother; he was Secretary to the Embassy in Paris; shortly after this date he was appointed Minister at Lisbon.

7 No doubt the portrait mentioned in Walpole's letter to Conway of 4 June 1758.

candlesticks, linnen, spoons, nothing struck his fancy; yet he was in no hurry, for he ransacked the offices, & every room of the first floor, and nobody knows when he came in or went out, tho he seems to have taken no precaution not to be heard. There were only the two Maids in town, who were waked by a Paſsenger that found the Street door open between five & six in the Morning. In Short, this is the first Virtuoso that ever visited a collection by main force in the middle of the night. Adieu!

yrs ever
H Walpole

P.S. Monday night.

I had sealed my letter, but am forced to open it again & put it in a cover, for I have this minute received yours & Thornhill.[8] The Likeneſs is well preserved & I shall not quarrel with the price, but it is too black, & the wig very hard—however as Worlidge's[9] style is fashionable, two or three more by the same hand may not displease, therefore pray trouble yourself to give the young Man two more, but none to Bannerman. Tell me how I shall send the money I owe you, besides a thousand thanks.

Addressed: To Mr Gray at Pembroke college Cambridge

547. MASON TO GRAY

Curzon Street:[1] March 27th [1771].

Dear Mr Gray

I FIND from Stonhewer that he has now £129 – 10 – 6, as appears by the acct[2] on the opposite page. If therefore it be not inconvenient to you I should be glad to borrow £100 of you, for a little pocket money during the present sequestration of my Ecclesiastical & temporal concerns.[3] I wish you would favor

---

[8] Sir James Thornhill (1675–1734), the painter. For the engraving in question, which is by Charles Bretherton, see *Works of Lord Orford*, vol. iii, p. 417.

[9] Thomas Worlidge (1700–66), painter and etcher.

LETTER 547.—First printed by Mitford in *Gray–Mason* (1853), pp. 445–8; now reprinted from original.

[1] Mason was staying here with Stonhewer, whose house was No. 14.

[2] See postscript.

[3] Mitford suggests that this probably refers to the expense Mason was incurring in building a new rectory house at Aston (see Letter 519 *ad fin.*). In a letter to Horace Walpole from Aston, written on 21 June 1777, shortly after he had received a visit from the new Archbishop of York (Markham),

me with a line as soon as may be on this matter, & if you do not object to my proposal I will immediatly send you my Note wch I have the vanity to presume is as good as My bond.

S is perfectly well. The forthnights rest wch his feverish complaint obligd him to take totally removd his other malady; so that he has never had occasion to recur to his former applications wch both you & I thought dangerous, & I always unnecefsary.

Wilson was with me yesterday. He has very gladly accepted the Tutoring of Mr Pierse,[4] & will write to Mr Brown shortly on that subject. I therefore turn the matter over entirely to him & the Master.[5]

The general opinion of what will be the businefs of the day is that the Lord Mayor[6] on acc^t of his Gout will not be sent to the Tower but committed to the care of Bonfoy;[7] whose pizzy-wizzy-ship will be horribly frighted on the occasion. The Mob is nothing in comparison of what you would [have][8] thought respectable when you interested yourself in those matters and attended them in Bloomsbury square.[9]

I am much amused at present in being privy to a great Court secret[10] known only to myself, the King, & about 5 or 6 persons more in the world. I found it out by a Penetration wch would

Mason said: 'His Grace praised my house and said it must have cost me a good deal of money. I said it did, and perhaps I was imprudent to lay out so much' (*Walpole–Mason Correspondence*, vol. i, p. 297).

[4] See Letter 535, nn. 1 and 2.

[5] Brown.   [6] See Letter 546, n. 5.

[7] Nicholas Bonfoy (see Letter 126, n. 11) who was Serjeant-at-Arms in the House of Commons. Mason's forecast was wrong. On Wednesday 27 Mar. (the day on which Mason wrote) 'At twelve at night, the ministers proposed to commit the Lord Mayor only to the Serjeant-at-Arms, on account they said of his ill-health, but, in truth to avoid extremities; he protested that he was perfectly well, and chose to accompany his brother alderman to prison; on which he was sent to the Tower' (Walpole's letter to Mann of 30 Mar. 1771).   [8] Omitted by Mason.

[9] Mason alludes to the siege of Bedford House by the mob in May 1765 (see Letter 403, nn. 4, 5).

[10] The secret is revealed in Mason's letter of 15 Apr. (Letter 548), where he describes it as 'the great State secret, that I and the King knew so well two Months ago'. In an unpublished letter to Alderson of 16 Mar. he wrote: 'I am going to communicate to you a most profound secret wch you must keep most religiously. I have the strongest reason to beleive that Lord H will soon be appointed Governor to the Prince of W. One, if not more of my friends will have honourable posts in the subsequent arrangement. But I shall be totally overlooked, or at best amusd by hopes of future favour wch I shall treat with becoming contempt.'

have done honour to a First Minister in the best of days, even in the days of S[r] Robert or Fobus.[11] When it is ripe for discovery I shall perhaps let you into some parts of it that will never be made public, in the meanwhile Mum is the word from

Your friend & Servant,
SKRODDLES.

I am glad the Master likes his Chairs[12] my true love to him

Rec[d] by M[r] Stonhewer of M[r] Barber⎫ for M[r] Gray ⎬		180 – 14 – 0[13]
Paid for M[r] Browns Patent[14]	49 – 1 – 6	
Given to M[r] Barber[15]	2 – 2 – 0	
	———	51 – 3 – 6
	Remains	129 – 10 – 6

Addressed (by Lord Jersey): Thomas Gray Esq[r] Pembroke Hall Cambridge *Franked:* Jersey *Stamped:* FREE *Postmark:* 27 M[R]

547*. Gray to Stonhewer
[*c. 13 April 1771*]

[In his letter to Gray of 15 Apr. 1771 (Letter 548) Mason refers to a letter from Gray which Stonhewer, with whom he was then staying in Curzon Street, had just 'this post rec[d]', and to a previous letter to him in which Gray had 'tifft at him'. These letters are not extant.]

548. MASON TO GRAY
Curzon Street April 15th
Dear M[r] Gray—   —71

STONHEWER has this post rec[d] yours but you tifft at him so much in a former Letter[1] that you are not to wonder he is so backward in answering it. however he means to write to you if

[11] The late Duke of Newcastle (see Letter 191, n. 16).

[12] These perhaps had been a presentation to Brown from the fund mentioned by Gray in his letter to Wharton of 2 Feb. (see Letter 542, n. 8).

[13] Gray's stipend as Professor was £400 a year; the sum of £180 14s. paid to Stonhewer on Gray's behalf presumably represents payment of the half year's stipend, less deductions for taxes or dues (see Appendix S).

[14] No doubt in connexion with his presentation by the Crown to the living of Stretham (see Letter 540, n. 5).

[15] Probably a Treasury official to whom Gray paid a customary gratuity.
LETTER 548.—First printed by Mitford in *Gray–Mason* (1853), pp. 448–53; now reprinted from original.

[1] These two letters are not extant (see Letter 547*); Gray must also have written to Mason in reply to Mason's letter of 27 Mar. (Letter 548), as Mason acknowledges Gray's loan below.

he survives the next subscription Masquerade for the superb Garniture of wch the Adelphi[2] are now exerting all their powers. Lovatini[3] cant sing for them to morrow. & it is thought Mrs Cornelys[4] will be happy if they allow her a third underground floor in Durham yard[5] to hide her diminishd head in. Well! & so the great State secret[6] is out, that I and the King knew so well two Months ago. But it may be well to inform you & such rusticated folks as you, that it is not my friend the Surveyor Jackson of Hornby Castle who is sub præceptor But a Jackson of Christ Church.[7] My Unkle Powel[8] may blefs his stars that he[9] is removd to Court. For he read such wonderfull Mathematical Lectures there; that if he had gone on a few years longer it is thought St Johns would have been eclipsd by the glories of Peckwater.[10] that Peckwater w^{ch}, in the days of Roger Parne[11]

[2] Mitford assumes that the brothers Adam, the architects, are meant. If so, they may have been designing decorations for the masquerade.

[3] Giovanni Lovatini, 'celebrated for the most beautiful tenor voice and for his most excellent acting', came to England in 1766 and left in 1779 (Burney, *Hist. Music*, vol. iv, pp. 489, 502).

[4] The allusion is explained by a letter of Walpole to Mann of 22 Feb. 1771. Theresa Cornelys (1723–97), a Venetian singer, in 1760 purchased Carlisle House in Soho Square, and made it 'a fairy palace, for balls, concerts, and masquerades'. She competed successfully with the Haymarket (see n. 2) and the theatres. On the information of Mr. Hobart that she was offending against the Act regulating theatres, her entertainments were stopped by the justices. She became bankrupt in 1772.

[5] Durham Yard, Strand, on the riverside in a part of the grounds of the former Durham House, on which the brothers Adam had begun in 1769 to erect the Adelphi Buildings.

[6] See Letter 547, n. 10. On 12 Apr. Lord Holdernesse had been appointed Governor, Mr. Smelt Deputy Governor, Bishop Markham Preceptor, and Cyril Jackson Sub-Preceptor to the Prince of Wales and his brother Prince Frederick.

[7] Cyril Jackson (1746–1819), of Christ Church, Oxford (M.A. 1771), of which he subsequently (1783) became Dean. He was appointed Sub-Preceptor to the Prince of Wales and Prince Frederick on 12 Apr., on the recommendation of the Preceptor, Markham, Bishop of Chester (see n. 14), one of whose favourite pupils he had been at Westminster when Markham was head master. In 1776 he fell out with Holdernesse and was dismissed from his office. Holdernesse and all the others holding similar posts about the Princes resigned their places (see Walpole to Mann, 5 June 1776).

[8] Mason calls him 'uncle' (in imitation of Gray) as having been his tutor at St. John's (see Letter 399, n. 32).

[9] Jackson.

[10] Meaning Christ Church, from the quadrangle of that name on the east side of the College.

[11] There was never a 'Roger Parne' at Trinity. 'Thomas Parne', who was a Fellow of Trinity from 1720 to 1751, had no distinguished position in the

was fain to bow even to Trinity. Then what say you of Mr. Smelt[12]—is it not a proof *that patient Merit will buoy up at last?*[13] In a word did you ever see an *arrangement* formd upon a more liberal & unministerial *ground*. To say nothing of the Governor himself, what think you of the Præceptor?[14] could any thing be more to yours & Lord Mansfields mind? Pray let me know if the New married Stephen[15] chuses to be seller of mild & stale to his royal highnefs[16] because I would put his name on the List of the Expectants I am to apply for, if agreable. I have a Baker a Locksmith a Drawing Master a Laundrefs an Arch-bishops cast-off groom of the Chamber already upon my hands. You must speak in time if you would have any thing. not that I beleive there will [be][17] a household these several years, even if we were rich enough to pay for one. Lord J[18] blabbd to Jack Dixon[19]

college, and was ultimately distempered in mind. Mason seems to have had an unaccountable lapse of memory. It is conceivable that he meant Roger Cotes (1682–1716), who was a most brilliant mathematician: Fellow of Trinity 1705, and Plumian Professor 1706.

[12] Leonard Smelt (*c.* 1719–1800), a member of an old Yorkshire family, Captain Royal Engineers, owed his appointment as Deputy Governor to the two Princes to his being a personal friend of Lord Holdernesse (their Governor), and a *persona grata* to the King. Mason did not like him, and his allusion to patient merit is ironical.

[13] Pope, *Essay on Criticism* (l. 461): 'For rising merit will buoy up at last.'

[14] William Markham (1719–1807), of Westminster School, of which he was head master, 1753–65; and of Christ Church, of which he was Dean, 1767–77. At the beginning of this year (1771) he became Bishop of Chester, in succession to Keene, translated to Ely (see Letter 540, n. 6).

[15] It is assumed that the reference is to Gray's servant, Stephen Hemp-stead (see Letter 439, n. 3), and that he had recently married and set up a public-house, possibly in Cambridge, as he was in attendance on Gray in his last illness (see Brown's letter to Wharton of 29 July 1771 in Appendix W). After Gray's death he was, on 28 Sept. 1771, appointed Butler of Pembroke College.

[16] The Prince of Wales. Mason, as Chaplain to Lord Holdernesse, the Prince's Governor, pretends that he would be in a position to dispense patronage.

[17] Omitted by Mason.

[18] Presumably Lord John Cavendish (see Letter 197, n. 5).

[19] One of seven sons of Jeremiah Dixon, a Yorkshire clergyman. Mason befriended the family, and Henry, one of the brothers, in 1780 married Mason's step-sister. John Dixon matriculated at Lincoln College, Oxford, in Jan. 1762; B.A. 1766; M.A. 1768. Mitford in *Gray–Mason Correspondence* (2nd ed., p. 500) prints the following note from the Rev. W. H. Dixon, Canon of York: 'John Dixon was my father's brother, and a very intimate friend of Mason and Palgrave, who left him his library. The statement that Mason was indifferent as to his blabbing some literary secret to the Czarina is

that Dr Hurd refusd,[20] & he blabbd it to Gould,[21] who will blab it to all the University & we shall be quite shent. Tell Gould if he Says a Word That Oddyngton[22] may again become vacant & I shall certainly serve him as I servd him before. Now I thought that Jack Dixon would have been at Petersburg before he could tell it to any body & I did not much mind whether the Czarina knew it or no. for I know shell get out all Jacks secrets in some of their amorous moments. But here am I writing nonsence when I should be thanking you seriously for Your £100 & sending you your security. Voila Donc! here it is. tear [it off and put it in your][23] strong box.

You say nothing of coming up, & Palgrave affects not to come up till the beginning of May I will prefs neither of you. I know you both too well. As to myself I mean to fly northward by the way of Northamptonshire & poor Hoyland[24]

cum Zephyris & Hirundine prima[25]

but as it snows at present you will think perhaps to find me here in June. & perhaps you may—well do your pleasure & beleive me

ever y^rs W M.

Congratulate me on the cefsation of all my fears about Kitchen garden Walls, &c. tis an ill wind that blows no body profit.

explained by his being at that time chaplain to the British merchants at Petersburgh.' Mason, in his will, made him one of the trustees of his landed property (see *Hurd–Mason Correspondence*, p. 162, n.), and he was responsible for the publication of the collected edition of Mason's works in 1811.

[20] This is explained by a passage in an unpublished letter of Mason to Alderson, dated 24 Apr.: 'As soon as the great secret was discovered, I went as in duty bound to congratulate my Lord [Holdernesse] on his promotion. I thought it necessary in the course of our talk to vindicate my friend Hurd's refusal of the Sub-præceptorship as a thing infra dignitatem suam.' Hurd was appointed Preceptor to the Princes in 1776.

[21] See Letter 392, n. 11.   [22] See Letter 486, n. 1.   [23] MS. torn.

[24] Francis Hoyland (b. 1727) matriculated at Magdalene College, Cambridge, in 1744. He graduated B.A. in 1748 and was ordained. He was a Yorkshireman and a protégé of Mason's. Walpole wrote to Mason on 11 May 1769: 'It is to you, Sir, Mr Hoyland owes everything' (*Walpole–Mason Correspondence*, vol. i, p. 10). Through Mason's good offices Walpole printed at Strawberry Hill, in Apr. 1769, 300 copies of his *Poems*, to be sold for his benefit. On 5 Apr. Walpole wrote to Mason: 'I enclose a short advertisement for Mr Hoyland's poems. I mean by it to tempt people to a little more charity, and to soften to him, as much as I can, the humiliation of its being asked for him' (*op. cit.*, p. 8). He may have been living in Northamptonshire, which would explain Mason's allusion.   [25] Horace, *Epist.* i. vii. 13.

549. NICHOLLS TO GRAY

Blundeston, 29 April, 1771.

Dear Sir,

IT is six weeks since I received De Bonstetten's letter, in conse-
quence of which I wrote to you;[1] I have long waited for your
determination, to enable me to answer it; my own was already
made when I wrote to you, only I cannot fix a time till I know
yours. I need not say whether it would be agreeable to me to
have your company in such a voyage; without it, I shall lose
half the pleasure and advantage I flattered myself with the
hope of, but I shall go at all events. I should think the first or
second week in June, at furthest, is quite late enough to begin
the journey; if so, it is high time, I think, to give notice to
De Bonstetten. I have provided both money and a curate, the
former, the sum I mentioned to you, two hundred pounds, and
the latter, from the beginning of June, to the end of October,
or a few Sundays longer, if I want him. I wrote to Wheeler[2]
(not about Berne) many months ago, but by a very uncertain
direction, I have not heard a word since and know nothing
about him, nor where to direct, so he is quite out of the question,
and if you don't go with me, I shall go alone.

As for Temple's matter,[3] I see it is troublesome to you, and
am very sorry I ever mentioned it; I did not understand, nor
did he mean, I think, that you was to have the trouble of form-
ing a complete list of authors, but only of pointing out a few of
the best and most necefsary in each period sufficient to make the
links of the chain, and continue it down unbroken and uninter-
rupted. Your sympathy with his distrefs drew this trouble on
you and encouraged my zeal to become impertinent.

I congratulate the ministry and the University on the honour
they have both acquired by the promotion of Mr. Scott;[4] may

LETTER 549.—First printed by Mitford (1835–43), vol. v, pp. 134–5.
[1] On 16 Mar. (Letter 545).
[2] John Wheler (see Letter 421, n. 18). Gray in his reply (Letter 550) says:
'Methinks I could wish that *Wheeler* went with you.'
[3] See Letter 545, n. 9. Nicholls must have inferred from Gray's silence
that he was unwilling to oblige Temple.
[4] James Scott (1733–1814), of Trinity College, Cambridge; B.A. 1757;
Fellow, 1758; M.A. 1760; B.D. 1768; D.D. 1775; a creature of Sandwich
(see Letter 390, n. 7), under whose inspiration he contributed in 1765 a
series of attacks on Lord Bute to the *Public Advertiser*, under the pseudonym
of 'Anti-Sejanus'. This year, through the interest of Lord Sandwich (at this

there never be wanting such lights of the church! and such ornaments of that famous seminary of virtue and good learning. I have found many insects, chiefly carabi and staphyli, great variety of the latter; this unseasonable season has put the months quite out of order, all of the vegetable tribe that should have looked gay and flourished early in March, just begin to peep up half starved with cold, and wishing themselves back again. Adieu! yours most sincerely,

N. N.

My mother desires me to make her compliments.

550. GRAY TO NICHOLLS

3^d May. 1771.
Pemb: Coll:

Dear S^r

I CAN not tell you, what I do not know myself; nor did I know, you staid for my determination to answer B:ˢ letter. I am glad to hear you say, you shall go at all events,[1] because then it is sure, I shall not disappoint you; & if (wch I surely wish) I should be able to accompany you, perhaps I may prevail upon you to stay a week or fortnight for me: if I find it will not do, you certainly shall know it.

Three days ago I had so strange a letter from B: I hardly know how to give you any account of it, & desire you would not speak of it to any body. that he has been *le plus malheureux des hommes*, that he is *decidé à quitter son pays*, that is, to pafs the next winter in England: that he can not bear *la morgue de l'aristocratie, & l'orgueil armé des loix*, in short, strong exprefsions of uneasinefs & confusion of mind, so much as to talk of *un pistolet & du courage*,[2] & all without the shadow of a reason afsign'd, & so he leaves me. he is either disorder'd in his intellect (wch is too pofsible) or has done some strange thing, that has exasperated his whole family & friends at home, w^{ch} (I'm afraid) is at least equally pofsible. I am quite at a lofs about it. you will see &

time First Lord of the Admiralty), he was presented to the living of Simon-burn, near Hexham, in Northumberland, which was in the gift of the Governors of Chelsea Hospital.

LETTER 550.—First printed by Mitford (1835–43), vol. v, pp. 136–7; now reprinted from original.

[1] Nicholls had decided to visit Bonstetten (see Letter 549).

[2] Gray has only partially underlined the last three French phrases, but he evidently intended them to be underlined throughout, like the first one.

know more: but by all means curb these vagaries & wandering imaginations, if there be any room for counsels. You aggravate my misfortunes by twitting me with Temple,[3] as if a pack of names of books & editions were any cure for his uneasinefs, & that I witheld it from him. I have had neither health nor spirits[4] all the winter, & never knew or cared, what weather it was, before. the Spring is begun here, Swallows were seen 23 April, the Redstart, on ye 26th,the Nightingale was heard on ye 29th, & the Cuckow, on 1st of May. methinks I could wish, that *Wheeler* went with you, whether I do or not! Adieu! I am

Truly Yours
T G:

Addressed: To The Revd Mr Nicholls at Blundeston near Leostoff Suffolk by London. *Postmark:* CAMBRIDGE 3 MA

551. NICHOLLS TO GRAY

Blundeston, May 14, 1771.

I HAVE just received the enclosed from my poor unfortunate Temple; it is a matter too nice for me to meddle with without your advice; you directed my interposition between the same persons before,[1] and with good succefs; pity I am sure will plead more strongly with you now, because the case is more important. I cannot bear to see such a sacrifice to filial piety in the person of one whom I esteem for that and a thousand valuable qualities, and whom his misfortunes have made me love; his mind and constitution too are too feeble for such struggles. I cannot bear to see him absolutely ruined, he is now nearer than ever, and cannot be saved but by the help of Lord Lisburne, or some one else who is able to help him; if I could be the means of awakening Lord Lisburne's humanity, it would be the action of my life I should reflect on with most pleasure. But it is too delicate a

---

[3] See Letter 545, n. 9.

[4] The letter itself bears evidence of Gray's ill-health and depression.

LETTER 551.—First printed by Mitford (1835–43), vol. v, pp. 137–9.

[1] The reference is to Temple and Lord Lisburne and to the differences between them at the end of 1767 (see Letter 456 of 17 Dec. 1767 and the letters of Gray to Nicholls during the six weeks thereafter). From the present letter and from Gray's reply (Letter 552) it appears that on this occasion Temple's troubles were chiefly financial, induced by his having again to come to his father's relief (Nicholls refers to his 'sacrifice to filial piety', Gray to his 'pious imprudence'). Help was to be sought from Lord Lisburne, and Temple had apparently hoped that he might be offered a chaplaincy abroad or preferment in Ireland.

matter for me to undertake unafsisted, when I may hope to have the benefit of your wise and friendly counsels; let me entreat you to send them speedily, he is waiting in an anxious suspense, which, if it last long, may too easily change to despair; I own I dread some desperate event; the silence with which he reproaches me was only occasioned by my waiting daily for an answer from you; this is a matter of so much greater consequence, and any little delay, any suspicion of neglect in me may work such fatal effects in a mind subdued by distrefs and on the brink already of despair, that I hope you will answer this directly, for I shall not write to him till I receive your answer.

I have writ to De Bonstetten to say I shall certainly be at Berne this summer, and that I am not without hopes of having your company thither; that, if I arrive not by the end of June, and he hear not again, he may conclude that I have waited for you, and that you come too. I have received a very civil invitation from Dr. Hallifax[2] to pafs some time at Trinity Hall; if (as I suspect) it is a civility which I owe entirely to you, I am very much obliged to you for it, but it will not be in my power to comply with the invitation, because I must go to town the other road and pafs a week with my uncle[3] in Efsex, whose son is now visiting me on that condition. I know nothing of Wheeler, nor in what corner of the globe he hides himself, he was to have been here this spring, but he neither writes nor comes, so I am not to blame.

Adieu! my heart is really full of poor Temple: you are too good to keep either him or me in suspense longer than is necefsary. Yours most faithfully.

N. N.

552. GRAY TO NICHOLLS

London. 20 May. 1771.
at Frisby's,[1] Jermyn-
Street.

I RECEIVED your letter inclosing that of poor T:[2] the night before I set out for London. I would by all means wish you to

---

[2] See Letter 409, n. 10.

[3] Presumably one of Nicholls's Turner uncles or great-uncles (see Letter 429, n. 7).

LETTER 552.—First printed in part (in a garbled text) in Mason's *Memoirs* (pp. 393–4); first printed in full by Mitford (1835–43), vol. v, pp. 139–41; now reprinted from original.

[1] Gray's address in Jermyn Street, so far as we have evidence, had hitherto

comply with his request. you may say many things to L^d L:[2] with a better grace, than he can. I trust to the cause, & to the warmth of your own kindnefs, for inspiration: there is little of management required, nothing to conceal, but the full persuasion (I trust) we both have, that L^d L: knows the distrefs of his circumstances at least as well as we do. this doubtlefs must be kept out of sight, lest it carry too keen a reproach with it. in all the rest you are at full liberty to expatiate on his good qualities, the friendship you have long had for him, the pious imprudence, that has produced his present uneasy situation, & above all your profound respect for Lord L:[s] character & sensibility of heart.[3]

who knows what may be the consequence? Men sometimes catch that feeling from a Stranger, wch should have originally sprung from their own heart. as to the means of helping him, his own schemes are perhaps too wild for you to mention them to L^d L: & (if they are to separate him from his Wife & family) what is to come of them in the mean time? I have a notion that the Chaplainship at Leghorn is still vacant by the death of a young Mr Byrom. at least I have never heard it was fill'd up. it depends on recommendation to the principal Italian Merchants, wch seems much in L^d L:[s] power. The B^p of Derry[4] (I apprehend) is at Nice, or somewhere in Italy, for his health: it is true he has a great patronage in Ireland, & sometimes (from vanity) may do a right thing. the other projects do not strike me as any thing, but (if L^d L: can be brought to mean him well) many different means will occur, by wch he may serve him.

I shall pafs a fortnight here, & perhaps within that time may see you in Town, at least I would wish so to do.[5] I am but

been at the house of Mr. Roberts, a hosier and hatter. He now changed his lodgings to Frisby's 'the oilman', as Nicholls described him (see Letter 176, n. 3).
    [2] 'T:' is Temple and 'L^d L:' is Lisburne (see Letter 551, n. 1).
    [3] Nicholls apparently wrote to Lord Lisburne. In Letter 554 he writes: 'I have done my best for poor Temple.' When the letters of Boswell to Temple were discovered at Boulogne, there were in the same bundle other letters addressed to Temple, including twenty-seven from Nicholls. These letters are for the most part missing, but a list of them was preserved (now owned by Professor Tinker) and this includes a letter from Nicholls: 'Jermyn St Thurdsay 11 June 1771', with the contents summarized: 'Copy of letter from Lord Lisburne concerning Temple's affairs, chaplaincy at Leghorn, preferment in Ireland. B. of Exeter. Lord Chancellor Yorke. N. going to Switzerland.'   [4] Frederick Augustus Hervey (see Letter 329, n. 5).
    [5] Nicholls in his reply of 27 May (Letter 554) wrote: 'I am coming to

indifferently well, & think, all things consider'd, it is best not to keep you in suspense about my journey.[6] the sense of my own duty,[7] which I do not perform, my own low spirits (to which this consideration not a little contributes) & (added to these) a bodily indisposition make it necefsary for me to deny myself that pleasure, which perhaps I have kept too long in view. I shall see however with your eyes, & accompany you at least in idea. write or come, or both soon. I am ever yours sincerely,

T G:

My respects to Mrs Nicholls. Clarke[8] (I hear) is in town at Claxton's.[9]

553. GRAY TO WHARTON

Dear Doctor

I WAS really far from well in health, when I received your last letter: since that I am come to Town, & find myself considerably better. Mason has pafs'd all the winter here with Stonhewer in Curson-Street, May-fair, but thinks of returning homeward in a week or ten days. he had your letter (wch had gone round by Aston) & was applying to Mr Fraser[1] & others for proper recommendations in case poor Mrs. E:[2] should be

town. . . . I design to be there Wednesday sennight' (5 June), and Gray's letter to him of 28 June (Letter 556) refers to his having been with Gray and having left some little time before.

[6] That is, the projected journey to Switzerland, in company with Nicholls, to visit Bonstetten. The rest of the letter has been torn off, carrying with it the address on the other side. The letter was intact when Mitford transcribed it, as he prints the remainder of the text without remark.

[7] As Professor of Modern History (see Letter 513).

[8] See Letter 513, n. 1.   [9] See Letter 483, n. 6.

LETTER 553.—First printed in part (in a garbled text) in Mason's *Memoirs*, p. 295; first printed in full by Mitford (1816), vol. ii, pp. 566–7; now reprinted from original.

[1] William Fraser, Under-Secretary of State (see Letter 195, n. 13).

[2] Mrs. Ettrick, Wharton's elder sister (Letters 401, 480). She was again suffering from ill-treatment by her husband. Mason had already written to Wharton, and his letter of 13 May (Egerton MS. 2400) explains the plans discussed by Gray: 'If you fix on Utrecht or any other place in Holland for the retreat of Mrs Ettrick, my friend Mr Fraser has already promised to write to M^r La Vale Secretary to Sir Joseph Yorke, & agent to the King at Rotterdam to take proper care of her & all her concerns. I will wait upon her in Boswell Court as soon as I can hear of her coming to Town; & do all in my power to assist her. But . . . would [it] not be rather better to settle her in some small town in Wales or any of the Western parts of England . . . (provided that she takes another name). . . .'

obliged to make use of them: but now you have given us some hopes, that these expedients may not be necefsary. I for my own part do heartily wish, you may not be deceived, & that so cool a Tyrant as her Husband seems to be, may willingly give up the thoughts of exercising that tyranny, when it is most in his power: but, I own, it seems to me very unlikely. however I would not have you instrumental (but at her most earnest intreaty) in sending her out of his reach. no persuasion or advice on this head should come from you: it should be absolutely her own firm resolution (before sure witnefses) for that is the only thing, that can authorise you to afsist her. it must have been her own fault (at least her weaknefs) that such a decision as that of these Delegates³ could find any grounds to go upon. I do not wonder, that such an event has discomposed you: it discomposes me to think of the trouble & expence it has brought on you!

My summer was intended to have been pafs'd in Switzerland: but I have drop'd the thought of it, & believe my expeditions will terminate in Old-park: for travel I must, or cease to exist. till this year I hardly knew what (mechanical) low-spirits were: but now I even tremble at an east-wind. it is here the height of summer, but with all the bloom & tender verdure of spring. at Cambridge the Laurustines & Arbutus kill'd totally: Apricots, Almonds, & Figs lost all their young shoots. St:ʳ⁴ has had a melancholy journey: tomorrow we expect him here. Adieu!

I am ever

Yours

T G:

at Frisby's, in Jermyn-Street, St. James's.
24 May. 1771.

Addressed: To Thomas Wharton Eˢᵠ of Old-Park near Darlington Durham
Postmark: 25 MA

554. NICHOLLS TO GRAY

Dear Sir, Blundeston, May 27, 1771.

I AM much mortified that you give me so little hopes of your company on my journey, but I do not quite despair of that point. I am infinitely more concerned to find you dejected as

---

³ See Letter 480, n. 3.
⁴ Mason, in the letter to Wharton quoted in n. 1, wrote: 'Stonhewer sets out early this morning for Durham having by this same post received an account of the Death of his Mother.'
LETTER 554.—First printed by Mitford (1835–43), vol. v, pp. 141–2.

you appear to be; I read your first letter[1] with concern, and your last[2] with greater. For God's sake how can you neglect a duty[3] which never existed but in your own imagination, which catches every alarm too quickly? it never yet was performed, nor I believe expected. I hope your want of health is not so great as you think it. Is it the gout, a return of any former complaint, or what? But you need not answer my question, I am coming to town to be satisfied. I design to be there Wednesday sennight, and you will do me a favour to bespeak for me the story above you at Frisby's[4] or some other lodging near you for a week. I have done my best for poor Temple.[5] I am now half distracted with trying to rescue myself from the oppreſsion of a mercileſs lawyer that is treating with me on Miss Allin's part about a lease of this house and estate;[6] I have my faithful Mr. Spurgeon[7] to counsel me, but all I believe will not do. Adieu! yours most faithfully.

N. N.

555. GRAY TO BROWN

Saturday. London.

Dear Sʳ   [June 22, 1771][1]

I WRITE just to tell you the reason of my stay here. the Gout has left me, but I have a feverish disorder, that seems to return regularly upon me every morning, & leaves me very weak & spiritleſs. another complaint has come upon me yesterday, that makes me unfit to bear the journey to Cambridge. Dʳ Gisburne advises me to take a lodgeing at Kensington for a week or two,[2] & I believe, I shall try this expedient

---

[1] Letter 550.   [2] Letter 552.   [3] See Letter 552, n. 7.
[4] Where Gray was staying (see Letter 552, n. 1).
[5] See Letter 552, n. 3.   [6] See Letter 537, n. 13.
[7] Mitford notes: 'Mʳ John Spurgeon was an attorney at Yarmouth, and Town Clerk of the Corporation. He died in 1810, aged 95.'
LETTER 555.—Now first printed from original.
[1] The date is determined by the reference to Gray's going to Kensington and by the postmark. 22 June was a Saturday in 1771.
[2] Walpole, writing to Cole from Paris on 12 Aug. just after he had heard of Gray's death, says: 'I saw him but four or five days before I came hither; he had been to Kensington for the air, complained of the gout flying about him, of sensations of it in his stomach, and indeed [I] thought him changed, and that he looked ill—still I had not the least idea of his being in danger.' To Mason he wrote on 9 Sept., after his return to England, that Gray told him 'he had been a month at Kensington for the air'. But as Gray did not move to Kensington till 23 June, and Walpole left England on 7 July, this is obviously a mistake.

tomorrow. my illnefs has prevented me from doing any thing about your carpet,[3] wch I hope you will excuse. pray, write to me & direct as usual in Jermyn-Street. I am ever

Yours

T G:

Addressed: To The Rev^d the Master of Pembroke Hall Cambridge *Postmark:* 22 IV

556. GRAY TO NICHOLLS

Jermyn-Street.[1] 28 June.[2]

1771.

Dear S^r

THE inclosed came a few days after you left us,[3] as I apprehend, from Temple. I continue here much against my will. the gout is gone, the feverish disorder abated, but not cured; my spirits much opprefs'd, & the more so, as I foresee a new complaint, that may tie me down perhaps to my bed, & expose me to the operations of a Surgeon. God knows, what will be the end of it.

It will be an alleviation to my miseries, if I can hear, you are well, & capable of enjoying those objects of curiosity, that the countries you are in[4] promise to afford you. the greater the detail you give me of them, the happier I shall be. Mr. Clarke call'd on me yesterday,[5] & desires to be remember'd. I know

---

[3] No doubt for the Master's Lodge at Pembroke.

LETTER 556.—First printed by Mitford (1835–43), vol. v, pp. 142–3; now reprinted from original.

[1] Though this letter is dated from Jermyn Street, it is evident from the previous letter that Gray was now staying at Kensington.

[2] On this day Gray proved Mrs. Olliffe's will.

[3] Nicholls had been lodging with Gray at Frisby's house (Letter 554).

[4] Nicholls, as appears from the address, was in Paris on his way to Switzerland. He wrote from there on 29 June (Letter 557).

[5] See Letter 513, n. 1. Clarke gave an account of this visit, and recorded the deep impression made upon him by Gray, in the following letter, written on 23 July 1772, to his friend Temple: 'I don't ask you, if you were shocked at Mr Gray's death or no? I declare I never was so affected in my Life. I was a little acquainted with him just before he died; Virgilium vidi tantum —I remember the last day I called upon him, he had just received a letter of yours to Nicholls, which he was going to forward to Paris to him. As much as I admired the Man for his Genius, so much more did I adore him when I saw him for his benevolence & humanity which I never saw so strong in any body in my Life, it shined out in every word, look, & motion—but, ipse Epicurus obit. I wish you joy of his Posthumous Works, which I think we shall have about Xmas, not that I think Mason will do him justice. Then

nothing new here, but that Mr. T: Pitt[6] is going to be married to a Mifs Wilkinson, the daughter of a rich Merchant, who gives her 30,000£ down, & at least as much more in expectation. Adieu! I am faithfully

Yours
T G:

Wilkes is like to lose his election.[7]

Addressed: [M]onsieu[r . . . . .][8] Mefs:ˢ Telluson & Neckar Banquiers, Paris France

557. NICHOLLS TO GRAY

Paris, June 29,[1] 1771.

HERE have I been since Wednesday last! not a word yet from you! are you worse? I hope not, better? why will you not let me know? It was Friday last[2] that I set out; that night I lay at Sittingbourne, the next day reached Dover by dinner time; after dinner I walked shivering with the East wind to Shakespeare's cliff, which is certainly dreadful enough to be improved by an imagination like his to what he has made it. I trembled, thought of you, collected a few plants, and returned to examine them. Sunday morning at six we embarked, and arrived at Calais at nine; from thence after haggling for a chaise, waiting for horses, &c. I set out in the afternoon in company with two Englishmen with whom I pafsed the sea. The total change of things in pafsing twenty miles struck me with astonishment the moment I set my foot on shore at Calais; we lay that night at Boulogne; the country as you know is not very agreeable,

[*MS. torn*] here, Salve! severi relligio loci! which vers[es I] saw when I was last abroad written by him[self at] the Grande Chartreuse—I am surprized, as he made his will the Year before he died, that he left Nicholls nothing—As to Nicholls, Claxton heard of him by chance t'other day; he is now at Naples & is to be at home in October.' (From an unpublished letter owned by Professor Tinker.)

  [6] See Letter 250, n. 12. He married on 29 July (the day before Gray's death) Anne, daughter and coheir of Pinckney Wilkinson, of Burnham, Norfolk. The lady was two years his senior, and survived him for ten years.

  [7] The poll for Sheriffs for the City of London and County of Middlesex, which began on 24 June, resulted on 1 July in the return of Wilkes at the head of the poll by a majority of 121, his colleague being his adherent, Frederick Bull, who had been the tenant of Gray's house at Wanstead, and had subsequently purchased it (see Letter 196, n. 9).

  [8] MS. torn.

LETTER 557.—First printed by Mitford (1835–43), vol. v, pp. 143–7.

  [1] Saturday.   [2] That is, Friday in the previous week, 21 June.

exactly like Cambridgeshire, uninclosed corn fields with a few hills with a tree or two on them. Towards Montreuil it mends, some pleasant valleys for this country wind among the corn land, several woods appear, and Montreuil itself, seated on a rising ground, is a good object. In going post there is not much time for observation.

The West front of the church of Abbeville struck me however as of the best and most beautiful gothic. At Amiens we arrived about three o'clock on Monday morning, at six we rose again and went to the cathedral, which was then full of people; a thousand different sorts of devotion going forward at the same time at different altars and in different chapels, little bells of different tones perpetually tingling for the elevation of the host, in short, the Boulevards since have put me very much in mind of it. The church is very handsome in itself, and adorned with a magnificence that pretends at least a zeal for religion, if it does not imply it. But all this was done in such haste and so much between sleeping and waking, that I reckon myself to have seen nothing in my journey. Tuesday we slept at Chantilly; there is a statelinefs in the Castle and its apartments, and their furniture very new to an Englishman. It was the finest evening pofsible, which added not a little to the spectacle; the castle seemed to come forward in relief from the purple and gold of a most glorious setting sun, which glowed in the water as well as in the sky; to this succeeded clear moonlight without a drop of dew. From Chantilly we reached Paris by noon next day, Wednesday—just giving a peep at St. Denis, but not at the treasury, for it was a wrong hour. Every thing that I have seen hitherto has been with the disadvantage of companions who see because they think they ought to see. In this manner I have run over le Palais Royal, but not in this manner the Cloister of the Chartreux,[3] where I pafsed part of this morning in admiration! The greatnefs of conception, the pure simple style so suited to the subject, the penetrating exprefsion, the dignity of attitude, and if I may be allowed to talk of colouring, composition, grouping, and keeping, the perfection of those too[4] make all that I have seen before trifling and little: there is besides an interesting solemnity on the subject if one forgets, as I did, entirely that it is only a silly legend; by that simple dignity peculiar to himself

---

[3] In his advice to Palgrave Gray singled out above all else in Paris the Cloister of the Chartreux with the pictures of Le Sueur (see Letter 400, n. 3).
[4] A probable correction for 'two' in Mitford's text.

he has contrived to make every part of the story interesting, even such as St. Hugo conferring the white habit, the Pope confirming the institution, &c. the death of St. Bruno, the interpretation of the dream, the resurrection of Raymond Diocre, and the figure of St. Bruno in the first piece, when he hears with deep attention and with a candour in his countenance open to conviction, the Doctor Raymond Diocre strike me most, at least I think so, but I wont swear till I have been again and again. In their chapter house too there is a fine picture by Le Sueur of the appearance of our Saviour to Mary Magdalen. Very much of the painting in the cloister is in perfect preservation, parts very much hurt, as it seems, by the dripping of water, there are doors to shut them in, but the mischief when it happens comes from the wall to which they are fastened. I saw the good fathers (for really they look so) at their devotions, deep devotion! accompanied with prostrations that had not the appearance of acts only of form or custom. I rather envied them for a moment, and felt myself 'une ame mondaine.'[5]

To-morrow (Sunday) I go to Versailles, and shall not return till Monday; Tuesday or Wednesday I set off; you will still direct if you please to me chez Mefsrs. Telluson and Neckar, à Paris.

The people here dare to exprefs their discontentment very loudly; it is the Chancellor[6] who is the chief object of their hatred; there is a competition for power between him and the D. D'Aiguillon,[7] the latter, it is thought, would be glad to put the most odious acts on him, and to see him ruined afterwards. Les pauvres princes, as the people call them, seem to be able to do little. All matters of property have been at a stand some time, criminal justice proceeds as usual. All complain, but seem to despair of a remedy. A fowl sells here for six or seven shillings.

Adieu! my best friend! if you have any friendship for me, take care of yourself, and let me hear that you are well, and think of me sometimes.

N. N.

[5] Nicholls kept a journal of his tour. It is stated in the *D.N.B.* that 'he is said to have printed for gifts to his friends an account of his travels'. No evidence is known to support this statement. It seems improbable, as Temple as late as 1795 records in his diary for 2 Sept. that he saw 'Nicholls Italian & Swiss Journals MS.' (*Diaries of W. J. Temple*, edited by L. Bettany, p. 140.)

[6] René Nicolas Charles Auguste de Maupeou (1714–92); he had been appointed Chancellor in Sept. 1768, and retained office till Aug. 1774.

[7] The Duc d'Aiguillon, First Minister (see Letter 533, n. 13).

APPENDIX A

The Case submitted to Dr. Audley

[Letter 28]

THE Case submitted to Dr. Audley on Mrs. Gray's behalf was published by Mitford[1] with a note prefixed:

'The following curious paper I owe to the kindness of Sir Egerton Brydges and his friend Mr. Haslewood. It was discovered in a volume of manuscript law cases, purchased by the latter gentleman at the sale of the late Isaac Reed's books. It is a case submitted by the mother of Gray to the opinion of an eminent civilian in 1735;[2] and it proves, that to the great and single exertions of this admirable woman, Gray was indebted for his education, and consequently for the happiness of his life.'

The Case, the Question submitted to Dr. Audley, and his Answer are as follows:

CASE

Philip Gray, before his marriage[3] with his wife, (then Dorothy Antrobus, and who was then partner with her sister Mary Antrobus,) entered into articles of agreement with the said Dorothy, and Mary, and their brother Robert Antrobus,[4] that the said Dorothy's stock in trade (which was then £240) should be employed by the said Mary in the said trade, and that the same, and all profits arising thereby, should be for the sole benefit of the said Dorothy, notwithstanding her intended coverture, and her sole receipts alone a sufficient discharge to the said Mary and her brother Robert Antrobus, who was made trustee. But in case either the said Philip or Dorothy dies, then the same to be assigned to the survivor.

That in pursuance of the said articles, the said Mary, with the assistance of the said Dorothy her sister, hath carried on the said trade for near thirty years, with tolerable success for the said Dorothy. That she hath been no charge to the said Philip; and during all the said time, hath not only found herself in all manner of apparel, but also for all her children, to the number of twelve,[5] and most of the

---

[1] As an appendix in *The Poems of Thomas Gray*, 1814, and in his editions of the *Works of Thomas Gray*, 1816 and 1835–43.

[2] The date should probably be 1735/6; see n. 10 below.

[3] The marriage is conjectured to have taken place in 1709.

[4] Robert Antrobus died on 20 Jan. 1729/30.

[5] Of the twelve children eleven died in infancy.

1195

furniture of his house; and paying £40 a year for his shop,[6] almost providing every thing for her son, whilst at Eton school, and now he is at Peter-House at Cambridge.

Notwithstanding which, almost ever since he hath been married, he hath used her in the most inhuman manner, by beating, kicking, punching, and with the most vile and abusive language; that she hath been in the utmost fear and danger of her life, and hath been obliged this last year to quit her bed, and lie with her sister. This she was resolved, if possible, to bear; not to leave her shop of trade for the sake of her son, to be able to assist in the maintenance of him at the University, since his father won't.

There is no cause for this usage, unless it be an unhappy jealousy of all mankind in general (her own brother[7] not excepted); but no woman deserves, or hath maintained, a more virtuous character: or it is presumed if he can make her sister leave off trade, he thinks he can then come into his wife's money, but the articles are too secure for his vile purposes.

He daily threatens he will pursue her with all the vengeance possible, and will ruin himself to undo her, and his only son; in order to which he hath given warning to her sister to quit his shop, where they have carried on their trade so successfully, which will be almost their ruin: but he insists she shall go at Midsummer next; and the said Dorothy, his wife, in necessity must be forced to go along with her, to some other house and shop, to be assisting to her said sister, in the said trade, for her own and son's support.

But if she can be quiet, she neither expects or desires any help from him: but he is really so very vile in his nature, she hath all the reason to expect most troublesome usage from him that can be thought of.[8]

QUESTION

What he can, or possibly may do to molest his wife in living with her sister, and assisting in her trade, for the purposes in the said articles; and which will be the best way for her to conduct herself in this unhappy circumstance, if he should any ways be troublesome, or endeavour to force her to live with him? And whether the said Dorothy in the lifetime of the said Philip, may not by will, or otherwise, dispose of the interest, or produce, which hath, or may arise,

---

6 The shop seems to have been in the house in which Philip Gray and his family resided. There is a reference below to 'some other house and shop'.

7 As Robert Antrobus was dead at the time, the reference is to William Antrobus.

8 The statement throws light on the furious temper of Philip Gray, whom Mason describes as 'morose, unsocial and obstinate'. (See *Memoirs*, p. 119.)

or become due for the said stock as she shall think fit, it being apprehended as part of her separate estate?

ANSWER

If Mrs. Gray should leave her husband's house, and go to live with her sister in any other, to assist her in her trade, her husband may, and probably will call her, by process in the Ecclesiastical Court, to return home and cohabit with him, which the court will compel her to do, unless she can shew cause to the contrary. She has no other defence in that case, than to make proof, before the court, of such cruelties as may induce the judge to think she cannot live in safety with her husband: then the court will decree for a separation.

This is a most unhappy case, and such a one, as I think, if possible, should be referred to, and made up by some common friend; sentences of separation, by reason of cruelty only, being very rarely obtained.

What the cruelties are which he has used towards her, and what proof she is able to make of them, I am yet a stranger to. She will, as she has hitherto done, bear what she reasonably can, without giving him any provocation to use her ill. If, nevertheless, he forces her out of doors, the most reputable place she can be in, is with her sister. If he will proceed to extremities, and go to law, she will be justified, if she stands upon her defence, rather perhaps than if she was plaintiff in the cause.

As no power of making a will is reserved to Mrs. Gray, by her marriage settlement, and not only the original stock, but likewise the produce and interest which shall accrue, and be added to it, are settled upon the husband, if he survives his wife; it is my opinion she has no power to dispose of it by will, or otherwise.

JOH. AUDLEY[9]

Doctors' Commons.
Feb. 9th, 1735.[10]

[L. W.]

[9] John Audley, admitted to Peterhouse from Eton in 1696, matriculated 1697, B.A. 1699–1700, M.A. 1703, LL.D. 1710. He was elected Fellow of Peterhouse in 1703, and was admitted as an Advocate in 1710. He was a contemporary of Robert Antrobus at Peterhouse, of which College both were Fellows, and it is not unreasonable to suppose that this association may have determined the choice of Audley to advise on the Case.

[10] If the date was correctly taken from the manuscript, it is probable that Audley, as he was writing a legal document, followed the old style, and that the year may be taken to have been 1735/6.

APPENDIX B

Gray's Tripos Verses

[Letters 35 &c.]

It was the custom at Cambridge every year, when the lists of the successful Tripos candidates were published, for the Proctors and Moderators to commission undergraduates to write Latin poems on subjects which they prescribed. These poems were printed for distribution,[1] and from the year 1748 the Tripos lists were printed on the back of the Tripos verses.

The Proctors were responsible for providing the verses issued with the 'First Tripos' paper, containing the list of the Wranglers and Senior Optimes, at the Comitia Priora, held on the day after Ash Wednesday, and the Moderators (who were the Tripos Examiners) for the verses issued with the 'Second Tripos' paper, containing the list of the Junior Optimes, at the Comitia Posteriora, held on the Thursday after mid-Lent Sunday.[2] On 29 December 1736 Gray wrote to Walpole (Letter 35), 'the Moderatour has asked me to make the Tripos Verses this year', that is one of the sets of verses to be issued with the Second Tripos list of 1736/7.[3] Mason tells us that Gray's subject was *Luna est habitabilis*, and his poem was printed in *Musæ Etonenses* (London 1755). From a letter of West to Walpole, dated 18 April 1737, it appears that Gray's poem had been sent to West by Walpole, with another poem *Planetæ sunt habitabiles*.[4] It may be assumed that this was the other set of verses issued with the Second Tripos list.[5] This poem, which was also

Appendix B.—[1] In a *Catalogue of the Sale of Books, Manuscripts, and Letters of the Poet Gray* sold by Sotheby and Wilkinson on 4 Aug. 1854, Lot 230 includes a printed copy of Gray's Latin poem entitled *Luna Habitabilis*. This was, no doubt, Gray's copy of his Tripos verses.

[2] For the First and Second Tripos see Adam Wall, *An Account of the Different Ceremonies observed in the Senate House of the University of Cambridge*, Cambridge, 1798. On the subject of the Tripos verses, see Wordsworth, *Social Life at the English Universities*, pp. 234, 235.

[3] Mason, *Memoirs*, p. 37, after quoting a letter of Gray to West of March 1737, says that: 'In the same letter he tells him "that his College has set him a versifying on a public occasion" (viz. those verses which are called Tripos) "on the theme of *Luna est habitabilis*".' It is doubtful whether Mason quotes Gray correctly; for it was not his College but the Moderator who had asked him to write, and the date assigned to the letter seems doubtful (see Letter 37, n. 1).

[4] See *Gray–Walpole Correspondence*, No. 57.

[5] Many of the Tripos verses are extant in the University Registry or Library. But the verses of 1736/7 are not to be found, nor is there any record of the subjects set.

Appendix B

printed in *Musæ Etonenses*, was written by Jacob Bryant,[6] then a freshman scholar at King's. Gray had contributed a Latin poem to the *Gratulatio Academiæ* on the marriage of the Prince of Wales, which was published in 1736, and perhaps on this account had been selected by the Moderators to write the Tripos verses.

The Moderators for the Tripos of 1736/7 were James Brown, of Pembroke, and Roger Barker, of Clare. We know that Brown was afterwards Gray's most intimate friend in Pembroke, and it is likely from the close association of Peterhouse and Pembroke (the Master of Peterhouse at this date, John Whalley, was an old Pembroke man) that Brown was the Moderator who asked Gray to write. This may have been the beginning of Gray's acquaintance with Brown.

[L. W.]

APPENDIX C

Gray's Corrections of West's Poems

[Letters 38, 106]

In Gray's Commonplace-book there are transcripts of ten English or Latin poems by West. Two of these, the elegy *Ad Amicos* and the *Ode* invoking May, were sent in letters to Gray, and the letters were printed by Mason. In both poems Mason's text has many and important variations from the text transcribed by Gray.[1] A comparison of the texts leaves little doubt that the text of each poem in the Commonplace-book is West's original version, and that the versions published by Mason had been corrected and improved.

In the elegy *Ad Amicos* (Letter 38) some variations (of which there are more than twenty) seem intended to improve the sound, as, for example, in line 9 'ye chuse' for 'you use'; in line 11 'Meantime at me' for 'At me meantime'; some to improve the sense or expression. One instance may be quoted. In the two lines preceding the last four lines of the poem the Commonplace-book has:

> Yet some there are (ere sunk in endless night)
> Within whose breasts my monument I'd write.

[6] The attribution of this poem to Horace Walpole in n. 1 to Letter 57 in *Gray–Walpole Correspondence* proves to be mistaken. Mr. R. A. Austen Leigh, *Etoniana*, p. 334, gives an 'Authors' List for Musæ Etonenses 1755' from a copy of the book in which the names had been inserted. *Planetæ sunt habitabiles* is ascribed to Bryant, as is another set *Recte Statuit Newtonus de Luce & Coloribus*. This very probably was a set of Tripos verses written a year or two later.

APPENDIX C.—[1] The texts of the poems, as transcribed, were printed by Tovey in *Gray and his Friends*, pp. 95–8, 165–6.

For this the later version has:

> Yet some there are (ere spent my vital days)
> Within whose breasts my tomb I wish to raise.

In the *Ode* (Letter 106) invoking May the version in the Commonplace-book has obvious faults, which needed correction. The *Ode* was written in six-line stanzas, but the last stanza had eight lines; 'you' and 'thou', 'your' and 'thy' were written indifferently. These faults are made good in the printed version, and the other variations (which are considerable) were manifestly designed to improve on the original text. There is a definite proof that the version in the Commonplace-book was that sent by West to Gray. When Gray replied to West on 8 May (Letter 107), he wrote, 'the exclamation of the flowers is a little step too far'. This must refer to

> And dyeing Flowers exclaim on you;

which, in the version printed by Mason, appears as

> Each budding flow'ret calls for thee.

It may be assumed that Gray made the corrections and improvements at some time after he had made the transcripts in his Commonplace-book; and a possible occasion may be suggested. Early in 1747 Walpole proposed to Gray that he should collect his own poems and West's for publication. Gray wrote (Letter 131): 'I much fear that our Joynt-Stock would hardly compose a small Volume'. He sent a list of all West's poems that he had. While he was considering the proposal, he may have undertaken to correct and improve some of them; and it is not unreasonable to suppose that he wrote his corrections on the original copies of West's letters. This hypothesis would explain how Mason came to print the corrected text, when he included the letters in his *Memoirs*.

[L. W.]

APPENDIX D

The Quarrel between Gray and Walpole and their Reconciliation

[Letters 97 and 116]

THE quarrel between Gray and Walpole, which occurred in the first days of May 1741, caused a breach in their friendship which was not closed for more than four years. Of the causes which led to the quarrel Gray gives no hint in any of his letters.[1] Walpole, when

---

APPENDIX D.—[1] Norton Nicholls in his *Reminiscences* (Appendix Z) gives Gray's account of his difference with Walpole. See also Letter 124, n. 2.

Appendix D

Mason was writing Gray's *Memoirs*, sent him an explanation to be included in the works, and a note to be added that Mr. Walpole charged himself with the chief blame.[2]

Walpole's statement goes far to explain how two men, both of difficult temper, with a diversity of tastes, who had been in each other's company for more than two years, should at last disagree so seriously that their relations came to a breaking-point. It is likely that there was some immediate occasion. Milford relates a story that Walpole, suspecting that Gray had spoken ill of him to some of his friends in England, clandestinely opened a letter of Gray's, which Gray discovered and resented.[3] The story has been generally rejected,[4] but a letter of Mann to Walpole, which has recently come to light,[5] written on 23 May, 1741, alludes to a letter of Gray's which seems to have been the cause of the quarrel. Mann wrote:

'From an horrid uneasiness I find & in justice to Gray (from whom I have reced no letter or wrote to, though I designed to have done it last Saturday but was prevented by my feaver) I cannot help adding two or three lines to assure you that in the late affair except writing that letter he was not so much to blame as on the sight of it you might imagine; I take the greatest part of the fault on my self. I am convinced of his regard for you, nay I have been witness to his uneasiness and tears when he suspected you had less confidence in him than his inward and real friendship for you made him think you deserved. This I think my self bound in justice to tell you, as I believd him sincere. [Two thirds of a line obliterated] and the particulars you mention and Bologna, they indeed surprised me much, and would almost induce me to give another turn to the whole.'

A second letter, written by Mann about the end of May, mentions 'the despair Gray is in', and begs Walpole 'to forget and forgive'. The two letters suggest clues which it is impossible to follow.

After giving Walpole's account of the disagreement, Mason continues his narrative in the *Memoirs* (p. 41): 'Mr. Gray went before him to Venice; and staying there only till he could find means of returning to England, he made the best of his way home.' Gray had gone to Venice with Chute and Whithed,[6] and, as Mason tells us (*Memoirs*, p. 116), he was there until the middle of July. But there is good

---

[2] See Letter 97, n. 7. Walpole's statement (repeated, with only verbal changes, by Mason, *Memoirs*, pp. 40–1) was sent to Mason in Walpole's letter of 2 Mar. 1773, with an explanation at greater length not intended for publication (*Walpole–Mason Correspondence*, vol. i, pp. 56–8).   [3] Mitford (1835–43), vol. ii, p. 174 n.

[4] See Letter 116, n. 8.

[5] The letters of Mann to Walpole have recently been acquired by Mr. W. S. Lewis.

[6] Walpole, in *Short Notes of my Life*: 'There [at Reggio] Mr. Gray left me, going to Venice with Mr. Francis Whithed and Mr. John Chute'.

Appendix D

evidence that for a month from about the middle of June Walpole also was at Venice, staying with Chute and Whithed, and therefore in the same house with Gray.[7] The difficulties of the situation for two men, who had cast aside all friendship, to be living for some weeks in each other's company, must have embittered their enmity. They left Venice, each on his homeward journey, about the middle of July, and from that time until November 1745,[8] there was no intercourse between them. At that date, in Walpole's words, 'a reconciliation was effected between them by a Lady, who wished well to both parties'. It may be assumed that the lady (whose identity is not known),[9] after conferring with Walpole, suggested a reconciliation to Gray, who proffered his goodwill. In October or November 1745 Walpole wrote to make the first overtures.[10] After Gray's reply other letters must have passed to arrange the date of a meeting. Gray's coming was not unexpected and his journey to town was made for the particular purpose of seeing Walpole.

The diary of his visit can be traced in his letter to Wharton of 16 November 1745 (Letter 116):

Thursday, 7 Nov. 'I wrote a Note the Night I came, and immediately received a very civil Answer.'
Friday, 8 Nov. 'I went the following Evening to see the Party.'
Saturday, 9 Nov. 'I supped with him next night.'
Sunday, 10 Nov. 'I set with him [Ashton] on Sunday.'
Monday, 11 Nov. 'Next Morning I breakfasted alone with M^r W: . . . such is the Epitome of my four Days.'

[L. W.]

[7] See Walpole's letter to Mann of June 1741 in *The Supplement to the Letters of Horace Walpole*, vol. i, p. 35: 'The Chutes are in the house with me, so I never want company.' For other evidence and a detailed account of the quarrel see 'The Foreign Tour of Gray and Walpole', by Leonard Whibley, in *Blackwood's Magazine*, June 1930.

[8] Walpole, in the letter to Mason of 2 Mar. 1773 (*Walpole-Mason Correspondence*, p. 58), gives the year 1744, which is certainly a mistake. See Letter 116.

[9] It has been conjectured that the lady was Mrs. Chute. Gray, in writing to Chute a year after the reconciliation, sends his compliments to Mrs. Chute, 'who once did me the Honour to write to me' (Letter 122, n. 8). But Gray's acquaintance with her seems to have been of the slightest, and a serious objection to the identification is that, when Chute returned to England in 1746, although Mrs. Chute was with him, he knew nothing of the reconciliation, until he learnt of it from Walpole (Letter 124). It is unlikely that Mrs. Chute, if she had 'effected the reconciliation' would not have told him.

[10] Gray, in writing to Chute in October 1746 (Letter 124), alludes to the reconciliation: 'I find Mr Walpole then made some Mention of me to you. yes, we are together again. it is about a Year, I believe, since he wrote to me to offer it.'

APPENDIX E

Gray's Standing as a Fellow-commoner at Peterhouse and Pembroke

[Letter 135]

A FELLOW-COMMONER, undergraduate or graduate, was a member of a College who had the privilege of dining at the Fellows' Table.[1] An undergraduate, admitted to this privilege[2] when he entered the College, paid higher dues than the Pensioners to the College. He was charged a higher matriculation fee by the University, and on ceremonial occasions he wore a gown trimmed with gold or silver lace, and a velvet cap with a gold or silver tassel.[3] Undergraduate Fellow-commoners were men of birth or wealth, for whom the rules of study and discipline were often relaxed, and many of whom did not proceed to a degree. Some were extravagant and disorderly; and from this class came 'the Bucks', whose excesses Gray described in 1747,[4] and the young bloods of Peterhouse,[5] whose persecution finally induced him to migrate to Pembroke.

But there were others, besides rich undergraduates, who, by admission to the Fellows' table, ranked as Fellow-commoners. It was a normal course for a resident on taking his Master's degree to be moved from the Bachelors' Board to the Fellow-commoners' Board,[6] and a Fellow, on vacating his Fellowship, was moved from the Fellows' Board to the Fellow-commoners' Board. And it is to be noted that these graduate Fellow-commoners had to have the Master or one of the Fellows (in practice usually a Tutor) as a sponsor.[7] The

APPENDIX E.—[1] Hence came the name 'Fellow-commoners' (*Commensales*).

[2] Such undergraduates were described in the Statutes of Trinity College as 'pensionarii in commeatum sociorum admissi'. Wordsworth, *Social Life at the English Universities*, p. 97.

[3] The status of Noblemen-commoners, who were also admitted to the Fellows' Table, differed in some respects and is omitted from consideration.

[4] Letter 135: 'the Fellow Commoners (the Bucks) are run mad', &c.

[5] Letter 213: 'my Neighbours every day make a great progress in drunkenness.'

[6] The Orders and Regulations passed in 1750 refer to 'such as enter into Fellows' commons after they have taken any degree'. Wordsworth, *op. cit.*, p. 491.

[7] At Peterhouse on 15 Mar. 1743 it was ordered that 'all Fellow-commoners and By-fellows should have the Master or one of the Fellows of the old foundation as a sponsor'. Wordsworth, *ibid.*, p. 648. In the Pembroke Register it is recorded on 15 Dec. 1763, 'At the desire of Mr Marriot, late Fellow of the College, his name was entered upon the board of the Fellow-Commoners, Mr Brown being his sponsor'. Gray, when he migrated to Pembroke, was entered on the Fellow-commoners' Board 'sub magistro Brown'.

sponsor was responsible for seeing that the Fellow-commoners on his list paid their debts to the College.[8]

Gray, when he returned to Peterhouse in 1742, was entered on the Fellow-commoners' Board. There is a certain ambiguity about his standing. He was still an undergraduate, and there are instances to show that an undergraduate who, during his residence, changed his status from Pensioner to Fellow-commoner, might be readmitted to his College and might even matriculate again in the University as a Fellow-commoner. There is no trace of this procedure in Gray's case, and it is possible that, as a senior man returning into residence, he was admitted to the Fellows' Table and entered on the Fellow-commoners' Board, without being *de jure* a Fellow-commoner.[9] As a Fellow-commoner he continued at Peterhouse after taking his degree as Bachelor of Laws[10] and on his migration to Pembroke his name was entered on the Fellow-commoners' Board.[11]

[L. W.]

APPENDIX F
Gray's Legal Studies
[Letter 114]

GRAY was destined by his parents to follow the profession of the Law, and on 22 November 1735, while still an undergraduate, he was admitted at the Inner Temple.[1] For the profession he lacked both inclination and aptitude: the prospect of entering the 'barbarous Halls of Strife' inspired him to write a Sapphic Ode to West (Letter 53), and he did not at any time allow the study of Law to interfere with his pursuit of Literature.

Mason says that, when Gray left Cambridge in 1738, his father 'had

[8] This regulation explains Gray's allusion to 'Birkett's old debt' in 1746 (Letter 127) and his requests to Brown, at the time of the College Audit, to let him know the amount of his bills (see Letters 281, 395, 414, 430, 454).

[9] Dr. Walker, 'Thomas Gray in Peterhouse' (*Athenæum* 27 Jan. 1906, p. 107) says: 'he reappears as "Mr. Gray". No formal record, such as on like occasions usually appears, has been found of his transference to the grade of Fellow-commoner, but his name is included amongst those of Fellow-commoners and Fellows in the Buttery Roll, and he could not have joined the table in any other character.'

[10] It may be noted that Gray never held a higher degree than that of Bachelor of Laws. He did not proceed to the Doctorate (see Appendix F, n. 7). Even when he held his Professorship he was merely a Bachelor.

[11] In the record of his admission at Pembroke there is no note of his status. The entry is as follows: 'Thomas Gray L.L.B. admissus est ex collegio Divi Petri March 6, 1756.'

APPENDIX F.—[1] The Admission Book shows his entry: 'Thomas Gray generosus filius et heres apparens Philippi Gray Civis et Draper Londini generaliter admissus est . . . vicesimo secundo die Novembris anno Domini 1735.'

hired or bought him a set of Chambers in the Temple'.[2] Whether he resided in chambers, or kept terms, then or later, we do not know, but he must have welcomed the respite offered by the foreign tour with Walpole. When, after nearly two and a half years' absence, he returned to England, he was probably still less disposed to apply himself to the serious study of the Law. We have little evidence to show how he spent the eleven months after his father's death, but we know that he was absorbed in Literature—reading, criticizing, and writing. But, as Mason tells us (*Memoirs*, p. 120), his mother and his aunt wished him 'to follow the profession for which he had been originally intended', and he, 'though he had taken his resolution of declining it', but wished not to hurt their feelings, found an ingenious means of escape. He 'changed, or pretended to change, the line of that study', and in October 1742 he returned to Peterhouse to take his Bachelor's degree in Civil Law.[3]

By so doing, he must have given up the intention of being called to the Bar at the Inner Temple and of qualifying himself to practise in the ordinary Courts. But the Ecclesiastical and Admiralty Courts were open only to Advocates who had graduated in Civil Law at Oxford or Cambridge;[4] and it must have been with the professed intention of qualifying himself for these Courts that Gray after attending the lectures of Dr. Dickins, the Regius Professor,[5] took the degree of Bachelor of Civil Law in December 1743.[6]

[2] *Memoirs*, pp. 4–5. Search has been made in the records of the Inner Temple, but Gray's name has not been found among those who purchased a set of Chambers. Chambers were sub-let by Members of the Inn who purchased them, and the possibility of Gray's father having hired a set for him is not excluded. (Information of Mr. Roy Robinson, Sub-Treasurer of the Inner Temple.)

[3] In July 1742, in a letter to Chute and Horace Mann (Letter 112), Gray made known his intention to return to Cambridge. The sentence, 'my sole reason (as you know) is to look, as if——', must refer to his pretence of still following the profession of law. In the same letter he talks of going to Trinity Hall, the special College of Civilians, but he returned to his old College.

[4] The pleaders in these Courts were 'Doctors of law, who having regularly taken their degree in either of the Universities, and having been admitted advocates in pursuance of the rescript of the Archbishop of Canterbury shall have been elected Fellows of the College [of Doctors' Commons]' (see Phillimore, *The Ecclesiastical Law of the Church of England*, 2nd ed., Lond. 1895). In 1768 'the College of Doctors exercent in the Ecclesiastical and Admiralty Courts' received a royal charter; but the rules of admission were doubtless the same in Gray's time.

[5] It was a condition of the degree of Bachelor of Law, often relaxed in practice, that the student should attend the lectures of the Professor. A note-book, in Gray's handwriting, now in the Cathedral Library at York, contains notes on the Roman Law of Persons and Property, which in form and in substance suggest that they were taken at lectures.

[6] In the University books Thomas Gray is entered as LL.B. designate on 16 Dec. 1743.

Appendix F

In a letter written to Wharton in this month (Letter 114), there is an ironical passage, which throws light on the purpose which he must have pretended to have in view:

'I am got half way to the Top of Jurisprudence & bid as fair as another Body to open a case of Impotency with all Decency and Circumspection.'

A case of Impotency would be tried in the Ecclesiastical Court, and, if a Doctor's degree was a necessary qualification to practise in the Court, the Bachelor's degree was half-way to the Doctorate.

But Gray never proceeded to the higher degree;[7] any pretence of practising in the Courts must have been henceforth abandoned. With his profound knowledge of so many branches of learning, in later years he declared his helpless ignorance of law,[8] and disclaimed interest in it, except where it touched questions of the Constitution.[9]

[L. W.]

APPENDIX G
Henry Tuthill
[Letter 120]

IN Gray's life, so generally devoid of incident, there was one event which, if we may believe Mitford, 'permanently affected his spirits'. This was the catastrophe which caused his friend Henry Tuthill to be deprived of his fellowship at Pembroke. In Gray's letters there are many references to Tuthill; at the time of his disgrace there are obscure allusions, which cannot be understood without some knowledge of the facts. These facts are the harder to discover because Mason did everything that he could to blot out all evidence of Tuthill's existence. Tuthill is never mentioned in the *Memoirs*; of the letters printed by Mason those parts which had any allusion to him were omitted. Probably Mason destroyed, or got others to

---

[7] Writing to Beattie in Oct. 1765 (Letter 413), Gray says 'formerly (when I had some thoughts of the profession) I took a Bachelor of Laws' degree; since that time, though long qualified by my standing, I have always neglected to finish my course, and claim my doctor's degree'.

[8] On 15 Mar. 1768 he wrote to Wharton (Letter 475): 'I am so totally uninform'd, indeed so helpless in matters of law.'

[9] Cf. Gray to Walpole, 30 Dec. 1764 (Letter 398).

Appendix G

destroy, letters directly concerned with his disgrace, and in letters addressed to Wharton Mason erased the name of Tuthill when Gray refers to him.[1] Henry Tuthill was admitted to Peterhouse from Felsted School in 1740; he was elected Cosin Scholar in 1740 and Hale Scholar in 1741, and graduated B.A. in 1743/4.[2] In September 1744 he was ordained Deacon, with a title to the Curacy of Alconbury, Huntingdon.[3] Alconbury is about four miles from Abbott's Ripton, the seat of Gray's friends, the Bonfoys, with whom Tuthill became acquainted.[4] Gray must have formed a friendship with Tuthill at Peterhouse,[5] and probably introduced him to Wharton and other members of the Pembroke Society. Wharton wished to get Tuthill elected to a Fellowship at Pembroke, and it must have been with this plan in view that Tuthill migrated from Peterhouse and on 5 July 1746 was admitted at Pembroke 'ad secundam mensam sub tutela Magistri Francis'.

His nomination to a Fellowship in October 1746, and the thwarting of his election by the Master's veto are discussed elsewhere (Appendix H).[6] It is not easy to explain why Tuthill, who had not

APPENDIX G.—[1] Mitford (1835–43, vol. v, p. viii) states: 'When Mason returned the Wharton correspondence it was found not only had he taken the greatest liberty with the text, but had cut out the names of several persons mentioned. . . . The name of Mr. Tuthill was in almost all cases erased.' We need not wonder that Mitford also says (ibid., vol. i, p. xi): 'The Editor has the very best authority for stating that Dr. Wharton was much displeased at the extraordinary liberties which Mr. Mason had taken with the volume that had been entrusted to his care.' As will appear below, some letters dealing particularly with Tuthill must have been destroyed.

[2] *Peterhouse Admissions*, p. 278. His place in the order of Bachelors is not known. The list preserved at the Registry has only the first 27 names, and does not include Tuthill. It must be assumed that he took a lower place among those who graduated *in comitiis posterioribus*.

[3] Information as to Tuthill's curacies was kindly supplied by Mr. A. E. T. Jourdain, Diocesan Registrar of Lincoln.

[4] Among Mitford's MSS. in the British Museum (32,562, vol. iv) are copies of anecdotes collected by Gray (printed by Tovey, *Gray and His Friends*, pp. 277 ff.). Among these are three marked 'T'. T. may be plausibly identified with Tuthill, and one anecdote is marked 'T from Mrs Bonfoy' and establishes his acquaintance with the family.

[5] It is possible that early in 1746 an effort was made to get Tuthill elected to a Fellowship at Peterhouse. From Letters 117 and 118 we see that Gray wished Walpole to influence Professor Turner to stay away from a College meeting, which was to be held for the election of a fellow. In Letter 118 he describes 'his young friend' as well affected to the Government. The young friend may have been Tuthill. If so, he was not elected; and this disappointment may have caused his migration to Pembroke.

[6] That Wharton was the prime mover is clear from passages in Gray's letters

taken a high degree, should have been so strongly supported for a Fellowship. It is possible that he had social talents and it was thought that he might attract men of birth to the College.[7] After his reverse Tuthill continued in his curacy[8] with brief visits to the College every term. Early in 1747 he graduated as M.A. For the time no fresh attempt was made to nominate him for a Fellowship and in March Gray was suggesting that it would be better for him to withdraw (Letter 135). After the equally unsuccessful attempt to get Mason elected in November 1747 Gray, in writing to Wharton, apparently alludes to some plan for Tuthill's election at Peterhouse.[9] In June 1748 Gray wrote that there was no hope of the Pembroke business coming to anything: ['My poor Tuthill] will be in a Manner destitute (even of a Curacy) at Midsummer' (Letter 145). He was not so unfortunate, for in September, after his ordination as Priest, he was admitted to the curacy of Brampton, a village within four miles of Alconbury.

It has been related elsewhere how Knowles, Mason, and Tuthill were elected Fellows in March 1749 (Appendix H). In October of that year Tuthill came into residence, and for the next seven years held a succession of College offices, Chaplain, Junior Treasurer, Dean, &c. There is nothing to prepare us for the entry which was made in the College Register on 5 February 1757:

> 'This day the Master in the presence of 5 Fellows, declared Mr Tuthill's fellowship to be vacant, he having been absent from the College above a month contrary to the Statutes which inflicts [*sic*] this punishment upon such absence.'

This entry, signed R^r Long, is followed by another:

> 'Since Mr Tuthill's absence common fame has laid him under violent suspicion of having been guilty of great enormities; to clear himself from which he has not made his appearance and there is good reason to believe he never will.'

What 'the great enormities' were there is no evidence to show. After a week's absence he had apparently returned to College for the

(see Letters 121, 135). In the latter Gray says, 'as you first made him a Competitor'.

   [7] Gray writes to Wharton in Aug. 1749 (Letter 150), after Tuthill and Mason had been elected: 'I have hopes, that these two with Brown's assistance may bring Pembroke into some Esteem.' Tuthill was private tutor to Lord Strathmore when he was admitted to the College in 1755 (Letter 196, n. 6).

   [8] Gray writes on 27 Dec. 1746 (Letter 129): '[Tuthill] continues quiet in his Læta Paupertas, & by this time (were not his Friends of it) would have forgot that there was any such Place as Pembroke in the World.'

   [9] After mentioning Keene, Master of Peterhouse, he says (Letter 143): 'I can never think of bestowing [Tuthill] upon him.'

festivities of Christmas and the New Year, and then left Cambridge. The scandal must have become known some time before the College meeting in February, and we may be sure that Gray wrote about it to Wharton, and probably to Mason also, early in the year. But any letters that he wrote must have been destroyed, and the first letter that we have after Tuthill's deprivation (written to Wharton) is dated 17 February.[10] It shows that Gray was deeply moved. Tuthill had been his intimate friend. He was concerned also lest the scandal should do serious harm to the College. His apprehension was relieved by the return to the College of Lord Strathmore and his brother: and Edward Southwell, who went to town in the middle of February, had assured Gray that he would not stay a week.[11] There follows in the letter a mysterious passage, which may refer to some explanation that had been put about in Cambridge to account for Tuthill's disappearance.

From Gray's next letter (Letter 234), of 3 March, it appears that Wharton had invited him to stay with him in London, and that Gray intended to go on the 5th. While he was staying with Wharton, he wrote to Walpole on 11 March (Letter 235), saying that he had 'a particular reason for desiring to see him'. It is not too improbable an hypothesis that Gray wanted Walpole's help or advice on some question connected with Tuthill. While in London he must have seen Mason,[12] and Mason, who was perhaps responsible for Southwell's being at Pembroke (Letter 220, n. 2), went to Cambridge and wrote from there a reassuring letter to Gray (Letter 237, n. 1). Gray on his return to Cambridge wrote to Wharton (Letter 236) and to Mason (Letter 237). But in the letter to Mason of 23 April he alludes to Mr. Bonfoy's not having done what Mason had recommended to him before he came out of town. 'Alas!', he writes, 'what may this delay occasion; it is best not to think'. This reference also suggests some anxiety about Tuthill's fate.

It is obvious that Gray was profoundly moved by the catastrophe, and Mitford, in one of his accounts of Gray's life, seems to attribute the melancholy, which was a lasting characteristic of Gray, to 'the

[10] In this (Letter 233) Gray thanks Wharton for a letter which must have been an answer to one of Gray's giving news of the crisis. Mitford's note, 'This letter will show the pain and suffering which were the consequences of Tuthill's unhappy history', is the only allusion to the scandal hitherto published.

[11] The College Books show that the Earl of Strathmore and Mr. Lyon, who had left Cambridge about the beginning of Jan., returned about 10 Feb., and that Mr. Southwell went away about 14 Feb. and returned about the 25th.

[12] Gray's reference in Letter 237, 'when I saw you last', refers probably to a meeting in town.

misbehaviour and misfortune of one whom he had called his friend'; and this friend must be identified with Tuthill.[13]

In none of Gray's extant letters of a later date is there any allusion to Tuthill, and nothing more is known of him except for a bald statement of Mitford, that he drowned himself.[14] Mitford gives no indication of date, and Tuthill's suicide may have taken place soon after his disgrace, or at a date which might have been after Gray's death. If he lived on in difficult circumstances it is possible that Gray helped him, and Mason's allusion to Gray's 'private charity when his means were lowest' may refer to Tuthill as one of the recipients. And in Gray's will the direction to his executors 'to apply the sum of two hundred pounds to the use of a charity, which I have already informed them of', might have been for the benefit of Tuthill.

[L. W.]

APPENDIX H
The Controversy between the Master of Pembroke Hall and his Fellows
[Letter 120]

FOR more than two years Dr. Long, Master of Pembroke Hall, was in conflict with his Fellows, who, under the leadership of James Brown, maintained a united front against him. In Gray's letters to Wharton there are many references to the course of this conflict and to the questions at issue. What these questions were is made clear by the College Register, which records the decisions taken at College Meetings, and by the Opinions of Counsel on Cases submitted by the Fellows, copies of which are still preserved in the College Treasury. The most important differences were connected with the right of veto claimed and exercised by the Master, and with the question of who was the proper Visitor of the College, to whom unsettled disputes should be referred.[1]

[13] See 'An original life of Gray', prefixed to the edition of Gray's Poetical Works published at Eton in 1847, p. xlvii. On p. xlix Mitford has the following note:
'Partly from the "Explanations of the late Archdeacon Oldershaw",—partly from his unpublished correspondence,—I believe that I am particularly acquainted with those circumstances that spread a considerable gloom over Gray's mind, and perhaps permanently affected his spirits . . . , but which it is quite useless to draw from the obscurity in which they have been placed, especially as Gray's character is totally unaffected by them.'

[14] In the Dyce Collection at South Kensington there is a letter of Mitford to Dyce, dated 31 Jan. 1828, in which he says: 'The name of Gray's friend, who drowned himself was *Tuthill*.'

APPENDIX H.—[1] Questions as to the Master's veto and the Visitor were raised

Appendix H

The first occasion of difference arose when it was intended to propose Henry Tuthill for election to a Fellowship. He had taken his Bachelor's degree from Peterhouse in 1743, and on 5 July 1746 he migrated to Pembroke Hall at the suggestion of Wharton,[2] in the hope of being elected Fellow. Wharton must have made sure of the support of the Fellows, but it was clear from the first that the Master would put his veto on the election, when it should be proposed in the Michaelmas Term. Already in July 1746 Messrs. Wharton,[3] Symonds Junior, Solicitors, had, on behalf of the Fellows, submitted to Dr. Andrew, of Doctors' Commons (Letter 120, n. 4), 'Queries on the Statutes of Pembroke Hall'. The queries touched the election of the Master and the method by which he might be deprived of his office, but the important question was: 'Has the Master a veto in the election of a Fellow?'; and the answer of Dr. Andrew was that 'the Master's consent is, I think, expressly required to make the election valid'. Gray, writing from London to Wharton at Cambridge on 10 August (Letter 120), describes Dr. Andrew's answers as being 'very unfavourable on the whole to our Cause' and wishes 'they might have been conceal'd, till the Attorney-General's [see Letter 120, n. 6] Opinion arrived'. This opinion, given on 13 August, was equally unfavourable. 'I conceive the Master has a Veto', wrote Sir Dudley Ryder. It is to this that Gray alludes in his next letter written on 11 September (Letter 121).

On 22 October, at a College Meeting, the Master and seven Fellows being present, Tuthill and Thomas Knowles, B.A. of Pembroke, were nominated for Fellowships. Tuthill received seven votes and Knowles four. In accordance with the Statutes the nominations were twice repeated. The result was the same, but before the Fellows proceeded to a formal election, the Master wrote in the College Register 'Ego non consentio', and nothing further could be done. There are no letters of Gray's on the subject until 11 December, when he wrote (Letter 127) of the ill feeling between 'Roger' and his Fellows. The Master was 'threatening them as usual with a Visitor'.

For some months no steps were taken on either side. In March 1747 Gray wrote to Wharton (Letter 135) that he thought it 'rather better for [T.] to give up his Pretensions with a good Grace'. The

---

at other Colleges in the eighteenth century: Christ's (see Letter 51), Peterhouse, and Clare (see Cooper's *Annals of Cambridge*, vol. iv, pp. 242, 259).

[2] See Appendix G, n. 6.

[3] The name suggests that some relative, possibly the brother, of Thomas Wharton, was a member of the firm.

Fellows meanwhile sought advice on the question of the Visitor. On 25 September they submitted a case to Sir Dudley Ryder 'concerning the Visitor and the course of Proceedings'. They stated that 'in the Statutes of Pembroke Hall there is no Visitor appointed, and no Heir to the Foundress'. In such a case, according to the Civilians, the King by his Lord Chancellor is Visitor; but King James the First had granted a charter to the University by which the right of Visitation was given to the Chancellor of the University. They therefore asked the opinion of Sir Dudley Ryder, whether King James's Charter had ever been confirmed by Parliament, and, if not, whether the Fellows should make application to His Majesty or the Lord Chancellor. The opinion given was that 'the Visitatorial Power is not either in the King or the Chancellor of the University; but the proper Remedy is by application to the King's Bench for a Mandamus to the Master to fill up the vacant Fellowships'.

On 7 November, at a College Meeting, William Mason, Bachelor of St. John's, was nominated for election by seven votes, and the Master again prevented an election by writing in the Register, 'Ego non consentio ut extraneus eligatur socius cum domesticos habeamus idoneos et dignos qui in ordinem sociorum cooptentur'. The Fellows again consulted Sir Dudley Ryder, who, in direct contradiction to his former advice, thought that the King had been Visitor, that the right of Visitation had passed to the Chancellor of the University, and that the remedy was not to be sought in application to the Court of the King's Bench. Gray, on 30 November, tells Wharton of the Attorney-General's change of opinion and thinks that the Fellows may consult Dr. Lee (see Letter 143, n. 15). And so, after another fruitless reference to Sir Dudley Ryder, they consulted Dr. Lee, and he, on 18 December, advised them that the Visitatorial power was in the Crown.

In May 1748 Dr. Long took the aggressive. Acting on the assumption that the Chancellor of the University had power of visitation, he lodged a complaint, and the Chancellor on 17 May appointed the Vice-Chancellor, as his deputy, to hear the cause of the Master of Pembroke. The Fellows next day sought the advice of Dr. Lee and Dr. Simpson,[4] who gave a joint answer that the Charter of James the First was not valid, and advised that the Fellows should protest in writing against the authority of the Vice-Chancellor as Visitor, and that if the Vice-Chancellor should proceed as Visitor, they should apply to the proper Court of Law for a Prohibition. It

---

[4] Edward Simpson, LL.D., Fellow of Trinity Hall.

was after this that on 5 June Gray wrote to Wharton (Letter 145):
'there is now, I think, no Hopes of the Pembroke Business coming to
any thing'.

The advice of Dr. Lee and Dr. Simpson was followed, and in June
and October the Court of the King's Bench stayed proceedings for a
Writ of Prohibition to be argued. On Monday 21 November 1748
it was argued 'upon the Motion of Sir John Strange',[5] and the Court
ordered 'that there issue a Writ of Prohibition to the Most Noble
Prince Charles Duke of Somersett Chancellor of the University of
Cambridge Francis Sawyer Doctor in Divinity Vice Chancellor
of the said University and Roger Long Doctor in Divinity Master of
the College or Hall of Maria de Valencia commonly called Pembroke
Hall in the said University of Cambridge to prohibit them and each
of them respectively from proceeding upon the Matter contained in
the Instrument or Citation Annext to the Affidavit of James Brown,
Clerk.'[6]

The Master was disappointed in his hopes of overruling the Fellows
by the power of the Visitor, and it was this defeat which probably
inclined him to make terms four months later. On 1 March 1748/9
a College Meeting was held and 'the Master proposed electing to
some of the vacant Fellowships', the Meeting was adjourned until
the next day, when 'Mr Brown declined making use of the presenta-
tion to Tylney given him the day before', and thereafter M^r
Knowles, Dominus Mason, and Mr Tuthill were elected Fellows
(each with five votes).[7]

Of this victorious result, and of the tactics which led to it, Gray, in
his letter of 9 March (Letter 148), gives a vivid account. James
Brown had a difficult part to play and was not sure of his supporters.
He entreated the Master, Gray tells us, to 'put an End to their long
Disputes himself, or else they would refer the whole to a Visitor'. The
Master now despaired of 'a Visitor to his Mind', and gave up without
further struggling. The Writ of Prohibition had worked effectually.
The Fellows elected their candidates, and the 'Peace of Pembroke',
as Gray describes it, was concluded.

[L. W.]

[5] Formerly Solicitor-General and afterwards Master of the Rolls.

[6] The extract from the King's Bench Entry Books of Rules was supplied by
Mr. Hilary Jenkinson, M.A., of the Record Office.

[7] The proceedings are recorded in the College Order Book.

APPENDIX I

The Composition of the Elegy

[Letters 121, 153]

THE date of the completion of the *Elegy* is known from Gray's letter to Walpole of 12 June 1750 (Letter 153); of its beginning and the process of composition we have little information that is trustworthy. If we could accept Mason's account Gray wrote the first draft of the poem in 1742. In the *Memoirs* (p. 157), after referring to other poems written in August 1742, he says: 'I am inclined to believe that the Elegy in a Country Church-yard was begun, if not concluded, at this time also: Though I am aware that as it stands at present, the conclusion is of a later date; how that was originally I shall show in my notes on the poem.'

Mason had in his possession two drafts of the *Elegy*. The copy in Gray's Commonplace-book is the finished version and does not differ substantially from the form in which the poem was printed. The other draft (now at Eton), which had the title 'Stanza's wrote in a Country Church-Yard',[1] was described by Mason in a note (*Poems*, p. 108) as 'the first manuscript copy'. In this manuscript twenty-two stanzas had been written continuously, and at a later time the last four of these had been bracketed for omission, and seventeen stanzas had been added.

In giving his promised explanation (*Poems*, pp. 108–9), Mason quotes the four stanzas, which were subsequently cut out, and adds: 'And here the poem was originally intended to conclude.' There can be little doubt, if we compare this explanation, with the statement quoted above, that Mason meant that Gray wrote the first draft of the poem in or about August 1742, and that in this sense the poem was then 'begun, if not concluded', and that 'the conclusion', that is, the final form of the later stanzas was 'of a later date'.

It is hard to believe that within a few weeks Gray, who had only recently begun to write original poems in English, should have written the *Sonnet on the Death of West*, the *Eton Ode*, the *Hymn to Adversity*, and the first draft of the *Elegy*. There is a hint of uncertainty in Mason's qualifying phrase 'I am inclined to believe', which suggests that he was drawing an inference, and not speaking from knowledge, and we are left in doubt as to the grounds of his belief.

APPENDIX I.—[1] Mason, *Poems*, p. 108, writes: 'He originally gave it only the simple title of "Stanzas written in a Country Church-yard". I persuaded him first to call it an ELEGY.'

Appendix I

Mason first made Gray's acquaintance 'about the year 1747' (*Memoirs*, p. 172), and there is no reason to suppose that at first Gray took him into his confidence about his poetical compositions.

There is, however, another statement which gives a later date for the beginning of the poem. When Mason was writing his *Memoirs* of Gray he sent his proof-sheets to Walpole, and on 1 December 1773 Walpole wrote (*Walpole–Mason Correspondence*, p. 109) to correct an error in the date, which Mason gave to the Elegy: 'The Churchyard was, I am persuaded, posterior to West's death at least three or four years, as you will see by my note. At least I am sure that I had the twelve or more first lines from himself above three years after that period, and it was long before he finished it.' Mason's reply is missing, but on 14 December Walpole wrote (*op. cit.*, p. 115): 'Your account of the Elegy puts an end to my criticism.' Walpole was sometimes more polite than sincere in expressing agreement with his correspondents: we do not know what the note contained that he sent to Mason, nor what was Mason's 'account'. But it is important that Walpole had been convinced that he had seen the beginning of the *Elegy*, three or four years after West's death, that is, at some time in 1745 or 1746. Towards the end of 1745 Gray and Walpole were reconciled, and in the autumn of 1746 Walpole took a house at Windsor and Gray saw him 'a good deal' (Letters 120, 121), and from letters written not long after (Letters 125, 128) we know that Gray had shown Walpole his poems, complete and incomplete.

If, in spite of Walpole's apparent acceptance of Mason's account, we may attach any weight to his original statement, Gray himself seems to add strong confirmation. In the letter of 12 June 1750 (Letter 153) in which he sent Walpole the completed *Elegy* he writes: 'Having put an end to a thing, whose beginning you have seen long ago, I immediately send it you.' Gray states that Walpole had, as Walpole wrote to Mason, seen the beginning of the *Elegy*, and this could not have been before the reconciliation of 1745, and probably not until their closer association in 1746. It is a further piece of evidence that in August and September of that year Gray had, for the first time since 1742, resumed the composition of poetry. On 10 August he wrote to Wharton (Letter 120): 'the Muse, I doubt, is gone, & has left me in far worse Company: if she returns, you will hear of her.' And in a letter of 11 September (Letter 121), after referring to his study of Aristotle, he says: 'this & a few autumnal Verses are my Entertainments dureing the Fall of the Leaf.' As Tovey suggested, we know of no poem except the *Elegy* to which Gray could be alluding.

Appendix I

If, in the conflict of testimony, it is impossible to attain certainty, there is a strong probability that Mason was wrong in saying that the first draft of the *Elegy* was written in 1742, and that, as Gray said, he showed Walpole the beginnings of the poem in 1746.[2]

[L. W.]

APPENDIX J

Gray's Removal from Peterhouse to Pembroke

[Letter 214]

MASON (*Memoirs*, p. 241, n.) gives the following explanation of Gray's departure from Peterhouse:

'The reason of Mr. Gray's changing his College, which is here only glanced at, was in few words this: Two or three young Men of Fortune, who lived in the same stair-case, had for some time intentionally disturbed him with their riots, and carried their ill behaviour so far as frequently to awaken him at midnight. After having borne with their insults longer than might reasonably have been expected even from a man of less warmth of temper, Mr. Gray complained to the Governing part of the Society; and not thinking that his remonstrance was sufficiently attended to, quitted the College. The slight manner in which he mentions this affair, when writing to one of his most intimate friends, certainly does honour to the placability of his disposition.'

Mason is referring to the letter to Wharton of 25 March 1756, in which Gray alludes to his 'having been taken up in quarrelling with Peterhouse, & in removing myself from thence to Pembroke' (Letter 214). This is the only mention of the affair by Gray which is extant. Mason, who was in residence at Pembroke at the time, and must have been acquainted by Gray with all the details, no doubt gave this colourless version of the affair in deference to Walpole's caution in his letter to him of 17 April 1774 (*Walpole–Mason Correspondence*, vol. i, p. 143): 'I would omit every passage that hints at the cause of his removal from Peterhouse. Don't you, or do you, know that that and other idle stories were printed in an absurd book called *Lexiphanes*! I would be as wary as the Church of Rome is before they canonize a saint.'[1] The 'idle story' was not

---

[2] For a discussion of the problem see *The Date of Composition* in the Introduction to the Edition of the *Elegy* by Mr. F. G. Stokes (Oxford, 1929).

APPENDIX J.—[1] Mason replied (*op. cit.*, p. 150): 'In a life so void of events, how is it possible to omit this, would not the omission make the world believe him more "wrong than he really was".' His reply suggests that the incident was not generally regarded as altogether to Gray's credit.

in *Lexiphanes* (which was a satire on Johnson) but in *The Sale of Authors, a Dialogue, in Imitation of Lucian's Sale of Philosophers*. The two pamphlets were published anonymously in the same year (1767) and were both written by Archibald Campbell (*c.* 1726–80), Purser of a man-of-war.

In *The Sale of Authors* Mercury, under the direction of Apollo, conducts a sale of authors, Gray, Macpherson, Wilkes, Churchill, &c. The passage in which Gray is put up for auction is as follows:

'*Mercury* [after an address to the audience]. You, waiter, bring out the poet in the watchman's coat, and set him up on the table.... Gentlemen and ladies, the first Author we exhibit is a poet of signal celebrity, and eminently possessed of plaintive powers.

*   *   *   *

Apollo [after explaining to the assembled booksellers the conditions of sale]. Now, Mercury, you may proceed with the sale.

Mercury. Here, gentlemen and ladies, we exhibit the *sweetly plaintive* G——,* the divine Author of Elegies in a Church-yard, and a Cat; who bids for the sweetly plaintive G——?

Apollo. I see this good company are not a little surprised, that so eminent a poet is wrapt up in a watchman's coat. Pray, Mercury, inform them how it happened. Besides I am really curious to know it myself.

Mercury. You must know, having made many unsuccessful attempts to catch this great poet, I was at last obliged to have recourse to stratagem. Though he has a great deal of poetical fire, nobody indeed more, yet is he extremely afraid of culinary fire, and keeps constantly by him a ladder of ropes to guard against all accidents of that sort. Knowing this, I hired some watchmen to raise the alarm of fire below his windows. Immediately the windows were seen to open, and the Poet descending in his shirt by his ladder.† Thus we caught him at last, and one of the watchmen, to prevent his nerves from being totally benumbed by frigorific torpor, lent him his great coat. Here you have him, watchman's coat, ladder of ropes, silver tea tongs and all. . . .

Apollo. You talk too much, Mercury; you'll never have done at this rate. Let the Poet exhibit a *specimen of his powers*.

M^r G——y. The Curfew tolls the knell of parting day,
>   The lowing herds wind slowly o'er the lea,
>   The plowman homeward plods his weary way
>   And leaves the world to darkness and to me.

Mercury. Admirably simple and elegant! Universally natural, Dorick, and pastoral!

>   With Kiltit coats when linkan o'er the lea,
>   I saw my Mag, but Maggie saw nae me.

You see, gentlemen, he imitates Allan Ramsay, the Prince of Pastoral Poets, *Weary way, plow man plods*. Happy alliteration! This line is worth

1217   z

a whole Dryden's Ode for St. Cecilia. Such are his Elegiac, now for his Pindarick *Powers*.

M^r G——y. Ruin seize thee Ruthless King!

Mercury. Better and better still. Only observe with what sublimity he has expressed the very vulgar phrase of Devil take ye. Come, who bids most money for the *sweetly plaintive* G——y?

Bookseller. Half a guinea for him.

Mercury. Fie, M^r D——,² fie for shame. Do but consider what a figure his Poems make in your admirable collection. Half a guinea only. Why, the ladder of ropes and the silver tongs are worth the money. Shall then all his plaintive poetical *powers* go for nothing!

Bookseller. Poetry is a mere drug now-a-days. It seldom pays for paper, print, and advertising. That I know both to my cost and sorrow.

Apollo (aside to *Mercury*). Knock him off. We shall get no more for him; and I do not know that he is worth much more.

Mercury. The sweetly-plaintive Grey a-going for half a guinea. A-going, a-going, once, twice, thrice.

(Here Mercury strikes his hammer)

Bookseller. Here's your money.

Apollo. And there's your Poet.

* An epithet generally given him in the Reviews. (*Author's note.*)

† The stories of the fire and ladder, and silver tea-tongs, are reported, though perhaps they have no other foundation than what may justify a harmless pleasantry, in a work of this sort, which attacks nothing but ridiculous oddities, affectation, and arrogance. (*Author's note.*)

The author, giving an obviously burlesque account, warns his readers that 'the stories of the fire and ladder . . . are reported, though perhaps they have no other foundation than what may justify a harmless pleasantry, in a work of this sort'. In spite of this warning, Gosse (in his *Life of Gray*, pp. 124–5) accepted the stories and amplified them with details, which were supplied by his own inventive powers.³

He relates that, after procuring a rope-ladder, Gray 'proceeded to have an iron bar fixed within his bedroom-window. This bar crossing a window which looks towards Pembroke,⁴ . . . marks Gray's chambers at Peterhouse. Such preparations, however, could

² In his copy of the *Sale of Authors* (now in the British Museum), Walpole filled in the name 'Dodsley'.

³ Gosse's account has gained more acceptance than it merited. Sir Leslie Stephen in his life of Gray in the *Dictionary of National Biography* follows Gosse and takes from him the mention of the tub (see n. 6).

⁴ Professor Temperley, the present occupant of Gray's rooms at Peterhouse (see Appendix K), in his article on this episode in the *A. W. Ward Memorial Volume* (pp. 104–11), points out that the iron bar is fixed outside (not inside) the window, and that the window looks not 'towards Pembroke', but into the churchyard of

not be made without attracting great attention in the latter College, where Gray was by no means a favourite among the high-coloured young gentlemen who went bull-baiting to Heddington[5] or came home drunk and roaring from a cock-shying at Market Hill. Accordingly the noisy fellow-commoners determined to have a lark at the timid little poet's expense, and one night in February, 1756, when Gray was asleep in bed, they suddenly alarmed him with a cry of fire on his staircase, having previously placed a tub of water under his window. The ruse succeeded only too well: Gray, without staying to put on his clothes, hooked his rope-ladder to the iron bar, and descended nimbly into the tub of water, from which he was rescued with shouts of laughter by the unmannerly youths. But the jest might easily have proved fatal; as it was, he shivered in the February air so excessively that he had to be wrapped in the coat of a passing watchman, and to be carried into the college by the friendly Stonehewer, who now appeared on the scene.'[6]

Of a very different character is another account (printed in Nichols's *Illustrations of the Literary History of the Eighteenth Century*, vol. vi, p. 805), which is given in a letter written on 12 March 1756 by the Rev. John Sharp, Fellow of Corpus (see Letter 290, n. 1), to the Rev. John Denne, a contemporary of his, who had in 1751 retired from a Fellowship at Corpus to the perpetual curacy of Maidstone. The account is as follows:

'Mr Gray, our elegant Poet, and delicate Fellow Commoner of Peterhouse, has just removed to Pembroke-hall, in resentment of some usage he met with at the former place. The case is much talked of, and is this. He is much afraid of fire, and was a great sufferer in Cornhill; he has ever since kept a ladder of ropes by him, soft as the silky cords by which Romeo ascended to his Juliet, and has had an iron machine fixed to his bed-room window. The other morning Lord Percival[7] and some

Little St. Mary's. The bar, which is fixed with stanchions, projects beyond the front edge of the window-sill, so that a rope-ladder hooked on to it would hang clear of the wall.

[5] The allusion to bull-baiting at Heddington (which Gosse must have derived from Wordsworth's *Social Life at the English Universities in the Eighteenth Century*, p. 181), refers to Headington near Oxford.

[6] On the foregoing account Professor Temperley observes (*loc. cit.*): 'There seems to be no authority for the water-tub at all, and the only one for the descent into the churchyard and for the wrapping in the watchman's coat consists in the rumours detailed in the *Sale of Authors*. . . . If Gray shivered at all, it was probably in the air not of February but of March, and, though Stonehewer was an eyewitness, there is no evidence that he carried Gray back into College.'

[7] John James Perceval (1738–1822), Viscount Perceval, who succeeded his father as Earl of Egmont in 1770. At the date of this escapade he was a Fellow-commoner of Magdalene.

Petrenchians,[8] going a hunting, were determined to have a little sport before they set out, and thought it would be no bad diversion to make Gray bolt, as they called it, so ordered their man Joe Draper to roar out fire.[9] A delicate white night-cap is said to have appeared at the window; but finding the mistake, retired again to the couch. The young fellows, had he descended, were determined, they said, to have whipped the butterfly up again.'

This account written, within a few days of the incident, by a Cambridge resident, with its absence of exaggeration and sensational details, may be accepted as substantially accurate.[10]

'The date of Gray's migration,' writes Dr. Walker (in the *Athenæum* for 27 Jan. 1906) 'can be fixed by the Peterhouse Butler's book. He was in residence during the week ending March 5, 1756. His name was entered on the list for the following week, but the Butler's pen has been crossed through it.'

The episode closes with the following entry in the Pembroke Admission Book:

'Thomas Gray, LL.B. admissus est ex Collegio Divi Petri. March 6, 1756.'[11]

[P. T.

L. W.]

---

[8] Mitford, in the *Life of Gray* written for the Eton edition of *Gray's Poetical Works* (1847), has a note (p. xxxiii): 'I have been told, on the authority of Dr Gretton, the Master of Magdalene [who was in 1756 an undergraduate of Peterhouse] that the young men of fortune [as Mason described them] were the late Lord Egmont, a Mr Forrester, a Mr Williams, and others; that Gray complained to the Master, Dr. Law [afterwards] Bishop of Carlisle; and he offended Gray by the little regard he paid to the complaint, and by his calling it "a boyish frolic".'

In an article in the *Athenæum* for 27 Jan. 1906, Dr. Walker identified Mr. Forrester and Mr. Williams as George Forrester and Bennet Williams, Fellow-commoners of Peterhouse, and pointed out that they (as is shown by a Bursar's book of the date) had rooms on the same staircase as Gray.

[9] Dr. Temperley (*loc. cit.*) explains: 'Joe Draper was doubtless sent round to the wooden stairs leading to Gray's rooms, while the huntsmen waited, hoping to see Gray descend his ladder into the churchyard.'

[10] William Cole, in a note on Mason's *Memoirs* (quoted by Mitford, 1836–47, vol. i, p. cviii), gives a brief account, which was probably the tradition twenty years after the event, and which is not inconsistent with Sharp's narrative: 'One of their tricks was, knowing that Mr. Gray had a dread of fire, had rope-ladders in his chambers; they alarmed him in the middle of the night with the cry of fire, in hope of seeing him make use of them from his window.'

In Percy's diary in the British Museum (*Add. MS.* 32339) there is a note headed: 'the story assigned me by my Cambridge friends for Gray's leaving Peterhouse.' The note starts with an allusion to the burning of Gray's property in Cornhill and, after an absurd story of the composition of the *Elegy*, mentions Gray's dread of fire and the 'ladder of ropes'. The narrative begins: 'Some young rakish Fellow-Commoners one night in a freakish mood'—and there it breaks off.

[11] In a blank page at the beginning of his pocket-diary for 1756 Gray

APPENDIX K

Gray's Rooms in Peterhouse and Pembroke

[Letters 213, 214, &c.]

WHEN Gray entered Peterhouse in 1734 the College consisted of one court, and we have no information as to the rooms which were assigned to him. But in the first letter which he wrote to Walpole from Cambridge there is a facetious description,[1] which suggests that he occupied a single large chamber, and another allusion implies that it was on the ground floor.[2]

When he returned to the College, as a Fellow-commoner, in 1742, the 'New Building' had just been built. This was a 'handsome and substantial pile of chambers in three stories, of brick, faced with Ketton stone on the south and east sides'.[3] Gray may at first have occupied some other chamber. We know that by Michaelmas 1755, at any rate, he was lodged in Set no. 1 on the top floor of the New Building.[4] This set is on the east staircase of the building, with windows on the south looking into the College court, and windows on the north looking over the churchyard of Little St. Mary's. On the sill of the north window in the inner room, which must have been Gray's bedroom, there is still an iron bar fixed on two brackets. The purpose with which this was set up and the circumstances which led Gray to leave Peterhouse for Pembroke on 5 March 1756 are discussed elsewhere.[5]

He was welcomed at Pembroke, and wrote to Wharton on 25 March:[6] 'I am for the present extremely well lodged here and as quiet as at the Grande Chartreuse.' For more than two years he did not have rooms assigned to him by the College. It may be assumed that some Fellow, who was not resident, allowed Gray the

recorded: Admitted to Pembroke, March 5 1756.' It was probably on 5 Mar. that he sought refuge in Pembroke, and his formal admission took place next day.

APPENDIX K.—[1] Letter 2: 'I am got into a room; such a hugeous one that little i is quite lost in it etc.' If the description that follows be taken literally, his bed was in his living-room.

[2] Letter 9: 'I got up, & open'd the door, & saw all the court full of strange appearances.'

[3] Willis and Clark, *Architectural History of the University of Cambridge*, vol. i, p. 35.

[4] Dr. Walker, *Athenæum*, 27 Jan. 1906, p. 108: 'A rough Bursar's book in the Peterhouse Treasury gives the names of the occupants of the six sets of rooms in the New Buildings at Michaelmas 1755.'

[5] Appendix J.   [6] Letter 214.

use of his rooms; and on grounds of probability, it may be inferred that he occupied Mr. Delaval's chamber. This was Chamber no. 42, described in the College Rent-book as 'South side of the New Court, West Staircase middle chamber over that in the passage to the garden with its bed-chamber on the same floor'. The rooms correspond with Gray's description, for they were on the first floor in the inner court of the College (then called the New Court) far from the streets that border the College on two sides. The windows overlook the court on the north, and the Fellows' 'Small Garden' on the south. Delaval was never in residence during the two years and more before Gray moved into rooms of his own, and when Gray did move, Delaval's chamber was assigned to another Fellow, Mr. Mapletoft.

The next chamber on the west was, between 1756 and 1758, assigned to Mr. Forester, but in June 1758 he gave it up,[7] and from that date it was transferred to Gray and entered in the Rent-book under his name. This chamber was no. 39, described as 'on the South side of the New Court over that on the right hand belonging to the Master'. It is on the staircase next the Hall at the west end of the Hitcham building, which had been erected in 1659. This part of the range is different from the rest and has 'an ornamental façade of stone in the Renaissance style'.[8] The rooms in it are of a higher pitch with larger windows; they were described as 'belonging to the Master', and rent was paid for them to the Master. It is probable that this part was originally built as an addition to the Master's lodge, and that Gray's rooms originally formed one large parlour, about 32 feet long by 20 feet 6 inches broad.[9] But a strip at the west end, 9 feet in depth, was at some time cut off to form a bedroom 14 feet long, and a small 'Study' of about 6 feet by 9. The sitting-room, measuring 24 feet by 20 feet 6 inches, has three lofty windows looking into the court, and one on the south side looking into what was then the Master's Garden. Wharton had occupied the rooms for some time, and when he gave them up in 1747 a considerable sum was spent in fitting them up, and putting in a new stone chimney piece. For these rooms Gray paid a yearly rent of £2 to the College (in consideration of their expenditure) and £6 to

---

[7] On 19 Dec. 1757 Gray wrote: 'Dick [i.e. Forester] is going to give up his rooms and live at Ashwell.' (Letter 259.)

[8] Willis and Clark, *op. cit.*, vol. i, p. 145.

[9] This suggestion is made by Mr. A. L. Attwater, Fellow of Pembroke, the present occupant of the rooms. The study was partitioned off from the bedroom with glass in the door.

the Master. From the end of June 1758 until nearly the end of 1761 Gray was out of residence, and except for the greater part of the summers of 1760 and 1761·only used his rooms for brief visits. In the Michaelmas term of 1761 he had a second chamber assigned ' to him, no doubt to provide for his servant[10] and his ever-growing library. This was on the opposite side of the same court, and in the next year it was exchanged for Chamber no. 40, which was immediately over his own rooms, for which a rent of £3 10*s.* a year was charged to him. These chambers (nos. 39 and 40) Gray occupied for the rest of his life.[11]

[L. W.]

APPENDIX L

Gray and James Macpherson

[Letters 310, 313, 315, 319*, &c.]

WHEN James Macpherson, a youth of twenty-three (Letter 313, n. 17), was preparing for publication his *Fragments of Ancient Poetry, collected in the Highlands of Scotland, and translated from the Galic or Erse Language*, he sent two specimens of his translation to Sir David Dalrymple. These Dalrymple sent to Walpole in January 1760, with a suggestion that they might interest Gray. Gray, with his enthusiasm for archaic poetry, was charmed with them and wrote to ask for further information, and expressed his wish to see a few lines of the original, but he seems to have thought it possible that some 'one now living in Scotland had written them to divert himself and laugh at the credulity of the world'.[1] A copy of Gray's letter was sent by Walpole to Dalrymple (Letter 310, n. 1), who must have communicated Gray's request to Macpherson. For in April Macpherson sent 'two short specimens of the Irish versification' to Dalrymple, who forwarded them to Walpole (see Letter 310, n. 3), and they were no doubt shown to Gray. The two pieces of translation Gray showed

---

[10] In July 1760, before he contemplated returning into residence, he asked Brown to have his bed aired and to speak about a lodging for his servant, and he hoped 'that if it were not contrary to the etiquette of the College . . . he might lie within your walls' (Letter 316). There are other instances of Fellows and Fellow-commoners having a second chamber for their servants.

[11] Chamber no. 39 was occupied by William Pitt, who entered the College two years after Gray's death.

APPENDIX L.—[1] See Letter 310 and notes. Gray's doubts persisted (see Letters 313 and 353).

to his friends, to Stonhewer and Mason,[2] and to Dr. Clerke.[3] He wrote to Scotland 'to make a thousand enquiries', and entered into correspondence with Macpherson himself. Macpherson's replies left him in uncertainty, as he told Wharton: 'The letters I have in return are ill-wrote, ill-reason'd, unsatisfactory, calculated (one would imagine) to deceive one, & yet not cunning enough to do it cleverly. in short, the whole external evidence would make one believe these fragments (for so he calls them, tho' nothing can be more entire) counterfeit: but the internal is so strong on the other side, that I am resolved to believe them genuine, spite of the Devil & the Kirk' (Letter 313). Macpherson sent a third specimen of his translation. This was 'merely description', a description of an October night by a Chief and five other Bards (Letter 315). This Macpherson sent also to Dalrymple who forwarded it to Walpole.[4]

The *Fragments of Ancient Poetry* were published at Edinburgh, apparently in June 1760, but Gray did not get them until about the end of July (Letter 317). Writing to Mason on 7 Aug. he expressed his opinion: 'I continue to think them genuine, tho' my reasons for believing the contrary are rather stronger than ever: but I will have them antique, for I never knew a Scotchman of my own time, that could read, much less write, poetry, & such poetry too!' (Letter 317). Early in August Gray seems to have written to a correspondent, who has not been identified,[5] a letter expressing his admiration for the *Fragments* and mentioning the suspicions which he still entertained as to their authenticity. His letter was communicated to Hume,

[2] Stonhewer and Mason were in town in April (Letter 311). In June Gray wrote to Wharton: 'If you have seen Stonhewer he has probably told you of my old Scotch (or rather Irish) Poetry' (Letter 313). In writing to Mason on 7 Aug. he alludes to Mason's 'affectation of not admiring' the fragments (Letter 317).

[3] Writing to Clerke on 12 Aug. he asks: 'Have you seen the Erse Fragments since they were printed' (Letter 318).

[4] Walpole, on 20 June, wrote to Dalrymple: 'I am obliged to you for the volume of Erse poetry . . . but I am sorry not to see in it the six descriptions of night, with which you favoured me before.'

The descriptions were first published by Macpherson, as a note to *Croma: a Poem* in *The Works of Ossian*, 3rd ed., 1765, vol. i, p. 350. Mason had the manuscript copy, which Macpherson sent to Gray, and in a note pointed out variations from the printed copy (see Letter 315, n. 13).

[5] Dr. Greig in *The Letters of David Hume* (Oxford, 1932), vol. 1, p. 328, suggests that Gray's inquiries had been addressed to Sir David Dalrymple, who had been in correspondence with Walpole since Jan. 1760 on the subject of the Erse poems. But the fact that it was Walpole who had communicated Dalrymple's information to Gray makes it the less likely that Gray should have written to him directly. Had he done so, it would have been still more unlikely that in quoting Hume's letter to Walpole, he should not have told him that he had procured it from Dalrymple.

who on 16 August wrote from Edinburgh a long letter, arguing for the authenticity of the poems.[6] Hume's letter was forwarded to Gray, who quoted parts of it in letters, written soon after, to Mason (Letter 319*) and to Walpole (Letter 320). He wrote to Wharton on 21 October: 'There is a second Edition of the Scotch Fragments,[7] yet very few admire them and almost all take them for fictions', and he repeated passages from Hume's letter (Letter 321).

Between this date and December 1761 (Letter 351*) there is no mention of Macpherson in Gray's letters.[8] This is the more surprising, as early in 1761 Macpherson was in London, and had shown Walpole the first book of *Fingal* in manuscript.[9] On 14 April Walpole wrote to Dalrymple expressing his admiration and saying that he had advised Macpherson 'to have the names prefixed to the speeches, as in a play'. He added: 'My doubts as to the genuineness are all vanished.' Gray was in London until June, and we may assume that he also saw the manuscript, and he may have met Macpherson.

Fingal was published on 1 December. Walpole's doubts returned. On 8 December he wrote to George Montagu: '*Fingal* is come out ... I will trust you with a secret, but you must not disclose it, I should be ruined with my Scotch friends—in short, I cannot believe it genuine.' Gray sent the book to Stonhewer and wrote: 'For my part I will stick to my credulity, and if I am cheated, think it worse for him [the translator] than for me' (Letter 351*). But he held his judgement in suspense, and on 11 January he wrote to Wharton: 'for me, I admire nothing but Fingal ... yet I remain still in doubt about the authenticity of those poems, tho' inclining rather to

---

[6] Hume's letter is printed below. Hume continued for some time to believe in the authenticity of the poems, and on 9 Feb. 1761 wrote to William Strahan, the printer, to introduce Macpherson and recommend him to his friendship (*Letters of David Hume*, edited by J. Y. T. Greig, vol. i, p. 342). Within a few years his opinion of Macpherson was completely changed (see his letters to Dr. Blair of 19 Sept. and 6 Oct. 1763 (*op. cit.*, vol. i, pp. 398, 403), and he wrote an essay (which he did not publish) to prove that the poems were forgeries (Burton's *Life of Hume*, pp. 471 ff.).

[7] A copy of the second edition with Gray's autograph on the title-page is in the Pembroke College Library.

[8] On a blank page at the beginning of vol. ii of Gray's Commonplace-book he wrote the titles of 'Gothic, Erse, and Welsh' poems. The entry may be dated about 1761, in which year he composed his Imitations of the Norse and Welsh poets (see Appendix M). Under the heading 'Erse' are entered the titles of four passages from Macpherson's Fragments, and 'Night described by six Bards', the passage sent to Gray in June 1760 (see Letter 313). It seems possible that Gray intended to put some of these fragments into verse, as specimens of early poetry, and would have done so, but for his doubts as to their genuineness.

[9] Walpole's letter to Dalrymple quoted above implies that Walpole had met and conversed with Macpherson.

believe them genuine in spite of the World. whether they are the inventions of antiquity, or of a modern Scotchman is to me unaccountable. je m'y pers.'[10] A year later in a letter to Brown, which he wrote to be forwarded to William Taylor How, Gray commended *Ossian, the Son of Fingal*: 'Mr How ... would there see, that Imagination dwelt many hundred years agoe, in all her pomp on the cold and barren mountains of Scotland' (Letter 367).

This is the last allusion to Macpherson and his works in any of Gray's extant letters. It is clear that from first to last he was consistent in his sincere admiration of the poems. He realized the objections to regarding them as genuine, and saw the force of general opinion against them. His doubts remained, but the difficulty of supposing that the poems were the composition of Macpherson seemed as great as the acceptance of Macpherson's claims. It is possible that his doubts became more positive before his death, and it is perhaps significant that in the letters he wrote after his journey to Scotland in 1765 there is no mention of Ossian, although he talks of the Highlanders at Glamis 'singing Erse-songs all day long' (Letter 412).

When Mason was writing his *Memoirs* of Gray in 1774, he sent some of the proof-sheets to Walpole. Walpole urged him to print nothing that might revive the Ossian controversy: 'In Gray's own letters there is enough to offend, your notes added will involve him in the quarrel.' He begged Mason: 'reserve the objectionable letters and your own notes to a future edition.' Mason replied: 'Only have patience with me and I will cancel every syllable that can offend Mr. Macpherson.' And so he stopped the press, and three or four months later wrote: 'I have employed myself since I came down in endeavouring to supply the chasms in the sheets where the objectionable notes &c occurred.'[11]

Mason does not say that he cancelled any letter of Gray on the subject; he printed the letter to Wharton of June 1760 (quoted above) in which Gray referred to Macpherson's letters in abusive terms. Mason expressed his own opinion in his notes: 'I suspected that, whether the Fragments were genuine or not, they were, by no means literally translated. I suspect so still' (*Memoirs*, p. 285). The 'objectionable notes' which he took out must have stated his doubts more plainly and more forcibly.

[L. W.]

---

[10] Letter 353. A few weeks later Gray wrote to Walpole: 'pray tell me . . . whether Fingal be discovered or shrewdly suspected to be a forgery' (Letter 356).
[11] *Walpole–Mason Correspondence*, vol. i, pp. 142–3, 148, 157.

Appendix L

Letter from David Hume on the authenticity of the Erse Fragments

Hume's letter (see n. 6), passages from which were quoted by Gray in letters to Mason, Walpole, and Wharton, was published in *The European Magazine* for May 1784 (pp. 327 ff.), having been sent by a correspondent signing himself 'J. W.'.

Sir,

I am not surprised to find by your letter, that Mr Gray should have entertained suspicions with regard to the authenticity of these Fragments of our Highland poetry. The first time I was shewn the copies of some of them in manuscript, by our friend John Home, I was inclined to be a little incredulous on that head; but Mr Home removed my scruples, by informing me of the manner in which he procured them from Mr Macpherson, the Translator. These two gentlemen were drinking the waters together at Moffat last autumn; when their conversation fell upon Highland poetry, which Mr Macpherson extolled very highly. Our friend, who knew him to be a good scholar, and a man of taste, found his curiosity excited; and asked whether he had ever translated any of them. Mr Macpherson replied that he never had attempted any such thing; and doubted whether it was possible to transfuse such beauties into our language: but for Mr Home's satisfaction, and in order to give him a general notion of the strain of that wild poetry, he would endeavour to turn one of them into English. He accordingly brought him one next day; which our friend was so much pleased with, that he never ceased soliciting Mr Macpherson till he insensibly produced that small volume which has been published. After this volume was in every body's hands, and universally admired, we heard every day new reasons, which put the authenticity, not the great antiquity, which the translator ascribes to them, beyond all question: for their antiquity is a point which must be ascertained by reasoning; though the arguments he employs seem very probable and convincing. But certain it is, that these poems are in every body's mouth in the Highlands, have been handed down from father to son, and are of an age beyond all memory and tradition. In the family of every Highland chieftain there was anciently retained a bard, whose office was the same with that of the Greek rhapsodists; and the general subject of the poems which they recited, was the wars of Fingal; an epoch no less celebrated among them, than the wars of Troy among the Greek poets. This custom is not even yet altogether abolished; the bard and piper are esteem'd the most honourable offices in a chieftain's family, and these two characters are frequently united in the same person. Adam Smith, the celebrated professor in Glasgow, told me, that the piper of the Argyleshire militia repeated to him all those poems which Mr Macpherson has translated, and many more of equal beauty. Major Mackay, Lord Rae's brother, also told me, that he remembers them perfectly; as likewise did the Laird of Macfarlane, the greatest antiquarian whom we have in this country, and who insists as strongly on the historical truth, as well as on the poetical beauty of these productions.

Appendix L

I could add the laird and lady Macleod to these authorities, with many more, if these were not sufficient; as they live in different parts of the Highlands, very remote from each other, and they could only be acquainted with poems that had become in a manner national works, and had gradually spread themselves into every mouth, and imprinted on every memory.

Every body in Edinburgh is so convinced of this truth, that we have endeavoured to put Mr Macpherson on a way of procuring us more of these wild flowers. He is a modest sensible young man, not settled in any living, but employed as a private tutor in Mr Graham of Balgowan's family, a way of life which he is not fond of. We have therefore set about a subscription of a guinea or two guineas a-piece, in order to enable him to quit that family, and undertake a mission into the Highlands, where he hopes to recover more of these Fragments. There is, in particular, a country surgeon somewhere in Lochaber, who, he says, can recite a great number of them, but never committed them to writing; as indeed the orthography of the Highland language is not fixed, and the natives have always employed more the sword than the pen. This surgeon has by heart the epic poem mention'd by Mr Macpherson in his preface; and as he is somewhat old, and is the only person living that has it entire, we are in the more haste to recover a monument, which will certainly be regarded as a curiosity in the republic of letters.

I own that my first and chief objection to the authenticity of these fragments, was not on account of the noble and even tender strokes which they contain; for these are the offspring to Genius and Passion in all countries; I was only surprised at the regular plan which appears in some of these pieces, and which seems to be the work of a more cultivated age. None of the specimens of barbarous poetry known to us, the Hebrew, Arabian, or any other, contained this species of beauty; and if a regular epic poem, or even any thing of that kind, nearly regular, should also come from that rough climate, or uncivilized people, it would appear to me a phenomenon altogether unaccountable.

I remember, Mr Macpherson told me, that the heroes of this Highland epic were not only like Homer's heroes, their own butchers, bakers, and cooks, but also their own shoemakers, carpenters, and smiths. He mentioned an incident which put this matter in a remarkable light.—A warrior has the head of his spear struck off in battle; upon which he immediately retires behind the army, where a forge was erected; makes a new one; hurries back to the action; pierces his enemy, while the iron, which was yet red-hot, hisses in the wound. This imagery you will allow to be singular, and so well imagined, that it would have been adopted by Homer, had the manners of the Greeks allowed him to have employed it. I forget to mention, as another proof of the authenticity of these poems, and even of the reality of the adventures contained in them, that the names of the heroes, Fingal, Oscur, Osur, Oscan, Dermid, are still given in the Highlands to large mastiffs, in the same manner as we affix to them the names of Caesar, Pompey, Hector; or the French that of Marlborough.

Appendix L

It gives me pleasure to find that a person of so fine a taste as Mr Gray approves of these Fragments, as it may convince us, that our fondness of them is not altogether founded on national prepossessions, which, however, you know to be a little strong.

The translation is elegant; but I made an objection to the author, which I wish you would communicate to Mr Gray, that we may judge of the justness of it. There appeared to me many verses in his prose, and all of them in the same measure with Mr Shenstone's famous ballad,

> Ye shepherds, so careless and free
> Whose flocks never carelessly roam, &c.

Pray ask Mr Gray whether he made the same remark, and whether he thinks it a blemish?

Your's most sincerely,
DAVID HUME.

Edinburgh
Aug. 16, 1760.

APPENDIX M
Gray's Studies of Welsh Poetry
[Letter 313]

IN his letter to Wharton of *c.* 20 June 1760 (Letter 313), Gray, after telling Wharton that he 'had gone mad' about Macpherson's supposed translations of Highland poetry and expressing his doubts as to their genuineness, proceeds: 'the Welch Poets are also coming to light:[1] I have seen a Discourse in Mfs. about them (by one Mr Evans,[2] a Clergyman) with specimens of their writings. This is in Latin, & tho' it don't approach the other, there are fine scraps among it.' The 'Discourse' was the *De Bardis Dissertatio*, which was afterwards appended to *Some Specimens of the Poetry of the Antient Welsh Bards, translated into English,* which Evan Evans published in 1764. A letter from Evan Evans to Richard Morris, the Welsh Scholar, written on 23 April 1760,[3] explains how the *Dissertatio* was brought to Gray's notice:

'I have waited on Mr Justice Barrington at Carnarvon with the Dissertation on the Bards, who approved of it. He has taken it and a copy

APPENDIX M.—[1] Gray's study of Welsh poetry had been begun some years before. In his Commonplace-book there are entries headed *Cambri* (parts of which were printed in Mathias, *Works of Gray,* vol. ii, pp. 50 ff.), which may reasonably be dated as early as 1758, when Gray was collecting material for his intended history of English poetry. There are notes on the 'Secret of the Poets', on the artistic devices of Welsh Poetry, and examples of their metres.

[2] See Letter 313, n. 19, and Letter 340, n. 5.

[3] *Collected Works of Evan Evans,* 1876, p. 164 (quoted in *The Celtic Revival in English Literature, 1760–1800,* by Edward D. Snyder, 1923).

of Nennius, both bound together to London. . . . He advises me by all means to translate more of the ancient Bards after the same manner I have done those odes I sent you, and make a small book of it by itself, which he says will sell well. He says that Mr Gray of Cambridge admires Gwalchmai's Ode to Owen Gwynned, and I think deservedly. He says he will show the Dissertation to Mr Gray, to have his judgment of it, and to correct it where necessary; so that I hope it will be fit for the press when I have it.'

Daines Barrington was a friend of Gray (see Letter 465, n. 8), and while Gray was living in London in 1759 and 1760, they must have had many opportunities of meeting. It may be assumed that it was Barrington who had given Gray the translation of the *Ode to Owen Gwynned*,[4] to which Evan Evans refers in his letter, and who now showed him the *Dissertation on the Bards*, which itself contained the specimens of their writings in a Latin translation. No doubt Barrington conveyed to Evans Gray's opinion of the Dissertation and the specimens, but there does not seem to have been any direct correspondence between them: in August of the next year Evans wrote to Percy: 'I have not the happiness to be acquainted with Mr Gray' (see Letter 340, n. 5, and Appendix N).

It was on the translations of Evan Evans that Gray based his imitations of Welsh Poetry. *The Triumphs of Owen, a Fragment* (derived from the *Ode to Owen Gwynned*), published in the 1768 edition of Gray's *Poems*, was described as 'From Mr Evans's Specimen of the Welch Poetry, London, 1764, Quarto', and three other fragments from the *Gododin of Aneurin*, published by Mason after Gray's death, were imitations of poems in the *Dissertatio de Bardis* (which formed part of the same work of Evans). It has usually been assumed that Gray's imitations of Welsh poems were not written until after the publication of Evan Evans's book, i.e. not before 1764, but as the poems which he imitated were known to him in 1760, it is likely that Gray's versions were written not long after he had first seen the translations.[5] There is positive evidence that they were not written later than 1761. In May of that year Gray had already written his imitations of the Norse poems,[6] and in his Commonplace-book, in which it was his

---

[4] This was, no doubt, the translation made by Evan Evans, which appeared in his *Specimens*, p. 25.

[5] Tovey has a note to Gray's letter to Wharton of June 1760: 'Though Gray in 1768 refers to the printed edition of Evans's book, it is possible that his versions from the Welsh were made not long after the date of this letter.'

[6] See Walpole's letter to George Montagu of 5 May 1761: 'Gray has translated two noble incantations from the Lord knows who, a Danish Gray, who lived the Lord knows when.'

Appendix M

custom to transcribe his poems, we find (in the third volume) four poems written consecutively: *The Fatal Sisters* (with the date 1761 appended), *The Triumph of Owen*, *The descent of Odin* (also with the date 1761), and *From Aneurin, Monarch of the Bards, extracted from the Gododin.*⁷ It can scarcely be doubted that the four poems were transcribed at the same time. The note '1761' appended to the Norse poems indicating the year when they were composed, not the date at which they were transcribed; but on other grounds it is probable that none of the entries in this volume of the Commonplace-book were made after the end of 1761. It seems reasonable to conclude, therefore, that Gray's imitations of the Welsh were written in 1760 or 1761, before he had given up his intention of writing the *History of English Poetry*, an intention which in 1768 he had 'long since drop'd'.⁸   [L. W.]

APPENDIX N
Gray and Thomas Percy
[Letters 340, 491*]

OF Gray's correspondence with Thomas Percy we have one letter of Gray (Letter 340) and a note, which was sent either to Percy or, more probably, to one of Percy's friends for Percy's information (Letter 491*). But in Percy's Diary and Correspondence there are many references to Gray, which show that for some years Percy was seeking to discover Gray's opinion of his works and looking to Gray for help.¹

On his visit to Cambridge in 1761 Percy made Gray's acquaintance on 1 September and drank tea with him in his chambers (see Letter 340, n. 2). Of their conversation on this occasion Percy made 'short minutes', which unfortunately have not survived,² but we have other

⁷ Mason, when he published this in the *Poems*, pp. 58–9, gave it the title *The Death of Hoel*.
⁸ In the 1768 edition of his *Poems* Gray prefixed an Advertisement to his Imitations of the Norse and Welsh, in which he says: 'The Author once had thoughts . . . of giving *the History of English Poetry*: In the Introduction to it he meant to have produced some specimens of the Style that reigned in ancient times among the neighbouring nations, or those who . . . were our Progenitors: the following three imitations made a part of them. He has long since drop'd his design' (see Letters 509*, 518).
APPENDIX N.—¹ For most of the references to the Percy Correspondence and for the explanation of the note on the 'Abbot of Mefx' (Letter 491*) grateful acknowledgement is made to Mr. A. Watkin Jones of Exeter College, Oxford.
² In the Percy manuscript, with Gray's letter and note (Brit. Mus. *Add. MS.*

1231

evidence of the subjects which they discussed. Their conversation ranged over early poetry, English, Welsh, and Erse. Percy had with him a 'Mſs Collection'[3] of old poems (presumably either the folio volume of his ballads or a transcript), and showed Gray *Death and Life in two fitts* and *Scottish Field*,[4] which were in the same measure as *The Vision of Pierce Plowman*, and it may be concluded that they discussed the early forms of English verse. They also talked of Welsh poetry: 'our discourse turned on you and the Welsh poetry', Percy wrote to Evan Evans (see Letter 340, n. 5). There is also evidence that Macpherson's *Fragments* came under review, for Shenstone in a letter to John Macgowan of 24 September 1761,[5] referring to them, wrote: 'It seems indeed from a former version of them by the same translator (which Mr. Gray, the poet, received from him, and shewed my friend Percy), that he has taken pretty considerable freedom in adapting them to the present reader.' The day following their conversation Gray wrote to Percy the letter in which he refers to a book and the letter of Evan Evans, which Percy had left with him (Letter 340).

It was probably not long after their meeting that Percy sent Gray a copy of the poem *Death and Life*, which he had shown him, with a glossary added, and requested Gray to supply emendations and explanations.[6] There is no further evidence of direct correspondence

32329), is a paper headed: 'Short Minutes of my Conversation with Mr Gray, the Poet,' with the note: '[Tho' dated at the time, they were not written till a Month after, when it was possible for some small particulars to have escaped my Memory, & some trifling Mistakes to have occurred to me.]' The Minutes are not extant.

[3] In a note obviously referring to this interview Gray mentions the 'Mſs Collection belonging to the Revd Thomas Piercy, which he had seen' (see n. 4).

[4] In Gray's Commonplace-book there is a series of entries under the heading 'Pseudo-Rhythmus' (printed by Mathias, vol. ii, pp. 31–43). The entries may be dated, in all probability, as written not later than 1758. In one of the entries, Gray, in discussing early alliterative verse, quoted in illustration a passage from *The Vision of Piers Plowman*; at some later time he added, in the margin, the following note: 'In the same measure is a poem called Death and Life in 2 fitts and Scottish Field. I read them in a Mſs Collection belonging to the Revd Thomas Piercy in 1761.' Percy in his *Reliques* (1st ed., 1765, vol. ii, pp. 260 ff.) in an *Essay on the Metre of Pierce Plowman's Vision* cites the same two poems as 'written in that species of versification'.

[5] Quoted in Nichols, *Illustrations*, vol. vii, p. 222.

[6] In the sale of the Percy MSS. at Sotheby's on 29 Apr. 1884, Lot 67 was described as follows: ' "Lyfe and Death—an ancient allegorical Poem written in the same Metre with Pierce Plowman's Vision." Transcribed by Percy, who adds a glossary and sent it to Gray with a request for emendations and explanations. Gray complies, and adds autograph notes.' It has not been possible to trace this manuscript.

between them, but in Percy's letters to Richard Farmer (see Letter 340, n. 3) and William Cole there are references to Gray and requests for his help. It is uncertain at what date Gray and Farmer became acquainted (see Letter 516, n. 1), but Percy's references to Gray in his letters to Farmer from 1764 imply that the two men cannot have been strangers to one another. Early in that year, what was then intended to be the first volume of the *Reliques*[7] had been printed and a copy was sent to Farmer, to whom Percy wrote on 12 February: 'You don't tell me what you think of ye 1st vol. of Old Ballads: give me your unreserved censure, that I may profit by it in what is yet unprinted. If you showed it to Gray, tell me what he says of it: I am afraid not much in its favour. However I can patiently hear my faults told me.' And in the same letter he referred to his version of *The Friar of Orders Gray*: 'if it should fall in your way, show it to Gray and ask him to inspirit it with improvements of his own' (Brit. Mus. *Add. MS.* 28222).

After the publication of the *Reliques* in February 1765, Percy showed the same curiosity to learn Gray's opinion. Writing to Farmer on 20 April he asked: 'whether my *old Reliques* are read much in your University and what is said of them. Pray what literary works are going on at your University? How is Mr Hurd at present employed? Has he seen the Reliques? Or Mr Gray? What faults do they find' (*ibid.*). On 19 August of this year Percy saw Gray at Alnwick, as he recorded in his diary (see Letter 412, n. 3).

On 7 June 1766 Percy wrote to Farmer, desiring him to ask Gray for information concerning a manuscript in the British Museum, which was described in Walpole's *Anecdotes of Painting*. Percy had applied to Walpole, who had referred him to Gray. Gray appears to have given no answer to Percy's question, for on 22 October Percy wrote to Farmer that he had 'got it answered from another Quarter' (*ibid.*). This neglect on Gray's part probably gave offence to Percy. For when in March 1767 Cole wrote to Percy that he thought Gray could furnish information, which Percy was seeking about Jane Shore, Percy wrote back on 28 March: 'I wish you c^d procure me from Mr Gray the Anecdotes you mention about Jane Shore: but then I must beg the favour not to have my name used to him: as I do not chuse to apply to him for any favour of any kind' (Brit. Mus. *Add. MS.* 6401, f. 157). The same ill-feeling was manifested a year later in a letter which Percy wrote to Farmer. Percy was interested in Surrey's works, and Farmer had mentioned that Mr. Mason

---

[7] In the course of printing the *Reliques* Percy transposed the first and third volumes. See L. F. Powell, 'Percy's Reliques', in *The Library*, Sept. 1928.

seemed to be well acquainted with the Surrey Manuscripts. Percy wrote on 28 March 1768 asking Farmer to obtain information for him: 'Yet not in my name if it is M.ʳ Mason the Poet. I would rather go a hundred miles in search myself, than ask a single Question either of him or his Brother Gray. . . . Have you seen the new Odes of the latter?' (Brit. Mus. *Add. MS.* 28222).

In connexion with another of his works Percy was still to be under obligations to Gray and Mason. For some years Percy was engaged in editing the *Northumberland Houshold Book.* In August 1768 the text was already in print, and on 22 August Percy wrote to Farmer[8] and sent him a copy. At some time within the next few months Gray was shown the text, presumably by Farmer, and at a date conjectured to be about January 1769, he wrote a note, dictated by Mason, to correct a statement of Percy's about Meaux Abbey (see Letter 491*, n. 2). This note was perhaps given to Farmer, for Percy's information, and it is now among the Percy papers. Gray's note was inserted, almost verbatim, by Percy as a correction of a footnote printed earlier in the book, but without acknowledgement of the source from which the information was derived.[9]

[L. W.]

[8] In his letter (Brit. Mus. *Add. MS.* 28222, f. 90) Percy wrote: 'I am told that in Pembroke Hall Library there is a Transcript of this very book or something like it: be so good as to make close Inquiry and let me know the result.' Percy does not mention Gray's name, but what information that he had about the book was in connexion with Gray. On 25 July 1767 Thomas Warton, to whom Percy had sent the first sheets of the *Houshold Book,* wrote to him: 'I think I saw in Pembroke-Hall Library, at Cambridge, a copy of your manuscript. At least it was a Book of the same kind. It was last Summer; and M.ʳ Gray was consulting it, I suppose, for anecdotes of ancient Manners, so amusing to the Imagination.' ('The Text of the Percy–Warton Letters', by Leah Dennis, *Publications of the Modern Language Association of America,* vol. xlvi, no. 4, p. 1191). The book in the Pembroke Library that Gray must have been consulting was the Duke of Norfolk's *Houshold Book* (for which see Letter 230, n. 25).

[9] After Gray's death Percy seems to have made further inquiries about Meaux Abbey, and among the Percy papers in the British Museum (*Add. MS.* 32329, f. 44) there is a letter from Mason to Percy repeating the information which Gray had given in his note. Apparently Percy sent Mason a copy of the *Northumberland Houshold Book* in recognition of his help, as in the same manuscript (fol. 68) there is a note from Mason to Percy of 8 Apr. 1773 thanking Percy: 'He is only sorry that his pretentions to so great a favour are founded on so slight an emendation.'

APPENDIX O

Gray's Correspondence with How and Algarotti

[Letters 369, 370, 374, &c.]

THERE are in the British Museum (*Add. MS.* 26889, 26890) two manuscript volumes containing letters to and from William Taylor How (Letter 366) with letters to his friend Thomas Hollis and transcripts of letters to or from Count Algarotti. A note in How's hand describes them as: 'Letters, Papers & Manuscripts chiefly while I was abroad and some since my return to England, which my Executors may peruse [or] burn as they please. Containing letters from Lord Chatham, Mr Gray, Mr Mason, Mr Conyers and others. Wm T. H.' They were given about the year 1816 to the Rev. Edward William Stillingfleet, a nephew of How, by his aunt Mrs. A. Taylor, How's sister; and Stillingfleet in 1865 presented them to the British Museum.

While on his travels in Italy, How made the acquaintance of Algarotti (Letter 366, n. 4). To him he showed the *Odes* of Gray and Mason's tragedies, and he became the intermediary of Algarotti's correspondence with Pitt, as well as with Gray and Mason. As Gray says, at the conclusion of his letter to Algarotti (Letter 374): 'I owe to Mr Howe the honour I have of conversing with Count Algarotti.' How's chief correspondent was Thomas Hollis (Letter 379, n. 8), who acted as a means of communication between How and his correspondents in England, and who received from How, and dispatched, the parcels of books which Algarotti sent as presents to Pitt, Gray, and Mason, and to other persons and societies in England.

How kept the letters he had received from his distinguished correspondents in England, as well as some letters of Pitt to Hollis; he also had transcripts made of letters received by Algarotti from Gray, Mason, Garrick, &c.: these as well as his own letters to Gray, which must have been sent to him by Mason after Gray's death, are in his collection. Mason printed parts of three letters from Gray to How (*Memoirs*, pp. 386 ff.), a letter of Algarotti to How (*Poems*, pp. 82 ff.), and an extract from another letter (*Memoirs*, p. 388). These were put at his disposal by How, as was Gray's letter to Brown of 17 February 1763 (Letter 367, also printed by Mason), which had been forwarded to How and remained in his possession.

Mason did not print Gray's letter to Algarotti of 9 September 1763 (Letter 374). This appeared first in the *Gentleman's Magazine* for January 1805 (vol. lxxv, pp. 9 ff.), together with Mason's letter to

Appendix O

Algarotti of 20 September 1763 and Gray's letter to How of November 1763 (Letter 382). The letters were prefaced by a letter to the *Magazine*, beginning: 'Through the kindness of a friend I am in possession of a packet of letters left by a relative long since deceased.' The letter is signed J. O., who is identified (by a letter of Stillingfleet to Mitford, dated 23 January 1816, now in the Harvard College Library) as the Rev. John Oldham, of St. John's College, Cambridge, Rector of Stondon, Essex, the parish in which How had an estate.

Gray's letter to Algarotti, which was in How's collection, was printed in the *Gentleman's Magazine* from the transcript which had been made for How. In October 1818 the letter was printed in *Blackwood's Magazine* (vol. iv, pp. 38–40) from the original. A note was prefixed: 'This letter is taken from the Correspondence of Count Algarotti, in the possession of M[r] Murray.' How the letter came to John Murray is explained in a letter written by Byron to Murray from Venice on 12 April 1818.[1] Byron wrote to introduce Signor G. B. Missiaglia, the principal bookseller and publisher of Venice, by whose hands Byron sent to Murray a collection of letters addressed to Count Algarotti. These letters were the property of Dr. Aglietti,[2] and they were purchased from him by John Murray. The letter of Gray to Algarotti and other letters are now missing from the volume, which is in the possession of Sir John Murray. The fate of Gray's letter is explained in a letter of 9 February 1832 from Pickering to Mitford (now in the Harvard College Library): 'M[r] D'Israeli . . . said that he once possessed a long and interesting letter of Gray's addressed to Algarotti on the Italian opera and that he was simple enough to send the *original* to Blackwood's Magazine where it is printed in one of the early volumes. . . the original is now probably lost.'
[P. T.
L. W.]

APPENDIX P

The Contest for the High Stewardship and Gray's Verses on Lord Sandwich[1]

[Letters 383, 385, &c.]

In November 1763 the first Earl of Hardwicke, who had been High Steward of the University since 1749, fell seriously ill and was not

APPENDIX O.—[1] *Byron's Letters and Journals*, ed. Prothero, vol. iv, pp. 222–4.

[2] Francesco Aglietti (1757–1836), a physician of Brescia; he edited Algarotti's Works (see Letter 366, n. 4).

APPENDIX P.—[1] A detailed account of the contest is given in Mr. D. A. Win-

expected to recover. The contest for the succession of his office was started with indecent haste. The Duke of Newcastle had been driven from the Government in 1762, and the King and his Ministers wished now to overthrow his influence in the University of which he was Chancellor. Towards the end of November the Earl of Sandwich, one of the Secretaries of State, informed the King of his desire to offer himself as a candidate. His life was scandalous, and only a week before he had made himself infamous by his denunciation of Wilkes. George Grenville, First Lord of the Treasury, saw how discreditable his candidature would be, and suggested that Lord Halifax should be the Government candidate, but he found that Sandwich had already dissuaded Halifax from standing.[2]

Before Newcastle knew of Sandwich's intention, he also had anticipated the probable vacancy and had decided that his candidate should be Lord Royston, Hardwicke's eldest son, whom he expected to succeed to the office without difficulty. He had no desire to announce his intention while Lord Hardwicke was alive, but when at the end of November Sandwich had begun his canvass, Newcastle was forced to declare himself, and to seek support in Cambridge and outside. Henceforth the contest was waged with bitter energy. It was greatly in favour of Sandwich that he was the candidate of the Court and the Ministry, with the power of patronage ecclesiastical and civil in his hands, while Newcastle was determined, with all his efforts and influence, to maintain his hold on the University.

Gray's first allusion to the contest is in a letter to Walpole of 27 January 1764 (Letter 383), in which he says of Sandwich: 'Yet he would be chose at present, I have little doubt, tho' with strong opposition, & in a dishonorable way for him.' A month later in a letter to Wharton (Letter 385) he expresses the same opinion of Sandwich's chances.

Hardwicke had rallied at the beginning of the year and for a time his recovery was expected, but in February he suffered a relapse and on 6 March he died. The heat of the contest was all the greater now that the election was in near prospect: the voting was at first fixed for 22 March, but on 15 March the day was postponed to 30 March. In a letter to Walpole, which was written probably on

stanley's *The University of Cambridge in the Eighteenth Century* (Cambridge, 1922), pp. 55–139, to which reference should be made. Grateful acknowledgement is also due to Mr. Winstanley for additional information concerning the negotiations of Charles Yorke (brother of the second Earl of Hardwicke) with George Grenville and Lord Sandwich.

[2] Here and elsewhere reference should be made to Mr. Winstanley's book.

18 March (Letter 386), Gray gives his forecast: 'the Anti-Twit-cherites are numerous & sanguine, & make themselves sure of throwing him out, whatever becomes of their own Candidate: but as they are nearly equal, I doubt his Lᵖ has some trick left to turn the scale.'

The event justified the forecast. The voting took place on a Grace submitting Lord Hardwicke's name to the Senate for approval or rejection. The Senate was divided into two 'Houses', the House of the Regents, the Masters of Arts of not more than five years' standing from their creation, and the House of the Non-Regents, the elder graduates; and the Grace had to be passed by each House separately. In the Non-Regent House the Grace was carried by 103 votes to 101; in the Regent House the Proctors at first differed as to the count of the votes, but in the end concurred in declaring the votes on either side equal. After some dispute as to the effect of this equality of votes the Vice-Chancellor dissolved the Congregation with the issue undecided.

Before further action was taken on either side it was discovered that Thomas Pitt,[3] Master of Arts of Clare Hall, had voted against the Grace in the Regent House, when he was already a Non-Regent, and but for his vote, which ought not to have been counted, the Grace would have been carried in the Regent as well as in the Non-Regent House.

On a declaration of the Senior Proctor as to Pitt's vote, Lord Hardwicke's solicitor called upon the Vice-Chancellor and the other Keepers of the University Chest, to put the seal of the University to a patent of Lord Hardwicke's election. The demand was refused, and on 28 June recourse was had to the Court of King's Bench, on a motion for the Vice-Chancellor to hold a congregation, the Proctors to make a return of the Grace, and the Keepers of the Chest to seal the patent. On 9 July Counsel for Sandwich obtained an adjourn-ment. It was on the next day that Gray wrote to Wharton (Letter 390): 'Our Election here is in Westminster-Hall: but it is not likely that any great matter can be done in it till Michaelmas-Term next.'

On 16 November affidavits were submitted on behalf of Lord Sandwich, but it was not until April 1765 that the Court gave judgement in Lord Hardwicke's favour, and he was declared duly elected. In the interval there had been intrigues and negotiations, to which Gray alludes in his letters. In October 1764 there had been a question as to who should be elected Vice-Chancellor in November, and Keene visited Cambridge to try to make terms in the

[3] Gray's friend, afterwards Lord Camelford (see Letter 250, n. 12).

interests of Sandwich: to this mission Gray may allude in a letter to Wharton at the conclusion of the business (Letter 401): 'I suppose you know by this time, that our Friend the B: of Ch: was the private Embaſsador of L^d S: to this place.' His visit seems to have started a rumour that there was to be a general compromise: Gray wrote to Brown on 25 October (Letter 394): 'To-day I hear the Cambridge affair is compromised, and Lord Hardwicke is to come in quietly.' Gray's information was wrong, as he himself inferred four days later (Letter 395). But in November Charles Yorke entered into conversations with George Grenville and Sandwich, as a result of which he and his brother gave up their opposition to the Ministry.[4] Efforts seem to have been made to arrive at an understanding with regard to University affairs. On 23 November Charles Yorke and Sandwich had a meeting, 'the remarkable interview', as Gray describes it (Letter 401) at which the Bishop of Chester was present. Of the terms proposed on either side some indication is given in a letter which the Bishop wrote to Charles Yorke on 1 December after he had again visited Lord Sandwich to communicate Yorke's views to him. The relevant part of the letter is as follows:

'I waited on Lord Sandwich by appointment yesterday morning, and that I might be certain of not having mistaken the terms he had proposed in the conversation of last week I desired him to repeat them which were that after the High Stewardship was settled Lord Hardwicke and he were to act *in concert* in the disposal of Cambridge preferments. . . .

'I told his Lordship that I came with a commission from you to express y^r opinion of the impracticableness of those terms, and to propose to him that each should support his friends separately and unconnected.

'His reply was that things stood on that footing at present and there was

---

[4] On 11 Nov. 1764 the Master of the Rolls died, and the prospect of promotion moved Charles Yorke to think that it was time to make terms with the Government. On 15 Nov. he had his first meeting with George Grenville. Charles Yorke wished to make terms for his brother about the contest at Cambridge, and on 22 Nov. at another meeting, of which Grenville gave an account in his diary (*Grenville Papers*, vol. ii, p. 530), 'another long part of the discourse was upon settling the affairs relating to Cambridge with Lord Sandwich with whom he had at first declined a meeting, but was now to have one next day, desiring Mr. Grenville to tell Lord Sandwich that he should expect him to give up Cambridge entirely and promise never to engage in any contest with Lord Hardwicke. Mr. Grenville told him it was a great deal too much to ask.'

Of the meeting with Sandwich on 23 Nov. our information is derived from the letter of the Bishop of Chester quoted above. What were the precise terms arranged we do not know, but at the beginning of December Charles Yorke accepted from the Government a patent of precedence over the Solicitor-General, and on 20 Jan. 1765 Walpole, writing to the Earl of Hertford, referred to the time 'when Charles Yorke left us'. He had definitely joined the ministerial ranks.

no occasion for any new stipulation . . . but continued to press the terms he himself proposed, as best suited to keep up a friendly intercourse, and to prevent disagreeable contests.

'With regard to the High Stewardship he said that his ideas of that matter remained as they were expressed in the conversation of last week. He repeated more than once that tho' he did not look upon himself as tied down to anything, you might be assured of his performing every thing that you might well expect from him towards accommodating the Cambridge affairs. . . .' (Brit. Mus. *Add. MS.* 35640, f. 179.)

What terms may have been arranged about the High Stewardship, or what further negotiations took place, we do not know. But the desire of accommodation may have led to the compromise concerning the elections to the Lady Margaret Professorship of Divinity and the Mastership of St. John's a few weeks later (see Letter 399, n. 17). It is possible also that Sandwich did not intend seriously to contest Lord Hardwicke's claim to the High Stewardship, and that the Court of King's Bench in April 1765 only sanctioned what had already been arranged in granting a mandamus for the appointment of Lord Hardwicke. Gray may have been justified in his statement to Wharton about the judgement (Letter 401): 'I do believe the two Pretenders had (privately) agreed the matter beforehand, for the House of Yorke have undoubtedly been long making up to the Court.'

Gray's allusions to the contest in its different stages are disdainful of the whole proceedings. He had no liking for Newcastle, but his sympathies were certainly not with Sandwich. Norton Nicholls in his *Reminiscences* of Gray, which he wrote forty years later (see Appendix Z), states: 'In the contest for the High Stewardship at Cambridge between Lord Hardwicke & Lord Sandwich Mr Gray took a warm & eager part, for no other reason, I believe, than because he thought the licentious character of the latter candidate rendered him improper for a post of such dignity in the University. His zeal in this cause inspired the verses full of pleasantry & wit which have been published since his death.'

It may be doubted whether Nicholls was right in saying that Gray took an active part in the contest. He was generally reticent and reserved in his conduct; as a Bachelor of Laws he had no vote in the Senate, and for three or four weeks before the voting he was kept in his rooms by illness. But the verses, which are included in his works with the title of *The Candidate*, remain to attest his bitter contempt for Sandwich and his clerical supporters. There is no evidence to fix the date when they were written, but their contents suggest that it was before the voting took place in the Senate. Copies of a fly-sheet containing the verses, with the heading 'The Candidate:[5] By Mr. Gray', are extant, and the suggestion has been made that it was circulated in Cambridge at the time. It is, however, not likely that Gray had the verses printed: it is still less likely that he circulated them under his own name. More probably he wrote them, as he did other of his satirical poems, to please himself, and made them known to a few of his closest friends. In September 1774, when Walpole lighted on a copy in Gray's handwriting, he seems to have thought it was the only copy in existence. When he sent a transcript to Mason, Mason wrote that Gray had repeated the verses to him, adding: 'for I never before saw them in writing'.[6] In his letter to Mason, Walpole wrote 'the devil is in it, if sometime or other it don't find its way to the press', and there are reasons, external and internal, to support the conclusion that Walpole had the verses printed at Strawberry Hill.[7]

[L. W.]

The verses, as printed in the fly-sheet, are as follows:[8]

THE CANDIDATE:

BY

Mr. GRAY.

WHEN fly Jemmy Twitcher had fmugg'd up his face
With a lick of court white-wafh, and pious grimace,
A wooing he went, where three Sifters of old
In harmlefs fociety guttle and fcold.
    Lord! Sifter, fays Phyfic to Law, I declare
Such a fheep-biting look, fuch a pick-pocket air,
Not I, for the Indies! you know I'm no prude;
But his nofe is a fhame, and his eyes are fo lewd!
Then he fhambles and ftraddles fo oddly, I fear—
No; at our time of life, 'twould be filly, my dear.
    I don't know, fays Law, now methinks, for his look,
'Tis juft like the picture in Rochefter's book.

[5] There is no reason to suppose that Gray gave the title of 'The Candidate' to his verses. When they were printed, as is assumed, by Walpole, he may have taken over the title from Churchill's verses on Lord Sandwich, which were published in May 1764.
[6] See *Walpole–Mason Correspondence*, pp. 160, 163.
[7] See 'The Candidate: By Mr Gray', by Leonard Whibley in *The Times Literary Supplement*, 21 Aug. 1930.   [8] From a copy in the Eton College Library.

But his character, Phyzzy, his morals, his life;
When fhe died, I can't tell, but he once had a wife.
They fay he's no Chriftian, loves drinking and whoring,
And all the town rings of his fwearing and roaring,
His lying, and filching, and Newgate-bird tricks:—
Not I,—for a coronet, chariot and fix.
Divinity heard, between waking and dozing,
Her fifters denying, and Jemmy propofing;
From dinner fhe rofe with her bumper in hand,
She ftroked up her belly, and ftroked down her band.
What a pother is here about wenching and roaring!
Why David loved catches, and Solomon whoring.
Did not Ifrael filch from th' Ægyptians of old
Their jewels of filver, and jewels of gold?
The prophet of Bethel, we read, told a lie:
He drinks; fo did Noah: he fwears; fo do I.
To refufe him for fuch peccadillos, were odd;
Befides, he repents, and he talks about G--.
Never hang down your head, you poor penitent elf!
Come, bufs me, I'll be Mrs. Twitcher myfelf.
D--n ye both for a couple of Puritan bitches!
He's Chriftian enough, that repents, and that --------.

APPENDIX Q

Advice to a friend travelling in Scotland

[Letter 451]

THE following notes, which give an itinerary from Durham to Glamis
(with some general directions about travel in Scotland), are now
first printed from the original. The manuscripts of these notes
and of three letters of Gray to Brown (Letters 403, 414, 555) are
in the Bodleian (MS. Montagu, d. 17). They formed Lot 629 in
the sale of Gray MSS., &c., in 1845. The association of the notes
with the letters to Brown makes it probable that they had belonged
to Brown, and that Gray wrote them in view of a possible journey
of Brown to Scotland. Brown went with Lord Strathmore to Glamis
in August 1767 (see Letter 451, n. 3), but the directions as to the route,
the inns, and the post-chaises suggest that the notes were written when
it was anticipated that Brown might travel to Scotland by himself.

When Gray went to Scotland in 1765 he wrote notes on his journey.
Some of these notes Mitford transcribed from a note-book of Gray's
(see Letter 412, n. 3), which must have been the source from which

Appendix Q

Gray drew parts of the notes which he wrote for Brown. Another note, which Mitford transcribed without indicating where he found it, has the heading 'Advice to a friend travelling in Scotland', and contains part of the directions given to Brown (see n. 9).

[P. T.]

Berwick-Road into Scotland

From Durham (thro' Newcastle, Morpeth, Alnwick, & Belford) to Tweedmouth. 77 miles.

All the East-side of Northumb:[d] is enclosed & cultivated, but unsightly & unpleasant. Morpeth & Alnwick are large neat & well-built Towns, seated in narrow valleys by the side of little rivers. Alnwick-Castle is well-worth seeing. from hence you have frequent views of the German Ocean to the right, & of Dunstan-burgh & Bamburgh Castles. the Farne-Islands, the Staples, Holy-Island with its Abbey & Castle, &c: from Belford to the Tweed you have the sea at a very small distance always in view, but ships are rare upon it. to the left you see Cheviot (pronounce *Chivitt*) Hills rising to a considerable height. Tweedmouth is divided from Berwick only by a bridge of near 1000 feet long:[1] in your journey back it will be a delight to lie at the inn at Tweed-mouth.

(the Marse, or Berwickshire)[1a]

From *Tweedmouth* over *Lemmer-Miur* (ugly dismal moors, hill & dale) thro' *Aiton* a miserable Town, to *Old-Cambus* as miserable an Inn. 16 miles.

From *Old-Cammus* to Belton-Ford, 13 miles. in the way you pafs the *Pese* (or Pethes of Dunglas) a steep hill, & a little farther at a place call'd *the Cove* the road winds much too near a precipice hanging over the sea, & pafses by Dunglas (S[r] J: Hall's[2] house) on the side of a hill cover'd with wood:

(East-Lothian, or Haddingtonshire)

then you come near *Tyningham* (the seat of the Earl of Haddington) with much wood round it, & of *Dunbar* a large Town on the coast.

From *Belton-Ford* to *Haddington* 8 miles, a fertile plain country. pafs

APPENDIX Q.—[1] In one of the notes transcribed by Mitford Gray refers to 'a bridge at Berwick, 325 of my paces (which makes 975 feet) in length'.

[1a] Here and in six instances below the names of counties have been inserted above the line, after the itinerary had been written.

[2] Sir John Hall (d. 1776), third Baronet of Dunglass, co. Haddington.

Appendix Q

by *Mr Charteris's*, a tall ugly fabrick of red stone.[3] Haddington is a large nasty town with the ruins of a handsome Gothick Church, tho' of reddish stone.

From *Haddington* to *Edinburgh* 16 miles, thro' an open flat well-cultivated country, spotted with many Gentlemen's houses, & plantations. before you appears the Isle of Bafs, & North-Ber-wick-Law, a lofty round hill, with the *Lomonds* (high hills in Fife) at a greate distance. you leave *Preston*—

(Mid-Lothian, or Edinb:^{shire})

[*Pans*][4] & the town of Preston on the right, & pafs thro' *Tranent* & *Mufselborough*, almost always in view of the *Firth*, & sometimes close to it. the view* of *Edinburgh*[5] at a few miles distance is very fine & singular. the principal things to see in the City are the noble view from the *Castle-Hill, & that (said to be still greater) from *Arthur's Seat, *Holyrood House, the Great-Church, & Parliament-Close, the Grey-Fryers, Herriot's Hospital, &c:

From *Edinburgh* to *Stirling*, 36 miles, thro' an agreable cultivated countrey to the Bridge at Kirk-Liston.

(West-Lothian, or Lithgowshire)

then over barren hills to *Linlithgow* (pronounce *Lithgow*) a city on an eminence with the remains of a *Palace, & a large handsome *Gothick Church: behind them is a *little Lake with terraces leading down to its banks. the same sort of countrey continues

(Stirlingshire)

to *Falkirk* (pronounce Fawkīrk) & somewhat farther changes to a pleasant cultivated plain leading over *Banock-burn* to *Stirling, wch like Edinburgh is seated on a rock, on the highest part of wch is the *Castle. thro' the plain below wanders the River *Forth with innumerable windings. on one side run the *Ochell-Hills*, on the other appear the Mountains of *Menteith*, & *Ben-Lomond* towering over them.

From *Stirling* to *Crief* 21 miles. before you leave the *Carses of Stirling* you see *Kears*, a great modern house of Mr Stirling, seemingly in a fine situation to the left, on a hill crown'd with wood.

---

[3] Gosford (now called Wemyss House), at that time in the occupation of Francis Charteris (see Letter 511 A, n. 18).

[4] MS. torn.

[5] Gray marked certain views and places with a * to indicate that they were specially worth visiting.

Appendix Q

(Perthshire)

then pafsing thro' a narrow valley near the Riv: Allan, & a house of Mr Rofs's with much wood near it, you come to *Dumblaine*, a poor City with the ruins of a considerable *Church in a good Gothick style. then crofsing *Sherry-Muir, a wild heath, & pafsing by Airdoch (where are great traces *of a Roman Encampment) over many hills & desolate moors you see *Drummond-Castle on an eminence with much wood, & arrive at *Crief*, a Market-Town, seated on the edge of *Strath-Erne*: here opens a *most striking view into the bosom of the Highlands towards Aberurgwhill (pronounced *Arbrookle*) the hill of Lagan, & *Beni-Voorlich*, a very lofty mountain, with the rapid river Erne winding its way thro' the valley.

From *Crief* to *Perth* 18 miles. very good road, at first among dismal rocks, & then thro' a fertile countrey. *Perth* is a large old City in a fine open valley on the River *Tay*, wch is here navigable, & about 550 feet over. here is a ferry.

(Angus, or Forfarshire)

From Perth to Glammifs, 27 miles. the road is every where good from Edinburgh hither.

~

If you go the shorter road from Edinburgh[6] you pafs the *Firth* at the *Queens-Ferry* (where it is 2 miles over) to *Inver-Keithing*, & go by *Kinrofs* & Sr *John Bruces[7] House seated at the head of *Loch-Leven, amidst extensive old plantations, thro' *Cowper* of Angus, & *Macgill* (pron: *Maggle*) to Glammifs. at *Maggle* in the Churchyard observe the old sepulchal stones with rude carvings on them. you will have seen the like on the road (east of Crief) at *Foules*, & near *Perth*: there are three more near Glammifs. Hector Boece mentions them all.

There are no regular post-chaises North of Edinburgh. at Beltonford is a very tolerable Inn. the Post-House at Haddington seems pafsable. at Edinburgh I recommend Mr Ramsey's in Cow-gate: the Driver's name is *John Black*: he is worth any money. there is a large good inn at *Perth*, wch My Lord sometimes uses. there is an inn with a very good bedchamber at Crief, where my Lady Dow:^r Strathmore lies.

---

[6] It was by this route that Gray went with Lord Strathmore (see Letter 412; the notes there may be consulted with reference to the places mentioned).

[7] Sir John Bruce Hope (d. 1766), commonly known as Sir John Bruce, seventh Baronet of Kinross.

See your sheets air'd yourself. eat mutton or hard-eggs. touch no fried things. if they are broil'd, boil'd, or roasted, say that from a child you have eat no butter, & beg they would not rub any over your meat. there is honey, or orange-marmalade, or currant-jelly, wch may be eaten with toasted bread, or the thin oat-cakes, for breakfast. dream not of milk. ask your Landlord to set[8] down, & help off with your wine. never scold at any body, especially at Gentlemen, or Ladies.[9]

From Glammifs to Dunkeld, about 27 miles. by *Cowper* crofs the R: of *Ila*, over a heath, by the Lakes of Kinloch. when you come to the *descent walk down the hill to Dunkeld. lie at Mr *Mac-Glashin's* at *Inver*, wch is just over the Tay. see the Duke of Athol's garden, walk to the *Hermitage*, & the *Rumbling Brig*, but do not come too near it.

2^d day.

From Dunkeld to *Taymouth* (Ld Braidalbin's) 25 miles, on the South side of the Tay. lie at Mr *Campbell's*.

3^d day.

From Taymouth to the *Blair of Athol* 27 miles. come back the same road to *Taybridge*, & continue North of the Tay to *Logie-Rait*. ferry over the Tummel (see *Mr Robinson's of Fascley) go up that river to the *Pafs of Gilliecrankie* & along the Garry to Blair. lie at Mr Mac-Glashin's Sen:^r

4th day.

Return on the North side of the Tay to Dunkeld by the most beautiful of roads.

5th day.

Come back to Glammis. the road is every where excellent, except that between Taybridge & Logie-Rait.

[8] See Letter 116, n. 10.
[9] Mitford (Brit. Mus. *Add. MS.* 32561, f. 204) transcribed a note, with slight variations of expression and order: 'Advice to a friend travelling in Scotland. Don't scold at anyone especially at Gentlemen and Ladies. and ask your Landlord to help you off with the Wine. Say from a child you have eat no butter, and they won't rub it over your meat . . . put Marmalade on yr bread &c.'

APPENDIX R

*Mason's Ode on Dr. John Brown and Lord Chatham**

[Letters 424, 427]

IN a letter, which may be dated about 26 August 1766 (Letter 424), Gray wrote to Mason concerning an Ode which Mason had sent to him. The Ode was to be transcribed by Gray 'in a print-hand', and sent to Dr. G[isborne], who was to take steps for its publication. 'You are,' wrote Gray, 'wise as a serpent, but the devil of a dove, in timing both your satire and your compliment.' The Ode referred to a man who 'stands on the very verge of legislation,[1] with all his *unblushing* honours thick upon him; when the Gout has nip'd him in the bud and blasted all his hopes at least for one winter; then come you buzzing about his nose, and strike your sting deep into the reddest angriest part of his toe, wch will surely mortify.' The Ode alluded also to another man, who 'has been weak enough in the plenitude of power to disarm himself of his popularity; and to conciliate a court that naturally hates him, submits to be deck'd in their trappings and fondle their lap-dogs; then come you to lull him with your gentlest hum, recalling his good deeds, and *hoping* what I (with all my old partialities) scarce should dare to hope, if I had but any one else to put my trust in'. Mitford overlooked the fact that the letter alluded to two men, and carelessly identified the first, the object of Mason's satire, with Lord Chatham. It is clear that Chatham is the second, who has disarmed himself of his popularity by accepting a peerage. This conclusion is confirmed by the discovery of Mason's Ode, in which also the identity of the first man is revealed.

In the Poets' Corner of the *St. James's Chronicle* or the *British Evening Post* of 26 August to 28 August 1766, there is a poem entitled *Extract from an Ode to the Legislator Elect of Russia on his being prevented from entering on his high Office of Civilization by a Fit of the Gout*. Within the next few days the poem was published (with some stanzas omitted) in the *Public Advertiser*, in *Lloyd's Evening Post*, and in the *London Chronicle*.

That this was the poem which Mason sent to Gray is proved by a comparison of the text with passages in Gray's letter, while the similarity of the style[2] to that of Mason's later satirical poems con-

APPENDIX R.—* Reprinted with alterations and additions from *The Times Literary Supplement*, 24 Sept. 1931.
  [1] Mitford, who was the first to publish the letter in *Gray–Mason Correspondence*, pp. 353–5, misprinted 'dissolution' for 'legislation'.
  [2] The metre is the same as that of Mason's *Ode to Mr. Pinchbeck*.

firms the conclusion that he was the author. The subject of Gray's
first allusion in the opening stanzas of the Ode is now revealed, as
Dr. John Brown, 'the Legislator Elect of Russia'; Lord Chatham is
the subject of the last four stanzas.

The poem, in the fuller version, as it was printed in the *St. James's
Chronicle*, is as follows:

> OH thou! who thron'd in priestly State
> Once took the Pains to estimate
> Our Manners and our Times;[3]
> Who held the Scales, like Epic Jove,
> Thy Country's Nothingness to prove,
> Accept these homely Rhymes.
>
> Yet, pitying its *Etourderie*
> Did teach it what was Liberty,
> What License and what Faction;[4]
> And shew'd it plain, past all Dispute,
> That not t' obey the Nod of B[ute],
> Was a rebellious Action.
>
> * * * * *
>
> This Russia heard—I'm much to blame,
> 'Twas *all the Russias* heard thy Fame,
> And prick'd their flapping Ears;
> Sent Compliments, and humbly ask'd
> You'd condescend to take the Task
> Of taming their He-Bears.
>
> 'Their Bears (you cry'd) why be it so,
> 'A Bear 's a Beast, as Times now go,
> 'Better to tame than Man.
> 'Men I have try'd with Prose and Ode
> 'And now am drawing them a Code[5]—
> 'The Bears shall have the Plan.
>
> 'A Preacher national I rose,
> 'Demonstrating to Friends and Foes,
> 'Our Troops could only dance;
> 'Spite of my Proofs they drew their Swords
> 'And merely to gainsay my Words,
> 'They *almost* conquered *France*.

[3] In 1757 and 1758 Brown published the two volumes of his *Estimate of the Manners and Principles of the Times*.

[4] In 1765 Brown published a pamphlet: *Thoughts on Civil Liberty, Licentiousness and Faction*.

[5] Perhaps a reference to *Principles of Christian Legislation*, which Brown announced in 1766, but which was never published.

'Yet still was my Compassion shewn;
'To save their Credit and my own,
  'I bruited through the Nation,
'That all their enterprising Spirit
'Was owing to th' inspiring Merit
  'Of my bold Exhortation.

'Vain were my Words, the Rabble-rout
'Did only sneer, and gibe, and flout,
  'As if they thought I ly'd.
'Therefore I gave each Mother's Son
'Up, as I've given up W[arburton],[6]
  'And half my Friends beside.

'Now fly abroad, ye red-stamp'd Hosts!
'Ye Chronicles! Ye Ev'ning-posts!
  'Proclaim thro' all the Land,
'That I in Russia's Cause engage,
'Ye Curates! Guard my Vicarage
  'And eke my Gown and Band.'

      *   *   *   *   *

'Meanwhile, dread Empress! I to thee
'Will Solon, will Lycurgus be,
  'And Montesquieu[7] also.'
And scarce these Words were well got out,
When lo! a Dæmon, call'd the Gout,
  Did tweak him by the Toe.[8]

Come, Patience, come invok'd full oft,
And in our Aid bring Flannel soft,
  To wrap the peccant Member;
Else, Grief of Griefs! he cannot go;
For who would trust a gouty Toe
  In Russia in November.

Not go! avert it gracious Fate!
What, not to save the Russian State,
  And be a Legislator!
Old Cincinnatus left his Plough
Tho' he had pecks of Wheat to sow,
  When voted Rome's Dictator.

---

[6] Warburton had befriended Brown, but Brown had quarrelled with him, and with others of his friends.

[7] In the *Estimate* (vol. i, p. 12) Brown described Montesquieu as 'the greatest of political writers'.

[8] This is 'the diabolical part' of the ode referred to by Gray in his letter.

'But Cincinnatus was not lame,
'The Case you see is not the same,
  'And cannot be laid Stress on.'
Quote we then Pitt, who once had Worth
Was wise—a Patriot—and so forth
  E'en by your own Confession.

How oft has he on Crutches twain
Upborn, and in extremest Pain
  Limp'd to St. Stephen's Chapel;
There fought for many an aching Hour
'Gainst all the Myrmidons of Power,
  Who ne'er durst with him grapple.

Forgetting all his Spasms and Cramps,
He lately in th' Affair of Stamps,
  Spoke like a very Tully,
Preserv'd the Colonies, convey'd
Fresh Spirits to expiring Trade
  And did his Duty fully.

And still I'll hope,[9] though Fools may flout,
That this same Pitt in spite of Gout,
  And what is worse, of Peerage,
Will do his best to save from Fate
That leaky Skiff we call the State,
  Now he is at the Steerage.

The circumstances in which Dr. Brown undertook to propose a scheme of legislation for the Russian Empire were briefly as follows:[10] In 1764 Dr. Dumaresq, who had retired from the Chaplaincy of the British Embassy at St. Petersburg, was invited by the Empress Catherine to return and prepare schemes of education for Russia. After he had done so he found that he was expected to include in his survey of reform, matters military and naval, civil and commercial. He was daunted by the magnitude of his task, when he received a letter from a lady suggesting that he should ask Brown to assist him. Brown was willing enough, and in October 1765 wrote that he had for years turned his thoughts to the general subject of legislation, and he sketched at great length a plan of reforms. He offered, if his plan should be thought worthy of the attention of her Imperial Majesty, to take a voyage to Russia at the proper season of the year.

Of his high hopes at the prospect before him we have further

---

9 In his letter Gray speaks of Mason's 'recalling his good deeds, and *hoping* what I (with all my old partialities) scarce should dare to hope'.

10 The account of Brown's intended journey to Russia is mainly derived from *Biographia Britannica* (2nd ed., 1780, vol. ii, pp. 653 ff.).

information from a letter which he wrote to David Garrick on 19 January 1766:[11]

'I have lately been invited to assist in the civilization of a great empire. I have had letters from Russia, which do me more honour than I can pretend to deserve; but which I have answered in such a manner, as may probably carry me to Petersburgh in a summer or two. The Empress is aiming at great things, but seems to me to be wandering in the dark. I have sent a general sketch of a plan, which by this time is laid before her Imperial Majesty. Whether the whole, or any part of it, may be adopted, I cannot yet say: if it should, you will probably some time or other see "A System of Legislation for the Russian Empire".'

Brown had further correspondence with Dumaresq, and early in 1766 received an invitation to go to St. Petersburg. On his acceptance funds were placed at his disposal by the Russian Ambassador in London, and in the summer he made preparations for his voyage: a post-chaise and a travelling bed were bought, and a servant was engaged. He wrote again to Garrick a letter, which is wrongly dated in the *Garrick Correspondence*, but which was written a week before he was intending to start, at a date probably towards the end of July.[12] Garrick had warned him not to be impetuous. Brown quoted part of his letter to the Russian Prime Minister and continued:

'Prudence herself! in theory,—yet I know by experience, that I have an unconquerable tendency to bolt out truths, independent of the consequences they may produce. . . . As to the point you speak of: it would certainly be dangerous to carry it so far, as to think of removing the seat of empire. That is certainly too much to think of: but to re-instate the City of Moscow in some degree of spendour, and to make it one of the two seats of art and science, I think is not so dangerous a proposal. However, nothing of this kind will I say to any soul living but the Empress herself, and that with great caution. But let me be fairly at home again, and then if I do not tell them my mind at large, in a general and connected plan of legislation, may I be knouted to death by the Metropolitan of Novgorod or Moscow!'

The letter showed that Brown was not ignorant of the problems to be solved; but his hopes were doomed to disappointment. On the

---

[11] See the *Private Correspondence of David Garrick with the most celebrated Persons of his Time* (1831, vol. i, p. 220).

[12] The letter is printed with the date 'London, Saturday night, 26th Dec. 1762' (*op. cit.*, vol. i, p. 154). The month and year are obviously wrong. Panin, the Russian Prime Minister, had written to Brown from St. Petersburg on 3 June 1766. Brown had answered his letter, and was intending to start in a few days. 'Saturday, 26th' (if the day of the week and month are correct) might be 26 July 1766. If so, Brown expected to leave England early in August.

eve of his departure he was attacked by violent gout and rheumatism. His friends took alarm and persuaded him to give up his journey for the time. On 8 August he wrote to the Russian Ambassador to excuse his change of plans, and on the 28th he sent a voluminous letter to the Empress, which gave in detail his scheme of education. He was not destined to be the legislator of the Russian Empire; for three weeks he lived with his hopes shattered, his body suffering, and his mind dejected, and on 23 September he put an end to his life by cutting his throat with a razor.

The news of Brown's death caused serious concern to Mason, as we learn from a letter of Gray's written on 5 October[13] (Letter 427). Gray wrote to reassure Mason. He had heard the news from Stonhewer and had written to him to make further inquiries. 'I suspect he knows our secret,' he says, 'tho' not from me.' And Stonhewer could hear of no appearance or cause of discontent in Brown. Gray continues: 'I think we may fairly conclude that if he had had *any other* cause added to his constitutional infirmity, it would have been uppermost in his mind—he would have talk'd or raved about it.'

Gray then refers to a suggestion that Brown never meant to go to Russia, but that 'he might have engaged himself so far that he knew not how to draw back with honour; or might have received rough words from the Ruſsian minister, offended with his prevarication. This supposition is at least as likely as yours, . . . if it be neceſsary to ſuppose any other cause than the lunatick disposition of the man; and yet I will not disguise to you that I felt as you do on the first news of this sad accident, and had the same uneasy ideas about it.'

There can be little doubt that Mason's 'supposition' was that Brown, if he had not been driven to suicide by the Ode, might have talked of it in his madness. If so, there was a danger that the authorship of the poem ('our secret', as Gray calls it) might have been discovered. How Brown was affected by Mason's satire we cannot tell. Miss Elizabeth Carter, in a letter[14] after Brown's death, wrote: 'I think it is very probable that the *cruel sarcasms* which were thrown out against him in the papers might exasperate the sufferings of a disturbed mind.' The satirical ode, which had appeared in so many papers, may have been in her thoughts. But Brown survived its publication for three weeks, and it is not likely that it was the determining cause of his suicide.

[L. W.]

---

[13] Gray had receivèd a letter from Mason which is not extant. In Letter 428 Gray again alludes to Mason's uneasiness and reassures him.

[14] Quoted by Mitford in *Gray–Mason Correspondence*, 2nd ed., p. 525.

APPENDIX S

Gray and the Professorship of Modern History

[Letters 478, &c.]

In the year 1724 his Majesty King George the First founded Professorships of Modern History at Oxford and Cambridge. On 16 May the King wrote to the Vice-Chancellors of the Universities,[1] and after stating that 'no Encouragement or Provision has hitherto been made in either of the Said Universitys for the Study of Modern History or Modern Languages', and deploring the fact that 'Persons of Foreign Nations' were 'often employed in the Education and Tuition of Youth both at home and in their Travels', announced that he had 'determined to appoint two Persons of Sober Conversation and prudent Conduct, of the Degree of Master of Arts or Bachelor of Laws, or of Some higher Degree in one of the Said Universitys, Skilled in Modern History and in the knowledge of Modern Languages, one for the University of Cambridge, and the other for that of Oxford, who Shall be obliged to read Lectures in the Publick Schools, at Such times as shall hereafter be appointed'. Out of their stipends each of the professors was 'to maintain with sufficient Salarys, two Persons at least, well qualified to teach and instruct in writing and Speaking the Said Languages: which Said Teachers shall be under the Direction of the Professors respectively, and shall be obliged to instruct gratis in the Modern Languages twenty Scholars of each University, to be nominated by Us'[2]. The stress laid on the teaching of modern languages is to be noted: the Professorships were founded to qualify young men for the public service, either at home or abroad, by instructing them in two foreign languages.

The stipend for each of the Professors was to be four hundred pounds per annum,[3] and at Cambridge the Senate expressed the gratitude of the University in an address, which alluded to 'an

APPENDIX S.—[1] See *Endowments of the University of Cambridge*, edited by John Willis Clarke, pp. 183 ff., and Cooper, *Annals of Cambridge*, vol. iv, pp. 182 ff.

[2] The teachers received a stipend from the Professor and were expected to teach twenty scholars gratis, and other scholars for a fee. When Gray, in July 1737, wrote to Walpole of Professor Turner's list 'vastly near being full', he may be referring to the 'twenty scholars'. Gray himself paid a fee to Piazza, the Italian teacher (Letter 29), who also instructed Cole and Walpole.

[3] The stipend of £400 was apparently liable to deductions. In the case of the Professorship at Oxford it is stated that it was 'reduced by fees of office to £371'. In the account of money due to Gray in Mar. 1771 the amount of £180 14s. may have represented half a year's income, after the deduction of such fees or of

Appendix S

appointment so ample, as well nigh to equal the Stipends of all our other Professors put together.'

On 28 September 1724 the Regius Professorship of Modern History was established at Cambridge; Samuel Harris, M.A., Fellow of Peterhouse, was appointed the first Professor, and delivered an inaugural lecture in Latin.[4] There is no evidence that, with this exception, he 'read lectures in the publick schools', but teachers of French and Italian, F. Masson and H. B. Piazza, were appointed and paid by him. The two Professors that followed, Shallet Turner and Brockett, did not regard their duties more seriously.[5]

Gray was qualified by his study of history to be Professor, and his knowledge of French and Italian fitted him to superintend the teaching of those languages. The Professorship became the object of his desire for nearly twenty years before he was appointed to hold it. At a date, which may be as early as 1748 and cannot be later than 1751 (Letter 147*, n. 1), on a false report of Professor Turner's death, Gray was hoping that his name might be put forward for consideration: 'I certainly might ask it with as much, or more Propriety, than any one in this Place', he wrote to Chute. He was regarded by others as a possible candidate, and in 1759 he wrote to Brown (Letter 294): 'Old Turner is very declining, & I was sounded by D^r G[reen] of Lincoln about my designs (or so I understood it). I afsured him I should not *ask* for it, not chusing to be refused.' In 1762, when Turner actually died, Gray had his name suggested to Lord Bute (Letter 363), but the post went to Brockett.

The circumstances of his appointment to succeed Brockett at the end of July 1768 are made clear in his letters at the time (Letters 477* ff.). The offer came to him 'unsolicited and unexpected' as he wrote to the Duke of Grafton (Letter 478). As the appointment rested with the Crown, Gray went to Court to kiss hands (Letter 483, n. 1): and on 9 September he was sworn and admitted to his office (Letter 485, n. 5).

The Professorship was subject to the conditions prescribed in the

taxes. The £2 2s. 'given to Mr Barber' was probably the customary payment to the Treasury official, who paid over the money.

[4] The lecture was printed (see *Historical Register of the University of Cambridge*, p. 88, n. 5).

[5] Cole, in his *Athenæ Cantabrigienses* (*Add. MS.* 5882), says of Shallet Turner: 'He never resided in the University, but only occasionally with Dr. Smith at Trinity College Lodge, being a great Acquaintance. As to reading Lectures, he never thought it incumbent upon him to do so: but allowed some small Pittance to the French and Italian Teachers in the University. I have often heard my old Italian Master Signor Piazza complain of him for the exility of his exhibition to him.'

1254

Appendix S

Statute by which it was created: the requirement that the Professor should read 'lectures in the publick schools at such times as shall hereafter be appointed' had not been defined; the former holders of the office had apparently given no lectures. At the outset Gray could not have been overburdened by a sense of the duties incumbent upon him. It must have come as an unpleasant surprise, when, within a few weeks of his appointment, he learnt (as he no doubt did) that the question of the duties to be attached to the Professorship of Modern History at Oxford had been raised in that University.

On 20 August 1768 Joseph Spence, who had been the Professor since 1742, died (Letter 485, n. 6). He had held the Professorship without lecturing or even residing in Oxford. This was apparently regarded as an abuse, and before his successor was appointed the Vice-Chancellor summoned the Heads of Houses to meet on 3 September, when a memorandum was drawn up for submission to the King.[6] It began as follows:

'The Vice-Chancellor, senior Proctor and twelve Heads of Colleges and Halls (being all that are present this day in the University) humbly conceive that it might be of signal service to the nation, if his Majesty would graciously be pleas'd to order that all his future Professors in Modern History should be subject to some such restrictions as the following. . . .'

The 'restrictions' required residence in full term, a course of fifty lectures in the year, and a payment of £100 a year to be divided between the teachers of modern languages. The Memorandum was submitted to the King, who, before the end of September, 'Signified his intentions that this office should never any more be held as a sinecure'.[7]

The Lords of the Treasury included Cambridge in the consideration of the duties to be expected from the Professors, and the Oxford memorandum was therefore submitted to Gray, as well as to the Rev. John Vivian, of Balliol College, who had been designated to succeed Spence. Vivian and Gray were apparently invited to submit their 'Proposals' for the conditions to be imposed upon the Professors.

Vivian's Proposal suggested considerable modifications of the conditions: a public lecture once a term, residence sufficient to direct the study of his pupils, and a reduction of the pay proposed for the teachers in French and Italian to £20 each. What happened at

[6] The memorandum together with the 'Proposals' of Mr. Vivian and Mr. Gray (in their own hands) are among the Liverpool Papers in the British Museum (*Add. MS.* 38334, ff. 149 ff.). Charles Jenkinson, afterwards first Earl of Liverpool, was at this time a Lord of the Treasury.

[7] Quoted from a letter of the Duke of Grafton to Bishop Warburton (see n. 8).

Oxford must be taken into account, so far as it may have affected Gray. The course of events at Oxford is not clear, and there are problems connected with it which have not been solved.[8] It appears that Vivian's answer did not satisfy the authorities at Oxford and that his appointment was held in abeyance so long as he declined to accept the stipulated conditions. For more than a year after the vacancy had occurred, he was hoping that the conditions might be relaxed, and he stood out against them until February 1770. Then he seems to have become *de facto* Professor[9] on terms that are not known; his formal appointment cannot be traced in the *Gazette* and is not recorded in the archives of the University.[10]

'Mr. Gray's Proposal is as follows:

'1. That the Profeſsor shall apply to the several Heads of Colleges, & desire them to recommend one or more young Gentlemen, who shall be instructed without expence in some of the modern languages, & attend such lectures as He shall give. the number (if each smaller College send one, and the larger two) will amount in the University of Cambridge to nineteen.

'2. That the Prof.^r shall nominate & pay two Præceptors, qualified to instruct these Scholars in the French & Italian tongues.

'3. That he shall reside the half of every Term at least in the University (wch half-terms at Cambridge make about a hundred & ten days, almost one third of the year) & shall read publickly once at least in every Term a lecture on modern History to his Scholars, & any others, that shall be present.

'4. That He shall besides at short & regular intervals give private lectures to his Scholars on the same subject, prescribe a method of study, direct them in their choice of Authors, & from time to time enquire into the progreſs they have made in the Italian & French tongues.

'5. That if he neglect these duties, he shall be subject to the same pecuniary mulcts, that other Profeſsors are according to Statute.'

[8] Besides the 'memorandum' and 'Mr. Vivian's Proposal' there are in the Liverpool Papers two letters from Vivian to Charles Jenkinson and a copy of Jenkinson's answer to the second letter (all three letters written in Nov. 1769) on the subject of the proposed regulations for the Professorship (*Add. MS.* 3826, ff. 143, 157). In Nichols's *Literary Anecdotes*, vol. v, pp. 655 ff., there are letters from Warburton to Thomas Warton, who was a candidate for the Professorship, written between 1768 and 1771, with a letter from the Duke of Grafton to Warburton, and a letter from Warburton to Archbishop Cornwallis, all referring to the Professorship.

[9] This is inferred from a letter of 22 Feb. 1770 from Warburton to Thomas Warton referring to the disappointment of his hopes and implying that Vivian was now Professor.

[10] Mr. Gibson, Keeper of the Archives at Oxford, states that: 'Officially Professor John Vivian has no existence. I can find no reference to him in the Archives in connexion with the Professorship.'

Appendix S

No indication of date is given on the 'Proposals' of Vivian or Gray: it is reasonable to infer that they were sent to the Treasury not long after the memorandum of the Oxford Vice-Chancellor had been 'received. This inference is confirmed by a statement of Mason (*Memoirs*, p. 397) that Gray 'drew up, and laid before the Duke of Grafton, just then chosen Chancellor of the University, three different schemes[11] for regulating the method of choosing pupils privately to be instructed by him'. If 'Mr. Gray's Proposal' was one of these schemes, the date would be fixed as soon after the Duke's election as Chancellor at the end of November 1768.

Gray had been appointed Professor under the Statute governing the Professorship at the time. He could not be made liable to fresh requirements imposed after he had been appointed. But he must have known that the acceptance of such requirements was a condition precedent to the appointment of a Professor at Oxford. His conscience was sensitive and he felt ill at ease. He had an enthusiasm in imparting his knowledge to individual pupils, as he showed in his converse with Norton Nicholls and Bonstetten, but the idea of giving public lectures must have been abhorrent to him.

He set himself to compose an inaugural lecture: Mason tells us (*Memoirs*, p. 396) that: 'immediately on his appointment, he sketched out an admirable plan for his inauguration speech, . . . and also wrote the Exordium of this Thesis.' The plan and the exordium are preserved in copies made by Mitford[12]; the plan consists of lists, one of 'Preparations and accompanyments' for the study of history (Geography, Chronology, Languages, Moneys, Antiquities, Law and Government, Manners and Education), the other of 'Sources of History' (Public Papers, Treaties, Letters of Princes and Ministers, &c.,

[11] It does not seem altogether probable that Gray submitted three different schemes to the Duke of Grafton. It might have been merely an inference from the fact that Mason found three drafts among Gray's papers. Nor need much importance be attached to Mason's statement that one of Gray's schemes 'was so much approved as to be sent to Oxford, in order to be observed by the new Professor then appointed in that place'. Mason (*Memoirs*, p. 398) quotes part of one of Gray's 'schemes' which must have been very different from his 'Proposal'. In this he discusses the value of 'public lectures': 'Lectures read in public are generally things of more ostentation than use; yet if indeed they should gradually swell into a book, and the Author should find reason to hope they might deserve the attention of the public, it is possible they might become of general service; of this we have already some instances, as Judge Blackstone's Lectures on The Common-Law, and the Bishop of Oxford's on Hebrew Poetry.'

[12] In Mitford's Note Book, vol. iii (Brit. Mus. *Add. MS.* 32561, ff. 170 ff.). In the Sale of 1851 one of the volumes of MSS. (Lot 53) included: *First Draft of a Latin Composition for his inauguration speech.*

Appendix S

Private Correspondence, Memoirs, Chronicles, Monkish Historians, with some indications of the methods of criticism). Of 'History itself', which forms a third heading, no details are given. The lists are sufficient to suggest the broad scope and the thorough method which Gray had in mind for the study. Of his 'inauguration speech' Mason says that Gray was at liberty to read it either in Latin or English: he 'chose the former, and I think rather injudiciously; because, tho' no man, in the earlier part of his life, was more ready in Latin composition, he had now lost the habit, and might therefore well have excused himself, by the nature of his subject, from any superadded difficulty of language.' The fragment of his speech confirms Mason's opinion. Gray had forgotten much of his Latin, there are errors of grammar; he was obviously embarrassed in expressing his thoughts, and as may happen in the difficulty of presenting ideas in a strange idiom, the thoughts themselves tended to be trite. He cannot have been satisfied with the composition, and probably on this account broke off at an early stage.

There is no evidence that Gray, as Professor, ever gave a lecture, public or private. He regarded residence in the University as a duty of his office;[13] he reappointed René la Butte[14] and Agostino Isola,[15] who had previously been the teachers of French and Italian; he may have supervised the studies of the young men who were studying history or modern languages. But he does not seem to have done more than his predecessors; and his professorship remained little more than a sinecure. So Bonstetten regarded it, who wrote to his mother: 'Le Roi lui a donné une pension de 400 guinées sous le titre de professeur en histoire moderne' (Appendix V).

Gray had an uneasy sense that he was failing in his duty. He wrote to Nicholls in March 1770: 'my own employment so sticks in my stomach, & troubles my conscience' (Letter 513), and a year later

[13] He wrote to Beattie on 31 Oct. 1768 (Letter 487), after mentioning his Professorship: 'As I lived here before from choice, I shall now continue to do so from obligation.'

[14] René la Butte, a native of Angers in Anjou, came to England as a printer and in 1744 went to Cambridge to work on the *Cambridge Journal*. Through the influence of Conyers Middleton he was appointed teacher of French, and continued to teach until his death in 1790.

[15] Agostino Isola, a refugee from Milan, was appointed teacher of Italian and Spanish in 1764 (*Cambridge Chronicle*, 3 Mar. 1764): he died in 1797, aged 84. See *The Letters of Charles Lamb, with a sketch of his Life*, by Thomas Noon Talfourd (1837), vol. ii, p. 141: 'Agostino Isola had been compelled to fly from Milan, because a friend took up an English book in his apartment, which he had carelessly left in view. This good old man numbered among his pupils Gray the poet, Mr. Pitt, and in his old age Wordsworth whom he instructed in the language.'

he wrote, also to Nicholls, of 'the sense of my own duty, which I do not perform' (Letter 552). Mason (*Memoirs*, pp. 398–9) states: 'Certain it is, that notwithstanding his ill health, he constantly intended to read lectures; and I remember the last time he visited me at Aston, in the summer of the year 1770, he expressed much chagrin on this subject, and even declared it to be his stedfast resolution to resign his Professorship, if he found himself unable to do real service in it. What I said to dissuade him from this, . . . had, I found, so little weight with him, that I am almost persuaded he would very soon have put this intention into execution. But death prevented the trial.'

No doubt Gray's ill health and the low spirits that it caused were in great part responsible for his lack of energy, but he was too old to turn himself to work to which he was unwonted, and he could not give to others the stores of knowledge that he had amassed for himself.

[L. W.]

APPENDIX T

*Gray's Verses on Lord Holland's Villa at Kingsgate**

[Letter 489]

WRITING to Mason on 29 December 1768 (Letter 489), Gray begins: 'Oh wicked Scroddles! there you have gone & told my *Arcanum Arcanorum* to that leaky Mortal Palgrave.' Mitford, in his note (*Gray–Mason Correspondence*, p. 425) said: 'This *arcanum arcanorum* must be an allusion to the lines written in 1766, on Lord Holland's villa at Kingsgate.' He had been informed by Sir Egerton Brydges (*Works*, 1835–43, vol. i, p. ciii) that the lines were written when Gray was on a visit to Mr. Robinson, at Denton, 'and found in the drawer of Gray's dressing table after he was gone. They were restored to him; for he had no other copy, and had forgotten them.'

Mitford was no doubt right in concluding that the arcanum referred to the verses on Lord Holland's villa, but wrong in following the tradition that they were written in 1766: they were almost certainly written in the summer of 1768, some six months before the date of the letter to Mason quoted above. Gray stayed with his friend William Robinson, at Denton in Kent, in the summers of both 1766 and 1768.

APPENDIX T.—* Reprinted, with alterations and additions, from *The Times Literary Supplement*, 9. Oct. 1930.

Appendix T

In referring to his visit in 1766, he wrote to Norton Nicholls (Letter 422): 'I did *not* go to Kingsgate, because it belong'd to my Ld Holland.' In 1768, as he wrote to Wharton (Letter 480), he passed a good part of the summer in Kent. He stayed at Ramsgate and, a fortnight later, at Denton (Letter 480, n. 1); and it may be reasonably assumed that it was at this time that he went to Kingsgate, and was moved by the sight of the villa[1] to write the verses. Another consideration, which supports this conclusion, is that in May 1767 Lord Holland wrote verses, entitled *Lord Holland returning from Italy 1767*,[2] which were privately printed in a broad-sheet. Gray had heard one line of these verses in June 1767 (Letter 443), and, within a little while, no doubt, saw the whole poem. There are allusions in Gray's verses which imply a knowledge of what Holland wrote.

The reason why Gray's editors attached the date of 1766 to his verses is obvious. Mason printed in the *Memoirs* part of a letter to Wharton, dated 26 August 1766, which referred to Gray's visit to Denton in that year (Letter 423), but did not print the letter which mentioned his stay in Kent in 1768 (Letter 480). In default of other evidence it was natural to assume that Gray wrote the verses in 1766. Their first appearance in print was in 1769 (as is explained below), but this was generally overlooked, and when the verses were sent to the *Gentleman's Magazine*,[3] some in 1777 and others in 1778, they were described as 'stanzas suggested by a view, in 1766, of the late Lord H——d's seat and ruins at Kingsgate'. Stephen Jones, who edited Gray's *Poetical Works* in 1799, and again in an 'enlarged and improved edition' in 1800, followed the text of the *Gentleman's Magazine*, (with some small variations in the edition of 1800). He printed as a title *Stanzas* (in 1800 *Impromptu*), *suggested by a View, in 1766, of the Seat and Ruins of a deceased Nobleman, at Kingsgate Kent*. The title could not have been chosen by Gray, who died three years before Lord Holland. Mitford adopted the title and the text as printed by Stephen Jones, and later editors have generally followed him.

They have overlooked the fact that the verses had been printed in Gray's lifetime, with a different title, and with variations in the

---

[1] Lord Holland's villa at Kingsgate was built in imitation of Cicero's villa at Baiæ, and the grounds were ornamented with sham ruins (see Tovey, *Gray's Poems*, p. 275).

[2] See J. H. Jesse, *George Selwyn and his Contemporaries* (1843), vol. ii, pp. 162, 163, where the verses are printed.

[3] The first three stanzas were printed in vol. xlvii (1777), p. 624, and the others in vol. xlviii (1778), part 2, p. 88. J. Nichols in *Select Collection of Miscellaneous Poems* (1780–2), vol. viii, p. 350, published a text almost identical with that in the *Gentleman's Magazine*.

text, which may be regarded as giving a more accurate version of what Gray wrote. Gray regarded the verses as his '*arcanum arcanorum*', but he made them known to some of his friends.[4] There is a copy of them in Wharton's hand,[5] with the title, 'On L^d H——d^s Seat near M——e. K^t'. He must have received the text from Gray, and it may be regarded as authentic. It need not be supposed that Wharton betrayed the secret, but from one or other of Gray's friends copies of the verses must have got abroad, and in 1769 *The New Foundling Hospital for Wit* (vol. iii, pp. 34–5)[6] published the verses, without the author's name, with the title 'Inscription for the Villa of a decayed Statesman on the Sea Coast'. The text varied very little from that of Wharton's copy.

It is strange that Wharton's copy, which may be accepted as giving Gray's own text, has not been preferred to the version of Stephen Jones. There are variants, some of which are noted below. One that is important deserves a separate consideration. In the fifth stanza Wharton's copy has:

> Ah, said the sighing Peer, had Bute been true,
> Nor Shelburn's, Rigby's, Calcrofts [*sic*] friendship vain.

The *New Foundling Hospital for Wit* had the same names, but the other printed versions had either blanks or various initials. Stephen Jones, after giving blanks in his first edition (1799), in his second (1800) printed: 'Nor M——'s, R——'s, B——'s', without explanation. Mitford, in his Aldine edition of Gray's *Poems*,[7] gave a note: 'These intitials stand for "Mungo's, Rigby's, Bradshaw's." See Heroic Epistle, v, 95.' Most editors since Mitford have printed these names in full. The initials and Mitford's identifications have no authority and cannot be right.[8] But Lord Holland in the verses, to which

---

[4] William Cole (Brit. Mus. *Add. MS.* 5821, f. 55) had a copy of the poem, with a note: 'These Verses on Lord Holland are said to have been composed by Mr Gray. Dr Glynn dictated them to me at Milton, May 1. 1777.'

[5] In the Egerton MS. 2400 with Gray's letters to Wharton, and manuscripts, in Gray's or Wharton's hand, of others of Gray's poems. Tovey read 'near W——e' in the title and interpreted it as Westgate, but Wharton wrote 'M——e' (i.e. Margate).

[6] There are allusions to the publication of the verses in Walpole's letter to Mason of 1 Dec. 1773, and in Mason's letter to Walpole of 17 June 1775 (*Walpole–Mason Correspondence*, vol. i, pp. 109, 195).

[7] *Works*, 1835–43, vol. i, p. 162. In his editions of the *Poems* of 1814 and 1816 Mitford had left the initials unexplained.

[8] The fact that Mason in the *Heroic Epistle* (written in 1773) happened to combine these names is no reason why Gray should have selected them. Tovey (*Gray's Poems*, pp. 74–5) (who otherwise followed Mitford's text) printed 'Shelburne's, Rigby's, Calcraft's', and argued (*op. cit.*, p. 276) that it is unlikely that Gray would attack

reference is made above, after an allusion to 'White-liver'd Grenville and self-loving Gower', chose for denunciation Rigby, Shelburne, and Calcraft. This confirms the text of Wharton's copy, and is evidence that Gray had Lord Holland's verses in his mind. The text of the verses in Wharton's copy is as follow:

On L⁴ H——dˢ Seat near M——e. K⁴
Old and abandon'd by each venal friend
Here H. took the pious resolution
To smuggle some few years and strive to mend
A broken character and constitution.
On this congenial spot he fix'd his choice,
    Earl Godwin trembled for his neighbouring sand,
Here Seagulls scream and cormorants rejoice,
    And Mariners tho' shipwreckt dread to land,
Here reign the blustring north and blighting east,
    No tree is heard to whisper, bird to sing,
Yet nature cannot furnish out the feast,
    Art he invokes new horrors still to bring.
Now mouldring fanes and battlements arise,
    Arches and turrets nodding to their fall,
Unpeopled palaces delude his eyes,
    And mimick desolation covers all.
Ah, said the sighing Peer, had Bute been true
    Nor Shelburn's, Rigby's, Calcrofts [*sic*] friendship vain
Far other scenes than these had bless'd our view
    And realis'd the ruins⁹ that we feign.
Purg'd by the sword and beautifyed¹⁰ by fire,
    Then had we seen proud London's hated walls,
Owls might have hooted in S⁴ Peters Quire,
    And foxes stunk and litter'd in S⁴ Pauls.

[L. W.]

those whom Mason called 'the minor plunderers of the age', and showed that 'Mungo' (as a nickname of Dyson), could not have been used before 1769.

⁹ Gray is describing the sham ruins at Kingsgate (see n. 1), and four lines above refers to 'mimick desolation'. He must have written 'ruins that we feign' and not 'beauties', which Stephen Jones, Mitford, and other editors have printed.

¹⁰ The commonly accepted reading is

Purg'd by the sword and purify'd by fire.'

Wharton's version is to be preferred. Gray is not likely to have written 'purg'd' and 'purify'd' in the same line.

APPENDIX U

Gray's Property in Hand Alley, Bishopsgate[1]

[Letters 439, 479]

ANN ROGERS, widow of Jonathan Rogers and aunt of Thomas Gray, at the time of her death in September 1758, was the owner of a ' Moiety of certain Messuages . . . and Premises in Hand Alley, in the parish of Saint Botolph Without, Bishopsgate'. The owner of the other moiety was Mr. Joseph Eyre, who is referred to in Gray's letters as 'Mr Eyres'.[2] By her will, dated 9 June 1757 and proved 6 October 1758, Mrs. Rogers left one moiety of this moiety to her nephew, Thomas Gray, and the other moiety of this moiety to her sister, Mrs. Jane Olliffe, for her life, and after her death to her nephew Robert Antrobus, his heirs and assigns.

Robert Antrobus, who was apparently an attorney at Great Hadham, Herts., died in March 1767. A will executed by him on 26 December 1765 left the reversion of the property in Hand Alley to his wife, Elizabeth Antrobus, for her life, and after her death to his sisters, Mary and Dorothy Antrobus. This will was proved in London on 3 April 1767. But he had realized, before he died, that he was indebted 'to divers and sundry Persons in several considerable sums of money', and made another will on 5 September 1766. This will was proved in London on 23 April 1767, 'probate of a will granted in the same month having been first brought in and declared null and void'.

Under his later will he left his freehold property in Great Hadham (subject to a mortgage held by his aunt Mrs. Jane Olliffe),[3] and the reversion of the property in Hand Alley to his sister Dorothy Antrobus and his 'good friend Robert Markland of Aldermanbury London Esq.' upon trust to sell these properties, and out of the money realized from them and from his other effects, to pay his debts, the residue to be paid to his wife. Dorothy Antrobus and Robert Markland were appointed joint executors.

Since the death of Mrs. Rogers, Gray and Mrs. Olliffe had enjoyed

APPENDIX U.—[1] Mr. George Tull, of the Solicitor's Department of the Port of London Authority, kindly supplied information as to the transfer of this property under the Deeds, which are quoted below.

[2] Joseph Eyre ultimately, in conjunction with Thomas Aylmer, became the purchaser of the moiety in which Gray and his relatives were interested.

[3] Mrs. Olliffe is described in the will as 'of Great Hadham', and may have been living with Robert Antrobus.

the income from their shares in the Hand Alley houses. It must have been a complicated business to manage their 'moieties of a moiety'. In Gray's pocket-diary of the year 1760[4] there are entries of payments to workmen, and commissions due to Worlidge,[5] and in a letter, which Gray wrote to Mary Antrobus in May 1767 (Letter 439), he gives a list of thirteen tenants with details of 'tax allowed', and a mention of 'M[r] Eyres', to whom a bill was due, and of a conveyance, which Worlidge ought to have got ready.[6]

In 1768 Gray was taking steps for the sale of the property, probably on behalf of Dorothy Antrobus and Robert Markland, the trustees of the will of Robert Antrobus, as well as for himself and Mrs. Olliffe. On 29 July he wrote to Mary Antrobus (Letter 479): 'I have found a man who has brought M[r] Eyres (I think) up to my price in a hurry; however he defers his final answer till Wednesday next. He shall not have it a shilling lower, I promise; and if he hesitates, I will rise upon him like a fury.'

The different stages in the transfer of the property are shown in documents now in the possession of the Port of London Authority. From these it appears that:

1. On 17 September 1768 a Deed of Transfer was executed, by which 'Henley and others representing William Singleton' conveyed the property to Gray and Mrs. Olliffe and to Dorothy Antrobus and Robert Markland. The explanation of this Deed appears to be that the property had not, up to this time, been legally transferred to Mrs. Rogers or her heirs. It is to this conveyance that Gray referred in his letter to Mary Antrobus of May 1767.

2. On 22 September Dorothy Antrobus, Robert Markland, and Mary Antrobus[7] sold their reversion to Joseph Eyre and Thomas Aylmer for £600.

3. On 14 and 15 November 'Deeds of Lease and Release' were signed by Thomas Gray by which his moiety of a moiety was transferred to Joseph Eyre and Thomas Aylmer for 1,000 guineas.

4. 15 November Mrs. Olliffe executed a 'Deed of Release' of her life interest in her Moiety of a Moiety for an Annuity of £80 a year.

---

[4] The diary is at Pembroke College, Cambridge.

[5] The will of Mrs. Rogers was witnessed by Philip and John Worlidge. It is a reasonable assumption that one of these is referred to by Gray, and that he was a solicitor acting for Gray and Mrs. Olliffe.

[6] What this conveyance was appears from the Deed of 17 Sept. 1768, referred to below.

[7] Mary Antrobus had no interest in the reversion. She was perhaps joined in the transfer to guard against any possible claim, owing to the terms of the earlier will of Robert Antrobus.

Appendix U

These transactions and their results are illustrated by letters of Gray to Norton Nicholls. On 8 November 1768 he wrote (Letter 488): 'So now I am going up to Town about my business, w^ch (if I dispatch to my mind) will leave me at rest, & with a tolerably easy temper for one while.' And on 2 January 1769 he wrote from Cambridge (Letter 490): 'Here am I once again, & have sold my estate, & got a thousand guineas, & fourscore pound a year for my old Aunt.'

Joseph Eyre, who had owned one moiety of the property in Hand Alley, and Thomas Aylmer, were thus the purchasers of the other moiety, and on 19 December 1768 they conveyed the whole property to the East India Company. From the Company, in course of time, it passed into the possession of the Port of London Authority, the present owners.

[L. W.]

APPENDIX V

Letter of Bonstetten to his Mother

PRINTED from a transcript kindly supplied by M. Frédéric Dominicé of Geneva, owner of the original. Extracts from the letter were printed in *The Times* of 12 Apr. 1929.

[P. T.]

[Letter 512]

de Cambridge 6 Février[1] 1770

Vous voulez donc, ma très chère Mère, que j'aille à Paris. Vous vous imaginez, sans doute, que je sais encore faire la révérence, saluer une jolie femme.—

L'on ne fait rien de tout cela à Cambridge, des traits allongés et roides, une démarche empesée et mesurée, des saluts avec le chapeau sur la tête, voilà ce que dans la patrie de Newton on appelle être décent.[2] L'on ne se voit ici qu'en cérémonie, l'on fait demander le matin la permission de se voir, le soir, ce sont des visites qui ressemblent assez à nos visites de 3 à 4. Vous trouverez trois ou quatre dames assises sur des chaises, des hommes en grandes robes noires occupent les canapés et les fauteuils, l'on entre en tirant le chapeau et en saluant chacun avec un: Votre serviteur, Monsieur; Votre serviteur, Madame. Tenir le chapeau sous le bras, avoir l'air riant, dire un compliment bien tourné à une dame, croiser les jambes, adresser ce que nous appelons des honnêtetés aux hommes, relever

APPENDIX V.—[1] Bonstetten had been in Cambridge since about 21 Dec. 1769 (see Letter 512, n. 1).

[2] See Bonstetten's description of Cambridge in his *Souvenirs*, quoted in Letter 512, n. 1.

un mouchoir tombé, prendre la tasse d'une femme, serait ici les manières du monde les plus ridicules et les plus indécentes; j'avais quelques fois des mouvements de tout cela, mais je les réprimais bien vite, de crainte que l'on me prît pour un sapajou bien dressé. En France et chez nous le silence dans un cercle est la chose du monde la plus embarrassante, j'en ai vu quelquefois qui causait des sueurs froides aux gens de la maison, nous n'avons pas honte de rompre un tel silence par un propos plat, ou par un . . . il fait bien beau temps. . . . Ce n'est qu'en Angleterre que l'on sait se taire; j'ai vu une quinzaine de personnes, hommes et femmes, assis en cercle, ne se rien dire durant un grand quart d'heure. On n'avait point cet air embarrassé que l'on aurait ailleurs dans une pareille situation, on ne le rompait point pour le rompre, mais parce que réellement on avait quelque chose à se dire. Vous pensez bien ma très chère mère, que ces personnes ont aussi une autre sorte d'esprit, un autre goût, une manière différente de penser et de sentir. Le genre d'esprit qui plaît le plus, c'est ce qu'ils appellent *humour*, il ne consiste pas à dire des saillies mais à voir les choses sous un point de vue nouveau, et cela dépend plus de la singularité du caractère que de la fécondité de l'esprit. Ils ont des auteurs pleins d'esprit, à qui ils n'accordent pas ce talent, tandis qu'il y en a sans esprit, fort admirés pour leur humour. Leur Congrève est plein d'esprit, leur Shakespear n'en a jamais, mais de l'humour dans toutes les scènes comiques.—

Je vous demande sincèrement pardon, ma très chère mère, de vous avoir parlé comme si vous entendiez l'anglais, mais vous me permettrez de ne pas déchirer cette longue page pour quelques mots.—Mon père sait sans doute le changement de Ministère et la chute du Duc de Grafton,[3] Milord Chatam remontera au premier grade dont un caprice l'avait fait descendre.[4] Mr. Norton le père[5] est Speaker ou Orateur de la chambre basse et ne tardera pas à avoir un titre, c'est le premier homme de loi. L'on a fait l'autre jour un membre pour le Comté[6] de Cambridge, je fus à l'élection, l'on me fit tous les honneurs que l'on pouvait accorder à un étranger.

---

[3] The Chatham–Grafton administration (July 1766–Jan. 1770) came to an end with the resignation of the Duke of Grafton on 28 Jan. 1770. A new administration was formed by Lord North in February.
[4] Chatham, who had been Lord Privy Seal, had resigned in Oct. 1768; he did not again take office.
[5] Fletcher Norton, who had been Attorney-General in the Grenville administration, was elected Speaker of the House of Commons on 22 Jan. 1770. His eldest son, William, was at this time Minister to the Swiss Cantons (1765–74); hence Bonstetten's reference to the Speaker as 'Mr. Norton le père'.
[6] Not the county, but the University.

Appendix V

Mr. le Vice Chancelier[7] préside dans sa robe pourpre et son mantelet d'hermine, les maîtres ès-arts écrivent leur suffrage et leur nom sur des petits billets qu'ils vont remettre à la table qui est devant le Chancelier.[8] Mr. de Gray, Procureur général,[9] fut élu; il était recommandé par le Duc de Grafton, l'Université qui suit aveuglément la volonté de la cour se vit presque embarrassée apprenant la veille même de l'élection la chute du Ministre. Les maîtres des collèges me traitèrent à tour; l'on est servi par des étudiants en grandes robes noires, à manches traînantes, dans des grandes salles gothiques. Dimanche je fus invité chez le Chancelier,[10] il n'y a pas de nation au monde plus hospitalière. L'amitié de Mr. Gray pour moi fait que tout le monde s'empresse à m'obliger; c'est certainement le premier écrivain et le premier poète de l'Angleterre. Le Roi lui a donné une pension de 400 guinées sous le titre de professeur en histoire moderne.[11] Je mange tous les jours chez lui, il vit fort retiré et a la bonté de témoigner un grand plaisir à me voir. Je vais chez lui à toute heure, il lit avec moi ce que je veux, je travaille dans sa chambre; pour m'amuser nous lisons de l'histoire naturelle. Ainsi je crois n'avoir point transgressé les ordres de mon père en donnant quelques semaines de plus au premier homme de mérite de ce pays. D'ailleurs que je ne pourrai jamais mieux employer mon temps que je ne le fais. Je ne m'arrêterai à Londres que pour aller au Parlement avec Mr. Pitt[12] et chez quelques seigneurs qui ont eu des bontés pour moi et qui, pour être attachés au nouveau Ministère ont perdu leur place; on trouverait très mauvais que je ne fisse pas des visites. Milord Huntington,[13] chez qui je devais aller à la campagne, a perdu sa place de grand-maître de la garderobe qui lui rapportait 3000 guinées, ce qui lui aidait à vivre, comme on parle ici. Mon père a toujours des Anglais l'idée des jeunes fous que nous voyons chez nous. Mr. Gray dit qu'il faut juger les anglais chez eux. J'ai vu des jeunes gens qui vivent depuis 10 ans à Londres, penser de même, mais je n'en étais pas surpris. Il y a mille étrangers à Londres qui ne con-

7 William Richardson, D.D., Master of Emmanuel College.

8 A mistake for Vice-Chancellor.

9 Sir William de Grey, who in Aug. 1766 had succeeded Charles Yorke as Attorney-General, was elected M.P. for the University of Cambridge on 1 Feb. 1770, to fill the vacancy caused by the appointment in January of Charles Yorke as Lord Chancellor.

10 Again a mistake for Vice-Chancellor.

11 See Appendix S.

12 Thomas Pitt, of Boconnoc (see Letter 250, n. 12). Nicholls had introduced Bonstetten to him (see Letter 508).

13 Francis Hastings, tenth Earl of Huntingdon; on the change of ministry he lost his office of Groom of the Stole, which he had held since 1761.

naissent pas un Anglais, ou qui ne voyent que les gens à mœurs françaises, tant tous les rapports des étrangers sont toujours suspects et tant il est difficile de voir au delà de ses propres mœurs.—Je vous rends mille grâces ma très chère Mère des vœux que vous daignez faire pour moi et de la bénédiction que vous me donnez; je me mets à deux genoux pour la recevoir, comme les enfants de cette Angleterre si prophane aux yeux de mon Père. Je suis fâché que vous ayez des regrets de me voir abandonner mon projet, je n'en ai pas moi, j'ai commencé à m'en consoler d'avance, c'est ce que je tâche de faire dans tout ce que j'entreprends afin de retomber sur mes pieds. Il y avait plus d'inconvénients que vous n'en pouviez voir.— Je n'en ai pas moins de reconnaissance pour ce que vous et mon père avez fait dans cette occasion.—Je trouve plaisant que Freundenrich[14] à qui j'ai écrit et qui ne m'a jamais répondu, s'avise de chicaner mon silence. Pour Gros c'est pour avoir de la contenance qu'il demande de mes nouvelles, je lui en ferai une révérence quand je le verrai. Il n'y a que les souvenirs de ma sœur qui me fassent plaisir, et je ne lui reproche que d'aimer en paresseuse. Je la crois plus heureuse dans son château que l'on ne l'est dans les Palais d'Angleterre, sûrement elle y rit davantage.—

On peut voir les grands sans envie quand on se compare à leur bonheur et tout le défaut qu'on en rapporte, c'est un mépris pour les gens qui ont leurs vices et leurs ridicules sans en avoir ni la grandeur ni les richesses qui pourraient les excuser. La seule supériorité des fortunes médiocres, c'est de nous donner les vertus si difficiles à acquérir dans l'élévation, mais j'ai toujours trouvé plus d'orgueil, plus d'entêtement, plus de fureur d'amasser, plus de sûreté, chez la plupart des gens d'une condition médiocre que chez les grands mêmes, avec cette différence que les grands qui jouissent de la fortune et de la grandeur sont plus aisément au dessus de l'un et de l'autre que ceux qui n'ont ni l'un ni l'autre. L'unique avantage que j'ai toujours accordé aux petits, c'est de s'ennuyer moins et c'est encore le secret des esprits vulgaires. Je n'ai guère trouvé que mon père qui ait véritablement les vertus de la médiocrité, je n'en veux d'autres preuves que l'estime universelle qu'on a pour lui dans tous les pays et sa modestie dans les circonstances du monde les plus propres à nous donner de l'orgueil, auquel si peu de nos magistrats sont réputés d'avoir échappés. Il y a un mois que nous avons le printemps, la verdure reste ici toute l'année. On a ses fenêtres ouvertes et des fleurs dans les jardins.—

---

[14] Mentioned as a friend of Bonstetten in Norton Nicholls's letter to Gray of 16 Mar. 1771 (Letter 545), where Mitford misprints the name.

Je partirai Lundi[15] de Cambridge et serai peut-être dans 15 jours à Paris.[16] Quand j'ai enfin trouvé un ami c'est pour le perdre et pour retomber dans cette sombre solitude où je reste la proie des vices et de toutes les misères humaines. Qu'un seul orage peut nous égarer loin et qu'il est dangereux de dévoyer d'une route où l'on va médiocrement bien, dans l'idée de nous faire aller mieux, comme si l'on restait toujours maître des vents, des mers et des orages.— La mort du Chancelier York[17] est remarquable. La veille de son élévation on avait dit à son frère Mylord H[18] (qui est dans le parti de l'opposition) qu'il avait courageusement dédaigné les offres de la Cour. Le lendemain le nouveau Chancelier se rend chez son frère, Mylord croyant qu'il avait refusé, court dans ses bras les larmes aux yeux, mais apercevant les marques de la dignité, il sort indigné et va brusquement s'enfermer dans son cabinet. Le chancelier York mourut peu d'heures après.—

Je vous prie mon très cher père d'adresser vos lettres à Mr. Lullin à qui j'ai coutume d'envoyer mes certificats de vie.—

APPENDIX W

Letters of James Brown and others relating to Gray's last illness and death

GRAY's last extant letter was written to Norton Nicholls from London on 28 June 1771 (Letter 556). On 22 July he returned to Cambridge, 'meaning', as Mason wrote (*Memoirs*, p. 399) 'from thence to set out very soon for Old Park . . . but on the 24th of July, while at dinner in the College Hall, he felt a sudden nausea, which obliged him to rise from table and retire to his chamber.' This was the beginning of the illness which caused his death on 30 July.

---

15 Feb. 12.

16 He did not finally leave England for Paris till 23 Mar. See Gray's letter to Nicholls of 4 Apr. 1770 (Letter 514).

17 Hon. Charles Yorke, second son of Lord Chancellor Hardwicke, on the dismissal of Lord Camden from the Chancellorship in Jan. 1770, was offered the post by the Duke of Grafton. As he was pledged to the Rockingham party not to accept office he at first declined, but under pressure from the King he was persuaded to accept (17 Jan.). The patent for his creation as Baron Morden was made out the next day, but before it could be authenticated he died (20 Jan.), either from rupture of a blood-vessel or, as was widely believed, by his own hand.

18 Philip Yorke, second Earl of Hardwicke; he had been a member (without office) of the first Rockingham administration (1766), and was consequently in opposition to the administrations of the Duke of Grafton and of Lord North.

Appendix W

The first three letters of Brown to Wharton, printed in this Appendix, and his first letter to Nicholls are concerned with the course of Gray's illness. The next letters of Brown announce Gray's death and give information about his will. These letters are followed by a letter of Cole to Walpole, a letter of Mason to Wharton, and a letter of Walpole to Stonhewer. These letters were written within seven weeks of Gray's death. A letter of Brown to Nicholls is added, written on 29 June 1773, the first opportunity which Brown had of communicating with Nicholls after he had returned from his foreign tour. With the exception of part of Cole's letter to Walpole and of Walpole's letter to Stonhewer the letters were printed by Mitford in *Works* (1835–43), vol. iv, pp. 203–15, vol. v, p. 157.

LIST OF LETTERS

	From	To	Date
I	Brown	Wharton	24 July 1771
II	Brown	Nicholls	26 July
III	Brown	Wharton	29 July
IV	Brown	Wharton	30 July
V	Brown	Wharton	31 July
VI	Brown	Nicholls	1 Aug.
VII	Brown	Wharton	17 Aug.
VIII	Mason	Wharton	18 Aug.
IX	Cole	Walpole	24 Aug.
X	Brown	Nicholls	6 Sept.
XI	Walpole	Stonhewer	16 Sept.
XII	Brown	Nicholls	29 June 1773

[*Note.* The letters from Brown to Wharton and the letter from Mason to Wharton are now reprinted from the originals in the British Museum (MS. Egerton 2400); the letters from Brown to Nicholls from the originals in the Eton College Library; the letter from Cole to Walpole from the copy which Cole made (Brit. Mus. *Add. MS.* 5833, f. 15); and the letter from Walpole to Stonhewer from the original in the Loyd Collection.]

[P. T.
L. W.]

I. BROWN TO WHARTON

Pembroke Hall
July 24. 1771.

Dear S.^r

Here is Mr Gray wishing to be well enough to take his journey to Old Park, but in truth he knows not when he shall be so happy. Tho' he does not give over the hopes of it, yet he thinks it is so

1270

uncertain when he can set about it, that he wishes not to alter any Plan you may have formed for passing away any part of your Summer. Some Complaints of the Gout he hath had; some feverish disorder which hath frequently returned & left him low and dispirited, and another complaint added to it which renders travelling very inconvenient. He had been for six or seven Weeks in London, and almost all the time out of order; he came hither the beginning of this Week; he had entertained great hopes that he shou'd have been with you before this time. I hope your Nephew[1] came safe into the North and that he is well; we much esteem him here.

The Weather is very fine at this time with us: I doubt not it is so with you and I hope your Daughters reap great benefit from it, and that they forget the severities of last Winter.[2] I join with M.ʳ Gray in sending to You and M.ʳˢ Wharton, to your Sons and Daughters our best Respects and heartiest wishes for their Health & yours. Don't forget my Compliments to your Nephew. I am Dear S.ʳ affectionately yours

J: BROWN

Addressed: To Thomas Wharton Esq. at Old Park near Darlington Durham by Caxton bag. *Postmark:* CAMBRIDGE

II. BROWN TO NICHOLLS

Pembroke Hall
July 26 1771

Dear S.ʳ

I am writing to you in M.ʳ Gray's room, and he is ill upon the Couch and unable to write to you himself. His illness is something like the Gout in the Stomach[1] but as D.ʳ Glynn[2] tells me there are many different degrees of that disorder, we may hope this is one of the less dangerous degrees, and that we shall see him well again in a short time. The last night passed over tolerably well but this morning after drinking Asse's Milk the sickness at the stomach has returned again. M.ʳ Gray has received from you one Letter from Paris dated June 29[3] and he has sent you a Letter from M.ʳ Temple inclosed in a very short one from himself.[4] You will give me leave to add my best Compliments to you and hearty wishes for your Health, and when there happens a vacancy in your conversation with M.ʳ Bonstetten tell him that I do myself the honour to think of

APPENDIX W.—LETTER I.—[1] Robert Wharton now an undergraduate at Pembroke College (see Letter 336, n. 3).
    [2] For the severe cold at the beginning of 1771 see Letter 542.
    LETTER II.—[1] See Letter III, n. 2.   [2] See Letter 461, n. 8.
    [3] Letter 557.   [4] Letter 556.

him often with esteem & admiration & wish him well.   I am your
faithful Humble Servant

J: Brown

Addressed: A Monsieur Monsr Nicholls Gentilhomme Anglois Chas Messrs Thelusson
et Neckar Banquiers à Paris *Postmark:* CAMBRIDGE 2⁵ IY POST PAID

III. BROWN TO WHARTON

Poor Mr Gray! my Dear S.^r I am afraid his friends at Old Park
will see him no more. Professor Plumptre[1] and Dr Glynn give us no
hopes of his recovery, they both attend him, and come together
three or four times a day. They say it is the Gout in the Stomach,[2]
& they cannot get the better of it. Stephen[3] his old servant is
very diligent and handy in his attendance upon him & Mr Gray is
well satisfied with it. He has very frequently convulsion fits. The
Physicians last night did not expect to find him alive this morning;
& this morning they did not think he wou'd live till the Evening.
They don't find him worse this Evening than he was in the morning,
yet they say tho' he may have strength enough to last a few days,
they think he has not strength enough to recover. He does not always
talk coherently and then recovers his thoughts again. I sent a special
Messenger yesterday to Mr Stonhewer, who wou'd probably find
him ten or twelve hours before the Post. Adieu and accept of my
best good wishes for yourself, Mrs Wharton, & your family.
I am affectionately yrs.

J. BROWN.

Monday Night
July 29. 1771.

Addressed: To Thomas Wharton Esq. at Old Park near Darlington Durham by
Caxton

IV. BROWN TO WHARTON

Dear S.^r,

Dr Gisburn[1] and Mr Stonhewer came here last night; were present
at three or four consultations and are gone away this Evening to

---

[5] Date partly defaced.

LETTER III.—[1] See Letter 391*, n. 2.

[2] It used to be held that when gout left the joints it might attack the stomach or
the heart. This theory of 'retrocedent gout' is now regarded as open to question:
the symptoms usually associated with it are thought to be due to uraemia, which
may accompany gout. Sir Humphry Rolleston, after considering the evidence
afforded by the letters as to Gray's illness, concludes that he suffered from chronic
kidney disease, which terminated in uraemia.

[3] Stephen Hempsted (see Letter 439, n. 3).

LETTER IV.—[1] See Letter 299, n. 10.

London without the least hopes of seeing our poor friend again. He told me, if I understood him right, where a Will wou'd be found, but I shall not look so long as he is alive. I have been told that you have had a Will in your custody; if it be so it is too probable that it will be wanted, and if one be found here it must be seen which of the two is the last. My best respects attend you and Mrs Wharton and your family. I am dear S^r affectionately y^{rs}

> J: BROWN

Tuesday Evening,
July 30. 1771

I think him dying and that he has been sensible of his approaching Death; nor hath he expressed any Concern at the thoughts of leaving this world.

He is still alive 9 o'clock.

Addressed: To Thomas Wharton Esq. at Old Park near Darlington Durham by Caxton *Postmark:* CAMBRIDGE

V. BROWN TO WHARTON

Dear S^r

You must expect what will give you great concern; Mr Gray died about eleven last night; there is nothing to be added about his Death but that the whole was peaceable and calm so long as he was himself; nor was there any thing violent afterwards: but we think that for some hours before he died tho' he appeared convulsed to us, yet that he himself felt no pain. This was the opinion of the Physicians. I found a Will in the place of which he had told me, dated 1 July 1770. I was concerned that Mrs Foster's[1] name is totally omitted. 500£ in the Stocks is left to her Daughter Lady Goring.[2] Mr Williamson of Calcutta a relation on his Father's side is a Legatee to the same value, & the Miss Antrobuses to a greater value. To Mr Mason he has left all his Books and all his papers, to be destroyed or preserved at his Discretion. he hath joined me with Mr Mason in the executorship. To Mr Stonhewer and Dr Wharton each five hundred pounds Reduced Bank Annuities and to each one of his Diamond Rings. He has desired to be buried near his Mother at Stoke near Windsor and that one of his executors wou'd see him laid in the Grave; a melancholy Task which must come to my share, for Mr Mason is not here and it will be necessary to proceed in a very

LETTER V.—[1] See Letter 163, n. 1.

[2] See Letters 163, n. 1; 480, n. 10. For the legacies to Lady Goring and George Williamson see Appendix X on Gray's will: for their relationship to Gray see Genealogical Table.

few days. This morning at eight, nine, ten, he was but little alterd. You haVe my best Wishes, you and your Family. I know they will grieve every one of them for the Loss of M.ʳ Gray. I am Dear S.ʳ very affectionately yrs
JAMES BROWN

Pembroke Hall
Wedn: July 31. 1771
I shall return as soon as I can.

Addressed: To Thomas Wharton Esq at Old Park near Darlington Durham by Caxton *Postmark:* CAMBRIDGE

VI. BROWN TO NICHOLLS

Pembroke Hall
Dear S.ʳ   Aug. 1. 1771

The night before last, between the 30 & 31 of July about eleven o'clock we lost M.ʳ Gray. My former Letter would give you some apprehensions but we did not think this sad event to be so near. He had frequently convulsion fits from the time I wrote to you, till the time of his death, and the Physicians thought he was past the sense of pain some hours before he died. On the Saturday he told me where to find his Will if there shou'd be occasion, I did not then imagine there would be occasion to look for it and he said no more to me upon that subject. He told Miss Antrobus he shou'd die and now, and then some short expressions of this kind came from him, but he expressed not the least uneasiness at the thoughts of leaving this World. He has left all his books to M.ʳ Mason and his papers of all kinds & writings to be destroyed or preserved at his Discretion.[1] His Legacies are to Miss Antrobus and her Sister, to M.ʳ Williamson of Calcutta, to Lady Goring, to M.ʳ Stonhewer, D.ʳ Wharton—he has joined me in the executorship with M.ʳ Mason. His Scritoire hath not yet been examined but upon opening it for the Will, I observed a Parcel sealed up and indorsed—*Papers belonging to M.ʳ Nicholls,* w.ᶜʰ we shall take care of. Your last Letter came too late for him either to read or to hear: I have it by me unopened and will take care of it. M.ʳ Bonstetten will be much grieved. Adieu—We shall miss him greatly! Cambridge will appear a very different place to you when you come again.—I am with my best wishes for your Health Your faithfull Humble Servant
JAMES BROWN

Addressed: A Monsieur Monsieur Nicholls Gentilhomme Anglois chez Messʳˢ Thelusson et Neckar Banquiers à Paris *Postmark:* CAMBRIDGE 2 AV POST PAID

LETTER VI.—[1] For the legacies generally see Appendix X.

Appendix W

VII. Brown to Wharton

Pembroke Hall

Dear S.ʳ   Aug. 17. 1771

Every thing is now dark and melancholly at M.ʳ Gray's Room, not a trace of him remains there, it looks as if it had been for some time uninhabited and the room bespoke for another inhabitant. The Papers are in good hands. M.ʳ Mason carried them with him to York, and his furniture he bequeathed to his Relations here. The thoughts I have of him will last, and will be useful to me the few years I can expect to live. He never spoke out,[1] but I believe from some little expressions I now remember to have dropt from him that for some time past he thought himself nearer his end than those about him apprehended it. I shall rejoice in the happiness of your family and desire my best respects to M.ʳˢ Wharton and all your Sons & Daughters, I am affectionately yrs   J: Brown.

Remember me to your Nephew: the bill you sent is in the hands of M.ʳ May[2]—Adieu.

Addressed: To Thomas Wharton Esq. at Old Park near Darlington Durham by Caxton

VIII. Mason to Wharton

Dear Sʳ   York. Augˢᵗ 18ᵗʰ 1771.

The best apology I can make to you for not writing to you sooner, will be to give you an accᵗ how I have been employ'd, since the sad event happend wᶜʰ now occasions my writing. I reᶜᵈ the melancholly news at Bridlington Key full ten days after it had happend. I crost the Humber immediately & got to Cambridge the day after in order to assist & relieve Mʳ Brown as soon & as much as I was able. He returnd not from Stoke & London till the Saturday.[1] On Sunday I set out with him for London to prove the Will & having done so returnd on Monday. this was a great & an unnecessary Loss of time. but nothing would satisfy his Cautious temper but our doing it personally. On Tuesday & Wednesday we delivered up the Furniture of the Rooms to the Antrobuss & in the meanwhile the

---

LETTER VII.—[1] The phrase has been misapplied to suggest a general characteristic. Tovey (*Gray and His Friends*, p. 21) wisely says: 'We cannot indeed believe that when good Mr. Brown said of Gray that "he never spoke out" he had anything in his mind but the fact that Gray did not acknowledge to his friends how near he felt his end to be.'

[2] Samuel May (see Letter 127, n. 7) was Tutor of Pembroke, and Wharton's 'bill' was presumably a bank bill in payment of his nephew's College charges.

LETTER VIII.—[1] 10 August. Brown and Mason went to London the next day, and the will was proved on Monday, 12 Aug.

Books were packed up & sent to the Lodge,[2] so that by this dispatch he will have nothing to take charge of but what remains to the Executorship. The Papers I brought all with me here yesterday. My first Business shall be to sort the Letters wch are numerous. I shall seal up those of the Living Correspondents & return them when convenient. I find a good many of yours, wch I shall return you with all fidelity.

You will perhaps wonder why I stayd so little a while with him. The time of my residence here began the very day after I reached Cambridge. Mr. Cayleys[3] Servants & goods were gone to his Parsonage. He stayd the Sunday over & that was all he could possibly do. so that it was impossible for me to prolong my stay another day. However the great Burthen i.e. the care of little matters, is now off his hands. You who know his attention to little matters, know how much he will be relieved by what is already done. You know too he could never have attended to other things till these had been done, & he would have been Months of doing without me, what I trust has been now done as effectually in three days. I purpose to return to him in November to transfer the Stock bequeathed, & to give up the title deeds of the House in Cornhill.

In the mean time My Dear Doctor Wharton shall not I assure myself of seeing you at York? Come I beseech you & condole with me on our mutual our irreparable Loss. The great Charge wch his dear friendship has laid upon me[4] I feel myself unable to execute without the advice & assistance of his best friends. You are among the first of these, & the first too whose counc[el][5] I would take on the occasion. As so[on] as the foolish hurry of this idle Week [is] over my house will be empty & my time my own. Come when it suits you, I shall take care to have a bed for you at the Deanery, if these rooms be too small. Mrs Wharton perhaps will accompany you & take this opportunity of seeing her Sister. My best Compliments to her & the young Ladies. believe me most Cordially yours

W Mason

Excuse great Haste & much confusion of mind. for I have been hurryd & concernd beyond expression.

Addressed: To Thomas Wharton Esq. Old Park near Darlington *Postmark:* YORK

² The Master's Lodge where Brown resided.

³ The Rev. William Cayley was Mason's colleague as a Prebendary of York.

⁴ Mason is obviously referring to the disposal of Gray's papers. He wrote to Walpole in similar terms on 28 Aug.: 'You will be informed I presume before this that I am entrusted with all Mr Gray's Papers "to preserve or destroy at my own discretion" an important charge which I shall find myself unable to execute without the advice and assistance of his other friends' (*Walpole–Mason Correspondence*, vol. i, p. 11).   ⁵ Here and elsewhere in the letter there are small tears in the paper.

Appendix W

IX. COLE TO WALPOLE[1]

For the Hon: Horace Walpole in Arlington Street London.

Milton. Saturday. Aug. 24. 1771.

Dear Sir,

Not satisfied with my late hasty Answer to your Letter from Paris,[2] after dining yesterday at our County Club, I waited on the Master of Pembroke in the afternoon, & drank my Tea with him, that I might from the Fountain Head give you a more authentic account of the subject of your Letter, which I gave him to peruse. He was very cõmunicative and obliging; shewed me Mr Gray's original Will, on a Skin of Parchment, which was executed July 2 1770; in which, after desiring to be put into a Coffin of well-seasoned Oak, without Lining either within or withoutside, & to be buried in a Vault contiguous to his dear Mother in Stoke-Poges Church Yard, and attended to his Grave, if at all convenient, by one of his Executors, he leaves 500£ to Mr Stonehewer, the like to the Master of Pembroke Hall, & the same Sum to Mr Mason,[3] the Precentor of York, to whom he also leaves all his Books, MSS, Coins, Medals, Music Books, both printed and MS, with a discretionary Power to do with his MSS what he thinks proper. To his 2 Cousins Antrobus of Cambridge, as well as I can recollect about 1000£ each, and to his Servant 50£. These, I think, are the most considerable legacies, & as far as I can judge, he died worth about 6000£,[4] having sold his Paternal Property[5] in Houses, not being made for Tenants &

LETTER IX.—[1] In vol. xxxiii of Cole's note-books in the British Museum (*Add. MS.* 5833) from folio 11 onwards there are many notes on Gray, including an account of his death, written presumably at the time (printed in Mitford, *Works* (1835–43), vol. i, pp. xcix f.). Cole also copied letters that he received or wrote at the time in connexion with Gray's death. Among these are letters to and from Walpole. The letter here printed faces folio 15.

[2] Walpole, who was in Paris, first learnt of Gray's death from the newspapers, which reached him about 10 Aug. On 12 Aug. he wrote to Cole, asking if the news were true. Cole wrote a hasty answer on 21 Aug. and followed it by this letter three days later. Walpole replied on 10 Sept.

[3] For the legacies see Gray's will in Appendix X. Cole's memory of some details was at fault. Brown and Mason were residuary legatees and were not left legacies of a fixed amount. The legacies to Gray's cousins were less than Cole states; these and the legacy to Stonehewer were not in cash, but in 'Reduced Bank Annuities', which at the time of Gray's death were considerably below par value.

[4] In a note which Cole wrote in his copy of Mason's *Memoirs* (quoted by Mitford, *Works* (1835–43), vol. i, p. cvii) Cole stated that Gray's property at his death amounted to about £7,000. Mitford (*ad loc.*) refers to an estimate of Sir James Mackintosh, which made Gray's property 'near the above sum'.

[5] Gray had sold his house at Wanstead many years before (see Letter 196, n. 9),

Repairs, & placed the Money in the Funds, with Part of which, as I was informed, he purchased an Annuity,[6] in Order to have a fuller Income. The Master and Mr Mason are left residuary Legatees. Mr Mason has been at Cambridge, &, as the Master told me, talked a good Deal about the Propriety of sending you an account of this Affair, from the long Friendship between you & Mr Gray: but as Mr Mason was acquainted with you, the Master put it upon him to do it: but he added that when Mr Mason left Cambridge, where This Business took up all his Thoughts & Time, he went to his Residence at York, where the Races were beginning, & where Lord John Cavendish was to take up his Lodgings with him: so that he doubted whether he had yet wrote to you, from his Multiplicity of Business; but made not the least doubt but you would soon hear from him; and on my expressing a desire that he should be acquainted with the Contents of your truly affecting Letter, he promised me to mention it in his first Letter, which would be soon.

All his Furniture he gave to his Cousins, who, on the Master's Representation, sent back a Piano Forte which had been given to him by Mr Stonehewer, but as the Master said, Mr Gray had taken it reluctantly, not liking to put his Friend to such an Expence, he thought it right that Mr Stonehewer should have it again. On the same principle Mr Mason designs to return an antique Seal[7] given to him by Mr Bedingfeild, a Roman Catholic Gentleman, Brother to the Baronet of that Name, & a great admirer of Mr Gray, on which was engraved the Figure of Justice.

Mr Gray was delicately scrupulous in taking it: but could not refuse it with good Manners. By a Memorandum the Master found since his Death, it appears that he was near 55 years of Age, being born Dec. 26. 1716. He went off pretty easily, considering the Nature of his Complaint, the Gout in his Stomach, which occasioned a Sickness & Loss of appetite neither would any Thing rest in his Stomach: he also complained for Want of proper Evacuations: & it was not till Friday before he died, that he had any Convulsions, when he was seized with the first, & had them occasionally till his Death on Tuesday night following, tho' not to any great

but the house at Cornhill was owned by him when he died. Cole probably had in mind Gray's interest in the property in Hand Alley, which he had inherited from Mrs. Rogers (see Appendix U); this he had sold in Jan. 1769 (see Letter 490).

[6] Cole was probably misinformed as to Gray's having purchased an annuity for himself. He had done so for Mrs. Olliffe (see Letter 490).

[7] See Letter 222, n. 1 a.

Degree; the Master being with him till half an Hour before his Decease.*⁸

As it was warm Weather, & the Distance considerable, it was impossible to comply with that part of his Will relating to his Coffin, which was wrapped in Lead. Mr Tyson whom I called upon Yesterday in my way to Pembroke, seeing me pass by, desired me to step into his Chamber, to see a Picture or Drawing⁹ he had just finished of Mr Gray, which, I have a notion, he intends either to send to you, or if he etches it, to inscribe to you; for I did not well understand him. It is very like him: but I think not more so than the Etching by Mr Mason which he would persuade me is very unlike: tho', in my opinion, his own is copied from it.

As my Sister goes for Bath on Monday having paid me a 2 months Visit, I shall take the opportunity of sending this, with Mr Essex's Plan of the Stone Cross, & his Letter about it: & wishing you once more a safe & happy Arrival I remain

Dear Sir

Your ever faithful & affectionate Friend & Servt.

WM. COLE.

* He retained his Senses to the last: but gave proof of their Decay a Day or two before his Death, which he expected, as he told one of his Cousins, saying, Molly, I shall die. The Decay I mentioned was this: Seeing the Master sit by him, he said, Oh, Sir! Let Dr Hallifax or Dr Heberden be sent to. He certainly meant for physical Assistance: Now Dr Hallifax, the Regius Professor of Law, his acquaintance, was a Divine, & no Physitian.¹⁰ He also gave another Proof, some few Days before his Death, of his Apprehensions of it: for being on his Sopha or Couch, when Professor Plumptre & Dr Glynn were in the Chamber, he gave the Master the Keys of his Bureau, & told him where to find his Purse, & to bring him some Gold, to fee the Physitians; which he did with his own Hands, & very cheerfully asked them, well, Gentlemen, what must this Complaint of mine be called after all? Certainly, answered the Professor, the Gout in the Stomach; but however, added he, don't be apprehensive as we make no Doubt to drive it from thence. When he told the Master where to find the Purse, he said, And, Master, if there should be any occasion for it, you will find something else in the same Drawer. Which was all that he said upon that melancholy Subject. I am thus minute and particular, as I judge you would like to know the most trifling Circumstances & Features that out of the whole a more striking Likeness may be collected.

---

⁸ The 'Footnote' was presumably a postscript in Cole's letter to Walpole.

⁹ Nothing is known of the drawing or painting by Michael Tyson (see Letter 534, n. 4).

¹⁰ Dr. Samuel Hallifax, the Professor (see Letter 409, n. 10), had a younger brother, Robert Hallifax, who was physician to the Prince of Wales. It was, of course, the physician whom Gray meant.

Appendix W

X. Brown to Nicholls

Pembroke Hall
Sept. 6. 1771

Dear S.^r

I thought it might be some satisfaction for you to know that I had disposed of the Letter¹ you mention according to your desire. You expressed yourself in the singular Number. I have seven or eight others by me; several of which I have read in company with Mr Gray, but be assured they are sacred; I have looked into none of them but with him, & shall still observe the same restraint. They may be kept till you come or otherwise disposed of, as you shall direct. I have received a Letter lately from Mr Mason; Mr Gray you know made memorandums in his pocket books of his transactions. In that for 1770 March 23 Mr M.ⁿ tells me, there is this Mem:—Lent M.^r de B:² 20£ and it appears further to be the day he set out for Dover.³ I venture to mention this to you as it makes a part of our Charge and perhaps it may be the best opportunity we shall have of hearing from Mr de Bonstetten how that matter stands. You will act in that matter as you please. No successor to Mr Gray is yet appointed Mr Symonds⁴ has been most mentioned; I believe indeed he does not himself apply for it, which makes his Success the more unlikely. I shall rejoice to see you and to see you well. I am your faithful humble Servant

JAMES BROWN.

Addressed: A Monsieur Monsieur Nicholls Gentilhomme Anglois chez Messrs Thelusson et Neckar Banquiers à Paris *Postmark:* DANGLETERRE 7 SE POST PAID

XI. Walpole to Stonhewer¹

Strawberry hill
Sept. 16. 1771.

I am very sorry, S^r, for all the trouble You have had about sending me Mr Mason's kind letter,² & very sensible to any attention from

LETTER X.—¹ No doubt this, and the 'seven or eight other letters' mentioned by Brown, were from Bonstetten to Gray. The letter Nicholls wished Brown to destroy may have been the one referred to by Gray in his letter of 3 May 1771 (Letter 550).
² Bonstetten, see Letter XII, n. 6. ³ See Letter 514.
⁴ John Symonds (1729–1807), originally of St. John's, B.A. 1752; Fellow of Peterhouse, 1753; M.A. 1754; Professor of Modern History, in succession to Gray, 1771–1807; LL.D. 1772.
LETTER XI.—¹ The name of the addressee does not appear, but it was obviously Stonhewer.
² Mason wrote to Walpole from York on 28 Aug.: 'I deferred writing to you on

two Gentlemen who valued so much & were so much valued by Mr Gray. The loss of Him was a great blow to me, & ought to be so to the World, as Mr Mason tells me he has left behind Him nothing finished, which might have compensated his death to them, tho not to his Friends. He was a Genius of the first rank, and will always be allowed so by Men of taste. You S^r will be honored by them for having done justice to his Merit; and as he was so averse to receiving favours, it will be a proof that He did justice to yours in consenting to be obliged to you.[3]

As I am not sure how long you Stay at Middleton,[4] I direct this to your House in town,[5] whence, if absent, I conclude it will be sent to you; & I shoud be sorry to seem careless in answering the favour of yours, as I am with great regard, S^r, your most obedient humble Sert

HORACE WALPOLE

XII. BROWN TO NICHOLLS

Pemb: Hall
June 29. 1773

Dear S^r

I received your Letter[1] in London; it is dated May 21 and I thought it a little unlucky that it came not to my hands before I left Cambridge, which was not till the 25. I might then have deliverd the parcel my self to Mr Turner.[2] I have now sent it by Mr Gillam[3] and put it into his hands yesterday. He is a trusty Agent, otherwise I shoud have thought your direction to Mr Turner rather too concise. Amongst M^r Gr's things we found some little Presents for his Friends which they might esteem as Memorials of him; for some of his Friends I mean. M^r De Bons: had sent him from Paris a little picture of himself;[4] we thought it wou'd be acceptable to you, and

the late melancholy occasion, till I heard you was upon your return from Paris. I hope this will find you in perfect health after your journey, and I have sent it under Mr Stonhewer's care that he may deliver it to you when he hears you are arrived in town' (*Walpole–Mason Correspondence*, vol. i, p. 11).

3 Walpole alludes to the accepted belief that the Duke of Grafton appointed Gray Professor of Modern History at Cambridge at the instance of Stonhewer, who was his private secretary (see Letter 480, n. 9).

4 Presumably Middleton Park, Oxon., the seat of the Earl of Jersey.

5 In Curzon Street.

LETTER XII.—1 Nicholls had recently returned from his tour in Switzerland and Italy.

2 Probably one of Nicholls's uncles (see Letter 429, n. 7).

3 The Cambridge carrier (see Letter 347, n. 1).

4 See Letter 540, n. 7.

therefore with Mr Mason's full approbation it is sent, and makes a part of your parcel. There are those of your Letters which we found, but the two or three journals, you speak of, are not there, unless possibly they may be inclosed in the parcel sealed.[5] Excuse me that I send no directions about the 20£:[6] you have wrote to M.^r De B: who will mention it, if it be as we imagine. I met Mr Barrett[7] twice in my walks in London, and should not have known him the first time, had he not been kind enough to know me. I was pleased to see him look so well. You will easily know what was the Subject of our discourse, whilst we stood together. I believe I was sitting by M.^r Gr: at the time he wrote you his last Letter to Paris[8] without feeling what it seems he suggested to you, how near he was to his end. It gives me a melancholly kind of satisfaction that my Letters cou'd be at all useful to you. The Report[9] you mention, I believe, was never utterd in England. Pray let me know, when you receive your parcel. I am with my best wishes for your Health and with much esteem your faithful humble servant

J: Brown

Addressed: To The Revd Mr Nicholls at Blundeston near Lowestoft Suffolk By Yarmouth *Postmark:* CAMBRIDGE

[5] In his letter to Nicholls of 1 Aug. 1771 (Letter VI) Brown mentions the 'parcel sealed up and indorsed—Papers belonging to Mr Nicholls'.

[6] This was the loan which Gray made to Bonstetten on the day he left England. Brown had written about it to Nicholls in his letter of 6 Sept. 1771 (Letter X), and left it to his discretion to mention to Bonstetten. From Brown's next letter to Nicholls of 24 July 1773 it appears that Nicholls had offered to pay the £20 to the executors and to recover the amount from Bonstetten. The loan was still unpaid in 1775, for on 4 July of that year Mason wrote to Nicholls: 'As to the money you mention, I should blush if it came into my part of the executorship through any other channel than that through which it ought long ago to have come voluntarily' (Brown and Mason's letters were printed by Mitford, *Works* (1835-43), vol. v, pp. 162, 165).

[7] Thomas Barrett (see Letter 357, n. 14) was a contemporary of Nicholls at Cambridge. In 1768 Barrett had proposed that Nicholls should accompany him to France and Italy. The invitation was declined (see Letters 482, 483), but during Nicholls's foreign tour he met Barrett and they had stayed together at Florence in 1772, as appears from letters of Nicholls to Barrett written in April and May of that year (Mitford, *op. cit.*, vol. v, pp. 167 ff.).

[8] Brown's letter to Nicholls of 26 July 1771 shows that Gray could scarcely have written to Nicholls after he returned to Cambridge. If Gray's 'last letter to Paris' was that of 28 June (Letter 556), written in London, it would appear that Brown must have gone to see Gray in London.

[9] The allusion has not been explained.

APPENDIX X
Gray's Will

GRAY's will was first printed in the 'New Edition' of *Poems by Mr. Gray* published by John Murray in 1778. From this time Gray's editors followed the tradition of adding the will to an account of his life (see Northup, *A Bibliography of Thomas Gray*, p. 202). Mitford printed the will as an Appendix in his editions of Gray's *Poems* or *Works*. Mistakes in the spelling of proper names and other typographical variations occur in the traditional text, which was probably derived from a transcript. The text is now printed from a photograph of Gray's holograph at Somerset House.

[P. T.]

THE LAST WILL AND TESTAMENT OF THOMAS GRAY

IN the name of God, Amen. I Thomas Gray, of Pembroke-Hall in the University of Cambridge, being of sound mind, and in good health of body, yet ignorant how long these blefsings may be indulged me, do make this my last Will & Testament in manner & form following.

First, I desire that my body may be deposited in the vault made by my late dear Mother in the church-yard of Stoke-Pogeis[1] near Slough in Buckinghamshire, near her remains, in a coffin of season'd oak neither lined nor cover'd; and (unlefs it be very inconvenient) I would wish, that one of my Executors may see me laid in the grave, & may distribute among such honest & industrious poor Persons in the said parish, as he thinks fit, the sum of ten pounds in charity.

Next, I give to *George Williamson*[2] Esq, my second Cousin by the Father's side, now of Calcutta in Bengal, the sum of five hundred pounds Reduced Bank-Annuities now standing in my name.

I give to Anna, Lady Goring,[3] also my second Cousin by the Father's side, of the County of Sufsex, five hundred pounds Reduced Bank-Annuities; and a pair of large blue & white old Japan-China Jarrs.

APPENDIX X.—[1] See Letter 176, n. 2.

[2] See Genealogical Table A. In an unpublished letter of Mason to Alderson, dated 2 Nov. 1771, in referring to his association with Brown in the executorship of Gray's will, he writes: 'I find by the papers that the Varelst East-india man is lost, in wch Mr Williamson one of Mr Gray's Legatees and his heir at Law was coming to England. Whether he be lost in her I do not yet know—this event however must retard our proceedings as nothing can be settled finally till we either know he is come home or is drown'd.' The fate of George Williamson has not been traced.

[3] See Genealogical Table A and Letter 163, n. 1. Lady Goring's husband was Sir Harry Goring, sixth Baronet, of Highden, Washington, Sussex.

Appendix X

Item I give to *Mary Antrobus*[4] of Cambridge, Spinster, my second Cousin by the Mother's side, all that my freehold estate & house[5] in the parish of St Michael, Cornhill, London, now lett at the yearly rent of sixty five pounds & in the occupation of Mr Nortzell,[6] Perfumer, provided that she pay out of the said rent by half-yearly payments to Mrs. *Jane Olliffe*[7] my Aunt, of Cambridge Widow, the sum of twenty pounds per annum during her life—& after the decease of the said Jane Olliffe I give the said estate to the said Mary Antrobus, to have & to hold, to her, her heirs & afsigns for ever. Farther I bequeath to the said *Mary Antrobus* the sum of six hundred pounds New South-sea Annuities now standing in the joint-names of Jane Olliffe & Thomas Gray, but charged with the payment of five pounds per annum to Graves Tokely,[8] of Stoke-Pogeis, in the county of Bucks, wch sum of six hundred pounds, after the decease of the said Annuitant does (by the Will of Anne Rogers[9] my late Aunt) belong solely & entirely to me, together with all overplus of interest in the mean time accruing. Farther, if at the time of my decease there shall be any arrear of salary[10] due to me from his Majesty's Treasury, I give all such arrears to the said Mary Antrobus.

Item I give to Mrs. *Dorothy Comyns*[11] of Cambridge, my other second Cousin by the Mother's side, the sums of six hundred pounds old South-sea annuities, of three hundred pounds four per Cent. Bank-annuities consolidated; & of two hundred pounds three per Cent. Bank annuities consolidated, all now standing in my name.

I give to *Richard Stonhewer* Esq, one of his Majesties Commifsioners of Excise, the sum of five hundred pounds Reduced Bank-annuities; & I beg his acceptance of one of my diamond-rings.

I give to Dr. *Thomas Wharton* of Old Park in the Bishoprick of Durham five hundred pounds Reduced Bank-annuities; & desire him also to accept one of my diamond-rings.

I give to my Servant *Stephen Hempsted*[12] the sum of fifty pounds Reduced Bank-annuities; and (if he continue in my service to the time of my death) I also give him all my wearing-apparel & linnen.

I give to my two Cousins abovemention'd *Mary Antrobus* & *Dorothy Comyns* all my plate, watches, rings, china-ware, bed-linnen & table-

---

[4] Mary Antrobus here and her sister Dorothy below are by some unaccountable mistake on Gray's part called *second* cousins (see Letter 283*, n. 1).

[5] See Letters 28, n. 3; 145, n. 2.

[6] *Kent's Directory* for 1770 (p. 131) gives 'Jacob Nortzell, perfumer, 41 Cornhill.

[7] See Letter 271, n. 3.   [8] See Letter 305, n. 10.

[9] See Letter 271, n. 2.   [10] As Professor of Modern History.

[11] See Letter 293, n. 3.   [12] See Letter 439, n. 3.

linnen, & the furniture of my chambers at Cambridge, not otherwise bequeath'd, to be equally & amicably shared between them.

I give to the Revd *William Mason* Precentor of York, all my books, manuscripts, coins, musick printed or written, & papers of all kinds to preserve or destroy at his own discretion.

And (after my just debts & the expenses of my funeral are discharged) all the residue of my personal estate whatsoever I do hereby give & bequeath to the said Revd *William Mason* and to the Revd Mr *James Brown*, President of Pembroke-Hall, Cambridge, to be equally divided between them, desiring them to apply the sum of two hundred pounds to an use of charity,[13] concerning which I have already inform'd them.

And I do hereby constitute & appoint them the said *William Mason* & *James Brown* to be Joint-Executors of this my last Will & Testament, and if any relation of mine or other Legatee shall go about to molest or commence any suit against my said Executors in the execution of their office, I do (as far as the Law will permitt me) hereby revoke & make void all such bequests or legacies as I had given to that Person or Persons, & give it to be divided between my said Executors & residuary Legatees, whose integrity & kindnefs I have so long experienced, & who can best judge of my true intention & meaning, in witnefs whereof I do hereunto set my hand & seal this second day of July, the year of our Lord one thousand seven hundred & seventy.

Sign'd, seal'd, publish'd, & declared by the said Thomas Gray the Testator as & for his last Will & Testament in the presence of us, who in his presence & at his request, and in the presence of each of us, have sign'd our names as Witnefses hereto.

Richard Baker

Thomas Wilson   Thomas (Seal) Gray

Joseph Turner[14]

12th August 1771

The Reverend William Mason Clerk Master of Arts and the Reverend James Brown Clerk Master of Arts the Executors within named were duly sworn

before me

And: Coltee Ducarel

Danl Williams for my Master ⎫   Surrogate
Mr Henry Stevens   ⎭

13 See Appendix G.

14 The witnesses were Fellows of Pembroke (see Letter 529, n. 1).

Appendix X

Thomas Gray Batchelor of Laws late of Pembroke Hall and Professor of Modern History in the University of Cambridge and died the 30th of July 1771.

Proved at London on the twelfth Day of Augt 1771 before the Worshipful Andrew Coltee Ducarel Doctor of Laws and Surrogate by the Oaths of the Revd William Mason Clerk Master of Arts and the Revd James Brown[15] Clerk Master of Arts the Extor̃s to whom Adm̃on was granted having been first sworn duly to Adm̃ster.

> John Stevens
> Henry Stevens   } Deputy Registers
> Geo. Gostling, jun.

APPENDIX Y

*Walpole's Memoir of Gray**

THE original of the following memoir of Gray by Horace Walpole is preserved in *A Common Place Book of Verses, Stories, Characters, Letters, etc., etc., with some particular Memoirs of a certain Parcel of People*, in Walpole's handwriting, dated 1740, in the Collection of the Earl Waldegrave, at Chewton Priory, Bath. The memoir, very inaccurately printed, was prefixed by Mitford to his edition of *The Correspondence of Thomas Gray and William Mason* (London, 1853), pp. xxxi–iv. In his Preface (p. xxviii) Mitford says:

> 'I present my readers with some brief notes on Gray by the hand of Walpole; I do not know the time when they were written. They are indeed very unfinished, and seem to have been composed in haste; but they have added something to our knowledge of the Poet's history, and they acquire an authentic value from the quarter from which they come.'

But he gives no indication of the source from which he derived them. Either he was supplied with a faulty transcript, or (which is more probable) the faults are due to his own carelessness as a transcriber. The text is now for the first time printed as it was written by Walpole.

[P. T.]

MR. THOMAS GRAY

He was son of a money scrivener, by Mary Antrobus a milliner in Cornhill, and sister to two Antrobus's who were ushers of Eton

---

[15] When Gray made his will Brown was President of Pembroke. He had become Master in December 1770.

APPENDIX Y.—* Reprinted from the *Modern Language Review*, vol. xxvii (1932), pp. 58 ff.

School. He was born in 1716, & educated at Eton College, chiefly under the direction of one of his uncles, who took prodigious pains with him, which answered exceedingly. He particularly instructed him in the virtues of simples. He had a great genius for music & poetry. From Eton, he went to Peterhouse in Cambridge, & in 1739 accompanied Mr H. W. in travels to France and Italy. He returned in 1741, & retired to Cambridge again. His letters were[1] the best I ever saw, & had more novelty & wit. One of his first pieces of poetry was an answer in English verse to an Epistle from H. W.[2] At Naples he wrote a fragment describing an earthquake & the origin of Monte Nuovo in the style of Virgil, & at Rome an Alcaic ode in imitation of Horace to Richard West Esq. After his return he wrote that inimitable Ode on a distant Prospect of Eton College; another Moral Ode, & that beautiful one on a cat of Mr H. W.'s drowned in a tub of gold fishes. These three last have been published in Dodsley's Miscellanies. He began a poem on the Reformation of Learning, but soon dropped it, on finding his plan had too much resemblance to the Dunciad. It had this admirable line in it,

And Gospel-light first flash'd from Bullen's eyes.

He began too a philosophical poem in Latin, & an English tragedy of Agrippina, & some other odes, one of which, a very beautiful one, intitled *Stanzas written in a Country Churchyard*, he finished in 1750. He was a very slow but very correct writer. Being at Stoke in the summer of 1750, he wrote a kind of tale, addressed to Lady Schaub & Miss Speed, who had made him a visit from Lady Cobham's.

The Elegy written in the Churchyard was printed by Dodsley Feb. 16 1751 with a short advertisement by Mr H. W., and immediately went through four editions. He had some thoughts of taking his doctor's degree, but would not, for fear of being confounded with Dr Grey, who published the foolish edition of Hudibras. In March 1753 was published a fine edition of Six of his poems, with frontispieces, head and tail pieces, & initial letters, engraved by Grignion & Müller after designs by Richard Bentley Esq. He lost his mother a little before this, & about the same time finished an extreme fine poem, in imitation of Pindar, on the power of musical poetry, which he had begun two or three years before.

In the winter of 1755, George Hervey, Earl of Bristol, who was

---

[1] From the fact that Walpole wrote 'were', not 'are', it is evident that the memoir was written after Gray's death.

[2] The piece in question was discovered in the Waller Collection, and was printed in *Gray–Walpole Correspondence*, vol. i, pp. 13–15.

Soon afterwards sent Envoy to Turin, was designed for Minister to Lisbon; he offered to carry Mr Gray as his secretary, but he refused it.

In August 1757 were published two odes by Mr Gray, one on the power and progress of Poetry, the other on the destruction of the Welsh Bards by Edward 1st. They were printed at the new press at Strawberry hill, being the first productions of that printing-house.

In Oct. 1761, he made words for an old tune of Geminiani, at the request of Miss Speed; it begins, 'Thyrsis, when we parted, swore' etc. two stanzas; the thought from the French.

APPENDIX Z
Norton Nicholls's Reminiscences of Gray

THESE *Reminiscences*, which were written in November 1805, were communicated by Nicholls to his friend T. J. Mathias, who availed himself of them freely in his account of Gray in the postscript to his edition of the *Works of Gray* (vol. ii, pp. 583–629). They were first printed, in an inaccurate text, by Mitford in *Works of Gray* (1835–43), vol. v. They are here reprinted from Nicholls's holograph, now in the John Morris Collection in Eton College Library.

[P. T.
L. W.]

1805 Nov. 18.

During the latter part of the life of Mr Gray I enjoyed the inestimable advantage of living more in his society than any other person whom I recollect, & on a footing of the greatest intimacy; during that precious time, never alas! to be recalled, it scarcely occurred to me that I might lose him, & I neglected to commit to writing opinions, & conversations of which tho' I remember some after an interval of 34 years, yet many have faded away from my memory & are gone; it is a small atonement for this neglect, but the only one in my power, to write now the little which I still can recall with certainty, & I promise not to hazard a syllable of which I am not certain.—I shall begin with what I knew of his moral character.— Ability, talents, genius, the highest acquisitions of science, & knowledge were in his opinion of little account compared with *virtue* which he often used to quote to me from Plato is nothing but 'the exercise of right reason.'—I remember in the early part of my acquaintance with him saying that some person was 'a clever man'—he cut me short & said 'Tell me if he is good for any thing?' In the choice of his acquaintances he certainly often preferred persons of excellent moral character to those of superior ability; & had an aversion for those who were vicious, profligate, & unprincipled which no admiration of their Genius could subdue, or even soften.

The great object of his detestation was *Voltaire*,[1] whom he seemed 'to know even beyond what had appeared of him, & to see with the eye of a prophet in his future mischiefs: he said to me 'No one knows the mischief that man will do.'—When I took my leave of him, & saw him for the last time, at his lodging in Jermyn Street[2] before I went abroad in the beginning of June 1771 he said 'I have one thing to beg of you, which you must not refuse.'—I replied you know you have only to command, what is it?—'Do not go to see Voltaire' & then he added what I have written above.—I said 'Certainly I will not; but what could a visit from me signify?'— 'Every tribute to such a man signifies.'—This was when I was setting out for Switzerland to pay a visit to Monsr de Bonstetten in which he would have accompanied me if his health had permitted.—I kept my word, for I passed a month at the Chateau d'Aubonne near Lausanne with Mr de Tcharner Bailiff of the district & did not go to Ferney.

This aversion to the moral character of Voltaire did not prevent Mr Gray from paying the full tribute of admiration due to his Genius.—He was delighted with his pleasantry; approved his historical compositions, particularly his 'Essai sur l'histoire universelle'—& placed his tragedies next in rank to those of Shakespear.—He said that the fame of Voltaire would have been higher if he had published nothing but his tragedies; in which I remember when I mentioned this to Mr Gibbon he agreed. He had an aversion to Hume for similar reasons; he thought him irreligious, that is *an enemy to religion;* which he never pardoned in any one, because he said it was taking away the best consolation of man without substituting any thing of equal value in its place.—He thought him likewise an unprincipled sceptick, refuted & vanquished (which the philosophers will not allow) by Beattie;—& besides this in politics a friend to tyranny.

In the contest for the High Stewardship at Cambridge[3] between Lord Hardwick & Lord Sandwich Mr Gray took a warm, & eager part, for no other reason, I believe, than because he thought the licentious character of the latter candidate rendered him improper for a post of such dignity in the University. His zeal in this cause

APPENDIX Z.—[1] It is not easy to decide whether the underlining of words in the MS. is due to Nicholls or to some other hand.

[2] See Letter 554.

[3] See Appendix P.

inspired the verses full of pleasantry & wit which have been published since his death.

He disliked Doctor Johnson, & declined his acquaintance; he disapproved his style, & thought it turgid, & vicious; but he respected his understanding, & still more his goodness of heart;—I have heard him say that Johnson would go out in London with his pockets full of silver & give it all away in the streets before he returned home.[4]—

After this, without endeavouring to arrange what I remember under heads, or in any order, I shall set down what occurs to me as it occurs.

I asked Mʳ Gray if he recollected when he first perceived in himself any symptoms of poetry; he answered that he believed it was when at Eton he began to take pleasure in reading Virgil for his own amusement, & not in school-hours, or as a task. I asked Mʳ Bryant[5] who was next boy to him at Eton, what sort of a scholar Gray was he said a very good one & added that he thought he could remember part of an exercise of his on the subject of the freezing & thawing of words, taken from the Spectator, the fragment is as follows

   . . . pluviæq loquaces
   Descendêre jugis, & garrulus ingruit imber.[6]

I will set down after this another little fragment, two verses made by Mʳ Gray as we were walking in the spring in the neighbourhood of Cambridge

   "There pipes the wood-lark, & the song thrush there
   Scatters his loose notes in the waste of air."

I asked him how he felt when he composed the *Bard*. 'Why I felt myself the bard.'

Spencer was among his favourite poets, & he told me he never sat down to compose poetry without reading Spencer for a considerable time previously. He admired Dryden, & could not patiently hear him criticised. Absalom & Achitophel & Theodore & Honoria

[4] Boswell (*Life*, vol. ii, p. 118) quotes the *Collectanea* of Dr. Maxwell, who had known Johnson for many years: 'He frequently gave all the silver in his pockets to the poor, who watched him between his house and the tavern where he dined.'

[5] Jacob Bryant (1715–1804), a contemporary of Gray, Walpole, and West at Eton. Nicholls alludes to him below (see n. 56). Mitford in the *Life of Gray*, which he wrote for the Eton edition of *Gray's Poetical Works* (1847), printed a long letter of Bryant, containing his recollections of Gray. Mitford states: 'It does not appear to whom this letter was addressed, but probably to some Person, who intended to publish memoirs of the Poet.' It is possible that the letter was written to Nicholls.

[6] This is quoted in Bryant's letter (see n. 5).

stood in the first rank of poems in his estimation; & Dryden's plays not as dramatick compositions but as poetry.

He placed Shakespear high above all poets of all countries & all ages; & said that the justest idea of the historical characters he treated might be taken from his plays.—He shewed me a manuscript which he had copied from the Museum containing the report of the Commissioners appointed & sent by King Henry VIII to endeavour to prevail with Queen Catherine to lay aside the title of Queen, & assume that of Princess Dow.ʳ of Wales which agrees not only with the sentiments, but sometimes with the words used by the same persons in Shakespear's play of H VIII.

He thought the Comedies of Cibber excellent; & commended his *Apology*, giving it as an instance of an author writing well on a subject he perfectly understood.

I asked him why he had not continued that beautiful fragment beginning 'As sickly plants betray a niggard earth' He said, because he could not; when I expressed surprise at this, he explained himself as follows; That he had been used to write only Lyric poetry in which the poems being short, he had accustomed himself, & was able to polish every part; that this having become habit, he could not write otherwise; & that the labour of this method in a long poem would be intolerable; besides which the poem would lose its effect for want of Chiaro-Oscuro; for that to produce effect it was absolutely necessary to have weak parts.—He instanced in Homer, & particularly in Milton, who he said in parts of his poem rolls on in sounding words that have but little meaning.—

He thought Goldsmith a genuine poet; I was with him at Malvern when he received the *Deserted Village*,[7] which he desired me to read to him, he listened with fixed attention, & soon exclaimed—'That man is a poet.'—

He allowed merit to Churchill.

He disliked Akenside, & in general all poetry in blank verse except Milton.

He thought Thompson had one talent beyond all other poets, that of describing the various appearances of nature; but that he failed when he ventured to step out of this path; & particularly when he attempted to be moral, in which attempt he always became verbose. He was much pleased with Gawen Douglas Bishop of Dunkeld the old Scotch translator of the Eneid, particularly with his poetical prefaces to each book in which he has given liberty to his muse, but

---

[7] First published in May 1770. Gray and Nicholls were at Malvern in the summer of that year (see Letter 530).

has fettered himself in the translation by the obligation he has imposed on himself of translating the whole poem in the same number of verses contained in the original.

The *Spleen*, a poem in Dodsley's collection, by Mr Green[8] of the Custom house was a great favourite with him for its wit, & originality.—Shenstone's School Mistress[9] likewise.—The fault of Young in his Night Thoughts[10] he said was redundancy of thought.—

Pope's translation of the Iliad stood very high in his estimation; & when he heard it criticised as wanting the simplicity of the original, or being rather a paraphrase than a translation, & not giving a just idea of the poet's style, & manner, he always said 'there would never be another translation of the same poem equal to it.' He liked the poetry of Pope in general, & approved an observation of Shenstone that 'Pope had the art of condensing a thought.'—He said of his letters that they were not good letters, but better things. He thought that Pope had a good heart in spite of his peevish temper.

Talking of Dr Middleton's style the elegance of which he admired he mentioned it as an object of consideration whether style in one language can be acquired by being conversant with authors of a polished style in another; whether for example Dr Middleton could have acquired his flowing diction from great attention to & study of the writings of Cicero.—

He placed Lord Clarendon at the head of our historians, & indeed of almost all modern historians; though I have heard him say that Macchiavelli's history of Florence is written with the simplicity of a Greek historian. He disliked Hume, as I have said before, & his political principles; but besides this he looked on his history of England[11] as meager in facts, as well as full of misrepresentations, in short not a proper source of information. Rapin's[12] he looked on as the only general history of England; & he said that by consulting his copious, & excellent marginal references, & referring to the original & contemporary authors, to the memoirs, state-papers & various authentic & curious documents they indicate a still better history might be formed with the advantage of a more agreeable, & brilliant style. That of Algernon Sydney[13] he admired, particularly in the delightful letters he wrote from Italy.

I think Warburton was not a great favourite; he said that his

---

8 See Letter 144, n. 8.   9 See Letter 144, n. 9.
10 See Letter 197, n. 4.   11 See Letter 292, n. 16.
12 See Letter 537, n. 6.
13 It is not clear to what work Nicholls is alluding, possibly it was to the Sydney papers published in 1746, which contained his letters.

learning was a late acquisition & did not sit easily on him, that he had a ὑστερομαθία.[14]

He thought Mr Harris a very dull man; & on my saying that I had just read his Hermes,[15] Mr Gray replied,—'Yes, that is what I call the shallow profound.' He dissuaded me from reading Butler's Analogy, & said he had given the same advice to Mason. I believe he liked Wollaston's Religion of nature.[16] He was surprised that Bishop Sherlock[17] who has given some specimens of Pulpit eloquence which are unparallelled in their kind should have given no more; & he was more surprised that Dryden should attribute the style of his Prose writings to the study of that of Tillotson.[18] He thought the Prose of Dryden almost equal to his Poetry.

Speaking of & criticising the architecture of Sir John Vanbrugh[19] he said his plays were much better than his Architecture.

He thought there was good writing & good sense in the sermons of Sterne[20] whose principal merit, in his opinion, consisted in his pathetic power in which he never failed, tho' he often did in his attempts at humour.—*Wit* he said had gone entirely out of fashion since the reign of Charles 2d.

Of the poetry of Mason Caractacus[21] was his great favourite, in comparison with which he said Elfrida[22] was the work of a child. On my saying that much of Mason's poetry appeared to me to be without force, & languid—He said no wonder, for Mason never gave himself time to think but imagined that he should do best by writing hastily in the first fervour of his imagination, & therefore never waited for epithets if they did not occur readily but left spaces for them & put them in afterwards. This Mr Gray said enervated his

---

[14] Apparently a coinage of Gray's for ὀψιμαθία.

[15] *Hermes, or a Philosophical Enquiry concerning Universal Grammar* (1751) by James Harris (1709–80).

[16] *Religion of Nature Delineated* (1724) by the Rev. William Wollaston (1660–1724).

[17] Thomas Sherlock (1678–1761), ultimately Bishop of London. His *Discourses at the Temple Church* were first published in 4 vols. in 1754–8.

[18] John Tillotson (1630–94), Archbishop of Canterbury. He made a great reputation by his sermons, a collected edition of which in 14 vols. was published in 1695–1704.

[19] John Vanbrugh (1664–1726), dramatist, architect, and herald. His first play, *The Relapse*, was produced at Drury Lane in 1697; his last, *The Journey to London*, which he left unfinished, was completed by Cibber and produced, as *The Provoked Husband*, in 1728 (see Letter 363, n. 29).

[20] See Letters 311, n. 36, and 313, n. 23.

[21] For Gray's criticisms of *Caractacus* see Letters 250, 284*, and 286.

[22] See Letter 158.

poetry 'for nothing is done so well as at the first concoction'—he said 'we think in words.'

He thought Mason a bad prose writer, & disliked the letters published with Elfrida.[23]—He mentioned the Poem of the Garden[24] to me with disapprobation, & said it should not be published if he could prevent it.—He said Mason had read too little & written too much. The last four lines of Mason's epitaph on his wife[25] were written by Gray, I saw them in his hand-writing interlined in the Mss which he shewed me The words of M[rs]. Mason[26] when she had given up all hope of life:

> "Tell them tho' 'tis an awful thing to die,
> 'Twas e'en to thee, yet the dread path once trod
> Heaven lifts its everlasting portals high,
> And bids the pure in heart behold their God."

I do not now remember the lines of Mason which were effaced & replaced by these which have the genuine sound of the lyre of Gray. I remember that they were weak, with a languid repetition of some preceding expressions. M[r] Gray said 'That will never do for an ending, I have altered them thus.'

There is no doubt however of Mason being the Author of the Heroic Epistle to Sir W. Chambers.[27] Palgrave, who probably derived his information from the source, affirmed it. D[r] Burgh[28] Mason's great friend, told me 'he knew the Author'—& Mason himself many years ago, when he was supposed to have taken particular offence at the K - - reflecting on him with severity on some occasion, I said, 'That is a trifle for you to say who are the author of

[23] See Letter 165*.   [24] See Letter 509*, n. 4.

[25] Mason's wife died on 27 Mar. 1767. The epitaph is inscribed on a tablet in Bristol Cathedral (see Letter 440).

[26] Nicholls wrote 'The words of M[rs] Mason, when she had given up all hope of life' as an afterthought on the opposite page of the MS., and marked the sentence with a Greek *a*, a similar mark being affixed to the place where it was to be inserted in the text. Nicholls describes these lines as 'the words of M[rs] Mason'. They are not her words, but the continuation of the apostrophe in which Mason calls on her to 'speak from the grave' an exhortation to the passer-by who reads the epitaph.

[27] It was first published (anonymously) in Feb. 1773, and eleven editions were published in that year (see *Satirical Poems of William Mason, with Notes by Horace Walpole*, edited by Paget Toynbee, Oxford 1926, pp. 31–71).

[28] William Burgh (1741–1808), an Irish landowner, M.P. for Athy, Kildare, in the Irish Parliament of 1769–76. Like Mason, he was one of the principal patrons of the York Association for Parliamentary Reform in 1780. He edited at York in 1783 (where he lived for nearly 40 years, and was thus in touch with Mason) a new edition of Mason's *English Garden*, with a commentary and notes. Mason left him, jointly with his trustees, all his manuscripts in prose and verse, in the hope that he would undertake a complete edition of his works, which Burgh failed to do.

the Heroic Epistle.' Mason replied instantly in a surly, nasal tone
which was not unusual to him, 'I am told the K - - thinks so, & he
is welcome.'—In spite of this admirable work, & Caractacus, his
mind certainly had not been strengthened & armed for poetry in the
temple of Apollo; He had not, like Gray, turned over, & ruminated
upon the 'exemplaria Græca,'[29] nor made his own

> "What the lofty grave tragedians taught
> In Chorus or Iambic, teachers best
> Of moral prudence."[30]

It is not pedantry but truth to say that the minds of those are best
cultivated who have cultivated them by Greek Literature; more
vigorous writers have written in that language than in any other,
& the language itself is the best vehicle that has yet existed for the
highest & noblest Ideas of which the mind of man is capable. M^r
Gray thought so; & had read, & studied every Greek Author, I
believe, of note, or importance:—Plato perhaps more than any other
person. He lost all patience when he talked of the neglect of his
favourite author at the University. He was astonished that its
members should in general read & admire Cicero, & yet not think
it worth while to pay any attention to him whom Cicero called
'Divinus ille Plato.'[31] What he admired in Plato was not his mystic
doctrines which he did not pretend to understand, nor his sophistry
but his excellent sense, sublime morality, elegant style, & the perfect
dramatic propriety of his dialogues.—I was reading Plato to him
one evening and stopped at a passage which I did not understand,
he said, 'Go on, for if you stop as often as you do not understand
Plato, you will stop very often.' He then added that finding what
he did understand so admirable he was inclined to think that there
might be a meaning in the rest which at this distance of time, & for
want of proper *data* we might not be able to reach.—He was a great
lover, & studyer of Geography as the ample collection in his Mss
Common Place books prove.—He placed Strabo[32] with reason at the

---

[29] Horace, *Ars Poet.* 268–9:

Vos exemplaria Graeca
Nocturna versate manu, versate diurna.

[30] Milton, *Paradise Regained*, iv. 261–3.

[31] The particular phrase has not been found in Cicero: but Gray may have had
in mind Cicero's phrases such as 'Plato . . . divinitus est locutus' (*De Orat.* i. 49) and
'quem [Platonem] omnibus locis divinum . . . appellat [Panaetius]' (*Tusc.* i. 79).

[32] Gray has many references to Strabo in his Commonplace-book, and cites him
as an authority for the geography of India and Persia, on which he made elaborate
notes. Mason states that: 'early in life he [Gray] had an intention of publishing an
edition of Strabo.' The statement lacks evidence and seems open to doubt.

head of all Geographers; & when, with a kindness, & condescension to which I owe all that is not bad in every part of my character, he undertook to be my guide and friend, long before I had arrived 'Al mezzo del cammin di nostra vita'[33] he plunged me into Greek, which I had not before entirely neglected; & said, 'When you have got thro' the two volumes of Strabo, then I'll talk to you further.' He advised me to miss the two first books & begin with the description of Spain. Strabo led the way,—Herodotus, Thucydides, Xenophon, Diodorus Siculus, Plutarch &c. followed. When I expressed my astonishment at the extent of his reading he said, 'Why should you be surprised, for I do nothing else.' He said he knew from experience how much might be done by a person who did not fling away his time on middling or inferiour, authors, & read with method. He congratulated himself on not having a good verbal memory; for, without it he said he had imitated too much; & if he had possessed such a memory all that he wrote would have been imitation, from his having read so much.—He had a memory however which served him accurately as to facts, & guided him infallibly to the source from which the information he wanted was to be drawn. From the deficiency of verbal memory he seldom quoted; but the spirit of Classic authors was always present to him, & breathed in every thought, & word of his compositions. He was a great admirer of Tacitus,[34] the result of whose deep thought strikes the minds of such readers as understand in pointed expressions which must be felt. Besides this, he possesses in equal perfection a power of a very different kind, that of painting a Scene, by judicious detail, as if it were on canvas. Mr Gray thought the narrative of Thucydides the model of history. He valued Herodotus as its father; & as an author of great veracity as far as he had the means of information himself, & never fabulous except when he gave the relations of others, which he careful[ly] distinguishes from what he relates on his own authority.

For Socrates, he had an almost religious veneration, & esteemed the Memorabilia of Xenophon as one of the most valuable books of Morality. & La Bruyére[35] likewise stood high in his estimation, & the Essays of Bacon. I remember part of a line among some juvenile Mss verses in his Common Place Book of advice to West, in which he recommends to him to rise early and

—read Plato, read Bruyére.[36]

33 The first line of the *Divina Commedia*, 'Nel mezzo del cammin di nostra vita'.
34 For Gray's opinion of Tacitus see Letter 101.
35 See Letter 58**, n. 12.
36 This sentence was added by Nicholls as an afterthought. Nicholls's memory

Appendix Z

My first acquaintance with Mr Gray was one afternoon drinking tea at the rooms of Mr. Lobb[37] a fellow of Peter-House.—The conversation turned on the use of bold metaphors in poetry; & that of Milton was quoted—'The sun was pale,[38] & silent as the moon' &c. when I ventured to ask if it might not possibly be imitated from Dante

mi ripingeva là dove il sol tace[39]

Mr Gray turned quickly round to me & said 'Sir, do you read Dante?' & entered into conversation with me.

He had a perfect knowledge of the Italian language & of the Poets of Italy of the first class, to whom he certainly looked up as his great progenitors; & to Dante as the father of all; to whose Genius, if I remember right, he thought it an advantage to have been produced in a rude age of strong, & uncontrouled passions, when the muse was not checked by refinement, & the fear of criticism. He preferred the Gerusalemme liberata of Tasso as a poem to Ariosto.

Petrarca he said appeared in his poetry to be two distinct persons of contrary characters; the one simple natural & tender; the other full of conceits & false thoughts; after this, tho' it can scarcely be necessary, it may not be improper, in order to obviate the possibility of any misconstruction or undue extension of the preceding criticism, to add that Mr Gray was a decided, and zealous admirer of Petrarca. He permitted me to copy from his edition the marks which he had used to distinguish the different degrees of merit which he assigned to the poems, & even single verses of this poet.

When I found in the Purgatorio of Dante the verses from which the beginning of the Elegy is imitated

s'ode squilla di lontano
Che paia 'l giorno pianger che si muore[40]

he acknowledged the imitation & said he had at first written 'tolls the knell of *dying* day' but changed it to *parting* to avoid the *concetto*. He thought that Milton had improved on Tasso's Devil by giving him neither horns, nor a tail. He admired Racine, particularly the Britannicus.[41] He disliked French poetry in general; but was much pleased with Gresset,[42] & extremely with his poem of the Vert-vert.

played him false with regard to the verses in Gray's Commonplace-book: they were addressed by West to Gray, not by Gray to West (see Letter 58**, n. 12).

[37] William Lobb, of Peterhouse, B.A. 1755; M.A. 1755; Fellow 1758. For the date of Nicholls's first meeting with Gray (11 June 1762) see Letter of Nicholls to Temple printed at the end of this Appendix.

[38] 'The sun to me is dark' (*Samson Agonistes*, l. 86).

[39] *Inferno*, i. 60.　　　　　　　　　　　[40] *Purgatorio*, viii. 5–6.

[41] See Letter 62, n. 7.　　　[42] See Letters 145, nn. 11–19, and 146, nn. 3–6.

The sly, delicate, & exquisitely elegant pleasantry of la Fontaine he thought inimitable; whose muse, however licentious, is never gross; not perhaps, on that account, the less dangerous. He thought that Prior, in the same kind, would not bear the comparison with la Fontaine. He liked the Art de Peindre of Watelet.[43] Hudibras, I think, he did not like.

He was much struck with the glowing eloquence, acute observation, & deep reflexion of Rousseau; & thought the Emile a work of great Genius;[44] tho' mixed with much absurdity, & that it might be productive of good if read with judgment; but considered it as ridiculous, & impracticable as a system of education; to adopt it as such he said 'you must begin by creating a new world.'

His contempt for the Nouvelle Heloïse,[45] is sufficiently known. He thought the story ill-composed, its incidents improbable, the characters unnatural, & vicious, & the tendency immoral, & mischievous:—& such faults as these could never in his judgment be redeemed, atoned for, or even palliated by any, the most eminent, & brilliant beauties of sentiment & diction, or interest of circumstances, & situation. Very different indeed was his judgment of the *Clarissa* of Richardson.—He said 'he knew no instance of a story so well told' & spoke with the highest commendation of the strictly dramatick propriety, & consistency of the characters perfectly preserved, and supported from the beginning to the end, in all situations, & circumstances, in every word, action, & look. In the delineation of the character of Lovelace alone he thought the author had failed; not having lived among persons of that rank it was impossible for him to give the portrait, from the life, of a profligate man of fashion. On the subject of Richardson I remember Mr Gray was pleased with an opinion of Dr Johnson related to me by Davies the player to whom Johnson had given it.[46] On being asked by him what he thought of the different, & comparative merits of Richardson, & Fielding. Johnson answered 'Why Sir, Fielding could tell you what o'clock it was, but as for Richardson he could make a clock, or a watch.' One could follow, & describe the motions of the human passions, but the other could trace their springs, & origin. He allowed great, but inferiour merit to *Sir Charles Grandison*.

When Boswell published his account of Corsica,[47] I found Mr Gray

[43] Charles Henri Watelet (1718–86); his poem was published in 1760.
[44] See Letter 373.   [45] See Letters 328, 330.
[46] See Boswell, *Life*, vol. ii, p. 49.
[47] For Gray's opinion of the book see Letter 471.

reading it. 'With this, (he said) I am much pleased, because I see that the author is too foolish to have invented it.'

He expressed regret at his want of Mathematical knowledge, & declared to me that he had still serious intentions of applying himself to the study of it.—At the same time he lamented that in the University it was usually studied to serve the purpose of taking a degree honourably, & generally laid aside afterwards, instead of being applied to the attainment of those useful, & sublime sciences to which it is the only guide, & conductor.

I had few opportunities of seeing Mr Gray in large, mixed companies, but in the year 1770 when I travelled with him thro' a part of England, & South Wales,[48] we went to Malvern with the situation of which place, & the extensive command of the two counties of Gloucestershire & Herefordshire from the summit of the hill (particularly the latter) he was delighted, but certainly not so with the numerous society assembled at the long table where we dined every day: tho' he staid there a week, most obligingly on my account, as I found some acquaintances whom I was glad to meet. He had neither inclination to mix much in conversation on such occasions, nor I think much facility, even if he had been willing. This arose perhaps partly from natural reserve, & what is called *shyness*, & partly from having lived retired in the University during so great a part of his life where he had lost as he told me himself 'the versatility of his mind.' In fact except during his travels he had never lived much (as the phrase is) in the world & even at that time the total want of congeniality, & similarity of disposition & pursuits between him & his companion, & the vanity, conceit, & airs of superiority in the latter never forgetting that he was son of the first minister could not inspire with much gaiety a mind not naturally prone to it, & probably contributed to depress his spirits. When I once endeavoured to learn from him the cause of his difference with, & separation from Walpole, he said 'Walpole was son of the first minister, & you may easily conceive that on this account he might assume an air of superiority' (I will not answer for the *exact expression*, but it was to this effect) 'or do or say something which perhaps I did not bear as well as I ought.' This was all I ever heard from him on the subject, but it is instead of a volume to those who know the independent, & lofty spirit of Gray.—Without considering the particular cause of difference mentioned above I agree with Mr Mason who once said to me that it was more surprising that two persons of characters so opposite to each other should ever have agreed than

---

[48] See Letter 530.

that they should finally have separated. A letter to West dated Florence, April 21. 1741[49] corroborates what I have said with respect to the effect which Mr Gray's travels had produced on his spirits. 'You must add then to your former idea, two years of age, a reasonable quantity of dullness, a great deal of silence, & something that rather resembles than is thinking; a confused notion of many strange & fine things that have swum before my eyes for some time, *a want of love for general society, indeed! an inability to it.*'

In London, when I knew him there, he certainly lived very little in society; he dined generally alone, & was served from an eating house near his lodging[50] in Jermyn Street.[51]

In one of the visits he made me at Blundeston I was extremely embarrassed because I had at that time with me an old relation,[52] & his wife who were so entirely different from any thing that could give him pleasure that I thought it impossible he should reconcile himself to their conversation, or endure to stay with me. I think he perceived this, & determined to show me that I had mistaken him; for he made himself so agreable to them that they both talked with pleasure of the time they passed with him as long as they lived.

Whenever I mentioned Mr West he looked serious, & seemed to feel the affliction of a recent loss. He said the cause of the disorder, a consumption, which brought him to an early grave was the fatal discovery which he made of the treachery of a supposed friend,[53] & the viciousness of a mother whom he tenderly loved; this man under the mask of friendship to him & his family intrigued with his mother; & robbed him of his peace of mind, his health, & his life.

After I had quitted the University I always paid Mr Gray an annual visit; during one of these visits it was he determined as he said to offer with a good grace what he could not have refused if it had been asked of him viz. to write the Installation Ode for the Duke of Grafton.[54] This however he considered as a sort of task to which he submitted with great reluctance; & it was long after he first mentioned it to me, before he could prevail with himself to

[49] Letter 97.

[50] Mitford (*Add. MS.* 32561, f. 188) quotes the somewhat malicious account which he heard from Samuel Rogers: 'Gray in London saw little Society. Had a nice dinner from the Tavern brought to his lodgings, a glass or two of sweet wine, and as he sipped it talked about great People.'

[51] Here follows in the original a passage of eight lines, which has been scored through, apparently by Nicholls himself. It is still decipherable and proves to be a repetition of what Nicholls had already said about his stay at Malvern with Gray.

[52] See Letter 488, n. 18.

[53] See Letter 83, n. 3.   [54] See Letter 493, n. 5.

begin the composition. One morning when I went to him as usual after breakfast, I knocked at his door, which he threw open, & exclaimed with a loud voice

'Hence! avaunt, 'tis holy ground.'

I was so astonished, that I almost feared he was out of his senses; but this was the beginning of the Ode which he had just composed. When one sees, and considers the persons who are *in fashion* in the world, caressed, courted, invited to dinners, & suppers as wits, authors, & men of letters, & then reflects on the neglect in which Mʳ Gray lived 'facit indignatio versum'[55]—Satire requires no effort, it is spontaneous, & involuntary.

Mʳ Bryant talking to me of Mʳ Gray seemed to think that he had taken something ill of him, & founded this opinion on some circumstance which appeared to me frivolous, & which I have forgotten. I never heard Mʳ Gray mention him but with respect, regretting only that he had turned his great learning into a wrong channel; what would Mʳ Gray have said if he had lived to see him endeavour to destroy with a stroke of his pen the famous city which besides a ten years' siege has stood that of so many centuries elapsed since?[56]

One day when I entered his apartment I found him absorbed in reading the newspaper: he said 'Here is such writing as I never met with before in a newspaper.' This was the first letter which appeared of Junius.[57] He thought that the abundance of Dictionaries of different kinds was a bad symptom for the literature of the age; because real, & profound learning is never derived from such sources, but drawn at the fountain-head; & they who are content to pick up the scanty, & superficial information which can be acquired by such means, have neither the spirit, nor the industry to study a subject thro' in the original authors; nor indeed! have they any further demands on literature than for a sufficient supply to satisfy their vanity. He thought the French Encyclopédie[58] best in its beginning, but carelessly executed afterwards.

Tho' I have mentioned that Mʳ Gray regretted his want of mathe-

---

[55] Juvenal, *Sat.* i. 79.

[56] Jacob Bryant (see n. 5) published in 1795 *Observations upon a Treatise . . . on the Plain of Troy*, and in 1796 *A Dissertation concerning the War of Troy*, in which he argued that no such war was ever undertaken and no such city as the Phrygian Troy ever existed.

[57] The first letter with the signature of 'Junius', which appeared in the *Public Advertiser*, was dated 21 Nov. 1768: the first of the continuous series was dated 21 Jan. 1769.

[58] See Letter 245, n. 4.

matical knowledge, yet he would never allow that it was *necessary* in order to form the mind to a habit of reasoning, or attention. Does not Lock require as much attention as Euclid? & what cause should prevent the mind unexercised in Euclid from severe attention to Lock? or from applying the powers it possesses to any other branch of knowledge? The study of Mathematics certainly requires strict attention, but does it *exclusively* produce the habit of it? & is not that habit to be acquired by application of any other sort?

I asked Mr Gray what sort of a man Dr Hurd was, he answered 'The last person who left off stiff-topped gloves.'

Mr Gray's love of, & knowledge in Gothic Architecture[59] are well known; he contended particularly for the superiority of its effect in churches; & besides, admired the elegance, & good taste of many of its ornaments. I remember his saying, tho' I have forgotten the building to which the observation was applied 'Call this what you please, but you must allow that it is beautiful.' He did not make the distinction which it seems now the fashion to make between Saxon and Norman; I never heard the latter term from him. And indeed! those who make this distinction have never, to my apprehension, explained the difference. He said that he knew no instance of a pointed arch before the reign of King John, in which I understand Carter,[60] the great Gothic critick agrees with him. All round arches, since the age of Roman architecture, he called Saxon with their zig-zag, & other well known appropriate ornaments, & these he attributed to a period not more recent than the reign of King John.— He was pleased at first with Strawberry Hill;[61] but when Mr Walpole added the gallery,[62] with its gilding, & glass he said 'He had degenerated into finery.'

The house of the late Mr Barrett[63] at Lee near Canterbury will

[59] In Gray's Commonplace-book there is a long note on 'Architectura Gothica' (printed by Mathias, vol. ii, pp. 98–103); see also Letter 399*.

[60] John Carter (1748–1817), draughtsman and architect, author of *Specimens of the Antient Sculpture and Painting now remaining in this Kingdom, from the earliest Period to the Reign of Henry the VIII*, 2 vols., fol., 1780–87, and of *Views of Ancient Buildings in England* (drawn and etched by himself), 6 vols., 16 mo., 1786–93.

[61] Walpole bought Strawberry Hill in 1748 and at once began to make additions and alterations, which he continued to do intermittently for the next 47 years. For Gray's favourable opinion of the earlier changes see Letters 192 *ad init.*, and 303.

[62] The gallery was completed in 1763: in a letter to Wharton of 5 Aug. 1763 (Letter 373) Gray described it as 'all Gothicism, & gold, & crimson, & looking-glass'.

[63] Thomas Barrett (see Letter 482, n. 2) had rebuilt his house, and had consulted Horace Walpole about the plans. Walpole described it as 'the quintessence of Gothic taste exquisitely executed'.

I hope remain longer than the frailty of its materials promises a monument of the superiour, & perfect taste of Mr James Wyatt,[64] in spite of malicious, & envious criticism, in that beautiful Species of architecture; which, tho' bound to certain rules like that of Greece, affords an ample space for taste, & fancy to range in.

Mr Gray disapproved the additions of Sir Christopher Wren, (the two towers) to Wesminster Abbey.

[64] James Wyatt (1746–1813). Walpole greatly admired his work and employed him on some of the later buildings at Strawberry Hill.

NOTE

The following letter, printed for the first time from the original in the possession of Mr. W. S. Lewis, fixes the date of Nicholls's first meeting with Gray (see n. 37 above):

My Dear Temple

Now I give you leave, nay insist on it, that you Envy me! Last Friday[1] I had the Happiness of drinking Tea with the great Mr Gray at Lobb's Room. I assure you after the first Quarter of an hour which was quite little enough for me to compose my Spirits, and get Courage enough to be happy I was as much so as it is possible for you to conceive me in such Circumstances. I did not find him as you found Johnson,[2] surly, morose, Dogmatical, or imperious. But affable, entertaining and polite. He had no other opportunity of shewing his superior abilities but such as naturally presented itself from the subject of Conversation, which however he never propos'd.

Conceive if you can how happy I find myself when he told me he hop'd to have the Pleasure of my Company some Afternoon at Pembroke. He has not yet fix'd on any. I am under a thousand Anxieties whether or no he will. But Lobb assures me I may depend on more of his Acquaintance. I assure you the whole afternoon, and eversince I have been employ'd with this Idea. That I should be acquainted with one of the greatest men who ever existed in the World! That he should (as it is probable he may) visit me at my own Room!

We had some Discourse about Dante and he seem'd very much astonished that I should have read any of it. He speaks of it in the highest Terms and particularly desir'd me to read one part of it the Story of Count Ugolino; as you may imagine, I read it the next morning, and found it what I expected one of the finest Things I had ever read in my Life.

[1] 11 June 1762, see n. 4.
[2] Presumably Nicholls is referring to Samuel Johnson, and Temple must have already met him. This would have been before Boswell was introduced to Johnson and many years before Boswell records (*Life*, vol. ii, p. 11) that on 15 Feb. 1766 he presented to Johnson his 'old and most intimate friend, the Reverend Mr. Temple'.

What I could chiefly observe in him, was vast politeness, great Good-nature, and the most elegant accuracy of Phrase in the World.

The Bell rings for Chapel and I can't bear to defer sending this by the Post. Adieu my most dear Friend!

N. N.

I was touch'd with your last Letter and Morris[3] was afraid of looking at it.

Sunday[4] [13 June, 1762]

Addressed: To Wm Johnson Temple Esq at No 10 opposite the Church in the Temple London *Postmark:* 14 IV

[3] This was probably Charles Morris, of Eton and St. John's; B.A. 1757, M.A. 1760. He was some years senior to Temple and Nicholls, but he may have continued to reside in Cambridge after taking his Master's degree.

[4] The date of the postmark, 14 June, is, no doubt as usually, a day after the letter was written. In 1762 13 June was a Sunday; Gray was resident in Cambridge during June of that year, and Temple had taken his name off the books of Trinity Hall in Nov. 1761 and lived in the Temple until June 1763.

GENEALOGIES

(*Compiled by* PAGET TOYNBEE)

A. Gray's Pedigree and Relatives on his Father's Side.

B. Gray's Pedigree and Relatives on his Mother's Side.

C. Antrobus and Nutting Families.

D. Pedigree of the Wharton Family.

E. Children of Thomas Wharton.

F. Mason's Pedigree and Relatives.

G. Pedigree of Edward Bedingfield.

TABLE A

Gray's Pedigree and Relatives on his Father's Side

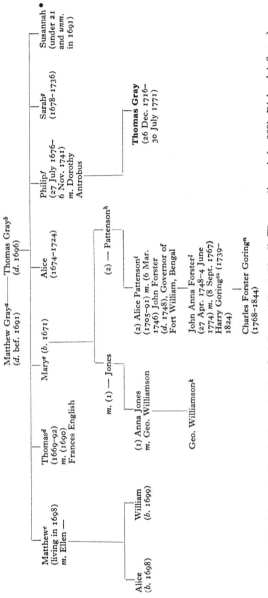

Matthew Gray[a] (d. bef. 1691) —— Thomas Gray[b] (d. 1696)

Matthew[c] (living in 1698) m. Ellen —

Thomas[d] (1669–92) m. (1690) Frances English

William (b. 1699)

Alice (b. 1698)

Mary[e] (b. 1671)

m. (1) — Jones

(1) Anna Jones m. Geo. Williamson

Geo. Williamson[k]

Alice (1674–1724)

(2) — Pattenson[h]

(2) Alice Pattenson[i] (1705–91) m. (6 Mar. 1746) John Forster (d. 1748), Governor of Fort William, Bengal

John Anna Forster[l] (27 Apr. 1748–4 June 1774) m. (8 Sept. 1767) Harry Goring[m] (1739–1824)

Charles Forster Goring[n] (1768–1844)

Philip[f] (27 July 1676– 6 Nov. 1741) m. Dorothy Antrobus

Thomas Gray (26 Dec. 1716– 30 July 1771)

Sarah[g] (1678–1736)

Susannah *
(under 21 and *unm.* in 1691)

* Omitted from the list children who died in infancy: Alice (1663–6), Thomas (*b.* and *d.* 1668), Richard (1672–3), William (1681–2).

NOTES TO TABLE A

Note.—The pedigree and notes are based, by permission of Mr. Charles Hall Crouch, of Hermon Hill, E., on his informative article on 'The Ancestry of Thomas Gray the Poet', in the *Genealogists' Magazine* for Dec. 1927 (vol. iii, no. 4), which throws a new light on the subject of Gray's family and connexions.

a. Died in H.E.I.C. service at Surat.

b. Citizen and cooper of London and Wanstead, Essex; Churchwarden of Wanstead, 1687; supplied wines to H.E.I.C., into the Freedom of which he was admitted in 1678, and had dealings with them in diamonds.

c. Merchant of St. Andrew Undershaft, London, in 1696, and of Wanstead in 1698; was co-security for his brother Thomas in 1687.

d. Elected a Factor at Fort St. George, Madras, 1687; died and was buried there, 1692.

e. Married twice; by her first husband, — Jones, she had a daughter Anna, who, it is conjectured, married George Williamson, and was the mother of the 'George Williamson, Esq. my second cousin by the father's side, now [2 July 1770] of Calcutta in Bengal', to whom Gray by his will left £500. This George Williamson arrived in India in 1756, and held various posts in H.E.I.C. service, up to that of Senior Merchant. He is described as the son of George and Anna Williamson, late of Calcutta; and was dismissed in 1770. (See Appendix X, n. 2.)

f. The dates of his birth and death are taken from a memorandum by Gray now in the John Morris collection at Eton. His death was announced in the *Daily Post* of 7 Nov. 1741, and in the *London Evening Post* of 5–7 Nov.: 'Yesterday died in Cornhill Mr Gray an Exchange Broker of Reputation and Fortune.'

g. By her will she left 'all my messuages, tenements, and houses upon London Bridge or elsewhere, and all ready money, goods, chattels, etc. effects and personal estate to my nephew Thomas Gray son of the said brother Philip'. Gray was executor, and proved the will on 16 Feb. 1735–6. The College books show that he was absent from Peterhouse *c.* 12 Feb. to *c.* 5 Mar., no doubt on account of his aunt's death and the settlement of her affairs.

h. He died before 1725, in which year his wife described herself as Mary Pattenson, widow.

i. See Letters 163, 282, n. 6, 285, 480. She was married, as Alice Pattison, on 6 Mar. 1746, at Fort William, Bengal, to the Governor, John Forster, who died there in 1748.

k. See n. *e.*

l. See Letter 480. She is named as 'Anna, Lady Goring, my second cousin by the father's side', in Gray's will, by which he left her £500.

m. Afterwards (Aug. 1769) sixth Baronet of Highden, Washington, Sussex.

n. He succeeded his father as seventh Baronet, 1 Dec. 1824.

TABLE B

Gray's Pedigree and Relatives on his Mother's Side

William Antrobus[a]
m. (20 Apr. 1675) Jane Goodwin[b]

Anne	Robert[e]	Jane	Mary	Dorothy	William[k]
(1676–Sept. 1758)[c]	(8 July 1679–	(1681–June 1771)[f]	(1683–5 Nov.	(bapt. 12 Aug. 1685–	(bapt. 8 Mar. 1688–
m. (1710) Jonathan	20 Jan. 1730)	m. William Olliffe	1749)[h]	11 Mar. 1753)[i]	22 May 1742)
Rogers[d] (1667–		(d. 26 Dec. 1726)[g]		m. Philip Gray	m. Elizabeth Nutting
21 Oct. 1742)				(See Table A)	(See Table C)

Thomas Gray

a. Citizen and Scrivener of London. He is said to have been a member of a St. Albans and London branch of the well-known Cheshire family of that name.   b. Daughter of Thomas Goodwin, Scrivener.   c. See Letter 271, n. 2.   d. Attorney, lived at Cant's Hill, Burnham, Bucks., where Gray stayed with him (see Letter 26, n. 3).   e. For 30 years Assistant at Eton.   f. See Letter 271, n. 3.   g. So Mitford, in Brit. Mus. Add. MS. 32561, f. 61.   h. See Letter 151.   i. See Letter 176, n. 2. k. Assistant at Eton; Rector of Everdon, Northants., 1726–42 (see Letter 283*, n. 1).

TABLE C
Antrobus and Nutting Families

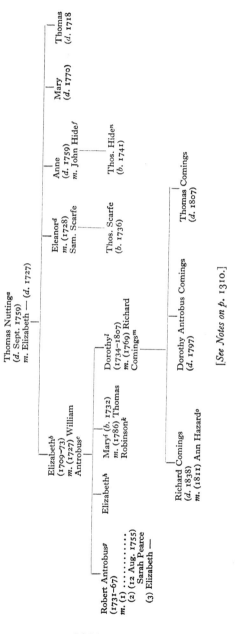

Thomas Nutting[a]
(d. Sept. 1759)
m. Elizabeth — (d. 1727)

Elizabeth[b]
(1709–73)
m. (1727) William
Antrobus[c]

Eleanor[d]
m. (1728)
Sam. Scarfe

Anne
(d. 1759)
m. John Hide[f]

Mary
(d. 1770)

Thomas
(d. 1718)

Robert Antrobus[g]
(1731–67)
m. (1) ....
(2) (12 Aug. 1755)
Sarah Pearce
(3) Elizabeth —

Elizabeth[h]

Mary[i] (b. 1732)
m. (1786) Thomas
Robinson[k]

Dorothy[l]
(1734–1807)
m. (1769) Richard
Comings[m]

Thos. Scarfe
(b. 1736)

Thos. Hide[n]
(b. 1741)

Richard Comings
(d. 1838)
m. (1811) Ann Hazard[o]

Dorothy Antrobus Comings
(d. 1797)

Thomas Comings
(d. 1807)

[See Notes on p. 1310.]

NOTES TO TABLE C

[*See p.* 1309]

Note.—Most of the above data are derived from an article by Dr. H. P. Stokes on 'Thomas Gray and his Cambridge Relations', in the *Cambridge Review* for 17 Jan. 1917.

a. Alderman, Merchant, and Postmaster of Cambridge (see Letter 293, n. 8).

b. See Letters 283*, n. 1, 301.

c. See Letter 283*, n. 1.

d. Cole says that Mrs. Scarfe kept the celebrated 3 Tuns Tavern, opposite the Market Cross, at Cambridge. He adds that she afterwards married a surgeon in Aldermanbury, London, of some repute, very amply provided for herself, and was a very agreeable woman.

e. Of Cambridge; they were married at Hildersham Church, Cambs., on 3 Oct. 1728.

f. According to Cole he was Alderman Nutting's book-keeper.

g. Referred to as 'Bob' in Gray's letter to Mary Antrobus of Nov. 1758 (see Letter 283*, n. 7).

h. A legatee under Mrs. Rogers's will (1757–8) (see Letter 283*, n. 1).

i. Mentioned in Gray's will as 'Mary Antrobus of Cambridge spinster my second [*sic*] cousin by the mother's side' (see Letter 283*, n. 1).

k. They were married by licence at St. Clement's Church, Cambridge, on 30 Dec. 1786. The portrait of Gray as a boy by Jonathan Richardson, now in the Fitzwilliam Museum at Cambridge, was originally in the possession of Gray himself, and was bequeathed by him to his cousin, Mary Antrobus, afterwards Mrs. Robinson. From her it passed to her sister, Dorothy Comings, mother of the late Richard Comings of Cambridge (d. 1838), who having inherited the picture from his mother, bequeathed it to his brother-in-law, Mr. H. Hazard, by whom it was presented to the Fitzwilliam Museum in 1858.

l. Mentioned in Gray's will as 'Mrs Dorothy Comyns of Cambridge my other second [*sic*] cousin by the mother's side'; she is referred to as 'Dolly' in Gray to Mary Antrobus, 3 May 1759 (Letter 293).

m. They were married by licence at St. Clement's Church, Cambridge, on 31 July 1769. According to Cole, this Richard Comings, who is described as of Little St. Mary's parish, Cambridge, was in partnership with the above-mentioned Thomas Hide (see n. *n*).

n. Referred to as 'your Cousin, T. Hide' in Gray's letter to Mary Antrobus of May 1767 (Letter 439). Cole describes him as a 'Common Council Man of Cambridge, in great Business as a Brewer and a Merchant, but a shatter-headed poor Creature from whom I can't expect any great Matters at last, tho' he makes no small Appearance at present; he is also a Lieutenant in the County Militia.'

o. They were married by licence at St. Benedict's Church, Cambridge, on 11 Mar. 1811.

TABLE D

Pedigree of the Wharton Family

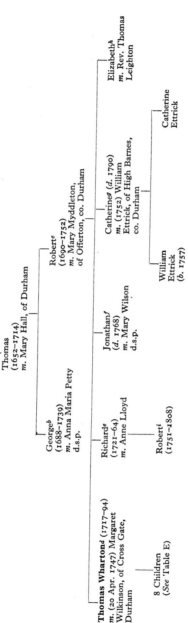

Thomas Wharton[a] (1614–73) of Old Park, Durham

Thomas (1652–1714) m. Mary Hall, of Durham

George[b] (1688–1730) m. Anna Maria Petty d.s.p.

Robert[c] (1690–1752) m. Mary Myddleton, of Offerton, co. Durham

Catherine[g] (d. 1790) m. (1752) William Ettrick, of High Barnes, co. Durham

Elizabeth[h] m. Rev. Thomas Leighton

Thomas Wharton[d] (1717–94) m. (20 Apr. 1747) Margaret Wilkinson, of Cross Gate, Durham

Richard[e] (1721–64) m. Anne Lloyd

Jonathan[f] (d. 1768) m. Mary Wilson d.s.p.

William Ettrick (b. 1757)

Catherine Ettrick

8 Children (See Table E)

Robert[i] (1751–1808)

a. Matriculated from Pembroke College, Cambridge, July 1638; migrated to Trinity College, Oxford; M.D. Camb. 1652; Fellow of Royal College of Physicians, 1650; Censor, 1658, 1661, 1666, 1667, 1668, and 1673; Physician to St. Thomas's Hospital, 1659–73; author of *Adenographia; sive glandularum totius corporis descriptio* (London, 1656).   b. Matriculated from Pembroke College, Cambridge, July 1706; M.B. 1712; M.D. 1719; Fellow of Royal College of Physicians, 1720; Censor, 1725, 1729, 1732, 1734; Treasurer, 1727–39.   c. Mayor of Durham; succeeded to Old Park on the death of his brother without issue. d. See Letter 79, n. 8.   e. See Letter 213, n. 1.   f. See Letter 116, n. 15.   g. See Letter 401, n. 1.   h. See Letter 420, n. 29.   i. See Letter 336, n. 3.

TABLE E

Children of Thomas Wharton

Thomas Wharton (1717–94)
of Old Park, Durham
m. (20 Apr. 1747) Margaret Wilkinson,
of Cross Gate, Durham

Mary[a] (1748–1802)	Margaret[b]	Robert[c] (1753–8)	Deborah[d] (b. 1755)	Robert (b. 1760)	Richard[f] (1764–1820)	Elizabeth	Catherine[h] (d. 1790)
				Richard	Robert		

Note.—The order in seniority of the eight children adopted above is partly conjectural. See Surtees's *Hist. of Durham,* iii. 300.

a. 'The little Doctress' of Letter 146 (see n. 1), the 'Lady Mary' of Letter 390; afterwards 'Miss Wharton' (see Letter 475, n. 15). She was for some years an invalid: she died unmarried in 1802.   *b.* 'Peggy' (see Letter 228, n. 5); she had artistic tastes (see Letters 453, 459). She was living (unmarried) in 1822.   *c.* 'Robin' (see Letter 177, n. 2); he died in 1758 (see Letters 270, 271).   *d.* 'Debo' (see Letters 209, n. 17, 294, 331, and Tovey, iii. 350, 356). She married Rev. Thomas Brand, and was living (as a widow) in 1822.   *e.* 'Robin' (see Letter 313, n. 3). He succeeded to the Myddleton estates in 1801, and assumed the additional name of Myddleton (see Letter 373, n. 8).   *f.* 'Dicky' (see Letter 459, n. 20); afterwards Fellow of Pembroke, Camb., and M.P. for Durham. In 1804 he published a volume of translations entitled *Fables; Consisting of Select Parts of Dante, Berni, Chaucer, and Ariosto. Imitated in English Heroic Verse.* He was Secretary to the Treasury from 1809 to 1814, and while holding that office published a poem (in 1812) called *Roncesvalles,* whence Scott speaks of him (to Morritt, 2 Mar. 1812) as 'the Treasury poet'. He married Henrietta, daughter of James Ferrers, of Lincoln's Inn.   *g.* 'Betty' (see Letter 414, n. 4, and Tovey, iii. 354 n.). She was living (unmarried) in 1822.   *h.* 'Kee', 'Kitty' (see Letter 459, n. 18). She married Major-General Anthony Salvin (d. 1844).

TABLE F

Mason's Pedigree and Relatives[a]

Hugh Mason, of Hull
(Controller of the Port, 1696)
m. Ann Lambert (1658–1726)

```
William Mason (1604–1753)          Mary Mason                    3 sons and 2 daughters
Vicar of Holy Trinity, Hull, 1722–53   m. Arthur Robinson,[b] of Hull
m. (1) Mary Wild   m. (2) Sarah Haynes   m. (3) Mary Ryles   Customs Officer at Sunderland
(d. 1725)          (d. 1741 s.p.)
```

```
                                          Arthur Robinson          Ann Robinson (1727–1814)
                                          Vicar of Hull, 1754–83    m. Josias Wordsworth,[f]
                                                                    of Sevenscore, Kent, and
William Mason[c]        Ann Mason (d. 1809)                         Wadworth, Yorks. (1719–80)
(1724–97)               m. 1780 Rev. Henry Dixon[e]
m. (1765) Mary Sherman[d]   1749–1820
of Hull (d. 1767)
```

```
                        William Henry Dixon[g]    Ann Wordsworth (d. 1835)   Mary Wordsworth
                        1783–1854                  m. (1771) Henry Verelst[h]  (1751–1817)
                        Canon of York 1826         (1731–85)                  m. (c. 1783) Sir Charles Kent,
                                                                              1st Bt. of Fornham
                                                                              St. Genevieve, Suffolk
                                                                              (1744–1811)
```

1313

F f

a. From Foster's *Yorkshire Pedigrees*, *D.N.B.*, and G. E. C.'s *Complete Baronetage*.   b. See Letters 209, n. 1; 438, n. 1.   c. See Letter 144, n. 33.   d. See Letter 408, n. 4.   e. See Letters 181, n. 8; 209, n. 1. He was a son of Jeremiah Dixon, a Yorkshire clergyman (see Letter 548, n. 19).   f. See Letters 209, n. 1; 438, n. 1.   g. Succeeded to Mason's landed property (see Letter 181, n. 3).   h. Governor of Bengal from Jan. 1767 to Dec. 1769, in succession to Clive. On his return to England in 1770 he purchased Aston Hall, near Sheffield, from Lord Holdernesse, where he settled and married in 1771 as above, having issue four sons and five daughters.

TABLE G
Pedigree of Edward Bedingfield

Sir Henry Bedingfield, 1st Bart. of Oxburgh (1614–85)
m. (1635) Margaret Paston (1618–1702)

Sir Henry Bedingfield, 2nd Bart. (1685–1704) m. (c. 1685) Elizabeth Arundell (1655–90)

Edward Bedingfield[a] m. Mary Fisher

Sir Henry Arundell Bedingfield, 3rd Bart. (c. 1686–1760) m. (1719) Lady Elizabeth Boyle (d. 1751)

Mary Bedingfield[b] (d. Feb. 1761) m. (1721) Sir John Swinburne, 3rd Bart.[c] of Capheaton (1698–1745)

Sir Richard Henry Bedingfield, 4th Bart. (1720–95)

Edward Bedingfield[d] m. (21 Mar. 1754) Mary Swinburne[e] (b. 1730) (b. 1729)

| John (1754) | Mary (1756) | Anne (1758) | Thomas[f] (1760) | Edward (1762) | Anthony (1764) | Peter (1765) | Frances (1768) | Helen (1770) | Isabelle[g] (1771) |

Note.—The pedigree and notes are based, in great part, on information kindly supplied by Sir Henry Paston-Bedingfield and Mrs. Paston-Bedingfield.

a. Barrister of Gray's Inn.   b. See Letter 183, n. 6; she was only daughter, and eventually heiress of Edward Bedingfield the elder.   c. Great-great-grandfather of the poet, Algernon Charles Swinburne.   d. See Letter 210, n. 1.   e. See Letter 210, n. 1.   f. Counsellor-at-law of the Inner Temple; author of a collection of poems, published in 1800; he died in 1789.   g. The names of his children and the dates of their birth were methodically entered by Edward Bedingfield in his Journal, owned by Sir Henry Paston-Bedingfield.

APPENDIX AA

37*. GRAY TO WEST

My good West   [*22 May 1737.*]

I AM qualified with full and ample powers to treat with you in
the names of H-W, and A̶;[1] but as you thought fit to begin
with me, I shall think fit to begin with myself: there can be no
excuse made for the backwardneſs of my payments, but Poverty;
alas! Master, times are so hard, and trading so bad, that now
& then a Pepper Corn is all [we] can pretend to; but if your
Worship would call, as you come this way [you] shall be as
welcome to a rasher of Bacon, & a pitcher of drink, as the
Lord Mayor of London—in short I depend upon seeing you
here next month[:] we have indeed nothing to shew you, but
three old faces, that you have been long used to, tho' perhaps
you may find something new even in them; as for me, I shall
be incefsantly painting my eyes, & tiring my head, & looking
out at the window in expectation of your wheels; so pray let
your driving, be as the driving of Jehu, the Son of Nimshi:
Mʳ Conway[2] has been here about a fortnight, & the little
Insensible was neither struck with Kings-Chappel, nor moved
with Trinity-Quadrangle, nor touched with the Senate-house,
& even talked of Oxford, as he was walking on Clare-hall Walks;
we expect you should be moved, struck, & touched with every
thing you see here; we have pulled down half my College,[3] that

LETTER 37*.—First printed by Leonard Whibley, *TLS*, 23 Oct. 1937,
p. 776, from the autograph MS. of three foolscap pages (two sheets) in
WSL. The margins are damaged. Here retranscribed from the original
by the permission of the Lewis–Walpole Library. Only the first and the last
lines of the poem were published in *TLS*. The complete draft is now printed
apparently for the first time. The following notes are largely drawn from
Whibley.

[1] Horace Walpole and Thomas Ashton, who, like Gray, were at Cam-
bridge. Richard West, then at Oxford, had in a letter to Walpole, 27 Feb.
1737 (*Yale*, xiii. 127), reproached the three for not writing to him. Con-
sequently, Gray has added to his own letter comic dummy replies for
Walpole and Ashton—asterisks for the former and 'Turn over' followed by
a blank for the latter.

[2] Evidently Walpole's cousin, Henry Seymour Conway (see Letter 44,
n. 9).

[3] '. . . it had been decided in 1736 to take down part of the first court at
Peterhouse, but the work was deferred, and Gray may be anticipating the
demolition' (Whibley).

you may have fewer Fibs to tell, when y[ou] begin to praise it;
you are to suppose the demolish'd to have been the best part of
it, & that, that is to be built, you may say all the fine things you
please about: we have put our trees in their best green Liverys,
[or]der'd the Sun to clear our Air, Walpole's Greyhound has
got a new Collar, [his?] Cat has learn'd to dance, and all this
against you come: we can't keep[our] best looks & manners long,
so make hast, I charge you: Leonidas,[4] to tell you all that I
think of it, not to conceal my judgement in any point, is really,
excessively —, I particularly admire that noble paſsage in the
—th Book, Line the —th, & then, then the Pathos in that speech
of — to —, & the Simile concerning the —, so applicable to
the present State of Affairs, and most people that I have met
with, I find perfectly of my opinion in this; for those who admire
it, & those, who do not; joyn in thinking the above-mention'd
paſsages perfectly fine: what think you of Mr Pope's, Cum tot
sustineas[5] &c: to me, much preferable to, Flore bono[6] &c: &
pray have you read, the Spleen,[7] publish'd sometime ago; bad
enough taken altogether perhaps; but if you pull it to pieces,
you may find pretty picking, & Scraps of great beauty: the
Essay on Conversation[8] is by no means contemptible: if you
direct letters to me out of malice, I will give you all poſsible
provocations; we excuse your Epigram[9] upon condition you
always fill up your backsides in the same manner; my backside
is too broad to be cover'd with an Epigram, so I'll tell you a
story; you must know, that Rinaldo[10] was lost, [so?] one Carlo
& Ubaldo went to look for him, they did not know where;
& so

[4] *Leonidas*, an epic poem, by West's first cousin, Richard Glover (see
Letter 109, n. 18). It is possible that in Gray's burlesque criticism of
Leonidas he has in mind the extravagant praise lavished on the poem in
Common Sense, or the Englishman's Journal, No. 10 (9 Apr. 1737), by George
Lyttelton, who thought Glover superior to Milton. West comments, without
enthusiasm, on this criticism in his letter of 18 Apr. See n. 10.
[5] Pope's *First Epistle of the Second Book of Horace*, published May 1737.
[6] Pope's *Second Epistle of the Second Book of Horace*, published Apr. 1737.
[7] *The Spleen* by Matthew Green (1696–1737), published Feb. 1737.
[8] *An Essay on Conversation* by Benjamin Stillingfleet, published Feb. 1737.
See Letter 311, n. 44.
[9] The epigram in Letter 22*, which thus should be dated 1737.
[10] Rinaldo d'Este, hero of Tasso's epic *Gerusalemme Liberata*. The follow-
ing lines are a translation from Canto 14, Stanza 32. A copy of them dated
1738 is in the Commonplace Book, i. 95–6, with some variations in word-
ing which are indicated in nn. 11–27. However, as Whibley points out, the

Appendix AA

Dismifs'd at length, they break thro' all delay
To tempt the dangers of the doubtfull way:
And first to Ascalon their steps they bend,
Whose walls along the neighbouring Sea extend;
Nor yet in prospect rose the distant Shore,
Scarce the hoarse waves from far were heard to roar;
When thwart the road a river roll'd his[11] flood
Tempestuous, and all further course withstood:
The torrent stream his ancient bounds disdains
Swoln with new force, & late-descending rains:
Irresolute they stand; when lo, appears
A[12] wondrous Sage; vig'rous he seems[13] in years,
Awful his mien, low as his feet there flows
A vestment unadorn'd, tho' white as new fal'n Snows:
Against the stream the wave[14] secure he trod;
His head a chaplet bore, his hand a Rod.

As on the Rhine, when Boreas' fury reigns,
And winter binds the floods in icy chains;
Swift shoots the village-Maid with[15] rustick play
Smooth, without step adown the shining way,
Fearlefs in long excursion loves to glide,
And sports, and wantons o'er the frozen tide.
So moved the Seer; but on no harden'd plain,
The river boil'd beneath, & rush'd into[16] the Main:
Where fix'd in wonder stood the warlike pair
His course he turn'd, & thus relieved their care.

Vast, oh my friends, & difficult's[17] the toil
To seek your hero in a distant Soil;
No common helps, no common guide ye need,
Art it requires, & more than winged speed:
What length of Sea remains, what various lands,
Oceans untried,[18] inhospitable Sands?[19]
For adverse fate the captive Chief has hurl'd
Beyond the confines of our narrow world:

1738 date in CB is almost certainly a slip by Gray, who was particularly
interested in Tasso in early 1737 (see Letter 37). Therefore Letter 37* was
probably written on 22 May 1737, especially since the publications men-
tioned (see nn. 4–8 above) were all printed in early 1737 and since West
finally left Oxford in March 1738. Furthermore, in the postscript to another
letter to Walpole dated 18 Apr. 1737 (*Yale*, xiii. 132), West mentions
Glover's *Leonidas*.

[11] its [12] The [13] seem'd [14] waves [15] in
[16] towards [17] difficult [18] unknown [19] Sands?]Sands!

Great things & full of wonder in your ears
I shall reveal;[20] but first dismifs your fears,
Nor doubt with me to tread the downward road,
That to the grotto leads, my dark abode.
  Scarce had he said, before the warriours eyes
When mountain-high the waves disparted rise;
The flood on either hand its billows rears,
And in the midst a spatious arch appears:
Their hands he seized, & down the Steep he led
Beneath th'obedient rivers inmost bed.
The watry glimm'rings of a fainter day
Discover'd half, & half conceal'd their way,
As when athwart the dusky woods by night
Th' uncertain Crescent gleams a sickly light.
  Thro' subterraneous pafsages they went,
Earth's inmost cells, & [caves o]f deep descent.
Of many a spring[21] they vi[ew]d the secret source,
The birth of rivers, rising t[o] their course;
How infant-springs in mazy wandrings stream
Pregnant of many a tide, & floods of mighty name;[22]
Whate'er with copious train its channel fills,
Floats into lakes, or bubbles into rills:
The Po was there to see, Euphrates'[23] Bed,
And Danube's[24] fount, & Nile's mysterious head.
  Further they pafs where ripening minerals glow,[25]
And embryon metals undigested flow,[26]
Sulphureous veins, & living Silver shine,
Which soon the parent Suns warm powers refine,
In one rich mafs unite the pretious Store,
The parts combine & harden into Oar.
Here gems break thro' the night with glitt'ring beam,
And paint the margin of the costly Stream:
All stones of lustre shoot their vivid ray,
And mix attempred in a various day:
Here the soft emerald smiles of verdant hue

[20] unfold
[21] flood
[22] How infant-springs . . . / . . . mighty name; *omitted from CB.*
[23] Danubius'
[24] And Danube's]Euphrates'
[25] flow
[26] glow

Here rubies flame with Sapph[ires] heavenly blew;
The diamond there attracts the wondring sight,
Proud in[27] its thousand dies, & luxury of light.

&c: &c:
yours,
T: Gray
Now for Walpole; he bids me tell you, as follows

*   *   *   *   *

yours,
H: Walpole.
Now for Ashton, he desires I'd send you word from him that
he

Turn over

Addressed: To Richard West, Esq. at Christ-Church in Oxford
Postmark: 23 MA

302. GRAY TO MRS. ANTROBUS

Madam   Sept: 8. 1759
  I am glad to hear from Molly[1] today, that there is no parti-
cular charge against you in your office, for if it is only the
greedinefs of the Corporation,[2] I will think it will be easily dis-
appointed, the afsurance Mr Shelvocke[3] has given you, that you
are secure weighs much with me: so much, that I doubt it was
hardly necefsary to speak to Ld Besborough[4] on that head, for
to petition before one is accused of any thing, may appear as
if we were conscious of having done somewhat amifs: however

[27] of
LETTER 302.—Now first printed from original in the Charles A. Brown
Collection of Autographs and Manuscripts, in the Rush Rhees Library of
the University of Rochester, New York. The postscript was printed in
Messrs. Sotheby's Catalogue of 8 July 1915 (Lot 380).
  [1] The letter of Mary Antrobus was evidently written, presumably on
7 Sept., in reply to Gray's letter conjecturally dated Sept. 5 (Letter 301).
  [2] In Letter 301 Gray refers to the attempt made to deprive Mrs. Antrobus
of her office. Here the attempt is attributed to the Corporation. There is
nothing in the records of the Cambridge Corporation to explain this.
  [3] See Letter 301, n. 4. There could scarcely have been time between
Alderman Nutting's death and the date of the letter from Mary Antrobus
(see n. 1) for application to be made to Mr. Shelvocke. Possibly he had
been written to before the Alderman's death.
  [4] In all probability Gray's letter to Lord John Cavendish referred to in
Letter 301 is meant.

my Letter is gone, & can not be recalled, if it is unne[cefsary][5] so much the better.

I believe & hope, you may continue ve[ry sure] on this head. let it only caution you to see the bus[inefs] of your office diligently executed, & to avoid even the least occasion of complaint, and then you have little to fear.

I am Mad^m,
Your Friend & Servant
T. G.

My love to the Girls.[6] pray tell Molly, I expect to *hear* from her again soon. she must direct At Mr Jauncey's in Southampton Row, Bloomsbury.

388*. GRAY TO BROWN

[London. c. June 1–7, 1764][1]

Dear S^r

I RECEIVED Mr Talbot's[2] letter from Bath, & hear today, that he is return'd to Cambridge. I should write to him, had I anything worth his notice, that I could tell him in a letter. I hope, he continues to feel the good effects of his journey.

[5] Here and below, owing to a small tear in the margin, words or letters are missing and have been conjecturally restored.

[6] See Letter 283*, n. 1.

LETTER 388*.—Discovered by William Powell Jones in the library of the late Frank Bemis of Beverly Farms, Mass., bound in an elaborate extra-illustrated edition of F. W. Hawkins, *The Life of Edmund Kean* (London, n.d.), v. 410; now in the Houghton Library of Harvard and printed for the first time from the original by permission of Harvard College Library. The letter is unsigned but unquestionably in Gray's hand. In a different hand there has been written at the bottom of the first page 'Gray, the poet' and in the same, or very similar, hand on the second page after the 'Yours' the name 'Gray'.

[1] At this time Gray was in London. His letters were usually written on the day they were postmarked or on the day before, but the sentence 'Clive embarks on Tuesday' (unless Gray's information was incorrect or 'embarks' was a slip of the pen for 'embark'd') sounds as if it referred to a Tuesday in the future. Yet, according to A. Mervyn Davies, *Clive of Plassey* . . . (New York: Charles Scribner's Sons, 1939), p. 370, 'Clive embarked on June 4' (which, incidentally, in 1764 was a Monday). If this is correct, Gray may have written the letter about June 1 to 3 and then forgotten to mail it for a few days. The events mentioned in the letter (see notes below) indicate the year 1764.

[2] William Talbot (see Letter 241, n. 15, and Index II). As Professor Jones has pointed out to me, this is the first indication that Talbot and Gray exchanged letters. It is therefore possible that Talbot played a more important role in Gray's life than biographers have realized.

Appendix AA

You probably know as well as I do, that the M: of Rockingham[3] has given a considerable living, Keeton (I think, is its name)[4] in Huntingd:ⁿ[s?] worth near 300£ a-year, tenable with his Mastership, to the V: Chancellour.[5] it is just under the nose of Hinchinbroke & Kimbolton, & comes very a-propos in all respects. I desire to know the policy of Trinity-Hall. there are 10 fellows (not insane) that elect, and I hear 5, if not 6, of them are Candidates for the Mastership, among wᶜʰ Mat. Robinson[6] is one. Dʳ Calvert[7] (I hear) has got the Chancellorship of Worcester.

I am sorry to tell you, that the tragical story of the Prisoners in India,[8] with those sad circumstances you saw in the Papers comes from Mʳ Pigot[9] lately return'd from thence. it is true, he had his intelligence from a Black Native of the Country concerning their fate: but it is generally believed here. Clive[10] embarks on Tuesday.

You will oblige me in sending Sally's account[11] (I mean the

[3] See Letter 394, n. 5, and Index II.

[4] J. C. T. Oates of University Library, Cambridge, writes: 'Keyston, as it is now spelt, is a small village about 12 miles west of Hinchingbrooke, former seat of the Earls of Sandwich, and 6 miles north-west of Kimbolton, former seat of the Dukes of Manchester. The Manchesters and Sandwiches were both members of the Montagu family, and the Manchesters held a property in Keyston known as Montagu Manor. The advowson of the parish church was attached to Keyston Manor and was acquired by Charles, Marquess of Rockingham, from the surviving co-heiresses of the family of Wingfield, which had bought the Manor in 1618. According to the *Victoria County History, Huntingdonshire*, iii. 74, there is in the church a shaped silver plate (hall-marked for 1775–6) inscribed "Keystone W. Elliston, D.D., Rector, 1776".' See n. 5.

[5] William Elliston (*c.* 1733–1807), Master of Sidney Sussex, 1760–1807; Vice-Chancellor, Nov. 1763–Oct. 1764; Rector of Keyston(e), 1764–1807.

[6] Matthew Robinson, Fellow of Trinity Hall.

[7] Peter Calvert was a Fellow of Trinity Hall, but the story Gray heard (unless it concerned a third and unidentified Worcester) must have been erroneous, for Worcester College, Oxford, never had a Chancellor and there never was a Chancellor of Worcester Diocese named Peter Calvert.

[8] Apparently a reference to the massacre in 1763 of 170 Europeans by Mir Kasim, Nabob of Oudh, at Patna.

[9] George Pigot (1719–77), created first Baron Pigot of Patshul 1766, resigned his office in the East India Company Nov. 1763 and returned to England.

[10] Robert Clive (1725–74), created first Baron Clive of Plassey 1762.

[11] See Letter 281, n. 8, and App. E, nn. 7, 8.

1321

sum total) as soon as you are able, for I know not how soon I shall leave London. Nicholls tells me, you are well, & walk to Ditton.[12] Adieu! I am sincerely

Yours.

Addressed: To the Revd Mr Brown President of Pembroke Hall, Cambridge.

Postmark: JV 7

388**. GRAY TO COLE

Pot pourri or perfumed Jar or Pot.

GET some coarse brown Bay Salt: this is the sine quâ non, & (by the way) is not to be had at Cambridge, where under the name of Bay Salt they sell a whitish Kind of Salt, that will never do for our Purpose, & will spoil all: at London the true Sort is common in every Shop, & a Pennyworth of it is enough to make a Bushel of Perfumes. Take a Peck of Damask Roses, pick'd from the Cups, Orange Flowers all you can get, Cloves (the Spice) a Quarter of an Ounce, cut small: scatter them in your Jar mixt in Layers about 2 Inches thick, & thinly sprinkle the Salt over them: repeat this, 'till the Vefsel is three Quarters, or more, full: cover it close down, let it stand 2 Days, & then stir it up well with a wooden Ladle or Skimmer: repeat this often, & it is made. If it is always moist to the Touch, it is right: if over-wet, you have only to put in more Flowers, & no more Salt. You may use, if you please, Tops of Lavender, Myrtle-Leaves bruised, Rose-Geranium, Angelica, Shavings of Orrice-Root, or (where Orange Flowers are scarce) young green Oranges sliced, or even the yellow Rind of Seville-Oranges: but of these Things a very little will do, least they

---

[12] A village near Cambridge.

LETTER 388**.—First printed in 'Coliana . . .', *Monthly Magazine*, xvii (1 July 1804), 550, with comments by 'Rosalba' and 'Rosarubra' in the 1 September and 1 November issues. Reprinted from William Cole's autograph MS. in the British Museum (Add. MS. 5825, ff. 283^b, 284^b, and identified as part of a Gray letter by H. W. Starr, [London] *Times Literary Supplement*, 30 Mar. 1951, p. 204. On Wednesday, 18 July 1764, Cole wrote to Walpole asking for some orange flowers to make a potpourri for which he had obtained the recipe from Gray. The editors of Walpole's *Correspondence with . . . Cole (Yale*, i. 67) thought Gray's formula was lost.

overpower the Rest. I can not be particular as to Quantities, because I observed none myself. Adieu Dear Sir, I am faithfully yours   TG.

Cambr July 7. 1764.[1]

[1] Cole appends to the recipe the following note: 'This I had by Letter from my Friend M*r*. *Gray of Pembroke Hall in Cambridge*, to whom I sent for the Receit, having seen & smelt the odoriferous Jar in his Chambers the Year before.'

INDEXES

In the following indexes all references are to the numbers of letters, but note numbers have been sometimes added where (1) the reference in the text is not clear, (2) the length of the letter makes reference difficult. The references in heavy type are to biographical notes.

INDEX I

THOMAS GRAY

For the events of Gray's life see the chronological table. For his birth and family see genealogical tables and Index II, s.v. Gray, Antrobus, Forster, Rogers, Olliffe.

Fire, fear of: 285, 303, 347

Friends, chief, (first reference to): Ashton 14, Balguy 234, Bonstetten 508, Brown 115, Chute 98, Clerke 79, Cole 26, Mason 144, Nicholls 397, Palgrave 273, Robinson 304, Stonhewer 120, Tuthill 120, Walpole 1, West 16, Wharton 79/

Health and spirits: allusions to his ill health 200, 213, 244, 245, 247, 385, 433, 533, 542, 550, 552, 555; allusions to gout 1755–71 *passim*; allusions to his good health 66, 249, 279, 284*, 321, 332, 352, 420, 531, 533, 534, 553; allusions to his melancholy and low spirits 110, 208, 218, 241, 246, 268, 278, 385, 433, 550

House property: Cornhill 28, 196, 409; Hand Alley 439; Wanstead 156, 196

Laureateship, offer of to Gray: 258*, 258**, 259, 261

Literary Criticism:

Addison: 'had not above two or three notes in poetry' 144

Akenside: 'often obscure and unintelligible' 115

Anstey: *New Bath Guide* 'a new & original kind of humour' 423; *The Patriot* 'I like it but little' 458

Aristotle: 'he is the hardest Author by far I ever meddled with. then he has a dry Conciseness . . . it tasts for all the World like chop'd Hay . . . thirdly he has suffer'd vastly by the Transcribblers . . . fourthly and lastly he has abundance of fine uncommon Things' 121

Bayle: 'Bayle's pedantic bawdy' 170

Beattie: 452, 529

Buffon: his weakness, a love of system; 'well worth turning over' 154

Collins: 'A fine Fancy, a bad Ear, great Variety of Words, and Images with no Choice at all' 129

Crebillon: *Le Sopha* 'Most people here are not such admirers of it as I was, but I wont give up an inch for all that' 109

Dodsley's Miscellanies: 143, 144, 161, 268

Dryden: 'No one more licentious' in inventing words 103; his own debt to him: 'be blind to all his faults' 413

Fielding: *Joseph Andrews* 'the characters have a great deal of nature; Parson Adams is perfectly well' 103

Frederick the Great: 'All the scum of Voltaire and Ld. Bolingbroke, the *crambe recocta* of our worst Free-thinkers toss'd up in German-French rhyme' 311

Froissart: 308, 'the Herodotus of a barbarous age' 540

Green: *Spleen* 'Scraps of great beauty' 37* (App. AA)

Home: *Douglas* 'The Author seems to have recovered the true language of the Stage, wch. had been lost for these 100 years' 244; *Agis* 'all modern Greek; an antique statue . . . dressed . . . by a Yorkshire mantua-maker' 268

Hume: 'a pernicious writer . . . has continued all his days an infant, but one that unhappily has been taught to read and write' 529

1324

Thomas Gray

Thomas Gray

Subjects of special interest and study:

Architecture 76, 191, 192, 273*, 320, 363, 365, 366, 374, 399*, 519

Gaelic Poetry 310, 313, 315, 317, 318, 319*, 320, 321, 322, 351, 367, 370, App. L

MSS. 230, 303, 314, 320, 458, 471, 472, 516

Music 86, 214, 238, 286, 294, 372, 374, 477, 499; musical instruments 'Acoustic warming-pan' 230, 'Haspical' 109, lyricord 373, musical glasses 309, 351, 352, 366, pianoforte 197, 212, 440; opera 3, 20, 24, 42, 60, 109, 128, 194, 212, 327, 330, 374, 397, 431; particular operas Adriano 20, Artaserse 20, Cefalo et Procri 109, Demofoonte 212, Mitridate 128, King Arthur 20 n. 14

Natural History: birds 94, 313, 331, 373, 420, 508*, 541*, 549; botany 331, 495, 512, 531, 533; calendars of flowers, fruit, crops &c. 296, 303, 306, 313, 331, 373, 420, 459, 511, 519; temperature and weather 296, 303, 306, 311, 313, 331, 373, 420, 423, 459, 502, 536, 537, 542

Painting 282, 285, 320, 321, 374

Romantic Scenery 71, 73, 74, 278, 279, 392, 412, 505 ff.

Theatre 3, 4, 20, 28, 42, 60, 63, 74, 109, 125, 165*, 357, 417, 510

Welsh Poetry 313, 340, App. M

Tours and visits: France and Italy 59–98; 'an excursion to Hampton Court' 120; Durham, &c. 177–82; Northants., Warwick, &c. 192; Portsmouth, Winchester, &c. 198, 199; Ely, Peterborough, &c. 271; Suffolk 335; York and Old Park 360–3; 'a little jaunt to Epsom & Box-hill' 373; 'a ramble away from Cambridge' 379–80; Winchester, Southampton, Salisbury, &c. 392–4; York, Old Park, Hartlepool 407–9; Glamis and the Highlands 411–16; Canterbury, Margate, &c. 421–3; Suffolk and Norfolk 425–6; Aston and York 445; Old Park, Carlisle, Keswick, &c. 446–54; Kent 480; Suffolk and Norfolk 488; Old Park and Hartlepool 503; Tour in the Lakes, Lancashire, and Yorkshire 504–511 A; Norfolk 517; Worcestershire, Gloucestershire, Monmouth, &c. 530–1

INDEX II

OTHER PERSONS

Richmond, Charles Lennox, 3rd Duke of: 345, **470 n. 9**
Richmond, Dr. Richard: **430 n. 20**
Ridlington, Dr. William (Fellow of Trinity Hall): **399 n. 13,** 409, 429, 432 n. 1
Rigby, Richard: **236 n. 9,** 237, 308, 373, 459, 488
Rinuncini, Marquis: **121 n. 4**
Roberts (hosier in Jermyn St.): 'my old Landlord' **176 n. 3,** 216, 424, 454, 488
Robinson, Mr., of Faskally: 412
'Robinson': 135 n. 21
Robinson, Rev. Arthur (Mason's cousin): 447, 449, **450 n. 2**
Robinson, Matthew: 388* (App. AA)
Robinson, William ('Billy': Fellow of St. John's): **304 n. 4;** his marriage 316, 317; Gray stays with him in Kent 421, 435   Letter to: 380
Rochefort, Mme de: **419 n. 13**
Rochford, Countess of: **206 n. 7,** 212
Rockingham, Charles Watson-Wentworth, 2nd Marquis of: **394 n. 5,** 395, 430, 443 n. 9, 459, 388* (App. AA)
'Rockinghams, The': 443, 459
Rodney, Admiral George Brydges: 296 n. 19
'Roger', *see* Long, Dr. Roger
Roger, Archbishop of York: **365 n. 2,** 366, 399*
Rogers, Mrs. (Gray's aunt): 26 n. 3, **110 n. 1,** 141, 145, 168, 176; has a stroke 183; 271, 277, 280; her death 281; her will 283*; 305 n. 6, 439
Rogers, Jonathan (Gray's uncle): **26 n. 3,** 110 n. 1
Rogers, Thomas (Fellow of Peterhouse): **149 n. 6**
Romayne, John (Archbishop of York): **366 n. 13**
Roper, Robert: **249 n. 5**
Ross, Mr.: 494
Ross, Dr. John (Fellow of St. John's): **149 n. 13,** 171 n. 10, 309, 380, 467; Dean of Ely 489, 490, 491
Rovezzano, Benedetto da: 324
Rowley, Mr.: 308
Royston, Lord, *see* Hardwicke, 2nd Earl
Rutherforth, Mrs.: 135 n. 19, **364 n. 8,** 479
Rutherforth, Dr. Thomas (Fellow of St. John's): **135 n. 19,** 288, 364; candidate for Mastership of St. John's 399, 479
Ryder, Sir Dudley (Attorney-General): 120 n. 6

Sackville, Lord George: at Minden 299*, 300; applies for a Court Martial 303; 308; his trial 309; declared unfit for command 311; in Parliament 420
Sackville, Lady George: 311
St. Albans, Duchess of: 345
St. André, Dr. Nathanael: **393 n. 14**
'St. Germain, Count': **313 n. 10**
St. Quintin, Sir William: **423 n. 19**
St. Simon, Marquis de: **206 n. 5**
Sallé, Mlle (opera dancer): **374 n. 7**
Sandby, Paul (landscape painter): **321 n. 12,** 322
Sandwich, Countess of: **332 n. 10**
Sandwich, John Montagu, 4th Earl of ('Jemmy Twitcher'): **331 n. 15,** 332; candidate for High Stewardship at Cambridge 385, 386 n. 6, 390, 395, 399 n. 22, 401; 430; Joint-Postmaster 459; 471, 472, 499, App. P
Sardinia, King of (Charles Emmanuel III): 71, 72, 73
Sardinian Ambassador: 307
Say & Sele, Viscountess: 345
Scarborough, Richard Lumley-Saunderson, 4th Earl of: **321 n. 15**
Scarlatti: 1
Schaub, Lady: **154* n. 2**   Letter from: 154*
Schoenfeld, Countess of: 206
'Scroddles' *or* 'Skroddles', *see* Mason, William
Secker, Dr. Thomas (Archbishop of Canterbury): **325 n. 18**
Selby, Bell: **230 n. 12**
Selwyn, George Augustus: **65 n. 1,** 66, 211, 470
Senesino, Francesco (opera singer): **81 n. 3**
Senhouse, Humphrey (Fellow of Pembroke): **230 n. 14**
Servius Tullius: 132
Sharp, Dr. John (Fellow of Corpus Christi College): **290 n. 1**
Shaw, Dr. Ralph: **473 n. 2**
Shebbeare, Dr. John: **263 n. 13**
Shelburne, Countess of: **416 n. 7**
Shelburne, William Petty, 2nd Earl of: 'Lord Fitzmaurice' **327 n. 13;** First Lord of the Treasury 373; resigns 376; rumoured divorce 416; Secretary of State 459
Shelvocke, George: **301 n. 4,** 302
Shepherd, Antony (Plumian Prof. of Astronomy): **484 n. 11**
Shepherd, Miss: 228
Shirley, Mrs.: **311 n. 25**
Shirley, Walter: **311 n. 21**

Index II

INDEX III

AUTHORS AND BOOKS

Index III

INDEX IV
PLACES

INDEX V

OTHER SUBJECTS